ALSO BY GERALD ASTOR

TERRIBLE TERRY ALLEN:
COMBAT GENERAL OF WORLD WAR II—
THE LIFE OF AN AMERICAN SOLDIER

THE BLOODY FOREST

THE GREATEST WAR:
AMERICANS IN COMBAT,
1941–1945

WINGS
OF
GOLD

WINGS OF GOLD

THE U.S. NAVAL AIR CAMPAIGN
IN WORLD WAR II

GERALD ASTOR

PRESIDIO
PRESS

BALLANTINE BOOKS
NEW YORK

A Presidio Press Book
Published by The Random House Publishing Group

Copyright © 2004 by Gerald Astor

Excerpts from *Wildcats over Casablanca: U.S. Navy Fighters in
Operation Torch* by Lt. M. T. Wordell and Lt. E. N. Seiler as told by
Keith Ayling. Introduction by Peter Mersky. Published by Brasseys Inc.,
Dulles, VA, in 2004. Used by permission of Brasseys Inc.

Excerpts from *Skipper*, by T. Hugh Winter. Used by permission
of T. Hugh Winter.

Excerpts from *Those Few Who Dared* by William C. Odell. Used by
permission of William C. Odell.

www.presidiopress.com

Library of Congress Cataloging-in-Publication data is available
from the publisher upon request.

ISBN 0-89141-853-9

Manufactured in the United States of America
Text design by Joseph Rutt

First Edition: June 2004

2 4 6 8 9 7 5 3 1

For Sonia, Ted, and Larry, and in memory of our Andy
and all those who wore wings of gold

ACKNOWLEDGMENTS

A major portion of this book came from interviews with a number of survivors who wore "wings of gold," and my deepest thanks go to them (see bibliography for individual names). I am also indebted to Paul Stillwell at the United States Naval Institute in Annapolis for his help and for the resource of the oral histories produced by that organization. The folks at the National Archives in College Park, Maryland, were also most gracious and helpful in pulling out the official records of the various units. Al Bolduc was kind enough to lend me his collection of photographs. I thank Ted Astor for his expertise and patience in retrieving photographs for use in this book. Finally, I am grateful for the support given to me by E. J. McCarthy and Bob Kane at Presidio Press, under whose aegis this work was originally commissioned and edited.

CONTENTS

WINGS
OF
GOLD

FIRST WINGS

Ed "Whitey" Feightner, who in 1940 was a student at Findlay College in Ohio and already held a civilian pilot's license, remembered, "The war was coming along, and it was pretty obvious that I was going to be drafted if I didn't do something. I immediately signed up in the Army Air Corps because I wanted to fly. But there were so many people that I was going to have to wait about eight months. One day, an SNJ [Navy air trainer] landed at the airport. This guy gets out of it, goes into the hangar. And he comes out and he's dressed in a Navy white uniform. A car comes, a convertible, and picks him up. This redhead is driving the car, and Mike Murphy [an instructor, barnstormer, oil company pilot, and reserve army officer] looks at this and says, 'Good God! How about you and Red [a friend of Feightner] take a plane up to Grosse Ile and find out what this Navy program is all about.'

"We flew up there and the Navy treated us royally. They took us in and they showed us what the program was. They showed us *Hell's Angels* [a spectacular movie featuring Navy pilots from the 1930s] and a little strip of this thing [*Hell Divers*] with Clark Gable and John Wayne." The pitch sold Feightner, who immediately enlisted.

David C. Richardson, as a youth in Mississippi during the early 1930s, was already oriented toward the Navy by his father's assurance that a naval officer had an easy life. "When I was about thirteen, William 'Stick' Sutherland, a naval aviator, came to an Easter party at our home. He was dressed in whites. He was a very good looking man. I took one look at him and said, 'That's for me.' "

Like so many young men of the 1930s and early '40s, Feightner and Richardson were entranced by the excitement and the romance of flight. The memory of Charles Lindbergh, the Lone Eagle, "Plucky, Lucky Lindy," who in 1927 flew solo from New York to Paris, remained vibrant. Barnstormers, with white scarves, leather helmets, goggles (the precursor of the sunglass look), wing walkers, air shows, and air races exuded glamour and excitement. For five dollars, kids, like Feightner, bought rides in rickety relics from World War I at small airports or from cow pastures.

While films such as *All Quiet on the Western Front* depicted the trench warfare of World War I in all its deadly misery, Hollywood glamorized aerial combat in the 1927 classic *Wings*, followed by productions of *The Dawn Patrol* and, as Feightner noted, burnished the image of the naval aviator in *Hell's Angels*. Magazines that spun tales of World War I dogfights circulated briskly, and boys built replicas of the earliest and latest airplanes out of balsa wood and tissue paper, powering them with twisted rubber bands or tiny, balky gasoline engines.

While the Army Air Corps attracted its share of recruits for a plunge into the wild blue yonder, the Navy, with its sparkling, brass-buttoned uniforms, aircraft carriers that promised seagoing adventures with voyages to exotic ports of call, and above all those golden wings, beckoned most seductively.

The Navy became interested in donning wings well before 1903, when at Kitty Hawk, North Carolina, the Wright brothers' contraption lifted off the ground and wobbled through the air a few hundred feet. Assistant Secretary of the Navy Theodore Roosevelt, in 1898, had recommended to his superior that a pair of officers meet with inventor Samuel P. Langley to discuss his plans for a flying machine with an eye to its possibilities as a weapon of war. In April of that year, the officers so charged reported that there was definite potential in Langley's ideas and suggested further investigation.

Ten years later, when the Wrights demonstrated their machine for the U.S. Army, observers from the Navy were on hand. That led to a recommendation that the Navy buy planes to be developed for the service's particular needs. Glenn Curtiss, an early manufacturer, built several flying machines, and in 1910, stunt pilot Eugene B. Ely, an employee of Curtiss, proposed to take off from a ship. He heard many a discouraging word. Curtiss himself thought it a bad idea.

Wilbur Wright decried the attempt as too dangerous. The secretary of the Navy refused to pay for such an experiment. It was noted that Ely could not even swim.

In spite of the naysayers, Captain Washington I. Chambers, the Navy's first director of aviation, supported Ely. Private contributions paid for a sloping eighty-three-foot-long platform built on the scout cruiser *Birmingham*, anchored at Hampton Roads, Virginia. The engine for the pusher-type Curtiss Hudson Flyer arrived aboard the *Birmingham* only the morning of the appointed day. Ely and mechanics, however, managed to install the motor and ready the plane, which had been salvaged from the wrecks of two other Curtiss aircraft.

"A strong wind was driving the rain in sheets," reported the *New York Times* correspondent. "His biplane rushed along the runway and the test began. He failed to elevate his plane properly as the biplane left the runway and the rudder and propellers struck the water some yards from the ship. There was a heavy splash and Ely was drenched."

Nevertheless, the pilot recovered and the Hudson Flyer lifted into the air. Originally, he had planned to travel fifty miles to the Norfolk Navy Yard, but the squall interfered. He initially lost his bearings and appeared headed out to sea before he changed course to land on the beach.

The triumphant Ely, despite a bent propeller blade caused by the near crash on takeoff, had demonstrated feasibility of airplanes in the service of the Navy. Captain Chambers remarked that the feat would have been easier had the *Birmingham* been moving. The authorities allowed that a plane might be used for "scouting purposes." While some of the brass scorned the "stunt," which required dismantling of some of the cruiser's guns, the Navy hedged its bets. A month later, Lieutenant T. G. Ellyson became the first naval officer assigned to undergo flight training at the Glenn Curtiss Aviation Camp.

Meanwhile, Ely, with the backing of Chambers, pushed the envelope further. He volunteered to land aboard a ship, the cruiser *Pennsylvania*, moored in San Francisco Bay. On January 18, 1911, Ely took off from an Army airfield thirteen miles off and headed for the cruiser. About fifty feet from the vessel, he cut his throttle and glided toward the specially constructed platform on the stern. The 1,000-pound plane touched down. As it rolled forward, hooks mounted on the undercarriage grabbed at a series of twenty-two ropes anchored by 500-pound sandbags. The final dozen lines snagged the hooks and Ely stopped, using only 60 feet of the 120-foot ramp. He did not require the use of a large canvas barrier erected at the end to prevent a slide into the sea, nor did he need the pontoons attached to the aircraft to stay afloat.

The *Pennsylvania* skipper became an instant convert, burbling about "the most important landing of a bird since the dove flew back to the ark." Following lunch, Ely took off from the ship and returned to the airfield. The *San Francisco Examiner* immediately grasped the significance of the round-trip. Its headline read, "Eugene Ely Revises World's Naval Tactics." And in England, a British aviator, Lieutenant Charles R. Samson, added to the possibilities when he launched himself from a moving ship, showing that planes could be carried to battle sites. Samson also innovated the first folding-wing aircraft, opening the way for convenient storage where space was always at a premium.

By 1912, a primitive catapult made it possible to launch a plane from a ship without a takeoff platform and in 1914 the Navy had created its own flying school at Pensacola. Navy flyers performed reconnaissance for Marine operations in Mexico near Vera Cruz during that country's revolution. World War I introduced the airplane as a serious weapon. While the land-based airmen specialized in reconnaissance and raids on ground forces, the naval service, relying on seaplanes, concentrated on antisubmarine campaigns, striking at U-boats and their bases. Occasionally, German pilots confronted the small American contingent. In the U.S. Navy's first air-to-air victory, Ensign Stephen Potter and his gunner shot down an enemy seaplane off the German coast in April 1918, but six weeks later his lone ship was jumped by seven foes over the North Sea and Potter was lost. Subsequently, Lieutenant David Ingalls, in a Sopwith Camel, a British-manufactured plane, became the Navy's first ace. In 1917, the British introduced HMS *Furious*, the first aircraft carrier, whose planes carried out a successful raid on a Zeppelin base in northern Germany. Unfortunately, the *Furious* lacked the means to recover its aircraft on board. It was a one-shot weapon, which reduced its contribution considerably.

A year after World War I ended, the Navy drew plans to convert a collier into its first aircraft carrier, named in honor of the prophet of the 1890s, USS *Langley*. At the same time, the Army's most fervent advocate of airpower, Brigadier General Billy Mitchell, had already begun his campaign to base American military strategy upon the airplane. Assistant Secretary of the Navy Franklin D. Roosevelt even invited Mitchell to meet with the Navy General Board to discuss future policy. Initially, the officers responded favorably, but those in the upper echelons dampened the enthusiasm. There was a growing suspicion that Mitchell intended to build an air force independent of both the Army and the Navy.

In 1921, Billy Mitchell sought to demonstrate the airplane's supremacy by bombing some captured German warships. The honors for the first attack went to the Navy, whose two waves of planes blew a German submarine to bits. The success raised some eyebrows, but old-line military salts noted that a thin-hulled U-boat on the surface could not compare with a thickly armored capital ship.

The next test, to find and sink the obsolete battlewagon *Iowa*, reddened Navy faces. Seaplanes could not locate the radio-controlled ship before Army blimps found her. And then the flying boats dumped eighty dummy bombs but scored a paltry two hits. While that discomfited the supporters of naval aviation, the seagoing traditionalists insisted it proved that their ships were invulnerable to any bombing attack.

Mitchell's crews, however, demolished a German destroyer and then the combined services, including the Marines, blasted a light cruiser. But the key test was the battleship *Ostfriesland* at 27,000 tons, as heavy as any warship then afloat. In increasingly poor flying weather, Navy and Marine flyers dropped 250-pounders that did little damage. Mitchell's people, with 600-pound bombs, scored a number of direct hits but apparently caused no critical destruction. On the following day, a return visit with 1,100-pound bombs, observers saw that the *Ostfriesland* had, in fact, taken on considerable water due to the previous attack. The renewed assault wrought further injury. For the coup de grâce Mitchell led a flight of eight bombers, each of which packed a 2,000-pound wallop. A series of near misses plus a direct blow on the point of the bow doomed the ship, and it turned on its side, then settled below the sea before the stunned eyes of a number of admirals and civilian Navy officials.

The surface-ship establishment recovered enough to dismiss the show, arguing that aircraft could never effectively target moving ships that would fire back in their own defense. The seeds of a rivalry, if not an internecine war, within the Navy between the aviation adherents and the big-gun, battleship-oriented were sown.

However, Admiral William A. Moffett, in charge of naval aviation but a determined opponent of an independent air force à la Mitchell, said, "The lesson is that we must put planes on battleships and get aircraft carriers quickly. We should have a minimum of eight carriers. The department has recommended only two." With military appropriations curtailed, the service, in 1922, decided to redesign a pair of unfinished cruisers into the carriers *Saratoga* and *Lexington*.

In 1923, Mitchell was granted a second opportunity to conduct tests against naval vessels. The targets were the obsolete battleships *New Jersey* and *Virginia*. Some three hundred military and civilian leaders, including the acting secretary of war, Dwight Davis; the Army chief of staff, General John J. Pershing; Admiral William E. Shoemaker; and the manufacturer and inventor of a new bomb-sight, Alexander De Seversky, boarded a naval transport, the *St. Mihiel*, to watch flights of heavily laden bombers pummel the pair of ships, and within minutes both disappeared under the water.

According to Mitchell's biographer Burke Davis, when Shoemaker read a report on the test he objected strenuously, "It's true, every bit of it, but my God, we can't let this get out or it would ruin the Navy." Others downgraded the experiment, noting again that the ships had been stationary and had offered no resistance, and that their watertightness had been compromised by removal of compartment sealing doors. The traditionalists, sometimes known as the black-shoe Navy (airmen wore brown ones) or the gun club, dominated Navy policy and strategic concepts. They did not entirely dismiss the value of aircraft but believed true strength lay in seagoing tonnage and inches of gun. The same sort of conflict wracked the Army. Mitchell's intemperate lobbying for his point of view forced his retirement from active duty.

Gerald Bogan, born in 1894 on Michigan's Mackinac Island and a graduate of a Chicago high school, was a member of the U.S. Naval Academy Class of 1916. During World War I he did convoy duty, assigned posts in engineering and gunnery. "I never saw a submarine or destroyer," he remarked. He volunteered for aviation duty in 1925 because he found battleships "uninteresting" and "aviation seemed the wave of the future." Bogan recalled, "When I first went into aviation, the black shoes had an adjective to describe aviators, just as the southerner had to describe Yankees—Goddamned Yankees, Goddamned-aviators."

Alfred M. Pride became one of the few early naval aviators who never attended the academy. An engineering student at Tufts University in 1917, Pride had joined the naval reserve because of the imminence of war. Facing a chemistry test on April 7, 1917, the day after the United States declared war on Germany, and certain he would fail, Pride rode a trolley to the Charleston Navy Yard and volunteered for active duty. He remembered, "It never occurred to me that I would be an aviator. But while on antisubmarine patrol in the harbor around Miami I saw airplanes flying about. It seemed like a good business to be in. I sat down at my father's typewriter and typed a letter from A. M. Pride, machinist's mate, second class, to somebody I'd heard about, the Chief of Naval Operations. I requested I be ordered to aviation duty." To his astonishment, a reply directed him to resubmit through the proper channels, and his request for flight training carried a stamp: "Approved."

Awarded wings after ground instruction at Massachusetts Institute of Technology and flight training in Miami, Pride became part of a team studying how to fly airplanes off large ships without disabling their guns. In 1919, Lieutenant Commander E. O. McDonnell, using a British Sopwith Camel, took off from the turret platform of the battleship *Texas*. Pride continued the experiments on the *Arizona* with a fifty-two-foot-long wooden platform that could be assembled quickly. "Until then," he recalled, "our observation from battleships was confined to the use of kite balloons. They obviously couldn't leave the ship." Three years later, catapults on cruisers and battleships, using either compressed air or gunpowder, launched planes. The ability to both scout and spot for capital ships increased the potential of aircraft, confirming in the minds of many that there was a place for naval aviation, as an adjunct to the main power of the fleet.

When the *Langley* went on active duty as the first U.S. carrier, there was still no satisfactory method to arrest a plane once it touched down on the flattop. Alfred Pride expanded on the methods used by Ely in his flight to the *Pennsylvania* in 1911. He applied engineering theory based on the potential energy involved and in place of sandbags substituted weights suspended in towers. When the *Saratoga* and *Lexington* joined the fleet, Pride's mechanics were installed. Because the planes of the 1920s and early '30s were relatively small and light in weight, one persistent problem was a tendency to skip over the wires. Said one veteran of the period, "We had barriers, of course, before the angled deck, and that saved us. We didn't have brakes in those days. We only had tail skags [hooks], and when we came on board the carrier they [installed] a wheel instead of the skags so you wouldn't tear the deck up." Not until 1931 were brakes standard equipment, and about the same time the first two-way voice radios became cockpit fixtures.

While these improvements added to the value of aircraft, to widen their influence and roles, flyers from both the services showed off their expertise. Robert B. Pirie, from the USNA Class of '26 and an aviator by 1929, recalled the public relations effort designed to enlist public support. "We went to the air races every year at Cleveland. One squadron would go, and we had some other air stunt teams. On the East Coast in 1930, we took all of the planes from the *Lexington* and *Saratoga* and flew them to all the large cities, New York, Boston, Philadelphia, Hartford, then stacked down over Washington, Baltimore, Richmond. They all got a chance to look at carrier airplanes. The public didn't know much about carrier aviation. The *Langley* was the first carrier and then the *Lexington* and *Saratoga*. We did the same thing on the West Coast, with San Francisco and at Seattle."

Navy pilots put on exhibitions with aerial torpedoes and dive-bombing, a technique successfully demonstrated in 1926. Aside from air races, the flyers challenged for speed and endurance records. Aviation became part of the program for cadets at the Naval Academy. They took at least one "familiarization" flight to acquaint them with the view from above. The seaplanes used the nearby Severn River. Although there was no pilot training, the midshipmen learned the rudiments of navigation. The resentment of the establishment, however, continued.

Chicago-born Dan Gallery, of the 1921 USNA Class (a three-year accelerated course because of World War I made him an ensign in 1920), said, "My interest in aviation didn't awaken until four or five years after graduation. Previously, I had been an engineer on the battleship *Delaware* and a destroyer before assignment to the *Idaho*." When he informed the executive officer he was headed for Pensacola, Gallery said the biblical response was "You're giving up your birthright for a mess of pottage." Gallery echoed Bogan: "Goddamn-aviators was a hyphenated word."

Fitzhugh Lee, whose father graduated from the U.S. Military Academy in 1901, earned a presidential appointment to the USNA from President Warren G. Harding. "I was thrilled with the idea of going there and getting out of the army." Following graduation, Lee served aboard a battleship and then the newly commissioned aircraft carrier *Lexington*. "I became imbued with aviation through the presence of the fighter squadron on the *Lexington*," said Lee. During Lee's sojourn at Pensacola, one of his fellow students was an older man, Captain William F. Halsey. "He was one of the senior officers brought back for indoctrination training as a pilot and then given their wings. This was not to make pilots out of them, but to give them some flight indoctrination to better fit them for aviation commands. Although I admired and liked Halsey a lot, he was awfully difficult to fly in formation with. When I read his biography subsequently, it [said] he was afraid to wear his glasses because he thought he wouldn't qualify for aviation if he did. Consequently, he couldn't read any of the numbers on the instrument panel. He didn't know how fast he was going, where he was going, nor his altitude."

Among other senior officers engaged in the flight indoctrination was the future chief of naval operations during World War II, Ernest J. King. Gerald Bogan, stationed as an instructor at Pensacola, remembered, "King was a man who always flew an aircraft into a landing faster than it needed to go. On occasion he ran out of field at the end of his landing."

After flight training Lee had joined Fighting Squadron Five, known also as the Red Rippers. "They wore fancy red scarves that waved in the wind, leather puttees, riding breeches, leather helmets and goggles." The studied appearance of those with wings of gold had become a hallmark of naval aviation. That could only have inflamed the rancor of the seamen.

George Anderson, Lee's USNA classmate, a Brooklyn native born in 1906 and a graduate of a Jesuit high school, saw a notice in the newspaper that Representative Ogden L. Mills could not find anyone to nominate for the academy. He promptly moved to Mills's district and received an appointment to the Annapolis institution. He recalled that it was after Lindbergh's feat that the Navy offered an aviation course upon graduation. He admitted that the extra $124 a month had been an incentive but added, "It seemed to me that aviation was the coming offensive arm of the Navy."

However, there was a two-year wait to be served aboard ships before one could apply for flight school. Furthermore, as with submariners, a candidate had to be unmarried to qualify. When Anderson, in 1929, received his orders to report to Pensacola, the skipper of the ship to which he was assigned said, "You goddamned fool! You're going to fly on one of those goddamned airplanes! I hope you break your neck." Nine months later, having completed the course in seaplanes, Anderson spent four years working on scouting maneuvers.

During the late 1920s, naval aviation, in spite of the disdain from powerful people, desperately needed more flyers to fulfill its needs. One program offered an opportunity for officers to attend a preliminary flight school at San Diego to determine whether they qualified for further instruction. Herbert Riley, a gunnery officer on the *New Mexico* and a 1927 alumnus of the USNA, found his requests for the training repeatedly rejected. "Three of us, all in the gunnery department," said Riley, "were always to go to the *next* class."

When their superior, William "Spike" Blandy, continued to postpone assignment of Riley and the others to the flight school for what was known as "elimination training" (disqualifying men who showed no aptitude for piloting an airplane) on the grounds that there were important exercises involving the *New Mexico*'s guns, Riley and his companions submitted official applications, Blandy wrote an unfavorable endorsement that was longer than Riley's request. Blandy obviously believed that battleship gunnery practice was far more important than the Navy's needs for more aviators.

However, the policy of aviation elimination training superseded the position taken by Blandy, and Riley attended a session at North Island, San Diego. Having successfully soloed, Riley and one of his two associates at North Island asked to be sent for the full course at Pensacola. "When we went back to rejoin our ship, I can assure you that Eddie Condra and I were the skunks at the garden party aboard the *New Mexico*. We were given every weekend extra duty, every dirty detail that any ensign could get on the *New Mexico* until the orders came through detaching us and sending us to flight training."

One of Riley's fellow alums from 1927, Arkansas son John "Jimmy" Thach, likewise left a battleship post for the so-called elimination course at North Island. Following five and a half hours of instruction, his instructor sent him up by himself. On the landing he bounced the ship rather hard, but his teacher announced, "Okay, that's fine. You've soloed, you've finished the course." From that uncertain beginning, Jimmy Thach would go on to be one of the principal figures in naval aviation during World War II.

The posture of the black-shoe people actually only enhanced David Richardson's desire to fly. "It really came home to me out in the fleet. In the attitudes and outlook of aviators there was an openness. With the surface commanders there was a tightly constrained atmosphere that I liked not at all. The general demeanor of the aviation community appealed to me."

Noel Gayler, upon graduation from the USNA in 1935, served five years on battleships and destroyers. While he was intrigued by the notion of flight, he said his decision to apply to Pensacola stemmed from an urge to have more responsibility and the sense that life in the surface fleet was "a pretty static society." By the time he attended flight school he was senior to his fellow novices.

Gayler also recalled a most congenial atmosphere. "Everytime we went into a port, the entire city would turn themselves out, I mean even big cities like San Francisco. We'd be guests of the city, and the debs would send invitations to the officers and the men would be entertained. They'd declare Fleet Week, with celebrations and visitors all over the place. In the peace time armed services . . . there just weren't that many of us, which made a difference. Then there was a social cachet about being a naval officer that was not inconsiderable. You were automatically of a social elite, wherever you went."

During the 1930s, military aviation drew increased interest because of the Great Depression. Young men saw a life in uniform as a career in an era of huge unemployment, and applications for the armed services academies swelled. David McCampbell, Alabama-bred and son of a West Palm Beach, Florida, hardware store owner, saw the family business plunge into bankruptcy. He entered Annapolis in 1929, but when he graduated in 1933, the Navy could fund only the top half of the class with commissions. He accepted an honorable discharge but a year later was recalled. And the 50 percent extra over base pay for aviation led him to pursue the wings of gold.

Willard Eder was born in a one-room log cabin on his father's homestead in Buffalo, Wyoming. His father was a civil engineer and part-time farmer and rancher. He graduated from the University of Wyoming in 1938 with an Army ROTC second lieutenant's commission in the infantry. "I needed a job. At the time, the Army Air Corps, and Army Infantry were feuding," said Eder. "My reserve Army C.O. recommended the Navy rather than the Air Corps for a job." Eder signed up with the Navy, and in May 1940 he joined Fighting Squadron Three, commanded by Jimmy Thach.

As in Eder's case, Jim Billo, born in Portland, Oregon, turned to military aviation because of the economy. He attended the University of Portland and Oregon State, studying engineering. "I got started in aviation in '39 when I couldn't get a full-time summer job and began civilian pilot training. I took two courses during school and got a commercial license. I received an appointment to West Point but turned it down to go to Pensacola for flight training." Graduated as a naval officer in November 1941, Billo remarked, "About a week later I got a good job offer, about December seventh."

Bill Anderson was two years into a chemical engineering course at the University of Rhode Island when the naval aviation recruiting team visited the school. "They put on a good show, promised us wings of gold, and furthermore if you did your four years of service you would get the large sum of five hundred dollars for each year in the Navy when you went back to college."

During the early 1930s, the airmen delighted in embarrassing their black-shoe rivals. Fitzhugh Lee, with the Red Rippers of Fighting Squadron Five, recalled maneuvers in which the carrier-launched planes attacked Pearl Harbor and the Panama Canal. "In both of these fleet problems it was pretty well shown that the defenses of these places were not equal to the potential of the carrier forces in destroying them."

Truman J. Hedding, USNA 1924 and an airman by 1926, as a pilot with Fighting Squadron Six, participated in the war games aimed at the Panama Canal and Hawaii. Flying off the *Saratoga* in 1932, he recalled, "We attacked Pearl Harbor in almost the identical way the Japanese did on the 7th of December, 1941. We came in from the north and made our attacks.

"We had no running lights on the planes; we had no radio. We decided we wanted to make a dawn attack on Pearl Harbor. We all had flashlights and we would flash them over our right shoulders so we could rendezvous in the dark. But we didn't rendezvous until practically over Diamond Head at dawn." The chagrin of the victims, however, had no influence upon the stances taken to defend American outposts.

During the 1930s, the Great Depression put the armed services on a near-starvation diet. The military, as David McCampbell's experience indicated, could not even absorb the graduating classes of their academies. Able to retain only a modest number of recruits for such highly skilled activities as pilot training, the Navy washed out all but the topmost candidates. Floyd Thorn, a Baptist minister's son who grew up in Oklahoma and Texas, left Baylor University in 1938 after three years to attend the flight school at Pensacola. He chose to enlist because "any idiot could see we were getting into war. Somebody was going to have to knock down that clown [Nazi dictator Adolf Hitler]." He added, "If you graduated from Pensacola, you were a cinch for anywhere you wanted to get a job. The airlines would hire you in a minute."

The catch was that because of the tight budget, the Navy would graduate only 10 to 12 percent of the class at Pensacola. "They didn't graduate us as ensigns," recalled Thorn, who had entered flight school with a leg up—he already held a commercial license. "They didn't have any vacancies so they sent us to the fleet as cadets, with our wings." Initially designated as a mine warfare officer (without the commission), Thorn joined VP-44, a PBY patrol squadron.

While the factions continued to quarrel over the role of airpower, there was no mistaking the drift of the world toward another large conflict. Although the Great Depression crimped America's pocketbook, defense-minded officials championed larger and larger budgets for the armed services. Along with fighting ships and submarines, the Navy drew appropriations to expand its aviation in terms of carriers, planes, and pilots.

The *Ranger* (CV 4) had joined the fleet in 1931. CVs 5 and 6, the *Yorktown* and the *Enterprise*, followed. In 1940, CV 7, the *Wasp*, was commissioned. That same year the Navy's first escort carrier, CV(E), the *Long Island*, a converted cargo ship, went to sea. In 1941, with the launching of the *Hornet*, the Navy achieved the level of eight carriers proposed by Admiral Moffett in 1921 after Billy Mitchell's first exhibition.

During the 1930s, the fighter aircraft gradually switched from biplanes to single-wing, all-metal machines. In 1941, the Navy was beginning to phase out the F2A Brewster Buffalo in favor of the sturdier Grumman F4F Wildcat as its basic fighter. Aside from superior protection for the pilot, the Wildcat possessed self-sealing fuel tanks. Its six .50-caliber machine guns provided heavyweight punches.

The SPD Douglas Dauntless had been adopted as the divebomber and the twin-engine PBY Consolidated Catalina and PBM Martin Mariner served as long-range patrol planes with limited offensive capability and a role in antisubmarine warfare. Battleships and cruisers could catapult the SOC float plane for scouting and gunnery spotting. The weakest item was the torpedo bomber, the Douglas Devastator, an agonizingly slow-moving machine. Aware of deficiencies in the air fleet, naval aviation experts had begun work on plans and prototypes for better fighters, dive-bombers, and torpedo bombers.

A. B. "Chick" Smith, whose forebears had participated in the American Revolution and whose family was deeply engaged in the textile industry, grew up in small-town North Carolina. When he entered the University of North Carolina in 1938, he enrolled in reserve officers' training with the Marine Corps. "I participated in mock battle exercises where my training platoons were attacked by Marine fighter aircraft. I concluded that the attacking pilots had a better deal than I did on the ground."

Smith and his contemporaries at Chapel Hill, unlike Americans at some other institutions of higher learning and elsewhere in the country, followed world events closely. "Political discussion were hot and heavy, very pro-Roosevelt, and sympathetic to England. In one such discussion, some fraternity brothers and I decided we would call the secretary of state to express our views. Mr. [Cordell] Hull actually accepted our call." (A highly unlikely possibility in post–World War II eras.)

His bias in favor of the British led Smith to a Navy cockpit. "At the end of my third year [1940–1941] a fraternity brother and I decided to help England by answering the call for naval aviation cadets. After some difficulty in getting out of the Marine Corps (with the help of my congressman) I found myself in flight class in Jacksonville, Florida. In February 1942, I received my wings of gold. I was twenty years old."

Jim Pearce, who grew up in Detroit, scented war. "I attended General Motors Institute in Flint, Michigan, where I studied mechanical engineering. After two years at GMI, in the spring of 1941, I sort of smelled a war coming and enlisted in the Navy's V-2 program to become a naval aviator. The war in Europe was well under way, and I saw no way the U.S. was going to stay out of it for long."

Both the Navy (Marines included) and the Army benefited enormously when Congress passed the Aviation Cadet Act of 1935, with appropriations targeted to radically expand the pool of reserve pilots for armed forces. This opened the avenue taken by Willard Eder. Additional funds for this purpose were approved during the period of 1936–1938. The Naval Reserve Act of June 1939 fixed the maximum number of reserve pilots at 6,000, who were enrolled in what was designated the V-5 program. Whitey Feightner was among those who entered through V-5. A second boost for aviation came from the 1938 Civilian Pilot Training Act, which would enlist 10,000 aviation-minded students at 460 colleges and provide ground and flight instruction to civilians. That was the avenue used by Jim Billo to get his wings. Alex Vraciu—the son of immigrants from Romania, who spent a year of his early schooling in the old country—while a student at DePauw University, Indiana, in 1940, his senior year entered CPT. "My instructor was a naval reserve pilot. They were starting to draft people and I had a low draft number and having CPT I declared myself for the navy."

To support the influx of pilots and planes, the service added schools for mechanics, radio technicians, ordnance experts, photographers, and parachute riggers. In February 1941, a program to produce engineering officers opened shop, recruiting civilians as commissioned specialists.

President Franklin D. Roosevelt had urged a crash growth of aviation. He had set a goal of 15,000 naval aircraft as of December 31, 1941. In June of that year there were only 3,600, and at the end of the year, some three weeks after the Japanese attacked Pearl Harbor, the usable total added up to 5,000. The figure covered not only combat planes but also trainers, transports, and utility machines.

With Europe already at war and Japan extending its reach into China, the tension between the United States and the Nipponese during 1940–1941 created the need to hurry the preparations for a conflict. Overseas American bases from the Philippines to Hawaii saw rapid increases in manpower and the machines of war. Intelligence sources monitored movements of the Japanese fleet, and air reconnaissance sought to pinpoint any shifts of significance. By December 1941, Patrol Wings 1 and 2, four squadrons of PBYs, operated out of Ford Island and Kaneohe on Oahu in the Hawaiian Islands. Short of spare planes, spare engines, spare parts, qualified men, and overhaul and repair facilities, they prowled the vast waters surrounding the islands on a limited basis. Army aircraft provided supplementary patrols, with a charter that covered up to twenty miles offshore. Navy combat aircraft were attached to the carriers. Responsibility for the implausible event of a raid on Hawaii lay with land-based Army and Marine squadrons.

Military flying was always a young man's game, and in 1941 the flyers were naturally junior officers, not privy to the high-level geopolitical interplay of world leaders. Their sources of information were largely the media of the day and scuttlebutt, the rumors inevitable to the armed services. They were hardly unaware of international tensions, but there was little sophistication to their understanding. For all of the excitement and the romance, those with golden wings played almost no role when the might of the Japanese crashed down first on the fleet at anchor in Pearl Harbor and then on the Far Eastern outpost in the Philippines.

John J. Hyland, Jr., from the USNA Class of 1934, a pilot with Patrol Squadron 26 stationed in Hawaii throughout 1940, said, "I don't recall any of the people seriously talking about a potential war with Japan and actually sitting down and preparing for it. I don't remember anyone ever studying a target folder or looking at the geography of Japan or talking about where their strengths were."

Assigned in 1941 to the Philippines, Hyland noted, "There was more of a sense of urgency in the Philippines because the Navy had evacuated dependents. But we had a number of alerts and we all thought it was crying wolf once too often. Right up to the day before the war started, we were not convinced that anything was going to come of it. At the officers' club, the night before Pearl Harbor, I made a little speech [saying] it was silly to imagine that Japan was going to attack the United States. It simply didn't make sense for a country with their strength to attack a huge country like the U.S."

Noel Gayler recalled, "The naval theory of the day was that of the fleet in being. The decisive encounter was to be between the battle lines. The destroyers were ancillary to that. The aircraft were very much ancillary to that. Even the very terminology—Aircraft Scouting Force—relegated aircraft to scouting." As a young fighter pilot he had participated in the two successive simulated attacks on Pearl Harbor. "We always came in from the south, rather than from the northeast as the Japanese did. [His memory of the direction of the mock attacks differs from that of Truman Hedding.] We almost always achieved surprise, even though it was a scheduled exercise. We almost had no difficulty penetrating to the ships, in spite of the fact that the Army Air Force were, first with their Seversky P-36s and then with their P-40s always there as a defending force. We fighters would tangle with them. We'd go around in a Dagwood [aerial dogfight] with the Army Air people but in the meantime, the torpedo planes and the dive bombers would go about their business beating up the ships.

"I thought that the higher command would see these things and take appropriate action more or less automatically. It didn't occur to me that what seemed to me to be obvious would be obvious to people with a different mind-set.

"I think that far more than either failures of intelligence or failures of awareness or the ins and outs of whether President Roosevelt did or did not want war with Japan, to me the 90 percent explanation of how something like Pearl Harbor could happen devolved from the mind-set of the commanders, all of whom had been brought up in the big-gun Navy, all of whom were identifying with battleships and believed that they were the decisive instrument, all of whom believed almost as a matter of faith that battleships were essentially invulnerable to air attack.

"I don't think any of them actually imagined that an air attack could be more than a raid. That was the terminology—air raids. The image of 'raid' suggests something that may be a nuisance, but that's it. I think it was that failure of imagination. When an officer has spent his career mastering one technology and then becomes a very senior person, he'd have to be a little bit more than human if he didn't have some reluctance to give away that and enter another technology that people vastly junior to him were the masters of." Old sea dogs, apparently, were of no different stripe than other ancients.

Whatever the talk that dominated the senior officers' messes, according to Gayler, the discussions in his junior officers' wardroom showed an interest in politics and a conviction that war with Japan was coming. David Richardson, with Fighting Squadron Five aboard the *Yorktown*, said there was a sense of the imminence of war. However, he ruefully remembered, "We did not have great respect for the Japanese, which was our mistake."

TWO

WAR BEGINS

In the early hours of December 7, 1941, as the Japanese armada steamed from the north, roughly the same course described by Truman Hedding, to within 275 miles of Hawaii, few of those who wore the wings of gold were on hand to greet the visitors. The carriers that housed the fighter units were busy elsewhere. The *Saratoga*, with Fighting Squadron Three, was completing an overhaul in San Diego. The *Lexington* had ferried a Marine scout-bomber squadron to Midway and was 425 miles southeast of that outpost. The *Enterprise*, part of a thirteen-ship task force, had completed a mission of delivering a Marine squadron to reinforce Wake Island.

On its return voyage, bad weather delayed by a day the refueling of the Big E's destroyer screen. When the morning of December 7 dawned, instead of being moored at Pearl Harbor, the carrier was plowing through the water some 250 miles west. All hands anticipated liberty in Honolulu and the airmen expected to get an early start. Pilots and crews from Scouting Six supplemented by a trio from Bombing Six manned their eighteen SBDs at 6:15 A.M. and revved their engines for a combat air patrol that would culminate in a landing at the Ford Island base on Oahu. These SBDs were early versions of the Dauntless. They lacked self-sealing fuel tanks and armor to protect the cockpit. Their weaponry was a .30-caliber machine gun for the radioman or passenger in the rear and a pair of either .30s or .50s forward. None of the planes carried bombs.

About 6:30 A.M., a lookout aboard the supply ship *Antares* spotted a small submarine barely a mile from Pearl Harbor. The *Antares* notified the nearby destroyer *Ward*, which quickly bore down on the interloper. Meanwhile, Ensign William P. Tanner of VP-14 (part of Patrol Wing 1), flying a PBY-5 on the routine morning surveillance of the waters around the islands, saw the destroyer swiftly bearing down upon the sub now in a dive. Tanner loosed a pair of smoke bombs to pinpoint the undersea vessel's location. When the *Ward* opened fire with deck guns and followed up with depth charges, Tanner, although uncertain whether the target was not American, chimed in with his own depth bombs. His attack was the first from the air by the Navy against the Japanese. Tanner radioed a description of the incident to his headquarters at the Kanoehe Naval Air Station.

When Tanner's message finally passed through channels to Commander Logan Ramsay, the CO for Patrol Wings 1 and 2, stationed in the islands, he drew up a search plan. But without authorization to set things in motion and dispatch his fleet of PBYs, Ramsay could only wait for the upper echelons to react. Catalina flying boats lay quietly at the moorings or in hangars and on the fields at Kanoehe and Ford Island. On the *Enterprise*, Air Group Commander Howard L. "Brigham" Young lifted off the deck at 6:18, and the last SBD rose into the air at 6:29. At about 6:00 A.M., due north of Hawaii, the Japanese fleet, which had closed to within 250 miles of Oahu, had dispatched the first wave of the 181 Japanese planes.

The earliest of the marauders swooped down upon the ships, parked Army and Marine planes, airfields, hangars, and barracks. At Kaneohe, four PBYs, separated from one another by about 1,000 yards, rode at anchor in the bay. Service crews in launches were being ferried out to the Catalinas when the first wave swept over the base. Machine guns sprayed the small craft in the water along with the airplanes. Within seconds, flames engulfed the quartet of planes and the four small boats were shattered. Dead and wounded lay in the water while other men struggled to swim to shore.

Arthur W. Price, an aviation metalsmith assigned to VP-14, one of the squadrons in Patrol Wing 1, said, "We had 36 airplanes at Kaneohe that morning, brand-new. Three were in the air. That left 33 at the base and we lost 33. We had two anchored in the bay that were sunk, strafed, and the others were up in the hangar or on the ramp. They were all burned, bombed."

James Ogden, an enlisted man in 1928 who earned an appointment to the Naval Academy in 1929 and completed flight training in

1936, was with VP-23, stationed at Ford Island, just across the water from where the huge battleships were anchored. Ogden was in the shower at the Bachelor Officers' Quarters shortly before 8:00 A.M. "In the shower I didn't hear very much but when I got out, airplanes were flying around and I thought the stupid doggone Army aviators didn't know enough to stay in bed on Sunday morning. There were some loud noises and vibration on the island and I went to the window with a towel around me. A bunch of black smoke was coming up from down near our hangars. They did have a trash dump there and I said it was very, very peculiar to be burning stuff on Sunday morning.

"I looked over towards Barbers Point and Ewa [site of the Marine airfield] and here was a TBD [U.S. Navy torpedo bomber] steaming up. I said, 'Good God, that guy's going against the course rules,' because we were all supposed to steer out that way but not come back that way. It kept coming, approaching Pearl City where the Pan Am [Pan American World Airways] docks were and the plane had a torpedo. Then he turned and headed right for me. He dropped the torpedo and I was in a three-ring circus, watching that torpedo track coming across. About the same time this guy ducked up over the *Utah* [a battleship] and banked by my window about 50 feet away. I could practically see the configuration of his eyes. [What] struck me was the great big round meatballs on each one of those wings. I was surprised. I decided it wasn't a TBD and I noticed that the *Utah* had received its calling card."

Ogden said that after he dressed, someone offered a ride to the ramp. "When I got to the squadron hangar, there was obviously much confusion. Most of our planes which were out in the open were damaged or destroyed. There was one plane, which I assumed had been in our undamaged hangar that was being prepared for flight. Our skipper Massie Hughes showed up. With his pants over his pajamas, he had dashed to wing headquarters for instruction. There he had been given a search sector from a plan drawn up by Logan Ramsay.

"Massie saw me and the plane ready to go and said, 'Come on, Jimmy, I've got this search sector so we'll go out and look for them. Pick yourself a crew.' I was looking for another pilot and some people to man the guns who could hit something. Fortunately, I was the gunnery officer so didn't have much trouble picking Swede [Theodore S.] Thueson [then an enlisted flyer] for the third pilot and bow gun position and a couple of sharpshooters for the waist gun positions.

"Normally, the skipper [Massie] would have been at the controls but for some reason protocol was bypassed and I made the takeoff and landing, and most if not all of the flying that day. As soon as the beaching gear was off, there was no thought of wind direction, channel or warmup—the throttles went on full and we headed general toward Middle Loch. I did notice some heavy timbers that caused me to do some juggling to avoid hitting them with my wing-tip floats. It was not our regular channel but I could see far enough ahead that I knew I could get off. I took off for Barbers Point at such a level that if the tail gunner wanted to, he could have cut cane all the way."

It was roughly a half hour since the enemy had struck when Ogden got his ship off the ground. "There seemed to be a lull. I did not see any fighters making their strafing runs. I assume they were otherwise occupied. We were at the opposite side of Ford Island from any torpedo planes or dive bombers. They wouldn't have bothered with me anyway, because they had something else to shoot at."

He dismissed any assertions that his had been the first Navy plane to take off. "There were people taking off in anything [utility planes, trainers] that was available. People were getting up in anything that they could throw a rock out of." Indeed, there were tales of men who flew noncombat aircraft, carrying a rifle as a means of defense. Some of the big ships, such as the cruiser *Northampton*, catapulted a pair of planes into the air. Ogden, following orders, flew out to sea in a vain search to locate the enemy fleet. He came upon the *Enterprise*, but he believed its crew recognized a PBY as a friendly and thus took no action.

Like others with families in the islands, he admitted to an initial high anxiety: "When you're sitting out there and you have a Japanese maid at home and a young bride and a year-old child, you start wondering what's going on back there. Then you . . . wonder who's in charge back at Ford Island. Nobody tells you anything and then you start wondering suppose we find this group. What then? I guess [we'd] be able to get off the plain language dispatch before we get shot down, but if we do, is anybody going to hear it? And if they hear it, what in the hell can they do about it?

"I knew that the *Enterprise* was not in a position . . . to launch even if we found out where [the enemy fleet] was. Even if we found

[them] they weren't going to send any planes until they found out where they were going to go. By that time they would be to hell and gone, and so what? It gave you cause to think, 'Why am I doing this in the first place? Suppose I do what I'm supposed to do?' But we didn't close our eyes. It [locating the Japanese] might have been a historical thing but it could have been a personal catastrophe." Ogden was absolutely correct. Had he found them, the condition of the Hawaii-based aircraft and ships would have precluded any response. And the *Enterprise* was not only too far away, but it would have been overwhelmed by the superior Japanese forces.

Floyd Thorn, whose VP-44 was also stationed at Ford Island, said he was sharing a room at the Moana Hotel with a young woman when they heard a rumbling sound. "I knew it was bombing, so we went down to the lobby to try to get back to the base. She had to get back to the hospital. I started off with a bad taste in my mouth when the cab driver wanted $100 to take me to the train. He saw the business end of my .45 pistol. If I would have had the time I would have marched him to the brig. But he took us to the train. We got on a flatcar and rode to the [end]. She got off and headed for Hickam Field, and I tried to get to Ford Island. But there were no boats—fire everywhere and oil.

"We got into the water and started swimming [the distance was about a quarter of a mile]. There were three of us from the squadron. As the skipper said later, that made it collective stupidity. But we were trying to get to our squadron office. Our planes were burning. Our standing orders were that if anything started we were to get to our squadron headquarters . . . to report for duty under any circumstances. A chief saw us [in the water] and sent a motor whaleboat to pick us up. We got to the island about the time the second pass came over, the tail end of it."

While the planes burned, civilians from the families of some of the Navy personnel tried to aid the wounded, who lay in rows on the ground. A dozen pilots from VP-44 reached their Ford Island headquarters, but with no aircraft to fly and the barracks destroyed, they were all taken by launch and then railroad into Honolulu. Thorn would again spend the night in the Moana Hotel.

A few Army fighters managed to get off the ground to engage the enemy. But there was little air resistance to the attack. Meanwhile, the SBDs from the *Enterprise*, having fanned out for their patrol, now strung out in no particular formation, approached the islands. In the rear cockpits of some of the planes, the radiomen picked up the

Honolulu broadcasts of popular music. Vice Admiral William F. Halsey, Jr., commander of the task force and aboard the *Enterprise*, was having breakfast with his flag secretary, Lieutenant H. Douglas Moulton, when the telephone rang. Moulton answered it, then turned to Halsey and said the staff duty officer had just received a message informing him of an air raid on Pearl Harbor.

According to Robert J. Cressman and Michael Wenger in their book *Stout Hearts and Steady Nerves*, Halsey responded, "My God! They're shooting at our own planes. Get the word to Kimmel [Admiral Husband E., commander of the Pacific Fleet and stationed in Hawaii]." Because of the requirement for radio silence from Halsey's task force, no signal had been sent to alert Hawaii to the arrival of the aircraft from Scouting Six. Halsey's confusion vanished moments later, when a second communication announced, "Air raid on Pearl Harbor. This is no drill."

Ignorant of what had occurred, the hapless flyers from the *Enterprise* now blundered into the midst of the furious assault upon the ships, planes, and airfields. At about 8:30, Commander Young, the leader of the group, and his wingman, Ensign Perry Teaff, passed over the Barbers Point landmark. Both noticed a group of planes wheeling in a column over the Marine base at Ewa. The Americans thought these must be Army fighters practicing maneuvers. The Navy pilots avoided them and descended toward Ford Island. Even more curious, puffs of black smoke from exploding antiaircraft shells dappled the skies.

Suddenly, a single fighter veered off and took a run at Teaff. The ensign figured an Army pilot wanted to play and obligingly offered no evasive action. The Mitsubishi A6M2, the famed Zero, opened fire with its 7.7-mm machine guns. At a range of only seventy-five feet, the bullets ripped through the horizontal stabilizer and grazed the wings and fuselage. Somehow, neither Teaff nor Radioman Third Class Edgar Jinks was hit. As the now clearly identified foe returned for a second assault, Teaff, aware this was a genuine threat, executed a sharp right turn. Meanwhile, Jinks unlimbered his .30-caliber machine gun and retaliated with a burst.

The Zero retreated but now focused on Young and his Dauntless. The air group commander yanked his SBD into violent gyrations, attempting to escape the enemy. According to *Strong Hearts and Steady Nerves*, Young yelled into the intercom to his passenger, Lieutenant Commander Bromfield B. Nichol, a staff officer carrying reports on the Wake Island situation, "For Christ's sake, Brom, get the gun out!" Unfortunately, Nichol had probably not worked with a free gun in a rear cockpit during the fifteen years since he had won his wings at Pensacola. For all of his frantic fumbling, he could not get the .30-caliber operational. Young controlled the fixed forward guns, but they were of no use against the quick-darting Zero.

Young and Teaff, believing they would never make it back to the carrier, now desperately tried to touch down on the Ford Island field. While they were momentarily free of their Japanese tormentors, they encountered a blistering barrage of antiaircraft fire from friendly forces who regarded anything in the sky as malevolent.

Young vainly tried to dissuade the gunners with recognition signals but he endured tracers all the way across Oahu. Not until the plane rolled to a stop at Ford Island did the firing cease. Nichols later recalled, "[We] went through the damndest amount of antiaircraft fire . . . that I have ever seen." Teaff, unable to land on his first pass, slipped through a second withering round of ground fire and joined his commander on the field. Both planes had been struck several times.

Others from the early-morning combat patrol were not so fortunate. Marines at Ewa saw an American plane collide with one of their Japanese tormentors. Flaming wreckage from both ships fell to the ground. SBD pilot John Vogt and radioman Sid Pierce did not survive the crash. Radios on the *Enterprise* picked up fragments of conversations. They heard a frantic message from the Dauntless piloted by Ensign Manny Gonzalez: "This is 6-B-3, an American plane. Do not shoot." Then followed an order to his radioman, Leonard Kozelek: "Stand by to get out the rubber boat." That was the final transmission from Gonzalez. A later action report from the Japanese carrier *Shokaku* described an encounter between an enemy two-seater and six Vals—dive-bombers—that blasted the American plane. Gonzalez and Kozelek disappeared.

Lieutenant Clarence Dickinson, with his radioman, William Miller, and their wingman, Ensign John McCarthy, with Mitchell Cohn in the rear seat, like the ill-fated John Vogt, neared Ewa. Miller, Dickinson's rear-seat companion, was on the final lap of his enlistment, and this would be his last flight before returning to the States and discharge. He had remarked to Dickinson that he was the only enlisted man in the squadron who had never suffered a water landing. As Miller climbed into the plane, he said, "I hope you won't get me wet today, sir."

When the pair sighted Ewa, Dickinson noticed splashes offshore, probably incorrectly fused antiaircraft shells. Figuring these must have been fired in error by a coast artillery unit, he remarked to Miller, "Tomorrow, the Army will certainly catch hell for that."

Indications of something askew increased. Smoke boiled up, all but obscuring the Ewa field. A towering cloud stood above the harbor area known as "Battleship Row." Black puffs of antiaircraft fire triggered greater alarm. As a precaution, Dickinson and McCarthy climbed to 4,000 feet. It was not nearly enough. Overhead, five Zeros, fighter cover for those working over Ewa and other installations, pounced on the two Americans. A 3,000-foot dive could not shake the pursuit. They poured bullets and shells into McCarthy's SBD, and it began to burn. Unable to shake them or recover, McCarthy wrenched open the canopy and bailed out. The stricken plane, with Mitchell Cohn wounded, dead, or unable to free himself from the rear seat, hurtled to the ground. McCarthy landed in a tree. He broke his leg climbing down.

The Japanese now savaged Dickinson's plane. While radioman Miller tried to deter them with his puny .30-caliber machine gun, the enemy overwhelmed the Dauntless. Already wounded twice, his ammunition all gone, Miller screamed in agony as pilot Dickinson got off a burst when an enemy ship crossed in front of him. Fire ate into Dickinson's left fuel tanks; control cables did not respond. As the plane began to spin, Dickinson yelled for Miller to bail out. The pilot himself then tumbled from the cockpit. Dickinson reached the ground safely, but his radioman perished.

A different but equally dismal experience befell Ensign Edward Deacon as he and wingman Ensign Wilbur Roberts approached Oahu around 8:20. With some astonishment, they viewed a flock of some thirty green-painted planes only 100 feet above the sea. Cressman and Wenger wrote that Roberts remarked on the dubious insignia, the red meatballs on the wings. He recalled thinking that it was stupid for the Army "to paint their planes like that for war games—someone might take them for Japanese." Although they were only some 400 yards apart, the American and Japanese flights acted as if this were routine, and both continued on their own courses.

A few minutes later, Deacon and Roberts saw smoke rising from Pearl Harbor as well as geysers erupting in the water. As they puzzled over the strange phenomena, Deacon's radioman, Audrey Coslett, tried to raise the tower at Ford Island for landing instructions. He heard a babble of voices that made no sense. But then Coslett and Donald Jones, the backseat occupant for Roberts, both listened to the ominous transmission from the doomed Manny Gonzalez.

In the two aircraft, the free guns were quickly mounted and loaded while the fixed ones were charged. Seeing smoke from burning planes at Ewa and some twenty Japanese planes headed for them, Deacon and Roberts changed their plans and flew toward the big Army base, Hickam Field. The course carried them directly over an Army post and the Fleet Machine Gun School, where trigger-twitchy Marines and GIs brought to bear anything that would fire on the two low-flying aircraft. A battery of the coast artillery eagerly focused upon the Navy planes. The ground forces spewed metal and lead from Browning automatic rifles, .30-caliber, bolt-action, single-shot Springfield '03s, .50- and .30-caliber machine guns, 20-mm anti-aircraft guns, and even three-inch shells.

To add to the peril, a pair of Zeros assayed a pass at Deacon, but the friendlies on the ground inflicted the real damage. Bullets ripped into Deacon's plane, inflicting a serious wound in Coslett's shoulder and neck. Deacon's left thigh was grazed; his parachute straps were severed. The Dauntless lurched, then plunged toward the water as the engine quit. Furious that his own side had brought him down, Deacon controlled the crash well enough to make a wheels-up landing in the shallows beside Hickam. He then bandaged the wounded radioman, broke out the raft, and assisted Coslett into it. As the pilot paddled toward the shore, soldiers directed sporadic rounds his way, but fortunately they missed. Seeing the white star insignia on the downed plane, an Army crash boat set out toward them. But even as it took them aboard and headed for the dock, troops on land fired at that craft before it finally reached the safety of the shore.

Although gasoline was leaking from his left wing, Roberts set down at Hickam with his seriously damaged Dauntless. However, neither the pilot nor radioman Jones had been injured. The pair, in fact, were able to repair their plane sufficiently for it to fly again.

Seven of the contingent that the *Enterprise* had launched that morning escaped injury. Scouting Six's executive, Lieutenant Wilmer Earl Gallaher, had gathered a half-dozen SBDs and led them to where they would be somewhat out of harm's way. During a lull, he tried to bring them in at Ewa, but after they touched down, the Marines asked them to leave, arguing that they would be strafed by the next wave. Back in the air, three of the SBDs waded through the ack-

ack at Ford Island and set down there. The other four elected to try Ewa again, and this time they were given refuge, their planes rearmed and refueled.

Unlike Jim Ogden, Tom Moorer, a member of the Class of '33 and assigned to VP-23, was scheduled to fly a routine patrol the morning of December 7. "I was leaving home when I saw the Japanese planes. My co-pilot was with me. We rushed out as fast as we could. We arrived while the first wave was striking Hickam Field and Pearl Harbor. We managed to commandeer a boat and went immediately to the location of our squadron on Ford Island. We arrived right in the middle of the activity that was laid on by the first wave.

"I had a grandstand view. I saw the torpedo attack on the battleships just a couple of hundred yards away. I saw both the *Pennsylvania* and the *Nevada* get hit. The *Cassan* and the *Downes*, two destroyers, were in drydock and I saw them get hit. I had a good view of many Japanese planes falling. About the time the first wave was through, the second wave arrived. At this time the defenses were much better organized, particularly the gun crews on the battleships and cruisers and destroyers. There were many planes shot down by the antiaircraft. It was so thick you could walk out on the parking area and scoop shrapnel up with your hands. It was just like snow around here, almost.

"[We felt] very helpless because we didn't have any aircraft that we could operate. Everyone wanted to retaliate. Our planes were out on the parking area and many, or most of them, for that matter, were shot up quite severely. Before they could take off," said Moorer, "it was mandatory that we make a very careful inspection to make certain that there was no damage to hydraulic lines or control wires, things of that kind." For most of the day, he busied himself with helping repair planes.

"Finally when we reported that we had a couple of planes flyable, Admiral Kimmel felt that the most likely sector or area in which we would find the Japanese was southwest [the enemy as it retreated was to the north]. In other words they would be going back to Kwajalein or Truk, somewhere like that."

Moorer's usual PBY happened to have been less damaged than others, and the practice was to fly one's own airplane. "It was an eerie experience to take off because there was about half an inch of fuel oil on the water from those battleships which had been struck with torpedoes and were still burning and smoking as we went by,

trying to get flying speed with all these ships just off the wing tips. It
was difficult [because] as soon as we hit a wave generated by the
boats—there were hundreds of boats going back and forth with the
wounded—oil splashed up on the windshield and I never did see
anything until I was well clear of the island. It was a 100 percent instrument takeoff.

"I headed right for the hills and had to make a 180 degree turn
and go out to sea. We managed to get some gasoline and get out and
clean off the windshields on the outside. You couldn't do that with
modern airplanes because you'd be going too fast. But in those days
you could stand up in the slipstream of those machines and get
away with it." Moorer completed his flight, an eighteen-hour patrol,
without incident but also without finding the Japanese fleet.

According to Jim Ogden, he spent in the neighborhood of twelve
hours prowling the skies while searching for the enemy. During this
period he heard not a word over his radio. "We came back around
8:30 in the evening. It was black as the inside of a cow. When we got
to Barbers Point, it was raining like hell and we tried to call somebody on the radio and got no answer. I don't know whether it was
because we weren't transmitting or because nobody was listening.

"We didn't have any recognition signals so the first thing to do
was to try to act as friendly as possible, turning on every light that
[you] would think of because only a damn fool would try to come in
in the dark. The next idea was where to land. Under normal circumstances the landing area closest to our ramp would have been the
Dry Dock Channel, but [it] had dredging rigs and long big pipes to
take the spoil, so that narrowed the channel in the dark. The only
light on the island was the *Arizona* burning, which wasn't much help
in making a night landing.

"We decided our best bet would be the Pearl City channel and
hope somebody had the foresight that day to clean up the debris in
the channel. This was a very fortunate decision because had we
elected to come in the other channel, which had a row of approach
lights right on the edge of the land as you were making your approach, the *Nevada* was beached alongside those landing lights. If
we had come in and hadn't see this in time, we'd have landed right
in the mast of the *Nevada*.

"We [headed for] the other place, and somebody had been
thoughtful enough to remove the debris. We went cheerfully along
our way, acting friendly as all get-out. At about that stage of the
game, four fighter planes from the *Enterprise* [actually, there were

six F4F Wildcats] did come in, and they didn't take the precaution of acting friendly. People got unfriendly on the beach and started the biggest fireworks display that has been seen in Hawaii, including all the Chinese New Years put together. We were only seeing one round in five, but the tracers lit up the sky like crazy. The shrapnel and everything was falling around like it was rain on the water. During the day, the guns for 35 airplanes had all been deployed around the parking areas and they had joined in the celebration. The Army was shooting off some of their small antiaircraft stuff.

"This got to be a very hairy operation. Every once in a while I got the impression that they were shooting at us. I turned off the lights so they didn't have a good aiming point. But then somebody would see our exhaust flames or hear the noise and start acting unfriendly, so I turned the lights back on again. Finally, we got to the ramp and were aboard."

Halsey, aboard the *Enterprise*, which had hoisted its battle flag, ordered a series of sweeps in hopes of finding the enemy task force. Luckily for the Americans, they missed the target. Badly outnumbered and vulnerable because of the lack of self-sealing tanks, they would not have survived an encounter. Along with aircraft from the carrier, the remnants of the group that had blundered into the Pearl Harbor attack went in search of the enemy. Nine planes scoured the sea north of Hawaii, finding nothing. To the dismay of the Japanese airmen, the admiral in command, Chuichi Nagumo, decided the first strikes had been sufficient. He ordered the fleet to head for home.

Distant sightings of unidentified ships and planes led to a late-afternoon search from the flight deck of the *Enterprise*. A strike group of nineteen torpedo planes, six dive-bombers, and six fighters roared off the flattop shortly before 5:00 P.M. It was one more fruitless effort. Darkness crept over the sea and the aerial attack group returned to the carrier. But the *Enterprise*, fearful that there might be an enemy sub lurking nearby, was reluctant to turn on its lights. On the other hand, the airmen in the torpedo planes, having prowled the area for almost four hours, felt they lacked enough fuel to safely navigate the Oahu mountain range on a night that one described "as dark as the inside of a goat's belly." The *Enterprise* acceded to their pleas. With a minimum of lights for a night recovery and with additional destroyer protection, the carrier began taking aboard the aircraft. The diarist for Fighting Six reported, "It was pitch dark and several of their pilots had never been up in a TBD before at night—

much less with a torpedo aboard! As the torpedoes were few and precious it was decided to land them aboard, torpedoes and all, dark as it was. They all got down and no trouble." It was well after 9:00 P.M. before the last Devastator came home.

While the *Enterprise* accepted its TBDs and SBDs, the half-dozen fighters flying cover for the mission were directed to put down at Ford Island. Aware of the confusion and friendly fire that had greeted his group from the carrier during the morning, Commander "Brigham" Young expected to direct the arrival using a low-powered transmitter at Ford Island. Army antiaircraft units and the still-viable ships in the harbor had been cautioned that a flight of Wildcats would be arriving. The advisory in at least one instance said that the Navy planes would show green lights.

As the six F4Fs passed over the first landfall, Barbers Point, they mistook their location. Repositioned, however, they flew toward the Ford Island field. The flight leader, Lieutenant (j.g.) Fritz Hebel, contacted the control tower, and Young instructed him to land immediately. For some reason Hebel announced an intention to circle left around the island before coming in. Because of the inadequate power of the transmitter, Hebel apparently did not hear Young insist that he land immediately. The problem was that, in their original passage, the Wildcats showed the green lights, but when they turned, their red lights on the port side winkled in the night.

As the planes, a mere 500 feet above the ground, flew over the battleship *Pennsylvania* in its dry dock, a gunner on that vessel opened fire. Captain James Shoemaker, the CO of the Ford Island Naval Base, in the cliché of combat, said, "All hell broke loose . . . countless machine guns firing thousands of tracer bullets back and forth across the field." Although all had been warned of the friendly arrivals, the reaction was "Those who are shooting must know something we don't," and they quickly added their firepower.

Ensign Jim Daniels, in one of the Wildcats, instantly cranked up his landing gear and sped out toward the safety of the sea. Over his radio, he heard Flight Commander Hebel cry out, "My God, what's happened?" A burst of antiaircraft fire struck the ship flown by Ensign Herbert Menges. His Grumman slammed into houses and buildings near the waterfront of Pearl City, setting numerous structures on fire. Four days would elapse before Menges's charred corpse was recovered.

Hebel, giving up on Ford Island, ran toward Wheeler Field. But at that Army installation, the gunnery there tore into his plane. The best Hebel could manage was a flat crash landing. At the time, U.S. combat aircraft were equipped only with lap belts, no shoulder harnesses. As the shattered aircraft bounced over the ground, the pilot's head banged against the gunsight, fracturing his skull. Soldiers extricated him from the wreckage, but he died of his injuries shortly after being brought to a hospital.

A five-inch shell knocked out Ensign Gayle Hermann's engine. Nevertheless he glided his aircraft through the continuing hail of fire to land at the Ford Island golf course. Ensign David Flynn had elected to escape out to sea, but when he turned back over land, his engine suddenly quit. At 1,200 feet in the air, he left his airplane to parachute into a cane field. Soldiers, convinced he was a downed Japanese aviator, heaped further humiliation upon him. They seized him as a prisoner, relenting only after his use of American profanity persuaded them of his origins.

Ensign Eric Allen, wingman for Jim Daniels, barely had time to abandon his F4F when ground fire set it ablaze and it exploded. As he dangled in his chute, he was hit by rifle fire and fell into the harbor waters. Pulled from the sea, he succumbed to his wounds a day later.

The last of the Wildcats, that of Jim Daniels, low on gas, contacted the Ford Island tower. After some back-and-forth chatter in which both Daniels and Brig Young in the tower cautiously attempted to confirm identities, Daniels was told, "Come in as low as possible, as fast as possible and with no lights." Traveling between 150 and 180 knots, Daniels streaked to the ground. Machine-gun bullets flew overhead as he rolled swiftly around tar barrels and parked trucks, obstacles to enemy landings. Still, as Daniels taxied to a ramp, a Marine in a sandbagged emplacement took some potshots at him. Gayle Hermann, in the area, purportedly halted the fire by slugging the Marine with a pistol butt.

The *Enterprise* entered Pearl Harbor on the afternoon of December 8 to take on fuel and recover the pilots and planes that had found refuge in Hawaii. Fortunately, the Japanese had not ravaged the vast oil stores, and the replenishing of the carrier and other vessels from the task force was swiftly accomplished. Back out to sea, the *Enterprise* and her planes searched for enemy in the vicinity of the islands. Diligence brought a morsel of revenge. On December 10, Perry Teaff, who withstood two encounters of friendly fire before landing at Ford Island in an SBD-2, sighted a U-boat and dropped a 1,000-pounder as it slid under the surface. Later, "Dick" Dickinson, who had parachuted from his flaming dive-bomber following an attack by a Zero and lost his radioman, tracked that same submarine on the surface. It opened fire on him with its machine guns while he began a dive from about 5,000 feet. At 1,700 feet Dickinson released his bomb, which struck the water near the sub. The U-boat sank almost vertically, leaving a spreading oil slick. A reading of Japanese accounts after the war confirmed the destruction of the I-70.

While the naval aviators in Hawaii and some from the *Enterprise* met the enemy over Hawaii, the *Saratoga* with Fighting Three had just completed its overhaul in San Diego. Noel Gayler recalled, "I was actually on the beach with my wife, and somebody said, 'Get back to your squadron right away.' We got back and the radio was blaring the news. We pilots and the squadron wives all sat around on ammunition boxes all afternoon while we belted up ammunition. We were so unready, we didn't even have the ammunition belted up."

In the Philippine Islands, some 5,000 miles west of Hawaii, word of the attack on Pearl Harbor reached naval headquarters in Manila at 2:30 A.M. local time when a radio operator intercepted the unencrypted Morse code message issued by the Honolulu-based offices of the Pacific Fleet commander: "Air raid on Pearl Harbor. This is no drill."

Because conflict with Japan had seemed almost inevitable, Admiral Thomas C. Hart, CO of the U.S. Asiatic Fleet, had ordered most of his ships to leave the islands and steam south, well out of range of any attack from land-based planes on Formosa. As in Hawaii, air defense of the Philippines rested with the Army, which had several squadrons of P-40 fighters and thirty-five of the Army Air Corps's latest weapon, the B-17 Flying Fortress, as well as some aging and obsolete bombers. The Commonwealth of the Philippines mustered its own air force, a ragtag bunch of trainers and badly outdated fighters and bombers.

Aircraft carriers were not part of the Asiatic Fleet, and the Navy's air arm in the archipelago consisted of Patrol Wing 10's twenty-four PBYs. Admiral Hart, on his own initiative, had dispatched the Catalinas to reconnoiter Cam Ranh Bay, an anchorage for Japanese naval vessels in what was then Indo-China. Patrol crews also examined portions of the ocean that lay between the Philippines and Japanese bases on Formosa and conquered territory in China.

John Hyland, who had thought that Japan would never have the temerity to attack the United States, flew regular patrols for VP-102. He remembered crossing paths with Japanese airplanes flying out of Formosa in the weeks before the war. While Hyland found a sense of urgency in the Philippines, he also recalled a number of alerts that led him to feel "It was crying wolf once too often." Hyland noted, "There was absolutely no relationship with the Army Air Corps." The isolation mirrored that of the other organizations within the Navy and Army.

Hyland had attended a party at the officers' club on the eve of the attack upon Hawaii and was awakened in the small hours of the morning with the news that war had begun. "As I recall it, the wording of one of the messages that came from Admiral Hart was 'We are at war. Conduct yourselves accordingly.' There was no one in the squadron, including the captain, who had ever been at war. We had no idea of how you conducted yourself and what that meant."

The enemy quickly dictated policy. Seven of the PBYs at Luzon Island's Olongapo base, sitting on the water, were strafed by a pair of fighters who set them afire, sinking every one. Within a week, Japanese raids had wiped out half of the PBYs. Hyland noted, "Our patrols were useless. If you saw any enemy forces, there was nobody left to do anything about them."

What remained of the patrol wing in the Philippines flew to the Dutch East Indies, where a unified ABDA (American, British, Dutch, Australian) command hoped to block the advance of the Japanese into these islands. Not only was the area rich in vital raw materials, but the location was of immense strategic value, posing a threat to Australia and indeed the entire South Pacific. One of the submarines that evacuated key personnel embarked all but two of the naval aviators and took them to Australia. Left behind in the Philippines were some ground crews and unlucky pilots from the squadrons of Patrol Wing 10 who could not be flown out. They served as ground troops during the last resistance on Bataan, where they were either killed or captured.

Hyland and those who did escape started to fly missions from the port of Ambon in the Molucca Islands, southeast of the Philippines and west of New Guinea. The slow-moving Catalinas—with a maximum speed of 115 to 175 mph and their puny waist guns, which could not deal with high-side attacks—were hardly much of an offensive threat. As the Japanese overran the Philippine Archipelago, Hyland led a section of six PBYs, loaded with 500-pound bombs, in an attack on Jolo, a port occupied by the enemy on the southern tip of the archipelago. "We took off at dusk [December 27, 1941] and flew through the night. As we got close to Jolo, I was absolutely astonished to be attacked by fighters. Four of our six airplanes were shot down on that one mission. I and one other airplane turned and ran once we started to get the fighter attacks. We were never over the target but I did see a cruiser there." On another mission, his three-plane section attempted to bomb a ship from 14,000 feet. "The captain of the ship watched the bombs and then made radical turns to evade them."

In addition to their long-range reconnaissance, the flying boats, as they would throughout the war, rescued downed airmen. While on a scouting mission, Hyland recalled a message about an Australian Hudson bomber that had ditched in the sea some thirty-five miles from him. "I headed over and sure enough there was the wreckage in the water. I could see one man waving his arm at us. It was a very still day and I decided I would try to pick him up. It was the only time I ever landed a PBY in open ocean. What I wasn't prepared for was that however smooth and nice it looked from the air it was really rough, big swells. I remember hitting like a ton of bricks on top of one swell. It seemed to me we bounced about a couple hundred feet.

"I taxied up and we picked up an Australian with a very badly broken leg. There were no other survivors. After we loaded him aboard and was ready to take off, word came that the plane captain [engineer], a chief named Schnitzer, was not aboard. He had gone into the water to help load the wounded man, but lost his grip on the plane and drifted off.

"My God, what a decision I had to make. I landed in the water and I almost lost my airplane because it's so rough and now I've lost my plane captain. I [was not] sure I could ever get off in this situation. Bobbing up and down in the swells and trough, we put a man on the wing and turned about looking for Schnitzer. It couldn't have been more than ten minutes of taxiing when I ran right into old Schnitzer. There he was floating in the water in his life jacket. He was completely unconcerned." Many months after Hyland returned with the rescued man and his crew intact, he received a Distinguished Flying Cross.

Along with the remnants of Hyland's outfit, VP-23, with Tom Moorer, originally ticketed for the Philippines, received new orders that directed it to Surabaya, on Java. Within a few days, Moorer was also working out of Ambon. "We would take off before day and come in after dark so the Japanese couldn't catch the planes on the water or strafe them. They would put beaching gear on [the aircraft] and tow them back into a big forest so they were not visible from the air.

Painfully aware of the vulnerability of his aircraft, Moorer said the basic technique was to avoid conflict. "The best defense we had was a sharp lookout and a big cloud. As soon as you saw a Japanese fighter, you'd go into the biggest thunder cloud we could find and there were many of them there. The Japanese would not come in there.

"We had one pilot, Ensign Dade who shot down a fighter. He went back to Surabaya and claimed it. They were going to give him a probable shoot-down. This made Dade mad as hell. The next day he shot down another one and it hit a spot on the water. He landed alongside of the plane, took his knife and cut the rising sun out of the tail. He took it back and said, 'How about this? Is this confirmed?' Unfortunately he was killed shortly afterwards. An awful lot of planes would go out and just never come back."

After MacArthur and the remnants of the Bataan troops retreated to the island fortress of Corregidor, off Manila, a pair of PBYs flew in from Darwin, Australia. Stripped of bombs and even ammunition for defense, the flying boats brought medical supplies, fuses, and ammunition for the defenders. For the return trip, the planes took aboard Army nurses, high-ranking officers, and other valued personnel. Unfortunately, although one lifted off successfully, on takeoff the other PBY ripped its bottom on a submerged rock. Its passengers traveled to one of the remaining outposts still held by the Americans in hopes of another route of escape but became prisoners. The crew of the damaged ship repaired it enough to fly to Darwin.

The Japanese rolled over the ABDA forces, and along with everyone else, the patrol units in the East Indies received orders to flee to Australia. "I finally left Ambon," said Moorer, "and I had four crews on my plane because the other airplanes were destroyed. I think I had something like thirty people in that airplane. You couldn't get from one end to the other. They were just packed in there. But we got everybody out."

THREE

THE ENGAGEMENTS BEGIN

When the Japanese turned the waters of Pearl Harbor into a killing sea, the *Saratoga* bearing Fighting Three was at San Diego, having just completed its overhaul at the Puget Sound Navy Yard. In the ready room, Onia B. "Bert" Stanley, Jr., an ensign through the Naval Reserve who had logged more than 1,000 hours in the air, learned of the devastating blow. He noted, "Our preparations for just another trip to Hawaii were altered and speeded by each additional news flash. 'Guam has fallen to the enemy—Wake, Midway, the Philippines, Singapore are being attacked—Transports are now landing troops on Oahu—Parachute troops are striking at many points—Most of the ships in Pearl Harbor are sunk or burning.'

"There was a bewildering mixture of truth and error in those first reports. Plans were changed abruptly and we assumed a war status. We drew two more planes available at the station and belted ammunition far into the night. Our planes were dispersed about the field at North Island, and the loading of the *Saratoga* was accelerated. Two squadrons of Army fighters landed in the afternoon and stood by while we were hoisted aboard."

Stanley's wife, Fay, was in Hawaii. Although she lived well away from military objectives, fear flickered in his mind. "A carelessly released bomb or a fanatical machine gunner. Oh, God, if I could only know."

Stanley reported that the flattop weighed anchor the following morning for a seven-day voyage of anxiety. "The ship was put in readiness for anything. General quarters were sounded at dawn and dusk. Personnel were to wear life jackets at all times. The scouts and bombers were on patrol from early till late. Fighters were standing ready every minute of the day. The laundry was closed to save water, and meals were served catch-as-catch-can."

When the *Saratoga* neared the Hawaiians on December 14, it launched its planes, with Fighting Three directed to Kaneohe. Said Stanley, "Our first glimpse of the damage showed the skeletons of the burned and bombed PBYs. They had been piled to one side in the weeks since the attack. The framework of a burned hangar still stood gauntly black in the sunshine. The wreckage of two or three machine-gunned and burned cars stood beside the road. Broken glass had been cleared away but bullet holes still scarred the plaster of the B.O.Q. [Bachelor Officers' Quarters]."

On Monday morning, the squadron flew into Pearl Harbor, Stanley recalled. "We protected the *Sara* while she entered the channel. A submarine was suddenly reported astern of the convoy. We raced there for frantic search. It was not to be found. The wreckage about Pearl Harbor was all that we had feared. Battleships and other showed blackened superstructures above the water—a few listing drunkenly. Only the broad bottom of the training ship *Utah* was visible."

After he landed, Stanley rushed toward a phone, and a pilot from Scouting Three yelled to him, "Have you heard from your wife yet?"

"No."

"She's okay. You can get her at 76875." Stanley quickly reached Fay, and her only concern was when he could come home.

There would be no immediate reunion. On the following day, the carrier shoved off for a 2,500-mile trip to Wake Island, ferrying a squadron of Marine fighters. Under the hastily cobbled-together plan, the *Lexington* and the *Enterprise* would join the *Saratoga* in reinforcing the beleaguered garrison on Wake while hitting nearby Japanese bases and enemy ships. Because the task force needed refueling along the way, the armada could travel only at the slow pace of the oiler. Rough seas delayed completion of the actual refueling, and by December 23, the ships were still six hundred miles from Wake. Meanwhile, an invading Japanese force, initially rebuffed by the unexpectedly strong resistance of the defenders, had begun a second landing bolstered by additional naval and ground forces. A pair of Imperial Navy carriers also contributed air support.

Fearful of wasting its few remaining assets in a losing cause, the

Pacific Fleet Command abruptly ordered a reverse course, pulling the task force back from succor for Wake. "We hovered in the area two days," recalled Stanley, "and then the attack was abandoned. Someday a historian or some admiral's memoirs will tell a disinterested world of the stupid mistake we made. With so powerful a force, we could not have failed." Indeed, naval historian Samuel Eliot Morison noted critically, "The failure to relieve Wake resulted from poor seamanship and a want of decisive action." But while the two Japanese flattops temporarily were not close enough to support the transports and ships attacking Wake, they were not so far off to dismiss their threat to the American carriers. The U.S. Navy at this point was far too weak to have seriously impeded the advances of its enemy.

As the *Saratoga* retreated to Hawaii, Fighting Three tried to hone its firepower. Noel Gayler, then flight officer of the squadron and responsible for training, said, "I was always very concerned that we practice intensively our gunnery, which was firing against a sleeve towed by another fighter. It had never been the custom to do that at sea. And here we were on this long sea cruise and no opportunity to keep our gunnery skills refreshed.

"So I lobbied and lobbied and lobbied, with Jimmy [Thach, the squadron CO] to do this aboard ship. [There] were difficulties. You had to launch with the sleeve made up and a towline in a special container under the wing. We didn't have to be catapulted. But you had to recover the thing to see whether anybody had hit it. We painted the bullets to see who had gotten what hits. [It] was a little dicey for a carrier skipper. He didn't much like the idea because you he'd have to drop the thing on deck. It had a big iron ring in the front that could have done some damage. Finally, I personally pledged that I would tow, and I would bring the damn thing back and put it on the deck. The skipper reluctantly consented.

"We got off and had a successful gunnery shoot, and then I came back to drop the thing on deck. The plan was to fly up the deck, about 20 feet off, and just drop it. Somehow or other, I'll never understand but there was an air bubble or something. Just as I came over the deck I dropped about ten feet and towed that damn tow through the parked airplanes. I damaged four. The next day, they had a ceremony on deck—a big cardboard rising sun and presented me with it for destroying four American planes."

It was one of the few moments of levity at this point in the war. The year 1942 began with the American forces in the Pacific stumbling in ignominious retreat. In the Philippines, General Douglas MacArthur had withdrawn his troops onto the Bataan peninsula for a campaign that doomed them to painful defeat and culminated in an even more agonizing surrender. The naval forces, packed off first to the Dutch East Indies, where they lost ships, planes, and men, scrambled for refuge in Australia or the expanses of ocean, well away from attacks by anything less than carrier-borne planes.

Like everyone else, those in naval aviation operated on a narrow margin. There was a severe shortage of trained airmen and effective aircraft. The first months of the war had demonstrated the superiority of the enemy's air might. Nothing in the American arsenal matched the quality of the basic Japanese fighter, the Zero. It traveled faster, maneuvered quicker, and outclimbed the Navy's F4F Wildcat and, for that matter, anything the Army Air Corps could put into the sky.

The Japanese torpedo planes were much better than the lumbering, 100-mph U.S. Devastators. A further handicap lay in their tin fish. As proved at Pearl Harbor, the torpedoes fired by the Japanese performed with deadly results. But as submariners and aviators both discovered, the standard American version, the Mark 14, frequently failed to run its calculated course or just did not explode even on direct contact. To save dollars and ordnance in the prewar days, the Navy had not tested live torpedoes.

The catastrophic destruction wrought by Japanese torpedoes at Pearl Harbor demonstrated that country's grasp of ordnance technology. Noel Gayler commented, "The notion was that you couldn't use torpedoes in Pearl Harbor because it was too shallow. The torpedoes the Japanese originally had would make a deep excursion when they were dropped. But the Japanese foresaw that, and fixed up their torpedoes with wooden shrouds so they couldn't dive. And the theory was that without torpedoes you couldn't do much to battleships. They sank the *Arizona* and *Nevada* with modified fifteen-inch SAP [semi–armor piercing] dropped from a high altitude."

Only the SBD-2, the Helldiver, measured up against the foe's dive-bombers. There was a disparity in the cockpits as well. Japanese pilots at the outbreak of the war, veterans of the country's China campaigns, averaged 700 hours of flight experience while their American counterparts clocked little better than 300. There were exceptions. Fighting Three's Jimmy Thach numbered 3,500 hours, his second in command, Don Lovelace, 3,200, and three others had better than 1,200.

A few flyers, bucking the common perception, foresaw the high quality of both the Zero and the men who manned them. In the spring of 1941, Thach, the 1927 Annapolis graduate, took note of intelligence documents that suggested the Japanese possessed impressive airpower. General Claire Chennault, a prophet without honor in the U.S. Army Air Corps and hired by China to battle the Japanese, had warned that the Nipponese Zero performed better than any existing American fighter. Chennault had even forwarded a manual from a downed Zero that detailed the qualities of the plane.

As Thach recalled, "The report described a new Japanese aircraft, a fighter, that performed far better than anything we had. Some of our pilots just didn't believe it and said, 'This can't be. It is a gross exaggeration.' I felt we should give it some credence because it sounded like a fighter pilot who knew what he was talking about it. As it turned out, this Japanese plane did have a climb of about 3,000 feet per minute. It could turn inside of anything and it did have a lot more speed than we did, even carrying more gasoline. This was the Zero. I decided we had better do something about this airplane." When the *Saratoga* docked at Pearl Harbor a week after the attack, Thach spoke with one of the few American pilots who managed to get off the ground. "He confirmed that a Zero could turn inside of anything we had. He said he had pulled up and was on this fellow's tail and was just about ready to shoot him and the Zero just flipped right over his back and was on his tail and shot him down."

During one of the *Saratoga*'s previous periods in port, Thach worked with matchsticks on his dining room table, trying to design tactics that would compensate for the slower speed and lesser rate of climb of the F4F Grumman Wildcat. He abandoned the standard three-plane V formation for a loose combination in which the Wildcats fought in pairs with a leader and his wingman.

In Thach's choreography, the F4Fs would fly parallel courses. When one was attacked, both planes would bank steeply toward each other. "The quick turn does two things to the enemy pilot," explained Thach. "It throws off his aim and because he usually tries to follow his target, it leads him around into a position to be shot at by the other part of the team. The Zero had us beat in three categories ... but I believed we had one advantage; if we could ever get into position to use it. We had good guns and could shoot and hit, even if we had only a fleeting second to take aim." Although he subsequently tested the potential through mock duels with a pair of future aces, Edward "Butch" O'Hare and James Flatley, the Thach Weave, as the maneuver became known, was not immediately accepted.

Noel Gayler, who reported to VF-3 in 1940, said, "Jimmy diagramed [the Thach Weave] like a football coach. We would go up and practice it with practice attackers. The idea was very much contingent on timing. You had to make the break at just the right time. If you did [this] you'd always wind up on the tail of anybody who was on the tail of your buddy. It was also a very good lookout position, because you could each watch 6:00 o'clock of the other fellow." To simulate the disadvantage of the Wildcat against the Zero, Thach allowed the team playing the Americans to operate at only half power.

Thach's partners in developing the tactic, Flatley and O'Hare, were both superior aviators. Flatley, an Annapolis alum, was small of stature but oversize in the minds of his associates. Whitey Feightner flew under Flatley with VF-10. "He was one of the most amazing people we had. A true leader, just sort of epitomizes what you think of as a squadron commander. He got along well with everybody in the squadron. He was a good aviator and had the respect of all in the squadron. He really thought a lot and felt deeply about the country. He was a very religious man. He felt that anything we did as a squadron should be done with an eye toward helping not only the squadron and the ship but also the country.

"He was concerned about such things as safety to the point that he invented the shoulder harness—although it was a chest harness. We modified all our airplanes and we were the first squadron ever to have it. He was a great man for sitting down with people, a small group. He would talk tactics. He would talk about the philosophy he thought the Japanese had and what we should expect from them."

Feightner remembered a game of volleyball in which one of the pilots, who towered over Flatley and weighed well over 200 pounds, tromped on Flatley's foot, breaking his arch. Flatley had a strap installed on the other rudder pedal, which allowed him to fly even with his broken foot.

Butch O'Hare's father, a Chicago politician with a working knowledge of the underworld, had been murdered by gunmen, probably at the behest of gangster Al Capone. A 1937 USNA graduate, O'Hare served his two years at sea before enrolling at Pensacola's flight school. When he came to VF-3 aboard the *Saratoga*, squadron leader Thach said, "We [had] established what we called the Humiliation Team. It was composed of myself, my executive officer, Don Lovelace, Noel Gayler, and my gunnery officer (Rollo Lemon). We would take the newcomers to the squadron up and give them all the altitude advantage they wanted. Then we'd fly toward each other and see if they could come down and get on our tails and stay there long enough to shoot. A pilot who has just achieved the wonderful accomplishment of getting his wings is usually rather full of himself and sometimes a little cocky. This was a good exercise to let them know that they didn't know everything right off the bat and to show them that they had a lot of work to do. We could even eat an apple or read a newspaper and lick these kids.

"This was true with one exception, Butch O'Hare, fresh out of the training command. The first time I took him up and gave him altitude advantage, he didn't make any mistakes and I did everything I could to fool him and shake him. He came right in on me and stuck there. He could have shot me right out of the air. I came down and I got hold of Rollo Lemon and I said, 'Well, I've had one of these new youngsters up but I want each member of the Humiliation Team to go up with him and give him a chance. He's pretty good, and I'll just wager a little bet that he'll get on your tail the first time and stay there.'

"Up they went and sure enough, Butch did it again. It wasn't long after that we made him a member of the Humiliation Team, because he had passed the graduation test so quickly. Butch O'Hare was a good athlete. He had a sense of time and relative motion that he may have been born with, but also he had that competitive spirit. When he got into any kind of a fight like this, he didn't want to lose. He really was dedicated to winning and he probably had worked a lot of this out in his own mind, then read as much as he could. When he first got to the squadron, he studied all the documents on aerial combat. He picked it up much faster than anyone else I've ever seen. He got the most out of his airplane. He didn't try to horse it around. . . .

"When you're in a dogfight, it isn't how hard you pull back on the stick to make a tight turn to get inside of him, it's how smoothly you fly the plane and whether you pull back with just enough turn on your aircraft so that it remains efficient and isn't squashing all though the air causing more drag. . . . Butch learned how to get around in the shortest time, to make the tightest turn consistent with not losing ground because of rough handling."

During the parlous days of early 1942, VF-3 was one of the

Navy's few assets. Without any question, Thach's leadership made a significant difference. Gayler said, "He led by leading. He was the first guy off the deck. He led by precept. Clearly understood what he was doing and why. Yet, at the same time he invited participation, ideas. He gave encouragement at the right time, occasionally the stick as well as the carrot.

"He was a perfectionist about being able to do everything, so we did do a lot of night tactical work, rendezvouses, intercepts—no radar [at the time] but intercepts under fighter direction, eyeball. A lot of attention to enhancing night vision. Absolutely mirror clean windshields. Jimmy was sort of ahead of the time on almost all the technical aspects and then we would learn how to pick up the target airplane against the night sky or by seeing the barely luminous exhausts and making an approach on that."

Although Fighting Three and a few other units were ready for combat, during the first months of 1942, American forces were too weak to mount offensive thrusts. The *Saratoga* sailed courses designed only to intercept a possible second strike or even an invasion of the Hawaiian Islands. During the somewhat aimless patrol, the carrier traveled at speeds of 7 to 12 knots, a pace that enhanced its ability to detect submarines but also rendered it highly vulnerable to U-boats. Significantly, the flattop's skipper was a nonaviator, not fully cognizant of the needs of a carrier or its weakness—a thin hull skin unlike that of cruisers and battleships, which offered stiffer resistance to torpedoes.

Jimmy Thach remembered idly sitting on a gun turret late in the afternoon when one of the ship's dentists walked by and, observing the slow movement, remarked, "Gee, if there was a Japanese submarine anywhere in this part of the ocean, it would seem like to me it could catch us easily."

Thach also professed surprise at the sluggish pace, noting that it would take a long time to launch an airplane if you had to get up speed to do it. He recalled, "That night I was sitting in the wardroom eating when it sounded like the bottom of the ship blew out, a whole big explosion, all the dishes went up in the air. I remember seeing my executive officer, sitting right by me, reach up in the air and catch a roll that was coming down."

On January 11, according to Bert Stanley, "We got the message our speed had been asking for. A little after seven that evening a submarine placed a torpedo neatly amidships on the port side. There could be no doubt in anyone's mind what had happened. The jar and explosion were felt throughout the ship. As the ship began to list to port, we manned our General Quarters stations quietly. There was no hysteria or fright, but as we sat in the Ready Room, we grew excessively gay and nonchalant. It was, I have since found, a very normal reaction. The ship listed several degrees to port and rolled a good deal, but the engineering crew worked with speed and accuracy. The ship was balanced and we turned in, still acutely conscious of every roll. Monday morning revealed some of the damage. Fuel oil covered the planes and deck aft of the stack. The explosion apparently struck the engine room or boiler compartments. The net and ladder near the explosion were torn up, and a part of the hole was visible in the blister at the water line. Six men had been killed in the flooded compartments below.

"We made all possible speed for Pearl Harbor and entered the channel before noon of the thirteenth. The squadron went to Ewa and the *Sara* went to dry dock. She was partially repaired there and then proceeded to Bremerton to finish the job and get some other work done. Fighting Two accompanied her while we went under Army Command at Ewa." After two weeks ashore, Fighting Three embarked on the *Lexington*.

Stanley expressed pleasant surprise at the transfer to the *Lexington*. "There was a different and better spirit aboard the *Lex*. The work on the flight deck went on with less noise and delay. The portholes were opened in the daytime so that fresh air entered the ship, and the evening meal was eaten in whites. The life jackets were put away—available, but not omnipresent. It was a good start, filled with promise for a happy cruise."

The ship was actually part of a task force assigned to swing one of the first counterpunches in the war against Japan. It had been preceded by air strikes from the sister flattops, *Enterprise* and *Yorktown*, which jabbed the enemy bases in the Marshall and Gilbert Islands, some 600 miles from the now-lost Wake. Stanley heard that eleven Navy planes from these forays had been lost, and wondered how many had been piloted by friends.

Noel Gayler recalled the frenzied efforts aboard ship to forge a carapace to protect pilots: "For years there had been provision for armor plate, but it wasn't installed. You were supposed to make airplanes lighter in peacetime. Here we were going into combat. Every night, they'd take one squadron of airplanes down in the incredibly hot hangar deck of the ships. Buttoned up, and off New Guinea, you can imagine how hot it was. The aviation mechs and metalsmiths would labor all night long to get the armor plate installed, one airplane at a time. They'd pass out, and they'd pull them out by the heels, and another guy would crawl in and work. As flight officer, I used to roll the bones [dice] to see who got the armored airplanes. So much for readiness and provision for armor plate."

As the *Lexington* crossed the equator, induction into the Realm of the Raging Main momentarily replaced the concentration on war. Appropriate ceremonies, under the hegemony of the shellbacks, baptized the pollywogs into the society.

The brief relapse into frivolity gave way to the business of combat, a raid upon the Japanese bastion of Rabaul on New Britain Island. According to Thach, the battle plan said, "The *Lexington*, with its few cruisers and destroyers, would steam in close enough for us to launch from the north, fly over New Ireland and go in to attack Rabaul. It was expected that there would be a number of heavy ships in the harbor and an unknown number of aircraft on the field. We realized that among them would be the famous Zero fighter, and we hoped to catch these airplanes on the field right at the crack of dawn, hoping they wouldn't have too many in the air. I was to lead the attack group and go in with the fighters and strafe the field and keep enemy fighters from taking off, while the dive bomber and torpedo planes were doing their job of bombing and sinking any ships in the harbor."

On the morning of February 20, Thach recounted, "I was on combat air patrol with Butch O'Hare leading another two-plane section and Bert Stanley leading a third. So, we had six planes on combat air patrol. [There] was real, honest to goodness, no-fooling radio silence. No one dared open up, because we figured if we did they might get a bearing on us. I almost jumped out of my seat when this loud voice of the *Lexington* fighter director came in giving me a vector and said there's apparently a snooper about 35 miles away. I started out after him and Butch O'Hare started to follow me. I turned around, looked at him and motioned him back. He didn't want to go back but inasmuch as I knew there couldn't be fighters in the area it could only be a large aircraft. I figured that my wing man and I could take care of that. So I made him go back. I also calculated that if there's one snooper, there'd probably be another. It was important to get these planes and knock them out before they could report the locations of the *Lexington* task group."

The directions given Thach sent him into a heavy thunderstorm, and when he queried his controller he was advised that the interloper was also in the squall. "Once we were in the soup, we couldn't see very much. We came into a rift, an opening in the cloud for just a second and right below me was this great huge Japanese insignia. I saw two engines on one wing and then just as quickly we were in the soup again. Here he was right below me, like about 20 or 30 feet. About that time the fighter director called and said, 'We have a merged plot [radar showing both planes in the same space].' I called back. 'We sure do. If we had been any more merged, we would have crashed into him. I just sighted him.'"

The snooper disappeared, but circling about, the American caught a vague outline of the Japanese plane. Within seconds, both aircraft broke into the clear and Thach readied for an attack. He directed his wingman to move to the other side, where the pair could bracket the target and guard against any turns. "I took what I figured was the proper lead on him and waited until I got close enough, coming in from the side, and opened up with all six of those guns. It was a really good blast of tracers. I took a good lead on him and on the engines on the right wing. Bullets would carry into the cockpit, through the engines or round the engines into the cockpit. I looked back and nothing happened. No smoke, nothing! I thought, have I got blank ammunition?" His partner maneuvered for a run when the wing of the victim burst into flame.

"This was an Emily [a four-engine bomber]. We'd never seen one. We had no intelligence that they had that kind of an airplane. I knew it was huge and I could tell it had a cannon because when the cannon was shooting, it would make smoke rings. I really felt sorry for him because here he was doing his job and obviously had gotten off a message on the location of the *Lexington* task group and I hadn't hit him soon enough because I couldn't find him in the soup.

"We didn't have to make any more attacks, just watched him. He started burning and six huge long bombs dropped in the water. A few minutes later his nose went down and in he went with a splash. Made a big cloud of smoke they could see all the way to the *Lexington*. I felt sorry for the crew because some of them, maybe all, had convinced themselves they could defend with all those guns against a fighter type aircraft. How else could they feel? It was the same sort of feeling when we were doing gunnery training and the same sort of propaganda that our big bombers were putting out to bolster their feeling of being able to survive against attack by fighters. I never believed it."

While Thach and his wingman, E. R. "Doc" Sellstrom, had pursued the bogey detected by the ship's radar, Bert Stanley and his companion, Ensign Lee W. Haynes, continued to fly combat air patrol over the *Lexington*. Suddenly their radios crackled a message from fighter control: "Orange Section from Romeo—Vector 343—Buster—Angels Six." The pair immediately acknowledged and headed north of the fleet.

Stanley wrote, "We had hardly gone twenty miles when Haynes's plane pulled alongside and began to dance energetically [radio silence between aircraft was the rule]. He had sighted our objective. I saw it then, sleek silver patrol boat, four engines, tremendous even at a thousand yards.

" 'Tally-ho from Orange Leader,' I transmitted gleefully. 'A big four-engine patrol plane.' As we climbed for attack position, I checked my plane: gas switch, prop, gunsight, gun switches—the patrol plane had spotted us. Black spindles of explosions fell from the fuselage to send up white geysers a mile below. They had jettisoned their bombs in hopes that the unloaded plane could escape.

"As we pulled into position, Haynes could see the cannon in the waist sending up its incendiary shells, seeking our range. I was already starting my attack. A half roll and the pull-through. The sights crept up and then held steady—now! I pressed the trigger and nothing happened. The motor continued its roar and the wind still tugged at my clothing, but only the fretful sparkle of the patrol plane's rear machine gun showed that someone was firing. I had missed the master gun switch. I was flying 3-F-7 and the switch was in a different place. [Pilots often used different aircraft.]

"Haynes had followed me closely and while I snapped on the switch and tested my guns, I noticed that the tail gun was no longer firing. Good shooting, Lee. From above and behind this time, and as the broad wing filled the gunsight, the guns responded to the switch. The red trail of the tracers could be seen to end abruptly as they passed from sight into the wing and the pilot compartment. Another burst, longer and more accurate now, and flame burst from the inboard engine on the port side. It disappeared and reappeared as I fired once more before ducking to avoid the tail. I looked back to see it become a solid sheet of fire flowing from the wing to the fuselage. Gray smoke traced the path of the plane as the left wing and nose began to drop. That last burst must have killed the pilots.

" 'Whee, we got it,' I couldn't resist reporting.

"Haynes had quickly followed to deliver the last blow. The nose had dipped lower until it was diving out of control—the smoke increasing with the speed. Nothing could save it—nothing could stop that dive. It crashed in a burst of red and a black pall quickly covered the spot. The great ball of smoke rose slowly to reveal a circle of flame on the gasoline-covered water, but the wreckage was already beneath the surface. Ten men were dead, and the plane, efforts of a hundred, was destroyed." Pangs of remorse like those expressed by Thach and Stanley were more common early in the war. Over time, as killing and death became more of a steady diet and word of Japanese atrocities spread, attitudes hardened.

After Thach landed aboard, he said, "Everybody wanted to know what it was like, what happened when we made the attacks, what kind of attacks, were they the same we did against the sleeve, and we said yes, the same thing you've been doing all the time. O'Hare was fit to be tied. He wanted to get in quick. This was the first enemy airplane any of us had seen."

Noel Gayler felt that he and his associates were eager to do battle. "We all felt Pearl Harbor very keenly. We all felt that we were about to get a chance to get our own back, and we were ready to go for it. Another mood is absolute confidence that we were going to win. We might get smoked as individuals, but America was going to win. . . . The reverse of Pearl Harbor didn't bother anybody at all in a strategic sense. It was a chance to get back at the bastards for a sneak attack."

O'Hare did not have to wait long before his opportunity for combat. Thach was studying charts and intelligence reports for information about the Emily when, he said, "The flight order sounded. 'Fighter pilots, man your planes.' I knew we had something coming and I figured it was an attack, or else another snooper." In fact, a large number of Japanese aircraft sallied forth from Rabaul intent upon destroying the task force. Other units preceded Thach, and for a time he sat in his airplane, watching. "It wasn't long before we could see from the flight deck, in the distance, some smoke and airplanes falling. I could see these bombers in close formation headed for us. The enemy was at about 8,000 feet. Later, I learned Noel Gayler [in command of a section] had called down, telling our own antiaircraft fire to please shorten their fuses to 8,000 feet because that was the altitude of the enemy bombers and he was being bothered by bursts of antiaircraft fire above them where he wanted to maneuver for attacks. We didn't have influence fuses [ones triggered by a target]. We had time-set fuses, so many seconds. This was the situation the first part of the war. We did half our fighting in the middle of our own AA fire and the other half in the middle of the enemy's."

Gayler was indeed involved with the attack by enemy aircraft. Flying combat air patrol, he said, "They came in two waves of nine. The first was Bettys [twin-engine bombers] and the second was Type 98s [another type of medium bomber]. Somewhat foolishly, I led my wing man, I think it was [D. W.] Peterson and I to a position for an overhead run, which entailed getting up and turning back toward and rolling over, firing almost vertically down, as opposed to a high-side run. I say foolishly, because it took me too long to climb into the attack position.

"In any case we did get into position. We did make an overhead run and a couple of high side-runs. I set one guy on fire, and the other guy started to burn while a couple of us were shooting at him. We got all but one and that one was the fellow that got close to the carrier when he was trying to kamikaze them. I was still airborne when the other group came but way out of position. That was when O'Hare and [M. W.] Dufilho went up after them."

The carrier had now dispatched Thach and Butch O'Hare with their wingmen. Said Thach, "I started climbing in the direction they were going so that if I ever did get to the altitude maybe I could get some of them, all the time watching these airplanes falling out of the air. Sometimes there were three or four falling at once, just coming down with dark red flame and brown smoke coming out. We didn't have a very high rate of climb, only 1,100 feet a minute when we were fully loaded with our 1,800 rounds of ammunition and full of gas. I managed to get up there and start working after I saw three of them still in some kind of formation. They split and were starting to run away individually. I made an attack on one from the low side because I didn't have enough altitude and it burst into flame and started down.

"About this time I saw one of my planes coming in dead astern [of another bomber] and a flash right on his windshield where, apparently a cannon had hit him and he went into a spin right on in. He made a bad mistake by coming in on the tail of a bomber that had a cannon [there]. I was pretty mad at this character who had shot down one of my pilots and I wasn't going to let him get home free. I managed to get a little bit above his level before starting the approach. I was amazed; I was definitely out of his range but he was shooting all kinds of stuff at me. You couldn't see it, looking right at it. You had to look behind to see it. I put what I thought was a real good burst into his wing root and fuselage and nothing happened. I got out and made another run, pulled out, looked at him again and all of a sudden he disintegrated, just blew up.

"I didn't have my wing man with me. We were a little disorganized because we never had a chance to join up after taking off. It wasn't really necessary because against bombers you didn't have to defend yourself with maneuvers. It was all right to just go hell bent for election and that airplane that can get there the first gets there. Then, over the radio I got the impression there was a second wave, another nine-plane group. . . . We didn't know what they were because they were entirely different from anything in our intelligence manuals.

"Butch was vectored out after these people and intercepted when they were about six minutes away. We had a practice, charge all your guns and fire a short burst to be sure you've got 'em charged and your gun switches are all on. His wing man [Dufilho] did this and nothing happened. He apparently had a short or some open circuit and couldn't get any gun to fire. Butch realized this and waved him back but he didn't want to go. Butch shook his fist at him but he came on and maneuvered to try to draw some attention to himself while Butch went in and made the attacks.

"They [the Japanese] stayed in rigid formation. That was the best thing for them to do. First they've got to have a bomb pattern if they want to hit the ship and [need] a whole proper formation for the right pattern. Furthermore, it gives all the guns from each airplane a chance to shoot to defend themselves. [O'Hare] got in, lined them up and apparently knocked down two in one pass. Then he went to the other side to work on that line back and forth. Inside of six minutes he had six down. At first he was given credit for only five. They thought antiaircraft had shot down one. Afterwards one of them came down and approached like he was going to crash into the *Lexington*. We got photographs of that airplane and one engine had completely fallen out of the wing. Butch had shot that engine out."

That afternoon of February 20, 1942, Willard Eder, who had held an ROTC commission in the infantry but on the advice of his inactive reserve CO had volunteered for naval duty because it offered immediate employment, had been with Fighting Three for almost two years. In an interview, he said, "[Butch O'Hare] was over the ship on combat air patrol. With my wingman [Ensign Ralph Wilson], I was on takeoff alert in my plane on deck. The radar spotted enemy planes at 80 miles. (Later we learned that this new radar gadget wouldn't spot aircraft 80 miles away at that low altitude.) We two were launched to intercept, sent out at 3,000 feet altitude. I spotted them, two-engine Bettys, at about 40 miles, well above us. I estimated 6,000 feet. Actually, they were at 12,000. I started climbing as fast as the old F4F Wildcat would take me. I left my wingman behind as he was only able to climb much slower.

"I fired my four guns when I got near, but saw I was still out of range. The tail gunners were firing back. [It's scary.] But I was too far away from them too. I ducked down to help pick up speed, then nosed up and fired long bursts against, that may or may not have been reaching the rear planes in the formation. Three guns jammed, and I pulled wide to clear them. About that time we were running into carrier's AA fire. As I pulled away, one spent seven-millimeter bullet from the planes hit my fuselage beside and below my seat. I hunted for my wingman by reversing course, but I never found him. His plane must have quit."

Bert Stanley expected to be a member of the group launched with Thach. However, when he rushed from the ready room to the deck, he discovered that another pilot, Peterson, had taken the Wildcat assigned to him. Temporarily grounded, he watched the action above. "I saw horizontal bombers beginning their final approach. The carrier was their objective. Already pilots of the second and third division [O'Hare was one] had sent four down in flames and as the AA began to dot the sky with its black bursts, the tiny fighters could be seen dodging in and out. Two more bombers came down to crash in pools of fire to one side before the three remaining reached the bomb release point.

"As the bombs splashed well astern, another came circling down. It was still partially under control and was going to attempt to crash the ship. The deafening fire of the five-inch AA batteries had been going for some time, but as the injured bomber came in range, the pom-poms and machine guns opened up with a racket that put all others to shame. The plane didn't have a chance. He crashed a hundred yards to starboard in a pool of red and yellow fire. He would have really made a mess of our flight deck if he had reached it. The two bombers that remained of the original nine had both been shot up but were still able to fly. A scout caught and finished one.

"Meanwhile, a second wave of nine had been reported and the

fighters who could started to intercept them. The ship continued to zigzag busily and the second division, their ammunition exhausted and their fuel almost gone, had to come aboard. It was an impossible situation. The four bombers that remained of the second group of nine were almost at the release point. For the ship to straighten out now would be fatal. And come aboard they did. The signal officer held his post despite the falling fragments from the AA bursts and the approaching bombs. As [R. J.] Morgan in the last plane hit the deck, the signal officer hit the net and the bombs hit the water a scant hundred yards astern. Their explosion, far below us, could be felt."

Stanley now took his turn in the air and later wrote, "Three of the second group [of bombers] had passed over the ship. One crashed a moment later ahead of the port destroyer. The ship turned quickly to avoid the flaming area. The other two headed for home but one fell before the pursuing fighters' guns before they were out of sight. One was found some distance away and was destroyed by a returning scout."

Said Thach, "Of the 20 aircraft we met that day, 19 were shot down." The Americans counted one pilot killed: Ralph Wilson, Willard Eder's wingman. Two aircraft were lost, with H. L. Johnson, who was slightly wounded, rescued by a destroyer. The success achieved by the airmen of the *Lexington* stemmed at least partially from the inability of the Japanese to provide air cover for their bombers. In their zeal to hit the task force well out to sea from Rabaul, the Japanese could not utilize their short-range fighters. Although the *Lexington* celebrated its aerial victories, the opportunity for a surprise raid on Rabaul had also been a casualty. The fleet aborted the proposed strike on the enemy base on New Britain.

FOUR

FROM TOKYO TO THE CORAL SEA

The modest successes of the U.S. carrier-based planes amounted to no more than a mosquito sting to the Japanese juggernaut. It rolled on, expanding its holdings in Southeast Asia on the mainland and islands of the area, wiping out the organized resistance in the Philippines with the surrender of the Corregidor bastion on May 6, and advancing the rising sun ever further into the southwestern Pacific.

A fortnight after Butch O'Hare earned recognition as the Navy's first ace, Japanese troops occupied the villages of Salamaua and Lae on the north coast of New Guinea, the large island that hovers between Australia and the Solomons. The bases being established there would seriously crimp shipments of men and material from the United States to Australia as well as threaten Australia's security. The *Lexington* and *Yorktown* were ordered to discourage the infusion of enemy resources into the new outposts of the empire.

Salamaua and Lae lay at opposite ends of a large horseshoe-shaped harbor. Thach said, "There was a harbor full of ships unloading, an unopposed landing, and there were a lot of cruisers, destroyers, et cetera. They didn't know about any airplanes, whether there were any there or not but it was an amphibious landing, with a lot of cargo and transports. When you're in there, you could be between [the two towns] and see each place."

The American task force plotted a course that would take it to the south shoreline of New Guinea via the Coral Sea and the Gulf of Papua. "With the Owen Stanley mountain range between us," said Thach, "[we could] fly up over the mountain range, then come down and hit them. It was planned to carry torpedoes on the torpedo planes."

As the most experienced of the tin fish squadron skippers, Lieutenant Commander Jimmy Brett led the pair of torpedo squadrons, VT-2 and VT-5. "They launched him last," said Thach, "because he was flying these TBD-1 Devastators and that was the poorest, oldest airplane we had at that time. They were absolute fire traps and they were underpowered, carrying a huge torpedo and all the gasoline. They could just barely get off the deck if they started from right at the stern and the ship was making 25 or 30 knots. I was to go along and protect the torpedo planes and stick with them all the way, because we didn't know what we were going to run into."

According to Thach, the lower end of the Owen Stanleys reached some 10,000 feet into the air. The raiders could not go around the jagged ridge because the distance would burn too much gas. "There was a lot of calculation done about whether or not the torpedo planes could get over the ridge carrying a torpedo, [with] a few bombs they could. But it was a question in everybody's minds, including the pilots of the torpedo planes.

"They climbed and climbed and got to the mountain range. They were still below, looking up at the ridge, and I was sitting right on top of them. It looked like they weren't going to make it. They went right at the ridge and then had to turn away. They milled around and tried to get more altitude but couldn't. In fact, it looked to me [as if] they were losing altitude.

"Jimmy Brett called me and said, 'You better go ahead. I don't think we're going to make it.' I said, 'No, I'll wait here a little bit. I've got enough gas.'

"He said, 'All right, hold it. I've got an idea.' He started to go parallel to this ridge. He'd seen a sunny spot over some lush fields. This young man had been trained as a glider pilot. He was one of the few that went through Pensacola when they had to take glider training before they got into powered flight training. He knew the glider pilot's business and he'd gotten real good at it. He saw the sun shining on the fields and he remembered that this is where you get a thermal updraft, and that's how gliders stay in the air so long. He headed for this [spot] and, sure enough, he started to rise. Just circled around there, rising and finally got enough [so] he just washed himself right over the ridge and yelled, 'Halfway House.'

"This was a signal [prearranged] everybody would recognize. Every naval aviator that went through Pensacola knows what halfway house means. It's a little place you get a cold glass of milk, a sandwich and soda pop, half way between downtown Pensacola and the Air Station. Everybody stopped there. Just a little roadside sandwich and cold drink place. Sometimes on a Saturday night they had a combo and dance. Everybody knew what halfway house was; they didn't have to be clued. He'd used up quite a bit of gas, but he was over and the glider pilot experience was what did it.

"It was about 8:30 or 9:00 A.M. when he got over. We went on into Salamaua and Lae and there were the cruisers. We saw them getting underway, pulling up the anchor chains and there were a lot of transports. He went in with his torpedo planes for the conventional anvil attack [planes striking from opposite sides]. I took my fighters in. I had Noel Gayler and Butch O'Hare. I left Butch upstairs. He didn't like that either. But we didn't know whether we were going to run into some Zeros and we went to go down and strafe just ahead of the torpedo planes to give them some chance.

"Butch didn't say anything but I think he was expecting that I knew there was some action he was going to get. If I was going to leave anybody up there, I want to leave Butch. I figured that no matter how many planes were coming, he could give them a busy time before they got down to us.

"We went in and did some strafing. The torpedo attack was beautifully executed. You could see the streaks of torpedoes going right to the side of these cruisers and nothing happened. I saw one or two go right on underneath, come out the other side and bury themselves in the bank on the shore. Some obviously hit the cruisers and didn't explode. What a heart-breaking thing after all of that effort, all of that training and use of wonderful experience. Jimmy Brett had to get over there and drop these torpedoes and they're practically all duds.

"There was a little float plane that came along, milling around, shooting a small-caliber gun at one of the torpedo planes. I saw it and looked up. Noel Gayler was coming down to strafe. He was strafing the cruisers and he turned out a little bit, gave a squirt at this airplane, blew it up, turned right back and went on the same run to strafe the cruiser. He was the only one that shot down an airplane. It was the only airplane anybody saw. Poor little float plane got mixed up with Noel Gayler, which was a bad mistake. The dive bombers got some hits on ships but I didn't see any roll over and sink, although some were on fire."

To counter the declining morale because of the unabated progress of the enemy, American strategists plotted a surprise coup, a raid on Tokyo mounted from a Navy carrier. Lieutenant Colonel James Doolittle, named to lead the mission, chose the two-engine B-25 Billy Mitchell bomber as the best plane for the task. To teach the Army Air Corps pilots how to take off from a carrier, the Navy assigned Lieutenant Henry L. Miller, USNA 1934, a pilot since 1938 and an instructor at Pensacola. Miller was not informed of the purpose of the training. Because of the top-secret nature of his duties, Miller's written orders directed him to report to the Air Corps base at Eglin Field, Florida, without mention of his responsibilities. Before Miller left for his new assignment, he spoke with the assistant training officer at Pensacola, who mentioned that the project had something to do with Lieutenant Colonel Doolittle. Miller was awed by mention of "the great Jimmy Doolittle," famous as an aviator for establishing a number of flight records, as well as for his performances at air races and air shows.

Miller then flew an ancient airplane to Eglin. "I reported to the colonel in charge of the base and I read him my orders. I said, 'Do you know what I'm down here for?' He said, 'No.' I explained I was an instructor at Pensacola, and I was a carrier pilot before and I was supposed to teach the Army Air Force [Corps] pilots how to take off from a carrier. He still said he didn't have any idea of why I came there. I was just getting up to say it must have been a mistake when I asked if he knew anything about Lt. Col. Doolittle's detachment there. With that he closed the doors, he practically asked me to talk in a whisper."

Neither Doolittle nor his executive officer was available when Miller checked in, but he immediately met with several of the B-25 pilots. He climbed into the cockpit of one of the Mitchells and, from the copilot's seat, explained the takeoff technique on a carrier. Miller had never flown a B-25; in fact, this was the first time he had even seen one. "I hadn't had time to look at it [the plane] except I had a feel for it. They told me the take-off speeds they'd been using, 110 miles an hour. The first take-off [relying on the technique detailed by Miller] they observed the air speed and it showed 65–67 miles an hour. They said it's impossible. You can't do that. I said come on back. We'll land and try again. The second take-off, the same way, indicated an air speed of 70 when we were in the air and they were convinced a B-25 could take off at that slow speed.

"Just before we finished up that first day, I was at this room they gave me, getting my flight jacket because it was chilly. I thought, gee whizz, here I am a lieutenant in the Navy and the Army Air Force [Corps] gives me a dirty, junky room. No carpet on the deck, just cold concrete and look at that crummy bed! I put on my jacket and wondered who else was staying in this little group of rooms, this little cell block. I went to see the name of the place and it said, 'VIP Quarters.' I thought they must be kidding. I went to the next room and looked at the name plate and it was Lt. Col. Doolittle's name. I went to the next one. Here was Mr. [Charles] Kettering of General Motors. I went to another one and it said, 'Major Johnson.' I [decided] this is pretty fast company I'm in. I better not complain about this horrible room they've put me in. Evidently these guys have the same kind of horrible rooms. That's the way the Army lived at that time. That's the way they lived all over the United States, in some places it was worse."

Miller ran his pupils through an intensive program: "I checked out all the pilots for light loads, intermediate loads, finally the maximum load they would take on the raid. Everybody did pretty well. We had extra crews. I took data on each one of the pilots. We had observers—I borrowed pilots to act as observers. We got a portable anemometer to find out how much wind they had. We measured the distance for each plane that got off. I recorded all that data. I observed techniques in the cockpit, because you get a feel for who's a good pilot and who isn't, no matter what his take off distance is."

Miller found one pilot's work unsatisfactory. "He was letting the plane fly him." The Navy expert arranged to personally check the man out. "He took off in a skid. He pushed into a harder skid and he didn't push the throttles to the floorboard. The plane settled right back down on the runway on its belly. We came to an abrupt stop. It didn't catch fire. We were lucky because we had gasoline all over that airplane."

Doolittle spoke to Miller about the accident, and the instructor explained, "There's nothing wrong with the technique or the airplane. What was wrong was Bates. He just wasn't flying the airplane."

Originally, the B-25s with their crews were to fly to California for further training under another instructor. Miller said he had spoken to Doolittle: "Colonel, it's a matter of professional pride with me. I don't want anybody on the West Coast telling you, 'No, let's start all over again with this technique.' If it's possible I'd like to go with you, if we're going to have time to do more of this practice out there." Doolittle arranged for Miller to accompany the group. At a Sacramento depot, the B-25s underwent a final overhaul and Miller continued to work with the pilots on their takeoffs.

Doolittle asked Miller to rate the crews on their expertise. He dutifully complied. However, he objected to the pilot who had narrowly escaped disaster back at Eglin. According to Miller, he related to Doolittle, "After we crashed, they [the pilot and copilot] were both going to jump out of the windows, right into those whirling props. I grabbed both of them and said, 'Sit down and wait until those props stop and turn off all your switches.' The switches were still on. I reached back to get my pencil, paper, notebook, came back. The props had stopped and they had jumped out. . . . When you get on over enemy territory and you have some of those Japs chasing you, you're going to have to be really sharp. You've got to be thinking all the time. If you panic, you're lost. I wouldn't take Bates. And they didn't."

Just before the contingent sailed on the *Hornet*, Doolittle asked Miller what he thought of the crews. Miller reassured him, saying he did not believe there would be any trouble. But for all of the practice that had been done, no one had actually flown a B-25 off a carrier. Miller made an offer. "Colonel, if you want proof, I've had less time in the B-25 than anybody. You can take an extra one along, a sixteenth airplane. When we get 100 miles out of San Francisco, I'll take it off. I'll deliver it back to South Carolina, to the Army and go back to Pensacola."

Doolittle said nothing at the time, but after he'd met with the *Hornet* skipper, Captain Marc "Pete" Mitscher, and the air officers, he announced to Miller, "I talked to them about your idea of taking an extra plane along and they go along with it. We'll take sixteen and launch you 100 miles out."

At sea, Doolittle invited Miller into the cockpit of one of the B-25s and said, "Gee, this looks like a short distance [the takeoff distance was 495 feet].

"I said, 'You see where that tool kit is way up the deck by that island structure?'

"He said, 'Yes.'

"I said, 'That's where I used to take off in fighters on the *Saratoga* and *Lexington*.'

"And he said, 'Henry, what name do they use in the Navy for bull shit?'"

The notion of launching Miller 100 miles at sea was aborted in favor of retaining the extra B-25 for the raid. The Navy officer said he was happy to continue the voyage.

The *Hornet* and its escorts proceeded smoothly toward the proposed launch site, about 400 to 450 miles from the target. However, about 650 miles out, the task force encountered picket boats set out as sentinels by the Japanese. Fusillades from the surface fleet and attacks by carrier-based planes destroyed the small craft, but fearful that they had reported the American presence so close to Japan, Doolittle and his now sixteen-plane armada powered up their engines. Miller had done his work well; every one of the B-25s lifted off and headed for Japan while the task force hastily steamed to safety. The Doolittle raid inflicted minimal damage, but it jarred Japanese self-confidence.

Intelligence, based on intercepted messages (the Navy had broken the enemy's naval cipher), indicated that the Japanese now plotted to solidify their New Guinea holdings by an end run aimed at Port Moresby on the southeastern coast of the island. Under the peculiar arrangements governing American forces in the Pacific, Admiral Chester W. Nimitz, Pacific Fleet commander, had responsibility for most of the Pacific. Nimitz had assumed the post of commander in chief, U.S. Pacific Fleet (CinCPAC), on December 31, 1941, the post formerly held by Admiral Kimmel. His territory stretched over the vast reaches of the central Pacific, from the Aleutian Islands to the north, down through Midway, the last bastion before Hawaii and Fiji, and Samoa, which lay along the route to Australia. To the west lay the Japanese strongholds dotting the ocean, islands grouped under headings as the Ryukus, Marianas, Carolines, Marshalls, and Gilberts.

A 1905 graduate of the Naval Academy, Nimitz had an excellent reputation among his peers, having served on a variety of ships from submarines through battleships and in staff jobs. President Franklin D. Roosevelt and Secretary of the Navy Frank Knox chose Nimitz over more senior men to replace Kimmel. Unlike some contemporaries such as Halsey, King, and others, he had never qualified as an aviator. As a consequence, he was initially viewed as favoring the gun-club establishment.

In contrast to MacArthur, Nimitz offered no showmanship; he was soft-spoken and patient. But beneath the placid exterior lay a determination that augured well for an aggressive approach. His subordinate Rear Admiral Raymond Spruance praised Nimitz's attitude: "The one big thing about him was that he was always ready to fight. . . . And he wanted officers who would push the fight with the Japanese. If they would not do so, they were sent elsewhere."

Nimitz's domain covered an enormous area with the one exception of the Southwest Pacific Theater, which was MacArthur's fief. Port Moresby fell within MacArthur's jurisdiction, and he had at his disposal all of the land-based aircraft in Australia and New Guinea. But deterring an advance through the Coral Sea, the avenue that led to Port Moresby, required the might of the Pacific Fleet under Nimitz. He dispatched the *Lexington* and *Yorktown* with their respective screens and support of cruisers, destroyers, and tankers to the Coral Sea. Additional naval forces sailed from Australia under orders from General MacArthur.

With the divided commands now forced to cross borders, Nimitz's ships and the vessels committed by MacArthur operated on MacArthur's turf but independently of his authority. Simultaneously, the Navy expected support from the Army Air Corps planes but had no control over them. It was a less than ideal arrangement for command and control.

Jimmy Thach, as leader of Fighting Squadron Three, expected to ship out on the *Lexington* for the coming confrontation in the Coral Sea. However, in Hawaii, Admiral Aubrey Fitch advised him, " 'We've decided that you better stay here at Pearl Harbor because there's a big training job to be done. We're getting more airplanes and more pilots coming out. There are not very many people who have had any combat experience, and you're going to have to stay back here and teach them how to fight.'

"That really hurt me. I begged him to take me with him. I said, 'I don't think you ought to go to sea without me, without my squadron.' He said, 'Oh, I'm going to take all your pilots and give them to Paul Ramsey [another squadron commander].' The point was that VF-2, Paul Ramsey's squadron was the *Lexington* squadron. He had a rest when we went down there [to Salamaua and Lae] and I was still basically in a *Saratoga* [still being repaired] squadron." Fitch added that Fighting Three would now be increased to twenty-seven planes even as it lost all its experienced flyers.

As the admiral indicated, the service was beginning to accelerate the production of men with wings. Henry Miller, speaking from his experience as an instructor, said, "There were still the same fundamentals of instruction in flying. They still had the same types of airplanes, getting a little bit more modern, but not much. They had a tremendous number of students to train and turn out. It was a speed-up program. There was a great hump of students and at one time we were flying seven days a week, and a couple of nights of night flying. We didn't mind. We knew that it had to be done and everybody turned to and did the job. In addition, the basic training centers in the country were so jammed that they gave us 500 civilians we had to train to be sailors, teach them the basic fundamentals of marching, carrying a gun and everything else."

While the task of Miller and his cohorts was vital to producing people who could fly, it was critically important that they possess the fighting skills. From the beginning, the Army and Navy both had recognized the value of experience in teaching the elements of combat. In developing the eventual superiority of the American naval aviators over their opposite numbers, the role played by the likes of Jimmy Thach cannot be underestimated. To their eventual detriment, the Japanese never embarked on a program that allowed their most experienced flyers to rotate home and pass along to novices the knowledge they had gained.

On May 1, 1942, the two task forces with the *Lexington* and the *Yorktown* rendezvoused. They paused for two days to refuel the array of ships. After a scouting mission conducted by the Air Corps reported the presence of enemy vessels moving toward the Coral Sea, Rear Admiral Frank Jack Fletcher, CO of the fleet that included the *Yorktown*, took his ships into the center of the Coral Sea while the *Lexington* and its accompaniment, still taking on oil, remained behind.

As part of their strategy for conquest of the area, the Japanese began with a landing on the island of Tulagi, part of the Solomon chain, just off the coast of the much larger Florida Island. Alerted to the move, Fletcher steamed to within 100 miles and then launched dive-bombers and torpedo bombers against the landing forces. Fletcher had prudently retained his fighters to protect the carrier, but in fact, the enemy, having no inkling of the Americans nearby, had withdrawn all air cover. Although they met no opposition, the Navy airmen inflicted only moderate damage, sinking three minesweepers and a few landing craft and damaging a destroyer.

While the destruction at Tulagi was minimal, it was enough to scare the remainder of the invasion fleet back to Rabaul. More important, the Japanese now knew that at least one U.S. flattop was in the vicinity. A pair of carriers that had been operating north of the Solomons now raced toward the position of the *Yorktown*. But the Americans departed before the *Zuikaku* and *Shokaku* could arrive.

It became a situation of hunters hunting hunters. They warily stalked one another across the trackless terrain, through skies sometimes diamond-like, shining clear and at other moments squall-line opaque. The Americans had radar, but this early in the war, its eye was myopic. Far more valuable was the knowledge of the enemy naval code. Both sides relied most heavily on the scout planes as they maneuvered through the Coral Sea.

Rabaul-based Japanese bombers sortied to pummel Port Moresby, from which Army B-17s located and attacked the light carrier *Shoho*, which had previously supported the Tulagi invasion. These were ineffectual jabs that only served to heighten the tension.

Leading a combat air patrol from the *Yorktown*, Lieutenant Commander Jimmy Flatley, the diminutive pilot who had worked with Thach to perfect the weave, noticed a Kawanishi flying boat (in U.S. naval terminology, "Mavis") leisurely observing the task force. He radioed the finding to the carrier, which replied, "Where is he?"

"Wait a minute and I'll show you," Flatley allegedly said. An explosion rent the clouds, and fiery wreckage tumbled through the air. On the way down, pieces narrowly missed Noel Gayler, who remarked, "That one almost hit me."

Flatley answered, "That'll teach you to fly underneath me."

On May 7, the U.S. destroyer *Sims*, along with the oiler *Neosho*, had the misfortune to be discovered by scouts from the two big Japanese carriers. Dive-bombers blasted the *Sims*; only sixteen of the crew survived. The attackers mortally wounded the tanker, which sat dead in the water. After retrieving her crew, an American warship delivered the coup de grâce.

That same day, searchers from the *Lexington* reported a pair of enemy carriers with four cruisers to the north. Fletcher immediately launched strikes from both the *Lex* and the *Yorktown*. Actually, the scouts, through an error in code, had mistakenly identified the small convoy of two old cruisers and some armed merchantmen. In a happy mistake, on their way to this lesser target, the dive-bombers and torpedo planes had discovered a carrier, cruisers, and destroyers off the Louisiades, a clump of small islands southeast of New Guinea.

Lieutenant Commander Jimmy Brett, who had led the daring but ineffective raid over the Owen Stanley Mountains, guided VT-2 from the *Lexington* to its attack. He said, "The approach was begun about 1135 and an attempt made to initiate an anvil or split attack. The two leading cruisers opened fire with AA guns and it was too accurate. It was decided to skirt the cruisers and approach from the beam of the CV [the carrier *Shoho*] in order to pierce the screen at its widest opening. This allowed the squadron to make a split attack from astern. During this interval, the squadron was intercepted by a number of . . . fighters; however the attack was pushed home without the loss of a single airplane.

"The divide into divisions of planes occurred about 1145 and shortly thereafter VB-2 [the dive-bomber unit] commenced their . . . attack. VB-2 had been ordered to coordinate their attack with the torpedo attack and this was done in an exceptionally fine manner. The Commanding Officer VB-2 [Lieutenant Commander Weldon L. Hamilton] judged the situation with such a nicety that their bomb drops covered the final approach and the retirement of the torpedo plane attack. The near hits of the 1,000-pound bombs caused billows of black smoke, which formed a very good smoke screen and allowed the torpedo planes to gain an advantageous position before dropping. This was the best coordinated dive-bombing–torpedo plane attack ever witnessed by the Commanding Officer, VT-2 both as regards to the tactical handing of airplanes and as to results obtained. . . .

"The first torpedo was dropped by Commanding Officer VT-2 about 1149 and the last one at about 1152. The observed results were nine torpedo hits [one of which was credited to Brett himself] on the CV which was the only vessel attacked. The ship was seen to settle slowly and to lose speed rapidly. When last seen she was dead in the water." Brett reported that his entire squadron returned home without casualties or damage.

The account by Hamilton, who commanded VB-2, differs on the question of who really blew up the carrier. In his presentation, he wrote, "As Bombing Two commenced its attack, the carrier was completing its second circle. There was no evidence of fire. High speed was being maintained. Five minutes later, the ship was a flaming wreckage, rent by tremendous explosions, slowed to nearly stopping— a spectacular and convincing pageant of destruction. The first 1,000-pound bomb struck the ship directly on the centerline aft, 250 feet forward of the ramp. A gigantic explosion followed and the entire after portion of the ship was immediately enveloped in smoke and flames. In the succession of 1,000-pound bomb impacts that followed, there were five direct hits upon the flight deck, all aft. These bomb hits provoked further disaster to a ship already doomed, culminating in a tremendous display as the resulting internal explosions tore the hull apart, and projected vivid flames hundreds of feet into the air.

"Torpedo Two pushed home its torpedo attack in the midst of the confusion created by the Bombing Two attack. As the ship had turned away from the torpedo planes in the process of circling left, the torpedo planes were able to utilize the vast clouds of smoke as a screen for their attack." He tactfully added, "I did not personally observed the torpedo hits, as I had retired eastward after my attack."

In addition to the punishment meted out by VB-2, Scouting Squadron Two, led by Lieutenant Commander Robert E. Dixon, contributed to the assault. Said Dixon, "It was obvious we had caught them by surprise. They had a number of planes on deck, and one was coming up from the hangar deck in the elevator. I could see them all clearly as I kept my eye on them sighting for the release point." Analysts confirmed two hits by his squadron.

VB-2 also engaged enemy fighters. The rear gunner of the CO's plane scored a probable as the Japanese plane fell off and descended rapidly toward the sea. Another from the squadron claimed to have seen its adversary crash in the water. While none of the dive-bomber crews was wounded, enemy fire damaged six planes. All returned safely to the *Lexington*.

Both Brett and Hamilton mistook the *Shoho* for a carrier by another name. But there was no doubt that an enemy flattop had been sunk. Dixon radioed the *Lexington*, "Scratch one flattop! Dixon to carrier. Scratch one flattop!"

The fighter group that protected the torpedo planes and the dive-bombers was commanded by Lieutenant Commander Jimmy Flatley, who had been ordered home to form a new squadron. He successfully begged to hang on for this battle and flew fighter screen. He said, "The sight of those heavy dive bombers smashing that carrier was so awful I was physically ill. They followed each other at three or four-second intervals, and those powerful explosions were literally tearing the big ship apart." Flatley had earlier knocked down a prowling Kawanishi flying boat.

From his position above the fray, he confirmed Dixon's version.

"The *Yorktown* dive bombing attack . . . scored at least six direct hits. The carrier was burning when the first torpedo was dropped about 1210. I made an effort to divert our torpedo planes to another target but they were already in their approach." When a quartet of Japanese fighters tried to intervene, Flatley said his people shot down three (one of which was credited to him), and the lone survivor fled. The opposition had consisted of both Zeros and Type 96 fighters (in U.S. naval parlance, Claudes), atavisms with fixed gear and open cockpits but still extraordinarily maneuverable.

As night started to fall over the Coral Sea, planes from both the American carriers and the two Japanese flattops flew patrols, protecting their ships while looking for the foe. In the blackness of the evening, one of the more bizarre incidents of the war occurred. The *Yorktown* switched on its landing lamps to aid its returning aircraft. A trio of planes appeared, winking their signal lights before coming aboard. As the carrier prepared to accept them, a speaker on a nearby destroyer messaged, "Have any of our planes got rounded wingtips?"

From the *Yorktown*, someone cried, "Wait!"

A destroyer voice yelled, "Damned if those are our planes." Antiaircraft guns fired across the *Yorktown*'s bow. The Japanese planes perceived their mistake and zoomed away. But shortly afterward, another three of the enemy made the same mistake and one was shot down.

The now jumpy antiaircraft jeopardized returning Americans. Noel Gayler, who had been flying CAP from the *Lexington*, entered the landing circle after conclusion of his mission. "They had a whole bunch of .50 calibers, independently operated on the catwalk. Somebody started shooting and in those days the fire discipline was very good, so everybody started shooting. The landing signal officer realized what was happening because he knew who he had in the landing circle. He turned around and hit the guy across the face with his signal flags and knocked him away from his gun. Gradually, the word went up the line and they realized. Christ, I had my wheels down and my flaps down."

The fleets were now so close that a showdown was inevitable. It came the following day as the two opponents almost simultaneously discovered the whereabouts of each other. Shortly after 9:00 A.M., a total of 122 U.S. planes headed north while 121 Japanese aircraft roared south. The dive-bombers and torpedo-bearing Devastators from the *Yorktown* and *Lexington* scored first. Around 11:00, they struck at the *Shokaku* while its sister, the *Zuikaku*, hid in a convenient squall. Unlike the assault on the *Shoho* the previous day, the Americans, hampered by poor weather and the prevalence of enemy fighters, were denied the opportunity to make a well-coordinated attack. (VB-2, for example, never even located the objective.) The *Yorktown*'s VT-5, according to Walter Karig in *Battle Report*, initiated the attack, which was followed by bombs from Scouting Squadron Five. "We dived on the starboard carrier," Karig quoted Ensign John J. Jorgenson as saying. "The skipper, Lieutenant Commander [William O.] Burch led and I followed. I saw the skipper's 1,000-pounder hit smack on the carrier's deck. After releasing my bomb, my plane lurched and started into a left spin. I pulled out and discovered a shell hole in the left aileron and wing, leaving the wiring and tubing protruded.

"I started climbing and three fighters jumped on my tail. Their bullets ripped into the plane, especially the wings and front end of the fuselage, passing over my right shoulder and tearing off the rear of the telescope and wrecking most of my instruments. Others hit the back of the armored seat. One bullet passed through the oxygen tube lying on my forearm and three grazed my right leg."

Jorgenson hid in the clouds, but another trio hammered him. He dueled one adversary head-on until the enemy veered off, trailing smoke. As his engine started to misfire, the ensign set the plane down in the sea, near enough to a destroyer to be picked up after only four minutes in the water.

Among those who smote the *Shokaku* was Lieutenant John J. Powers, who had sworn he would hit a carrier "come hell or high water." He was fatally intent on carrying out his pledge. He flew so close to the flattop before letting go of his bomb that the resultant explosion consumed him. He received a posthumous Medal of Honor.

Despite claims from the torpedomen, none of the torpedoes that were dropped hit home, but three bombs appeared to strike the flattop. Afire and trailing smoke, it halted flight operations and withdrew. The ship maintained its headway, having no damage below the waterline.

Noel Gayler flew a VF-2 fighter that accompanied the dive-bombers and torpedo planes. "The visibility was very bad. You couldn't see much. Big towering columns of rain clouds, sort of like pillars. You'd go around them and all of a sudden you'd see the carrier. Here he is, and there he's gone." Gayler, focusing on the Zeros in the sky, said he had paid little attention to the antiaircraft fire. "The Americans [AA] were a lot closer than the Japanese [who] were just plain lagging. It was shoot, shoot, shoot, about a half mile behind."

Gayler got into a dogfight with a Zero. "I think the guy I tangled with was a much better pilot than I. He got on my tail pretty promptly and he was a very good shot. He had his wing men all way out here and they went by on both sides. As soon as I saw them I took the stick with both hands and [pushed it down in a steep dive]. I did something violent.

"I came around and found another one, made a big hairy, climbing turn, taking a long shot at him and fell out of it for lack of air speed. Just before I fell out, I saw him starting to burn. It was just such an incredibly confusing, mixed-up, screwed-up situation. Poor visibility and people yelling on the radio." Gayler splashed two of the Zeros and, on his way home to the Lexington, knocked down another pair of enemy patrol planes.

Willard Eder, one of the fighter pilots transferred to the Lexington's VF-2 while Jimmy Thach remained behind to train a new squadron, had his second encounter with the enemy during the struggle to protect the carrier. After flying high cover for the attack on the seventh, the next day he was in the clouds over the Lexington. "My wingman and I headed for two Jap planes, which ducked into a cloud. We lost them in the clouds. Then he and I became separated and I turned out and saw below me this fighter. He turned up toward me. I headed down toward him and we met head-on. I was firing four .50-calibers in a down slant and he was firing in an up slant. I could see his 20-mms were falling quite short of me. His 7.7-mms were doing better when my .50-caliber began hitting him. Almost immediately his plane sort of snap-rolled, then spiraled downward, uncontrolled. My emotion was 'scored,' and I'm glad my .50-calibers were more adequate than his guns."

Now it was the turn of the Japanese. They fell upon the Lexington in a furious, coordinated assault that the American fighter screen could not disperse. Short of fighters, the Lex's combat air patrol enlisted pilots from a squadron of Douglas Dauntless dive-bombers. They were terribly overmatched, roughly 100 miles an hour slower than the Zeros and with only two guns firing forward. A dozen Zeros jumped a flight of six SBDs and immediately dispatched two in flames. Lieutenant Stanley "Swede" Vejtasa, piloting one SPD, maneuvered to enable his radioman in the rear seat to fend off enemies on the flanks while he lined them up in his front sights. He put three Zeros in the Coral Sea. Dauntless pilot Lieutenant John Leppla, with his gunner, D. K. Liska, credited with four of the foe downed the day before, added three more. Flatley brought several F4Fs to the aid of the Dauntless pilots.

One of the fighter pilots, Lieutenant (j.g.) Richard Crommelin, killed off two Zeros before ditching his shot-up Wildcat. Crommelin would become one of the most admired Navy flyers of the war. Both Vejtasa and Leppa would subsequently be drafted for the fighter squadron that Jimmy Flatley was to command. Lieutenant (j.g) Paul Baker, a former enlisted pilot recently commissioned with three confirmed kills and one probable, collided with a Zero. The flaming wreckage of both planes spattered the sea.

But the defenders were overwhelmed by superior numbers and skilled pilots. Two torpedoes smashed into the *Lexington*'s side. The thousands of tons of water induced a serious list that required counterflooding to maintain an even keel. The tactic, while successful, reduced the *Lexington*'s speed and maneuverability, making it an even easier target. Fire erupted from bombs. The *Yorktown* also reeled from the explosion of an 800-pounder close by its island. Temporarily, it lost power.

Gayler, with eight victories now the Navy's top ace, said he did not know that the *Lexington* had sustained a torpedo hit. "She was making twenty-five knots, operating airplanes. She looked okay from the air. It was only when I landed, I noticed nobody paid any attention to me contrary to before. All the sailors would come up and [ask] 'How did you do?' I looked around and some of the faces were looking sort of strange. Then I saw flecks of fire-fighting foam all over the deck and I knew she had been hit."

When Gayler reported to the captain, Frederick "Ted" Sherman, he asked him to look over the side and see where the torpedo had struck. "I got my plane captain [crew chief] to hold onto my heels and leaned way out over the side of the nettings. I counted five big holes, maybe 20 feet in diameter." Since the *Lexington* still seemed able to function, Gayler tried to organize another strike at the *Zuikaku*, the carrier untouched by the earlier attacks. But there was no way to fuel the aircraft. It was impossible even to save the *Lexington*'s planes by sending them to the *Yorktown*; thirty-nine remained on the carrier, although nineteen had been taken aboard the *Yorktown*.

Willard Eder's group had also been brought in and landed. "We were to refuel, rearm and relaunch from the carrier's flight deck, which seemed intact. However, before the replenishment was accomplished, the below-deck fires were reaching close under the flight deck." The conditions barred any takeoffs. Optimistic reports initially filed by Admiral Fletcher could not disguise the outcome of the Battle of the Coral Sea. The battered *Shokaku* extinguished its fires and steamed toward home for repairs. Some of the first American aviators to return from the attack on the enemy, unlike Gayler, were so low on fuel they had to pancake-land. Several slid over the side. The number of U.S. planes lost added up to sixty-six.

Although the wounded *Yorktown* snuffed out its blazes and could continue flight operations, the *Lexington* was in grave condition. Leaking fumes wrought a huge blast, and a second spasm ignited flames beyond the capabilities of damage-control parties. After a ten-hour battle to save the carrier, Captain Sherman gave the order to abandon ship. "We were driven by the fire," recalled Gayler, "to the extreme end of the ship, astern. The ship's service ice cream plant was in the extreme port quarter. Some clown passed the word that there was free ice cream. Sailors who were abandoning ship lined up for free ice cream. Of course, they puked it up as soon as they had been swimming in salt water a little while. There was no panic. No worry about being picked up. I felt comfortable; the water was warm. Destroyers moved in with cargo nets." Gayler spent about ninety minutes in the water. Torpedoes from a destroyer later sank the still-burning hulk.

Eder said, "After the 'abandon ship' signal was given, I sort of waited my turn and then descended on a knotted [1½-inch] line into the warm water. I wore an inflated life jacket, waited to grab on to a life raft, and I hung on the outside. In the raft were maybe eight CPOs [chief petty officers], most quite old. We paddled away from the *Lex* and waited while the DDs [destroyers] picked up lone swimmers. The DD *Dewey* finally stopped to pick us up, threw a line to our raft and helped the CPOs up lifelines. I, being the 'young' one, held the line to the boat to the last and then grabbed one of the DD's lifelines. I was too exhausted to climb it. A sailor came down with a line to a winch, and I was winched up."

Flatley later drafted a critique of the attack on the *Shoho*. He noted that had someone exerted tactical command at the scene, elements could have been diverted to strike other enemy ships. He remarked that the dive-bombers had arrived in a cluster and circled before breaking up. "If the enemy VF had been on the job or if the A.A. had been more effective, such tactics would have been disastrous." He then offered specific details on distance and altitude that would have provided the best results, pointing out that the technique had already been successfully adopted by those on the *Enterprise*.

He had a number of hints for fighter pilots: "Gain plenty of altitude before contact with enemy VF. You can lose altitude fast but you can't gain it fast enough when up against enemy VF. Use hit and run attacks diving in and pulling out and up. If your target maneuvers out of your sight during your approach, pull out and let one of the following planes get him. If you attempt to twist and turn you will end up at his level or below and will be unable to regain an altitude advantage. If you get in a tough spot, dive away, maneuver violently, find a cloud.

"Stay together. The Japs' air discipline is excellent and if you get separated you will have at least three of them on you at once.

"You have the better plane if you handle it properly and in spite of their advantage of maneuverability you can and should shoot them down with few losses to yourselves. The reason for this is your greater fire power and more skillful gunnery. . . . Watch out for ruses. The Japs have a method of creating smoke from their exhaust which doesn't mean a thing. Set them on fire before you take your guns off of them. They also have a method of releasing a gasoline cloud from their belly tanks.

"Never hesitate to dive in. The hail of bullets around their cockpit will divert and confuse them and will definitely cause them to break-off what they are doing and take avoiding action." Other fighter commanders like Jimmy Thach made less sanguine comments on the chances of the Wildcats against the Zeros.

Lieutenant Commander Paul Ramsey, CO of Fighting Two, advised, "The Jap pilot is a well disciplined, determined, resolute, tenacious and dogged individual and none that was encountered by pilots of this squadron showed any disinclination to fight at any time. It was noted [that] . . . a Jap formation in close order did not break up that formation in order to launch an attack on our flyers unless provoked by specific attacks on themselves."

The Battle of the Coral Sea, the first in naval history in which the entire action between opposing forces on the high seas featured only aerial attacks, could be seen only as a statistical victory for the

Japanese. They suffered one lesser carrier sunk, repairable damage to another, a destroyer and some small craft sunk. The American losses included destruction of the *Lexington*, the *Yorktown* seriously wounded, an oiler and a destroyer sunk. However, the fight soured the Japanese on the Port Moresby invasion and canceled their invasion plans.

FIVE

THE MIDWAY SIDESHOW

Although the Japanese aborted their attempt to capture Port Moresby, they had a much more ambitious scheme on the drawing boards. A few weeks after his devastatingly successful foray upon the U.S. fleet at Pearl Harbor, Japan's Admiral Isoroku Yamamoto, commander in chief of Japan's Combined Fleet, plotted a follow-up seizure of the westernmost outposts of the rapidly shrinking American zone of control, the tiny islands of Midway, Johnston, and Palmyra, as a prelude to the invasion and conquest of Hawaii itself. Stocky, with an education abroad that included studies at Harvard, chess devotee Yamamoto believed that at the very least, bold moves toward the U.S. assets might bring out the remnants of the Pacific Fleet for a shoot-out with the superior forces of the empire. But before Yamamoto could implement the strategy, Japan's policy makers directed their resources not only to the Philippines and the Dutch East Indies but also to the Asian mainland: Burma and China.

By March 1942, however, Yamamoto's proposed thrust to the east had won approval from the high command. The Doolittle raid early in May, while inflicting only minor damage, added impetus to the desire for a wider sphere of dominance. American aircraft carriers would lose the freedom to sail within range of the home islands.

While the media had celebrated Doolittle's foray, a miasma of anxiety sifted through the halls of the U.S. government. Early in March, four "Emily"-type four-engine flying boats with ranges of

4,000 miles flew over Hawaii, dropping a few inconsequential bombs but jangling nerves. Fearful of widespread sabotage and espionage, Washington decreed that those of Japanese ancestry be herded into relocation camps, an undertaking enthusiastically supported by jingoists and people who profited materially from the removal of farmers, store owners, and workers. Secretary of War Henry L. Stimson met with Army Chief of Staff General George C. Marshall and his subordinate General Henry "Hap" Arnold to discuss the danger of a retaliation for the Tokyo foray with a carrier-based hit on the West Coast, a most unlikely possibility. A Honolulu newspaper warned that Lieutenant General Delos C. Emmons, the military governor of Hawaii, was anticipating further assaults upon the islands.

More to the strategic point, Admiral Chester Nimitz foresaw the vulnerability of Midway, 1,100 miles from Hawaii to its east and the same distance from Wake, now a Japanese base. Floyd Thorn, the pilot with VP-44 whose aircraft had been destroyed during the Pearl Harbor attack, had become a member of VR-1, a jerry-built utility squadron that took to the air in anything that could get off the ground. He flew Nimitz in a four-engine flying boat to inspect Johnston Island, a tiny outpost southeast of Midway. On another trip Nimitz toured Midway itself. As a result, he instigated steps to strengthen Midway's defenses. (The atoll actually consists of two islands, Sand and Eastern.) An influx of Marine ground troops soon crowded both parts of Midway. Seabees carved out additional landing strips and improved the existing ones.

There was also a wild card that complicated matters for Nimitz: the Japanese appeared poised to strike in the Aleutians, the island chain that points a finger from Alaska deep into the Bering Sea toward Japan and the Soviet Union. There was some worry among the Japanese that the United States might try to invade via a string of their bases established in Alaska and the Aleutians. The notion was preposterous, considering the climate, geological conditions, and distances. Some American strategists, equally foolishly, considered the Aleutians a potential springboard for a Japanese drive toward the continental United States.

Japan's Northern Force fleet operations offered several possible rewards. Occupation of the westernmost islands could block raids, originating in Alaska, upon the homeland in the event the Americans arranged to land in the Soviet Union. The presence of the Japanese fleet in the area might draw out enemy warships, providing an opportunity to destroy them. At the very least, the Northern Force could divert ships and planes from the defense of Midway. Even with information gleaned from message intercepts, the Americans could not determine whether the task force headed toward the Aleutians was a bona fide invasion force or merely a tactic designed to siphon naval assets away from the enemy's real goals.

On June 3, with a dim ceiling of 700 feet, the carriers *Ryujo* and *Junyo* launched thirty-five aircraft bound for the American installation at Dutch Harbor on Unalaska, in the Aleutian clump known as the Fox Islands, relatively close to the Alaskan peninsula. Only about half of the raiders actually reached the target; the remainder aborted because of weather problems. But those that persisted arrived during a period of clear visibility. The Americans on the ground at first thought the incoming flight belonged to an Army P-40 outfit that had buzzed the base a few days earlier while en route to a base farther west at Umnak. Sighting of the wing insignia, however, brought orders to open fire.

Unmolested except for ground fire, the bombers blew up a barracks, killing twenty-five and injuring the same number, and wrecked several other structures at Fort Mears. With no U.S. fighters present, the Zeros strafed a lone Catalina as it started to taxi out of Dutch Harbor. Machine-gun bullets killed two crewmen and wounded another pair. The PBY pilot beached his heavily damaged airplane. As the attacking force rendezvoused for the return to the flattops, according to James Russell, VP-42's CO, a lone Catalina hove into view. The Zeros promptly attacked, shooting down the American patrol plane. But before it crashed, a waist gunner apparently winged a Zero. All hands were lost including the waist gunner, who was later found, machine-gunned to death while floating in his life jacket.

That crewman's achievement brought an unexpected dividend, Russell explained. "The bullet [that hit the enemy fighter] went in from the top and severed the oil pressure gauge line behind the dash of the Zero. This cut off the oil pressure from the gauge and Flight Petty Officer Tadayoshi Koga [from the *Ryujo*] who was flying the airplane saw his oil pressure drop to zero. [He] radioed the *Ryujo*, saying, 'I expect my engine to freeze up momentarily. I've lost my oil pressure and I will make a forced landing on Akutan Island. Please send a submarine to pick me up.' [That island had been previously chosen for such emergencies.]

"His plan was to land on the island, destroy his airplane by burning it, and walk down to the beach on Akutan to be picked up by a submarine which they had cruising in the vicinity of Dutch Harbor. What he didn't realize was this lovely mountain meadow which he picked out to make his landing was a bog, as most level places in the Aleutians are, and he lowered his wheels. If he'd left his wheels retracted I think he would have gotten away with it very handily. But he didn't. He lowered his wheels; these immediately caught in the bog, flipped him over on his back. He broke his neck and was killed." The flight leader, watching, estimated the plane to be heavily damaged and the pilot probably dead or wounded. A patrol submarine did check out the island but could not locate the wreck.

Although several other aircraft were shot down or crashed, this would be the most noticeable loss to the Japanese. Five weeks later, an American search party looking for a missing Catalina flew over Akutan. Said Russell, "They were amazed to find this airplane with red apples on its wings bottom up in the marsh. A salvage party [put together at Dutch Harbor] went over to the scene of the wrecked Zero and disassembled it enough to get it down to the waterfront and load it on a lighter. Towed to Dutch Harbor, it was put aboard a freighter and brought to the naval air overhaul facility at North Island, San Diego." The rebuilt plane underwent intensive flight tests and studies that revealed its strengths and weaknesses, extremely valuable information for aerial combat.

Members of VP-41 had begun to routinely search the surrounding waters to detect the expected onslaught from a Japanese amphibious force. After one prowling airplane disappeared, Russell said they were convinced that it had been a victim of the enemy fleet. A PBY under Lieutenant Lucius D. Campbell, who in prewar days had been a chief petty officer rather than a commissioned officer, had just landed at Umnak to refuel when word of the attack on Dutch Harbor came. He took off without pausing for more gas. In the air, Campbell and his crew peered through the thick cloud banks.

As Walter Karig reported in *Battle Report, Pacific War: Middle Phase*, Campbell had already started for the Umnak base when, he said, "two small float-type planes appeared on our starboard quarter. I knew we were very near the Japs then, because these were catapult observation planes."

Both of the seaplanes fired on the PBY. They missed during the first pass but scored some hits on the Catalina on their second run. Campbell hid in a cloud, and when he broke out into a patch of open sky, he looked down to see two carriers with cruisers and destroyers. "I was so engrossed in those ships down below," said Campbell, "I didn't see the Jap Zero. It came from above and we heard the yammering of its guns before we saw the plane. It lasted only a moment but he gave us everything he had." The damage included perforation of the already low fuel tanks, hits on the rudder controls, and a cannon shot that blew away a wing strut. One bullet wounded a gunner. In the midst of a report to the home base, the radio quit. Although the message was garbled, the skipper of Patrol Squadron Forty-two realized that Campbell had seen the enemy.

With his controls crippled and out of gas, his radio transmitter not functioning, Campbell desperately looked for a place to set down. He pushed the nose down and entered into a rapid glide. Somehow he guided the powerless aircraft into a fairly soft landing. While the crew frantically plugged the holes in the fuselage to keep the plane from sinking, the radioman tinkered with his set. For a brief interval it worked, long enough to send a report on the fleet sighting to Dutch Harbor. Campbell and his people spent three fretful hours drifting in the frigid sea before a Coast Guard vessel rescued them.

Because of constant snow squalls, widespread fog, and the almost perpetual haze that hovers over the frigid waters, sorties from Patrol Wing Four hunted in vain for the Northern Force until June 4. That day, the Japanese attacked Dutch Harbor a second time, wrecking fuel tanks, a new hangar, and some construction equipment. Air Corps P-40s, operating out of a well-concealed field at Umnak, intercepted the air group on its way back to the fleet and shot down four dive-bombers while losing two fighters.

The surprise appearance of the P-40s infuriated the Japanese air group commander. It happened that the PBY whose loss had convinced Russell of the approximate location of the enemy task force had crash-landed in the water. "When they were shot down," explained Russell, who after the war interviewed a navigator, Lieutenant (j.g.) Wiley Hunt, "they landed and got out the big rubber boat which held seven men and the little one which held two. The big raft was riddled with bullet holes and it didn't float too long. The men swam over and hung onto the little raft. Hunt tried to get them to come aboard but they wouldn't because they knew it wouldn't support all of them. He watched them slowly get numb, lose their grip, and drift away.

"The three of them who were in the raft survived, two enlisted

men and Hunt. They were picked up by the Japanese heavy cruiser
Maya, and immediately the commissioned officer and two enlisted
men were segregated. They were so far gone that the Japanese had
to put a line on them and haul them up on the deck. They couldn't
climb under their own power. Hunt was interrogated but not severely until the second day."

His treatment changed radically because during this second day,
the P-40s suddenly jumped the Japanese as they rendezvoused. The
air group commander from the *Junyo* came to the *Maya*, seeking information on the source of the opposition. Hunt told Russell they
started to beat him while asking questions. "They rigged a device to
make him open up. They tied his hands behind his back and a deep
sea lead, which weighs considerable about his waist (you couldn't
swim with it, particularly with your hands tied) and they put him
out in the leadsman's chains. They took the life line down, so he was
on a platform over the sea. A burly seaman had his hand on his
shoulder to push him over the side. The interpreter thrust a paper at
him saying, 'Answer these questions or you will die.'

"They were about Umnak, from which he'd taken off with his
amphibian that morning. But he was so imbued with the idea that
you said nothing but your name, rank and serial number that he generated a cock-and-bull story that he'd flown up in forced marches
from down in the States, that he'd taken off from Dutch Harbor that
morning and he didn't know anything about this fighter field.

"The air group commander was in a rage and he wouldn't take
that for an answer. If a pilot was flying from Dutch Harbor, he must
know more than that. He must know where there are fighters." Russell said Hunt told him, " 'I thought pretty fast. I said I have told you
I flew up in great haste from the United States. I flew out of Dutch
Harbor and I don't know anything about this field that you mentioned.' They thrust the questions at him again. 'This time,' he said,
'I thought maybe I had better stall a bit, and I said to the interpreter,
'Is there a priest or minister on board?' [The idea was to administer
the last rites.] The interpreter didn't know 'minister' or 'priest' so he
ran down to his stateroom to get his English-Japanese dictionary.
Meanwhile, Hunt was standing there with a hand on his shoulder
ready to be pushed over the side. The interpreter came back up and
said, 'No, no priest or minister on board.' He stood there for some
time and finally they said, 'Okay, you will live.' "

In weather so poor that the Japanese could not launch any fighters, a PBY piloted by Lieutenant Marshall C. Freerks finally spotted

the task force. Subsequently, Freerks turned over the job of shadow to another PBY. Unfortunately, the skies cleared enough for the task force to send up some fighters, which shot down the PBY. Patrol Wing Four's Catalinas were not effective in their sporadic attempts to torpedo the enemy. A pair of Army B-26s also failed to have any impact on the marauders. One of them had borrowed a torpedo from the Navy and actually dumped it onto the deck of a carrier. But the Army pilot did not realize that the tin fish needed to spin its propellers in the water to arm the device.

Two days later, the Japanese shifted their attention much farther west and landed troops on the islands of Attu and Kiska. Both were undefended, and the only American military presence was on Kiska, where ten enlisted sailors operated a weather station. The Japanese now owned the two islands, but none of their realistic desires was fulfilled. Nimitz refused the bait. He neither sent ships and planes away from Midway to deal with the threat, nor was he provoked into committing any forces to a sea and air battle with the enemy. A week passed before Patrol Wing Four aviators even discovered that the enemy was now installed on Kiska and Attu.

Notwithstanding the slowness to find the Japanese occupation in the Aleutians, intelligence was the vital element in the U.S. defense of Midway. In Hawaii, a team of code breakers, working under canny Commander Joseph Rochefort, a veteran cryptanalyst, were reading the entire message traffic of the Japanese fleet. From these intercepts, Rochefort, chief of the combat intelligence office, and his cohorts tracked the enemy fleets. Rochefort deduced that frequent references to a place designated as AF meant Midway. Furthermore, he believed that AF was the target of the enemy ships steaming through the Pacific. His certainty as to the Japanese objective had convinced Nimitz, but to persuade any doubters, Rochefort concocted a trap.

Around May 10, he arranged for Midway to send a message in the clear to Naval Headquarters in Oahu reporting that the saltwater distillation system had broken down and freshwater was in short supply. Within forty-eight hours, Japanese naval radio messages spoke about AF as having water problems.

Under Admiral Yamamoto, the forces committed to the Midway campaign consisted of three separate armadas. Four aircraft carriers with a pair of battleships, several cruisers, and twelve destroyers led the fleet. Planes launched from the flattops would pulverize the island defenses and take out warships. Behind this task force steamed Yamamoto's Main Body, an assortment of heavyweights that included powerful battleships. Yamamoto himself sailed in the Main Body aboard the world's largest battlewagon, the 72,000-ton *Yamato*, which packed 17-inch guns. The Main Body would smash any American vessels that escaped the torpedo planes and dive-bombers or rushed from Pearl Harbor to reinforce Midway. A small portion of the Main Body split off to head north and support the Aleutian adventure. Bringing up the rear were the ships carrying a landing force. Augmenting the massive flotilla were submarines, expected to be a prime source of intelligence on enemy ship movements and even conditions on Midway.

Nimitz ordered three carriers, the *Hornet*, the *Enterprise*, and the *Yorktown*, to meet the threat. The *Yorktown* departed Hawaii only after a Herculean effort by workers to repair the injuries received during the Coral Sea battle. Jimmy Thach and his fighter squadron landed aboard the patched-up *Yorktown* when it was 50 to 100 miles out of Pearl Harbor and on its way to join the task groups that included the carriers *Enterprise* and *Hornet*.

Thach's unit had barely completed their combat instruction in the first week of June 1942 before being ordered onto the *Yorktown*. The arrival of VF-3 was anything but propitious. "I had given Don Lovelace [an old comrade] the pick of wing men. I'd already landed aboard and was in the ready room and Don Lovelace brought his division in. He landed and he had taxied across the barrier [which] had just been lifted behind him. His wing man landed too hard, bounced clear over the barrier and landed right on top of Don Lovelace and cut his head off. It was an especially difficult thing to accept at that moment. We'd all been briefed on what was coming along. It was a sad thing to lose the life of a good friend but to lose his ability and leadership was a doubly bad blow." Some replacement pilots who had never practiced the Weave also joined the squadron as it boarded the carrier.

When Thach mentioned "what was coming along," he was referring to the critical struggle shaping up around Midway Island. The outpost's land-based Army and Marine flyers would be overwhelmed by the enemy's superiority in quality and number of aircraft. The Navy task force that included the *Yorktown* hoped to add its strength to the defenses. When he took off from Hawaii, Thach knew only of an impending big fight in the Pacific. Once aboard the

Yorktown, he listened to a complete briefing on the opposition. Thach was reassured after a visit with his engineering chief, who promised that all the planes would be ready.

While the carrier was some 400 miles out of port, two newly commissioned pilots, right out of flight school, were assigned to join the flattop. "I was still just a cab driver in VR-1," remembered Floyd Thorn. "They were afraid that [these two pilots] wouldn't find the carrier. They wanted somebody to take them out there. I flew a fighter and took them. I had gone through fighter school in Pensacola. I was really proud of those two kids. They got down on that deck just as slick as a whistle. I talked to an ol' chief about that [saying] 'Those kids made a real nice landing.' He said, 'They always do when they're scared.' " Thorn learned that not only had he served as a guide but he was also now considered available for fighter duty aboard the *Yorktown.*

Gordon W. Prange et al.'s *Miracle at Midway* reports, "On paper, the American carrier force racing westward looked like a sea-going David going forth to tangle with a salt-water Goliath." The comparison of assets puts the number of Japanese fighting ships at eighty-six compared to the puny twenty-seven mustered by the United States. Yamamoto had four heavy aircraft carriers and two light ones. In this category, the attackers would be opposed by a mere three carriers. Nimitz had no battleships to ante up, only six heavy cruisers, one light one, and seventeen destroyers. But like the enemy, a number of American submarines prowled the Pacific, collecting information and hoping for a shot at one of the many targets.

Only in aircraft did the numbers suggest an edge to the defenders. The land-based Marines and Army possessed an assortment of 115 torpedo bombers, dive-bombers, fighters, scout seaplanes (including the PBYs), Army B-26s, and B-17s. From the three carriers, Nimitz could count on 223 combat aircraft: torpedo bombers, dive-bombers, and fighters. That gave the Americans a total of 348. The enemy's available planes added up to 325.

But the statistics were deceptive. Initially, the air defenses consisted of Marine Air Group Twenty-two, which included Scout Bombing Squadron 241 and Fighter Squadron 221. The latter flew the obsolete F2A-3 Brewster Buffalo and the former the marginally suitable SB2-U3 Vindicator. But in May, VP-44, with a dozen PBYs, arrived to supplement the patrols flown by the Marines. The Army brought in twenty-seven B-17s, and then Marine Air Group Twenty-two arrived with seven F4F-3 Wildcats and nineteen SBD-2s Dauntlesses, improvements over those flown by the brother air group. However, in a major failing, no one drafted measures that would enable the flyers from the three American services to coordinate their actions.

One unplanned reinforcement came in the form of a six-plane detachment from Torpedo Squadron Eight. A member of the oufit, Ensign Albert "Bert" Earnest, a graduate of Virginia Military Institute who had held an Army reserve commission in the field artillery, had decided he would prefer to fly. He had transferred to naval aviation in February 1941 but had been disappointed by his assignment to VT-8. "I had wanted to fly fighters," he told writer Rich Pedroncelli in an interview published in *Naval History* magazine. "I had never flown torpedo planes before, not even during flight school, but I knew what they did and it sounded pretty hairy to me."

Earnest thought the Devastator "a very easy plane to fly." When the Navy decided to replace it with the new TBF-1 Avenger, he and five others were temporarily detached from VT-8 to train on the new aircraft. They were left behind at the Norfolk Naval Air Station while the *Hornet*, with the rest of the squadron aboard, sailed for the Pacific. Earnest and his mates reached Pearl Harbor too late to join the carrier. Instead, equipped with extra fuel tanks, they flew 1,200 miles to Midway. Said Earnest, "Everywhere you looked there were planes. I was impressed there were so many B-17s; they were parked all over the place. There were so many airplanes there was almost no place to park." The torpedo plane detachment's commander, Lieutenant Langdon K. Fieberling, consulted with the Marine dive-bomber people about a possible joint attack.

Japanese fighters remained superior to the best the United States flew. The first radio-transmitted IFF (identification, friend or foe) system was starting to appear in American cockpits. At the time of the Battle of Midway, however, only a few Navy aircraft boasted IFF. During the Coral Sea fiasco, it had been the absence of IFF that caused sailors to believe that the Japanese planes preparing to land on the carriers were friendly. The Navy also used radios that were far better than those of their Japanese counterparts.

Japanese intelligence underestimated the number of planes based at Midway, but a far more critical error was overestimating the previous U.S. carrier losses. Radar had not been installed on the main elements of the Japanese fleet—with the exception of the armada that would sail to the Aleutian Islands. Absent radar, the intelligence sources open to the Japanese at sea consisted of sightings by submarines and aircraft patrols. The U-boats, however, provided little of value. A key group never got close enough to file useful information. The single exception was I-168, whose inspection of the Midway area found extensive construction and a near-constant air patrol out to a distance of 600 miles, which suggested that the Americans foresaw a threat to the island. Sightings of U.S. submarines trying to track Yamamoto's fleet confirmed to the Japanese that their adversary was aware of their approach.

Still of limited capability, American shipborne radar could see some 50 miles or so. The distance increased for detection gear on land bases such as Midway. Radar permitted more effective direction of fighters, but the early versions of the device were not accurate in showing altitude. And the ability to read the Japanese naval messages provided the Americans with an enormous advantage: knowledge of where the enemy planned to strike. However, the question of whether the defenders could exploit this information was quite another matter.

Both sides relied heavily on reconnaissance by air. The Japanese, however, labored under a handicap. With Wake their nearest base, their land-based patrols required long-range aircraft. A plan called Operation K tried to overcome the disadvantage. A pair of Emilys, four-engine flying boats, were to rendezvous with a submarine at French Frigate Shoal, some 500 miles northwest of Oahu, refuel from submarines, and then fly as far as Hawaii while reconnoitering the waters between Oahu and Midway. But when the submarine reached French Frigate Shoal it saw two U.S. warships there. Operation K was canceled.

Although Rochefort and his team could read the Japanese navy's radio messages, Yamamoto prudently ordered radio silence. The Americans had the luxury of using the Army B-17s, some of which were rushed into recon work within a day after their arrival. The Flying Fortresses obediently headed for a predicted enemy meeting place 700 miles out to sea. But before they traveled half the distance, the big Army planes became lost in near-ceiling zero weather, and they barely got home. Scout planes from the *Hornet* and *Yorktown* also traversed sectors of the sea, seeking the oncoming fleet.

On June 1, some 500 miles or so west and southwest of the island, a two-plane Catalina search team bumped into a pair of Japanese bombers intent on a similar mission. One of the Navy planes radioed Midway that it was under attack, and the enemy continued to pursue and snap at the amphibian for more than an hour. The PBY staggered back to its base with three injured crewmen.

Among the Navy people now engaged in the search for the enemy was Jim Ogden, one of the few people who got aloft during the Japanese attack on Pearl Harbor. "When we got out there [Midway], we expected the attack to come on the 3rd of June and therefore we would find to the southwest the landing force at a distance of 600 miles bearing 260 degrees. And we should [find] the striking force to the northwest.

"On the 2d of June search, nothing was found in either area where the Japanese were expected to be. The northwest was completely covered with a fog bank. On the 3rd of June, however, the landing force was sighted by VP-44, which had the southern half of our sector, bearing 261 degrees, distance 600 miles. This is how good our information was. [Ogden's memory was off by one degree and 100 miles.] The striking force was not sighted again because of weather, although we felt sure that it was there."

The pilot from VP-44 who picked up the landing force was Ensign Jack Reid. In letters to Gordon Prange after the war, Reid reported that he and his crew had awakened at 3:00 on the morning of June 3. After a breakfast of bacon, eggs, toast, and coffee and a briefing for the twenty-two-plane reconnaissance mission that stressed the possibility of an invasion of Midway, Reid took off for the daily twelve-hour surveillance. Some six hours out of Midway, as he prepared to turn in to the dogleg route that would bring him back to Midway, Reid acceded to requests from Chief Radioman Francis Musser and Navigator Ensign Robert Swan to extend the flight another ten minutes. The crewmen, apparently, were not thinking in terms of finding the Japanese ships so much as hoping for an encounter with an enemy plane. They had borrowed from the Army Air Corps some new explosive bullets that the B-17 gunners swore would destroy anything they hit.

The extra minutes expired, and Reid began to swing his PBY toward its homeward route. Suddenly, he spotted some specks on the horizon, which at first he thought were dirt on his windshield. Prange wrote, "He stayed on his original course, then did a quick double-take and shouted to his co-pilot, Ensign Gerald Hardeman, 'My God, aren't those ships on the horizon? I believe we've hit the jackpot.'"

Hardeman peered through his binoculars and concurred with Reid. "Then, within a few seconds, Ensign John Gammell, the second co-pilot and bow gunner, set up a shout. 'I've spotted ships dead ahead approximately twenty-five to thirty miles.' "

Reid sent off a message to Midway: "Sighted Main Body." He added a few minutes later, "Bearing 262, distance 700." The news galvanized the commanders on the island. But before they committed their forces, they wanted to know more about the oncoming ships. Reid cautiously maneuvered to approach the task force more closely. Undoubtedly, the Japanese could dispatch fighters if they saw a snooper, and a PBY, even with explosive bullets, could hardly dogfight a Zero.

Dropping down to well under 1,000 feet of altitude, he opted for a course that brought him behind the fleet, where, tracking the wakes, he could report with some precision, "Eleven ships, course 090, speed 19 . . . one small carrier, one seaplane carrier, two battleships, several cruisers . . . and several destroyers." At the point of no return in terms of fuel, Reid gladly obeyed orders to return to Midway.

Although he had categorized the group as the "Main Body," Reid actually had come across, as Ogden noted, the Midway Invasion Force. And at that he had seen and reported only a portion of that flotilla. Captain (later Rear Admiral) Edward Layton, the fleet intelligence officer, reminisced in his book *And I Was There*, "I happened to be in Nimitz's office when this message came in. His eyes lit up like searchlights.

" 'Layton,' he said excitedly, 'have you seen this?'

" 'What is it, sir?'

" 'The sighting of the Japanese forces,' Nimitz replied, giving me a dazzling smile. 'It ought to make your heart warm.' "

Although Reid's report used the term "Main Body," Nimitz, clued in by Rochefort and Layton, in code advised Rear Admirals Frank J. Fletcher, CO of Task Force Seventeen aboard the *Yorktown*, and Raymond Spruance on the *Enterprise* (he had replaced Vice Admiral William Halsey, who was temporarily hospitalized) differently: "That is not repeat not the enemy striking force—stop—That is the landing force. The striking force will hit from the northwest at daylight tomorrow."

Regardless of which part of the combined enemy forces had been located, the command at Midway acted. Commander Logan Ramsey had been invested as the head of air operations. Under his aegis, the Army Air Corps's B-17s had been engaged in recon missions, and now nine of the Flying Fortresses, laden with four 600-

pound bombs, under Lieutenant Colonel Walter C. Sweeney, roared down the runway and headed west toward the enemy. Ramsey was quoted as having said that this was "the most experienced group of B-17s and its effectiveness, resolution and communication efficiency and discipline were outstanding."

The big bombers found the landing force in the late afternoon. The Japanese opened up with antiaircraft from a cruiser and destroyers convoying the troop transports. After a brief interval of evasion in the clouds, the B-17s unloaded from altitudes of 8,000 to 12,000 feet. A number of bombs failed to detonate. Although the Air Corps claimed five or six hits on battleships, cruisers, and transports, in fact there was no damage or casualties. For that matter, the heavy ack-ack from the ships also registered a complete miss.

While the B-17s droned back to their Midway base, Ramsay and Commander Cyril Simard, the naval air station boss, organized a special mission, a night torpedo attack by PBYs. Lieutenant William L. Richards, the exec of VP-44, would lead the all-volunteer expedition Taking off around 8:00 P.M., the flight immediately encountered bad weather. As Richards said in *Miracle at Midway*, "What had begun as a night merely as black as the inside of a coal mine, got really dark." One PBY soon lost contact with the group and groped unsuccessfully through the night to find the target. Eventually, the crew abandoned the quest, jettisoned their torpedo, and flew home.

A second plane, piloted by Ensign Gaylord D. Probst, also separated from the others, but Probst, nicknamed Dagwood, came upon the invasion force convoy on his own. He picked out the biggest vessel he could see and, only 50 feet above the sea, unleashed his torpedo. "As we swung away," he reported, "the sky began to light up like Coney Island on the Fourth of July." Probst evaded the antiaircraft gunnery by entering the clouds.

The flight leader, William Richards, also located the quarry. In one account, he supposedly thought his target was a carrier, but in Prange's book he is quoted as describing the vessel as "a large transport or cargo ship of about 7,000 tons." Gliding down, Richards dispatched his tin fish, and when he banked above his victim, two of his crew claimed "a huge explosion and heavy smoke." Richards then flew toward a rendezvous point.

Lieutenant (j.g.) Douglas C. Davis, who had stuck with Richards, made two runs over a ship, seeking a better approach. On his second try, he met a blizzard of machine-gun fire while he launched his torpedo. A waist gunner sprayed the enemy with .50-calibers, but his Catalina absorbed considerable damage from the Japanese shooters.

Postwar records found that while Richards's torpedo exploded, the sole hit of the day belonged to Probst. The blast killed or wounded twenty-three sailors on an oiler. Individually, all four PBYs sought to return to base but detoured to the tiny island of Lisianski upon the news that Midway itself was now under attack.

SIX

THE BATTLE FOR MIDWAY

The opening salvos of the battle for Midway had begun with the total misfire of the B-17 expedition and the minimal damage inflicted by the VP-44 raid. But, however inconsequential the American attacks, when coupled with the appearance of the PBY flown by Reid, they notified the Japanese that their enemy knew about their presence and, more important, their location. These events confirmed to Yamamoto and Vice Admiral Nagumo, commander of the First Air Fleet, that the moment for their attack had arrived.

It was shortly before 3:00 A.M. on June 4 when the engines aboard the four Japanese flattops of the strike force coughed to life. At 4:30, the Midway attack forces started to lift off the decks as the first Zero zoomed off the floodlight-illuminated *Akagi*, and within fifteen minutes the 108 aircraft from *Akagi*, *Kaga*, *Hiryu*, and *Soryu*, the first wave, started forming up for the assault upon Midway. Left behind were eighteen fighters to supply cover for the flattops should any American planes attack. Simultaneously, the Japanese assigned seven aircraft to search for segments of the U.S. Navy. The carriers contributed a pair of planes, and the rest catapulted off accompanying cruisers and battleships. Considering the size of the area, the effort was well short of the need. One of the weaknesses of the Nipponese air arm lay in a lack of training in search techniques. But much more deadly, in a major miscalculation, the Japanese believed that any enemy forces were still well east of Midway and would be unable to intervene until the island had been conquered.

About the same time as the Japanese commenced their operations, half a dozen Marine fighter pilots in the cockpits of Grumman Wildcats rose from the island for combat air patrol. Simultaneously, eleven PBYs slowly lifted off for their reconnaissance task. Certain that the enemy was continuing to steam toward Midway, the American commanders felt that their eyes in the sky would locate the oncoming carrier force. Sixteen B-17s also roared off the runways, hoping to find and bomb the Japanese troop transports, vessels that lacked the air cover of the striking force. On the tarmacs waited a handful of Army B-26s, six Navy torpedo-armed TBF-1s from VT-8, the Marine combined bomber and torpedo squadron VMSB-241, and the remainder of VMF-221, a puny assortment of the hopelessly inadequate Brewster Buffalo fighters.

For reasons never explained, the thin Japanese search for possible enemy carriers became even more anemic when a number of planes assigned to the task never got into the air. U.S. Task Forces Sixteen, under Rear Admiral Raymond Spruance, and Seventeen, under Rear Admiral Frank Jack Fletcher (neither of whom had qualified as aviators), remained invisible to the Japanese as their flattops also began to scour the seas for the enemy strike force.

Shortly before 6:00 A.M., one of the patrolling PBYs sighted two groups of forty-five planes boring in on Midway. Lieutenant (j.g) William A. Chase radioed in the clear, "Many planes heading Midway bearing 320 degrees, distance 150."

In another Catalina, ducking the rain squalls, Lieutenant Howard P. Ady broke through a cloud, and there, a heart-stopping vision, spread out below, streamed the striking force under Admiral Nagumo. Chase, adjacent to Ady's area, also sighted the massive force. He radioed, "Two carriers and main body ships, carriers in front, course 125, speed 35."

On Sand Island, radar now detected incoming bogeys. They were 93 miles off and at 11,000 feet. Alarms rang and antiaircraft gunners sprang to their posts, while every fighter that could took off from the Midway strips at about 6:15 A.M., with the attackers only 40 miles off. What followed was a slaughter of the valiant but hopelessly underequipped Marine squadron. They were unable to match the speed, rate of climb, or maneuverability of the Japanese fighter cover. Although the Americans knocked down several bombers and Zeros, the enemy virtually destroyed all of the fighters based on Midway. With no air cover to protect the island, Japanese bombers blasted gun emplacements, hangars, support buildings, fuel dumps, and ammunition pits, carefully avoiding the runways, which they expected to use after the invasion. Between the antiaircraft gunnery and the resistance offered by VMF-221, the Japanese listed a total of eight aircraft lost; no figures on damaged planes were recorded. But most significantly, the heavy ground fire indicated to Admiral Nagumo that the island would require a second attack wave.

The first U.S. Navy strike, on June 4, came from the tiny six-plane detachment of Torpedo Squadron Eight, which included Ensign Bert Earnest. Around 6:00 A.M., with the search planes reporting the position of the enemy fleet, the Avengers took off from Midway, expecting to join fighters and dive-bombers already in the sky. They thus left Midway just before the enemy struck. Earnest noted that his turret gunner, Jay Manning, looked back and saw the guns of the island offering a reception to the Japanese raiders.

Instead of waiting for the Marine dive-bombers, the commander of the six Navy aircraft, Lieutenant Langdon Fieberling, elected to proceed alone. The group flew for an hour before Earnest recalled, "I saw a large force ahead of us with at least two carriers. It was the first fleet I had ever seen." But even as he spotted the target, Manning spoke through the intercom: "Here come the Zeros." His machine gun started its chatter. Earnest identified one of the enemy as a Messerschmitt 109, but he was in error, as no German aircraft were operating off Japanese carriers.

Fieberling led the Avengers in a dive toward the water, leveling off at 200 feet. Said Earnest, "When the fighters attacked, we held formation pretty well. The first thing we did as we dove was open our bomb bay doors." The technique ensured the ability to launch the tin fish even if hydraulic systems failed, but it slowed the Avengers to fat-target speed. The Zeros persisted while Earnest marveled at their skill: "There were so many of them they were getting into each other's way. You couldn't help but be impressed by how maneuverable they were."

Their guns ravaged the torpedo planes. During a lull following the third fighter pass, Earnest noticed that Manning's gun was no longer sounding. His radioman/tunnel gunner, Harry Ferrier, saw Manning hanging lifeless in his harness. Their plane itself absorbed terrible damage as cannon shells ripped into the wing and the frightened pilot felt machine-gun bullets pelting the armor plate behind his seat. He lost elevator control and began to glide toward the water; the hydraulics shut down, and now Ferrier's gun fell silent. A piece of shrapnel pierced the canopy and gouged Earnest's cheek. "Blood spurted all over the place, covering the control panel. I could feel blood going down my neck."

Earnest, convinced that his crewmen were both dead, and with his aircraft badly maimed, abandoned his hope of hitting a carrier with his 2,000-pound torpedo and picked out the nearest ship, a light cruiser, as his one chance to strike a blow. Moments later he dropped the missile, but he said, "Doubt if I got a hit. I didn't get much of a lead on it." He had no time to observe because a pair of fighters closed in on his crippled ship. "They just peppered me. I did everything I had ever heard of to throw them off. I kept trying to turn into them—I heard this might work. It didn't seem to bother them a bit. They pounded me at will." For some reason, his tormentors withdrew. The beating absorbed by the TBF, which continued to fly, testified to its durability.

While not many controls remained viable, the engine droned on, and Earnest set a roundabout course for Midway that would steer him around the carriers and out of harm's way. To his surprise, he now heard Harry Ferrier, his radioman, addressing him. A bullet had grazed Ferrier's skull, knocking him unconscious, but he had come to his senses. At Midway, with only one wheel willing to be hand-cranked down, Earnest rejected a wave-off on his second try to land. He set down and ground-looped but was home, the only pilot from his detachment not lost.

Although Chester Nimitz had instructed the Midway command to deploy all of its fighters in the battle against the enemy carriers, leaving the defenses against aerial bombardment to antiaircraft, Captain Cyril T. Simard, the commander, chose to retain the fighters as part of the island's shield. Therefore, the six TBFs sortied without air cover. They were, however, part of a mixed bag of raiders; the four B-26s, plus some B-17s and Vindicators, went off on the same mission. Only two of the four B-26s that attacked the striking force limped back to Midway. Except perhaps for a few casualties inflicted by machine gunners, the Martin Marauders had nothing to show for their losses.

However ineffective the initial sorties against the Japanese carrier group, the harassment, coupled with the stubborn Midway defenses, interfered with the grand strategy envisioned by Yamamoto and Nagumo. Aboard the carriers *Akagi* and *Kaga*, crews had already armed the torpedo bombers with tin fish in anticipation of a confrontation with enemy ships. But with no sign of these and with the report that Midway would require another battering before the landing force could be committed, the air fleet commander felt he had no choice but to replace the torpedoes with bombs. An hour or so would be needed for the change. Nagumo also envisioned that his second strike would probably catch the pesky handful of Navy and Army aircraft that had futilely poked at his armada on the ground.

At 7:28 A.M., a Japanese scout launched from the cruiser *Tone* finally spotted Spruance's Task Force Sixteen with the *Enterprise* and *Hornet*. When he radioed word to Nagumo, the Japanese admiral became becalmed. He halted the conversion from torpedoes to bombs while awaiting further information. The planes that had already been switched had returned to the flight deck, and the two flattops now held ten to fifteen aircraft ready to resume the battering of Midway. Otherwise, the decks remained empty, in anticipation of the return of the aircraft that had attacked Midway. When the *Tone*'s patrol plane checked in again, he reported the disagreeable news that there was at least one carrier among the Americans.

As the Japanese pondered their next move, the land-based VMSB-241, sixteen SBD-2 Dauntless dive-bombers, hove into view. Unfortunately, most of the green pilots were also unfamiliar with their aircraft. Instead of using the more deadly dive technique, they embarked on a combined glide-dive method. Before the Marines could even draw a bead on the targets, fighters from another Japanese carrier, *Soryu*, fell upon them with devastating results. Among the first to flame into the sea was Major Lofton Henderson, the squadron leader. When the gunfire, explosions, and smoke died away, eight of the Dauntlesses and their crews had been lost, and those that staggered back to Midway were badly damaged. The best they had achieved were near misses.

Lieutenant Colonel Walter Sweeney, again leading the Flying Fortresses, first headed for the landing force. But before takeoff he had been told that if the Navy found the carriers, he should divert to that target. When advised of the location of the striking force, Sweeney obediently changed course. At altitudes in the neighborhood of 20,000 feet, the B-17s dropped their ordnance but at best they scored near misses. They, unlike the other Americans raiding the fleet, easily fended off the few Zeros that tried to shoot them down. The ample guns and high-altitude characteristics of the four-engine bombers apparently discouraged Japanese fighter planes, in contrast to the fierce confrontations staged by the Luftwaffe in Europe.

Nagumo, bedeviled but unhurt by all of this Midway-based hostility, had received an erroneous message that claimed there were no carriers among the enemy ships. In a final frantic blow at its tormentors, Midway dispatched a dozen Marine SB2-U3 Vindicators. Intercepted by Zeros, the "Vibrators" scored not even a scratch on the Japanese and straggled home bereft of a third of their original number.

At 8:30 A.M., to the dismay of the perplexed Nagumo, a reconnaissance plane confirmed the presence of at least one enemy carrier among the oncoming Americans vessels. It was a most inopportune moment, for at the same time, the aircraft that had first attacked Midway, their fuel low, were now ready to be retrieved. An impatient Yamamoto advised the air fleet commander to launch the available planes for bombing Midway, but Nagumo was unwilling to send them off without fighter cover. Nor did he want to risk having most of the returnees from Midway ditch at sea while the flight decks were occupied by planes taking off. Furthermore, he believed it preferable to neutralize the American task force first. Therefore, he ordered the harried crews of the flattops to move the bomb-armed planes below and change back to torpedoes, while on deck the recovery process could begin.

Admiral Fletcher, the senior officer for Task Forces Sixteen and Seventeen, issued orders to commence an attack on the Japanese striking force. Spruance, aware of the enemy snooper, launched the squadrons on the *Enterprise* and the *Hornet* into the air beginning around 7:00 A.M. Fletcher with Seventeen, farther away from the foe, waited two more hours before the pilots of the *Yorktown* started to roll down the flight deck. The two American admirals concurred in their strategy. Gordon Prange, who interviewed both, quoted Fletcher: "I figured that if I were going to hit the Japanese, I should hit them with everything I had. We couldn't afford to wait. We had to strike first, strike swiftly and strike in great force."

Spruance's chief of staff, Captain Miles Browning, an aviator, figured out that the Japanese attack force would be homing in on their carriers around 9:00 A.M., which would be the optimum moment to strike. Because the Japanese vessels, temporarily abandoning Midway as a target while they confronted the American ships, abruptly changed course, almost the entire contingent from the

Hornet, thirty-five dive-bombers and twenty-seven F4F fighters, never found the enemy. Every one of the Wildcats ran out of fuel during the search. After they ditched, the pilots were rescued, and thirteen of the dive-bombers could leg it only as far as Midway. The remainder also landed in the water.

Ten fighters from the *Enterprise* missed their rendezvous with the torpedo planes of VT-6. While these outfits never arrived for their meeting, VT-8, the torpedo squadron from the *Hornet*, divorced from its fighter cover by cloud layers, had the bad luck to zero in on the enemy fleet.

Lieutenant Commander John C. Waldron, who commanded VT-8, had handed out a message to his torpedo men the previous evening: "Just a word to let you know I feel we are all ready. We have had a very short time to train, and we have worked under the most severe difficulties. But we have truly done the best humanly possible. I actually believe that under these conditions, we are the best in the world. My greatest hope is that we encounter a favorable tactical situation, but if we don't and worst comes to worst, I want each one of us to do his utmost to destroy our enemies. If there is only one plane left to make a final run-in, I want that man to go in and get a hit. May God be with us all. Good luck, happy landings, and give 'em hell."

The grim truth is that VT-8 was most unready for what it faced. Pilots such as Ensign George Gay, while schooled in theory, had little practice or experience in their craft. When Gay launched that morning, it was the very first time he had ever taken off and flown bearing a torpedo. In fact, he had never even seen it done. In VT-8, Gay's background was far from unique.

Furthermore, as VT-8 started to descend for its attack, it faced the nadir of tactical circumstances. There were no American fighters to protect the slow-moving, hapless birds from an estimated thirty-five predatory Zeros. Gay, who was among the final element making its run, watched in horror as the first two Devastators plunged into the sea. Then he saw flames erupt from Waldron's fuel tank. The squadron commander stood up in a vain atttempt to extricate himself from the cockpit before he too crashed. More and more of the TBDs succumbed to the enemy until Gay realized that he alone was still airborne.

Through his intercom, Gay heard his radioman, Bob Huntington, murmur, "They got me." When the pilot swiveled his head for a quick glance back, he saw Huntington's head lolling lifelessly. As he would later tell a writer from *Life*, he felt a stabbing pain in his upper left arm and a hole appeared in his jacket sleeve. With his right hand, he ripped the garment and pulled out a machine-gun bullet sticking out of the wound.

Additional shrapnel slashed Gay as he guided his damaged plane by gripping the stick between his knees. Some 800 yards from the *Soryu*, he dropped his torpedo. He believed that an explosion followed, but actually the missile slipped past the carrier without making contact. As Gay flew over the bridge, he said, he "could see the little Jap captain up there, jumping up and down, raising Hell." A quintet of Zeros pounded on him, shooting out his remaining controls and ailerons. The Devastator slid into the ocean. A wing ripped off and the fuselage quickly sank, but not before Gay clambered out with his rubber life raft and seat cushion.

He was in the midst of the enemy fleet and he concealed himself from sight by ducking beneath his black rubber seat cushion. Some of the sailors on the ships noticed his presence, but they ignored him, as more American aircraft were now menacing their vessels. The latest arrivals, fourteen Devastators of VT-6 from the *Enterprise*, scored no better than their doomed compatriots. Only four rattled back to the flattop, including one so shot up that it was jettisoned over the side.

Ten fighters from the *Enterprise*, scheduled to rendezvous with VT-6 and then come to their aid on a prearranged signal, missed their connection with the torpedo men. Instead, they wound up shadowing TBDs from the *Hornet*. These Devastator crews, ignorant of the coded call that could summon aid, floundered helplessly. The Wildcats from the *Enterprise* could only act as observers before being forced to return when gas ran down.

On the *Yorktown*, the leaders of the dive-bomber and the torpedo squadrons, none more senior than a lieutenant, regretfully agreed with Thach, who could deploy only a portion of his fighters (the bulk of the Wildcats would remain behind as protection for the *Yorktown*) to escort the torpedo planes. He explained, "If you had enough, you would stack your fighters up to and including the dive-bombers. The torpedo planes were old fire traps that were so slow and awkward and [had] no self-sealing tanks. They needed protection more than anyone else, so that governed our decision in this case."

Shortly before takeoff, Thach, as commander of VF-3, was dismayed to learn that even fewer than the expected number of

Wildcats—only six—could accompany the TBDs. The rest of the squadron would fly cover for the carrier and the other vessels. Thach reminded his tiny contingent that one enemy trick was posting a lone plane as an inviting target. "But there were his friends waiting topside to come down and pick you off if you pulled out alone. Nobody was to be a lone wolf, because lone wolves don't live very long under the circumstances we were going into."

Thach faced high noon off Midway with considerable trepidation: "I was very concerned about whether the torpedo planes could get in or not. I knew that if the Japanese were together in one formation and had a combat air patrol of defending fighters from all the carriers we would be outnumbered. We were also quite concerned that the Zero could outperform us in every way. We had one advantage in that we thought we could shoot better and had better guns. But if you don't get a *chance* to shoot, better guns matter little."

He was disturbed that only six fighters could make the mission, thus violating the basic weave structure, which was predicated on sets of fours. Because the Americans divided their forces into two groups, Task Force Sixteen, under Spruance, and Task Force Seventeen, commanded by Admiral Frank Jack Fletcher, a gap of more than 25 miles separated the *Yorktown*, with Task Force Seventeen, from the *Enterprise* and *Hornet*, part of Task Force Sixteen. The distance between the flattops reduced the opportunities for a mutual protection fighter shield.

The half-dozen Hellcats led by Thach followed the Devastators until Thach spotted ships spread over the ocean. "Several antiaircraft bursts [exploded] in our direction, one red and another orange." He wondered at the firing because the U.S. planes were well out of range. He soon learned that the colored bursts signaled the enemy combat air patrol of the American presence. Now about twenty Zeros, lurking overhead, dived onto the interlopers.

As the vast array of Japanese aircraft hummed toward the Americans, Thach recalled, "More torpedo planes were falling but so were some Zeros. We thought, at least we're keeping a lot of them engaged." However, the Devastators from the three U.S. carriers, *Lexington*, *Enterprise*, and *Hornet*, were being slaughtered, particularly as Thach's handful of Hellcats became embroiled in combat with the Japanese fighters, some of which Thach glimpsed still taking off from the enemy vessels.

"The first thing that happened was that [Ed] Bassett's plane was burning. He was shot down right away. I didn't see the Zero that got to him but I realized that they were coming in a stream from astern. I was surprised they put so many Zeros on my six fighters. I had thought they would go for the torpedo planes first. They must have known we didn't have the quick acceleration to catch them the way they were coming in at high speed in rapid succession and zipping on away. But then I saw a second large group that were now streaming right past us and into the poor torpedo planes. That first attack on us and the torpedo planes was beautifully coordinated. It was something I had to admire. It was beautifully executed. This was their first team and they were pros."

Thach was preparing to inaugurate a weave when he noticed that a Wildcat from another section, manned by a pilot named Brainard Macomber, was too close. Thach tried to raise him on the radio, but there was no response because the radio in Macomber's F4F was dead. To further complicate matters, Macomber was among the newcomers who never had practiced the weave. Frustrated, Thach contacted Ram Dibb, his own wingman, and ordered a modified version of the weave. "Pretend you are a section leader and move out far enough to weave. He said, 'This is Scarlet Two, Wilco.' His voice sounded like he was elated to get this 'promotion' right in the middle of a battle."

Even as he did, he watched below him the massacre of the torpedo squadron. Thach said, "Several Zeros came in on a head-on attack on the torpedo planes and burned Lem Massey's plane right away [Massey commanded VT-3]. It just exploded in flames. And beautifully timed, another group came in on the side against the torpedo planes. A number of them were coming down in a string on our fighters; the air was just like a beehive. It didn't look like my weave was working, but then it began to. I got a good shot at two of them and burned them. One had made a pass at my wing man, pulled out to the right and then came back. We were weaving continuously, and I got a head-on shot at him. About the time I saw this guy coming, Ram said, 'There's a Zero on my tail.' He didn't have to look back because the Zero wasn't directly astern which gave me the head-on approach. I was really angry because this poor little wing man, who'd never been in combat before, [had] very little gunnery training, his first time aboard a carrier and a Zero was about to chew him to pieces.

"I probably should have decided to duck under this Zero but I lost my temper a bit and decided I'm going to keep my fire going into him and he's going to pull out. He did and just missed me by a few feet. I saw flames coming out of the bottom of his airplane. It was like playing 'chicken' with two automobiles on the highway headed for each other, except we were both shooting as well. This was a little foolhardy, but I think because I hit him—the first reaction on being hit is to jerk back—he pulled his stick back and his nose went up.

"I had wanted him to pull out. I was going to force him to pull out, which is foolish. I didn't try that any more. You don't need to because if you haven't hit him by the time you get there, you certainly can afford to duck under and get away.

"I kept counting the number of planes that I knew I'd gotten in flames going down," he remembered. "You couldn't wait for them to splash, but you could tell if they were flaming real good and you saw something besides smoke. If it was real red flames, you knew he'd had it.

"I had this little knee pad and I would mark down every time I shot one that I knew was gone. Then I realized that this was sort of foolish. Why was I making marks on my knee pad when the knee pad wasn't coming back? I was utterly convinced then that we weren't any of us coming back because there were still so many of these Zeros and they'd already gotten one of us. I couldn't see Tom Cheek or Ed Sheedy [two other pilots]. The only others I could see were Macomber and Ram Dibb.

"Pure logic would convince anyone that with their superior performance and the number of Zeros they were throwing into the fight, we could not possibly survive. So I said, this counting is foolish. It takes a second or two to look down to your pad and make the mark. 'A waste of time,' I said, still talking to myself. 'We're going to take a lot of them with us if they're going to get us all.' We kept on working the weave and it seemed to work better and better.

"How much time this took I don't know and I haven't the slightest idea how many Zeros I shot down [one naval history credits him with six]. But I was absolutely convinced that we weren't coming back and neither were any of the torpedo planes."

The duels among the fighters slacked off enough for Thach to watch the remaining torpedo planes make their runs. He believes that one scored a hit, but that was denied by both Japanese and American historians. "Then I saw this glint in the sun and it just looked like a beautiful silver waterfall, these dive bombers coming down. I'd never seen such superb dive bombing. It looked like almost every bomb hit. Explosions were occurring in the carriers."

The aircraft wreaking devastation upon the Japanese flattops were from the *Enterprise's* VB-6 and VS-6, two squadrons of Dauntless dive-bombers. The plans for all attackers to arrive simultaneously had gone awry when the torpedo units and the bombers had lost contact with each other in the air. Because the Devastators found the target first and initiated their runs without a coordinated attack, they were doomed.

Initially, the entire mission seemed bound for failure as the thirty-two SPDs searched unsuccessfully for the target. Air Group Leader Lieutenant Commander Wade McClusky, although his fuel began to run dangerously low, set a course bearing his aircraft northwest. Later, Nimitz himself characterized McClusky's choice as having been "one of the most important decisions of the battle and one that had decisive results."

The squadron executive officer, Lieutenant Clarence E. Dickinson, with VS-6, who had parachuted from his plane after a covey of Zeros had mugged him six months earlier over Hawaii, said that McClusky had spied the fleet some 45 miles off. Dickinson told writer Boyden Sparkes, "What McClusky had distinguished first, almost halfway to the far horizon, on that dense ocean blue were thin, white lines, mere threads, chalk-white. He knew those must be the wakes of the Japanese ships. . . . Because I was less high, it was not until about five minutes after McClusky saw them that I could see them too."

Dickinson was awestruck by the vision. "Among those ships I could see two long, narrow, yellow rectangles, the flight decks of carriers. Apparently they leave the decks either the natural wood color or possibly they paint them a light yellow. But that yellow stood out on the dark blue sea like nothing you have ever seen. Then further off I saw a third carrier. I had expected to see only two and when I saw the third my heart went lower. The southwest corner of the fleet's position was obscured by a storm area. Suddenly another long yellow rectangle came sliding out of that obscurity. A fourth carrier!"

He said he was puzzled as to why enemy fighters had not swarmed over his squadron, but for the moment he saw no opposition: "each battleship, cruiser and destroyer advertised itself as Japanese with this marking painted on the forward turret. The turret top appeared as a square of white with a round, blood-red center. But on the deck of each carrier, bow or stern, the marking was exactly like that which appears on their planes. . . . On the nearest carrier I could see that this symbol probably would measure sixty feet across; a five-foot band of white, enclosing a fifty-foot disk of red. An enticing target!

"There were planes massed on the deck of each carrier and I could see that the flight decks were undamaged, in perfect condition to launch." He advised his radioman-gunner, Joseph DeLuca, to stand by for the inevitable rush of fighters. Like Dickinson, DeLuca was a veteran of the December 7 fiasco. He had spent the night of the attack on Pearl Harbor manning a machine gun on the island of Kauai, prepared to repel landing attempts.

Through his headphones, Dickinson heard McClusky crisply issue orders to Lieutenant Wilmer Earl Gallaher, CO of VS-6, and Lieutenant Richard H. Best, CO of VB-6, designating which carriers they should strike. Because VB-6 launched first from the *Enterprise* and therefore operated with a shorter deck, its aircraft carried only 500-pound bombs. VS-6, having the latitude of a longer runway, packed 1,000-pounders. McClusky elected to head one run and advised, "Earl, follow me."

Actually, missed communication between McClusky and Best led the latter to believe that he should focus on the *Kaga*. Only when McClusky suddenly dived past the startled Best, narrowly missing a collision, did Best decide to shear off and aim at the other flattop, *Akagi*. Best was further dismayed to see that only two others from VB-6 followed him.

From his vantage point, Dickinson now understood why fighters had not yet come after the bombers. "I saw some of their fighters milling about close to the water . . . they were finishing a job, our torpedo squadrons." As McClusky and those taking their cue from him now nosed over and dived toward the ships, Dickinson kicked his rudders back and forth, the ducklike twitch of his tail the signal for his division to attack. "I pulled up my nose and in a stalled position opened my flaps. We always do this, throw the plane up and to the side on which we are going to drive, put out the flaps as brakes and then peel-off. I was the ninth man of our squadron to dive."

Down, down he plunged. "I was making the best dive I ever made. The people who came back said it was the best dive they had ever made. We were coming from all directions on the port side of the carrier, beautifully spaced. Going down I was watching over the nose of my plane to see the first bombs land on that yellow deck. . . .

I felt sure I recognized her as the *Kaga* and she was enormous. [Dickinson and the other flyers had studied models of the main elements of the Japanese navy, and in fact it was a flight of Zeros from that vessel that had shot him out of the sky on December 7.]

"The *Kaga* [26,000 tons] and the *Akagi* were the big names in the Japanese fleet. Very likely one, or more of their newer carriers was better, but to us those two symbolized that which we had trained ourselves to destroy. The carrier was racing along at thirty knots, right into the wind. She made no attempt to change course. I was coming at her a little bit astern, on the left-hand side. By the time I was at 12,000 feet I could see all the planes ahead of me in the dive. We were close together but no one plane was coming down in back of another. . . . The target was utterly satisfying. The squadron's dive was perfect. This was the absolute. After this, I felt anything would be just anticlimax.

"I saw the bombs from the group commander's section drop. They struck the water on either side of the carrier. The explosions probably grabbed at her like an ice man's tongs. Earl Gallaher was the next man to drop. I learned later that his bomb struck the after part of the flight deck, among the parked planes and made a tremendous explosion which fed on gasoline.

"As I was almost at the dropping point I saw a bomb hit just behind where I was aiming, that white circle with its blood red center. . . . I saw the deck rippling and curling back in all directions, exposing a great section of the hangar below. That bomb had a fuse set to make it explode about four feet below the deck. I knew the last plane had taken off or landed on that carrier for a long time to come. . . .

"I dropped a few seconds after the previous bomb explosion. After the drop you must wait a fraction of a second before pulling out of the dive to make sure you do not 'throw' the bomb, spoil your aim as certainly as when you jerk, instead of squeeze the trigger of a rifle.

"I had determined during that dive that since I was dropping on a Japanese carrier I was going to see my bombs hit. After dropping, I kicked my rudder to get my tail out of the way and put my plane in a stall. So I was simply standing there to watch it. I saw the 500-pound bomb hit right abreast of the island. The two 100-pound bombs struck in the forward area of the parked planes on that yellow flight deck. Then I began thinking it was time to get myself away from there and try to get back alive."

As a holocaust enveloped the reeling *Kaga*, the *Akagi*, which became the object of the attentions of Richard Best and his two wing-men, prepared to launch the second wave on Midway. At least one Zero had roared down the deck when a lookout screamed the alarm. Although Lieutenant Best insisted that he had secured a hit, the first bomb appears to have been a very near miss. But the second one crashed near the amidship elevator, and a third one penetrated the port flight deck. The explosions ignited fierce fires that cooked off the nearly 2,000-pound bombs stacked up for loading aboard air-craft. The plane's fuel tanks burst into flames. The violent tremors aboard the *Akagi* pitched two hundred sailors over the side.

Just before the *Enterprise* squadrons swooped down upon the *Akagi* and *Kaga*, seventeen planes from VB-3, the sister squadron of VT-3, under Lieutenant Commander Maxwell F. Leslie, arrived on the scene. A twenty-year veteran of the Navy and an aviator for twelve of these years, Leslie, on attaining an altitude of 20,000 feet, had executed the prescribed drill for arming his bomb, tripping a newly installed electrical switch. His bomb had instantly released and plopped harmlessly into the sea. When the same mishap oc-curred with three others of the squadron, Leslie broke radio silence to warn the remainder of his outfit to use the manual switch rather than the electrical one.

On sighting the Japanese fleet, although he no longer had any-thing lethal to drop on the enemy, Leslie nevertheless chose to lead his squadron down. He still had his machine guns for strafing. He picked out a carrier, which he believed was the *Kaga* but actually was the smaller, 10,000-ton flattop. He screamed down, peppering the bridge with his forward guns. Even that effort was limited, because the weapons jammed and the frustrated Leslie could only pull out.

Behind the squadron commander, his wingman, Lieutenant (j.g.) Paul Holmberg, who had nearly crashed on takeoff when his wing had brushed a gutter on the forward catwalk, led the pack. Holmberg dived to a bare 200 feet before he released. As he roared over the carrier, he saw a flaming explosion. Ensign R. M. Elder, next in line, reported that Holmberg's bomb had blown away an enemy plane starting its takeoff. A total of three solid strikes re-duced *Soryu* to a burning hulk in thirty minutes.

George Gay, occupying a soggy ringside seat, peeked out from under his black seat cushion to cheer lustily. "The [Japanese] carri-ers during the day resembled a very large oil-field fire. . . . The fire coming out of the forward and after end looked like a blowtorch, just roaring white flame and the oil burning. . . . Billowing big red flames belched out of this black smoke . . . and I was sitting in the water hollering Hooray! Hooray!"

In a wisp of time, perhaps three minutes, the American dive-bombers had destroyed the heart of the Japanese strike force. Their success lay not only in their determination and technique but also in the unwitting sacrifice of the torpedo pilots who had preoccupied most of the Japanese fighters and the diversion created by Thach with his mere six fighters, only one of which was lost.

The battle of Midway was not over despite the havoc achieved by the Navy. *Hiryu,* the carrier that VT-3, under Lem Massey, futilely sought to blast, launched its contingent of aircraft against the American carriers. A force of eighteen dive-bombers and six fighters, all that could get airborne while respotting the raiders recovered from the forays against the island, took off. No torpedo planes were available.

Earlier, aboard the *Yorktown,* Floyd Thorn, who had guided two fighter pilots out to the flattop, was in effect shanghaied until the battle for Midway ended. On the night of June 3–4, he said, he was sleeping when around midnight, Dixie Kiefer, the executive officer of the ship, woke him up. "He said, 'You're gonna be flying picket [combat air patrol] in the morning.' That was the first I knew of it." Thorn explained that it meant "flying around pylons—if you were good at it, you'd spend a lot of time going in really tight circles where the sun was behind you, so he [an enemy pilot] is looking into the sun if he's going to try to get to you. You could keep him from attacking out of the sun by getting 'up-sun' on him."

As a member of a two-plane section with Kiefer in the lead, Thorn acted as wingman. They circled the carrier in a racetrack pattern for perhaps ninety minutes, landed, refueled, and then resumed patrolling. The blips on the *Yorktown's* radar indicated bogeys 45 miles out. "I don't remember the exact time but it must have been around 1:00 P.M. or 2:00 when we got jumped." According to Thorn, he had studied the Thach Weave, even if he had never drilled in it. He and Kiefer executed the maneuvers as the enemy attacked. When Kiefer made a climbing turn with his belly up, Thorn explained, "That guy [a Zero pilot] saw the belly and headed for him. That laid him wide-open for the guy [Thorn] behind Kiefer." Thorn said he had shot down the first Zero and then, when another one of the enemy was "suckered" into the same move, Thorn hit him also.

"We both got our planes shot up. . . . The engine was running fine. It didn't act like there were any problems. I came to land, caught the second [arresting] wire, which was a soft wire. The tail stayed on the wire and the rest of the airplane rolled up in a ball. I hit the wall of the island. A gentleman in an asbestos suit came out and said, 'Don't get excited. We're gonna get you of there.' " Pulled from the wreckage, Thorn would be hospitalized four months with a broken back and smashed knees.

The Wildcats knocked down as many as ten of the enemy, but they continued to bear down on the flattop. Gunners on the ship shattered the lead dive-bomber, which still deposited its ordnance on the flight deck. The bomb penetrated down to the hangar deck, igniting several fires. A second missile tumbled through the carrier's innards and knocked out three boilers, rendering the *Yorktown* dead in the water. A third blow lit several more blazes. Damage control crews and engineers brought the flames under control and restored power to the engines.

While the ship was under attack, Leslie and his cohorts formed up to return to the carrier. They were waved off and directed to the *Enterprise*. A number of the participants in the attacks upon the strike force, because of damage from enemy fire or empty gas tanks, were forced to ditch. Both Leslie and Holmberg circled the area looking for anyone who needed rescue. They consumed all of their fuel, splashed down, and were quickly picked up.

Over the Japanese strike force, Thach hung around the battle scene, a spectator now that the Japanese were preoccupied with the destruction wrought upon their fleet as dive-bombers from the American carriers hammered their opposite numbers. "I could see three," said Thach, "burning pretty furiously. I picked up one torpedo plane and flew back to the *Yorktown* with it."

On his return to the mother ship, Thach said, "I felt my shoes were a little squashy. I reached down and felt this slippery liquid all over my leg. I thought it was blood. It felt like blood. I didn't want to look at it and didn't for a while. I wiggled my legs and they felt all right. I picked up my glove and looked at it. It was oil."

After Thach landed on the *Yorktown*, a mechanic saw a hole in his gas tank. When he removed the tank for repairs, he discovered a half-burned incendiary bullet inside. What had saved Thach from a fire was the richness of his fuel mixture. The bullet had lodged at the bottom of the tank, and the thickness of the fuel had snuffed out the flames of the incendiary. Thach also learned that the oil on his feet and legs had come from a line shot away by another bullet. However, his Hellcat's engine continued "ticking" until after he touched down on the carrier deck.

Bleeding profusely, one of his pilots, his cockpit riddled by bullets and shrapnel, dropped in on the first carrier he saw, the *Hornet*. Said Thach, "He came in and his guns went off and killed an officer and two enlisted men." According to Thach, subsequent inspection discovered that the wounded pilot's master switch had been welded shut by bullets and would not switch off, even if turned to that position. "The circuit was complete and when he hit the arresting gear wire he jolted forward. His hand was on the stick where the trigger is and he fired a burst into the island."

A second wave of bombers, fighters, and torpedo planes left the *Hiryu* under orders to destroy the other American carriers. Perhaps due to faulty communications, the Japanese headed directly for the battered *Yorktown*, which was limping along at only 19 knots. The combat air patrol intercepted the assault team fifteen miles out and reduced its numbers considerably. But five torpedo planes escaped both the fighters and the antiaircraft. Two tin fish pierced the thin-skinned hull and exploded, inflicting fatal damage. Water flooding into the ship canted the flight deck until it almost touched the sea. The skipper issued orders to abandon ship. The crew began an orderly evacuation; they carefully dragged the wounded on stretchers across the slippery, tilted deck, then lowered them to life rafts and rescue boats. Able-bodied sailors climbed down cargo nets and swam for safety. Only six planes, including the one Thach had flown, would go down with the carrier. Others that had not been forced to come down in the sea found refuge on the *Enterprise*.

The *Hiryu* now readied a third strike: five bombers, five torpedo planes, and an escort of ten fighters. This final thrust would aim at what the Japanese believed to be the sole remaining American carrier. They mistakenly assumed that two separate flattops had been destroyed, when in fact both of their onslaughts had been against the *Yorktown*.

But while the commanders finalized their plans, scout planes from VS-5 pinpointed the *Hiryu*'s location. Air Group Commander McClusky's wound prevented him from leading his troupe, so Earl Gallaher assumed command of the composite group comprised of VS-6 and VB-6, including Richard Best. Augmenting this force, the remaining fourteen dive-bombers from the *Yorktown*'s VB-3, under Lieutenant Dewitt W. Shumway, joined up.

Late in the afternoon, Gallaher and company caught up with the *Hiryu*. Initially, Gallaher directed Shumway's flight to target a battleship while he led the others against the flattop. But when Gallaher and the first dive-bombers that followed him missed, Shumway abandoned the quest for the dreadnought and shifted his attention to the *Hiryu*. Four quick detonations by bombs dropped by the Americans near the bow brewed a fiery cloud.

With all four of the Japanese carriers blazing corpses, the Americans took some shots at the cruiser *Tone* and the battleship *Haruna*. Neither the Navy bombers nor some B-17s sortied from Midway could land a blow. Admiral Spruance, aware that he no longer faced any threats from the air, nevertheless chose to withdraw to the east rather than pursue the enemy. Although Task Forces Sixteen and Seventeen controlled the skies, they would be far outgunned in a possible surface battle against Yamamoto's main force. Furthermore, Spruance worried that the enemy might still press ahead and seek to invade Midway. Early in the morning of June 5, however, with three of the Japanese flattops already sunk and the sole survivor, *Akagi*, awaiting the coup de grâce from her destroyer escorts, Yamamoto approved a message to all of his forces: "The occupation of AF [Midway] is canceled." The radio advised all ships to proceed westward, a full retreat.

Planes from both the *Hornet* and *Enterprise* continued to look for the enemy fleets. Spruance believed that there could be other carriers that might imperil Midway. When one scout radioed that he had seen a flattop with destroyers, Spruance ordered a strike from the *Hornet*. The flock of dive-bombers with a small fighter escort was already in the air when the information was corrected to indicate two heavy cruisers with three destroyers. The *Hornet* aircraft stung both of the cruisers, and thirty-one dive-bombers and a dozen fighters from the *Enterprise* descended upon the ships. The *Mikuma*, which weathered the first assault relatively well, now buckled as five bombs tore into her, knocking out guns and setting off some torpedoes. Nearby, another cruiser, the *Mogami*—seriously damaged herself—assisted in the rescue of some three hundred sailors who had either leaped into the water or been blown there.

A third strike from the *Hornet* followed and ignited a huge fire on the *Mikuma*, forcing the crew to seek refuge in the water or other ships. The cruiser soon slid under. The dive-bombers also hammered a destroyer, killing many sailors, although the ship remained afloat.

While the order to abandon ship had been issued in the mid-afternoon of June 4, the *Yorktown* refused to go down. Salvage parties boarded the stricken vessel. They pumped out water, dumped heavy equipment over the side, including gun installations, and snuffed out the fires. They even conducted burial services for thirty-five dead sailors. The destroyer *Hammann* bound herself to the side of the stricken ship, furnishing power for the teams working to save the *Yorktown*.

Undetected, however, a Japanese submarine I-168 lurked in the depths, evading the screen of destroyers while seeking a clear shot for torpedoes. In the early afternoon, the U-boat captain felt the moment propitious, and four torpedoes streaked through the water. Lookouts sounded the alarm, and the guns of the *Hammann* and the few still operating on the *Yorktown* desperately tried to blast the tin fish out of the water. One torpedo blew up the destroyer, breaking it almost in half. Depth charges on the destroyer's deck rolled into the sea and began detonating at different levels, killing many of the floundering crew. Two torpedoes that flashed under the *Hammann* struck the wounded *Yorktown* and doomed the ship. She lasted another night but at dawn disappeared beneath the water. The I-168, although aggressively hunted, somehow escaped the avenging destroyers.

The fortunes of other battered combatants varied. George Gay from Torpedo Squadron Eight drifted unmolested in the water for a day before a PBY spied him bobbing in the now-tranquil water and rescued him. He was the sole survivor of the VT-8 flyers who had taken off from the *Hornet*. Altogether, in the ten days following the battle for Midway, PBYs skimming the waves rescued twenty-seven airmen from their rafts.

From VT-6, Machinist Albert W. Winchell, an enlisted pilot, and his gunner, Douglas M. Cossett, having unsuccessfully dispatched their torpedo, fled the scene with fuel pouring through holes in their aircraft's tanks. Winchell ditched some miles away from the conflict. He and Cossett then embarked on a life-raft ordeal. The pair exhausted their emergency rations. Desperate, they ignored the curse described in Samuel Taylor Coleridge's *The Rime of the Ancient Mariner* by slaughtering a curious albatross that came fatally close. The bird provided little sustenance, and the pair was starving. After they endured a dozen days at sea, a Japanese submarine discovered them. The U-boat crew and its captain inspected them, judged them too paltry a catch to imprison, and left them to die. On the seventeenth day, however, a PBY rescued them; they had each lost sixty pounds.

Even uglier, on June 4 a Japanese destroyer plucked a pilot and gunner from the *Enterprise* found floating on their life raft. They were interrogated about Midway and the American ships for several days. When it was decided that the two could provide no more useful information, they were taken on deck, blindfolded, bound to cans filled with water, and hurled overboard to their deaths.

Years later, Thach recalled, he had felt quite depressed at the time. "These torpedo pilots were all my very close friends, Lem Massey especially. I felt pretty bad about this. I felt like we hadn't done enough, that if they didn't get any hits this whole business of torpedo planes going in at all was a mistake." The seeming chaos of the day concealed the fact that the Americans had executed, in Thach's words, the "classic, coordinated attack that we practiced for so many years, with the torpedo planes going in low and the dive bombers coming in high, pretty much simultaneously, although it's usually better if the dive bombers hit first, then the torpedo planes can get in better among the confusion of bombs bursting. I realized that these people hadn't given their lives in vain; they'd done a magnificent job of attracting all the enemy combat air patrol, all the protection that the Japanese carriers had were engaged and were held down. We did do something, maybe far more than we thought at the time. We engaged the enemy that might have gotten into the dive-bombers and prevented them from getting many hits."

As the two combatants separated, they counted their casualties. The American defense of Midway and counterattacks on the enemy fleet had cost 307 lives, 150 planes, and the *Yorktown*. But the Japanese paid an extraordinary price: the total destruction of four carriers with all of their planes, a cruiser and a destroyer, more than a thousand sailors, and, perhaps most critical, a sizable number of their top pilots. Any notion of the rising sun advancing farther east across the ocean vanished with the battle for Midway, which historians later would characterize as the turning point at least in the naval war if not in the entire conflict in the Pacific.

The defeat of the Japanese hardly hid from Jimmy Thach the weaknesses in U.S. naval aviation. He wrote a blistering memorandum about his experiences: "Six F4F-4 airplanes cannot prevent 20 or 30 Japanese [fighters] from shooting our slow torpedo planes. It is indeed surprising that any of our pilots returned alive. Any success our fighter pilots may have against the Japanese Zero fighters is *not* [his italics] due to the performance of the airplane we fly but is the result of the comparatively poor marksmanship of the Japanese, stupid mistakes made by a few of their pilots and superior marksmanship and team work of some of our pilots. The only way we can ever bring our guns to bear on the Zero fighter is to trick them into recovering in front of an F4F or shoot them when they are preoccupied in firing at one of our own planes. The F4F airplane is pitifully inferior in *climb, maneuverability* and *speed* [all his italics]. The writer has flown the F4F airplane without armor and leak proof tanks. Removal of their vital protection does not increase the performance of the F4F sufficiently to come anywhere near the performance of the Zero fighter. This serious deficiency not only prevents our fighters from properly carrying out an assigned mission but it has had a definite and alarming effect on the morale of most of our carrier based VF pilots. If we expect to keep our carriers afloat we must provide a VF airplane superior to the Japanese Zero in at least climb and speed, if not maneuverability."

What happened at Midway signaled the limitations of surface gun power. The Japanese Main Force bound for Midway could never steam close enough to bring its big guns into play because of the presence of the U.S. flattops with their dive-bombers and torpedo planes (despite the latter's ineffectiveness). The brief campaign also demonstrated the weakness of land-based, high-altitude bombing, the basic concept of the Army's strategic warfare policy. The B-17s and even the lower-flying B-25s could not achieve hits against moving targets, which could often avoid bombs with adroit maneuvers.

That lesson was obscured in the first news about what happened. Nimitz's first communiqué on the battle attributed the successes to the "armed forces of all branches in the Midway area." However, the *Honolulu Advertiser* ran a story that said, "The Army pilots who actually dropped the eggs reported personally that they made hits on three Japanese carriers, one cruiser, and one other large vessel which may have been either a cruiser or a battleship, one destroyer, and one large transport." A mild caveat added that these were "incomplete reports." Navy brass and aviators fumed when newspapers including *The New York Times* carried headlines such as ARMY FLIERS BLASTED TWO FLEETS OFF MIDWAY. The erroneous claims even fogged the minds of Washington's military authorities. Secretary of War Henry L. Stimson, basing his statement on preliminary information, attributed the victory to "mainly land based air forces," a position reiterated by Adolf A. Berle, the assistant secretary of state. The unhappiness caused a near riot when frustrated Navy veterans of Midway refought the battle at Honolulu's Moana Hotel with a group of celebrating Army aviators.

Months later, Jimmy Thach, having completed temporary duty in Hollywood making training films at the Disney and Warner Bros. studios, was awarded two Navy Crosses and a Distinguished Service Medal in one ceremony. A press conference followed. The talk turned to Midway, and Thach said he was asked, "Weren't the enemy carriers already hit before our carrier pilots got there?"

Tongue in cheek, Thach replied, "If they were, they were repaired. They showed no damage because they were steaming at high speed into the wind." At the time that Thach remarked on the difficulty of hitting a ship with high-level horizontal bombing, he was accompanied by Noel Gayler, who supported his argument.

Thach pointed out that the Norden bombsight had originally been a device created for the Navy. "I was well qualified to discuss the problem of horizontal bombing because I had corns on my knees from kneeling over a Norden bombsight and undoubtedly had more experience with that kind of bombsight than any of the bombardiers in the B-17s." In his remarks, Thach stressed, "We gave up horizontal bombing and I think the torpedo planes took the bombsight out of the planes because they could do better otherwise."

After the Boston newspapers ran an account of Thach's remarks, the Washington press corps demanded to know why it had not been invited to listen to such newsworthy statements. For their benefit he was given a chance to face the reporters again. Thach reiterated his comment about the enemy fleet not having been damaged and the ease with which a ship captain could avoid a high-altitude, horizontally dropped bomb. "They said, a lot of ships have been sunk by the B-17s. I said 'No, I don't think so.' As a matter of fact, not one major ship has been sunk by horizontal bombing in this whole war, either in the Pacific or the Atlantic."

A newsman persisted, citing the case of Captain Colin P. Kelly, who had been awarded a posthumous Medal of Honor for sinking the Japanese battleship *Hiruna*. That had supposedly occurred during the Japanese invasion of the Philippines. Thach gracefully ducked by paying tribute to Colin Kelly for his courage and sacrifice but refused to concede that the Army pilot's B-17 had actually sunk the *Hiruna*. In fact, that battlewagon had been part of the Japanese fleet attacking Midway. Postwar investigation showed that at best the bomb from Kelly's Flying Fortress had damaged a large cargo ship.

For all of the efforts of Thach and others, the misplaced credit for the defeat of the Japanese at Midway would persist until after the end of World War II.

SEVEN

GUADALCANAL

While the Japanese navy retreated, the Nipponese army had been consolidating its grip on its holdings in the Pacific Theater. Although the strategy for a seaborne expansion of Nipponese-controlled turf on New Guinea through the capture of Port Moresby had been denied in the Battle of the Coral Sea, the goal would be pursued via an overland march from Buna on the southeast coast. Protection of these ground forces and of the New Britain base at Rabaul called for possession of the Solomons, a stretch of tropical, junglelike, mountainous, rain-sodden, mosquito- and bug-infested islands north of Australia. Allied reconnaissance flights had taken notice of the first incursion there, the seizure of Tulagi. However, that island's terrain proved inhospitable to airfields. By contrast, neighboring Guadalcanal was better suited as a base, and the Japanese military began construction of facilities on that island.

Well south of the Hawaiians and about equidistant to the east from Australia, the Allies in turn had created bases in the Fiji Islands, the Samoan group of Tonga and Bora Bora. Had the Japanese overcome the Americans at Midway, in short order the Rising Sun would have fluttered over these outposts. Instead, they provided stops for aircraft shuttling from the United States to Australia, naval refueling, and resupply. But they were too far away to act as platforms for amphibious operations or offensive strikes against the enemy.

While the defeat at Midway had rocked the Japanese, in the

summer of 1942 the American forces were hardly robust. Nimitz, in a June 15 statement, noted that to date the production of aircraft and introduction of skilled pilots had only balanced out losses. In addition, Operation Torch, the invasion of North Africa scheduled for November, would drain off planes, flyers, and ships. Nevertheless, it was deemed imperative to knock the Japanese out of Tulagi and take possession of Guadalcanal, particularly after the discovery of enemy forces engaged in building an airfield there.

The order of battle designated Task Force Sixty-one as the spearhead of the U.S. invasion of the immediate objectives in the Solomons. In this vanguard sailed the *Saratoga*, *Enterprise*, and *Wasp*, each toting four air groups with a mixture of fighters, dive-bombers, and torpedo planes. American Marine, Navy, and Army aviators, along with Royal New Zealand Air Force units stationed in the New Hebrides outpost of Espíritu Santo, Fiji, Samoa, and other places in the vicinity, augmented the seaborne airpower. To the utter dismay of Rear Admiral Richmond K. Turner, however, Vice Admiral Robert L. Ghormley, commander of the South Pacific Force, Pacific Fleet, specified that the carriers would remain off Guadalcanal to support the Marine invaders for only two days. Kelly vigorously protested—in vain—that his amphibious forces required air cover while cargo ships and reinforcements continued to be unloaded beyond Ghormley's deadline.

A providential weather front obscured the movement of the American task force, and the invasion force achieved total surprise. On the morning of August 7, from off Guadalcanal, barrages from cruisers and destroyers thundered down upon what were thought to be Japanese defensive positions. When the first combat team waded ashore on Guadalcanal and secured a beachhead, the troops encountered neither resistance nor mines. Some units slogged inland while supplies piled up on the beach.

Instead of the predicted 5,000-strong savvy jungle fighters, the leathernecks learned that little more than 2,000 Japanese were in residence and almost all were from naval construction units. The Marines quickly acquired the airstrip still under construction. It would be named Henderson Field in honor of the Marine officer who was among the first casualties during the Battle of Midway.

At 5:30 A.M., sixteen pilots from Scouting Three (VS-3) gunned their motors and left the deck of the *Saratoga* bound for the north coast of Guadalcanal and the area surrounding the Lunga River. They commenced a series of glide-bombing runs on antiaircraft emplacements near Lunga Point, dumping 1,000-pound demolition bombs. Fires blazed up from small buildings as the marauders strafed huts and tents, expending almost 3,000 rounds of .50- and .30-caliber ammunition.

Lieutenant Commander Dewitt Shumway led eleven SPDs from VB-3, taking off at 7:10 A.M. Assigned to bombard the southeast section of Tanambogo Island and the nearby Bungana Island, they hurled 500-pounders at the former. The explosions ignited several buildings, but no personnel were seen. Blows at Bungana produced similar results. Six aircraft from VB-3 assumed station over Guadalcanal until instructed to bomb and machine-gun enemy installations and vehicles in dense woods about a mile south of Lunga Point. The raiders believed they had demolished a number of trucks but could not discern whether they had inflicted casualties on troops.

During the remainder of August 7, planes from the *Saratoga* repeatedly pummeled the vicinity of Lunga Point. They carried out their missions with no interference from enemy planes and against ineffective ground fire. The reports from the airmen spoke of starting fires, but the thick vegetation prevented any precise information on what they accomplished. The rather vague descriptions of what they targeted hints at the paucity of information on the enemy positions. That conclusion is supported by the guarded comment of Dewitt Shumway in his action report: "In analyzing the . . . operations it is believed there is need for closer and more rapid coordination between responsible commanders of the various forces involved in occupational operations in regard to the type aircraft bombs needed for objectives as the land occupation progresses and as enemy opposition increases or decreases. It seemed that bombings were sometimes ordered on indiscriminate objectives in order to rid aircraft of bombs prior to the time necessary to leave station."

Between Guadalcanal and Tulagi lay the narrow, eighteen-mile-wide channel that would become known as Iron Bottom Sound because of the many ships sunk there. The Tulagi area included smaller enclaves on Gavutu, Tanambogo, Makambo, and Halavo. The turf on Tulagi was invested with 1,500 well-dug-in Japanese troops who were awaiting any assault. Again the warships offshore delivered cannonades. The First Marine Raider Battalion, commanded by Lieutenant Colonel Merritt Edson, slipped onto Tulagi's Blue Beach easily enough, but as they advanced they met heavy fire.

At 5:30 A.M., Air Group One, from the *Wasp*, with sixteen Wildcats from VF-71 launched and headed for Tulagi and its environs.

Lieutenant Commander Courtney Shands, leading the expedition, reported, "I saw several VFs [fighters] moored off the NW tip of Makambo Island, about 30 yards from the deck or jetty. . . . These planes were discernible only against the early dawn reflection in the water. I immediately broadcast their location on the radio and made a sharp left turn to attack, setting one afire while Ens. Ferrer set another afire. Two other planes were shooting simultaneously above (apparently Ens. Reeves and Ens. Conklin), setting two others afire. The two sections were making a simultaneous divided attack. . . . The light of the four burning planes revealed that there were seven Kawanishi 97, 4-engine flying boats, moored in this area. One plane apart from the others appeared to be taxiing in a circle. This was immediately attacked and set afire by Ens. Reeves and Ens. Conklin. The sections then reversed course, one section (Shand and Ferrer) concentrating on one plane while the other section (Reeves and Conklin) destroyed the remaining plane. At this time all seven planes were burning with heavy flame and smoke. Oil fire appeared to be spreading toward the dock at the tip of Makambo Island. The sections then separated and proceeded upon a search of the remaining area. Intermittent AA machine gun fire was observed. . . . Ens. Conklin received a bullet hole in one wing. No other damage was sustained.

"At about 0620, it was fairly light and the sections had reached Port Purvis on Florida Island without locating any other aircraft. Upon returning from this area, I noticed what appeared to be burning planes on the water at Tanambogo, northeast of Gavutu-Tanambogo. I spotted seven more fighters on floats, moored in a line about 25 feet off Halavo Beach and about 50 feet apart. They were immediately attacked and set afire (Shands 4, Ferrer 3). Several persons were seen to be running on the beach toward the planes and a few in the water. An AA machine gun nest was silenced by Ens. Ferrer in one run. Firing runs were made toward the beach, setting a plane afire with a burst of about ten shells from each gun, quickly pulling up to avoid the palm trees and volcanic hills, circling back of the beach to avoid AA fire, then out over the water at high speed and back at the beach. Being almost out of ammunition after several runs, I called for assistance from other planes in the vicinity, which soon arrived and destroyed what appeared to be a fuel dump and an airplane on the beach.

". . . At about 0655 the planes of flight 101 departed for the *Wasp*, inspecting Savo Island, and Cape Esperance on Guadalcanal en route for possible enemy dispositions. None were located. Ens. Reeves landed on the *Enterprise* due to shortage of fuel. All other planes returned to the *Wasp* on schedule, landing aboard at 0715." Shands claimed the destruction of nineteen enemy seaplanes and one motorboat.

Around noontime, the first Japanese reaction by air showed, as bombers from Rabaul flew over the American fleet. Shipboard guns boomed as dive-bombers struck at the destroyer screen. Bombers also headed for the American beachhead on Tulagi, and they were greeted by eight F4Fs from the *Enterprise*'s VF-6. During the scrap that followed, the Americans shot down one of the bombers and damaged four others before a coven of Zeros interrupted them. In the ensuing melee, the Zeros drove off the Wildcats.

The pace of action in the sky quickened. *Enterprise* dive-bombers dueled with Zeros while an assortment of Japanese fighters and bombers focused on the transports unloading their wares and men. Half of a six-plane Navy combat air patrol confronted the bombers, and the remainder took on the Zeros. The Americans gunned down a pair of the Japanese, but three F4Fs crashed in the water, the pilots of two of which were rescued. When a group of Wildcats off the *Saratoga* started their climb toward a formation of bombers, a passel of high-flying Zeros roared down and shot down five defenders while the damaged surviving three limped back to the carrier. Only one of the American flyers was pulled from the sea.

On the same afternoon, another division of eight F4Fs from VF-5 pounced on eleven unescorted Aichi Type 99 dive-bombers. The squadron claimed that its .50-caliber guns had destroyed all but one of the would-be attackers. As the day ended, the task force counted eleven F4Fs and one SBD-3 lost.

Just before noon of August 8, the second day of the invasion, a flock of twenty-six Mitsubishi medium bombers (Bettys) droned over the eastern end of Florida Island, targeting the American armada with torpedoes. The Combat Air Patrol (CAP) from the *Enterprise* cut down four, but the remainder were proceeding on their final approach, a scant 20 feet above the water, when they met a blizzard of antiaircraft fire from the ships. Only three of the Bettys actually passed among the deployed vessels. One torpedo struck the destroyer *Jarvis*, which subsequently sank. A handful of dive-bombers arrived. They also reeled from the onslaught of shipboard guns; their only hit came from an already flaming plane that crashed into a transport, a precursor perhaps to the kamikazes of the future.

As night swallowed the craggy Solomons, the Marines ashore had achieved their objectives. But on the beaches, their equipment heaped up, and the ships standing by had to wait for opportunities to unload their cargo. Admiral Fletcher succumbed to fears of heavier Japanese air attacks, perhaps from some of the Imperial Navy's remaining carriers. His available fighter planes had shrunk from ninety-nine to seventy-eight. He obtained approval from Admiral Ghormley to remove his flattops, and they steamed away, twelve hours shy of even the minimum forty-eight promised the amphibious forces. One account claims that Fletcher misled his superior, lying that the flattops needed to refuel. To no avail, Admiral Turner protested. Although intelligence indicated that a Japanese naval flotilla was headed for Guadalcanal, intent on ravishing the vulnerable cargo and transport vessels, he refused to release them. They remained on station, delivering vital supplies and equipment. The desertion of the flattops also angered Lieutenant General Alexander Vandegrift, the Marine commander, whose troops desperately needed support. Samuel Eliot Morison, the naval historian, who rarely criticized commanders of that service, pointed out that Fletcher had at his disposal more fighter planes than had been on hand when the Midway battle had begun, as well as sufficient fuel. He commented, "His force could have remained in the area with no more severe consequence than sunburn."

American intelligence derived from an Australian search plane had indeed found a bunch of enemy ships headed toward the Solomons, but the information undercounted the strength, listing the components as three cruisers, three destroyers, and a pair of seaplane tenders. The group actually consisted of five heavy cruisers, two light ones, and a destroyer—no aircraft carriers. Fletcher would seem to have had enough strength to deal with that flotilla. Poor weather grounded the land-based search planes, preventing a more accurate count. The apparent presence of seaplane tenders misled the Americans into the assumption that they were facing a daylight assault by seaplanes.

Vice Admiral Mikawa Gunichi, in command of the Japanese, seemingly ignored the possibility that his vessels might be victims of American air. He counted on his ships and sailors, who were well versed in night action, to overcome any numerical superiority in the American surface seapower. His explicit orders read, "Destroy the American landing and cargo vessels at Tulagi and Guadalcanal."

Undetected by prying eyes, the Japanese steered into the Slot (a stretch of water between the Solomons), bound for their objectives, determined to strike the invasion force and its seaborne support. American and Australian cruisers prowled the entrances to the narrow waters between Florida and Guadalcanal, unaware of the imminent threat steaming toward them at 24 knots. None of the Allied vessels sighted Mikawa's warships as they penetrated Iron Bottom Sound, and the primitive Allied radar provided no early warning.

A destroyer sounded the alarm at 1:30 A.M. just as star shells lit up the sky and salvos from big guns and torpedoes blasted the nearest target. The very first barrage left the Australian cruiser *Canberra* afire, motionless in the water, already on its way to the bottom. The second wave stuck a torpedo into the USS *Chicago* and then devastated three more American cruisers, *Astoria*, *Quincy*, and *Vincennes*. Ronald Spector wrote in *Eagle Against the Sun*, "It was the worst American naval defeat since 1812."

Satisfied with the havoc he had wrought, Mikawa reversed course and sped out of the Slot. Although the Japanese had wiped out all five Allied cruisers and a pair of destroyers, the admiral, unaware of the departure of the U.S. flattops, feared that by the time his fleet reached Guadalcanal, daylight would provide American planes with easy, unopposed pickings. The ground troops and the ships unloading materiel on the beach escaped an attack only because of the Japanese lack of information about the carriers. Even then, with the last of the cargo ashore, the Marines were in short supply of many necessities, down to four days' ammunition and skimping on two sparse meals daily.

Every day the troops scanned the skies, fearful that they would be deluged by bombing and strafing. Not until August 20 was Henderson Field ready to receive a Marine fighter squadron with nineteen planes and a dozen Marine dive-bombers that flew in from the escort carrier *Long Island*. Five P-40s and some substandard P-39 Airacobras, manned by Army pilots, joined them. At this moment, the small seed of what became known as "the Cactus Air Force" ("Cactus" was the designated code name for Guadalcanal) provided the only air shield against whatever the Japanese could muster from their land bases or their carriers.

Only one day after Henderson Field became operational, Japanese Zeros tangled with the Marine fighters on Guadalcanal. Unexpected help arrived for the besieged elements of the Cactus Air Force. By sheer happenstance, eleven SBDs launched from the *Enterprise* to hunt for a Japanese carrier never found their quarry and landed at Henderson after dark. The Navy pilots with their machines were pressed into service with the Cactus Air Force.

For some two weeks after the start of the Guadalcanal invasion, Japanese warships steamed down the Slot and unloaded against the American ground forces. They proceeded unchallenged while the U.S. Navy recuperated from its stunning defeat in Iron Bottom Sound. Further disquieting to Nimitz and company was the growth of Japanese naval air assets throughout the South Pacific.

Again, faulty intelligence plagued the Americans. Word circulated that the enemy carriers had traveled north of Truk in the Marianas, a substantial distance away from the Solomons. Hearing the news, Admiral Fletcher, now in charge of Task Force Fox, felt able to send the *Wasp* two cruisers and seven destroyers south for refueling. But he acted on incorrect information. Three flattops accompanied by strong support, rather than being north of Truk, were speeding toward Task Force Fox.

A routine dawn search by SBDs from the *Enterprise* stretched out some 200 miles from the Solomons. At 10:17, one plane reported sighting an enemy carrier with three more warships. They were only 281 miles from the *Enterprise* and *Saratoga*, well within range of bombers, torpedo planes, and fighters. A second scout confirmed the seagoing formation. Later in the afternoon came more dire news: spies in the sky reported a huge fleet that included carriers, cruisers, destroyers, and transports. The principal actors took the stage for what became known as the Battle of the Eastern Solomons.

Having found the quarry, several of the *Enterprise*'s Bombing Squadron Six seized the chance to unload 500-pound bombs on one of the carriers. They succeeded only in creating large splashes near the flattop.

David Richardson, who as a boy had been enthralled by the vision of a naval aviator in his dress whites and then graduated from the USNA in 1936, took off from the *Saratoga* as a pilot with VF-5. "I was launched with my division about noon for combat air patrol. My former wing man, now section leader, [Ensign] Frank Green led the second section. Intercept control directed us to close a bogey at 20,000 feet. We were at 15,000. I tally-hoed a large seaplane. It commenced a full-speed descent to the south. We chased it for 55 miles before closing to shooting range. I closed straight in from astern. Green flew out to the left to close from the beam.

"The rear gunner in the four-engine plane opened fire. I could see his tracer shots falling well short of me as I closed. I selected the starboard, inboard engine as my aim point and opened fire with six .50-caliber guns. The engine broke out in a long trailing fire immediately. I pulled up, then rolled over to my left side to see what happened. [Describing the incident Richardson vigorously gesticulated with his hands.] The seaplane, which had been flying only a few feet above the surface, had crashed and burned. A large fire burned on the ocean surface. It was *Saratoga's* first shoot-down, nine months into the war."

At 2:30 P.M. that day, the *Saratoga* dispatched aircraft from Bombing and Scouting Three along with TBFs from the reconstituted Torpedo Squadron Eight. Most of the pilots had spent the previous day in fruitless missions hunting for the enemy and because of darkness had been forced to spend the night in the primitive facilities on Guadalcanal. They had only just returned to the carrier when they sortied. The attackers, however, now found the carrier *Ryujo*, the heavy cruiser *Chikuma*, one light cruiser, and two destroyers.

Lookouts on the *Ryujo* spotted the oncoming Americans, and the carrier started to launch aircraft. Scouting Squadron Three, the spearhead of the assault, nosed over from an altitude of 16,000 feet to begin their dives. The SPDs screamed down to 2,000 feet for the release of the 1,000-pounders. They pulled out at top speed to escape the sporadic and largely ineffective AA. But the best the fifteen Dauntlesses could achieve were some near misses. VB-3 followed its brother squadron, and the first division also registered no hits. The second division of the squadron had originally been ordered to strike the cruiser but was redirected to the *Ryujo* because of what Air Group Commander Harry Felt labeled "poor marksmanship." Four of the bombs struck the flattop. Smoke and flame billowed up from the *Ryujo*, which eventually foundered.

As the torpedo planes commenced their approach, four planes that the now-burning *Ryujo* had launched attempted to attack the TBF Avengers. Two were shot down by the rear-seat gunners from VS-3. When the Americans retired from the scene, they rendezvoused. In formation they suddenly encountered a flight of four Aichi 99 dive-bombers. They were returning from a mission against the *Saratoga*. The overwhelming force of some twenty U.S. planes immediately shot down three of the enemy.

Just as the Americans had scouted out the enemy armada, Japanese reconnaissance had located their adversary. Vectored toward a target by the fighter director, Lieutenant Richard Gray from VF-5, leading a flight of four F4F-4s, caught up with a large Japanese flying boat and set the plane afire. Only eight miles from the *Enterprise*, it had been shadowing the American fleet.

The Japanese, now cued in on the position of their foe, retaliated for the siege of the *Ryujo* as an estimated seventy-five planes—thirty-six dive-bombers, a dozen torpedo planes, and twenty-seven fighters—targeted the U.S. forces. VF-5 claimed an impressive number of victories. Lieutenant (j.g.) Hayden Jensen, part of a combat air patrol, intercepted oncoming dive-bombers about fifteen miles from the carrier and destroyed a trio before fighter cover drove him off. Another Wildcat pilot, Ensign K. Kleinman, not only insisted that he had shot down a pair of dive-bombers but also claimed an "ME 109 type fighter." Whatever he hit, it was not a German-made Messerschmitt.

After he blew away the flying boat, Richardson landed aboard the *Enterprise* rather than his home carrier, the *Saratoga*, because its flight deck was busy sending up aircraft. "The *Enterprise* rearmed us," remembered Richardson, "and flew us off when the Japanese were coming in. I was not launched with my division but instead with three other pilots—transplants to Fighting Five. I had been upset earlier with their normal leader because his wing men didn't stay close in. They spread out a lot. He said, 'Don't you worry. Whenever there's combat, they get right in there close, but they take it easy the rest of the time.' But they didn't.

"The four of us took off and I was the division leader. We were climbing, headed due west. I spotted planes up to the right coming in—they were the Japs—so I made a sharp turn to the right to close. I looked around and these guys were way behind me. They hadn't closed up on me. I figured, 'I'll cut across. They'll close on me.' Two of them were shot down. The other one survived. He said that right after I made that turn, they encountered a flight of Zeros that come in head on from above. If I hadn't turned, I would have been right in that thing too. I never saw them. I never knew they were there. So we lost two of the pilots."

Such CAPs performed valiantly, disposing of some attackers, but still some thirty dive-bombers bored in upon the *Enterprise* and the battleship *North Carolina*. Shipboard guns blew away as many as thirteen of these, and the battleship escaped injury, but three bombs struck the flattop, inflicting considerable damage.

David Richardson's seaplane victim was a Mavis, and the seeming ease with which he disposed of it belied its relative strength. The intelligence officer of Bombing Three advised the squadron commander, "Caution should be taken in attacking new reconnaissance enemy flying boats . . . not only do these planes possess greater speed (270 knots indicated) in 15 degree dive than our SBDs but also greater fire power, possibly carrying two 20 mm guns in rear turrets."

Far more critical, the intelligence specialist reported that the fighter director on the *Saratoga* had mistakenly advised two sections, totaling twenty, Wildcats of bogeys detected in one sector. "These 'bogeys' were discovered to be . . . two TBFs and three SBDs. In both cases the pilots had not turned on their I.F.F. [the friend-or-foe identification device now installed in all combat aircraft]. While the fighters were out investigating these 'bogeys' the Jap dive-bombers came in comparatively unopposed . . . and were not subject to the full potential strength of our fighter opposition. Moreover, the false bogey SBDs, planes originally ordered to attack enemy CV carriers (*Shokaku* and *Zuikaku*), were instructed to jettison their bombs and repulse enemy torpedo-bomber attack which of course was non existent."

Following the clash of August 24, the carrier-based warfare slackened, although the Japanese continued to control the sea. The Imperial Army tried vigorously to land sizable ground troops on Guadalcanal while the Americans poured in reinforcements, including Army troops for their beleaguered forces. The Cactus Air Force, aided by Army bombers from other bases and some Navy flyers, sparred with aerial raiders and threw punches at the transports seeking to unload enemy soldiers.

On September 11, Fighting Squadron Five, with twenty-four pilots and an equal number of Wildcats, took up station on Guadalcanal for operations with the First Marine Air Wing. Scouting Squadron Five, using SBD Dauntless dive-bombers, also moved to Henderson Field. The Marines who directed plans and operations worked closely with VS-5, assigning them to both reconnaissance and attacks against nearby enemy ground or amphibious forces. In contrast, VF-5 remained on the alert at Henderson, scrambling when the Japanese headed there.

"I was shot down my second day there, September 12th by a plane I never saw," said David Richardson, one of VF-5's Guadalcanal-based pilots. "An explosive bullet hit right behind the seat and exploded in the cockpit. It hit the oil line between two oil coolers, one of which was in each wing. It severed that line. The engine rotation had to be cut way back on and I had to make a power-off approach coming back into Henderson Field. But in the meantime, my calves froze on me, in fact, I probably still [in 1992] have probably 100 tiny bits of metal in the calves. I could not work the pedals to brake.

"I couldn't control the brakes so it ran off the side of the runway. At that point it was so slow it didn't do any damage. Out came a Jeep. They leaped up on the plane. They had to pull me out of the cockpit because I couldn't get out and they took me to the little hospital there on the field. That night we were three deep [there were, said Richardson, twelve to eighteen spaces in the hospital] and I was in the bottom bunk. A fellow in the bunk right above me complained because the man in the top bunk was urinating on him. Finally, he got one of the corpsmen over. The corpsman said, 'Urinating, hell! He's hemorrhaging!' "

On the following day, a DC-3 flew Richardson, temporarily suffering from paralysis of his legs, to a hospital at the Efate base in the New Hebrides Islands. He recuperated there for about three weeks before returning to the squadron on Guadalcanal.

In mid-October, surface vessels hammered Henderson Field with heavyweight shells, demolishing as many as forty-five planes, gouging enormous holes in the strip, and shredding many of the base's fragile buildings. Richardson endured the offshore barrages. He recalled, "During the period of the twelfth to sixteenth of October, the shelling was at its highest level. There were two 14-inch [gun] battleships and a number of cruisers. They would come down in the evening and turn, and from about 2200 to 2230, they'd shell the area and then turn around. There would be about a 15-minute respite around midnight or a little after. Then about 2:30 it would be over and they'd be getting the hell away before dawn permitted aircraft to launch.

"We were in little dugouts, and there was no water. You just picked yourself out a hole somewhere. We had quarter-inch or three-eighths-inch steel plate over the tops of our holes in the ground that were deep enough to sit [in] and bend over. They probably were about two and a half feet deep and you had to crawl when you went in and out. We'd go out to urinate, then come back in. On one occasion I went out and it was all wet when I [returned]. Somebody in our little hole didn't have guts enough to go out, so he urinated in the entrance.

"There was a corpsman that probably wasn't over 17 or 18 in

that dugout. There were maybe five or six of us in this one hole. The corpsman was shaking with such an amplitude, vibrating his whole body, that I laid on top of him to try to calm him down or constrain the magnitude of his shakes."

Richardson scrounged a few moments of comparative comfort. "I had a close friend, company mate and platoon mate at the academy. His name was Dick Wallace, and he went into the Marine Corps [Richard Wallace was a captain]. Lieutenant Colonel Robert Luckey had what they called the Special Weapons Battalion. [It] was made up of a few 3-inch guns that he'd haul down to the beach to battle the battleships and cruisers. But he had a luxurious dugout. It was a hole with coconut logs across the top and you could stand up in it. Once or twice before the shelling, I went down and spent the night with Dick because there was a cot in the place.

"One morning after one of the shellings, Dick and I went out and there were four 8-inch shells around the dugout, none of which exploded, and none of them were more than 10 or 12 feet away, spaced like symbols on a 5 card with our dugout in the middle. They probably wouldn't have hurt us if they'd exploded but they sure would have given us a thrill. Anyway, it was comfortable sleeping there the one or two times I was able to.

"After several days of shelling in our area, we said, 'The hell with this. Let's get out.' We went in different directions. Four or five of us in Fighting Five went up with the 7th Marines to the southeast of the field, up along the ridge line. We dug ourselves little foxholes on the leeward side, and that's where we would stay. We stayed up there maybe three nights.

"On one occasion, there was a Japanese night attack up the ridge on the other side. The Japs were yelling and a number of the Marines turned and ran. The colonel said, 'The ones who run one night are the ones who stand the next.' Courage is a funny thing. It has as much to do with whether you had a good night's sleep or a reasonable night's sleep and food as with anything else. Courage is a variable. Enough stayed to hold."

According to Richardson, by the time he rejoined VF-5, it had none of the planes with which it had started operations on the island. "We were reinforced one time by pilots from VF-72, which came up with about twelve planes. We must have lost some forty that were burned out or destroyed in air combat or ship shelling."

He celebrated his return on October 12. "I had just come back from the hospital and [Lieutenant (j.g.) Hayden] Jensen led the strike. We were up at 28,000 feet when the Bettys came over. I was number four, with three ahead of me. I saw three planes burned. And then I opened fire. I was a good gunner and zapped the wing tank and it went into flames. I had time to kick up and open fire on a second plane and did. Those bullets out of the six fifty caliber machine guns just played hell. The one thing that the F4F-4s had, was a lot of firepower. If you got anywhere near them, you were going to kill them. We shot down five of eight Bettys, although Japanese records don't confirm this. I wonder if their records of losses were just inaccurate or maybe 'cooked.' I saw them diving down aflame." Richardson notched his third Guadalcanal victory against a Zero just before VF-5 pulled out.

"When we left," recalled Richardson, "I had four pistols that I had brought up. As it turned out we didn't need them. I had kept these four pistols in my bag. When we were about to leave, we asked the Marines, 'Well, what do you want?' Mostly they wanted those pistols. They took three of them and I kept my fourth one. We left everything else—all our spare underwear, socks, you name it, everything except what we wore."

Operations of the Cactus Air Force had a helter-skelter quality. A pilot for each available plane always stayed on the alert in the ready tent while the plane captains—chief mechanics—stood by the dispersed aircraft. When the order to scramble sounded, the pilots sprinted to their machines and rolled down the strip in no particular order. First man off the ground acted as leader until the assigned commander could take over. The guiding principle established an altitude of 26,000 to 30,000 feet as mandatory prior to the attack. The Wildcat's slow rate of climb required a potentially deadly thirty-five to forty minutes for the ascent.

For the Navy personnel, the sojourn on Guadalcanal exposed them to a life unlike that aboard a flattop. VF-5's commanding officer sent a memorandum to Nimitz that noted, "The operations at Guadalcanal presented the first opportunity for the Navy to observe pilots under stress of continued action. The most important single contributory factor to pilot fatigue is lack of sound sleep. The stress of day-to-day combat, plus being bombed when on the ground during the daylight, or bombed and/or shelled during the night will render any pilot ineffective to the point of danger within three weeks."

The report insisted that two pilots were necessary for every plane. It noted that land-based operations "are far more intense and difficult for VF than carrier-based operations." It reiterated the complaints about the Wildcat's deficiencies in rate of climb, speed, and range, arguing that half of the enemy bombing attacks reached their objective prior to interception because the F4F lacked the capability to grapple with them early enough.

The stint on Guadalcanal concluded the tour for much of Fighting Five. The outfit remained on the island for more than a month and claimed to have shot down forty-five enemy planes with six more listed as probables. Its losses included two Americans known dead, three missing, and four wounded in action. The squadron counted a total of twenty F4F-4s as destroyed during aerial action, by mechanical or other noncombat malfunctions, and by enemy bombardment.

Richardson recalled that he and three others from the squadron had been the first to reach Honolulu. "We had nothing, no change of clothes, no pay records. We were put into the BOQ on Ford Island in Pearl Harbor and were invited by Lieutenant Commander Bob Pirie [an aviator since 1929] to a cocktail party at the O club that night. We bathed and brushed our only clothes off. But when we arrived, we were still wearing beards and looked like street people. We went to the party, the four returning 'heroes.' The admiral took one look at us and said, 'Get those four clowns out of here.' We were invited back to the BOQ. There were women at the party. We looked disgraceful. This wouldn't have happened a year later nor with other admirals. Bob Pirie was outraged, but he was a lieutenant commander so there wasn't much he could do."

While the brass in Hawaii piddled over decor, in the Solomons a desperate situation demanded an iron fist. President Franklin D. Roosevelt told his Joint Chiefs of Staff that Guadalcanal must not be lost. Nimitz sacked Robert L. Ghormley, Commander South Pacific, as being insufficiently aggressive and replaced him with William "Bull" Halsey, who sounded a mantra: "Kill Japs! Kill more Japs!"

Both Halsey and the Japanese looked for propitious situations that would enable a significant thrust. The opportune moment for a confrontation arrived, starting October 25, in the vicinity of the Santa Cruz Islands, well to the east of the southern Solomons. Having deposited a fresh supply of soldiers and supplies on Guadalcanal, a fleet of some forty Japanese ships, including a pair of battleships and three carriers, *Shokaku*, *Zuikaku*, and *Zuiho*, with appropriate escorts, swept toward the Solomons.

During the interval after the encounter in the eastern Solomons, the *Enterprise* had retired to Pearl Harbor to take aboard fresh

squadrons—VB-10, VS-10, and VF-10—and on October 16 it sailed
for the South Pacific battle area. The carrier was the nucleus of the
Enterprise group, which, with the *Hornet* group, made up Task
Group King. While half the strength of the Japanese force, it was
much stronger than that posited by enemy intelligence, which knew
only of the presence of the *Hornet*.

The *Enterprise* air group included the newly formed fighter
squadron VF-10, which mixed a few veterans, such as the former
dive-bombers Swede Vejtasa and John Leppla, with a batch of men
right out of flight school under the leadership of Jimmy Flatley. Jim
Billo, almost immediately after the attack on Pearl Harbor, received
orders to join a torpedo squadron. But a shortage of TBFs prevented
him from carrier qualification and he switched to fighters for his
Carquals (carrier qualifications). "With a lot of fancy footwork, a few
small lies, and a lot of luck, I got assigned to Fighting Two instead of
Torpedo Two," said Billo. The fighter unit became VF-10 under Flatley, who tried to build esprit de corps by giving his new squadron the
moniker "Grim Reapers."

Just before the carrier shipped out of Pearl Harbor, three more
men joined the Reapers. Edward "Whitey" Feightner, as a fighter pilot training in Hawaii under Butch O'Hare, had been scheduled to
sail aboard the *Yorktown*, but after it had sunk he and two others
from VF-3 had drawn VF-10 and the *Enterprise*. "The day before the
battle actually started we had reports that the *Zuikaku* and the
Shokaku were up north of us and coming in. They organized a
search and attack group. We had about four TBMS with torpedoes.
I think there were six SBDs, all carrying 1,000 pound bombs. I think
we had eight fighters.

A far-ranging PBY had spotted a pair of enemy flattops some
360 miles off but approaching at a brisk 25 knots. Air Group Ten
launched dive-bombers, torpedo planes, and a fighter escort to meet
them halfway.

Feightner remembered, "We headed off 175 miles in late afternoon, along about 3:00 when we got launched. We got off the end of
175 miles and it was one of those days you could see for 100 miles,
and we were flying around 15,000 feet. The group commander [Dick
Gaines] said we'll fly one more leg, a little bit further east. We still
weren't getting any reports; we still didn't have a carrier in sight. The
sun's getting kind of low behind us and [Gaines] said we would fly
one more leg, a little bit further east.

"We flew another 75 miles east; when we got to that point, we should have been landing aboard. I was completely lost. I thought I was a navigator; I had my plotting board and by this time we made those two turns. There was no radio transmission at all; they didn't permit it. If somebody had said, 'Go home,' I would have had a hard time finding my way. I was flying wing on Swede Vejtasa." A fuel malfunction forced Lieutenant Frank D. Miller to bail out over the ocean. No one could remain to watch over him because they were all running out of gas.

"All at once," recalled Feightner, "the group commander started to circle. This was where the carrier should have been. It's now dark and there's nothing visible down there. Still no radio transmission; apparently there were submarines all over the area. We started to spiral down and there was a ceiling of broken clouds, maybe 600 to 800 feet. You could see under it. The moon wasn't up yet; it was really black.

"I see the clouds going by me. We're down under this cloud deck. We've got twenty or so airplanes, all stooging around. No carrier visible. The bomber skipper decided—they were still carrying their bombs on the SBDs—to drop them. That was the biggest flash you've ever seen. One of those bombs didn't safe and when it hit the water it blew. The next thing, SBDs were going into the water. Two of them, apparently, survived the initial blast but they went in the water shortly thereafter.

"About this time, I noticed—my gosh—I could see the water in my wing lights. Swede Vejtasa was down there, making small turns, and all of a sudden he just straightened out and headed off. What he had done was find a slick [oil] from the task force with his wing lights, down on the water. We were ten to fifteen feet off the water. I turned around and everybody is following us. Swede's leading the way and I'm on his wing. Forty-five miles away, we found the task force. He did it just by [finding] a bearing from that leak.

"They decided that since the fighters were lowest on fuel, we ought to get aboard first. Swede went around and I was right behind him. That was my first night carrier landing and it didn't even bother me in the least. I'd done it on the field but I'd never landed aboard the ship at night. That's how short we were on training those days. The group commander was up there still circling in his TBM, but the other TBMs started dropping in the water. Most of them made good water landings and survived. We lost eleven pilots, ten days after we left Pearl Harbor," said Feightner, "but most of them [including Miller, the man who had parachuted from his plane during

the return flight] were actually picked up later." But in a grim footnote, Miller and nearly a dozen pilots and crewmen perished when
Zeros pounced upon a PBY ferrying them to safety.

Early the next day, both sides swung knockout blows. Three waves
of attack groups roared away from the two American carriers while
sixty-five Japanese planes with equally deadly intent raced toward the
Big E and the *Hornet*. The raiders passed each other on their courses
toward their respective targets.

For the Americans, the vanguard consisted of Scouting Eight
and Bombing Eight Dauntlesses, followed by Torpedo Six Avengers.
Fighters from VF-72 shepherded the flock, all of which departed
the *Hornet* around 8:30 A.M. Perhaps half an hour later, Bombing Squadron Ten, Torpedo Squadron Ten, and Fighting Squadron
Ten started out from the *Enterprise*. Working from hastily cobbled-
together plans, the entire attack lacked coordination, not only between the two separate carrier forces but even within the strike
groups. Training had instilled in the bomber pilots formation flying
that provided mutual support through their machine guns, but the
tactics did not include the best way to integrate torpedo planes into
the flow. The inherent weakness of the F4F-4, which required it to
maintain a high altitude, tended to separate the guardians from
their charges.

At 9:30 A.M., aboard the *Enterprise*, eleven F4F-4s from VF-10
took off to augment the dozen Wildcats already engaged in CAP over
the American fleet. Vejtasa and his companions observed dive-
bombers starting their pushover to attack the *Hornet*. Vejtasa almost
immediately essayed a high-side run, and his guns sent a would-be
bomber down in flames. Other attackers, however, had already completed their runs, scoring significant hits on the *Hornet*. "We [he
used the editorial first-person-plural pronoun] picked up two enemy
dive-bombers which were retiring and shot them both down in
flames. They attempted no defensive maneuvers."

A wing tank problem forced Vejtasa to temporarily abandon the
fray, but he dumped the tank and climbed to 10,000 feet in search
of more bogeys. "I heard Ensign [Hank] Leder give 'Tally-ho, nine
o'clock down.' We were then at 13,000 feet and I sighted the enemy
torpedo planes below at about 7,000 feet. There were very easy to
distinguish by the smooth dark paint on the wings and fuselage. I
believe there were eleven planes in this group, flying in a step-up column of 3-plane sections and one 2-plane section.

"My second section, Lieutenant [Stanley] Ruehlow and Ensign Leder, who had pulled away and dove on two Zeros a few minutes before, already were attacking the torpedo planes. We picked up about 350 knots in our dive and were able to place ourselves in position for a steep, high side run. I estimated the torpedo planes to be making about 250 knots. They were already in a high speed approach about to deploy beneath a large cloud and attack the task force. Lieutenant [L. E.] Harris and I attacked one 3-plane section and each set a torpedo plane on fire. As I broke away, I saw another F4F-4 attacking. The formation then broke up [and flew into a cloud]. I followed very close behind a 3-plane section and blew the number two man up with two short bursts. I then fired at the leader and shot the rudder off before the plane caught fire. The third plane started a shallow turn and caught on fire after I fired a rather long burst into it. These three attacks were no deflection runs directly from astern in a heavy cloud.

"Pulling up, I saw another enemy plane above me and I tried a low, side attack, but missed him badly. Following him out of the clouds, I saw he was too high and much too fast for an effective drop on our carrier. The A.A. guns opened up in one direction, so I broke away. The torpedo plane continued on in almost a straight line and hit a destroyer. There was a tremendous explosion near the No. 1 turret forward."

Vejtasa circled around the protective screen formed by the ships below. He spied a pair of torpedo planes passing through the anti-aircraft fire and beginning their withdrawal close to the surface of the sea. Seeing another F4F drawing a bead on one of the enemy, he attacked the nearest. "My ammunition was about gone, and I emptied my guns into the plane. As I fired, the Jap pilot skidded his plane violently in an attempt to evade my fire. The plane caught fire, but proceeded about five miles before diving into the water."

Harris, Leder, and Ruehlow, their ammunition expended like Vejtasa's, joined him in an approach to the *Enterprise*. The flattop, however, could not land or launch aircraft because of an imminent renewed assault by the Japanese. "We circled just outside the screen for an hour and twenty minutes, out of ammunition and low on gas. While circling, we observed an F4F-4 pilot parachute from his plane at about 7,000 feet and land in the water about twelve miles from the carrier. At 1320, all Reapers were told to pancake and my flight landed aboard the *Enterprise*."

After action reports confirmed Vejtasa's astonishing bag of two dive-bombers, five torpedo bombers, and an assist on another—altogether seven and a half enemy aircraft—Flatley, who ordinarily disdained medals, recommended Vejtasa for the Medal of Honor, but the decoration was reduced to a Navy Cross.

Jim Billo, whose flight experience amounted to less than 500 hours and fewer than twenty carrier landings, went into combat on October 26 as part of a section led by Lieutenant Bobby Edwards. "Shortly after takeoff," said Billo, "Bobby's prop went into high pitch and he had to return to the carrier, and he took his wingman with him. That left me and my wingman sitting up there wondering what the hell to do. The fighter director in charge of all this—sitting down on the ship—went stark raving crazy and issued all kind of crazy orders and direction for us in the air. For instance, we were up about 20,000 feet milling around and he would say, 'There's a whole bunch of them coming in on the port bow.'

"Who in the hell knew where the port bow of the ship was? We couldn't see the ship. If we could [see], it was in a complete turn, which would put the port bow doing a circle. So he was no help.

"My wingman and I proceeded out in the direction we had started and found a large group of Zeros picking on a lone F4F, and we joined in that and did some damage. The first one I made a pass at blew up on me and went down. But we were sadly outnumbered, and we dove out of that mess.

"We went back around the ship and found some other fighters of ours milling around and joined up with them. They were principally from the *Hornet* [already stricken by enemy marauders], which was operating with the *Enterprise* at that time. My wingman didn't come with me. I lost him someplace. This group I was trailing around with wasn't doing any good, so I left them and went back over the ship area, [where I] joined up with another *Hornet* fighter. We got into the pattern of the dive-bombers coming off their runs and ruined some of their trips home by splashing some of those as they came out of their runs low on the water.

"I was soon running out of fuel, and I tried to get aboard the *Enterprise*, which was trying to take planes. The forward elevator had been blown up by a bomb; the *Hornet* was dead in the water. Everything in the air was trying to get aboard the *Enterprise*. For everyone that got a cut [waved in to land] there were five that couldn't get aboard because of a fouled deck."

In the melee of attacking and defending aircraft gyrating over the fleet, the shipboard antiaircraft gunners banged away without restraint. Billo recalled, "After being shot at by the USS *South Dakota*, which shot at anything regardless of friend or foe, I eventually went into the water. I, of course, had my canopy jammed shut and went down with the plane and had the fun and games of trying to get out. I came to the top of the water, and no airplane in sight. I got into my raft and a friendly airplane made a few passes at me, which alerted the carrier screen. A few destroyers came over and looked at me. All but one pulled out as they approached. Finally, one [*Preston*] kept coming, threw me a line, didn't slow, and I was lucky enough to tie it around me. They dragged me about awhile and eventually got me aboard.

"I reported to the bridge, and the skipper made my day by saying, 'If I had known you were a pilot, I wouldn't have come after you.' I learned later why he said that. The *Porter* [another destroyer] had stopped to pick up a torpedo plane crew that had landed in the middle of the fleet, and a Japanese sub which was operating in our fleet sunk the *Porter* right in the middle of the fleet. The skipper of the *Preston* didn't bother to explain that. I learned it months later."

One member of VF-10, Lieutenant Albert Pollock, who commanded a four-plane section, shot down two attacking bombers before he saw the torpedo speeding through the water toward the *Porter*. Pollock dived on the tin fish, spraying machine-gun bullets to explode it. The targeted destroyer and surrounding warships, unable to distinguish Pollock from the enemy, showered him with antiaircraft shot and shell. Undaunted, he made two desperate runs at the torpedo. But the missile found its mark; the explosion hurled a 100-foot tower of seawater into the air as it mortally wounded the destroyer. Subsequently, Pollock was awarded a Navy Cross.

Although the *Enterprise's* aircraft left the flight deck after those from the *Hornet*, they encountered the Japanese first. Disaster enveloped a VF-10 section led by Lieutenant John Leppla, escorting dive-bombers and torpedo planes. Some 70 miles out from the carrier, nine Japanese fighters dived out of the sun upon the formation. They knocked out a number of SBDs and a TBF before focusing their guns on Leppla's section. Three of the four Wildcats absorbed fatal wounds. The lone survivor of the quartet, Ensign Willis "Chip" Reding, his F4F-4 hit several times, rendering his electrical circuits inoperative, escaped the pursuing Zeros and made it back to base.

Post-action reports credited VF-10's Leppla, Raleigh Mead, and Al Rhodes each with taking out an enemy fighter. Both Mead and Rhodes were seized as prisoners by the Japanese.

Whitey Feightner recalled, "They threw together a strike force and launched us [as escorts for the attack group]. I was flying with Flatley, that morning, in the second division. John Leppla and his group were on the left side. We were about 20 miles from the carrier [Reding had estimated a greater distance], had just formed up and were headed out. Flatley told us to check our guns; everybody was essentially checking to make sure that their guns were charged. Somebody yelled, we looked up and here came Zeros all over us. They had gotten up about two hours before we did, and they were that close to the task force. They came pouring down. They took out Dusty Rhodes, John Leppla, and Al Mead. And they took out four dive bombers and one torpedo plane out of that group with one pass. Those early Japanese pilots were good."

According to Eric Hammel in *Guadalcanal: The Carrier Battles*, bullets from the Zeros ignited a fire in Rhodes's wing tank and riddled his cockpit, smashing his instrument panel and even clipping his goggles. Although the fire subsided, his engine conked out. Even as another enemy poured machine-gun fire into him from his rear, he shoved away his shattered canopy, stood up, and pulled the parachute ring. It opened and whipped him free of the Wildcat to a watery landing. Mead made an even quicker departure from his F4F-4, drifting down to the sea under the silk. Before he went down, Rhodes glimpsed Leppla in a chute that failed to deploy fully. He apparently did not survive the plunge into the water.

Feightner said his group never wavered. "Flatley didn't let us turn away a bit. He just said, 'Keep going.' The Zeros made that one pass and went on to the task force. And we headed off on to their task force. . . . We found [it] and we made an attack out there." While the torpedo planes and dive-bombers struck at the Japanese with their ordnance, Flatley and his companions strafed the ships to discourage their antiaircraft gunners. Somewhere in the engagement, Feightner disposed of an Aichi bomber and scored a probable on a torpedo plane. Flatley added another Zero to his list of victims.

The spearhead from the *Hornet* had just come upon the enemy task force when the inevitable Zeros struck. They feasted upon the torpedo planes as the fighter escort frantically rushed to their aid. The dogfights brought casualties on both sides, but they also delayed the American fighters from accompanying the Dauntless dive-bombers. Their first sight of the enemy revealed only battleships and cruisers but no carriers. The VB-8 commander was tempted to abort the mission, but a few minutes more of flight brought two flattops into view. Lieutenant Commander William J. "Gus" Widhelm, a man who kept five dollars' worth of nickels handy for Coca-Colas aboard the carrier and played an expert game of badminton on the hangar deck during nonalert periods, had said, "This attack is going to separate the men from the boys." He led the attack. Noticing one of the targets, *Zuiho*, trailing smoke, Widhelm turned the attention of his posse to the larger carrier, *Shokaku*.

Standard tactics prescribed a coordinated approach with the torpedo bearers, but the Avengers had missed the rendezvous. While Zeros rose to drive them off, the dive-bombers, at a height of 12,000 feet, closed up their formation to greet the foe with maximum firepower. Widhelm reported he had seen a Zero coming toward him. "I pulled my nose up and put my head just about half a cowling above him and held fire right there until he flew into it. He burst into flame."

However, another interceptor severed the cooling system in Widhelm's ship. A former stunt pilot, he threw the plane into a corkscrew dive to evade further pursuit, then set down in the water. He and his gunner, George Stokely, clambered out and onto their raft. Other fighters sought to rupture the integrity of the formation, but the Americans refused to disperse. Although several Japanese fighters succumbed to the concentrated machine guns, they knocked out four of the dive-bombers, including Widhelm's.

As the interference slackened, the surviving VB-8 aircrews, now under Lieutenant Moe Vose's direction, doggedly pursued the *Shokaku*. Vose planted a 1,000-pounder on the flight deck, and then another Dauntless hit blew the carrier's elevator into the air. Altogether, Widhelm, from his nearby raft, counted six bombs on target. He believed that the burning vessel could never recover. Enemy destroyers flashed by Widhelm and Stokely close enough for the pilot to observe grins on the faces of the Japanese sailors, but he and his companion remained unmolested.

Also from the *Hornet*, a half-dozen Dauntlesses swooped down upon the heavy cruiser *Chikuma*. Explosions blasted the bridge and then consumed portions of the engineering area. All three of the enemy vessels—*Shokaku* (in spite of Widhelm's prediction), *Zuiho*, and the cruiser *Chikuma*—retired from the scene under their own power, but many months would pass before they could return to battle. Widhelm and Stokely floated on their life raft for three days before a patrol plane set down and rescued the pair.

Feightner described the conditions when he returned to his seagoing base: "I'll never forget the sight. I looked on the horizon and the first thing I see, is our happy home is leaning over, smoking like mad. It turned out it was the *Hornet* and not the *Enterprise* [which was] another 30 miles beyond.

"We got back to the *Enterprise* and we were really low on fuel. We get in the traffic pattern and looked down. Here go these torpedo wakes. That ship is zigzagging; it's S-turning like mad. But they're taking us aboard—there were airplanes stacked up clear back across the barricade. Signal officer Robin Lindsey was standing out there, giving us the cut. We'd come around and he'd take us aboard. They were in a terrific right turn when I came aboard. Here I am in a left-hand pattern and they're making a right turn. I came around and got on the stern. He gave me a cut, so I landed.

"They taxied me forward and I got out of the airplane. There was no number-one elevator on the ship. The elevator was completely gone. I got down to the hangar deck. I was wading around in water, fuel and dead bodies. It was about halfway up to my knees down on the hangar deck. Something had burned; you could smell it all over the place. They'd taken a bomb back on the starboard quarter. It knocked out the first three wires [arresting gear] on the ship. In the mean time not only are these torpedoes going by but there's a dive-bombing attack going on at the same time.

"I went back to where the ready room was supposed to be and it wasn't there. The last SBD landed aboard. I got back up to the flight deck in time to see Robin Lindsey in the back seat of that SBD and he's got those twin .30s and he's shooting at an airplane coming across the fantail of the ship. And he actually got it; the guy went in.

"The *Hornet*, what was left of their air wing, was now aboard the *Enterprise* or else were flying and airborne. We had so many airplanes that we had to keep some of them airborne all the time—we kept cycling the deck."

In the chaos of the Battle of Santa Cruz, Billo, among others retrieved after a water landing, did not immediately rejoin his squadron. "I stayed on the *Preston* two or three weeks until we got down to Noumea, New Caledonia for some ship rework. It wasn't until I got back to my squadron that I learned that on October 26th we had 11 of our squadron go down that day. Four of us were picked up by the U.S. fleet. We learned later that two more, Rhodes and Mead

[Ensigns Al and Raleigh] were picked up by the Japanese and five were lost. This included my wingman, Jim Caldwell, my roommate Jack Leppla, Gerald Davis, Gordon Barnes and Lyman Fulton. That brought our losses to seven because we had lost Robert Von Lehe in Hawaii [through an accident] and Frank Miller, the night before the battle of October 26th."

The *Hornet* could not be saved and succumbed to torpedoes and shell fire from her associates. The *Enterprise* limped away from the fight for repairs. The destroyer *Porter* was sunk. One bomb exploded on the battleship *South Dakota*'s forward turret. A flaming Japanese torpedo plane slammed into the bow of the destroyer *Smith*, doing major damage, and bombs mauled the cruiser *San Juan*.

Although at the time, the United States appeared to have lost more ships, the records for the Battle of Santa Cruz eventually revealed a subtle advantage to the United States. While seventy-four American planes were lost, the Japanese figure totaled twice that number. Even more telling, thirty-three American aviators were casualties, but the enemy mourned the deaths of more than a hundred. As U.S. factories manufactured an ever-increasing amount of new and better aircraft and the flight schools pinned wings of gold upon a growing body of young men, a widening gap in strength and experience now jeopardized the future of the Japanese war effort. Furthermore, by withstanding the enemy fleet at Santa Cruz, the Americans secured their base at Guadalcanal, a key installation for coming campaigns.

EIGHT

TAKING THE OFFENSIVE

For the embattled aviators, the sailors aboard the still grievously wounded Pacific Fleet, and the besieged Marines and soldiers on Guadalcanal, the last half of 1942 seemed like the ultimate struggle. To the Allied chieftains plotting the overall war effort, however, the main show lay half a world away, in the West. There the Soviet armies tenaciously staved off the Wehrmacht in spite of the huge inroads into their territory by the Nazi military machine. Moscow demanded a second front to relieve the pressure on the embattled Soviet forces. In North Africa, the British staggered backward as the Rome-Berlin Axis bested their Eighth Army. The advances in the desert, coupled with the unfriendly Vichy French rule in French Morocco, Algeria, and Tunisia, threatened to shut down the Mideast oil resources.

Recognizing that their forces were too weak to open up a second front through an invasion of Europe, the Allies had drafted Operation Torch, a plan to invade North Africa. Not only would that protect the oil supplies, but control of the territory would open an avenue into Italy, mistakenly perceived as a soft route into the Axis mainland. While not fully satisfying the Soviet call for a second front, Torch landings in Morocco and Algeria would squeeze the Italian and German armies between troops advancing from the west and east, draining assets that might otherwise be deployed against the Red armies.

Despite delicate clandestine negotiations, no one could ascertain with surety the reaction of the French colonial military, whose forces included naval and air units along with ground troops. Furthermore, the Mediterranean harbored untold numbers of hostile submarines. The nearest Allied air bases at Malta and Gibraltar lay out of range to provide air support of the invasion. The strategy, therefore, assigned the Navy through its carrier planes the tasks of shutting down air strikes against Operation Torch, tactical interdiction on enemy ground forces, neutralizing any French warships that might resist, and antisubmarine action.

All of the big American carriers, with the exception of an occasional voyage to ferry planes to England, were not available, as they were engaged in the Pacific war. In fact, only the incompletely repaired *Enterprise* remained fit for combat. The *Saratoga* remained in its West Coast port, recuperating from its injuries. At the bottom of the sea lay the *Lexington*, *Yorktown*, *Wasp*, and *Hornet*. For Torch, the Navy could offer only the dowager *Ranger*, a smaller flattop creaky with age, and four light or escort carriers, *Sangamon*, *Santee*, *Suwannee*, and *Chenango*. This quartet had originally slid down the shipbuilding ways as oil tankers but because of the acute shortage had been converted to aircraft carriers.

Commonly referred to at first as "Jeep carriers" and then as escort carriers (CVEs), they had short flight decks and limited speed. Fitzhugh Palmer, Jr., detached from VF-8 to serve as executive officer of VF-26, stationed on the *Sangamon*, said, "Standard speed was fifteen knots, and sixteen was full. Our 'flank' speed of 18½ could be achieved only when going downhill with a strong wind at our backs." The usual pace for the bigger carriers was 25 to 30 knots, as the higher speeds aided the aircraft's liftoff.

The air group on the *Sangamon* consisted of a dozen F4F Wildcats, nine TBF Avengers, and nine SBD dive-bombers. According to Palmer, when the fighter squadron formed in May, only the CO and he had undergone Carquals. The remainder of the pilots were all fresh out of flight school. He remarked, "In a way these frisky young fellows had an advantage when it came to flying their F4F Wildcats on and off the *Sangamon*'s deck. Since they'd never been on the bigger carriers, they didn't know what they were missing. For me it was quite an adjustment to go from an 800-foot-long deck with 30 knots of wind to 550 feet of deck and the hope for 20 knots of relative wind."

The flyers compensated for the deficiencies with a special launch technique. The ships' engines were revved to full bore before release of the brakes. They kept their wing flaps up while building speed, but near the forward end of the flight deck, the pilots lowered them for extra lift. With a high wind, the F4Fs could get off after a mere 300 feet, but if the wind fell, the deck run had to be extended. Eventually, the Jeep carriers relied more and more on their catapults.

To the *Chenango* fell the obligation to transport seventy-six Army Air Corps P-40s, and the pilots expected to start operations as soon as the ground forces captured airfields. The initial support in terms of fighter, bomber, and torpedo squadrons would launch from the other four carriers. Altogether the Navy could count on 172 planes against what intelligence reported as 168 French aircraft. The vast majority of the Navy's air arm assigned to Torch lay in 108 fighters. The defenders owned a motley collection of machines, some the equal of the attackers', but many were quite obsolete, purchased by France from the United States but long ago discarded from the American arsenal. With a single exception, the German Luftwaffe, which was equipped with formidable fighters, would fortunately not be immediately on hand.

Because of the enmity of the French toward the British—due to a Royal Navy assault upon French warships in the port of Oran and the distrust of Charles de Gaulle's Free French forces by the colonialists in North Africa—the role of spearhead devolved upon the Americans. The scenario laid out three separate areas for invasion. In the center sat the French Moroccan city of Casablanca, with the landings plotted for Fedala, about fourteen miles north. Some eighty miles farther north, a task force would seek to put almost ten thousand troops ashore near Media with the immediate goal being the French airfield at Port Lyautey. The carriers *Ranger*, *Suwannee*, and *Sangamon* would host the air cover for these two operations. One hundred and forty miles south of Casablanca, the third element of the invasion was to strike at Safi. *Santee* steamed off the coast here with her air group.

The pilots were not combat-experienced, and many had limited time at the controls. Chick Smith, the Anglophile who had quit the Marine Corps reserve in favor of wings of gold, had originally trained in F2A biplanes with open cockpits and then the inadequate F3Fs before making the transition to the Wildcat. He reported to VF-9 with only 300 flight hours. On the other hand, he said, the squadron commander, Jack Raby, was an experienced fighter pilot; the executive officer, Lieutenant T. Hugh Winters, was a veteran dive-bomber man; and the third senior officer, Lieutenant (j.g.) Jake Onstott likewise brought many hours as a dive-bomber. "Under our skipper's strong leadership we learned fast. We flew lots of gunnery and tactical flights."

D-Day for Torch arrived on November 8, 1942, with still no firm answer to the question of whether the French military would greet the invaders with open arms or firearms. Fear of provoking a hostile reception generated orders not to fire unless fired upon. On board the *Ranger*, airmen from VF-9 and VF-41 assembled in the ready rooms at 4:00 A.M. to ensure that they would react immediately. According to M. T. Wordell and Edward Seiler, pilots with VF-41, in their book *Wildcats over Casablanca*, the chaplain led them in the Lord's Prayer and "we stumbled through the Act of Contrition." The padre explained that the latter was principally for Catholics but added, "I will let you non-Catholics in on it. It won't do you any harm."

The sky, said the authors, loomed "pitch black with cold pale pinpoints of stars overhead" when their squadron leader, Lieutenant Commander C. T. "Tommy" Booth, offered final instructions: "Boys, as I've said before, our primary mission is to cover the landing. I'm taking my formation to Cazes first. We'll take the first attacks. You are to make for Fedala and hang around until we need you." *Wildcats over Casablanca*, first published in 1943, indicates that the pilots seemed fearful they would not get an opportunity to fight. "There may be no resistance in our sector," the writers quoted a "pessimist" as saying. "That meant that as our tasks were over Casablanca and Fedala, we wouldn't see any action."

While the fighter pilots restlessly awaited their signal, at 6:45 A.M. the Dauntless bombers had already taken off. The book reported, "They assembled over their targets at Casablanca at 10,000 feet, circling like dark birds of prey. Until the defenders attacked they would not 'play ball.' "

Shortly after dawn, as the fleet hovered in the vicinity of Fedala, coastal artillery battalions suddenly spurted exploding orange blobs and antiaircraft gunners threw up shells toward the Dauntlesses. One of the pilots, Max Eaton, told Wordell and Seiler, "We turned for Casablanca and, as we approached, black puffs of smoke blossomed out in front of us. That was flak, but it seemed unreal and entirely without menace. . . . Dawn came fairly quickly as if someone had turned up the lights on a stage setting, and there was Casablanca suddenly gleaming in the daylight. We went around in a wide circle. There were no fighters yet, so we hugged in formation. The antiaircraft puffs were getting closer and closer as the gunners found the range and deflection. Two of them jolted my plane but I didn't worry because we were straightening out for a dive. I could see the planes ahead starting down. The harbor beneath us was a mass of twinkling lights. . . . It reminded me of Coney Island. Then as another shell burst near and jolted my wing, I realized it wasn't Coney Island. Those weren't lights, they were machine guns, spitting at us.

"We had no trouble finding the submarines moored against the Jetée Delure. The *Jean Bart* [a battleship] began to throw up everything she had. The stuff was going wide. I took my aim at the sub formation, and held it all the way down. As I came near, red tracer was coming right for my nose and streaking by over the wings. You get a strange feeling of aloofness as the stuff goes by." Eaton loosed his ordnance and pulled out while gunners continued to dog his track. He noticed several French fighter planes watching the dive-bombers, but they did not interfere.

The initial strike sank three merchantmen and, more important, three submarines. However, eight U-boats slipped out to sea, a deadly serious threat, especially to the thin-hulled Jeep carriers, which stored copious supplies of fuel.

The first fighters off the *Ranger* had come from VF-9 under Lieutenant Commander Jack Raby. As they approached Fedala at an altitude of 10,000 feet, they observed sixteen enemy planes in two equal sections 1,000 feet or so beneath them. Raby targeted the leader of the second group of eight, opening fire from 150 yards above and astern. Tracers poured into a French Curtiss 75A and it disappeared in a cloud, presumably destroyed. Raby, still in pursuit, entered a cloud, and as he emerged, a different Curtiss 75A appeared less than 100 yards ahead. Raby opened up with all six .50s. It caught fire, blew up, and fell to earth in pieces.

Ensigns M. J. Franger and A. E. Martin jointly attacked another enemy plane, which started to burn. Lieutenant K. C. "Casey" Childers discovered a foe on his tail and threw himself into a tight spiral and controlled spin. At 1,000 feet he came out in a tight, nose-high turn. His pursuer passed into Childers's sights and a crush of machine-gun bullets. Smoke trailing, the aircraft plummeted to the ground. Ensign L. A. Menard picked off one of three adversaries trying to intercept his section. His guns ripped the plane to pieces. Another Curtiss 75A wobbled and flamed, vanishing in a cloud after Lieutenant (j.g) H. E. Vita caught it in his gun sight.

Raby and company now followed a course in the direction of Port Lyautey. A French Leo 45, a twin-engine bomber, hove into view a bare 400 feet off the water. The Navy F4Fs quickly turned toward the plane. Raby, aiming at the left engine, caused it to burst into flame. Ensign M. J. Franger then scored direct hits on the right engine, inflicting similar damage. The Leo 45 exploded as it struck the sea.

Wordell and Eiler reported the reaction on their ship upon news of the first salvos: "There was pride in the Padre's voice. . . . We heard it over the plane-to-ship radio. The news that Pete Carver of the scout-bomber squadron had encountered opposition was the signal we were in action. Carver called back, 'Batter up.' 'Play ball,' answered the ship."

Seiler remarked on the initial lack of noise, except for the clatter from shoes as pilots ran across the deck and then climbed into the cockpits. "The handling crews winding the intertia starters for the scouts' bombers yank out their cranks and stand clear. Starter cartridges are inserted in the fighters, and we wait for 'Start engines.' Four dozen airplanes engage their engines and the quiet of the deck is gone. . . . One by one the planes began [sic] to creep forward to their positions for the take-off."

From the air, the fighters saw shells from the battleship *Massachusetts* supplemented by smaller ones from destroyers smash into the *Jean Bart* and other Vichy warships. The French battleship, still under construction and moored to a berth, retaliated briefly before an explosion jammed its main battery turret.

Tommy Booth guided his section to the Cazes airport. The Wildcat pilots spotted French aircraft. Fighters and bombers on the field were dispersed, and antiaircraft guns greeted the interlopers. Booth ordered one section to remain above to ward off any enemy opposition while the remainder of the squadron went for the antiaircraft pits. They succeeded in silencing their targets, but other emplacements continued to shower the American flyers.

The waves of dive-bombers and fighters destroyed a number of French aircraft on the ground, but some rose to engage in aerial combat. The best of the French planes, the Dewoitine 520, posed a formidable threat, while the Curtis 75A, identified by some Americans as a P-36, was overmatched. Ensign "Windy" Shields, in the section assigned by Booth to guard the strafers, saw a pair of Dewoitines moving in for an attack. Above him lingered what he labeled as two P-36s. He focused on one of the Dewoitines but overshot him on his first run. "As I went past I saw he was coming around on my tail. I pulled up and came back over in a quick turn that brought me with my nose toward him. I was too far away and much too anxious. I gave him a burst for quite a long range. These .50 calibers got him. I could see him, standing still in the air as if something had jerked him up by the tail. He looked as though he was going to stall to take evasive action, and he fell over to starboard, his wing fluttering. The plane's nose went into a sharp dive. I followed him down, too excited to think of doing anything else. He hit the ground, bounced, and with his motor still running ricocheted across the field till he came to a stop in a water hole."

Shields and another VF-41 F4F accounted for two Curtis 75As and then blew up a Douglas DB-7 bomber as it attempted to get off the ground. But his luck ran out as a French fighter came out of the sun and spewed bullets that ripped his fuel lines, filling the cockpit with fumes. Three more aircraft zeroed in on his now-crippled Wildcat. In *Wildcats over Casablanca*, Shields said, "the machine was still flying. Then an incendiary bullet started a fire. A great lick of flame came up at my face and I knew it was the end. I pushed back the hood and tried to turn the plane on her back, but she wouldn't have it. The tabs and aileron surfaces were not working. How the heck was I to get out? I decided to stall her, and at the moment when she lost flying speed I braced my knees and jumped for it. I got clear. The parachute opened, and I floated down feeling angry and frustrated. A French plane came at me. I thought he was going to shoot me up but he just flew past me, wagging his wing tips and waving his hand and laughing like hell. I waved back."

From the ground, however, the reception was less friendly. Infantrymen pegged several shots at him. He took out his pistol and fired back. When he slammed into a barbed-wire fence, the riflemen stopped shooting. He said he saw German officers hastily boarding transports to flee the scene. Shields himself temporarily became a prisoner of the local French.

During their rampage, the team under Booth caught a column of tanks on the Fedala-Rabat road and punished it severely. The members of VF-41 quickly returned to the *Ranger* for replenishment of fuel and ammunition. In his action report, Squadron Commander Booth reported that his people had seen as many as sixteen enemy fighters airborne and approximately the same number of aircraft on the ground. He claimed nine of the Vichy airmen shot down and some fourteen on the airfields either burned or badly damaged.

Lieutenant Mac Wordell commanded sixteen fighters from VF-41 and VF-9 for the mission in support of the landings at Fedala. Launched at 7:10 A.M., the group formed up and arrived at its objective in less than half an hour. Circling at altitudes of 9,000 to 10,000 feet, they sighted a French naval force—two cruisers and four destroyers—leaving the Casablanca harbor to engage the U.S. warships and transports.

Under heavy flak from the ships, the Wildcats dived on the six ships, hosing the turrets, batteries, bridge, and sailors on deck with a mix of tracers, incendiary, and armor-piercing machine-gun bullets. The assault ignited sizable fires aboard the cruisers. Trailing thick black smoke, both of them reversed course, seeking shelter in the Casablanca harbor. The pack of destroyers, two also in flames, followed the bigger vessels back to port. No fighters rose to challenge the raiders.

In his first strafing run, antiaircraft struck Wordell's F4F, disabling his engine. While three associates guarded him, Wordell picked out a flat area a few miles south of Fedala and set his ship down. In the soft dirt the plane nosed over. Wordell immediately radioed his anxious squadron mates, "I'm all right. Will try to make it to Fedala. Go back and get those bastards. I'm going off the air now." The airmen saw him leave his Wildcat and begin walking. He too became a short-time captive.

Outstanding aid to the U.S. warships pummeling the shore batteries came from spotter aircraft. On the second day of Torch, the battleship *New York*, guided by a plane it catapulted, destroyed a coast artillery position that would have prevented the use of the Safi harbor. The heavy cruiser *Philadelphia* put up its spotter, who flew low enough to locate a well-camouflaged battery of three 155-mm guns near Safi. When the *Philadelphia*'s bombardment registered no hits, the ship dispatched its own float planes. Their bombs knocked out the battery.

Fighters and torpedo bombers from Air Groups Twenty-seven, Twenty-eight, and Thirty aboard the Jeep flattops worked in conjunction with the *Ranger* complement on the central site of the invasion. Some of the bombers bludgeoned the submarine pens in Casablanca while fighters dueled with the opposition in the air. Lieutenant H. L. Johnson and Ensign P. M. Henderson, of VGF-28, saw a twin-engine bomber approaching the carrier *Sangamon*. They identified it as a French Leo 45. Bursts from their machine guns sent the bomber into a diving crash in the water. Later the pilots and the

Navy were chagrined to learn that the victim had been a British Hudson. Unfortunately, no one had been advised that there would be such aircraft in the vicinity.

American intelligence believed that the French would not resist in the vicinity of Safi, the southernmost landing area, if their airfields went unmolested. That information was incorrect, but acting upon it, the command assigned the carrier *Santee*, home of the least experienced air group. The pilots taking off from the *Santee* also contended with a particular difficulty, very light winds. When the first bunch took off at daybreak on D-Day, one plane disappeared and another splashed down, its pilot rescued after nearly three days in the water. Four aircraft, unable to find their way home, landed at an airstrip, where they became prisoners. A second flight, after running out of gas, attempted to touch down at the Safi field, which was excessively soft and bumpy. Before anyone could be waved off, the mushy ground wrecked nine Wildcats. The pilots scrambled aboard small boats that returned them to the *Santee*.

Only one flyable plane remained available. In the hands of the air group's lieutenant commander, Joseph A. Ruddy, it performed reconnaissance for eight hours the first day and nine the second, with time out only for refueling. The absence of the *Santee's* airplanes influenced the *New York* and the *Philadelphia* to rely on their own catapulted machines for the work against the shore batteries. With replacement planes, the squadron sortied again, wrecking a dozen or so planes on a field at Marrakech and shooting up a truck column.

On November 10, Lieutenant Commander Jack Raby led the VF-9 squadron against the Port Lyautey air base. Lieutenant T. Hugh Winters, a 1935 USNA graduate and the exec of VF-9, said, "I was able to average three missions a day, and actually felt safer in the air than on the ship, as the antique gasoline system leaked so badly you could sometimes smell high-test gas." VF-9 would lose three pilots during the brief North African campaign, and Winters saw two of them go, including a member of the party that rampaged over the Port Lyautey air base. "The first was my own wingman, Willie Wilhoite, who had flown with me all summer. We were strafing fighters on the Port Lyautey field and I had just exploded a gas truck between two fighters refueling, and pulling out over them I heard Willie call, 'They got me, Pedro.' He glided steeply into the ground about a mile from the field. I did a wingover and went back at ground level to the machine-gun nest and got hit myself, but not seriously. Ex-

pensive lesson learned—never in the heat of rage do a wingover at
close range."

His wounds from the ill-conceived maneuver over Port Lyautey
required tending from the flight surgeon. Only after intervention by
squadron commander Raby did Winters receive permission to fly
again. "When you work so long getting a squadron ready you don't
want to miss any of the fighting. The bench is no place for the first
string. As a tree on the golf course is 95% air, even more so, war is
98% waiting and 2% shooting, and at times it can be long and boring.

"Next day," reported Winters, "we were burning bombers on another field and Eddie Micha exploded one with bombs attached just
as he passed over it at 20 feet altitude. The blast converted his little
Wildcat into a large ball of fire bouncing along the runway. The loss
of Willie, and then right away Eddie, added some to my 29 years."

Ground forces complained of having been strafed by a lone as-
sailant coming over the beach at Fedala, seemingly timing his attack
for when the area was clear of American fighters. The marauder
quickly received the nickname of "Phantom Raider." On November 9,
two F4Fs from VT-41, manned by Lieutenant (j.g.) Glen D. Wood
and Ensign Hank Weiler, suddenly interrupted the Phantom in his
rounds. The incident was reported in *Wildcats over Casablanca*. "It
was quite different from any other plane we had seen," said Wood.
"As far as we could make out, it was an ME-109 [Messerschmitt]. It
was painted dull black all over and seemed very fast. It was the
meanest, dirtiest job I've ever seen. Hank made a pass at him, but
missed. I crammed on full power and made a shallow high-side run.

"I opened fire from 150 yards and gave him all guns. It was a
long burst. I felt this was a job that had to be done extra well. I kept
firing until he disintegrated in my face. As a matter of fact, I was
forced to pull up very violently to avoid pieces of the plane and the
flames." Wood could consider himself fortunate that he had not dog-
fought with the ME-109, whose flight characteristics made it quite
superior to an F4F.

After having its main turret jammed by a shell from the *Massachusetts*, by November 10, the *Jean Bart* had restored its 15-inch
cannons and resumed its duels with U.S. warships. Lieutenant Commander Ralph Embree and his cohorts from the *Ranger* took 1,000-
pounders over the harbor in their Dauntlesses. They deposited nine
of them, two of which smashed into the battleship. It suspended its
cannonades.

From the start of Torch, the Navy flyers constantly scanned the water for signs of submarines. Ensign Gilbert Peglow from Air Group Twenty-seven, based on the *Suwannee* and flying a TBF, took off on antisubmarine patrol on November 10. He suddenly noticed a torpedo speeding straight for the carrier. To his astonishment, it passed just under the stern, continued on, and actually bounced into the air, then exploded harmlessly after it hit the battleship *New York*. On hearing of the incident, three more Avengers searched for the U-boat. Ensign D. Hill discovered a sub starting to submerge and dropped eight depth charges. A destroyer confirmed the destruction of the undersea predator.

One day later, three torpedo bombers left the *Suwannee* near dawn during a fog that restricted the ceiling. From beneath the mist loomed a large submarine moving through the water with its conning tower exposed. The fog bank had kept the Americans concealed, and they were able to start their attack before the vessel could submerge. The first depth charge struck just as the conning tower began to slide under the sea. Another eight depth charges fell close enough to either hit or impact upon the submarine. An iron bar erupted from the water into the air, and a large oil slick that bubbled for forty-five minutes spread over the surface while the TBFs hovered above. The submarine was believed to be destroyed.

Chick Smith of VF-9 flew nine combat missions, fighter sweeps against Vichy French airfields. "I did not have any encounters with enemy aircraft," said Smith. "But Fighting Nine lost four pilots to AA."

By the morning of November 12, the invaders had secured almost all of their objectives. No aerial opposition existed; the entire complement of the Vichy air armada had either been knocked out of the skies or else blasted useless on the ground. The colonial forces capitulated, and a handful of Navy pilots such as Wordell and Shields were liberated. With Army Air Corps pilots now ensconced at the local airfields, the carriers departed, taking with them the Navy pilots and planes. There was still a "wings of gold" presence. As the flattops sailed off, Patrol Squadrons Seventy-two and Ninety-three began to fly out of French Morocco, performing antisubmarine operations and keeping eyes on Axis shipping in the Mediterranean. Fleet Air Wing Fifteen assumed responsibility for these duties beginning on December 1.

During the opening month of Operation Torch, across the globe in the Pacific Theater, the Guadalcanal pot continued to boil. By November, the Americans had solidified their once slight and uncertain beachhead. At the same time, the enemy had, in spite of considerable losses, put ashore as many as 20,000 fresh troops. While Henderson Field still lay under the guns of land troops, additional strips housed a growing number of aircraft. The base at Espíritu Santo served as a backup from which Navy planes of all types and heavyweight Army bombers could operate.

Whitey Feightner, with VF-10 on the *Enterprise*, recalled that after the Santa Cruz Island battle, the ship traveled to Espíritu Santo at a slow pace, the voyage consuming almost thirty-six hours. Some of the torpedo planes and dive-bombers went in advance, allowing sufficient space to retain all of the planes, including those left from the *Hornet*, aboard. At Espíritu Santo the shops performed emergency repairs on the flattop, which then moved on to the bigger base at Nouméa for more complete refurbishing over a period of several weeks.

Air reconnaissance soon discovered another major thrust from the Japanese in the form of a heavyweight battle fleet that not only expected to deliver more soldiers but also planned to bombard the American positions. The task force included a pair of light aircraft carriers, two battleships, a batch of cruisers, and a bevy of destroyers. The nearest U.S. surface vessels were badly outgunned. The *Enterprise*, in a group with two battlewagons and some destroyers, was too far off for the first round, which occurred in the early-morning darkness of November 13. The Japanese sank the cruiser *Atlanta* and the destroyers *Laffey*, *Cushing*, *Barton*, and *Monssen*. Two cruisers, *San Francisco* and *Portland*, reeled under heavy shell fire, and then the enemy guns raked the light cruiser *Juneau*, which sank. Only ten sailors from a complement of nearly seven hundred survived. The casualties included the five Sullivan brothers. Their deaths led to a directive that forbade assignment of siblings to the same unit or ship. Also killed in the engagement were two American admirals. U.S. guns added two Japanese destroyers to the Iron Bottom Sound inventory and pummeled the battleship *Hiei* severely.

The American fleet with the *Enterprise* headed for the contested waters. "We started up toward Guadalcanal," said Feightner, "with the concept that we were to search and find. We knew this bunch of transports were coming down to reinforce Guadalcanal, but that's all the information we had. We were sent to intercept the transports.

Red Carmody, flying an SBD, ran across them. We immediately got this attack group—everything we had on the ship that could go which we put into one big strike force."

The attack group, numbering eight SBDs with a twelve-fighter escort, flew under the command of Jimmy Flatley. Before Flatley, Feightner, and the mixed bag of Dauntlesses and Wildcats got on-stage, the *Enterprise* had launched some Avengers and fighters to precede the carrier in the defense of Henderson Field. En route, they came upon the wounded *Hiei*. The torpedo bombers struck at the target of opportunity, and now the battered battleship could only steam in circles within a screen of destroyers. The Navy pilots landed at Henderson, refueled, and rearmed. Reinforced with Marine bombers, they returned to further torment the enemy battleship, which eventually gave up the ghost.

"We were cruising at about 25,000 feet," said Feightner, "and we've got the bombers with us. All of a sudden we looked up and here comes about 40 Zeros, right at us, up above us maybe 5,000 feet. I've never heard anybody so calm in my life. Jimmy Flatley got on the radio and said, 'Don't anybody flash any wings or canopy. Just sit still. Our mission is to attack the ships down there.' With these airplanes going overhead, he was saying, 'Okay, Carmody, you take the one on the front. I don't want any duplications on this.'

"We had only nine bombers with us. And he assigned every bomber a separate target, with these 40 Zeros sitting over our heads, going over. Fortunately, they didn't see us and we pressed right on in. We dove down and were strafing them; they had eleven transports. We went in and strafed the decks. There were people all over those decks. [After] we strafed a transport, Flatley pulled up and we strafed a destroyer. That destroyer started smoking and today [2002] that destroyer is still beached on the north side of the island.

"We had no more finished that than we had Zeros all over us. We managed to get the bomber group together and covered them all the way back to Guadalcanal. That was typical of his [Flatley's] aggressiveness. If he had a mission, that came first. We got all but three ships. I have vivid recollections of during our strafing attacks, seeing people leaping over the sides of the ships, rather than stay there. Four airplanes strafing down the deck of a transport, with people all over topside, it must have been devastating." As he left the scene, Feightner observed three of the transports, burning and beached.

Despite the destruction of seven troopships, the Japanese commander loaded as many soldiers as possible aboard other vessels and continued to set his course for Guadalcanal. The Americans, reduced to a handful of destroyers, now brought into Iron Bottom Sound two new battleships, *Washington* and *South Dakota*. Both mounted 16-inch guns, compared to the sole and weaker enemy capital ship, *Kirishima*, which, like the *Hiei*, was an elderly vessel that had been refitted. In the night action that boomed through the Slot, the Japanese again demonstrated a superiority in the ability to fight in the dark. Of the four American destroyers that confronted the Imperial Navy's nine similar warships, two sank in the encounter, another would never fight again, and the fourth suffered moderate damage. Only one Japanese destroyer received any wounds.

The enemy firepower concentrated upon the *South Dakota*, illuminated by Japanese searchlights, blasting her superstructure. But the focus on that vessel permitted the *Washington* to beat up the *Kirishima*, which eventually sank and also forced the crew of a fatally struck destroyer to abandon ship. In terms of warships, it was another victory for the Japanese, but only a fraction of the reinforcement troops ever got ashore and with precious little in supplies. The air losses to the Japanese had also been substantial. In fact, the air and sea battles around and over Guadalcanal were not a standoff. Japan was not geared to what had become a war of attrition. While U.S. industry began to launch hundreds of ships, turn out thousands of planes, and school tens of thousands of pilots, the Japanese output was not even enough to compensate for their losses.

At the conclusion of the brawl, the naval aviators, instead of returning to the *Enterprise*, landed at Henderson. While the SBDs enjoyed the luxury of the bomber strip covered with a Marston mat, the VF-10 pilots used a grass field set aside for fighters. Feightner recalled, "I landed and off to my right a big geyser of dirt went up. It turned out the Japanese had a six-inch gun on the side of the hill and they were shelling the airfield. I looked around and there was a Marine beckoning me to come over under the trees. I taxied over there. They grabbed the tail and pulled it around underneath the trees. I jumped out of the airplane and had the shock of my life. There was a hole, about two and a half feet across, in a big winding spiral down into the ground. It was an 18-inch shell hole, where the battleships had been shelling the place.

"They took us over to a tent area, back under the trees. This guy is still shelling the field and it's the first time I ever saw Joe Foss [then a Marine captain, whose twenty-eight victories was the highest number among the leatherneck pilots]. Right in the middle, this guy with a campaign hat and smoking a big cigar come strolling across the middle of the strip. I'd never seen him [before] but this was him, strolling along across the area, saying hello to all these people and he welcomes us. We became part of the 1st Marine Division, Reinforced. At the time we landed, the Marines had three airplanes that were operational. That night, the guy up on the hill managed to bag a couple more airplanes; both of them were new ones we had brought in. I guess we ended up with about twenty fighters left out of the whole melee."

Feightner's first morning on the island provided a chilling experience of conditions. "We're about to get up when this Marine came by and said, 'Stay in your tent.' The next thing we hear all this automatic fire. They're out there and they're machine gunning the tops of the trees. The Japs had infiltrated during the night and they're sitting in the tops of these coconut trees, waiting for us to come out. They got a couple of them in the trees and we [left the tents]."

Supply remained a critical problem for the Americans, even though the enemy's attempts to restock and reinforce its troops had been blocked. Army B-26s ferried torpedoes for the Marine and Navy planes because the Martin Marauders could not be properly fitted to use the tin fish. The weapon continued to frustrate its users. Feightner and the other F4F pilots joined up with torpedo planes, seeking to knock out the battleship that plagued them with its enormous shells. "We'd go steaming out there, and it's only thirty miles to this thing. We strafed ahead of the torpedo planes and then those guys went through all this stuff. A couple of them got shot down. . . . They'd go in there and drop, and those torpedoes ran up against the side of that ship, bounced off and didn't go off. I've never heard so many unhappy people."

Jim Billo, who was tormented by the loss of his wingman, Ensign James Caldwell, and who had rejoined the squadron after his rescue by a destroyer with a less than hospitable skipper, recalled his first stay as a Guadalcanal reinforcement: "We lived in tents, used nearby foxholes during a night bombardment. Marines serviced our aircraft." Like many who served in the South Pacific, he caught malaria, which would periodically flare up. "The ship's doctor gave each of the departing pilots a pint bottle of Schenley's Black Label. On our arrival at Henderson Field, the Marines first stole the airplane clocks while our engines were still cooling, then started bartering for our valuable cargo. Flags, knives, guns and up to $50 cash were offered. A night-time bombardment of our tent city convinced me that nothing was worth acquisition. I drank mine."

On his second day out, Feightner flew wing for Lieutenant David Pollack, who had been awarded a Navy Cross for his efforts to stop a torpedo directed at the *Porter*. As the flight commenced its attack, several Zeros interrupted them. "One of them got through and fired at us and hit the hub of the electric propellor on Dave's [F4F]. His airplane went into flat pitch and couldn't maintain airspeed. He started down, turned and headed toward the strip. Like a good wing man I followed him. Soon his prop just stopped turning.

"He made a water landing. His head hit the gunsight and it put a great big gash in his head, knocked him silly enough so he wasn't entirely conscious. He got out of the airplane. I circled around watching him and he was swimming on his back. The only problem was he was swimming right toward those three ships that were on fire over on the beach about a mile away. About this time, the Zero made a pass at him. I was busy driving that guy off. I never could get a shot at him but I kept making runs at him.

"By the time I finished that, here's Dave—getting close to the beach and the Japanese are coming out in rubber boats to get him. I got over and started strafing them. All but one turned and went back. I was going to come around and make another run . . . and a couple of Marines in a rubber boat came out and the Japanese started shelling them. I went over and did some strafing. The Marines finally got ahold of Dave, got him in the boat and took him back.

"I went in to land about the time the rest of the group was coming back. The field was in such bad shape from being shelled that they told us to go and land in this cow pasture. The third guy to land flipped over on his back in the middle of the strip. It was hard to find a place to land. A couple of guys tried and ground looped. Finally, they told us to land on the beach; the beach was pretty wide. We all go over and land on the beach. We were getting along just fine." However, Army flyers using P-39s also tried to put down there. "One of the P-39s landed, and with that nose wheel they had, it dug into a soft spot in the sand. He went flipping down the beach. Fortunately, he didn't burn but it really closed up the beach." Meanwhile, bulldozers had filled in the holes at Henderson, enabling the remainder of those still in the air to get down.

The short stay at Guadalcanal provided the aviators with a grim glimpse of the stress for those condemned to fight on the ground.

"You just feel completely helpless," Feightner commented about the nightly outbursts from offshore. "We had some kind of coconut-covered dugouts there. It was impossible to live in these. It was sweltering hot, so that's why we were out in tents. The minute that shelling started, we all went piling into those things." He recalled a group of Marine dive-bomber pilots about fifty yards away. When the barrage began one night, they all climbed into one of the dugouts, which was covered with coconut logs and quarter-inch iron plates, more logs and dirt. A direct hit wiped out nine people.

Feightner saw a young Marine suddenly go berserk, wildly firing his weapon until another leatherneck "managed to cold-cock him." On edge from the nocturnal cascades of shells, the fighter pilot heard enemy soldiers slithering through the nearby woods, endeavoring to climb trees to gain a sniper's perch. "I have a lot of empathy for those ground troops."

In the air, the Navy flyers worked closely with their Marine counterparts. "Anybody who was available flew together," recalled Feightner. "We all used the Thach Weave. We flew a four-plane formation. We split out to about double the turning radius of the airplane. When we caught somebody, we split around them and then we'd make one run from here and one from here, so we were always protected, even while attacking. It was a really effective technique. The Japanese hadn't learned how to counter it. Jimmy Thach and Jimmy Flatley both deserve an awful lot of credit for it; they saved a lot of lives.

"We had such a tenuous hold that it was touch and go whether we were going to survive and stay there. The Japanese were flying, and there was a row of hills just to the west of the strip. They would circle over there behind the hills, and if you extended your landing pattern down there, man, they'd pop over the hill and bag you. You never saw so many tight turns to landings in your life."

The ill-performing P-39s were, in Feightner's words, flying coffins. "Air-to-air they didn't have a chance against the Zero. They were hanging bombs on them and when these guys would set up these six-inch guns up in the hills, they would go up and just dive bomb them from low altitude, practically skip bombing is what they were doing. They were pretty effective." Indeed, the Soviet Air Force found the P-39 an excellent ground-support tool.

He was impressed, however, with the Lockheed P-38 Lightning, which began to operate in the Pacific. He noted, though, that the Army pilots had precious little time to train on the twin-engine fighter. "I talked to one guy who had never fired the guns in it," said Feightner. "Somebody stuck him in a P-38 and said, 'Go!' "

Alex Vraciu, who would become one of the Navy's top aces after Guadalcanal, offered an explanation of why the Americans had bested the Japanese in the air. "The Zero was the dominant plane out there early in the war. It was such a capable plane, compared to what we had, that it took control of the air. Although they had aerial superiority in numbers, they didn't seem to use them properly for escort work. Instead of escorting—as we would—up close—they'd have the fighters flying far aft of the bomber groups when they were attacking us at Guadalcanal.

"[They] had good pilots. You could be on the tail of a Zero, down low, and it was *so* maneuverable, they told us, that inside of two turns it would be on your tail. It was half the weight of your plane. They were about 6,000 pounds, and we were at 12,000 pounds in the Hellcat [the new Grumman fighter that replaced the Wildcat and that Vraciu flew]. The Wildcat was lighter than the Hellcat—and it was somewhat maneuverable—but it had frequent gun trouble and was grossly underpowered. At Guadalcanal, if it wasn't for the coast watchers to give the Wildcat a chance to climb when they spotted the planes coming in to make raids on Guadalcanal, the F4Fs wouldn't have been able to get to an altitude to counter the attack.

"The Japanese never adapted like the Americans on tactical warfare. They could have accomplished a lot more if they had done so. Maybe it was the long flights that they had from Rabaul to get over to hit Guadalcanal and other places. They would go 500 miles outbound. My God! That's 1,000 miles total both ways, plus any air action over the target area. That's a lot of time. Fighter pilots don't like to sit on their seat for too long a stretch. Three hours in a combat air patrol is enough."

Vraciu noted that because everyone in the Navy underwent similar tactical training when a replacement joined up or a fighter pilot found himself alone, he could quickly pick up another lone survivor to be integrated into the familiar Thach Weave for mutual protection.

After about a week on Guadalcanal, the Navy pilots from VF-10, leaving all their airplanes for the Marines, embarked on a 500-mile voyage to the Espíritu Santo base. A Jeep carrier met them with a new set of F4Fs.

One last-ditch effort to reinforce the embattled Japanese soldiers on Guadalcanal on November 30 brought another after-dark exchange off Tassafaronga, near the site of the October clash. No carriers participated in the gun duel, which sank a U.S. heavy cruiser and reduced three others to floating wrecks. But the enemy fleet, bearing fresh troops, could not penetrate the American naval defenses. The situation for the Japanese garrison on Guadalcanal was hopeless, and when Imperial Navy ships ran the gauntlet early the next year, the purpose was to withdraw soldiers instead of reinforcing them.

NINE

FLIGHTS BACK, ESCAPES, AND RESCUES

At the close of 1942 and the beginning of the New Year, both the American and Japanese naval forces appeared to require a respite from the furious action of the preceding months. Jim Billo, with VF-10 on the *Enterprise*, recalled the parlous state of naval aviation at the time: "The ship [*Enterprise*], being the only carrier left in the Pacific, was at risk. The tactics were not morale builders. The tactics of the ship were to stick its nose into every place it could in the South Pacific and not proceed once sighted but to turn and run. It was not a great way to fight a war, but we couldn't afford to lose the *Enterprise*. [Toward the end of January 1943, the *Saratoga* returned to the war.]

"We operated with the home base of Espíritu Santo, where the ship would pull into the harbor and we'd go ashore into the fighter strip, sometimes the bomber strip. We did such things as stand a combat patrol over the cruiser *Chicago* when it was hit in January and drove off a bunch of Bettys that came in to sink it, which they did.

"We were also used to supplement the Guadalcanal fighter squadrons by launching a group of eight, flying from the *Enterprise* to Guadalcanal, staying a few days, flying patrols, then flying back, either to the ship or down to Espíritu Santo. This was an interesting trip because it's about 500 miles over water with no markers. So when we'd leave Cactus, they'd send out a DC-3 ahead of us, and we'd take off and fly until we overtook it, then hold his heading until we got to Buttons—Espíritu Santo. It was just not fun."

Whitey Feightner, a member of VF-10, recalled the sinking of the *Chicago:* "There were twelve Bettys that came after the *Enterprise* and we managed to turn them around and they were headed for the *Chicago.* We shot down six of them before they got there, but six of them bunched up together and they could outrun us; we couldn't catch them. They dropped their torpedoes which went into the *Chicago,* which was under tow [an earlier raid had blown off the bow] and they sank it."

Feightner said that he had been flying wing for Flatley and after the Betty group loosed their tin fish, the two of them pursued a trio still airborne. "We were very slowly overhauling this one. [Flatley] pulled his nose up, fired, put tracers in front of the guy which panicked him. He turned and headed for a cloud layer at maybe 2,500 feet. Being a dumb ensign, I went after him, in the cloud right after him. He turned and the next thing I saw—in the cloud—was this big thing in front of me. I fired, managed to miss him somehow, broke out on top and he didn't come out. I went back down below, joined up on Jimmy Flatley, and he wags—the big thumbs up—'You got him.'

"When he got back he would take no credit for that airplane at all, gave me full credit. He said, 'All I did was turn him around. You shot him down.'" Feightner received a Distinguished Flying Cross for knocking down three of the Bettys. The engagement, known as the Battle of Rennell Island, marked the completion of Flatley's command of the Grim Reapers. He had been named to take command of a new air group.

In his farewell message, in which he spoke fondly of his associate, characteristically, Flatley added a cautionary note: "Take care of yourselves. . . . One parting word of advice. There is a definite tendency on the part of every one of you to throw caution to the winds every time you meet the enemy. We've been lucky so far. But it's dumb. We've spent hours and hours on tactics, designed not only to destroy, but also to protect ourselves. Keep that thought foremost in your minds. Rip 'em up and down, but do it smartly." William "Killer" Kane assumed command of the squadron.

Upon completion of their assignments for Operation Torch, the four Jeep carriers involved had voyaged to the South Pacific. The route for the *Suwannee* took it to Bermuda and then a brief stop at Hampton Roads. The flyers from Air Group Twenty-seven drew a week of liberty before the flattop headed, via the Panama Canal, toward the waters around Guadalcanal. The script had called for the aircraft on the *Suwannee* and the *Chenango* to contribute to the aircraft protection for Task Force Eighteen, in which the *Chicago* sailed. For reasons best known to him, Rear Admiral Robert C. Giffen, in command of the task force, strayed from the textbook. He failed to ensure that the two escort carriers rendezvoused with the cruisers. By the time Giffen ordered the pair into position, the *Chicago* had gone down. The aviators of the *Suwannee* did get in some licks in support of the landings on Rennell.

Mindful of the vulnerability of the warships to undersea predators, antisubmarine patrols constantly occupied the aviators. Ensign Benton J. Skuda from the *Suwannee* took off in the late afternoon of February 27, 1943, with his crew of Gunner John Boosalis and Radioman Lawrence O'Neal, for a routine AS patrol. For an hour they simulated bombing and torpedo attacks on the task force before heading out to their assigned sector. As Skuda maneuvered the TBF for a meeting with the *Suwannee* some 45 miles off, the engine suddenly quit and refused to restart.

"I jettisoned the bombs and all hands prepared for a forced landing at sea," said Skuda. "The bombs dropped from about 500 feet and exploded well clear. I closed the bomb bay doors and put down my flaps. The wind was about 10 knots and the landing was effected comfortably. On landing, we launched our rubber life raft and procured sundry articles from the plane before it sank."

After getting clear of the drowning aircraft, the crew took inventory. Their possessions included two parachutes, a pistol, ten eleven-ounce cans of water, and one standard-issue canteen full of water. They had twenty-four cans of emergency food—Spam in a can—five Hershey chocolate bars, seven cans of malted-milk tablets, one can of crackers, and a first-aid kit. The latter held four tins of battle dressing, four sulfa packages, iodine, six morphine syrettes, a tube of chlorine tablets for water purification, tannic acid jelly, energy tablets, and capsules containing spirits of ammonia.

The first night drifting in the sea, Skuda said, no one slept. With the stars as a reference, they set a course for an island they deemed to be about 25 miles away. Paddling with oars and using a sea anchor, the downed airmen figured they had traveled 5 miles. Both of his crew retched after swallowing saltwater. When day broke, a dead calm, under a torrid sun, settled over the area. "We took turns manning the oars," reported Skuda, "and fairly good progress was made. Although we opened a few tins of rations, we couldn't force the food down and it eventually spoiled. [Because of] continuous rowing and hot sun, we required much water, and as our supply was limited, I systematically rationed out small quantities. By noon, a shark that was following us disappeared and Boosalis and I got into the water and tried to push the boat along while O'Neal rowed. This did not work out successfully and we went back to our original plan."

That night a strong wind whipped up the sea, pushing the raft back toward the open sea. To defeat the elements, the trio set up a rotation of two at the oars while one rested. "Our water being very critically low," said the ensign, "our bodies became dehydrated, and our mouths were very dry. Even though this strenuous work called for more water, we had to be satisfied with merely wetting our tongues. We kept this up all night, several times almost giving up from fatigue. The next morning found us still rowing but with little enthusiasm. Our hands were badly blistered and our skin was inflamed from the hot sun, but this was only secondary to our thirst.

"All the previous night we were kept going mainly by the thought of cold mountain springs that we could duck our head into once we reached the island. We were sadly disappointed. By noon the wind luckily changed, helping us along with the make-shift sail we rigged up. In mid-afternoon we maneuvered our boat through the breakers and touched shore, too dejected to experience any joy.

"On the beach we found two small coconuts and [drank] the last few ounces of our water. Too tired to move we spread out on the beach but found we couldn't sleep. Our thirst was more acute than our tiredness. We set out in search of water. We left our boat and other articles on the beach, taking with us our rations, first aid kit, empty water canteen and a strip of parachute which could be used as a netting against insects. Walking along the beach was very difficult. It was [a] jagged lava bed, full of holes, gullies and cliffs. After a few hours of walking, we observed that many holes contained stagnant water, and on tasting several, we found, much to our relief, that they were free from salt. These puddles had been formed by a recent rainfall. Even though the water was stagnant and had a strong taste of lime, we filled our canteen and added chlorine tablets from our first aid kit. Then we drank to our hearts content. The effect of water produced extreme fatigue and tiredness but not hunger. In fact we could not eat food of any available kind. We stretched out on the beach and soon fell asleep."

On the following morning, the men began a search for fresh water and perhaps civilization. Because of their swollen, blistered, and lacerated feet, they trekked at a slow pace. The razor-sharp lava rock slit open their shoes, requiring them to use their parachute shroud lines to bind them. Salt that clung to their clothes irritated their sunburned skin. Blisters and sores blossomed. They noticed, lurking amid the lava, numerous highly poisonous coral snakes. Steep cliffs along the beach eventually forced them to try to penetrate a jungle. But cliffs and dense undergrowth blocked their progress. By nightfall they again faced a critical shortage of water. Too exhausted to return to the beach, they bedded down for a sleepless, insect-hectored night.

In the morning they retreated back to the beach, climbing down from a cliff using vines for the descent. The aviators discovered a cave that gave respite from the pitiless sun and set up camp there. For a day they rested their sore, cut feet, sleeping much of the time.

"The second day in the cave," said Skuda, "our first pangs of hunger were felt. We opened a few tins of rations and killed and roasted a crab found on the beach. We decided to go back to our point of landing, uncover our boat and paddle along the shore line. We noticed the hot sun was rapidly drying up the fresh water puddles." The boat trip, however, gave them their first hopes of rescue. That afternoon, they came across a beach that appeared to have been used for fishing. Stopping there, the airmen scouted about until they found a path leading inland. It led to a garden with orange, lime, lemon, and papaya trees.

"With the green fruit we gathered from the trees," reported Skuda, "and a few more crabs found along the shore, we succeeded in having quite a nourishing meal. We stayed overnight but a steadily falling rain prevented us from getting much sleep. That night heavy seas and breakers came up, barring progress along the beach the next day. During the night, salt water spray ruined most of our fresh water puddles, except those that were further inland. We stayed here two days in all. As our water was again diminishing rapidly, we had to hurry to reach our boat, which we estimated was about seven miles along the shore.

"A few hours after starting the return journey to our boat, we ran across a native on the beach who was searching for his lost pigs. He proved to be very friendly and that afternoon took us to his village. There we were treated very hospitably by the natives. We were fed, bathed and had our clothes washed. In their gardens the natives had food and fruits of all sorts. That evening a few natives returned from the hunt brought back a wild bullock and a wild pig.

"During the evening natives from other villages came to see us. Some of them knew a little English and consequently were able to get the gist of our story. We learned from the natives that we were on Eromonga Island, in the New Hebrides group. We also learned that an Australian rancher was living on the other end of the island. After living in the native village for a few days, several native guides escorted us to his home. We arrived there still in very bad physical condition, and it took most of our stay to get our wounds under control."

During the second week at the Australian rancher's home, Skuda's shipmates broke out with serious cases of malaria. Their host, however, proved skilled at treatment, and he fed them well. On March 26, a month after they had taken off, a small interisland cutter that toted supplies to the rancher learned of their presence. It forwarded the information to a district commissioner on another island. He radioed Naval Headquarters, and two days later a seaplane retrieved the trio.

In a report to the *Suwannee* skipper, Skuda acknowledged making errors in not taking precautions against sunburn and husbanding their energy and water. He also noted his error in not digging a water hole for storage when it rained.

The remnants of Japanese forces, their survival on Guadalcanal rendered hopeless by the repeated defeats of attempts to reinforce or resupply them, continued to stubbornly resist the U.S. ground forces. But with that island and neighboring Tulagi firmly in the Allied bag, attention turned toward the obstacles to further advances up the Solomon string. To deter American notions in that direction, the Japanese constructed a large air base at Munda Point on the western corner of New Georgia Island, about 200 miles northwest of Guadalcanal. Munda Point would become a most familiar name to the naval aviators. Girdled by coral shoals, the site discouraged invasion. It was only partially susceptible to bombardment from the sea, and any air strikes against Munda Point required flying over enemy-controlled territory. To buttress their residence on New Georgia, the Japanese constructed a second installation on Kolombangara Island. In addition to these obstacles to U.S. ambitions, other prime targets during the first half of 1943 included installations on the large island of Bougainville and Japanese shipping plying the waters around the Solomons and New Guinea. Almost all of the actions taken against these targets were preliminaries for eventual invasions, with the conquest of New Georgia at the head of the list.

Still believing that the enemy intended to retake Guadalcanal, the U.S. Navy assembled a massive fleet composed of no fewer than six task forces with five carriers, seven battleships, a dozen cruisers, and more than thirty destroyers. Nimitz and company calculated that their armada could defeat any further attempts to oust the United States from Guadalcanal. Contrary to such an operation, the foe deftly executed a feint that distracted the Americans enough for a collection of landing barges to remove most of the remaining Japanese soldiers on the island.

On the heels of the extrication of the embattled Japanese troops, the Allies took one step forward, occupying the Russells, a small cluster of islands between Guadalcanal and New Georgia. The invasions passed unopposed. Construction crews hacked out another airstrip to bolster those on Guadalcanal and give easier access to the objectives farther up the line.

In March, Air Group Twenty-seven, nominally aboard the *Suwannee*, received the unenviable duty of supplementing the ground-based Marine and Army units at Henderson Field and the new field in the Russells. The first combat mission for the TBFs attached to the air group departed from Cactus on March 16 for a night raid. The bomb loads were 1,600-pound magnetic mines, with the harbor at Kahili on the southern end of Bougainville, the target. The flights lasted a tiring five and a half hours over water.

On April 1, a galaxy of Japanese fighter planes smeared the sky above the Russells. Some seventy enemy fighters, broken into groups of forty and thirty, sped down the Slot. They met a smaller contingent, thirty-four Marine, Navy, and Army aircraft—Corsairs, Lightnings, and Wildcats. Pilots from the *Suwannee* tangled with both batches of Zekes—versions of the Zero. Lieutenant (j.g.) George Seel picked out a target and began to chase him. Suddenly, Seel realized that a Zeke had seized an opportunity to position himself on Seel's tail. Tracers flashed by his cockpit; the plane shuddered from the impact of those that found their mark. Seel pushed over, then abruptly yanked back on the stick to pull out. The hard-charging Zeke overshot him, and Seel now sat on his tail. A single burst exploded the enemy.

Seel resumed his attacks on other airplanes. Before he fired all of his ammunition he splashed another and received credit for two probables. Cecil Harris, a former South Dakota schoolteacher who had been with Air Group Twenty-seven during Operation Torch, participated in the aerial battles of Guadalcanal and registered his first two knockdowns. He would add many more in future actions. The scorecard at the end of the affair, according to the Americans, was eighteen Japanese and six American planes downed. Some of the naval aviators who survived crash-landed at Guadalcanal because of wounds to themselves or to their aircraft.

That same day, Henderson Field on Guadalcanal welcomed Torpedo Squadron Eleven, under Lieutenant Commander Frederick Ashworth, USNA 1933 and a naval aviator since 1936. Ashworth developed expertise with different aircraft, flying patrol biplanes and the Boeing F4B two-wing fighter. Both of these featured open cockpits. After a stint specializing in aviation ordnance, Ashworth, to his surprise, had received orders to train VT-11. In addition to his many hours as a pilot, Ashworth brought his advanced education in tin fish to the task. He had also studied the reports on the successes achieved in the Coral Sea and the disaster event that had befallen the torpedo squadrons during the Battle of Midway.

Remarking on the deficiencies of the TBD Devastator and its speed and altitude limitations, Ashworth said, "If only the dive bombers and the torpedo planes could fly together and approach the target together, then there might be a better chance of making the coordinated attack. But as long as the TBDs were the best we had, this would be impossible.

"Then I was saved, because . . . the torpedo plane Grumman TBF Avenger came along. These planes had the performance to keep up with the SBDs and the air group could proceed to the attack together. It would then only be necessary that the torpedo plane leader so maneuver as to complete the desired coordination at the target area."

Still Ashworth faced a daunting responsibility: "Along with the job to train torpedo pilots, they gave me twelve or fourteen young naval aviators right out of flight training to make into torpedo pilots. These were kids who had either recently been college graduates, or who wanted to get into the war before finishing college and all commissioned ensigns in the Naval Reserve. They were the best group of young men I would ever want to meet." (Author's note: My conversations with Navy veterans and research indicates that, unlike in some circles in the Army, there was little or no conflict between reservists and graduates of the Academy.)

Resolved not to throw these novices into battle without practical experience, Ashworth arranged with an acquaintance supervising the overhaul and repair of torpedoes to receive a steady supply of practice tin fish. He drilled his squadron in techniques and boasted that while training, his pilots unloosed more than eighty torpedoes.

When Ashworth learned that the Navy, having lost all interest in horizontal bombing, planned to close the school for teaching that tactic, he requested that the instructors be posted to his squadron. Ashworth explained that the TBF was designed to permit installation of the Mark XV bombsight and its associated Stabilized Bombing Approach Equipment (SBAE). "It was my view that horizontal bombing could be a useful capability for my squadron and furthermore I knew that the SBAE made an excellent automatic pilot."

Something of a savant when it came to equipment, Ashworth heard that squadrons had rejected a plan to put airborne radar—the ASB-1—aboard the SBD scout planes. He immediately requested the devices for his squadron. His became the first carrier unit with the ASB-1. "I believed we would be doing night flying when we got into combat and these would be invaluable. Indeed they were. I owe my life to the thing."

VT-11 had arrived on Guadalcanal on April Fool's Day, 1943, and life for those stationed at Henderson Field was much improved over the early days when David Richardson and Whitey Feightner had cringed under offshore shelling and ducked snipers. "The last few Japanese," said Ashworth, "were being cleared out of the hills and jungles. The dirty work was all done and it was altogether a peaceful operation. There was a Carrier Aircraft Service Unit (CASU) that provided servicing for the squadrons based there, assisted by our own assigned enlisted personnel. The CASU operation was pretty well relaxed. I remember the CO of the CASU spent most of his time growing a vegetable garden. We got a little benefit from that . . . [and] in the local mess where all the squadron people were fed with reasonably good food of the dried eggs and Spam variety.

"Shower facilities were outside and with cold water only, which was hardly a hardship because the weather was usually warm and a cool shower was welcome. The enlisted men were billeted nearby and had their own outdoor shower facilities. We lived in pyramidal tents with wooden decks, again with officers in their own camp area. The others in our tent slept on canvas cots. I had brought along with me a down sleeping bag and air mattress which I spread on the floor. In the middle of the tent was a table around which there were four folding chairs." The earlier residents from carriers had slept on the ground, and at times the only meal of the day had been a cup of hot cocoa in the morning.

It was not entirely a summer camp situation, however. "Washing Machine Charlie," a single Japanese plane, paid regular evening calls in what Ashworth labeled a "heckling operation." The intruder would drop a few bombs, none of which caused serious damage but necessitated retreating to a foxhole if the plane came close.

VT-11 had the good fortune to operate from Guadalcanal during a dry period. Ashworth noted that mud was not a problem. Takeoffs and landings were noisy because of the use of the Marston matting, perforated metal rugs.

On one occasion, the nocturnal visit occurred just as VT-11 began to taxi out to the operation runway. The red alert sounded, and Ashworth ordered everyone to shut down his engines, leave the planes, and take shelter in revetments. He noticed his own gunner still in his turret and shouted at him to get out. "He said, 'I'm okay, Captain; I can see fine from here!' "

In the beginning, Ashworth and company concentrated upon the Munda stronghold. "There was an operating air field on the Jap held island of Munda. And there was a bivouac area close by where some 6,000 or 7,000 troops were located. The air field was operational, but I don't recall any Japanese air from there bothered us. What we did expect was anti-aircraft fire. Our attacks on Munda became sort of milk run in nature. We would drop bombs by glide bombing on either or both the air strip and the bivouac area. Putting the air strip out of operation was a bit futile because the six or so bombs we would put on it were soon bull-dozed over and the field was back in operation.

"I learned there was a move afoot to step up the attacks on Munda and on the neighboring island of Kolombangara [in] preparation for landings soon to come. I went to see General Schilt, Marine Corps, who was the 'Strike Commander' for Admiral [Marc] Mitscher's operations from Guadalcanal. I told him of our horizontal bombing capability, and if he would let me, I would guarantee 2,000 pound bombs on the runway more or less simultaneously. We had been exercising our bombardiers and I was confident of my proposal. The General, reluctantly, I thought, agreed to let me do it. A day or two later he called me to Strike Command and told me, 'I'm sorry about this but I know what your boys can do with glide bombing, but I don't know anything about your horizontal bombing, so scratch it and do your regular attacks.' So that was the end of my horizontal bombing performance."

Oddly, however, the gospel of Ashworth on the possible effectiveness of horizontal bombing spread to other organizations. On April 15, the Avenger pilots from Air Group Twenty-seven practiced masthead bombing runs on the hulks of ships beached at Tassafaronga. The TBFs dived down, then leveled off to a near-horizontal flight at a height of 150 to 300 feet. From a distance estimated at 300 to 400 yards, the bombs were then lobbed toward the near side of the ship, with the expectation of a hit or a very near miss. The technique supplemented the dive- or glide-bomber approaches.

One day later, the TBFs carried out the first attempt to use masthead bombing against shipping in Kahilion Tonoley Harbor on Bougainville Island. The raid, which began with a two-hour-plus flight over water during dusk, combined Army B-17s and B-24s with TBFs and a joint assault on a nearby airdrome as well as the vessels at anchor. Eight of the Avengers executed a standard dive-bomber maneuver over the airfield, and the four-engine Flying Fortresses and Liberators followed.

Working from a coordinated timetable, the other four TBFs dropped on two cargo ships. Lieutenant Commander R. C. Jones, skipper of VC-27, led his companions, but the results were inconclusive, as searchlights and antiaircraft fire prevented the airmen from determining whether they had done any damage.

Ashworth's squadron inherited some of the responsibilities for mine laying. The assignment to shut off access to the Bougainville harbor required three missions, each one flown by eighteen aircraft with a single mine. The task was extremely hazardous since calculations determined that when planting a mine, on the longest leg, the Avengers fly at an altitude of only 100 feet, crawling at 60 knots for as long as ninety seconds. Ashworth nominated himself for this most perilous route.

"The first night's operation turned out to be relatively easy," said Ashworth. "The guns were alerted and firing, but not until we were well into the mission. But what we saw that night worried us as to what would happen the second and third time around when undoubtedly they would be waiting for us." Again he turned to General Schilt to ask if Army B-25s might precede the TBFs, suppressing the small-caliber fire with bombs and strafing. Unfortunately, the Army partners for the venture failed to show, and the second stage of the mine laying proceeded through a hail of hostility. Ashworth contacted Schilt about the no-shows, and on the third run the B-25s pounded the shore batteries, allowing the torpedo planes to perform without losses. Valiant as it was, the effort was basically for naught as the Japanese swept channels through the harbor entrance, allowing their ships to move freely.

As Ashworth indicated, the Japanese usually did not intercept or defend the strikes at Munda. On the other hand, when VT-11 participated in an all-out air group assault on shipping anchored south of Bougainville, they encountered strenuous opposition from Japanese Zeros. Ashworth remembered, "There was intelligence information that there would be two or three cruisers, several destroyers and some smaller ships anchored on the south end of Bougainville. Probably the Japanese also had information that there might be amphibious landing operations against New Georgia. These ships constitute some sort of defense force. Our squadron had mined the area some days before. It was one of our toughest operations and one in which we lost some planes.

"As a result of the strike, one cruiser was sunk, one damaged so badly that it was last seen proceeding north, steaming slowly astern. Since the group was at the limit of range for the aircraft there was no opportunity to pursue and try to sink that one. If I recall correctly a couple of the destroyers were also sunk. It was quite a successful operation. I have to confess that my four, five hundred pound bombs released in salvo all missed. Torpedo planes aren't bombers and we didn't do well."

In hindsight he observed that his TBFs had been pressed into mine laying and glide bombing as a matter of expediency. They would have been more effective had they been carrier-based, but the imminent amphibious operations required the sort of tasks assigned. Later, the PB4Y, the Navy equivalent of the Army's four-engine B-24 Liberator, would handle most of the mining missions.

The TBF, said Ashworth, was a comfortable airplane to fly and "certainly rugged." He recounted, "On that raid we made against shipping in Bougainville, one of my planes came back with one side of his horizontal tail surface gone right up to the fuselage and with a big hole in his rudder. He was hit during his glide bombing attack. He pulled out of that and flew back to Henderson Field and landed with no trouble. Furthermore, on the way home he was jumped by a couple of Zeros and he played games with them in and out of the clouds. At one point, one of them flew along side, apparently out of ammunition, and gave him a signal which meant he wanted him to land. The pilot, Bill Hirsch, gave him the finger, flew home and landed with no trouble at all, with more than half of his tail surfaces shot away and a lot of bullet holes too.

"On that same raid, when I got back home, my plane captain climbed up on the wing to unhook me and told me, 'You got hit, didn't you?' I said, 'Oh, did I?' I had a hole in my engine cowling. Closer examination showed that the bullet passed between a couple of rocker boxes and struck one of the major joints in the engine mount where several of the members are welded together. It tore up the joint, was deflected and passed out through the side of the fuselage and through the wing. It looked to have been a twenty millimeter, which fortunately did not explode. If you were to trace its path until it hit the engine mount, it was headed right for my head."

On another occasion at Bougainville, however, Ashworth did not miss. "We had word, probably from a coast watcher, that there were merchantmen anchored close in to the shore on the south coast of Bougainville. We sent a six-plane group to strike. I was in the lead. The south end of the island was a hill or slope, probably about 1,500 feet high, going down to the water. The ships, two or three of them, were anchored close in to the shore, maybe not more than 100 yards from the beach. It would be impossible to make any kind of a glide bombing attack from the sea side because there was no way to retire after the attack. Land was too close to make a turn away and it sloped up to add to the problem. The only thing was to fly inland over the island at about 2,000 feet and attack gliding down the slope of the hill. Then it would be okay to retire out to sea.

"I told the crewman in the bilge of the plane where the bomb selection was made to line the system up to drop one bomb on the first run. I charged down the hill, pickled off the bomb, looked back when clear and saw I had made a hit for there was a small fire on the ship that I was attacking. It didn't look like I had done much damage, so I decided to go around and make another run. We flew down the side of the hill. I pickled off the bomb and retired far enough to look around to see what happened. Three splashes in the water beyond the target. But why three? I expected to drop one bomb at a time. When I asked the crewman why there were three bombs, he said, 'Captain, I distinctly heard you tell me to drop in salvo.' I am sure that he had had enough of that game.

"On the first run there was no anti-aircraft reaction but on the second, every small-caliber gun along the shore was alerted and started shooting. I started to jink violently and was pleased to see the tracers going by. If you can see them, they won't hit you. For no good reason I glanced at my altimeter and it read ZERO. I was about to fly into the water. I yanked back on the stick, zoomed to about 5,000 feet and headed home. I couldn't understand why I was so cold. All I had on was a pair of skivvies and an old flight suit. I realized that they were wringing wet from sweat."

As a squadron skipper, Ashworth found the loss of men under his command highly stressful. At one point, the outfit received the seeming blessing of rest-and-recreation leave in Australia. His trusted operations officer, six officers, and twelve enlisted men from VT-11 aircrews, as well as a handful of others, including the air group commander, were all killed when a C-47 carrying them to Australia crashed. "What happened was simply devastating. I was in Sydney when told about it. I am not sure what I was looking for but when I learned about it, I found a cathedral, went in to pray, and I suppose, mostly just to think. The resident pastor found me there and we talked for quite a while.

"I think that had this taken place in a combat operational situation, the trauma would not have been quite as bad. These things happen and you lose people. But the way this accident happened. It is very hard to rationalize the loss of so many fine people."

Replacement pilots filled the roster. "I had to reassign some of the crew members to the new guys. One was the group commander's gunner. Then they order an all-out squadron effort to lay mines at night [the Bougainville mission]. You can't say, 'Look, Boss, these six pilots do not have adequate training. They just arrived as replacements and we haven't had them long enough to train them.' Two or three didn't come back from one of those operations due to weather and darkness. They weren't trained for night flying. In one of those planes was the [former] group commander's gunner. They just disappeared. There were two weather fronts to fly through. The old hands had no problem. We were trained for it.

"It is just possibly a harder situation to accept when I was required to send out six new guys at night, untrained, at least to the level that we were, knowing that there was a good chance that some of them wouldn't be able to hack it. And you knew that if they couldn't then there would be two others who would go who had no control over their destiny."

The routine for personnel losses directed the squadron commander to write a letter to the next of kin. As in some organizations, the personnel officer actually drafted the message, but the COs, such as Ashworth, signed them.

Machine guns and cannons spitting lethality at pilots in their aircraft seem a deadly enough description of the war in the air, but it could be even more terrifying. On June 7, 1943, a covey of Wildcats rose from Guadalcanal to accompany a strike force of dive-bombers and torpedo planes for a New Georgia foray. The bomb-laden planes, on seeing bad weather ahead, returned to the airfield. However, some of the Wildcats decided to proceed and see what mischief they could perpetrate.

A four-plane division under Lieutenant (j.g.) Cyrus Cady approached the target area. When Cady tallyhoed a formation of twenty-four Zeros, the four Americans ducked into a cloud as the Zeros chased them. The two sides played hide-and-seek within the clouds. At one point an enemy plane crossed Cady's bow, 300 yards off. He instantly opened fire, and the Zero fell to the water in flames. Zeros tried to close in on Cady, who popped in and out of clouds, throwing rounds at anyone who came near, until he reached Henderson Field.

Ensign Daniel Hubler, Cady's wingman, was not so fortunate. He reported, "I was flying wing in the second section when we sighted the 24 Zeros. . . . At the same time I saw about 12 more Zeros directly over us. I followed the rest of the division as they turned for the cloud. I was last in the turn and before I had completed it, I saw 7.7 mm tracers going by me and could hear them hitting the armor plating behind the seat. Then there was a pause of a few seconds and more came past, followed by two 20 mm shells which exploded in the cockpit. The cockpit filled with smoke, my wrists were burned and the plane shuddered off to the left. Throwing back the canopy I started to jump but was held in by my safety belt, which I had forgotten to unbuckle. Finally, I made the jump and fell free. I was then above 10,000 feet and delayed opening my chute until I was about 1,000 feet since I knew the Japs would strafe me if they could.

"I tried to undo my leg straps before I hit the water but was unable to do so. After I hit the water and [had] gotten out of chute, but before I could inflate the life jacket or raft, I saw a Zero skidding toward me and ducked under the water as he opened fire. When I came up, I saw another Zero coming in low and ducked down again. The next time I came up, a third Zero was coming over and the bullets were hitting the water all around me. Finally, all was quiet and I inflated my raft and started paddling toward East Island. In a short while I noticed that a small boat was overtaking me. At first I thought they were Japs but it was soon apparent that the men in the boat were natives. They took me in their boat and after a short stop at East Island, we reached Segi that night. A PBY returned me to Guadalcanal the next day."

Lieutenant (j.g.) Terry H. Holberton told a similar tale. "We had made one turn and were headed for the cloud when two bursts of 7.7 went by me. Each time I skidded violently to the left, and the tracers went over my wings. Then there were several cannon shots, one of which hit my right wing root and knocked my cockpit hood off the runners and put my gunsight out. Several pieces hit my right arm and the cockpit filled with smoke. The engine quit and when I tried to throw back the hood I found it had jammed. After I got into the cloud, my engine caught again but was very rough and the instrument panel was vibrating as if it were about to tear loose. I made several turns and came out of the other side of the cloud to see a Zero at the top of a wing over about to start down on an F4F-4. I pulled up on him but my guns wouldn't fire and the Zero passed over me without firing.

"I went into a second cloud where my engine quit cold and dove out of the bottom of [the cloud] at 4,000 feet to find myself over mountains. Selecting a deep ravine in case I had to jump, I followed it to the sea and made a water landing. As I was breaking out my raft, I saw a parachute descending in the mountains of Vangunu. Turning the blue side of my raft up, I started to paddle toward a small island. I dressed the wounds on my leg and on my forehead, which had been gashed when it hit the gunsight as I landed."

Holberton threaded his way through lagoons toward the settled island of Vangunu. But when he reached his destination he was mystified to find a deserted village, although there were signs of recent life. As night enveloped the island, he saw two figures silhouetted against the moonlight and heard dogs bark. He slept under a church.

"At dawn I took another look around the village and saw two loin cloths outside a hut. I went to the door and looked in and saw two men sleeping. They woke up and it is a question of who was the most frightened. I explained as best I could who I was and they became very friendly, explaining that all of the other villagers had taken to the jungle when two Jap barges passed by the day before."

Holberton was fed and then guided to a place where a plane, accompanied by no fewer than sixteen fighters, picked him up.

The flyer in the parachute descending in the mountains of Vangunu was the fourth man in Cady's division, Lieutenant (j.g.) Edward Johnson. He recalled of the encounter with the Zeros, "I looked back for Hubler and could see his plane stagger as a stream of tracers went into him. He was flying very wide of me at that time and that is the last I saw of him. Looking forward, I could see that at least three planes were firing at Holberton and one was firing on Cady from above. At this time I could see tracers going by my plane and could actually hear the bullets hitting the wings and fuselage. After two or three minutes I made the cloud cover, although I knew I was badly hit, as the engine cut out several times. I went quickly through this first cloud and was immediately jumped on the other side by two or three Zeros before I could turn in to another cloud.

"The cockpit began to get exceedingly hot, and I was almost sure the plane was afire. My left oil cooler had definitely been hit and I could see oil streaming out of the wing. I'm sure that at this time my engine had been badly hit. At different times I heard violent explosions, which could have been cylinder heads blowing off or exploding 20 mm cannon shells.

"Every time I came out of a cloud I was subject to heavy fire from enemy fighters; they seemed to be everywhere, flying around like a swarm of bees. I turned back toward the clouds and found two Zeros directly in front of me. I chose the one on my right as he was [nearer] and closed in for a head-on attack. I opened fire as soon as I was in range, but the Zero refused to continue [his] attack. He pulled up sharply, and I followed him with all six of my guns firing but I could not pull with him. It is my belief that I did not hit him badly, if at all. I pulled straight up. . . . I was very slow. It is quite possible that the other Zero to my left, which I had lost sight of, shot my engine out completely at this time. I wobbled off into cloud cover again with oil pouring out of every hole in the airplane."

Johnson checked his instrument and saw his manifold pressure sinking, his engine barely turning over. As he fell below 3,000 feet, the engine gave out. "I nosed the plane down to hold my speed, opened the hood, unlocked my safety belt, and jammed the stick full forward. I was thrown up and out and felt a hard blow on my right leg. As far as I know, I had not been hit [in my body] by any fire to that time. I pulled my rip cord with both hands almost upon leaving the plane, as I figured I was between 1,000 and 1,500 feet above the side of the mountains. My chute opened with an extremely hard jerk, as I had been diving fast when I got out. I heard my plane crash into the mountain side almost immediately.

"It seemed that I hung motionless in the air for some time, because I could see two fighters about two miles to the south. Finally, one of them saw me and turned toward me. But by that time I was nearing the tree tops. The Zero dove at me, firing just as I dropped below the tree tops. Fortunately, I dropped right into a hole among the trees, which were at least 150 feet high. The chute snagged in the higher branches just enough to slow my fall, and I hit the ground without too much of a jolt. I unsnapped my harness immediately, got clear of the parachute and moved around behind a large tree as the plane or planes were still making passes at the spot where I had gone in. They fired at the spot twice, pulling up sharply off the trees. After five or ten minutes, all planes had moved on."

Johnson took time to examine his leg. He had a clean four-inch gash, an inch and a half deep, below the back of his knee. When the bleeding stopped, he could clearly see the muscle tissue. Unfortunately, he mistakenly decided he had come down on New Georgia rather than Vangunu. Unknowingly, he was very near an enemy camp of 250 soldiers. Johnson committed a second error. He discarded both his life raft and his life jacket because he wanted to travel light. Furthermore, he reasoned that their yellow coloring, designed to make downed flyers more visible to rescuers, could make him conspicuous to enemy eyes. He carried with him his .45 automatic, a jungle knife, a compass, his first-aid kit, and the sparse issue of survival rations.

He walked in the direction that he thought would lead to the village of Segi on New Georgia. Hampered by his painful wound and heavy jungle growth, he was forced to take detours around deep streams and a cove, bodies of water he could easily have crossed had he taken either his life jacket or the inflatable raft. He managed to reach the coast and travel on the beach, coming across several wrecked lifeboats. He noted that one had some flotation cans with only a few bullet holes in them.

On his second day marooned, Johnson's passage along the beach came to an abrupt halt when he stumbled upon a thicket of mangroves that extended all the way to the beach with a lagoon six or seven feet deep. He had no alternative but to retrace his steps back to the shattered lifeboat in hopes of salvaging the flotation cans for a raft. It was a slow, almost agonizing ordeal, pushing through vines and thorny bushes and over fallen trees.

"I got the best two cans out of the boat and carried them up the shore to a cleared place on the beach. I proceeded to plug up the bullet holes with wooden plugs, using my undershirt as caulking. I cut two saplings about ten feet long and cross pieces to hold the cans in place. I bound the whole frame together with vines and tied the cans into the frames with more vines." At this point he regretted not having had the foresight to take the shroud lines from his parachute for just such a purpose. With a few nails retrieved from the abandoned boat, he constructed a paddle from a stick and a small board. For the second time, he dressed his wounds with sulfa powder.

At dawn the following day he climbed a tree to look for local people and observe the water beyond the beach. "I heard a loud voice call out and I saw two large craft which at first looked like native war canoes. Casting caution aside, I called as loudly as I could. The men stopped paddling and looked around. It was evident from their indecision that my voice had echoed, and they were not sure where I was. I saw at that time that the craft were not canoes, but barges. They were being sculled, poled and paddled—moving slowly. I suspected that they were Japs and went back to get my automatic.

"I decided to wait where I was and keep a sharp lookout. The two barges had passed behind a small island off shore and seem to have come to the main island and moved northward. I waited until 1000 and decided to move northward. I paddled my raft past the mouths of the lagoons which I had had so much trouble getting around. As the small island seemed to have coconuts on it, I paddled over to it. I was tying my raft in among the mangroves [when I] turned to look behind me. I received a real jolt, because the two barges were about 300 yards away, crossing open water. The men had camouflaged the boats but I could plainly see the yellow skins bared to the waist. I dropped into the water among the mangrove roots. I was positive that they had seen me and although my automatic was wet and somewhat rusted in spite of my attempts to keep it in working order, I got it clear and waited for them to come over and get me. I did not feel brave or afraid. I only knew that if my gun worked I would shoot as many as possible. I did not intend to be taken alive."

To his great relief, the occupants of the barges continued on their course, toward the large island, where they paddled up and down the shore looking for the source of the voice that had called to them. When they finally departed, Johnson decided to remain on the small island and take advantage of a barrel full of rainwater and the coconuts. He came across a small shack left by natives and appropriated a pair of one-inch-thick mats for use with a bed he had rigged up. His bower lay deep in the brush, inaccessible even to him except by crawling on hands and knees. To add to his discomfort, he had open sores on his left heel, his right ankle, and both legs. Although he wore gloves, his hands and wrists had many cuts on them. He avoided the worst of the mosquitoes by using a head net, wearing gloves, tucking his pants into his socks, and leaving only his wrists exposed.

Refreshed by a good night's sleep, he returned the mats to the hut, dined on meat and milk from the coconuts, and started to paddle south, away from the direction taken by the barges. Eventually he beached his raft and began to walk the shoreline because on foot he could travel faster. He came across taro roots, which suggested that indigenous people must be nearby. Unfortunately, in his travels he also noted bootprints in the sand, which suggested an unfriendly presence. He was also discomfited by the absence of geographical landmarks characteristic of New Georgia, where he mistakenly believed himself to be. In his travels he came across more and more bootprints, and in a hut he found cloth disks bearing the insignia of the Japanese navy.

By his sixth day on the island, the desperate Johnson had plunged into the jungle, hoping to evade the Japanese near the coast and perhaps find local residents in the interior. As he worked his way through a watery jungle, he said, "I heard a pounding or chopping sound. I hoped that it would be natives but I was almost sure that it was not. Natives have almost no metal tools like axes. I wormed my way noiselessly through the swampy undergrowth until suddenly about 100 yards ahead I saw a wooden shack. I remained motionless and watched. I saw two men at first. They were stripped to the waist and obviously yellow. One had a sort of turban wrapped around his head. Through a window I saw a huge man roll out of a bunk and walk out of and around the shack. This fellow was well over six feet tall and moved like a cat. There were five men in the vicinity of the building and others working in the jungle on the far side.

"This convinced me that further progress in this direction was out of the question. My immediate problem was to get clear without being detected. I worked my way through the mud on my hands and knees and on my stomach when necessary. I went right back up the coast, picking up two coconuts and drinking my fill of water [from a river]. On the way I picked up a wooden box with good nails and a long flat board for a spare paddle."

With his found hardware, Johnson reinforced his raft, adding vines, nailing strips of wood across it, and even making himself a kind of seat. He gorged on coconut juice and meat and polished off two blocks of the chocolate in his emergency rations. He stored more coconut meat in his backpack and set out to paddle across open water toward the larger island. When he found himself in open water, he realized he could not be between New Georgia and Vangunu. He sought refuge on another small island, where he built a shelter and then slept.

Once again he headed out to sea, convinced that on one of the many islands he would find natives. After a long day under a broiling sun he stepped ashore on one of the islands as night approached. Buoyed by a coconut repast, he started inland. "I found myself in a small banana plantation with some papaya trees intermingled. I walked [until I found a] small shack in which a fire had been recently burning. On the ground there were bare foot tracks. I knew they must be fresh because it had rained the previous evening. A sudden movement in the jungle caught my eye, and I thought I saw a black person. I called out, and the boy started to run. I called again and started after him. I said, 'Hello, I'm a pilot.'

"When I said this, they [apparently there was more than one] started toward me. I was so happy that I was almost overcome. One of the boys came up and saluted me smartly. They all shook hands with me and grinned happily with relief, because as they told me later they saw me before I saw them and thought possibly I was a Jap. I asked them what day it was and though they could speak very little English, they knew it was June 15. That was the first that I knew exactly how long I had been out. I still had a full bar and two blocks of chocolate and part of my third pack of sulfanilamide. With what sulfathiazole I had I believe I could have gotten along in good shape for six or seven days longer."

His hosts took him to their village, where they fed him boiled taro and fish, which he ate "almost ravenously." One of the men said they would take him to Segi, and indeed, in a war canoe with six men at the paddles, Johnson traveled across the water for seven hours to that settlement. On June 19, he returned to Guadalcanal. "It looked as good as my own front yard in Coronado, except my wife was not there."

The experiences of the downed flyers, enduring protracted days at sea before being rescued, and being aided by the indigenous population while evading Japanese forces, were replicated many times over. The Americans of that era, like Johnson, often demonstrated a remarkable resilience, self-reliance, and talent for survival. Their accounts also raise one of the more controversial issues of World War II—the attacks on men helpless in their parachutes or in the water. Propagandists often capitalized on the "barbarity" of those who would machine-gun a pilot who had bailed out, or strafe sailors who had abandoned ship. But the truth is that in many cases these highly trained individuals, if left unharmed, would return to the war.

TEN

ANTISUBMARINE WARFARE

Both the Allies and the Axis powers regarded submarines as prime weapons against their adversaries. The big aircraft carriers *Saratoga*, *Yorktown*, and *Wasp* and the smaller escort and Jeep flattops *Liscombe Bay* and *Block Island* were all victims of Japanese subs, to say nothing of other warships ranging from battleships through destroyers. While they could and did sink tankers and cargo ships, Japanese submarines more often than not targeted naval vessels rather than threatening supply lines.

In the Atlantic it was another story. For the first two years of the war, German submarines rampaged against shipping in the Atlantic, destroying vessels faster than they could be replaced. In January 1942, subs ravaged forty-six Allied and neutral merchant ships, gross tonnage 270,348. The following month, the figures rose to seventy-two and 427,733. Except for some temporary dips, the ravenous appetite of the U-boats consumed ever-higher totals, hitting peaks of more than 100 vessels in a month four times. Gerald Bogan, then an instructor at Pensacola, said, "All through the summer of 1942, the Gulf Stream off Miami was a sea of fire at night from flaming tankers. You'd see three or four at a time, 10 miles off shore burning." Convoys of cargo carriers and transports, shepherded by warships and protected by patrolling aircraft based on the farthest reaches of North America and Europe, lessened the losses somewhat, but the depredations seriously threatened the Allied war effort.

Dan Gallery, whose choice of aviation for his speciality had provoked the sneer "You've given up your birthright for a mess of pottage" from a superior on the battleship *Idaho*, joined the Battle of the Atlantic almost from its beginning. After commanding scouting and observation squadrons, he served as the CO of the *Langley*, the very first carrier commissioned by the Navy. In January 1941, Gallery checked in as assistant naval attaché for air at the U.S. Embassy in London, where the British had already been engaged in a sea war with German U-boats.

Briefly reassigned to a Washington staff job in aeronautics, Gallery returned to England, where a huge seaplane base was secretly under construction. "We were building the seaplane base there and I was designated to be the commanding officer," said Gallery, "when and if we got in the war. The role of the seaplanes was to take part in escorting convoys in the Battle of the Atlantic . . . at that time we were losing the Battle of the Atlantic hand over fist." The entire plan went up in the smoke and fire of the Japanese raid on Pearl Harbor. Instead, Gallery became commanding officer of the Fleet Air Base on Iceland.

"I had a squadron of PBYs, the old work horse PBY amphibian. We were escorting convoys past Iceland. We'd go out for thirteen-hour hops and pick the convoys up 500 miles south of Iceland and escort them for three or four hours. If you'd pick them up at 500 miles, it took you about five hours to get out there and five hours back, and that only left three or four hours." Theoretically, the RAF then took over the duty, but between the farthest air cover extended from North America through that supplied from Iceland and the British Isles lay a thousand miles or more of seas protected only by the limited resources of escort warships.

The situation was desperate for the Allies. At the height of the Battle of the Atlantic, the Germans were sinking ships faster than the United States could build them. In a convoy of 100 ships, as many as 20 might be lost, and during the disastrous July 1943 Convoy PQ-17 run to Murmansk more than half went down. Escort vessels were unable to destroy more than a few members of the ravenous wolf packs.

"The RAF Coastal Command was the outfit I was working with," said Gallery, "and they were extremely effective. Their main mission was escort of convoys, antisubmarine warfare. And they were damn good at it and did a fine job." However, the Americans were frustrated by their inability to hurt the enemy. Gallery continued, "After we had been there several months we had several chances for attacking subs and we muffed them for various reasons: one, maybe buck fever on the part of the pilot, or maybe the bomb rack hung up and didn't work, or various things of that kind. We missed our first three or four chances. So I laid down the law to the boys and said: 'From now on we're closing the bar in the officers' club until we get a sure kill,' which was a cruel and unusual punishment. Anyway, we closed the bar.

"Then a couple of weeks later this lad Hopgood went out and caught a German sub and attacked it with depth charges and damaged it so that it could not submerge. Hopgood was on the way to a convoy which was about a hundred miles from the spot where he attacked the sub. After he had expended all his depth charges he then saw that the sub was surfacing and couldn't submerge. He then flew from the spot to the convoy and told them about the sub and they broke off a couple of destroyers to go over and get the sub. He circled back and forth between the disabled sub and the oncoming destroyers, coaching them on. The submarine came across an Icelandic fishing vessel. They went alongside and boarded it, abandoning the sub, opening the scudding valves on it, sank the sub and headed for Germany with the fishing vessel. Hopgood saw all of this; he kept circling around reporting it to these destroyers and they kept coming. Eventually they came alongside the Icelandic fishing vessel and went aboard and got the whole German crew and took them prisoners."

In Iceland and at RAF headquarters, radio sets listened to the play-by-play unfolding of the action. All of the messages were in officialese and coded, but when the British destroyers removed the submarine sailors from the fishing boat, Gallery remembered, "Hopgood's last report came in to me in plain English, no code, he said: 'Sank sub, open club.' And we did. We damn near blew the roof off the joint."

At the height of the celebration it was proposed that the fleet air base deserved a trophy. "The most suitable one," said Gallery, "would be the skipper's pants; . . . we'd caught him with his pants down. I wrote a letter to the first lord of the Admiralty [who had visited the base recently] and explained the American expression, 'caught with your pants down' and said we would like to have the skipper's pants to hang in the bar room of our officers' club. 'In order to avoid leaving the skipper in an embarrassing position, I am sending herewith a pair of my own khaki pants which you can exchange with him for his.' "

Gallery received a polite letter back saying the matter would be submitted to the proper authorities. "About two weeks later," said Gallery, "I got a very stiff letter from the head of Naval Intelligence quoting the Geneva Convention on the business of humiliating prisoners and so forth. . . . 'In view of this it is impossible to send you the skipper's pants.' I didn't mind the malarky about the Geneva Convention so much as I did the outrageous fact that he didn't even send my own pants back."

As satisfying as that incident was, the enemy submarines continued to run up the score. The Allies began to introduce new means to combat the menace. Aircraft such as the four-engine Consolidated bomber, the Army's Liberator, and the Navy's PB4Y added range to the land-based air patrols. Radar improved, and so did depth charges. But the most significant weapon introduced was the CVE, Jeep carrier, a pint-sized 11,000-ton, 19-knot-top-speed replica of the 27,000-ton flattops bearing the brunt of the air war in the Pacific. Built to merchant-ship standards like the vessels launched under the auspices of the company headed by Henry J. Kaiser, they were designed to serve as carriers from the keel up. Most of them went to the Pacific, mainly to haul replacement planes for the fast carriers.

In one of the earliest ventures from a CVE, on June 12, 1943, the CVE *Bogue*, first of its class, launched Lieutenant R. L. Stearns in a TBF and, as his wingman, Lieutenant R. J. Johnson in an F4F-4. They sighted a U-boat on the surface early in the afternoon. Immediately upon seeing the enemy, Stearns radioed Johnson to begin a strafing run while the Avenger pilot maneuvered into position for his attack. Johnson dived on the stern, spouting machine-gun bullets from 3,000 feet down to a mere 15 feet above the water as he swooped over the sub from stern to bow. Meanwhile, Stearns moved in, firing his fixed forward .30-caliber gun. The Avenger was only about 100 feet over the water when the pilot leveled off for an instant before making a shallow dive. The depth bombs, dropped in pairs, straddled the U-boat, which tried to submerge. In the clear water, Stearns saw the sub go down to about conning-tower depth before the depth charges exploded.

It resurfaced, its decks awash and trailing oil. Johnson renewed his machine-gun assault just as the sub slipped below the water to about twenty-five feet. Other planes from the *Bogue* now struck at the sub, which emerged from the water again. Lieutenant (j.g.) W. S. Fowler, who had previously made two attacks on U-boats, dumped four more depth charges while his wingman in an F4F-4, Lieutenant Tennant, hammered away with his machine guns. Like a pack of hounds besetting a wolf, Avengers and Wildcats from the *Bogue* lunged, snapped, and ripped at their prey.

With their vessel unable to escape by diving or even moving, the submariners attempted to man the deck guns. Machine-gun fire from Tennant and Fowler, working from opposite sides, drove them to seek refuge in the lee of the conning tower. They donned life jackets but did not leap overboard. Another TBF, flown by Lieutenant (j.g.) H. E. Fryatt, arrived and deposited a cluster of depth bombs. Only the heavy traffic in the air prevented Fryatt from taking a second crack at the sub. When he finally saw his way clear, Fryatt realized that the U-boat's stern was so low in the water that it appeared doomed, and he held his bombs.

Some of the sailors began to jump into the water. As other aircraft rallied to inflict more damage, a few valiant Germans managed to shoot off a couple of bursts of antiaircraft fire. Then Lieutenant (j.g.) R. S. Rogers bored in to administer what was the coup de grâce. The U-boat simply blew up in a geyser of metal, oil, and water. The sea was littered with bobbing bodies, some dead, others still alive. Fryatt, in a gesture of mercy, threw them his rubber boat. The men in the water acknowledged his gesture with hands clasped above their heads and waved in gratitude. Rescuers on a destroyer subsequently plucked out seventeen men alive, leaving four dead in the sea. All of the officers had been killed in the conning tower. Altogether, the planes from the *Bogue* expended sixteen 325-pound depth charges, 4,410 rounds of .50-caliber and 800 of .30-caliber.

A surface submarine was by no means, however, a tame beast. Later that year, Composite Squadron One's Lieutenant (j.g.) Asbury H. Sallenger flew a TBF off the CVE *Card* with Ensign John F. Sprague in a Wildcat as a wingman. Sallenger reported, "I was flying a routine submarine search in company with Ensign Sprague. There was a solid overcast with occasional rain squalls and poor visibility, so we were ducking in and out of the base of the clouds.

"At about 0811 we came out of a cloud flying at 800 feet and on my port bow, I saw two U-boats not more than one or one and a half miles away. They were pretty close together, about 150 yards and on slightly different courses. . . . When sighted, their decks were awash and there was no bow wave or wake visible, indicating a speed of 2–3 knots.

"It all happened so fast that I had no time to advise the ship of the contact before the attack. I had turned on my transmitter to warm it up, figuring on reporting immediately after my first run. I signaled Ensign Sprague to attack. He slid under me and we made a split attack on the nearer of the two subs, coming in from bow to stern, the fighter from the port bow, the TBF from the starboard bow. Ensign Sprague made a beautiful strafing attack, working over the deck and conning tower methodically. When I was a little more than halfway in on my attack, range about 1,000 yards, my plane was hit by at least one 20 mm explosive shell up through the bomb bay into the tunnel compartment. This knocked out my radio, interplane communication, and other electrical equipment. Later I learned that the vertical fin and rudder had also been hit in this barrage. I saw the bomb bay light go out right after the first shell hit. The plane took several more hits in the tunnel and something began to burn in the bomb bay. During this run my speed was about 185 knots. . . .

"As a result of the electrical system being out, my bombs did not drop on the first pass. I turned for a second run, coming in this time from the starboard quarter, target angle about 170 degrees. The engine was popping and cutting out during this attack. My speed was reduced to 160 knots. . . . During this run Ensign Sprague was working over the other sub. Again he was doing an excellent job, but the enemy AA fire seemed even heavier. On this run, the plane was hit in the left main gas tank at the wing root (it had about 30 gallons in it at the time), tearing a hole about a foot wide and immediately bursting into flames. There were other less effective hits. I proceeded on in and dropped two depth bombs manually (the bombs, of course, dropped in salvo). I looked back to make sure they exploded and the explosion [seemed] to go off right next to the submarine, covering it with water. I'm sure it was a good drop.

"By now my wing tank was burning badly, so I jettisoned the MK 24 Mine on armed, about one half mile ahead of the course of the U-boat. I then turned directly into the wind and landed in the water with flaps up and bomb bay doors open because the hydraulic system had been punctured, making it inoperable.

"The fire in the wing was put out on landing. I was unhurt, my gunner [James Henry] O'Hagan popped out of the turret and together we got the rubber boat out. I then realized Chief Downes was missing. I swam to the other side, [dived] under and opened the tunnel door. I was halfway in the tunnel when the plane started to settle. I estimated it sank within 30 seconds." Sallanger was never able to reach Downes.

"I saw Ensign Sprague going in for another strafing attack while we were inflating the rubber boat. After that, I don't remember seeing the plane or hearing the engine again. After hitting the water, we paddled as fast as we could down wind, thinking one of the U-boats might surface near us. Though we did not realize it at the time, this took us right back over the scene of the action. We actually paddled through a large oil slick that must have been left by the attacked submarine as it submerged. It was so new we could smell the fresh oil."

Sallenger reported that while he had not actually seen the U-boat guns, he believed that they each had at least six 20-mm ones and the fire had come from a platform aft of the conning tower. He ruefully remarked, "The U-boats seemed to recognize the TBF as the striking power and concentrated on it till we had been shot down." Not until he was picked up several hours later by a destroyer did Sallenger learn that Sprague, his companion, had probably been shot down and was missing in action.

Gunner O'Hagan confirmed his pilot's account but added, "Our electrical system was shot up and I could not work the turret or get in contact with Mr. Sallenger. I called to Downes, our radioman, to ask him to help me turn my turret around as it was stuck. I looked down in the tunnel and he was lying on his face. The radio equipment was on the deck by his feet, the camera by his side smashed up."

Dan Gallery was assigned to serve as CO of the Jeep carrier *Guadalcanal*, and early in 1944, the flattop joined the Battle of the Atlantic. "We had twelve TBMs, the so-called Turkey Martin torpedo planes. And I believe we had eight single-seater fighters. I tried to get rid of the fighters and get other torpedo planes to replace them but I never could sell that idea. The fighters were no use to me at all. But they kept saying the Germans had got the Focke-Wulf, a very long-range plane which theoretically could get out more or less to a ship like the *Guadalcanal* . . . but we never did encounter any Focke-Wulfs."

According to Gallery, while his ship would sail at about the same time as a convoy, it was not tied to escort duty. "The admiral simply told us to operate in the vicinity of the Azores [a nesting area for U-boats]. Those were the orders and gave you plenty of elbow room to write your own ticket." For intelligence about the locations of submarines, Gallery depended on a daily message from the Tenth Fleet. "They would pinpoint the location of all submarines that they'd had reports on in the past twenty-four hours. They would estimate where other submarines were, that is that they knew a submarine had been [at] a certain point . . . three or four days ago. They would estimate where he was going and where he was today.

"I treated this COMINCH [commander in chief] daily estimate as Bible truth every day and we based our operations on it completely. One reason why I did was that the very first thing that happened on this first cruise was we got a special message from COMINCH from the Tenth Fleet saying, 'There is going to be a refueling rendezvous of submarines off the Azores at a certain point at sunset on a certain day.' . . . We were going to be reasonably close to it so I laid off about a hundred miles from that point until about four in the afternoon. Then we launched eight torpedo planes to search that area. And right at sunset we caught the refueler with a sub alongside, hoses stretched across and another sub standing by waiting his turn. We caught them and we blasted the hell out of the refueler and the guy alongside of him." The TBMs sank the refueler and thought the U-boat was taking on oil, but the undersea boat was able to limp back to the harbor at Brest.

Flush with the word of victory, the crew of the *Guadalcanal* prepared to recover its torpedo bombers. However, the attack had occurred at sunset and the flyers all wanted to take a gander at the site, even though only three of them had actually been in on the kill. In spite of Gallery's warnings that the planes should return immediately, by the time they reached the carrier, darkness was rapidly obliterating the scene. None of the pilots had flown at night with the small carriers.

"The first three got aboard all right," said Gallery. "The fourth one went off the side of the flight deck and nosed down in the gallery walkway. We had to get this guy out of there. We were a brand-new ship then. We just got butter-fingered and clumsy that night and we couldn't get that plane out of the gallery walkway. We tried everything, but we couldn't budge it. I even tried to flip it over the side by turning the ship real sharp and putting a list on it and then shoving it over but we couldn't get rid of it.

"I called the guys in the air—there were four of them—and I made a pitch to them and said, 'Now, look, the tail of that plane sticks out a bit on the flight deck but not much. If you guys will land just the least bit over to the port side you won't hit the tail.' I got some very skeptical and reluctant 'rogers' back from the air.

"Then we started making passes and trying to bring those guys in. We were lit up like a barroom on a Saturday night because we had to. But it was black. And the boys had not done any night flying. They were jittery and they made some of the wildest passes I have ever seen. We had to keep waving them off, waving them off. Meanwhile they were burning up their gasoline. We finally in desperation gave one guy a cut and he came down, hit his wheels on deck, bounced in the air, rolled over on his back and dove into the water. Our plane guard destroyer picked up all three of the guys in that plane and saved them. But that was enough of that. I told the other three, 'Now you land in the water. We'll have our destroyer turn the search lights on. We'll pick you up.' They landed in the water and we did pick them up but . . . I decided we were going to learn to fly at night."

Not only did Gallery inaugurate a night flight training program, he also ordered the crew to spend two weeks practicing the techniques to dump a crashed plane off the carrier. When a new squadron came aboard to relieve the old one, he insisted they drill in nocturnal takeoffs and landings. His diligence paid huge dividends.

"On the first half of [a] cruise from Norfolk to Casablanca, we flew all day long every day, bringing the last planes in just before sunset. We never did get the kind of weather I wanted to start the night flying. Then on our way back . . . there was a nice calm sea the night of the full moon and we started our night flying. That very night we got the U-515. We caught him on the surface charging his battery and drove him down. Then we hounded him all night. Every time he'd pop up, we'd nail him again and chase him down again. Making a depth charge attack on a sub at night, or even in the daylight, is not a 100-percent thing. You don't get the kill every time and especially at night you don't."

Destroyers summoned by Gallery arrived in the morning, and for six hours they worked the area over. Although the veteran sub skipper knew all the artifices of his trade, he could not escape, and eventually the badly damaged U-boat surfaced right in the middle of the warships, which promptly opened fire. When the U-boat turned on end and sank, the Americans rescued most of the crew.

"This was the very first night we'd been flying. During that same night we made another contact or thought we made another contact on another sub. We sent out a search for the second sub. And we got

[him] the next night. . . . These two were old-time U-boats. We caught the U-68 right at sunrise, the planes coming in out of the west, with the sun rising in the east. They were coming in out of the dark. They had been out all night hunting for him. They caught them [*sic*] completely unaware on the surface with only three lookouts up on the conning tower.

"We plastered them with machine guns, rockets, depth charges and a homing torpedo. We broke them in two, so down he went and left the three lookouts swimming around in the water." The circling planes dropped a raft, and one remained on the scene to guide the *Guadalcanal* on a rescue mission. Only one man of the entire sub crew was still alive.

"We got two kills the first two nights we flew," said Gallery. "We had gone three weeks before, flying in the daytime, with no kills at all. The subs simply did not come up in the daytime. They came up at night. If you wanted to do business out there, you had to fly at night. When we came back from the cruise and reported this, all the other CVEs started night flying."

The Germans extracted a small measure of revenge for the sack of their U-boat fleet in May 1944, when a torpedo sent the escort carrier *Block Island* to the bottom of the South Atlantic.

The imperative to drop depth charges close to the target meant bombing from a very low altitude, and that could lead to dire consequences. In June 1944, Ensign George Edwards took off shortly after daybreak from the USS *Solomons* on a routine antisubmarine patrol. Some three hours later, Edwards radioed the *Solomons* that he had detected a U-boat about 50 miles from the carrier. When Edwards failed to check in further, about two in the afternoon, Lieutenant Commander Howard Avery launched from the carrier in search of both the missing pilot and the sub he had reported. Three hours into his flight he sighted a wake, and when he closed in he saw a fully surfaced submarine traveling at about 15 knots.

The U-boat suddenly started to run in circles, successfully keeping Avery on its stern. The crew had obviously noticed the plane, and intense AA fire erupted from the deck. The sub made no effort to submerge, and Avery prudently remained at a distance of more than two miles while waiting for reinforcements.

Additional hunters from the *Solomons* arrived a few minutes after sunset. Directed by Avery, two fighters and two torpedo bombers, armed with rockets, savaged the quarry. The F4F pilots, Ensigns Wadsworth and McMahon, poured machine-gun fire on the sub to suppress its antiaircraft capacity and perhaps inflict other injury. Wadsworth began his run at 2,000 feet and amid a thicket of AA pulled out less than 100 feet above the victim. A damaged wing tank forced him to return to the *Solomons*. McMahon executed a steep dive from 3,000 feet, abruptly ending at 500 feet as he soared away, making way for the first rocket attack.

Ensign Spear, who had coordinated his approach with the strafers, came in from the starboard beam of the U-boat at an altitude of 2,000 feet. At a range of 800 feet, Spear launched four pairs of projectiles. Six of these, said observers, struck a vital area a few feet forward of the conning tower. When Spear began his dive, Avery homed in on the port side, unleashing three pairs of missiles. Four exploded near the previous ones. As the two torpedo bombers roared away, their rear gunners unloaded on the sub's still-active but slower-firing deck guns. The crews were well protected by armored shielding.

Lieutenant (j.g.) William F. Chamberlain, who had been in on the sinking of the sub a year earlier aboard the *Bogue*, now in concert with Lieutenant (j.g.) Weigle, added his ordnance to the fight. Weigle, instructed by Avery and preceded by another strafing from McMahon, dispatched eight rockets, six of which slammed into the deck. The U-boat's pace dropped to a mere 3 knots, and an ominous, large, greenish-yellow oil slick spread over the sea surface.

Avery directed Chamberlain to finish the task with depth bombs. Ignoring the bursts of AA fire, Chamberlain swooped in at less than 50 feet above the conning tower and released two bombs. When they hit forward of the conning tower, a violent explosion erupted. It engulfed Chamberlain's plane, starting a fire in the bomb bay and center cockpit. He was able to keep control of the torpedo bomber as he turned sharply and then landed in the water about 500 yards from the U-boat.

As Avery, Weigle, and McMahon maneuvered for still another assault, the submarine went down by the bow. The flyers could see thirty to forty men in the water. The entire confrontation actually lasted only seven minutes.

Almost six hours after the U-boat sank, the destroyer *Straub* rescued twenty-one German sailors. Neither Ensign Edwards, who had originally located the sub, nor Lieutenant Chamberlain and his crew were ever found. The captured submariners told interrogators that Edwards had made a series of runs at them in the face of withering antiaircraft opposition. On his fourth attempt the plane had been hit and crashed into the water.

According to Gallery, the Allies began winning the Battle of the Atlantic by April 1943, when losses fell to forty-four ships and 276,790 tons, followed by May's figures of forty-one and 211,929. He credited the shift of the tide to the advent of longer-range aircraft that could reach out to the middle of the Atlantic from strategically placed bases, as well as to the Jeep carrier, improved radar, better depth charges, and homing aircraft torpedoes. "All these things came to a head at once and when they did we slaughtered the U-boats for three months, April, May and June 1943, when we sank a hundred U-boats and just rocked the U-boat fleet right back on their heels."

Antisubmarine duty was not always grim. Jim Pearce, the one-time student at General Motors Institute in Flint, Michigan, who had smelled war coming and volunteered for naval aviation, began his military career flying the Vought OS2U scout plane. "I was assigned to VS-52, stationed on the island of Bora-Bora [in the Society Islands, northwest of Tahiti], in 1942 and early 1943. There was no war for thousands of miles around, and we did our duty keeping on the lookout for submarines, which we thought might be snooping around the island. None of us in VS-52 ever saw a sub, and life was a gas. About once a week we were slated for 'dawn patrol,' which consisted of being waked up early by a steward with a cup of hot coffee in his hand, climbing in your pajamas up the ladder of an aircraft made ready for flight, being handed the coffee and maybe a donut, if the steward liked you, starting the engine, and taking off (from the water). Usually, sometime after takeoff, as the sun came into your eyes, you really woke up and did your hundred-foot tour of all the islands in the local group around Bora-Bora, waving 'good morning' to the bare-breasted wahines who came out on their docks to wave their appreciation for the protection we were providing them from the agonies of war." Pearce's stay in paradise ended, and he entered into the shooting war.

The current had definitely turned against the Japanese in the Pacific as well. While the combat, except for occasional spasms such as the Rennell Island encounter, may have been conducted at a less feverish pitch, the Americans began to introduce a compelling new character, the F6F-3 Hellcat. Alex Vraciu, the DePauw University graduate who went on active duty in October 1941 and became one of the Navy's best-known fighter pilots, said of the new Grumman, "It had the best kill ratio of any plane in the war—any war—19 to 1. The Hellcat was not only a perfect carrier plane but it was terrific for landings. It was good for the old guys as well as young kids. It was stable, and it was a beautiful gun platform. It would outgun, with the six .50-calibers—three on each wing—the Zero. It could outdive the Zero and outclimb the Zero above 10,000 feet. If you maintained a speed of about 250 knots and fought them on a vertical plane, then you could handle the Zero. Their stick forces at high speeds were such that they couldn't turn with you, and you could follow them down and get them. If they're on your tail, you could pull away from them and outturn them and get away."

Like its predecessor, the F4F, the F6F-3 was a rugged piece of machinery, able to endure the slashes of shrapnel and the punctures of cannon shells and bullets. Unlike their opponents, the Americans continued to be protected by self-sealing gas tanks and armor around the cockpit. In Vraciu's words, it was not a "hangar queen," an airplane frequently deadlined for repairs.

The Navy accepted the Hellcat after trials of the first versions of the F4U, the Chance-Vought Corsair, revealed difficulties in carrier landings. Among other problems, the landing gear of the Corsair tended to collapse. Although the Navy temporarily rejected the F4U, the plane debuted as a Marine ground-based weapon in February 1943 and quickly asserted its superiority over the Zero. Another welcome addition to the fleet air arm arrived in the form of the Black Cat, a refined model of the PBY with airborne radar for night searches and even after-dark attacks on shipping.

For a short period of time, however, the American air arm consisted of a mix of the old and the new. On June 12, 1943, Fighting Squadron Eleven, based temporarily on Guadalcanal, took off from the Fighter One airstrip to accompany a PBY mission to southeastern New Georgia. The task accomplished, the F4Fs headed home. Fighter direction notified them of a bogey in their vicinity, and its radar vectored them on several courses. Initially no enemy planes were sighted, but a Marine group of F4U Corsairs appeared nearby.

Suddenly a large flight of aircraft showed up and engaged in a series of maneuvers that suggested preparation for a combat encounter. The dozen Wildcats, led by Lieutenant William N. Leonard, having already been in the air for a considerable time, averaged about 50 gallons of fuel remaining. Leonard reported, "The flight of planes sighted was at varying altitudes, some below and some above our altitude of 26,000 feet. I estimated that there were 20 to 30 planes but it was hard to tell." In fact, there were thirty-six of them. "We had been airborne about three hours and 15 minutes and, as far as the Wildcat is concerned were in excellent shape for a short fight.

"As we closed the contact, I passed the order to make one pass and retire as we did not have gas enough to remain and fight. It was still not certain that all of the planes sighted were enemy or not . . . due to the great resemblance between the P-40 and the Zero in color and outline at certain angles, [I] withheld a perfect shot at a Zero until it was too late to do any damage.

"As my division flew into the rat race and the planes could be seen clearly, it was first established that they were all Zeros. We tangled with the Zeros at our level and those below, while the Zeros above came down and were engaged by others in my flight as well as by P-40s and F4Us, which arrived on the scene.

"Owing to the fact that our target was maneuvering in all directions, the situation immediately developed into a free-for-all with our planes fighting singly in the same general area and supporting one another as opportunity permitted." Obviously, the careful design of the Thach Weave could not always be maintained when large numbers of planes became embroiled in a chaotic affair. "I made passes at three or four Zeros and saw two of them explode in flames. This was a typical action; a pass at one target—flames or a miss . . . a pass at another target—flames or a miss . . . 5,000 feet lost in each pass . . . all gas in main exhausted, 27 gallons left in the reserve . . . several Zeros, 3,000 to 7,000 feet above . . . one or two friendly fighters at the same level.

"When I completed my runs and was at 16,000 feet, another F4F-4 joined me and we returned to Fighter One. I would have preferred to land at the Russells, but decided not to when I saw Zeros diving in that direction." Leonard actually landed with eight gallons of gas left. Postcombat analysis credited him with two Zeros definitely shot down.

Lieutenant (j.g.) Robert L. Gilbert from Leonard's division said, "When we started down I was 'tailend Charlie' and had counted up to 20 Zeros. I saw a plane cross in front of me to the right as we were turning left and I opened up on him using a no-deflection shot from the stern. Then I paused momentarily because he looked so much like a P-40, but as he pulled up in a climbing turn I saw the red balls on each wing. I said to myself, 'Thank Goodness,' and let him have it until he caught fire. Breaking away to the left, I found myself on the tail of another Zero and gave him a squirt until he burst into flame. As I was making a run on a third Zero, another pulled right into my sights and I fired on him until he began to emit black smoke and fell off. Being low on gas, I headed for home. Two more Zeros flew through my sights and I opened up on them, saw my tracers going into their fuselages but neither burned. Just then I ran out of ammunition and pushed over to get home. I heard the Russells radio report Zeros between there and Esperance and seeing eight of them I made a slight detour." When Gilbert shut off his engine he had three gallons of gas and no more bullets. The evidence indicated that he had destroyed three Zeros.

Lieutenant (j.g.) Vernon E. Graham, a section leader in Leonard's division, recalled, "We [Leonard's division] with two other planes were in a loose formation when we moved in on the fight at 26,000 feet. A Zero got on either Leonard's or [Lieutenant (j.g.) Claude] Ivie's tail and did a slow roll. I came in on him with an overhead, fired a short burst and he broke into flames. All the F4F-4s had split up and single combat were going on all around. There were some F4Us up above. Suddenly I saw a Zero on my left and a little below. I made a high side attack and set him afire. Looking down I saw another Zero about 150 feet below coming around toward me in a climbing turn. I pulled up and the Zero rolled over on his back and pushed his stick forward to meet me head on. This maneuver put my pipper [gun sight marker] dead on him and I opened fire. He exploded. I don't think he'd even fired on me.

"At this time Captain [Kenneth] Ford of VMF-121 came by and gave me the joining up signal. Another F4U was with us and we went over to take on four Zeros. We were scissoring on one another when one of the Marines draw a Zero on his [the Marine's] tail right across my path and I gave him a burst. The air was filled with flying pieces of his plane when my six .50s went in him and some of them were so close I thought they would hit me.

"By now, I was close to the Russells and almost out of gas. I saw another Zero ahead and above me so I pulled up and opened fire at about 350 yards. He began to smoke, rolled over and headed down. I did not see what happened to him but Captain Ford reported that this Zero crashed in the water. Then I ran out of gas and two Zeros jumped on my tail. The Marines shot one down off my tail and chased the other one off.

"I came on down to the Russells strip and because my plane was so light, all my gas and ammunition being gone, I over ran the runway and cracked up." In the crash, Graham fractured his skull. He was unconscious for several days, but after intelligence officers interviewed him and the Marine pilots who had been with him, Graham was acclaimed an ace with five victories that day. The squadron's summary of the confrontation recorded fourteen Zeros downed with a loss of four planes.

After many weeks in which the Japanese air arm seemed dormant except for fighter patrols, on June 16, 1943, a major strike force came hurtling down the Slot. From 105 to 115 Zeros and dive-bombers appeared bound for an attack on the shipping in the neighborhood of Tulagi and Guadalcanal. Most of Fighting Squadron Eleven was at lunch when the alarm sounded. Within fifteen minutes the pilots were standing by in flight gear, and at 1:10 P.M., Fighter Command ordered sixteen planes scrambled to climb and orbit the anchorage around Tulagi and Guadalcanal.

When the route of the approaching Japanese became clearer, Lieutenant Commander Raymond W. Vogel led the F4F-4s to intercept them. Another eight F4Fs, two more divisions, led by Lieutenant Frank B. Quady, were dispatched to patrol the skies. About the same time an additional four Wildcats, under Lieutenant Commander Clarence M. White, which had landed at Henderson Field after a recon mission, refueled and took off. Fighter Command continued to advise on the positions of the oncoming raiders.

Quady and his people made the first contact with the bogeys, eighteen to twenty dive-bombers chaperoned by thirty Zeros over the mountains of Guadalcanal. Quady's division dived out of the sun, making overhead and stern runs of the spearhead V of the dive-bombers. Quady blew away two of them and then smoked a Zero that sought to interfere. His wingman, Lieutenant (j.g.) Charles H. Schild, definitely shot down one Zero and probably another.

A second division, led by Lieutenant (j.g.) John W. Ramsay, approaching from another direction, pushed over and fell upon another flock of dive-bombers with the fighter escorts. Ramsay got one of each, and his wingman, Lieutenant (j.g.) Vernon Gaston, accounted for a Zero. Their two companions brought down a pair of enemy fighters.

White's division, which had taken off separately from the others, caught up with the bombers just as they were starting to form a diving column. White and his wingman, Lieutenant (j.g.) Teddy I. Hull, interrupted the procession. White reported that the frenzied action, which included a diversion by a Zero, prevented him from following everything that occurred. However, he saw two of the dive-bombers start to smoke and fall out of formation. When he reached the bottom of his dive, he noticed for the first time that Hull was no longer with him. The wingman was not seen again. Two others from the division, Lieutenant (j.g.) James S. Swope and Lieutenant (j.g.) Charles R. Stimpson, followed their leader into the melee. Stimpson flamed four of the enemy dive-bombers, while Swope destroyed three more.

The group commanded by Vogel caught up with the swirling, roaring, smoking, burning maelstrom, which some pilots described as "a gigantic aerial circus." The conflict engaged a wide inventory of aircraft—Zeros, Aichi 99s, Nakajima 97s, P-38s, P-39s, P-40s, F4Us, and F4Fs—as Army and Marine flyers joined with the Navy pilots. The near anarchy of the combat brought the only three casualties suffered by VF-11. One pilot reported seeing a pair of F4Fs chasing a Zero 150 feet off the water when they collided and crashed. A P-40 and a Wildcat smashed into each other, and the F4F probably was that of the missing Lieutenant Hull.

Altogether, some eighty of the attackers were believed shot down, with VF-11 claiming thirty-two positively and four more probably. A postaction critique said the success was "undoubtedly due to the initial altitude advantage which they [the F4Fs] had. The armor of the F4F undoubtedly saved the lives of many of the pilots. Many of the planes had a number of 7.7 hits in them and several received 20 mm bursts in the wings and fuselage. One plane received three 20 mm bursts in the wing and fuselage but landed safely." The report concluded that even a small number of Navy fighters could disrupt an attack by a numerically superior enemy.

The June 16 battle demonstrated that the Japanese could no longer generate a sustained successful offensive air operation against American installations. By mid-1943, Japan could only fight a defensive war.

ELEVEN

INVASION HAWKS AND BIRDS OF THE NIGHT

On July 10, 1943, the Allies invaded Sicily under the rubric of Operation Husky. With the ouster of the Axis forces from North Africa, the Army Air Corps established air bases from which it could support the invasion without need for the carrier-based planes that had been vital to Operation Torch. Nevertheless, a handful of Navy flyers played vital roles. A heavy bombardment from offshore preceded the landing of the troops. In the absence of any ground observers to pinpoint shore batteries, gun emplacements, enemy tanks, and other strongholds of resistance, the cruisers did the shooting, relying upon spotters catapulted off their decks.

Lieutenant (j.g.) Paul E. Coughlin, from the *Philadelphia*, achieved distinction on Husky's D-Day. Flying an SOC Kingfish, he noticed enemy troop movement near where the Americans were coming ashore. Coughlin dropped a pair of 100-pound bombs on the Axis soldiers. Neither exploded because of incorrect fusing. However, the threat intimidated the men, and when Coughlin and Richard Shafter, his radioman, started strafing, the Italian soldiers hoisted white flags.

The pilot flew low enough to gesture for them to march toward the landing parties. Shafter encouraged them by spraying bullets behind them. When his gun jammed, Shafter kept the parade going by shooting off his .45 pistol. Fully engaged in the proceedings, Coughlin failed to notice a pair of Messerschmitts creeping up on his tail.

A observer on the *Philadelphia*, however, arranged for some five-inch shells to explode behind the Americans, and the fighters broke off their attack. Coughlin and Shafter returned safely to the cruiser, having rounded up about 150 prisoners.

Again, following the capture of Sicily, the warships softened up defenses on the mainland of Italy with aerial scouts from the cruisers directing fire where it would do most good. Most notably, the *Savannah*, guided by an SOC (Seagull), lambasted an enemy tank column that threatened the invasion force. However, the Seagulls were far more vulnerable here because of the proximity of enemy airfields with high-performance fighters. The job of spotting for warships was turned over to Sicily-based aircraft that could hold their own against the enemy.

Along with more and improved planes, the Navy had begun to add ships, particularly aircraft carriers. The Pacific fleet welcomed lighter flattops—*Independence*, *Princeton*, and *Belleau Wood*—as well as faster, bigger ones: *Essex*, a reborn *Lexington*, and *Yorktown*. Originally named the *Bonhomme Richard*, the latter loaded aboard Air Group Five, under recently promoted Commander James Flatley. Lieutenant Commander Charles L. Crommelin took charge of VF-5, one of the new forty-plane fighter squadrons. Charles Crommelin was one of five brothers who had graduated from the USNA, and he was recognized as an outstanding flyer and leader.

Fighting Five benefited from the experiences of Crommelin, his executive officer, Edward Owen, and pilot Melvin "Boogie" Hoffman, all of whom had been involved in the initial tests of the F6F Hellcat. They brought a wealth of knowledge about its performance, its pluses and minuses. The trio had also worked on the restoration of the Japanese Zero recovered in the Aleutians, accumulating expertise on that opponent. Boogie Hoffman, who had been a member of the prewar VF-2, the Flying Chiefs, in which all of the pilots except for the squadron commander and a few other senior people had been enlisted personnel, actually flew the Zero across the country. He engaged in simulated combat with Navy pilots, exercises that helped flyers understand what they were up against.

On August 31, 1943, Task Force Fifteen, which included the new *Yorktown*, *Essex*, and *Independence*, brought the war to Marcus Island, a scant 1,000 miles southeast of Tokyo, as a reminder of the ability of the United States to carry the battle to the Japanese. The four attacks over a period lasting from 6:00 A.M. to 2:00 P.M. bombed and strafed with no opposition in the air. VF-5 lost two pilots and had one seriously wounded from ground fire in its virgin endeavor. Marcus Island, weakly protected against air raids, became, in subsequent months, the site for initiating novice aviators to the experience of combat strikes.

The *Independence* served as home for a composite squadron, VC-22, under Lieutenant Commander J. M. Peters, and VF-6, a fighter squadron with the new F6F Hellcats, headed by Lieutenant Commander Butch O'Hare. On the final day of August, the bombers from VC-22, protected by O'Hare and three more fighters, flew 130 miles to an enemy air base on Marcus Island.

Peters's group dropped on a number of buildings and shot up portions of the airfield. O'Hare and his subordinates strafed various structures at the airfield, leaving behind several demolished bombers. On the way home, the TBFs rendezvoused, then sought out an enemy tanker reported dead in the water and set afire by a patrol plane. One TBF had been loaded with a torpedo for this ship, and Peters had saved one bomb. When the tanker came into sight, the F6Fs subjected it to their .50-caliber machine guns. As Peters and his torpedo-bearing associate maneuvered for the kill, the ship exploded, sending flames a thousand feet into the air before it cracked in half and rapidly sank. The target, instead of carrying oil, apparently was full of munitions.

Although the ability of the Japanese to offer offensive action faded, their defensive ring of island bases remained puissant. Cognizant of this strength, for the first time in the war, the Navy organized a task force with six carriers to lead Operation Galvanic, the conquest of Tarawa in the Gilbert Islands. On September 19, 1943, VF-16, numbering thirty-six F6F-3s, took off at 3:30 A.M. and seventy minutes later arrived over the atoll of Tarawa. The objective was the destruction of enemy aircraft, AA installations, and shipping, all preparatory to an invasion by the Marines.

Broken into two waves, the Hellcats pounded the island in the face of heavy AA fire. Because they were operating in darkness, the flashes of the ground guns enabled the fighter pilots to see their locations and silence them. The Navy flyers claimed to have destroyed six aircraft on the ground, a PT boat, and some small vessels, and perpetrated other damage. One F6F disappeared into the sea during the combat, and seventeen others absorbed hits requiring, in many instances, considerable repair.

Altogether, the task group built around the *Lexington*, *Princeton*, and *Belleau Wood* mounted seven strikes against Tarawa and nearby Makin. Half of the eighteen planes on Tarawa's airfield were destroyed, a number of installations smashed, and a substantial number of soldiers killed or wounded. The raids upon Marcus Island, Tarawa, and subsequently Wake Island also featured a new rescue service, lifeguard submarines that stood offshore to save flyers who ditched.

Al Vraciu, following his postcommission training, heard that a squadron was being formed under Butch O'Hare. He successfully campaigned to join the unit, originally VF-3, subsequently changed to VF-6. "Butch O'Hare selected me as his wingman. I felt that it was an honor. I was pretty committed. After Pearl Harbor, I had a big mad on. But I felt that I owed to him to be dedicated and to do my very best. That provided me with much of the education and training that I needed. I learned my trade from one of the best! He had a very quiet demeanor and he didn't have much to say. We just absorbed what he did say.

"From Butch I learned how to conserve fuel, conserve ammunition, get in a little closer in firing, aim at the wing roots, and to look back over your shoulder for possible enemy planes before starting a dive on strafing runs. I feel it may have saved my life several times."

Vraciu was in on the original strike at Marcus Island. "I felt it was kind of tame. There was no air-to-air action, but our division did sink a small ship. We strafed it and blew it up. The torpedo guys were a little disturbed with us because we didn't give them a chance to get in a little practice."

The gung ho Vraciu had to wait a month or so before his first air-to-air combat, October 5 over Wake Island. By that time he had moved up to section leader. "I didn't have radio reception on that mission. I would have to respond in my actions by the way he [O'Hare] was flying or maybe by a few of his hand signals. We were on a combat air patrol and we caught a group of three Zeros coming in to land at Wake Island. We had altitude on them—perfect position. Undoubtedly Butch was getting some report from the fighter director, which I wasn't privy to. But he had me trained as a section lead on what to do. In other words, we used two planes in that division that would fire on our high-side pass. In a lot of divisions, the leader would be the only one firing and the other guys wouldn't get a chance to fire. But in this case, where you're shooting going down on a Vee of three planes, I was to take the inside guy, and the division leader would fire at the outside guy. Some leader would try to break up an attack by going after the lead plane, but that would scatter them like ducks, and you don't get nearly as many planes that way. And our purpose was to clear the air of enemy aerial opposition. That was the job—shoot down as many of them as possible.

"We dove on down. This was the first time I'd fired a gun at an enemy plane. I'd strafed Marcus Island, and I survived that strafing run on the airfield. But this time I was firing at a Jap plane. Butch got the Zero wingman on the left, but it took him down below a broken cloud layer. I got the Zero wingman on the right, and it felt damned good. I practically flew through the pieces.

"I pulled up and I realized Butch had disappeared below the clouds with his wingman. I found out later that they ran into more planes down below. Here I am, looking for him, but I'm keeping my eye on that lead enemy Zero. I saw him land at Wake and skitter off to the side of the runway. I thought, 'I'm going to go down and strafe that sucker!' And I did. I burned the Zero and while doing evasive maneuvers across the field, I noticed a parked Betty near the runway, so I pulled around, and my wingman, Willie Callan, and I went in and burned the Betty.

"I caught a little hell, when I got back, for not going below the cloud with Butch, but I didn't see him go down. But I learned that this is what can happen in combat. Sometimes there is separation, but you learn a lesson."

Flatley himself had led the Hellcats of V-5 from the *Yorktown* to Marcus Island. But he was reassigned, and Crommelin succeeded him. As part of the six-carrier force punishing Wake, VF-5 would also visit the island. The evening before the mission, Air Group Commander Crommelin promised a bottle of Old Crow whiskey to the first pilot who destroyed an enemy plane in the air. During a predawn arrival over Wake, Ensign Robert Duncan and Lieutenant Boogie Hoffman spotted several Zeros approaching them with hostile intent. Duncan quickly disposed of one with a full deflection burst into the cockpit. When he saw another enemy seeking an advantage over a fellow American, Duncan intercepted him. According to the former ensign, writing in the third person, "the Jap pulled up sharply as only a Zero could, did a wing over and bored in . . . upside down. His bullets hit aft of the cockpit. As the Zero pulled out of his pass, he pulled up into a loop with Duncan following. At the top of the loop, Duncan opened fire. The Zero began to flame and went spinning in on fire. The pilot made no attempt to bail out." The entire action occurred before dawn, when little more than the silhouettes of the airplanes could be distinguished.

With Hoffman, Duncan made machine-gun runs on grounded planes. They each destroyed a pair of twin-engine bombers. When a Zero happened by above them, they gave chase. Both loosed a burst, but Duncan's ammunition was now gone. He could only fly wing while Hoffman shot down his second Zero. From then on Duncan swore he would save his two inboard guns "to come home on" and fire only the four outboard ones at targets.

Duncan said he had originally been mystified by the reactions of his second victim. Only an inexperienced pilot would make such a stupid move. But later he learned that his adversary actually was a veteran with nine U.S. aircraft destroyed. Then he realized that the Zero pilot had never seen a Hellcat before and had mistaken it for its predecessor, which could not follow a Zero in a tight loop without spinning out on top. But a Hellcat could match the Japanese fighter in that maneuver. Crommelin awarded Duncan the Old Crow trophy.

Fighting Squadron Nine, blooded over North Africa and re-equipped as a Hellcat squadron skippered by Lieutenant Commander Philip H. Torrey, shipped to the Pacific on the *Essex*. They were among the forty-seven F6Fs that roared toward Wake. Some 50 miles out, twenty-seven Zeros tried to intercept them. In the ensuing dogfights, Torrey knocked down one Zero, and Lieutenant (j.g.) Hamilton McWhorter, a veteran of Operation Torch, pounced upon a group of enemy fighters and exploded one for his first aerial victory.

On November 1, American troops waded ashore at Empress Augusta Bay on Bougainville, in the Solomons. Seizure of the base by the Allies would isolate New Britain and Rabaul. The strategy expected a counterpunch by the Japanese, who would support their forces on Bougainville from Rabaul. Accordingly, the Navy and Army bombers pounded that site, where enemy warships had gathered for the purpose of thwarting the Americans invading Bougainville.

On November 5, the *Saratoga* launched twenty-two dive-bombers from VB-12 that formed up with fifty-two fighters and a group of torpedo planes, including some from the carrier *Princeton*. Air Group Commander H. H. Caldwell, as senior officer, coordinated the entire attack on forty to fifty ships in the harbor. The Imperial Navy's eight cruisers and twenty destroyers, just getting under way, plus some shore batteries, tossed up a screen of heavy but inaccurate antiaircraft. Enemy fighters attempted to drive off the bombers and torpedo planes but with little effect. The Americans claimed hits on six heavy cruisers as well as a destroyer.

When pulling out their dives, the raiders dodged between, around, and over ships, jinking, skidding, and altering altitude to avoid the surface response and the forest of masts. When it was over, the toll in U.S. aircraft added up to four F6Fs, two TBFs, and one SBD. Eight of the dive-bombers returned badly shot up, including one with a dead gunner killed by a 20-mm that had exploded in the cockpit.

Henry Miller, who had tutored Doolittle's Tokyo busters in the art of lifting a B-25 from the deck of a flattop, commanded Air Group Twenty-three on the *Princeton*. "We heard," said Miller, "that the Japanese had sent a big cruiser and destroyer force that was sitting at Rabaul and they were going to wipe out our forces that were landing in Empress Augusta Bay in the Solomons. So we were ordered to go up and hit Rabaul, the *Saratoga* and the *Princeton*. Admiral Halsey told us later that he didn't expect to get the *Saratoga* and the *Princeton* back after these raids. He expected to lose us in that raid.

"We went to about 150 miles away [from Rabaul] and launched aircraft. It was a beautiful clear day. For fifty miles we could see Japanese fighters taking off from all the fields around Rabaul to intercept us. It was quite a battle. We had to save that Empress Augusta Bay operation and I think they made a very wise decision because we went in that day and got a lot of Jap planes. We hit the cruisers and destroyers, and the Japs had to send that force back to Japan and to Truk to get fixed.

"They always considered me the old man in the fighter squadron. I and a whole bunch of young kids. I was about thirty-one years old, the old guy, couldn't see. When we got into combat, if there was anything in the air, I was the first to see it. When we got in to Rabaul, we were the top cover and I saw four Jap Zero airplanes coming toward us and to the left. I assumed that everybody saw them, so I swung right around behind them with my division of four and I started shooting.

"One airplane blew up right in front of me. I pulled up to the right to get at the other one and start shooting at him. My three other planes in that division were all shook up because they hadn't even seen anything yet. They got quite a ribbing when they got back.

"We had about seventy-five planes involved and everybody did a marvelous job. They really carried the attacks home. Our own group lost several pilots. But we got the hits and we shot down seventeen Jap planes from our little squadron."

The campaign to sterilize Rabaul introduced another new American machine, the SB2C Helldiver, as a replacement for the SBD Dauntless. Unlike the Hellcat, it did not draw unanimous raves—although naval historian Clark Reynolds, in *The Fast Carriers*, claimed that "the new SB2C Helldiver won the praise of earlier doubters; even the skipper of Bombing Nine on *Essex*, which still flew the SBD, remarked that 90 per cent of the bomber pilots were now 'all for them.' " Kent Lee, who graduated from flight school in 1943, volunteered for dive-bombers, and became an instructor, demurred: "The Helldiver was the dog of all dogs. It was big, clumsy, had a low climb rate, poor design for dive bombing, and poor maneuverability." Lee admitted that the SBD had one weakness: it was underpowered. However, in spite of what Reynolds said, many longed for the SBDs after the substitution of SB2Cs.

In a postaction report, Air Group Nine complained that the new planes received by the carrier groups were not combat-serviceable. A number of the aircraft could not participate in the attack, and some aviators doubted that their guns had been properly boresighted. Flattops, at the time, lacked the ability to make such adjustments. The need for quick replacement of lost aircraft and pilots frequently outstripped the capacity to produce satisfactory facsimiles of the originals.

One of the new flattops, the *Bunker Hill*, hosted a recently activated unit, VF-18. Jim Pearce, who had so enjoyed tootling around Bora Bora in a scout plane, had been reassigned to VF-18 as a Wildcat pilot. But the squadron shifted to Hellcats, and then, with only 30 percent of their training completed, VF-18 was sent to sea on the *Bunker Hill* after VF-17, equipped with the new Corsairs, discovered that their aircraft had flunked carrier operation tests.

Admiral Bull Halsey was determined to neutralize Rabaul. He ordered aerial assaults from two separate task forces. "Five air groups," said Halsey, "ought to change the name of Rabaul to Rubble." On November 11, Pearce led a division of Hellcats assigned to escort two TBFs carrying torpedoes plotted for use against some ships in Simpson Harbor, Rabaul. "As we approached Rabaul," said Pearce, "we could see the Jap fighters taking off in clouds of dust from the dirt runways around the harbor. Soon they were all around us, some doing slow rolls and playing around out of range. Our instructions were to stick with the TBFs unless we, or they, were under attack and strafe the ships they were attacking to help tone down the AA from the ship, then escort them back home.

"Some of the Jap fighters moved high up over us and began dropping what appeared to be phosphorous bombs trailing white smoke. These things were ineffective and didn't particularly bother us. Then they started coming down at us. A Zeke [a variation on the Zero] worked himself onto the six [rear] of my wingman, Dave Mandt, I called a 180 to Dave, and we turned sharply toward each other. I got a good head-on shot at the Zeke. I do not know what happened to him, because we were closing at a rapid rate and our mission was still to protect the TBFs.

"We immediately rejoined the TBFs. The Zeke was scored a probable, even though I saw pieces flying off the machine in the brief seconds we closed. By this time we were approaching the harbor, and there were several Jap warships steaming to get out of there. Our torpedo guys picked out a cruiser and began a shallow dive toward it. As instructed, we fighter guys strafed in front of the TBFs and realized for the first time that this was a hell of a dangerous thing to do. The cruiser seemed to have a thousand guns blinking at us. But we got through the AA somehow and pulled up to watch the action of the TBFs. They dropped two torpedoes and both hit the side of the ship, but neither exploded.

"Thanks to the Grumman Iron Works [the nickname for the manufacturer because of the hardiness of the aircraft], all of us got in and out, but the torpedo maker, whoever that was, had better go back to the drawing board. I had pulled up just under a broken overcast to watch the dismal torpedo show and wham, I got hit big. I learned at that moment that it was dumb to park just under an overcast when AA was around. The gunners knew the height of the overcast and set their fuses accordingly. The hit I took severed both rudder cables, knocked off my goggles, set the hydraulic fluid on fire, and blew over 140 holes in the aft fuselage behind the armor plate. Much smoke in the cockpit until the fire burned itself out behind me, but I had no rudder control, both pedals were [jammed] up against the cockpit forward bulkhead. And I would have no rudder control, no flaps to land, and one chance to get the gear down with the emergency air bottle if I got back to the ship.

"But the tough old Hellcat was still running, and back to the ship we went. When we arrived, I was instructed to remain in the air until all the 'usable' aircraft were recovered. Then I could be permitted to try a landing. My landing was only partially successful. My tail hook bounced over the arresting wires, and I ended up in the 'barrier,' a cable 'wall' between landing aircraft and the parked planes forward. The ship's crew pushed the aircraft over the stern of the ship, after I got through counting the 140-plus holes. So much for my first combat experience."

Ensign Thomas S. Harris, a University of Illinois engineering student until Navy recruiters arrived in early 1942 and enticed a score of collegians to volunteer as aviation cadets, listed Rabaul in his logbook as his first combat mission. Harris, from VF-18, inscribed in the book a red-ink replica of a Rising Sun flag and the word "Val," to indicate his first victory. The line beneath notes, "Lost Charley Austed over Rabaul." It would be the first of a series of such laconic notations in Harris's log.

There were a few combat veterans with VF-18, notably Ram Dibb, who had flown as wingman for Thach, and Jim Billo, who had been rescued after ditching by a less than friendly destroyer skipper a year earlier. Billo recalled that after a tour on the *Enterprise* that had included flying ground-based missions from Espíritu Santo and Guadalcanal, he had come home with malaria only to find himself ticketed for redeployment. He recalled, "One of our early actions was over Rabaul, which was not a nice place to take a brand-new squadron, but that was the way it worked. My division flew high cover over the bombers right over the port, pushed over with the bombers, and was jumped by multitudinous Zekes at the top of the pushover.

"In our weaving I shot two fighters off my second section's tail before we got into the dive, then as we pulled out, and after a strafing run in the harbor, got another one, chasing him off a torpedo plane." Billo's first section turned sharply to aid the second section with a Zero on its tail. Their guns smoked the enemy, who pulled up and jumped. "We did *not* [his emphasis] strafe the pilot in the chute," said Billo.

Chick Smith of VF-9, and his wingman, Bill Blackwell, were two of the shepherds guarding Air Group Nine's attackers. "As we approached Rabaul, some 30 or so Japanese fighters started shadowing us, flying 2000–3000 feet higher than our formation of dive-bombers, torpedo bombers and fighters. They had altitude advantage but for some reason did not use it. They did not attack until our torpedo and dive-bombers started their attack run-ins and dives. During the attack, I shot down one Zero attempting an attack against our planes. As we were retiring, I shot down another as it made a run at an SBD."

Hamilton McWhorter from the same squadron started after a cruiser seeking the open seas at high speed. On his strafing run, he felt as if every weapon aboard was concentrating on him, and he actually saw the eight-inch shells as they streaked toward him. At a distance of 2,500 feet, he unloosed a four-second burst at some unprotected antiaircraft guns, then sprinted over the ship. On his way home to the rendezvous point, he intervened in a massive dogfight between about a dozen Hellcats and more than thirty enemy fighters.

McWhorter picked out a target and promptly set his engines aflame. Engrossed in the action, he was startled by a sound "like when someone throws a handful of large rocks on a galvanized tin roof." His F6F, of course, was that roof and the noise came from bullets banging into his plane. McWhorter executed a split-S dive that brought a Zero into his sights. He blew up that one, and in the space of forty-five seconds had destroyed two fighters.

At the time of the November 11 strike, VF-6 was actually divided among three different carriers. Alex Vraciu, with those on the *Independence*, escorted torpedo bombers and, except when strafing the ships as a diversion from attention on the TBFs, stuck with the Avengers. On the way home, a Hellcat from another carrier sidled up to Vraciu and pointed in the distance to a gaggle of forty or fifty Zeros performing loops and other stunts. Mindful of his responsibilities, Vraciu refused to snap at the bait and leave the returning bombers. Others, however, could not resist the lure and challenged the enemy fighters.

While VF-17, the F4U-equipped squadron, was deemed not fully ready for carrier operations, it could and did fly combat from the Ondongo base on Bougainville. In the steamy heat of the island, the pilots lived in tents that squatted over mud, worried about an occasional enemy sniper in the jungle, and flew wearing a pair of shorts, a summer flight suit, and tennis shoes. One of the young ensigns with VF-17 was Ira Kepford, a former Northwestern University football blocking back, who, along with a number of other students, had been inducted into the Navy during the halftime of the 1941 Northwestern-Purdue game.

The squadron, under Lieutenant Commander Roger Hedrick, drew two assignments for the assault upon Rabaul. Starting at dawn, twenty-four F4Us plus twelve F6Fs flew combat air patrol over the task force. Three carriers, *Bunker Hill, Essex,* and *Indepen-dence,* launched their own aircraft for the strike. Once the raiders all left, the CAP, including the Corsairs, which had been modified for carrier use, landed on the *Essex* and *Bunker Hill.* Refueled and rearmed, they took off again to cover the task force during the recovery period.

They were thus in position when the Japanese force counter-punched against the fleet. The three carriers nearest Rabaul, *Bunker Hill, Essex,* and *Independence,* were shielded only by the limited resources of the combat air patrol. They could not halt the entire land-based attack of 120 planes—the Japanese had shifted aircraft and pilots from their flattops to help in the defense of Rabaul.

The divisions and sections of VF-17 skirmished with the waves of Zekes, Vals, Hamps, and Tonys, destroying a number before having to return to their land base for refueling or due to damage. Ira Kepford, with three other Corsairs, was about to head for Ondongo when they saw the ships firing and entered the fight above the task force just as a formation of dive-bombers pushed over. Kepford and his wingman each picked out a column of the Vals. On a high-side approach, he blasted a dive-bomber. When the others sought refuge in a rain cloud, Kepford caught one with a short burst that exploded the victim. Two Zekes tried to gun him down but missed, and the former football star chased another dive-bomber into a squall. With a full deflection shot Kepford blew up his third dive-bomber. Coming out of the rain, he found a fourth Val nearby and sprinkled his wing with bullets.

The action over the task force continued, and Kepford attempted to intervene. He rocked his wings to persuade gunners that he was friendly and then homed in on a Kate seeking to hit the *Bunker Hill.* The AA bursts continued to come uncomfortably close, bumping the F4U when they detonated. But he finally closed to a mere 50 feet and put the Kate in the water.

Along with the defenses provided by VF-17, the American carriers wheeled, veered, and swung to avoid falling bombs and slithering torpedoes. With a limited screen of destroyers, they threw up a torrent of antiaircraft. None of the seagoing vessels suffered a hit while knocking down more than two dozen of the enemy. In one of those common random moments of modern war, events that make the difference between life and death, the *Independence* catapulted Ensign J. B. Thomas in a TBF just as the enemy attacked the carrier. Thomas was at an altitude of only 75 feet, turning left, just as a Val completed its dive 200 yards from him. As the dive-bomber pulled up, it exposed its belly. Thomas's top turret gunner raked the Val with bullets along the fuselage and into the engine. It burst into flames and crashed.

The Marcus, Wake, and Rabaul onslaughts put the Japanese back on their heels, inflicting damage on their ships and bases while weakening their air arm further. But further steps on the road to Tokyo required control of the islands that led west. While MacArthur, with the aid of the fleet under Halsey, moved in the southwest Pacific through the Solomons and New Guinea, Nimitz in the central Pacific was confronted by the Micronesian barrier of the Gilbert and then the Marshall Islands. At the top of the list beckoned Tarawa, bolstered by a new airfield on Betio, one of the two atolls that made up Tarawa. The secondary objective in the Gilberts was Makin, a home for seaplanes and subject of an ill-conceived hit-and-run raid by Colonel Evan Carlson's Marine Raiders in August 1942.

Alex Vraciu participated in the softening-up exercises preparatory to Operation Galvanic, the invasion of the Gilberts. "For three days at Tarawa we escorted the TBFs, strafed and flew combat air patrols in support of the Marine landings." During one of his days on CAP, Vraciu outran his associates in pursuit of a Betty frantically trying to escape notice by skimming the waves. He caught up to it in a tail chase. "Somewhere in my first burst I must have gotten the tail-gunner, because I didn't see his cannon shooting 20 mm shells." Later Vraciu said he had learned to respect the "stinger" [tail gunner] when approaching from astern. He and his mother ship, the *Independence*, left the scene, however, when the flattop took a torpedo. Under its own power but with an escort, the carrier retired to a base at Funafuti, 700 miles away.

With the Empress Augusta Bay landings now established, the carrier *Nassau* launched VF-1 at the start of Operation Galvanic, the invasion of Tarawa. In its action report on the strafing mission, the squadron said that while general instructions were given to hit 40-mm positions, there was a need for specific locations. The pilots saw no personnel, and the defensive positions were well camouflaged. "The only visible targets to shoot at were gun flashes." They also complained that too many planes were over the target and the heavy traffic risked midair collisions. Radio channels were clogged with transmissions, indicating a need for a separate channel devoted solely to air support.

There was clear evidence of fatigue with two pilots who flew three missions, logging eight and a half hours in the cockpit in a single day. The majority of VF-1 averaged about six hours during two flights for three straight days. This did not include the time spent in the ready room awaiting the announcement "Pilots, man your planes."

Henry Miller said of Tarawa, "They were too optimistic. From the aviation point of view, they thought they had just beaten the place to death, that there were probably very few living Japs there, that they [the Marines] were just going to walk ashore and take over, because they'd really pounded it with airplanes, bombs, strafing and those battleships and cruisers pounding away. The Japs had done a beautiful job in building solid fortifications in that bit of sand and dirt on Tarawa.

"That was the first time that the United States had run into the tough fortifications that the Japs set up in a great many places in the Pacific. We didn't have the aerial reconnaissance in those days that we have today [50 years later] or that we had at the end of the war. We thought we were pretty doggone good with our bombs and bullets but it didn't turn out that way.

"Pilots would come in as low as possible, depending on the bomb load. Normally they'd level out at a thousand feet to give them greater accuracy. Some were misses, some faulty ordnance. In a great many instances, bombs don't do the job you think they're going to do. If they get a glancing blow, they don't do the job. You've got to put it on target to be sure everything works.

"We used to work like the devil to support those Marines who were on the beach. We knew they had to have all the support in the world. We worked a little harder to give them that support. We lost more airplanes in close support of troops than we did on big strikes."

Jim Pearce recalled his ground support missions at Tarawa, Makin, and other sites as a mixed bag: "These missions seemed to take two forms, ones where you could really see what you were shooting at and ones where you were directed to fire into a particular grid section where, often, you couldn't really see what you were shooting at or bombing."

VF-9 supported the Marines at Tarawa. While engaged in that duty, Mac McWhorter downed a float plane off the island on November 18 and then a Betty the following day. In splashing the latter he fired only eighty-six rounds, earning him the nickname "One slug." McWhorter, as a result of his achievements at Tarawa, became the first Hellcat ace.

A critique in the fiftieth-anniversary book published by men from the *Suwannee*, which supplied planes for prelanding strikes and CAP, said, "While the fast carriers provided most of the air support for Betio, the escort carriers learned a lot from the problems of the fast carriers. Many of the attacks were poorly executed. Bombs were off target and strafing was done haphazardly. Poor communications, poor coordination and poor training all combined to reduce the effectiveness of the big carrier missions. Things improved dramatically with our CVE [escort carrier] pilots after they began close and immediate communication with the target land coordinators."

The experiences of aviators from the *Bunker Hill* indicated limitations in the effectiveness of aerial bombardment. The combat action report told of five- and six-inch coastal defense guns mounted in turrets with circular concrete emplacements some thirty feet in diameter. "No substantial damage to the coast defense guns . . . occurred from the air bombing . . . destruction of any of the gun positions would have required direct hits from the planes within areas averaging only about twenty-five to thirty feet in diameter. Such accuracy seems not within the capability of the dive-bomber."

VF-18 filed its own appraisal of air support missions. The report began with comments on the technical aspects of dive angles and speed that limited firing time, concluding that the gun sight must be "pretty exactly 'on,' " which in turn required detailed knowledge of the defensive installations, data that intelligence should supply prior to takeoff.

"Strafing was conspicuously successful chiefly against personnel. Gun crews and troops above ground were the most profitable targets . . . [but] the mass of the Japs never showed themselves—or exposed themselves to .50 caliber fire—until they came above ground to oppose the landings.

"Japanese opposing the landing forces were strafed. But it appeared that closer and more detailed collaboration between VF and ground troops *after* the landing would pay greater dividends— perhaps by relatively continuous use of smoke pots or other devices to mark front lines so repeating strafing to within twenty yards of own troops . . . would be possible.

"In this operation, each strike was in great force; so there were real traffic problems over the island during the attack." As the factories rolled out more and more planes and the training schools graduated ever-larger numbers of pilots, the services began to cope with a new problem, a superabundance of aircraft working within a limited airspace. Queuing up for a shot at the enemy, whether on the ground or sea, and even competing for a crack at an airplane, became more common, creating the attendant risk of midair collisions.

At the same time, sporadic massive strikes brought intervals during which the defenders went about their business unmolested. The VF-18 memorandum suggested spreading out the raids to inflict almost continuous strafing. "No attacks were made at night," noted the author of the paper. "If operational difficulties could be overcome, some surprise very low altitude strafing sweeps at night, when the Jap is above ground patching up his defense and moving between position, might prove surprisingly effective." The technique, it was argued, could be effective on smaller islands, even if there were no specific targets.

"For attack missions upon ground targets," the paper proposed, "the effectiveness of the F6F might be enhanced if, in addition to strafing, each plane carried two 137 pound incendiary bombs on wing racks. Carrying larger bombs in lieu of belly tanks is less practicable; it reduces the effective radius of the F6F." That last comment, however, would shortly be refuted. Whatever the failings of operations, no one could deny that both the offshore naval barrages and the aerial attacks did not prevent the defenders from offering fierce opposition to the invasion forces. For much of the war, complaints about ineffective prelanding softening up and tactical support would be reiterated.

As a footnote to the torturous mission of Operation Galvanic, in his logbook, Tom Harris inscribed the melancholy notations, "Strafe Tarawa [twice]. Jim Forman shot down."

On November 23, off Tarawa, a combat patrol from VF-16 relieved VF-5, hovering over the amphibious fleet. Within minutes, a horde of enemy attackers approached the task force. Lieutenant Commander Paul Buie's squadron shot down seventeen of the nineteen raiders. On the following day, VF-5 took up station at roughly the same time as the air battle the previous day. The Japanese, reputed to be creatures of habit, however, failed to show. But no sooner had VF-5, having flown its required hours, yielded the responsibility to VF-16 than the enemy reappeared. On this occasion another dozen Japanese planes went into the water. The leaders of Air Group Sixteen frequently teased VF-5 that in two days they had destroyed twenty-nine enemy planes, while Fighting Five was, in the word of Bob Duncan, "skunked."

As the statement from VF-18 following its experiences in Galvanic demonstrated, the air Navy lacked the ability to wage war at night. For nearly two years since Pearl Harbor, naval aviation had operated in daylight hours except for some missions with takeoffs that began before dawn or an occasional sortie such as that against Marcus Island, which depended upon reaction from the enemy to illuminate targets. Some flyers, such as Henry Miller, had landed after dark, but that was not standard practice. As Dan Gallery discovered, the lack of experience in recovery after dark could be disastrous. Similar experiences had disturbed commanders in the Pacific when squalls blocked plans to set down at Henderson Field or Espíritu Santo and the pilots were forced to ditch because they could not risk a return to the carrier after dark.

The Japanese had shown themselves adept at nocturnal operations, on the sea surface, and in the air, where they frequently dispatched bombers or snoopers. (American ground troops, mostly unschooled in night maneuvers, learned that the Japanese often attacked in the dark.) Washing Machine Charlie, who bedeviled the residents of Guadalcanal, was a harbinger of more serious forays against installations and ships. With the advent of improved radar available for cockpits, American experiments for night action began. Butch O'Hare, promoted to air group commander aboard the *Enterprise*, involved himself in the development of carrier-based night fighter operations and created what he dubbed "Bat Teams."

Because the radar was too bulky to fit in a Hellcat, O'Hare and his associates worked out an arrangement where a larger TBF Avenger would carry the device and partner with fighters. In theory, vectored toward a bogey by the carrier's fighter director officer (FDO), the Avenger, using its radar, would lead the F6Fs to a position behind the oncoming enemy. The Hellcats would be guided close enough for the fighter pilots to see the exhaust flames from the Japanese raiders and then shoot them down.

Bill Odell, an Army Air Corps pilot who flew on the very first mission against occupied Europe on July 4, 1942, and subsequently became a night fighter expert, reported in his manuscript *Those Few Who Dared*, "This was precisely the same 'innovation' tried and discarded in 1940 by the Royal Air Force using a radar-equipped Havoc acting as the search element for a pair of Hawker Hurricanes. . . . The method required close coordination using strict flight procedures, precise communications and considerable daytime practice to perfect the coordinated attack.

The aircraft carrier age dawned in 1910 as barnstorming pilot Eugene Ely lifted his Curtiss biplane off an improvised flight deck on the cruiser USS *Birmingham* at Hampton Roads, Virginia. *(Photograph from U.S. Naval Academy)*

As World War II approached the United States in 1941, the elderly USS *Ranger* crowded more than fifty obsolete biplanes, Grumman F3Fs, on its flight deck. *(Photograph from U.S. Navy)*

Scouting Squadron Six pilots vainly scoured the Pacific on December 7, 1941, in search of the armada that had destroyed the Pearl Harbor installations. This group photo was taken on January 24, 1942, and four of the pilots would be dead within a week, shot down in the vicinity of the Marshall Islands. *(Photograph from National Archives)*

John "Jimmy" Thach developed a "weave" as a tactic for fighters, and the technique enabled the slower, less maneuverable Navy planes to successfully duel with the enemy. *(Photograph from National Archives)*

Edward "Butch" O'Hare became the first American ace in February 1942 over Rabaul, New Guinea, when he shot down five bombers as they tried to attack the carrier *Lexington. (Photograph from National Archives)*

Noel Gayler, who led a flight of four Wildcats from the *Lexington* during dogfights over the Coral Sea in May 1942, saw three of his mates shot down. *(Photograph from U.S. Navy)*

Jimmy Flatley commanded VF-10, the Grim Reapers, one of the most successful fighter squadrons, which made its home on the *Yorktown*. *(Photograph from National Archives)*

Grim Reaper John Leppla began World War II as an SBD Dauntless dive-bomber pilot, then switched to a fighter in VF-10. He shot down seven Japanese Zeros, but in October 1942 he disappeared during the Battle of Santa Cruz. *(Photograph from* Chicago Tribune*)*

Jim Billo, an ace, flew two tours as a fighter pilot, first with the Grim Reapers of VF-10 and then with VF-18. *(Photograph from Jim Billo)*

A torpedo exploded against the Japanese carrier *Shoho* during the Battle of the Coral Sea. *(Photograph from National Archives)*

As a Douglass Dauntless dive-bomber and scout pilot, Stanley Vejtasa knocked down three enemy planes with his fixed guns during the Battle of the Coral Sea and then joined the Grim Reapers as a fighter pilot. *(Photograph from U.S. Navy)*

Pilots from Torpedo Squadron Eight posed on the deck of the *Hornet* shortly before every one of them except for Ensign George Gay (front row, third from left), along with their crews, was killed on June 5 during the Battle of Midway. (*Photograph from U.S. Navy*)

The Japanese aircraft carrier *Hiryu* burned before sinking after an assault by American dive-bombers during the Battle of Midway. (*Photograph from National Archives*)

Badly damaged by enemy bombers during the Battle of Midway, the *Yorktown* listed heavily to starboard but remained afloat until a Japanese sub slammed two torpedoes into her hull. (*Photograph from National Archives*)

Henderson Field on Guadalcanal served as a base for the Navy, Marine Corps, and Army Air Corps. *(Photograph from National Archives)*

During the Battle of the Atlantic, planes from the escort carrier *Bogue* battered the German submarine U-118. *(Photograph from National Archives)*

A Douglas SBD launched its bomb as it dove toward a target. *(Photograph from National Archives)*

VB-12's SB2C Helldivers lined up for a launch. The Helldiver, unlike the slower SBD Dauntless deployed at Midway, carried an internal bomb load to lessen drag. *(Photograph from National Archives)*

A flight of Avengers, Grumman torpedo bombers, headed toward the Japanese island bastion of Truk. *(Photograph from National Archives)*

An exuberant Alex Vraciu held up six fingers to indicate how many Japanese planes he shot down during the Great Marianas Turkey Shoot. It was Vraciu's second tour. Altogether he was credited with nineteen victories in the air and claimed another twenty-one aircraft destroyed on the ground. *(Photograph from Alex Vraciu)*

After plucking Lieutenant (j.g.) George Blair, of VF-9, based on the *Essex*, from Truk Lagoon, an OS2U-3 landed beside its mother ship, the cruiser *Baltimore*, which hoisted the plane aboard. *(Photograph from National Archives)*

Vice Admiral Marc Mitscher, commander of Task Force Fifty-eight, personally congratulated Alex Vraciu for shooting down six Judy bombers during the Great Marianas Turkey Shoot. *(Photograph from Alex Vraciu)*

A galaxy of aces from VF-15 with more than three hundred enemy planes downed, lined up in front of the Hellcat flown by David McCampbell (front row, fourth from right). McCampbell finished the war with thirty-four planes shot down, the highest score for both the Navy and Marines. To McCampbell's immediate right is Norman Berree, to whose right is Walter Lundin. *(Photograph from Walter Lundin)*

LeRoy "Robby" Robinson earned the title of "ace" while flying an F6F with VF-2. After the war he traded his wings of gold for those of an airline pilot. *(Photograph from LeRoy Robinson)*

Ken Hippe, with VC-3, encountered enemy planes only once, but on that occasion he knocked five kamikazes out of the sky. *(Photograph from Ken Hippe)*

As a member of the fighter squadron with Air Group Fifteen aboard the *Essex,* Walter Lundin flew missions against twenty-three enemy bases, participated in the two Battles of the Philippines, and won ace honors. *(Photograph from Walter Lundin)*

Willard Eder reported to Fighting Three in May 1940, and some of his fellow pilots on the *Lexington* included Jimmy Thach, Noel Gayler, and Butch O'Hare. Eder rose to command of two fighter squadrons based on the carrier *Cabot*. *(Photograph from Willard Eder)*

On the flight deck of the *Randolph*, just before takeoff, a Hellcat pilot awaited the signal from the checkered flag. *(Photograph from National Archives)*

A dive-bomber piloted by Ralph Embree, skipper of VB-12, erupted in flames during a hard landing. Embree switched to fighters and was later lost to antiaircraft fire over Okinawa. *(Photograph from National Archives)*

Hamilton McWhorter, who flew missions during operations off North Africa in 1942 and then became a member of VF-12 in the Pacific, received a Distinguished Flying Cross from Commander Charles Crommelin after knocking down ten enemy planes. Crommelin was later killed in a midair collision with another F6F. *(Photograph from U.S. Navy)*

Vice Admiral Marc Mitscher (right), commander of Task Force Fifty-eight, plotted action in the waters off Okinawa with his deputy, Commodore Arleigh "31-knot" Burke. *(Photograph from National Archives)*

Commander T. Hugh Winters, with VF-9 in the North Africa campaign, led VF-19 stationed on the *Lexington* during attacks on Japanese installations in the Philippines, 1944–1945. *(Photograph from National Archives)*

The *Randolph* launched its fighters for an air strike against targets on Japan itself. *(Photograph from National Archives)*

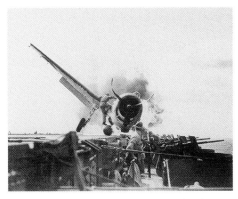

An F6F burst into flames during a landing. A member of the crew climbed up to help the pilot escape. *(Photograph from National Archives)*

During the Battle of Leyte Gulf, the carrier *Kitkun Bay* scrambled its fighters to defend against the kamikazes. Three months later, in January 1945, a suicide plane damaged the *Kitkun Bay* so badly that it was withdrawn from sea duty. *(Photograph from National Archives)*

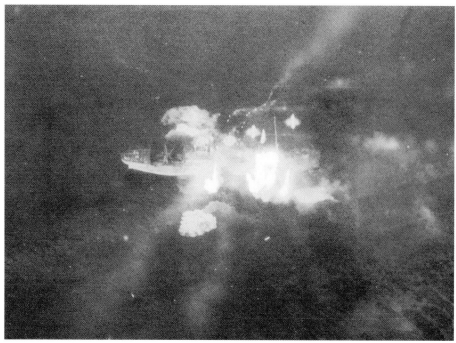

A hapless enemy freighter staggered from a storm of exploding bombs and machine-gun bullets. *(Photograph from National Archives)*

In Manila Bay, one Japanese ship lay half submerged as Navy planes relentlessly attacked vessels in the harbor. *(Photograph from National Archives)*

Ensign Harry D. Jones, age twenty-two, the pilot of a torpedo bomber, was flanked by turret gunner Jack T. Meyer (left) and radioman-gunner Herman R. Canada. Assigned to VT-17, they attacked the Japanese battleship *Yamato* as it headed toward Okinawa. *(Photograph from Harry D. Jones)*

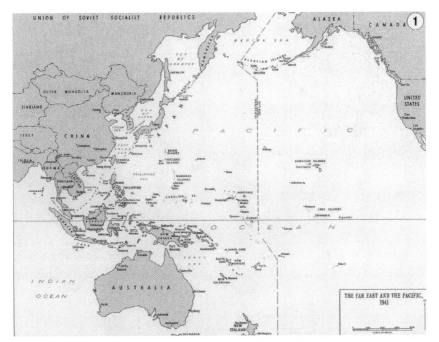

Wings of gold spread over the vast arena of the Pacific Ocean, from Hawaii southwest to Santa Cruz and the Coral Sea, northwest to Tokyo and more than 5,000 miles due west as far as Saigon. *(Map from National Archives)*

Jim Pearce, assigned to VF-18, led a division (four fighters) near Okinawa when eighteen Japanese twin-engine Betty bombers headed toward the U.S. fleet. Pearce and his mates helped knock all of the enemy aircraft down. *(Photograph from Jim Pearce)*

Jim Pearce (far left) celebrated with (left to right) Chili Crawford, G. C. Johnson, and "Windy" Winfield after their squadron, VF-18, helped destroy all eighteen Japanese twin-engine Betty bombers attempting to attack the U.S. fleet off Okinawa. *(Photograph from Jim Pearce)*

Bob Murray, a member of VF-29, stationed on the light aircraft carrier *Cabot,* shot down 10.33 planes (a shared credit on one) and claimed six probables in the air and seven destroyed on the ground. He earned a Silver Star, three Distinguished Flying Crosses, and five Air Medals. *(Photograph from Bob Murray)*

"The faults of the TBF/Hellcat combination were identical to the flaws found in the RAF experiment. The TBF, like its RAF Havoc counterpart, although it also had the advantage of radar, lacked speed, fire power and maneuverability, all three of which were built into the Hellcat and Hurricane. . . . Having missed this point, the Navy reasoned: send an Avenger out to find the enemy and give it a Hellcat on either wing to help out when the shooting starts."

After practicing, O'Hare and his Bat Team had gone on one actual mission but never contacted any intruders. On the night of November 26, 1943, the *Enterprise* scrambled two sections of three planes. O'Hare, who was afflicted with a severe head cold that might have grounded someone else, and his wingman, Ensign Warren "Andy" Skon, left the deck first at 6:00 P.M. Lieutenant Commander John E. Phillips, CO of VT-6, with more than 1,000 hours of instrument flight, then took off in his radar-equipped Avenger. Lieutenant (j.g) Hazen Rand, a graduate of Massachusetts Institute of Technology and the Navy's own Airborne Radar School, operated the controls for the homing device. In the TBF's ball turret, Aviation Ordnanceman First Class Alvin B. Kernan kept an eye out for anyone trying to attack them from the rear.

The fighter director signaled a heading for the bogey. There was still a bit of daylight, which would allow a purely visual interception if the enemy could be found. By the time Phillips had joined up with the two fighters, darkness was beginning to creep over the sea. According to Odell, the *Enterprise* reported to O'Hare that he was within a mile of the bogey, but neither O'Hare nor Skon saw anything. Phillips flew in their vicinity, but he could not see them nor they him. His radar scope flashed the movements of a Japanese plane, but the image kept disappearing.

"As the end of an hour," wrote Odell, who drew on Edward Stafford's *The Big E*, "the *Enterprise* FDO reported O'Hare's two-plane element 'in the midst of many bogeys' but had also reported 'no contact.' Their only hope of locating the target lay in joining up with Phillips. The FDO steered the Hellcats within a few miles of the Avenger. But Phillips was busy. Rand had finally locked onto a bogey. Flying entirely on instruments, Phillips closed on the enemy. The blip on Rand's scope moved down the face of the tube and crossed the range circle. Two miles . . . a mile and a half . . . one mile. At the mile mark, Phillips looked up from the dimly red-lighted gauges and searched the darkness ahead. He could make out the flickering blue flame from exhaust stacks and added a little throttle to close. His eyes swept back and forth between his instruments and the engine outline ahead while Rand switched to a larger scope scale. He kept calling out ranges over the intercom.

"Phillips and Rand were working as a true night fighter crew now," wrote Odell. "At 400 yards, Phillips could make out the dark shape of a Betty bomber. His altitude was 1,200 feet. He was in nearly level flight closing at 190 knots. His two fixed .50 calibers were armed. At 200 yards Phillips held the trigger down and bored in to 50 yards. Fires began to burn along the dark wings. He pulled up and to the left, leveling off as Kernan in his ball turret fired down over the starboard side into the burning plane. Phillips lifted his eyes from his instruments and looked around. To his amazement, he saw tracers lancing through the sky coming from both sides ahead, none directed at him. In the surprise and confusion he had caused, enemy bombers were shooting at one another."

Three miles to the northeast, O'Hare and Skon saw a burning object fall into the sea, spreading a pool of fire that burned on for half an hour. They turned toward it and the TBF, still hoping to join up. Rand had found another bogey a few miles south. This time, because his night vision had deteriorated due to the flash of his tracers and the light of the burning Betty, Phillips did not see the enemy until he was in to three quarters of a mile away. Rand's instructions to Phillips over the intercom were interrupted by O'Hare's voice: "Phil, I figure we're about a mile to starboard of you. Can you turn on recognition lights to help us join up?"

Odell wrote, "Philips answered, his eyes still on the enemy shape ahead, 'I've got another one of the bastards in sight, Butch. Don't like to use lights, but I'll flash a couple of times for you.'

"The Avenger recognition lights flashed, alerting the Betty, which banked abruptly left and then right again with Phillips following like a wingman on an aerobatic team and continued to close. At 200 yards, in a gentle turn, Phillips opened fire and hung on for almost a minute until the Betty began to burn. It dropped toward the sea and must have landed nearly flat because it left a narrow streak of fire on the surface for a long time with bright red flames like the first Betty. Kernan fired a burst at another blacked-out enemy plane crossing under the Avenger's tail.

"O'Hare and Skon were close enough to see Kernan's tracers. They closed in at once to help. With no targets in sight for the moment Philips turned on his navigation lights, and on order from the

FDO, began a left-hand orbit at 1,200 feet to facilitate the rendezvous. The Hellcats also lit up, hesitantly, because of the possibility of enemy planes nearby and slid in toward the TBF. Skon was on O'Hare's left wing. The torpedo plane was to the left and ahead of the two fighters, so Skon was elected to take Phillips' left wing and O'Hare his right. Skon slid under the Avenger's tail, taking up a position about a hundred feet to the left and slightly below. O'Hare moved in to fly in the right wing position. The shifts were made with a minimum of radio communication. Rand and Kernan heard none of it; both remained on the intercom circuit.

"With O'Hare still some 300 feet out of position something went terribly wrong. Kernan in the TBF's ball turret opened fire. Skon thought the tracers passed between his plane and O'Hare's. Kernan reported that he fired at another unlighted plane which appeared near Skon and then crossed over near O'Hare. Whatever happened, five to ten seconds after Kernan ceased firing, Skon saw O'Hare's plane with its lights still on slide down and to the left. He thought Butch was making a run on an enemy below in the vicinity of the burning wreckage of the two downed Bettys, and dutifully tried to follow him down, but O'Hare's Hellcat lost altitude so fast that Skon did not see it after the first few seconds. Kernan thought he saw a parachute blossom in the night. Reluctantly, and with difficulty, Skon rejoined the TBF. The two planes circled the area for forty-five minutes, calling O'Hare by radio and providing a good navigational fix on the position for rescue purposes. Admiral [Arthur] Radford dispatched a destroyer which searched all night.

"At first daylight . . . six planes from the *U.S.S. Enterprise* and a rescue PBY criss-crossed the calm, clear sea and found nothing. No one knows what happened to Butch O'Hare. He could have been killed by Kernan's .50-caliber guns. But lighted up in the midst of the enemy he could conceivably have been caught by non-tracer fire from a darkened Betty or his head cold could have pushed him into vertigo at the moment of rendezvous." Another suggested explanation is that O'Hare flew so low he might have dragged a wingtip in the water.

Sometime later, Alex Vraciu spoke with John Phillips, subsequently lost in a raid on Truk. Vraciu understood from Phillips that a fourth plane had tried to join up with the three Americans, causing Kernan to open fire. "Apparently," said Vraciu, "Butch got caught in the crossfire." Whatever the cause, his loss underlined the perils of night missions.

Distraught when he heard the news, Vraciu said, "When I found out on the *Essex* that he was killed, and I heard it was a Betty that did it, I did tell my wingman, Willie Callan, 'I'm going to get ten of those bastards! Ten Bettys!' I was only able to get a total of five. It made a *big* [his emphasis] difference to me. Between the vow on Butch and Pearl Harbor, I think that probably was the biggest single motivator—driving force—in my life as to why I preferred to be out there rather than back home. I'd rather be in combat."

The bloody struggles to subdue the garrisons on Makin and Tarawa notwithstanding, the Navy stepped up its campaign for the next objective, the Marshall Islands, a chain that stretched 150 to 500 miles northwest of the Gilberts. VF-5's skipper, Charles Crommelin, led a raid on Mili, one of the Marshalls closest to Makin. As Crommelin dived on a Mitsubishi bomber on the ground, a 40-mm antiaircraft shell exploded in his cockpit, knocking out most of the F6F's instruments. Crommelin himself sustained serious wounds in his head and foot, losing all vision in his left eye and retaining minimal sight in the right. His right wrist was fractured, and he was bleeding from his mouth and chest.

Though the canopy had not shattered, it was frosted over by multitudinous cracks. With his blurred vision, the only way he could see was to open the canopy and peer out the side of the cockpit. Others in VF-5 surrounded him in an effort to lead him back. Ensign Murray "Tim" Tyler flew alongside, talking to Crommelin to keep him conscious and encourage him. In spite of his pain, the battered commander kept his badly crippled ship airborne for 120 miles back to the *Yorktown*. Duncan happened to be standing on the catwalk and watched Crommelin come in. He said, "[I] never saw a better approach and landing during [my] entire naval career. After landing, in a magnificent gesture he taxied his aircraft out of the arresting gear and forward of the barriers to its parking spot. He tried to climb out of the aircraft and walk away. Only then did he collapse."

Crommelin returned to the United States for a long period of hospitalization and recuperation. Coincidentally, only a few hours after Charles's narrow escape from death, his brother John, aboard the carrier *Liscombe Bay*, bolted stark naked from the shower and went over the side as the flattop succumbed to a torpedo from a Japanese sub. He too survived.

TWELVE

ACES AND ADVANCES

As December 1943 unfolded, the Navy brass intensified the operations for their next objective, the Marshall Islands, with Operation Flintlock the code name for the invasion. The major air base for the Marshalls was on Kwajalein, and the anchorage at Kwajalein reportedly held a number of ships. Six carriers, split into two task forces, sailed to within 125 miles of the objectives, approaching from the northeast, a surprise direction to the defenders. In the predawn darkness of December 4, the flattops swung into the wind and launched their combat air patrols. Under a ceiling of fighter wings, the dive-bombers, torpedo bombers, and their escorts now lifted off for the journey to Kwajalein. A secondary strike was scheduled for Wotje. Following up on attacks upon Mille and Jaluit, heavier salvos from the fast carriers struck the Kwajalein atoll, which consisted of an island by that name along with two smaller ones, Roi and Namur.

The script called for a batch of Hellcats to work over a bomber-laden field on Roi. But Japanese camouflage, according to naval historian Samuel Eliot Morison, befuddled the attackers, who lacked photographs to guide them. The damage inflicted amounted to three bombers and sixteen fighters, but many more aircraft stored in revetments escaped notice. Dauntlesses and Avengers from the *Essex* and the *Lexington* hunted vessels in the lagoon. A munitions transport disintegrated in a tornado of fire and smoke. A light cruiser wobbled from a hit that wrecked her rudder, but most of the Japanese ships maneuvered smartly to avoid injury.

Teams from the *Enterprise* and *Yorktown* hammered another naval site. They sank some small freighters, damaged a light cruiser, and wiped out eighteen float planes at a seaplane base. The overall results fell short of expectations, although an estimated fifty-five enemy planes had been destroyed.

While the approach to Kwajalein temporarily fooled the Japanese, interceptors soon scrambled. They were in the air to meet the incoming air armada near the targets, and ground installations commenced vigorous ack-ack. Boogie Hoffman, leading a division from VF-5, encountered an observation plane. Hoffman swiftly disposed of it, even though all but one of his six machine guns jammed. The fighters then descended upon the ships, shore installations, and antiaircraft positions in the Kwajalein area. When a cargo ship spewed shells from its battery at Bob Duncan as he finished his run on the vessel, he returned for a second strike, this time aiming for the antiaircraft position. His bullets exploded the ammunition stores for the guns, and the ship itself blew up and sank. The squadron, however, lost Lieutenant Herb Gill, who was last observed parachuting into the lagoon after his F6F had apparently been hit. He was never seen again, nor was there ever word about his fate.

On the return trip to the *Yorktown*, VF-5 met big trouble. The four-plane division under Hoffman, climbing through 4,000 feet, suddenly encountered a host of Zeros—as many as twenty—diving on them from out of the sun. The post-action report said, "This was a first line team of Japanese fighter pilots and they knew exactly what they were doing. From our intelligence, we believe that they were a shore-based squadron of Navy pilots. Six Zeros positioned themselves on each of our two-plane sections, with two of their planes always firing in section on each of our sections. When we headed toward them to counter their attack, they would make a violent pullout and climb at a sixty-degree angle back into the reserve force above. Two more would feed off from the reserve group and take position for attack on each side. Then two more would come at us.

"Our Hellcats went into a protective 'Thach Weave,' each section (Hoffman and Duncan; [Karl "Si"] Satterfield and [Denzil] Merrill) scissoring back and forth to protect the other section. It was a case of hit them with all you had, reverse and do the same thing over again. We were giving them everything we had with no quarter asked on either side. There wasn't time to see what happened to the enemy aircraft we hit. We would have given anything for more altitude to work with and Boogie would have given ten years of his life for another gun (he only had one gun operating and his gun sight was out of commission). Duncan's radio transmitter wasn't working and although he originally spotted the Zeros sometime before the others he had to fly forward of the division and indicate by hand signals that the Zeros were dropping their belly tanks and getting ready to attack.

"The attack continued for several minutes with the Japanese squadron commander utilizing his aircraft to the optimum advantage. Evidently, he figured out a counter attack to the Thach Weave. The Japanese sections began to feint an attack and when we would initiate our counter turn into them they would zoom up into the reserve group. Two more would catch us on the outside of our turn before we could get back for our other section to take them off. They caught Duncan on the outside of one of these turns and 'stitched' his left wing with bullets from the outer wing tip at the leading edge back through the entire length of the wing into the cockpit, just aft of the armor plate, and out the starboard side. These were all highside approaches and if one could have become completely detached and to one side of the action as an impartial observer he would have seen the epitome of enemy aerial fighter attack; it was a pure and simple, graceful and beautiful aerial display of the best in fighter attacks.

"This continued until they caught Si Satterfield and Den Merrill on the outside of their weave where they hit Si's plane setting it on fire. The last observation of Si was with both wing tanks burning, flames reaching half way down the fuselage, apparently out of control. However, just before he went into the water, it looked like he was trying to pull it out. He hit the water at almost a flat angle. Maybe with a little more altitude he could have set it in.

"Why they didn't shoot us all down is a mystery. We would have destroyed them if the situation had been reversed. The one thing we did learn was that they weren't as good gunners as we are."

Other VF-5 members ran a gauntlet of hostile fighters. Crommelin's replacement as squadron boss, Lieutenant Commander Ed Owen, rushed to aid a fellow Hellcat beset by two Zeros on his tail. Owen picked off one, but the action steered him near a cloud layer housing a passel of Zeros. They jointly doused him with shot and shell. With one aileron gone and no control of the other, his instruments shot away, one wheel hanging down, and oil leaking from his engine, Owen crawled to a position over the task force. His engine then conked out and Owen bailed. A destroyer gathered him from the sea.

Among those on the scene for this Kwajalein venture was VF-6 with Alex Vraciu. The squadron had remained on the *Independence* as it labored to Funafuti for repairs after the torpedo hit. Following several days in port, the carrier off-loaded the Hellcats and the pilots flew in stages to a Tarawa airstrip.

"We arrived at Tarawa," recalled Vraciu, "where they were still shooting at us. At night they'd come out of their caves. We were supposed to sleep in our planes that night, but, hell, shooting was still going on from time to time. So we all huddled in a tent as low as we could get. During the day, I roamed around, and the Seabees and Marines would tell you, 'Don't touch anything! It may be booby-trapped.'

"I learned that they used to knock the gold teeth out of the jaws of some of the dead Japs that were around—there were plenty of them. I was given a souvenir gold tooth, and later I had the dentist on the ship drill a hole in it, clean it up. I had it hanging on a gold necklace and gave it to my niece when I came stateside. Are we ghoulish or are we not?"

With their usual home laid up, VF-6 received assignment to the *Essex*. But according to Vraciu, the command on the carrier favored its regular air group. "This," said Vraciu, "was where I really tended to dislike combat air patrols, because, obviously, we were only guests—visitors—on the *Essex*, and they had their full complement of pilots. Naturally they got all the action. We never got to hit anything on the shore or in the air."

The Kwajalein assault unfortunately left an abundant number of enemy torpedo planes unscathed. Even as the Navy carried out its mission against Wotje and then recovered the planes, the surviving Japanese stalked the task forces. The first predators arrived before dark, and American planes splashed several and broke up the attack. But under cover of night, twin-engine Betty bombers and torpedo planes harassed the ships, which still lacked night fighter capacity—O'Hare had been lost only a few weeks earlier. While shipboard anti-aircraft downed a couple of planes, one unleashed a torpedo that killed nine sailors, wounded thirty-five, disabled the *Lexington*'s steering mechanism, and jammed the rudder. Emergency repairs enabled the carrier to steer while she fended off further insults through her own antiaircraft fire.

The temporary loss of the *Lexington* did not seriously diminish the strength of the naval operations, however. Rear Admiral Marc A. Mitscher now commanded Task Force Fifty-eight, a fast carrier fleet broken into four separate groups. His armada included six big carriers and six light ones, backed up by eight fast battleships, six cruisers, and thirty-six destroyers. Mitscher's air arm featured about 700 planes.

Lieutenant Commander Harvey Feilbach from VF-60, following some experiments, persuaded the brass that the F6F-3 could carry and drop bombs without compromising its role as a fighter. The so-called oil slicks, the *Suwannee, Chenango,* and *Sangamon,* converted to carriers from tanker hulls, subsequently traded in some of their torpedo bombers and dive-bombers for more Hellcats. Instead of operating a dozen fighters, the flattops boosted their complements to twenty-two. Standard procedure mandated that the 100-pound bombs immediately be jettisoned in the face of aerial combat.

Another versatility experiment, a precursor to napalm bombs, flopped. Several pilots from VF-16, flying at low level, targeted large buildings with their belly tanks, releasing them just short of the mark. When they smashed into structures or the ground, the tanks saturated the area with 150 gallons of gasoline. Tracers then ignited the volatile puddles. But examination after the missions discovered that release of the belly tanks while traveling at high speed severely damaged the fuel lines, and this pre-napalm type of weapon was discarded.

By the end of January, VF-6 had left the *Essex* for a more permanent berth aboard the *Intrepid,* and the squadron engaged in waves of knockout punches aimed at Kwajalein. "I was not scheduled for the first two flights," said Vraciu, "because they were rotating the good hops—the early ones. Mine happened to be the third of the day—a 10 A.M. mission to Kwajalein—a target CAP over the Roi airfield.

"The first two strikes ran into some air action, but I wasn't too hopeful of any action continuing until it was our turn. I hadn't had a chance to see a Jap in my gunsight for some time. Arriving at the Roi airfield, there did not seem to be any enemy planes airborne, so we prepared to strafe targets of opportunity—most probably parked aircraft. I sighted a nice large, fat transport on the field and I pointed down toward the airfield to my wingman, Tom Hall. I had hardly started my dive, when, all of a sudden, I saw a string of Bettys flying low over the field. They had just arrived from Lord-knows-where. I immediately stopped my dive and started to position my section for a high-side run on the tailender. I remember thinking, 'My prayers are being answered.' I doubt whether he had even seen us.

"I got into position and I had just a perfect run—a flat, high-side run—and he was flying straight and level. I fired out at 300 yards, and I normally didn't fire that far away. Perhaps I was a little anxious. But it just seemed right, and I had the perfect shot. I barely touched the trigger, and he started flaming around the starboard wing root and almost immediately crashed into the sea.

"I looked up ahead and saw another Betty flying at about 300 feet. He dove down to 100 feet and I came in on his stern. On my first burst the port engine and wing exploded, and the Betty crashed into the lagoon. I probably caught a round in my hydraulic system from his tail-gunner because it affected my ability to fire at the next plane. But this one made number two. Just before he crashed, I saw bodies dropping out of the plane into the water—they were down that low. I guess it was probably burning so badly that they had no choice.

"Again I looked up ahead—two more in line. I headed after the nearest one and Tom Hall pursued the farthest. The Betty that I was approaching started turning west, down low on the water, and pouring on the coal. I pulled up abeam—out of range—and I could see the tail-gunner already shooting at me. I had to be respectful of that 20 mm cannon—that stinger—back there. I did what I had practiced against friendly planes [while carrying squadron mail] going from island to island in the Hawaiians. But this time it was for keeps! I pulled up alongside, intent on making high-deflection runs from one side to the other, trying always to be on the move. I made a run with no visible effect. On the second run, I found that only one of my guns was firing. I continued to make runs, using flat high-sides, with the Betty jinking and turning in toward me. On one run my guns failed to fire at all. Even with constant charging, only one of my guns was operative for the rest of the attack.

"I'd get out about one or two rounds, and the firing would stop. It was exasperating for me because I could see his damned tracers heading my way practically each time I made a pass. But I didn't want him to get away. I would have chased him back to Eniwetok [a Marshall atoll about 325 miles northwest of Kwajalein]. I think I made about seven, eight runs. I don't know whether I was just lucky, but after my last run, the Betty nosed toward the sea and crashed from an altitude of about eighty feet. I believe the Betty's pilot must have been hit.

"I returned to the carrier. I had 'notched' three. They were all Bettys, and that made me feel good—really good. I thought, Okay! Good start on my vow! [to avenge O'Hare]." The three confirmed victories, added to his earlier two, established Vraciu as an ace.

Unfortunately, his wingman, Tom Hall, one of the handful trained for a Bat Team, was killed the very next day during a predawn launch. "He was spotted ahead of me," said Vraciu, "and took off ahead of me. His left wheel seemed to hit a stanchion off the bow of the *Intrepid*. His belly tank blew up in the collision. His plane ended up in a fireball off the port side."

The Japanese knew the invasion of Kwajalein was imminent. They attempted to reinforce the atoll by loading troops from some of the adjacent islands aboard assault boats similar to the American Higgins. Several divisions from VF-5, carrying out CAP over Kwajalein, fell upon these hapless small craft, jammed to the gunwales with soldiers. According to Bob Duncan, the merciless strafing sank the assault boats, and those men not killed by bullets drowned because of their heavy gear. He said, "The carnage was so extensive the Japanese soldiers' blood colored the water of the lagoon. Americans would have halted the launches and waited until dark, but the Japanese, with their suicidal bent, continued to send wave after wave." Rather than questing for self-destruction, more likely the Japanese command, as was often observed during the war, rigidly adhered to orders even when circumstances indicated an urgent need for a change.

James Ramage, who as a boy had seen his family's Iowa farm auctioned off, chose naval aviation after drinking in the spectacle of Admiral Richard E. Byrd, the polar explorer. Ramage remarked about Byrd's "white service uniform and I recall he wore those wings of gold. I thought, pretty neat." Ramage, a 1939 USNA graduate, had qualified as a dive-bomber pilot after a tour in the "black-shoe Navy." For his first combat assignment, he drew Scouting-Bombing Ten on the *Enterprise* and the Kwajalein operation. Whether one flew recon or attack missions, the plane used was the same SBD.

"Our first strike was against Taroa, an island in the Marshalls, and one of those so-called unsinkable aircraft carriers the Japanese bragged so much about. It had crossed runways. It had various facilities, but the unsinkable aircraft carriers had one problem, they don't move. We could concentrate our ten or twelve carriers on these guys one at a time and it was no match. The fighter sweep was to take off pre-dawn and the strike group which I led was to take off at just about first light. The planes were all manned. The fighters took off directly into a rain squall and it was probably the fourth and fifth of our fighters that had a mid-air collision with a tremendous explosion. It wasn't very reassuring.

"But we went in and found the target very easily. By that time the fighters had knocked down anything that was in the air. My specific target was a torpedo storage area. I think I got a hit or close to it. We did a good job and came back."

Ramage flew four strikes over Kwajalein, which was invaded on February 1 in support of the Army's 7th Infantry Division. (The Marines captured Roi and Namur.) "We had people on the ground with the Army and this was all handled through the command ship. As the airborne coordinator [a post held by Ramage on occasion] you would dig out targets of opportunity and report back to the command ship what you saw, and if there was anything needed. By the end of this time [the island was declared secured on February 6] we had so many planes in the air that you just couldn't use them all.

"When those battleships and cruisers and the air had been [working over Kwajalein] for four or five days got through with that place, it looked like the moon. It was plowed ground. I don't think there was a stick of anything standing. It looked just completely beaten up. We had certainly learned our lesson at Tarawa [the prelanding barrage had been curtailed] where we lost so many Marines and rather than underdo it this time, they certainly overdid it."

Ramage pointed out that earlier, as at Midway, the carriers had loaded three attack aircraft—dive- and torpedo bombers—for each fighter. "Later on, when we re-formed," said he, "we had to get more fighters on the carriers because we simply did not have enough to escort our strike groups into the target properly." He explained, "We had a base element generally of twelve dive-bombers and six torpedo planes and twelve to sixteen fighters overhead, depending upon what the opposition. The procedure as we approached the targets the low combat air patrol, which was weaving just over the bombers, would start in to the target just before the bombers. The bombers would then go in, and the torpedo planes simultaneously would pull out to either side and do a spiral and come on in low for their torpedo attack or from about 5,000 feet in the event they were going to drop bombs. We could get the full strike group on and off the target in less than two minutes' time. It was quite a devastating shot. Of course, the fighters would strafe ahead and then the high cover, providing there was nothing up there, would come on down and strafe afterwards."

Kwajalein provided the venue for two newcomers to combat, the light carrier *Cabot* and Air Group Thirty-one. Arthur Hawkins, a Texan who had enlisted at age twenty and had earned his wings and commission on New Year's Day, 1943, became a pilot with VF-31, the fighter squadron. "My first combat hop," said Hawkins, "actually started out easy. We had started flying combat air patrol on the way to the Marshalls. These were considered combat hops because the Japanese planes might come out to meet you. My first [actual] combat was supporting the landings going ashore at Kwajalein." The addition of ordnance to the Hellcats had quickly progressed beyond the small packages of explosives promoted by Harvey Feilbach. Hawkins reported, "With an F6F they could put 250- or 500-pound bombs on. We would be loaded with 500-pounders and drop them, then strafe as necessary. [We were] assisting the troops on shore, and covering them while they were going in. We'd assist them under our grid system."

The escort carriers *Suwannee* and *Chenango* added their offensive power through Air Groups Sixty and Thirty-five. Fighters and bombers struck at gun emplacements, ammo dumps, radio facilities, barracks, and other components of the enemy installations. The concentration of aircraft in the limited airspace over the atoll led to casualties in the air. A TBF from the *Suwannee* chewed off the tail of another torpedo bomber with its propeller. Some crewmen were rescued after both made watery landings, but a pilot and two gunners were lost.

A flight from the carrier *Belleau Wood* by VF-24 hit an ammunition dump. A section leader set it ablaze, but when his wingman followed close behind, his Hellcat was caught in a blast that tore off part of his wing. He spun into the lagoon at high speed. Recommendations were drafted for additional spacing between strafers over ammo stores.

The base and harbor at Rabaul continued to pose a threat to the Allied forces operating in the southwestern and central Pacific waters. On January 25, the Japanese had reinforced their potential by flying in from Truk, a bastion in the Mariana Islands, a number of dive-bombers previously housed on carriers. During the intense campaign against Rabaul, the top Marine ace, Lieutenant Robert Hansen, with twenty-five victories, crashed after a strafing run. Major Gregory

"Pappy" Boyington, with twenty-two planes shot down, was himself knocked out of the sky near Rabaul and taken prisoner.

On February 19, Lieutenant Commander Roger Hedrick led the VF-17 Corsairs from their field at Bougainville in a sweep over Rabaul that targeted military installations. The twenty F4Us took off at about 8:00 A.M. to accompany the bombers and cruised at 170 knots toward the target. Ira Kepford, now a lieutenant, was flying with Ensign Don McQueen as his wingman. When McQueen developed engine problems, he turned back. Ordinarily, the rules of the game said that one never flew solo, and that meant Kepford should also abort the mission. However, under the circumstances, McQueen was unlikely to be accosted by hostile aircraft, and the flight leader agreed that Kepford could stay with the bombers, at least until they approached the target area.

The former Northwestern blocking back dutifully began to head for home at the appropriate moment. However, as he passed over tiny Buka Island, he noticed an aircraft far below, just above the water and coming in his direction. Kepford dived down, and when he opened up with his machine guns, the enemy float plane flew right into the machine-gun bullets. Kepford pulled out of his dive, and as he looked back, the smoking Japanese machine crashed into the sea.

Kepford resumed his trip to Bougainville only to see a large formation of Zekes blocking his way to the VF-17 base. He immediately radioed Squadron Commander Hedrick, alerting him to the presence of the fighters, and then tried to hide by dropping down near the water. However, a quartet of Zekes peeled off and dived on him. The leader aimed a burst at the F4U, but in his eagerness he overshot Kepford, affording the American an opportunity for a deadly counterpunch. The Zeke fell off into the water.

The three remaining fighters now boxed Kepford in, and he saw tracers streaming past. Furthermore, his course now took him away from Bougainville. His only chance lay in outrunning his pursuit. The Corsair engine was equipped with a water injection system that could increase the aircraft's speed for a few minutes. (A similar mechanism subsequently was installed in Hellcats.) Kepford resorted to this emergency power, and his plane surged forward. The enemy, however, continued to hang on, more tracers whizzed by, and something slammed into the rear of the aircraft.

He had no opportunity to turn because that would bring him directly into the firing line of the foe, but with his added speed from the water injection he began to stretch the space between him and the Zekes. Kepford gambled on a couple of feints that induced the pursuers to lose more ground when they executed changes of direction. Two of them lagged well behind, but one continued the chase. The two planes skimmed the waves. Finally, with his engine now in danger of overheating, Kepford threw the Corsair into an extremely violent turn that nearly blacked out his vision. When the enemy pilot again began to fire, Kepford yanked his F4U into another abrupt change of direction, stalling. The Japanese fighter sought to come about and hold his advantage, but his left wing touched the water and the Zeke cartwheeled into the water. An exhausted Kepford limped home, the gull wing of his Corsair full of holes and both flaps and elevators similarly perforated.

Meanwhile, Hedrick and company, along with fighters from other units, feasted upon the Rabaul-based aircraft, taking a heavy toll on the shrinking forces available to defend the base. Australian troops seized Green Island, only 100 miles from Rabaul, shutting off further reinforcement. After the February 19 debacle, the airplanes stationed at Rabaul fled to Truk, to bolster that island's defenses as the American offensive now threatened the Marianas.

In fact, three days before the last big attack on Rabaul, an all-fighter sweep bashed the facilities and aircraft stationed on Truk. Altogether, seventy-two F6F-3s from five different carriers—the *Essex*, *Bunker Hill*, *Enterprise*, *Yorktown*, and *Intrepid*—set a course for Truk, less than 100 miles from the flattops.

The Truk atoll consisted of a number of islands—Moen, Dublon, Uman, Tol, Fefan, and seventy-eight lesser-known ones—entirely surrounded by coral reefs with only five narrow openings, a most forbidding target for an amphibious invasion. The lagoon surrounding the atoll spread over 500 square miles.

Alex Vraciu exulted, "Our squadron's first fighter sweep, boy, we all loved it—just the idea of it. Being on the *Intrepid*, we were on a large carrier, so we got a bigger piece of the action. What was significant was the apprehension that everybody seemed to have about the place. It was a big unknown bastion. Some people said, 'My God! Truk!' One of the stories that came out afterwards was that Admiral Mitscher one time had said, 'The only thing we knew about Truk was in the *National Geographic*.'

"Apparently, a Marine Liberator [PB4Y4] several weeks before staged a daring high-altitude reconnaissance flight over Truk and furnished some information and pictures on the harbor. There were a lot of ships in there. Our main purpose was to take control of the air because it was supposed to be pretty heavily loaded with planes. They were using it as a staging area for other operations. We hoped to catch some carriers and support ships in there, also. Our mission was the destruction of enemy aircraft in the air over Truk Atoll and the airfields at Moen, Eten and Param Islands."

The flyers with VF-5 held similarly dire anxieties about Truk. When the squadron received word on the objective, according to then Lieutenant (j.g.) Bob Duncan's account, "As one pilot put it, 'My first reaction was to jump over the side and start swimming back to Pearl Harbor.' " For this operation, the Navy slotted only its biggest and fastest attack carriers and left the escort flattops behind.

Lieutenant Commander William "Killer" Kane, who had been rescued after being shot down over the ocean in October 1942, led the VF-6 contingent from the *Intrepid*. Kane's group held a rendezvous with the Hellcats from the *Essex* and then proceeded toward the atoll. From an altitude of 1,000 feet the group traveled about 45 miles and then started to climb. Truk hove into view, and the two squadrons formed a circle to gain more height. Below them they saw VF-10, the low cover, and they presumed that VF-18 occupied the skies above them. Around 8:00 A.M., the fighters maneuvered into position for a strafing attack on the Moen Island airfield and its bombers.

On the ground, two Bettys rolled for takeoff while other aircraft remained spotted around the base. Antiaircraft fire signaled the enemy's awareness of the American presence. Ten of the VF-6 fighters pushed over and spiraled toward their targets. The last two planes in the formation, piloted by Vraciu and Ensign Lou Little, were about to follow. Vraciu suddenly noticed they had company, unfriendly aircraft that intended to interrupt the Americans.

"I remembered to look back over my shoulder," said Vraciu. "It was a good thing I did. It may have saved a few of our lives. I tallyhoed but the others in our flight had already proceeded far down toward the airfield. The leader of the enemy planes, by then known to be Zekes by Lou and me, and his group started to head downward. I could see the enemy leader was already firing by the light flashes from his guns.

"I turned my section into the attack, getting bursts fired at their leader, causing him to break off his attack and head downward. From that moment on, there were enemy planes all around our Hellcats. We had built up enough speed—a good 250 knots—so that when we pulled up in a steep chandelle [a crack-the-whip-like maneuver to transfer some of the excess speed of a dive, enhancing the rate of climb] and then rolled over and dove back down on a Zeke that tried to stay on our tail, the Zeke pulled up into a climbing turn, but spun out at the top. We jumped him, but had to let him dive on down because of the other Zekes preparing to strike from above. By scissoring [Thach Weave] with friendly planes, we were able to work all the enemy fighters down to our level and below.

"Until this time," said Vraciu, "we hadn't had much opportunity to press home the attack. From then on the picture changed. We noticed that the Japs weren't reluctant to attack, but once they were cornered, they'd dive steeply toward the water or cloud cover. We began to follow them down. I was able to follow three planes in this manner and set them on fire. All of them hit the water inside Truk Atoll."

It was a free-for-all with a frenzy of gyrations punctuated by bursts from machine guns and 20-mm cannons. "There were dog fights all over the place," recalled Vraciu. "I even saw one of our Hellcats shoot another Hellcat down. It was a *great* deflection shot but . . . One of our guys just shot first before being sure and this other poor pilot was forced to parachute out. In the course of the action, I saw a number of Japanese parachutes in the air."

Lieutenant Ed Owens from VF-5 described the scene as a "a Hollywood war." Said Duncan, "The two sides were almost evenly matched with dogfights, smoke, flame and burning, hurtling aircraft all over the sky." Lieutenant Elwood "Smoky" Stover, a recruit to VF-5 after serving earlier with the original Fighting Five aboard the old *Yorktown*, was engaging in his first air-to-air combat since he had knocked down four enemy planes eighteen months earlier. Stover, in fact, according to Duncan, had never actually received orders to VF-5. Instead, he had been aboard the *Yorktown* as a combat information center officer. But he had pleaded with everyone for a chance to fly with VF-5 and earn a rating as an ace.

When the section with Duncan and Stover approached Truk, the former, as Stover's wingman, received a serious hit in his engine, just as he arrived over the target. Oil and smoke poured from his engine, and he retired back to the *Yorktown*. Just as he taxied out of the arresting gear and across the barriers, the engine seized up completely due to oil starvation.

Behind Stover and Duncan, Denzil Merrill led a second section as they dived upon enemy vessels fleeing the anchorage. Flak thrown up by the warships smashed into Stover's F6F-3. He pulled up while Merrill pulled alongside to inspect the damage. Merrill advised Stover that his Wildcat was grievously injured. The pilot bailed out, splashing down just beyond the lagoon. He inflated his life raft and flashed Merrill a thumbs-up. Merrill remained overhead, keeping an eye upon the downed flyer while trying to call in a rescue ship. But Stover was never recovered.

Messages sent by Stover before he was forced to abandon his plane alerted Admiral Raymond Spruance to the deployment of the enemy ships. A fast surface attack force, led by a pair of battleships and two cruisers, steamed at full speed to intercept the Japanese. Simultaneously, the *Yorktown* mounted a mission to slow or even destroy some of the vessels fleeing Truk until Spruance's heavyweights could reach the area. Fighters from VF-5 accompanied the bombers.

Lieutenant John Gray led one division of F6F-3s, Lieutenant Ted Schofield another, and Bob Duncan a third, all of which stayed with the bombers until they were over the lagoon. Then the first two flights of Hellcats strafed the ships, diverting their attention from the bomber runs. Duncan's batch flew high cover against a possible enemy foray. A fourth division of fighters flew cover for bombers seeking to pummel any vessels that had left the lagoon.

From an altitude of 14,000 feet, Duncan and company saw ten to fifteen Zeros coming out of the sun at 20,000 feet. Gray and Schofield heard the tallyho from Duncan, followed by "Get up here fast. We have more than we can handle." While the F6F-3s hurried to aid their besieged squadron mates, Duncan's wingman reeled from a 20-mm shell that had smashed into his elevator. In the melee that followed, Duncan's division shot down eight Zeros. The leader himself added four to his two previous knockdowns, establishing him as an ace. Six others from the squadron emerged with double victories, one a triple, though several had to be content with a single kill. Schofield not only destroyed two in the air, but in one action, the enemy pilot tried a forced landing on an airstrip. Schofield followed him in, lacing the crippled plane with more fire until one of the wings hit the ground. Totally out of control, it tumbled end over end, careening through a row of parked torpedo planes, sparking a gigantic pyre, and stopping just short of a four-engine aircraft. Schofield, when he returned to the *Yorktown*, in Duncan's words, "complained bitterly" because he could not tack this machine onto his total.

Before they roared up to enter the brawl above them, the ten fighters from the *Intrepid*'s VF-6 stuck to their assignment, making more than forty runs on the Moen airfield planes, a dozen strafings on Param field, and a few blows at a seaplane base. They reported some twenty-four aircraft, including fifteen bombers and eight fighters, exploded and burned.

With its work complete, VF-6 made for the rendezvous area and a return to the *Intrepid*. En route, Vraciu spied a Zero skirting a thin cloud. "I made a pass at him. He promptly headed for a thicker one, and after playing cat-and-mouse with him for a while, I climbed into the sun and let him think I had retired. When I came down on him for the last time from five o'clock above, he never knew what hit him. His wing tank and cockpit exploded." That made four more downed by Vraciu.

"There was one more plane [in which I was] involved. But I let Lou Little have it. I asked him about the fifth when we got back aboard the carrier. Since he got in a good burst on that bird also, I said, 'Okay, you take it.' Some squadrons split up credit for victories on a regular basis but I thought he deserved full-credit for that one. A good wingman often doesn't get all the action or credit he deserves."

Arthur Hawkins, with VF-31 from the *Cabot*, carried out a different sort of mission. "We had a bombing flight. I took in a 1,000-pound bomb on that strike and the bombs were to pit the airfield. They were set for two hours, four hours, nine hours, twelve hours—various time fuses on these bombs. We would take them in and stick them in the runway. Then they would go off just to keep the field from being used."

For this fighter sweep, VF-6 counted eight more enemy planes knocked out, with Lieutenant (j.g.) Chambers scoring the same number as Vraciu. Lieutenant G. C. Bullard, hit by AA fire from a cruiser, crashed in the sea but his companions saw him swimming in his life jacket. He was later rescued by a seaplane. That was the only F6F-3 lost by VF-6 during that morning sweep. When Vraciu landed, the plane captain found two machine-gun bullet holes behind the cockpit.

His day was not over, however. He flew two more missions. "On one we escorted our bombers going out to strike Japanese ships just north of Truk. Memorable was one of their cruisers listing badly—dead in the water. I still cringe a little thinking of how we strafed the hell out of it. Our six .50-calibers were ripping into hundreds of their sailors.

"On another mission that afternoon, I was on a CAP over our forces while a group of our support ships—including a battleship—were deployed to strike a few Japanese combat ships that had escaped out of the North Pass. One of our task force flight missions, flying ahead, mistook our surface [ships] group detachment for Japanese ships and started to align his flight to attack our own ships. Somebody yelled out on the air [radio], 'They're *our* ships, Goddamn it!' Fortunately, a friendly-fire disaster was averted."

Although the fleet escaped an assault by the Navy airmen, at least one pilot succumbed to friendly fire. A formation from VB-6 shadowing portions of the flotilla steaming away from Truk happened to pass over the American warships hot in pursuit of the enemy without incident. After dive-bombers sank one cargo vessel and injured another, they returned by the same route. Lieutenant Paul E. TePas, the leader, radioed his companions that he would advise the battleship *Iowa* of what they had seen. He flew toward the *Iowa*, planning to drop a message. The fire control officer on the battleship recognized TePas as an American and instructed his gun crews to track but not fire. When the dive-bomber was only 100 yards off, a single machine-gun section, apparently misunderstanding the orders, opened up. The bursts were deadly accurate, and the plane turned wing over wing and spun into the water. There were no survivors.

Torpedo Ten, aboard the *Enterprise*, seized the opportunity to put into play an idea originated by the squadron CP, Lieutenant Commander William I. Martin. He believed the latest radars installed in the Avengers could make it possible to carry out low-altitude night attacks. Lieutenant Van Eason commanded the twelve Avengers, each bearing four 500-pounders, which took off after dark, flying low enough to avoid detection by enemy radar. A hospital ship in the lagoon suddenly lit up the sky with flares; their presence was no longer a secret. Antiaircraft spattered the night, but the defenders had no idea of the altitude of the TBFs.

The cockpit radars fingered the ships in the anchorage, and bombs started to fall with telling effectiveness, thirteen direct hits that destroyed eight merchant ships and damaged five, according to author Walter Karig in *Battle Report: The End of the Empire*. The ratio of hits to bombs dropped far surpassed that of the average for daylight expeditions, which exposed aircraft to much more deadly AA. Only in a night foray could the planes have roamed the lagoon at such a low altitude with added accuracy. At that they still endured considerable punishment. One TBF went down, and flak ripped into seven more

VSB-10 was part of the first strike group that followed the early fighter sweep. Jim Ramage remembered, "By the time we got in there, there were a few Zeros around but not enough to bother us. Our strike group was standard size, escorted by probably sixteen fighters. The only problem is that we were down to only two or three SBD squadrons in the fleet at that time. The SB2C had begun to come out by then. We'd get tally-hoed from time to time as Zeros because the SBDs had rounded wingtips and kind of looked like the Zero. I'd have to get on the air and say, 'No, we're your friendly SBDs. Leave us alone,' which they did."

When he flew over the atoll, Ramage said, good bright sunlight lit up the scene. "An ammo ship had just erupted. I understand that a fighter had strafed it and blown himself up at the same time. It was, I think, the biggest explosion I've ever seen—other than the atomic bombs. It was just an enormous blast. As we got into the lagoon area, there must have been forty-five ships in there—unfortunately, only one or two combatants—but it was a good bunch of targets. I picked out the biggest ship which was in there, a tanker, and put our guys on it. We got some hits."

Ramage had spoken of the intense feelings against the Japanese, and an event in the Truk harbor demonstrated the hatred. "There was a hospital ship in there. I'm afraid probably we had banged it up a little bit but it was under way and had two escorts with it. They were smaller than destroyer escorts, probably about PC [patrol craft] size, on either side of it. We had dropped our bombs on other ships on the way out. There was nothing against cleaning out those escorts, so we immediately went to work and chopped them up pretty badly with our forward .50s to the point that both of them were sinking. They had a lot of people in the water, life boats, rafts, people in life jackets. But most of our .50s were out of ammo by that time so I put all the SBDs into a circle and let the rear gunners kill all the rest of them. I don't know how many were in the water. If any of them lived, it wasn't our fault."

The shattering of the Japanese air arm during the Gilbert and Marshall campaigns may have given some Americans a sense of omnipotence. James Ramage said he was unaware of any loss of danger. "I was interested in kicking the hell out of as many Japs as I could possibly get to and I think that was the main desire. There was still a lot of hatred."

While the fighter sweep and the subsequent bomber attacks devastated the Japanese air forces on Truk, the record indicates that a total of 204 enemy planes was destroyed by the carrier aircraft, 127 of them on the ground. By two in the afternoon not a single Japanese airplane appeared in the sky. While the first sortie against Truk went without a fatality for VF-6, later missions cost the Americans. Vraciu mourned, "Our ill-fated night-fighting 'Bat Team' was literally decimated at Truk. Air Group Commander Phillips—flying a Hellcat on an afternoon flight with one of our fighter squadron pilots, John Ogg, never returned to our carrier. We figured that they must have been jumped by enemy planes. Lieutenant James Bridges, of VT-6, and the other torpedo plane Bat Team pilot, dropped his bombs on an enemy ammunition ship anchored in the harbor. A blast of fiery black smoke erupted, in an explosion that blew up the target and his own plane [the incident mentioned by Ramage]. With Tom Hall and the torpedo plane pilots gone, our night-fighter capacity would have been useless to our ship, if the *true* night fighters had not arrived in the fleet on time."

In contrast, only twenty-five U.S. planes were lost, and eight of these occurred because of accidents. More than half of the air crews were saved. VF-9's CO, Lieutenant Commander H. N. Houck, had written a memorandum earlier in which he cited the case of a pilot shot down during a dawn strike. Although the flyer was seen by his companions during the day, there was no specific doctrine that planes stand by until a rescue. When a seaplane finally reached the area, it searched but could not locate the pilot. Houck urged a system that would assign several aircraft to remain in sight of anyone in the water to pinpoint the exact position for a savior.

As they gained experience, the airmen learned to hover over downed flyers, fending off the Japanese and providing an accurate fix for rescue planes or destroyers. Hellcat pilot Lieutenant (j.g.) Relly I. Raffman, from the *Cowpens*, was jolted by flak, and his engine began to labor. After completing his strafing run, he advised those around him that he doubted he could make it back to the carrier. Three planes then rode shotgun for him, but forty miles away from the target he began to lose altitude.

Raffman's F6F-3 slapped the water. A few seconds after he evacuated the cockpit, the plane sank. But he had his Mae West and his raft. He used a green dye marker to pinpoint his place in the ocean. Word of his plight had already been sent to the task force, and within thirty minutes a seaplane catapulted off the *Massachusetts* ferried him to the battleship.

Lieutenant (j.g.) George M. Blair, from VF-9 off the *Essex*, wound up floating in the Truk lagoon after he was downed. A nearby Japanese destroyer approached, but nine F6F-3 from VF-9 repeatedly discouraged their interest. When the last of his protectors reluctantly left because of a low supply of gas, the enemy warship also departed, seeking its own survival. A pickup for Blair arrived in the form of a catapulted aircraft from the cruiser *Baltimore*. The rescue pilot, Lieutenant (j.g.) Denver Baxter, won the honor of being the first American to intentionally land at Truk.

North of Truk, the submarine *Searaven*, on lifeguard station, fished three *Yorktown* torpedo crewmen out of the water. On similar duty, the *Darter*, lurking to the south, received no business.

What the carrier pilots had begun, the surface warships finished when they overwhelmed those elements of the Japanese fleet that had slipped out of the lagoon. Ramage, flying outside the atoll, saw an enemy cruiser that was down at the stern and going very slowly in circles. "We had no bombs left. I called 'Bald Eagle,' who was Mitscher over there in the *Yorktown*, and told him that we had this cruiser out here which apparently was damaged. If they'd send a strike group over, I'd stay on station and we'd take care of him too. I got an immediate call back. 'Cease and desist. You are not to hit the cruiser.' It turned out later that Admiral Spruance had called the carrier planes off the cruiser because he wanted to give the battleships an opportunity to kill this poor little bastard. So the big battleships finally drew blood against a cruiser that was almost dead in the water. It must have been a great victory." The antagonism between the air Navy and the seagoing one remained virulent.

The Navy records declare that between the air offensive and the sea encounter, as many as thirty-two enemy vessels were sunk, including two light cruisers and four destroyers along with a bevy of cargo transports and oilers. Another seventeen ships, formerly residents of the Truk anchorage, were damaged.

THIRTEEN

MITSCHER SHAMPOOS AND NEW GUINEA

For those who wore wings of gold, life aboard the carriers was relatively comfortable. A few of them, such as Whitey Feightner, Jim Billo, and David Richardson, briefly sojourned in foxholes and tents, ate field rations, and tasted the miserable circumstances of frontline land life. Kent Lee, a former farm boy who had grown up in South Carolina without a telephone at home and no car until 1937, and went from enlisted man into pilot training, said, "Ships at sea are like a big prison, except there are no handcuffs. We had movies. There were bridge clubs, reading and we did have an exercise room. Relations were surprisingly good aboard ship. We had a lot of professionals aboard, both USNR types and regular Navy types. I thought living conditions were great aboard ship [the *Essex*]. I lived in a bunk room, so-called 'boys' town.' We had clean sheets every night, no foxholes and stewards took care of our laundry. I thought the food was excellent, a lot of rice. Sometimes we ran out of fresh provisions but that was no great hardship. Fighting a war from an aircraft carrier is fighting a war in style."

Between missions or campaigns, Vraciu recalled card games—acey-deucey a favorite—reading, coffee in the wardroom, or just sacking out. "Everybody thought we were being pampered, but I thought it was a good thing to do, because you're on adrenaline all the time in the forward area, you're getting up at all crazy hours, you're eating crazy."

Religion alleviated the anxiety for some. The carriers all had

Navy chaplains who conducted services, consoled grievers, and pitched in to help with casualties. David Ramage spoke for many when he said, "I came from a very religious family, and I did pray, but I never prayed for myself. I thought it would be a very arrogant thing for me to pray that I would live and somebody else would die. That wasn't in my way of thinking. I did pray from time to time that I would do a good job. I didn't think of praying for the longevity of myself or anybody else. We were out there to do a job and everybody else knew somebody was going to get killed. It's a fact of life during war. I think everybody had about the same feeling. I don't know anybody that was too damned concerned about himself."

Ramage remarked that going into combat, he had no more fear or apprehension "than any other carrier takeoff. You always take your nervous pee just before you man your plane and when you get in your plane, you wish you could do it again. I can remember sitting back and seeing the carrier swing into the wind and the planes gradually take off but you're checking, looking around to see what's going on. There really isn't any great apprehension, at least in my case. Everything went just as briefed. We were well trained. As base element commander, I rendezvoused my bombers, then gathered up the torpedo planes and fighters. We were always last off because the SBD had fixed wings. We didn't have folding wings, so consquently we were always on the stern. That was fine because we were the base element and it gave the other two squadrons an opportunity to get themselves organized."

Kent Lee expressed similar emotions: "The night before the first flights following a period of rest and recreation, I was always very nervous and didn't sleep very well. Once we manned the airplanes, revved up the engines and were ready to go, it was all business. You're so busy that you don't have time to be afraid."

While all Navy personnel could look forward to liberty when in a port, the airmen in particular could relax and enjoy themselves. Except for the few hours in exercises or training designed to keep their combat skills sharp, they had no responsibilities. In Hawaii in particular, the aviators were welcomed by the affluent and enjoyed the hospitality of plantation owners. For the less discriminating, Honolulu offered ample opportunities to indulge the pleasures of the flesh. Under the governance of the Army provost marshal, bordellos flourished until late 1944, when the champions of virtue finally prevailed over the purveyors of vice. Australia's major cities also offered many divertissements. At smaller island bases, more innocent activities such as swimming, fishing, and even occasionally hunting were available. Unlike the ground forces, airmen benefited from rotations back to the States, where civilians lionized those with gold wings.

Although some lucky ones left the combat areas, the pace of the American advance quickened. The assault upon Truk presaged the next move for the central Pacific campaign. The Carolines, with Truk as their centerpiece, lay due east of the Marshalls. These outposts would be largely bypassed in favor of those to the northwest, the Marianas. This particular clutch of islands attracted American interest because of their suitability for advance naval bases and airfields within striking distance of the Philippines and eventually even Japan (the B-29 bomber, with its huge range, was now rolling out of the Boeing shops). Sentimentally, there was the additional factor of the former American turf of Guam. The three other major pieces of real estate in the Marianas were Saipan, Tinian, and Rota.

On the heels of the thrashing administered to Truk, Vice Admiral Marc Mitscher's fast carriers opened the campaign against the Marianas. Task Force Fifty-eight split itself in two, with 58.2 concentrating upon Guam and Saipan while 58.3 attended to Tinian and Rota. The war was now moving so rapidly that some routine matters, such as detailed intelligence on targets, fell by the wayside. According to Samuel Eliot Morison, "American ignorance of the Marianas at that time was so complete that the pilots could not even be briefed on where to find airfields."

The approach of the Americans was no surprise to the Japanese. A recon plane saw the armada, and during the night of February 22, four separate air attacks threatened Mitscher's ships. The first carrier-based night fighter squadron VF(N)-101, a four-plane F4U-2 unit, had reported January 16, aboard the *Enterprise*. For this encounter, however, the task forces depended solely on their own fierce antiaircraft batteries and the skilled maneuvering of the vessels in harm's way. The combined efforts completely frustrated the enemy, who scored not a single hit and lost ten twin-engine bombers to the shipboard gunners.

When the sun rose, the Japanese made one more effort. Not only did the ships knock down four more, but a sunrise CAP put away a pair of dive-bombers that imperiled the *Yorktown* and the *Essex*. Unfortunately, one F6F-3 fighter pilot pursued the foe with such zeal that he flew directly into the intense flak thrown up by his own side. He was killed and flung into the sea.

Now it was the turn of the task forces. The target for Jim Billo, with VF-18 on the *Bunker Hill*, was supposed to be Saipan. "The first attack, the skipper [Lieutenant Commander Sam Silber] led the fighter sweep. My division was one of three, which included the skipper. We got up over an overcast going in, and the skipper turned and found a hole. We all poured through the hole, found an island that had airplanes flying around and an airfield. We attacked and destroyed all kinds of things on the ground and some in the air. Then we finally figured out where we were; we found we were over Guam. It wasn't our target, but it didn't hurt anything. That was the first flight over Guam since the war had started, the first attack [there] since the war had started. We lost Pete Foreman on that action. Now the squadron score was up around seventy airplanes we had shot down."

In Silber's account, as reported by Karig, "We saw a couple of fighters just ready to land. They apparently hadn't seen us and we waited until both of them had their wheels and flaps down before we strafed them; they had just about hit the ground when we polished them off." When a pair of Bettys similarly blundered in for a landing, VF-18 followed a similar drill.

Unlike VF-18, VB-9, using TBMs that carried radar, found Saipan even though a 12,000-foot overcast hid the ground. The bombers correctly inferred they were in the right location after they saw one of their escort fighters shoot down an enemy plane. Lieutenant Commander Arthur Decker reported, "We circled for twenty minutes before we could see a hole large enough to warrant going through it. We had a general idea where the airfield was and [Lieutenant Commander] Phil Torrey, the group commander, said, 'Go ahead and attack.' We couldn't dive; we couldn't split our flaps and really push over as we like to, so we went through in a glide. We hit the airfield very throughly and the hangar and installations around it, although the weather was so bad around the island we were very lucky to get everybody together in a rendezvous. It was solid right down to the water with visibility about twenty yards in spots."

In the afternoon, the raiders from the *Bunker Hill* caught the Japanese with some seventy aircraft scattered around an airfield on Tinian. Most of them were destroyed. Postwar investigation revealed that the base had served as a training site and the pilots were simply not ready to take off and confront the Americans.

While degrading the defenses in the Marianas before actually invading, the Navy simultaneously had the obligation to aid the southwest Pacific operations under General Douglas MacArthur. His strategy foresaw an advance up through New Guinea toward the lowest rung of the Philippine archipelago, Mindanao. The operations of Nimitz's Pacific Fleet and MacArthur's forces, which included the Army Air Corps. protected each other's flanks.

In early 1944, MacArthur focused on the Dutch New Guinea stronghold of Hollandia as the next step for his march toward the Philippines. Any move on Hollandia, however, risked a counterpunch from a small clutch of islands known as the Admiralties, which sat at the mouth of the Bismarck Archipelago. However, if the Admiralties could be seized, in MacArthur's phrase, "the bottle would be corked," with the enemy forces in the Bismarck Archipelago and the remnants of Japanese troops in the Solomons, a total of 100,000 men, totally shut off. Instead of going to carrier aircraft, the job of ground support and control of the skies went to the Fifth Air Force of the Army. After some bloody ground battles and heavy cannonades from warships offshore, the Admiralties passed into American hands.

This success lined up the next objective, the Western Carolines, known as the Palaus, which included an island by that name along with about a hundred others, including Yap, Ulithi, and Woleai. The Palaus had served the Japanese well, providing bases to stage the initial assaults upon the Philippines and New Guinea. Army bombers spent much of March rocking the defenses of the Palaus, and now Task Force Fifty-eight, swollen to eleven carriers, hoped to catch elements of the enemy fleet that had departed from the caldron at Truk. When a scout plane from Palau reported the American heavyweight armada steaming toward the islands, the Japanese warships prudently evacuated the area.

Jim Ramage now led VSB-10, while Killer Kane had become the air group commander. Ramage played a prominent role in trampling the remaining Japanese holdings. "There were thirty to thirty-five ships in there, mainly tankers, and the old Mitscher Shampoo sank them all the first day. The Mitscher Shampoo was an attack that would start with a fighter sweep on the first day, then deck load launches throughout the day, depending upon target distance, usually about eight carrier deck loads off each carrier. It was a pretty good process. Once you cock the ship and start the first deck load, and then you shoot the second deck load off and land the first, and then it just keeps going until you've either run out of ammo or run out of targets."

VB-10's first strike off the *Enterprise* brought a dozen SBD-5s, the latest version of the Dauntless, to the harbor of Palau. Unmolested, the dive-bombers cruised the scene until they observed a destroyer attempting to make for open sea. One division unloaded five 1,000-pound bombs with "one hit being registered causing ship to jump out of water." A second division attack inflicted more injury, and the vessel started to founder. A subsequent torpedo sent it to the bottom. One of the SBDs never came out of its dive, plunging into the ocean with the loss of both airmen. Antiaircraft fire from the destroyer struck the first division's leader during his dive. He finished his run, then headed his smoking aircraft for the carrier. Forced to make a water landing, he and his crewman were picked up by a destroyer three hours later. When he was returned to the *Enterprise*, the carrier, honoring what was now a tradition, passed along to the rescue ship fifty gallons of ice cream churned out in its galleys.

A second strike by VB-10 blasted a tanker and a cargo ship. On the third visit to Palau by the squadron, one of the trio of SBDs included a photo plane. In addition to the pictures it took, the Dauntless blew up a warehouse with its 1,000-pounder.

A partial source of the success enjoyed by Ramage's unit and similar ones lay in a preattack mining mission carried out from the air. This was the largest tactical use of the devices from the air to date and penned up the vessels, which were hammered by subsequent waves of bombers. As a bastion for operations against American interests, Palau lost relevance, its 150 airplanes eliminated, its fuel storage and supply facilities and barracks all destroyed. Yap, Ulithi, and Woleai, much weaker in resources, crumbled under additional assaults.

"We had enough carrier power to make it stick," said Ramage. "We had enough fighters to defend ourselves, mainly because of the CVLs [light carriers]. They were fighter heavy. They had twenty-four fighters and twelve torpedo planes. The CVLs at first were supposed to be used mainly as defensive forces. Of course, the CVL guys bitched like the dickens about being on the second team, so later they got a good crack at the strikes as well as being the combat air patrol."

Air Group Commander William Killer Kane flew a Hellcat with the Grim Reapers of VF-10, who annihilated several more aircraft. Included in the bag were a float biplane and a Nate, a lightweight fixed-gear fighter that depended upon its maneuverability. That such obsolete specimens were being used indicates that the Japanese war machine was faltering.

The *Hornet* fielded Air Group Two, which included VF-2, the squadron that had trained under Butch O'Hare for the Gilbert Islands campaign but since his death had reconstituted. For many of the pilots, the Palau raids were the first experiences under fire. In the squadron's official history, *Odyssey of Fighting Two*, Lieutenant (j.g.) F. T. Gabriel is recognized as having been the first to shoot down an enemy. The entry for March 30 reports, "As we feared the Jap fleet had evacuated Palau. Throughout the day we pounded the islands from tip to tip and encountered negligible opposition. Mike Wolf got a Zero, the only interception made. Skon [Andy, O'Hare's wingman on that ill-fated night] exploded an oil or ammunition ship.

"Our torpedo squadron lost two planes and the crew of one of them in the pre-dawn take off. They later lost a third over the islands. Our bombers have suffered heavily. The day has been a dark one for Air Group Two."

According to Bob Duncan with VF-5, during the Palau campaign, the enemy air forces did not show up until the second day. Lieutenant John Gray, who now commanded the squadron, said of its adversaries, when they finally appeared, "They were bright and shiny, as though they had come right out of the factory. We were over Palau a little over an hour chasing them around. The hardest part of the fight was to beat some other Hellcat to getting a Zero."

Gray, leading a four-plane division, spotted a similar number of Japanese fighters below his echelon. He dived down after releasing his belly tanks. Within a short spate of minutes, Gray earned the title of ace, knocking down his fifth enemy and adding two more shortly after. The fourth unlucky Zero fell victim to Ensign Robert "Rocky" Aldrich. Lieutenant Daniel "Dapper" Nelson tacked on two more to the three victories achieved at Truk.

The Hellcat again demonstrated its durability. A 20-mm shell pierced Gray's engine; smoke and oil gushed out. The hydraulic system balked, and as he touched down on the carrier, he could not lower his tail hook. He hand-cranked down his landing gear, and his craft rolled swiftly down the deck into the barrier, where it finished with its nose to the deck; Gray himself emerged unhurt. Ensign R. Black returned to the *Yorktown* with his F6F-3 liberally punctured and most of his controls disabled. He banged into a gun turret, shearing off a wing and all of the fuselage aft of the cockpit. Black, with the remainder of his plane—half a wing, the cockpit, the engine and prop—jounced to a stop. Cut atop his head by the canopy, Black climbed down to the deck on his own power.

Flak tore up the plane flown by replacement pilot Ensign J. J. Brosnahan as he strafed an airfield. He pulled up to 1,500 feet as flames spurted from the crippled aircraft. Lieutenant Ted Schofield, flying behind him, barked over the radio, "Bail out, bail out!" Brosnahan did not reply, nor did Schofield see him leave the Hellcat. Back on the *Yorktown*, the squadron had already conceded his loss when word came that he had been pulled from the water by a lifeguard submarine. Altogether, the squadron claimed twenty-nine planes destroyed during the two days over Palau.

After the *Intrepid* swallowed a torpedo during the February assault on Truk and limped back to Hawaii for repairs, Air Group Six was ordered back to the States. But Alex Vraciu said, "Not wanting to go home at this time, I requested permission from the skipper to go to the Commander Air Forces Pacific to see if I could effect a transfer to another squadron still in the combat area. I had a feeling that a fighter pilot should be where the action was. The Navy accommodated me, but not before a Captain Callan took me in to see an admiral. He told the admiral, 'This man wants to stay out here.' I think they thought I was crazy."

Vraciu transferred to VF-16, a squadron stationed on the *Lexington*. He was involved in the support campaign for MacArthur. "At Palau I remember destroying thirteen aircraft on the ground, parked alongside the runway. In bombing, I remember one time missing a small enemy boat by an embarrassingly large margin while experimenting with skip-bombing. Recognizing that my technique could use some practice, I arranged for my division to get some much-needed practice at the earliest opportunity."

For some time Admiral Nimitz had wrestled with the conflicts in strategy and tactics between the seagoing admirals and the air admirals. In a definite shift of course, he decreed that task force commanders, if they were nonaviators, would have an aviator as chief of staff and vice versa. Nimitz believed that would allow a more rounded approach in the decision-making process. One result: Captain Arleigh Burke, nicknamed "31-knot Burke" because of his penchant for pushing his destroyers at flank speed, became Vice Admiral Mitscher's chief of staff.

Truman Hedding, who had earned his wings in 1926 and was a senior officer on Mitscher's staff aboard the *Lexington*, said that after the Navy obtained control of the air he suggested to Arleigh Burke,

" 'How about flying in and taking a ride around and see what's going on in there [Hollandia]? That'll be fun.'

"He hitched a ride in the back seat of a scout bomber with the squadron commander. He went on a typical strike with these bombers but apparently got a little lower than intended and fragments came up into the wing. When he got back, he looked kind of funny. When he landed, Captain Burke announced, 'I believe the airplane is here to stay.'

"I wrote up this dispatch from Admiral Mitscher to the task force. It said, 'The task force commander is pleased to report the safe return of his chief of staff, "31-knot Burke" from a harrowing flight over enemy territory.' "

With the Palaus neutralized and the Admiralties under his control, MacArthur proceeded with his moves on Hollandia. The operations were mostly supported by the Army Air Corps, which accepted additional air cover contributed by escort carriers. According to Ramage, when generals from MacArthur's staff approached Admiral Mitscher with a request for aid from his task force, he said, "Tell me what time you want how many planes and we'll put them there."

"I can remember this general in the Army," said Ramage, "he was very surprised because he said, 'You mean that you will do what we tell you to do?'

"And the admiral said, 'Absolutely. What time do you want them?'

"And the general then said, 'You know, we don't get the same kind of cooperation out of the Army Air Corps.' "

Ramage believed that the Hollandia operation "was another case of overkill. We stood off the beach and launched aircraft. The main target area was completely fogged in, which is unusual in the tropics. The three airfields in the area were on Lake Sentani, back of a mountain called Cyclops Mountain. Somehow the fog had gathered there the evening before, so when our fighter sweep and the first strike were over the target, there was nothing in the air.

"Gradually, the Japs would try to come up through the overcast and our fighters would knock them down one at a time. Then the fog lifted all of a sudden and they got jumped on by about 200 airplanes. It was a massacre. That was the end of all air opposition in Hollandia. I had three strikes into Hollandia. Other than planes on the ground, there wasn't much in the way of targets. The landing took place and it was virtually unopposed."

Daniel Rehm, after spending three years at Loyola University in New Orleans earning a private license through the Civilian Pilot

Training Program, remarked that when the moment for enlistment had come, he had preferred the Navy uniforms to those of the Air Corps. After graduating from Pensacola with his wings in 1943, he joined VF-50 aboard the *Bataan*. He experienced one type of incident, typical of combat, while the carrier was still on its shakedown cruise in the Gulf of Paria off Venezuela.

"I was forced to bail out of an F6F on a training mission at 20,000 feet over mountainous areas when my engine stopped for no good reason. I tried to make the water. However, at the last moment I decided to bail out and when I stood up in the cockpit my parachute got caught on the canopy so I lunged over the wing and pulled the ring as I cleared the aircraft. The chute popped open and I almost immediately went into the water. That was very close. I was picked up by a fishing boat and brought back to the naval station."

His first encounter with the enemy occurred during the invasions of Hollandia and the surrounding areas. Rehm recalled, "I was flying the second division behind the Executive Officer who had spotted a twin engine bomber Betty, and shot it down. As it was going down and before it hit the ground, I let go with a couple of shots just to wet my feet. I was excited, as was everyone else to finally have contact with the enemy."

When VF-5 took its turn at Hollandia, he said, "Something was funny. The Army Air Force bombers had been getting plenty of air opposition earlier in the month on each of their missions into the area. On the 3d [April] twenty-six Jap interceptors were shot down and on the 7th, some seven more. But the morning of the 21st, although there were enemy planes in the air, VF-5 fighters destroyed ten single-engine and twenty twin-engine aircraft on the ground plus twenty-three probables."

Only one division, under John Gray, met the enemy in the air. As the F6F-3s started to attack, they noticed two bombers, one of which was already smoking. Evidently, a fighter from another squadron had scored some hits. Gray's group quickly finished off the crippled plane and then pursued the second. Gray reported, "I pulled up right over him and tailed after [him]. I got so close that he didn't just fill the gun sight—he filled up my whole windshield. He wasn't more than a hundred feet away. I couldn't miss. I could see the bullets going in all over, riddling him. He was burning everywhere but there wasn't any explosion. He just bounced on the water once—twice— then turned over and burned."

MacArthur's invasion forces advanced steadily, reducing the need for air support. However, the Japanese scraped together one after-sunset attack upon the fleet. From the *Enterprise* VF(N)-101, Corsair night fighters patrolling the darkening skies located a twin-engine marauder. The squadron head, Lieutenant Commander Richard E. "Chick" Harmer, moved in toward the stern. The tail gunner ex-changed machine-gun fire with Harmer before the Betty started to burn. It ditched in the water and was the first confirmed kill by car-rier-based night fighters since the experiment that had cost Butch O'Hare his life.

With their help no longer needed by MacArthur, Task Force Fifty-eight sailed northeast. "We stopped by," said Ramage, "and gave Truk another Shampoo [April 29–30]. This time there were no ships. We were to destroy shore installations, fuel tanks, the shipyard and any-thing that was in there. This time the Triple A opposition was really heavy. [Reports indicated that this was the most intense AA met by the Navy to date.] We cleaned out about everything that was worth-while the first day.

"A friend of mine was ferrying an F6F [replacement aircraft were being brought from Jeep carriers to the big flattops] aboard *Enterprise*. He asked me if I thought I could get him a strike into Truk. I said I was sure I could. I went to see Killer Kane and said, 'This guy wants to fly with you today.'

"Killer said, 'Okay, get him in here. He's going to be on my wing.'

"After the flight was over, this guy came to me. He said, 'That's the last time I'll ever do that. This man is a mad man. We were down at the streets looking in the windows, shooting up everything we could possibly find. I've had my strike. I'm going back to the Jeep.' "

Ramage himself flew two strikes the first day and then returned on the following one. "The area was overcast with clouds at about 1,000 feet. I took my strike group under the overcast and there was antiaircraft firing at us down out of the hills. They were higher than we were, going through the shipyard area. We were bombing straight and level, which isn't good bombing. We had a lot of bomb damage from our own fragments." His squadron had little practice with this technique, but as Ramage explained, "We certainly didn't want to throw our ordnance in the general direction of the enemy like some of the sister service people did [the sniping between the airmen of the Army and Navy raged unabated despite the common foe]. As long as we were carrying these 1,000-pounders, we want to do something with them. We didn't lose anybody but we got quite a bit of damage to the aircraft from our own stuff. As I pulled out, I don't know how many airplanes of ours that I saw in the water—ten to fifteen that had the same problem—and also from the Triple A fire. We had the SOCs [Curtiss-Wright Seagulls] inside the lagoon, picking up people. We had the rescue subs off the atoll and they were picking up people. It was really not a very good day. I don't know how many planes were lost that day but I'd suggest maybe twenty or thirty." Officially the toll added up to twenty-seven aircraft with twenty-eight of the forty-six airmen who ditched being rescued.

Combined efforts from carrier pilots, scout observation seaplanes catapulted off the bigger ships, and, above all, the submarine *Tang*, deputized as a lifeguard, saved the downed flyers. A Zero pilot attacked Lieutenant (j.g) Bob Kanze, on duty as escort for a TBF photo plane. The two fighters wound up in a head-to-head duel, spitting bullets at each other. Both planes burst into flames, and both airmen bailed out. The onshore water currents, while carrying the the Japanese flyer to safety, endangered Kanze with capture at the very least. The *Tang*, conned by Commander Richard O'Kane, sought to retrieve Kanze, but the tide slewed the downed pilot's raft within range of a Japanese shore battery, eager to take potshots at an enemy sub. The *Tang* swapped a few shells with the coast artillery and then quickly escaped from the scene, leaving Kanze bobbing in the water.

Early the next morning, the battleship *North Carolina* catapulted a Kingfisher piloted by Lieutenant John Dowdle and a crewman, R. E. Hill, to rescue Kanze. Dowdle set the OS2U down in the choppy lagoon and taxied over to Kanze. Just as Kanze hauled himself up on the wing, a cross-chop wave capsized the float plane. Now three Americans were in the water. Another Kingfisher from the *North Carolina*, flown by Lieutenant (j.g.) John A. Burns with enlisted man Aubrey Gill in the rear seat, observing the struggle, landed in the lagoon. The rough water and the heavy load reduced the possibilities of a successful takeoff. Burns taxied carefully to a rendezvous with the *Tang* and transferred his three passengers. He then lifted off from the water to search for more survivors.

During these operations, Henry Miller, as Air Group Twenty-three commander, and others in similar leadership roles answered a summons to the Task Force Fifty-eight flagship, where Captain Jimmy Flatley, Mitscher's air officer, announced, "We're losing too many air group commanders. I don't want you guys going in and dropping any bombs. You stand off and you run the show." Miller recalled that this was due not to the enemy picking out group commanders as primary targets but to the fact that they perhaps were taking too many chances. Miller added, "You really can't [fly missions without carrying ordnance] if you're a squadron commander or air group commander [and] say, 'Okay kids, you go in there and give it the old college try. I'll stay out here and watch.' You can't fight a war that way." Nevertheless, Captain Flatley emphatically warned the leaders not to ignore his admonition.

"I went back to the carrier," recalled Miller, "and told them about this. I said, 'He threatened the whole bunch of us.' We had a big operation the next day or day after. I was up before [the air group] and said, 'Now here's the plan of attack.'. . . Somebody said, 'We took the bomb off your airplane.' You could have heard a pin drop. I said, 'You put that bomb right back on.'" According to Miller, the air commander of the Pacific was unhappy when he learned that Miller had disobeyed orders.

The *Yorktown*'s air group had also feasted on Truk. The top-scoring pilots from VF-5, Gray, Duncan, and Nelson, all stood down while others received a chance to raise their totals. Bob Duncan said, "The opportunity of finding enemy aircraft in the air is best on the first fighter sweep of the day. The term 'fighter sweep' means that all enemy aircraft were to be literally swept out of the sky before the next flights were to arrive over the target. This unofficial policy was fair and popular. The Navy was not out to build up 'big names.'"

After the VF-5 fighters reached the target, the bombers left the deck. Just about then, four Jill torpedo planes, having evaded the combat air patrol, bore down on the task force. Shipboard antiaircraft blasted three out of the sky but one homed in on the *Yorktown*. The carrier poured murderous fire on the Jill. Still, it continued on a course toward the port side. Just when it seemed the plane would crash into the flattop, it passed over the flight deck before falling into the sea. It was a harbinger of what lay ahead in the time of the kamikazes.

Aboard the *Cabot*, Arthur Hawkins was on standby. "You go on various stages of standby," explained Hawkins, "because of feasibility and closeness of a raid or other reasons. We were in our cockpits on a catapult, our standby position. A raid of twelve torpedo bombers came in from Truk. The planes were low on the water and they didn't pick them up until they were about fifteen miles from us. They launched us. I was on the starboard cat. As they launched me, the ships opened up with their guns at these torpedo planes. As I went off the cat, I turned into the flight coming in, and then I was head-to-head with a Judy [carrier-based dive-bomber]. I opened up on him and splashed him, then pulled up in a short chandelle, getting my gear up.

"Then I turned and followed the remainder while these eighteen destroyers, two cruisers, two battleships and three carriers were firing at these planes coming through." Hawkins's pursuit had carried him into the middle of the fleet's antiaircraft. "I didn't get hit. Luckily I was over [the Japanese]. I was a little higher than they were. They were right on the water, dropping their fish at the ships, and everybody was shooting. We had a few ships shoot up each other in this particular case. I followed [the Japanese] all the way through the fleet, out the other side. The kid who went off the other cat had turned and gone back through. I joined him on the other side and we pursued them under radar control. He got one more of the planes."

While Hawkins defended against the intruders, the pilots from VF-5 exploited their opportunity in combat, scoring heavily. Two from the outfit advanced to the rank of ace. One of them, Lieutenant (j.g.) Harry Hill, however, had little time to savor his achievement. On the final strike of the day, the AA winged him and the best he could do was make a forced landing east of Truk, just beyond the lagoon. Not only was he in the water, but the prevailing winds blew him steadily toward the reef and potential capture. Hellcats from VF-5 circled overhead to register his position and if necessary foil any efforts by the garrison at Truk to capture him.

When fuel ran low and darkness neared, the watchers returned to the *Yorktown*. In the ready room, the pilots of VF-5 held what might be called a council of rescue. Duncan said, "They had watched too many of their fellow pilots land in the sea alive [Stover among them] only to be deserted and left to die, either by the elements or torture and death at the hands of the Japanese."

They decided to mount an early-morning fighter sweep that would clean out any enemy planes or ships that might be prowling the area. That objective accomplished, the aircraft would form a scouting line at low altitude to search for Hill. The submarine *Tang*, acting as a lifeguard, had remained in the vicinity, and the idea was to locate Hill and keep an eye on him until the *Tang* could bring him aboard. Awareness that their tour was about to end fortified their resolution. The VF-5 members did not want to leave anyone behind.

At the same time, the demands of war militated against an all-out effort. The air officer or air boss of the *Yorktown*, new to his job, had other ideas in mind. He decreed that all flights would be limited to two and a half hours rather than the normal four, thereby dispatching more sorties to the target. Duncan explained that there was a goal to carry as much ammo, bombs, and ordnance as possible to the target, setting a record for ordnance expended in a single day's operations. The VF-5 pilots, however, cared more about saving Hill than establishing new marks.

On the following morning, four divisions of sixteen Hellcats from VF-5 made sure that no enemy fighters were aloft and then formed their scouting line. They found Hill a few miles south of Truk, near a smaller atoll. Hill had paddled vigorously during the night to prevent the wind currents from driving him into the Truk reef. The choppy water added seasickness to his discomfort. Duncan and three others, having the most fuel, stood the first shift, watching over the downed pilot. As their gas dwindled, another pack of four relieved them, and the routine continued through until the afternoon of April 30, when some of the F6F-3s contacted the *Tang* and led it to the exhausted Hill. Not long afterward, Ensign Bob Cole also wound up in the drink. A *Yorktown* bomber saw him and marked his position. The *Tang* retrieved Cole, who had only his life jacket and no raft. He joined Hill and three others aboard the sub.

That same day, Burns, in his Kingfisher, had found seven airmen in the water. The aviators hung on to the wings and clung to the fuselage as Burns sloshed through the hard slaps of the surging sea until he reached the *Tang*. The submarine took everyone in, including Burns, whose OS2U now was so badly battered it could not fly. The *Tang*'s deck gun disposed of the plane. In its lifeguard role at Truk, the sub rescued twenty-two naval airmen. For his efforts, Burns received a Navy Cross.

That night a contretemps sputtered aboard the *Yorktown*. The air boss placed all of the division leaders who had overstayed the two-and-a-half-hour limit on report for disobeying his orders. They were informed, recalled Duncan, "it isn't your responsibility to assume the rescue of Hill. We have rescue units assigned that task."

According to Duncan, Lieutenant Commander Bob Jones, the CO of VF-5, won the hearts of his pilots for staunchly defending the pilots during a hearing. The skipper of the *Yorktown*, Captain Ralph

Jennings, dismissed the report charges with a statement: "It is my view that these pilots have been in continuous combat for too extended a period of time, almost eleven months, and as a result are suffering from pilot fatigue which has affected their judgment. The report is dismissed."

Actually, although VF-5 pilots overstayed their airtime, the carrier did set a record for what it threw at the Japanese in a single day. On that same day, the squadron registered its final victory. A division led by Duncan happened upon a two-seater torpedo plane darting between the clouds. Duncan's wingman, Engisn D. O. Kenney, burned it, and the total for the unit reached 95 aircraft shot down in the air plus 15 probables. Another 195 had been destroyed on the ground, along with 117 damaged. Only Si Satterfield was counted as lost due to aerial combat; the other casualties had all been seen alive after their F6F-3s had gone down but had either perished at the hands of the enemy or had not been rescued at sea. On the *Yorktown* the evening after Hill was saved, the ship's band played "California, Here I Come." The shooting war was over for the men of VF-5.

From the *Lexington*, Alex Vraciu and VF-16 escorted bombers on a morning raid on Truk. "Our flight," he said, "was attacked by a small group of enemy fighters. We simply pounced on them quickly and destroyed them at *their* [his emphasis] best performance altitude—down low. It was a no-contest affair after we had them boxed in. I was fortunate enough to down two Zeros from the six o'clock position.

"We preferred not to fight the Zero at low altitudes but we had no choice when escorting SBDs at 3,000 feet on the return leg home to the carrier. One could not help being impressed with the Zero's maneuverability at low altitude, but their pilot also had to remember his altitude. [One] started to go into a loop at a ridiculously low altitude just at the time that I got in a good burst. It seemed to stop him dead, and he went into the water smoking.

"Unfortunately, in the same engagement, one of my squadron mates tried to follow one of the Zeros in a loop. Again, it was a case of not thinking of the altitude. He went into the water right after the Zero."

The afternoon mission for Vraciu turned out more exciting than he would have preferred: "I was on an escort mission and while I was setting up at 9,000 feet for a strafing run on one of the Truk Atoll airfields, my Hellcat was hit by medium altitude AA fire. Part of the flak passed through my cockpit just in front of my face, showering the cockpit with Plexiglas. My hydraulic system was riddled and the landing gear dropped down part way.

"Aborting my run, I was escorted back to the task force by my wingman. Being unable to lower my landing gear, I was given the choice of parachuting over the fleet or ditching in the water alongside one of our destroyers." He elected to land in the sea. "I had learned to lower the tailhook to feel the wave and this time it was with 'power on.' The other one [his previous ditching] was 'power off'—different entirely. Even though the waves were kind of heavy, I landed on the backside of the wave rather than hitting it head-on.

"Funny thoughts can cross your mind [on such an occasion]. You're in the water and the first thought you have is, 'My God! It's deep down there!' On the first ditching the destroyer kept overshooting me on his approach. I had my fighter boots on, and I didn't want to lose those boots. The toggles on my Mae West were both jammed so I was treading water for a long time until they threw me a life preserver. After the third missed pass, I yelled up to them, 'What's the matter? Don't you want the ice cream?' Eventually, I was hauled aboard."

On the first occasion of ditching, Vraciu quickly returned to the carrier, but this second time, rough seas and the coming of night prevented his transfer. Anxious to get back to the *Lexington*, Vraciu prevailed upon the destroyer skipper to let him send a message to Gus Widhelm, the air operations officer for Marc Mitscher. "I said, 'Gus, get me off this danged roller coaster, or I'll vote for MacArthur, so help me.' MacArthur was being touted as a presidential hopeful [in the 1944 election] back home. He had upset the sensitivities of the Navy by saying 'My Navy' in reference to the ships assigned to him in the South Pacific. That went through the Navy like wildfire." Vraciu thought his jibe might trigger faster action to retrieve him.

Widhelm sent a message to the destroyer skipper that read, "Captain, in order to conserve aircraft, desire you retain my 'birdman' until we reach Ulithi, at that time we will transport him back via rubber boat." Vraciu wondered if he had gone too far, but soon semaphore flags waved the destroyer to the vicinity of the flattop. "I was high-lined [transported in a basketlike device] from the destroyer to the carrier." Widhelm greeted him and immediately took him to Admiral Mitscher on the bridge, announcing, "Admiral, here's the character that sent that message." Mitscher took it all with good grace.

Vraciu remarked, "Amazingly, although some Plexiglas had embedded itself into one of my eyes, I never felt it until the middle of the night. The ship's doctor deadened the eyeball and scraped out the offending glass." Since Vraciu had ditched for the second time within a five-week period, he was teased as being "Grumman's best customer."

James Ramage said he had gone to see Rear Admiral John Reeves, commander of Task Force 58.1, and Captain Mathias Gardner, skipper of the *Enterprise*. "I told them as far as I could see that we'd done about all the damage that was worthwhile. I pointed out that we'd lost an awful lot of airplanes. Admiral Reeves turned to Captain Gardner and said, 'I think we've run into the law of diminishing returns. I'm going to recommend to Admiral Mitscher that we cease this operation.'"

The Truk Shampoo amounted to a total of 2,200 sorties that just about emptied the carriers' ammunition and ordnance magazines. The planes obliterated more than four hundred buildings, barracks, canneries, refineries, and offices, along with six hangars. Another ninety-three Japanese planes were obliterated. Truk no longer figured as a factor in the Pacific War.

While MacArthur carried out his strategy, Chester Nimitz had been plotting Operation Forager, the taking of the principal islands at the southern end of the Marianas: Saipan, Tinian, Rota, and Guam. The overall command for the invasion, scheduled for June 1944, went to Admiral Raymond Spruance with Mitscher's Task Force Fifty-eight, now burgeoned to fifteen carriers, a key component. The ground forces would include Marines and Army troops. The rough coincidence with Operation Overlord, the D-Day landings in France, bespeaks the tremendous increase in U.S. military forces. However, since the distance from the Normandy beaches to the airfields in Great Britain was scant, there was no need for carrier-based aircraft to assist over the English Channel.

In the Marianas, the Japanese girded their resources for stout resistance. Having captured a pilot from a crashed B-29 performing a test flight over territory they controlled, the Japanese had learned of the extraordinary range of the Super Fortress. They foresaw how the weapon could be deployed against the home islands from bases in the Marianas. To stave off the Americans, the dwindling Imperial Navy husbanded its ships for a defense of the territory. The Japanese First Mobile Fleet, hanging about mostly in the Philippine waters, included nine carriers, five battleships, twelve heavy cruisers, and four divisions of destroyers. The armada could count on about 540 land-based aircraft to bolster them. The stage was set for a major confrontation between the two navies. Reconnaissance by the Japanese in the second week of June established that Task Force Fifty-eight was bearing down on the Marianas. Further scouting determined that the Americans were readying for an onslaught on Saipan.

FOURTEEN

THE MARIANAS OVERTURES

The Japanese, despite their setbacks, were still unwilling to concede control of the sea to the Americans. The Imperial Command created Operation AGO, which combined a fleet of capital ships, carriers, and destroyers with Army land-based bombers from the Philippine Islands and the Marianas, in the hope of reversing the course of the Pacific War. The Philippine Sea between the two sets of islands would be the venue for this decisive battle—if the Japanese could dictate the script.

In the central Pacific, the United States had mustered its own huge armada of 644 ships. Though Admiral Raymond Spruance held overall command of the Fifth Fleet, its lead element, Task Force Fifty-eight under Vice Admiral Mitscher, would need to cleanse the skies of enemy aircraft before the invasion of the Marianas. With the first troops scheduled to hit the Saipan beaches on June 15, Mitscher pushed forward the schedule for the fighter sweeps to D minus 4 for fear his task force had been discovered by the inevitable snoopers.

Japanese reconnaissance aircraft, roaming the central Pacific, had apparently spotted Mitscher's ships. A division of four fighters from the *Yorktown*'s VF-1, on station over the fleet, learned from fighter direction of bogeys. The Hellcats tracked an Emily—a four-engine flying boat—and then struck in a coordinated assault. Lieutenant (j.g.) G. W. Staeheli jockeyed into position from above and ahead of the Emily. His first burst missed, but then he poured tracers into the starboard wing and outboard engine. On his third run he saw his bullets pierce the fuselage belly.

Lieutenant R. H. Shireman, Jr., the wingman to Staeheli, also approached from above and ahead. His .50s chipped pieces from the wing, and he observed tongues of fire licking an engine. Lieutenant (j.g.) W. P. Tukey's stream of machine-gun bullets penetrated the area directly behind the pilot. Ensign Hogue, the fourth assassin, hit the wing root, even as tracers from the Emily passed beneath him. The Americans saw their victim start a slow turn before its wing dipped into the ocean and then the big patrol plane flipped over on its back. One survivor emerged from the wreckage.

Another division from VF-1 performing CAP received similar information on a bogey from fighter direction. It picked up the twin-engine enemy some 25 miles from the fleet and promptly maneuvered into position for an attack. Lieutenant (j.g.) Martin, in the lead, opened fire, and the aircraft blew up, spattering Martin's windshield with oil as it disintegrated.

The *Bunker Hill's* CAP, Hellcats from VF-8, put one division directly over the fleet, while a second flight under Whitey Feightner meandered through the skies some 25 miles off. They came under direction of the *Yorktown*, which vectored them toward an intruder 45 miles away. The Betty spotted them and tried to run. Feightner and his wingman, Lieutenant (j.g.) Richard Rosen, peeled off for their beam attack. It was Rosen who apparently triggered the fatal blows as the starboard engine flamed and then exploded. The bomber dived straight into the water.

Although the spy planes all seemed to have been splashed, Mitscher felt he could not take the chance that they had not radioed his presence to the Japanese fleet and therefore ordered the attack to begin on June 11.

From 200 miles east of Guam, the southernmost of the islands, the task force, at 1:00 P.M., dispatched a deckload strike: 208 fighters and eight torpedo bombers against the enemy airfields. VF-2, based on the *Hornet*, contributed sixteen fighters and a pair of VB-2's SB2C-10 Helldivers with extra life rafts also sortied.

According to James Ramage, "The only aircraft in the air other than fighters were some planes that carried extra life rafts. The submarines that we normally used as lifeguards off the target area apparently weren't in position by that time."

As Fighting Squadron Two struck at Guam's airfields, AA disabled the F6F-3 flown by Lieutenant (j.g.) Howard Duff, Jr., who radioed

Lieutenant Arthur Van Haren, "I am going down five miles north of Orote [a town on Guam]." Lieutenant (j.g.) Daniel Carmichael, Jr., immediately began to search for Duff. Carmichael saw smoke coming from the distressed fighter. "He made a beautiful water landing," reported Carmichael. "I was coming down from 5,000 feet and made a steep turn around him. By the time I got back around him, he was out and in the water. His plane was just sinking then and he was safe. I rolled my hood open and waved to him because the skipper [Commander W. M. Dean] had called and said, 'We will take care of you.' The captain called 41 Ripper [the rescue SB2C with extra life rafts] which earlier had been chased by Zekes. I heard him answer that he was seven miles west of Orota and coming in at 7,000 feet and would like someone to meet him. The skipper couldn't contact him and kept calling. I went down and found myself flying around Duff alone."

Just about the moment that Duff went into the water, a flock of nearly thirty enemy aircraft had charged onto the scene. Squadron Commander Dean noted, "My first contact was made at 1,000 feet while we were circling in search of Duff. Tracers started to go over us. Two Zekes came down behind us. Dan [Carmichael] and his wingman were below us at the time. [Lieutenant (j.g.)] Davy Park and I did a chandelle to the right and to the left respectively and each of us turned into one. We shot them down and they burst into flames."

Dean turned his attention to the other interceptors. "This plane was heading toward the field at 1,000 feet and I was at 2,000 feet on an opposite course. I rolled to the left and made a high side run. I got this one while I was one thousand feet above him. He burst into flames and crashed. Three Tojos came by at 3,000 feet. I used water injection and 65 inches of manifold pressure and chased one which I had singled out. It climbed to 7,000 feet and I closed on it in the climb. I gave it a burst. It did a diving turn to the right and headed toward the clouds. I closed on its tail at 6 o'clock, firing. It burst into flames and crashed." A tight dogfight with a Zeke followed, and with the last of his 1,800 rounds of ammunition, Dean scored his fourth victory.

Dean's wingman, Davy Park, first became aware of a hostile presence when tracers zipped by. He executed a quick turn and then relied on a chandelle to ascend speedily. "I saw a Zeke making a run on the Captain while the Captain was firing on another. We exchanged a few shots and I got him in the belly and he started burning.

He came for me and I went over on my back, did a roll and followed him on down, squirting him. He crashed into the water."

Park said that while attempting to meet up with Dean, two Tojos bored in. Park's guns ignited a fire in one that ended with another crash. "[Lieutenant (j.g.) Charles] Carroll called us about three Zekes in the clouds and said, 'I got one and there are two more up here.' The Captain and I climbed into two Tojos. I worked one over and the Captain the other. I gave him two long bursts. I hit him. He went into a long glide toward Orote field." With no confirmation, Parks could claim only a probable.

Carmichael, trying to stay near his fallen comrade, said, "I was making a tight turn around Duff. A Zeke was coming at me. It went by Carroll and I leveled out and went straight for it. I pulled up in a chandelle as he leveled off and he rolled across in front of me. I shot at him from an altitude of 1,500 feet, full deflection, at 9 o'clock. He burned when he hit the water.

"Van Haren and I were circling Duff and I saw a plane coming over for me. I pulled up as he was in a sharp turn. I got a full deflection but I did not see any flame. He rolled over on his back and went into the water from about 1,800 feet. I then went back and couldn't find Duff. I looked for ten minutes. After rendezvous [for return to the Hornet] I got permission to go back and make one more search but still I could not find him."

Altogether, the D-minus-4 sweeps cost the Japanese 147 aircraft. Other units reported signal success. VF-31, from the Cabot, claimed thirteen destroyed in the air, four on the ground, and other damaged or probables. VF-2 reported a total of twenty-three of the enemy shot down without a single loss in aerial combat. The unfortunate Duff, forced to ditch because of flak, became one more name on the lengthening list of "missing in action."

Leading up to the June 15 scheduled landing on Saipan, various complements of Navy aircraft struck the major Mariana Islands. Ramage, with his bomber squadron, flew five strikes off the Enterprise with Task Group 58.3 over three days. Promoted to full commander, Killer Kane led VF-10's Hellcats to Saipan. A dozen Japanese fighters confronted them there. When the dogfights ended, the Americans had felled five Zeros and an Army Nakajima Oscar.

Ensign Lee Gray, after disposing of the Oscar, rushed to assist another Hellcat pursued by a pair of Zeros. A burst from his guns ripped into one of them, and the other quit the contest. Later, Gray, who shot down another Zero a few minutes later, received confirmation of a kill from the pilot, whom he aided. The thankful flyer happened to be Whitey Feightner, a plank owner (original member) of the Grim Reapers and now a lieutenant in VF-8 aboard the *Bunker Hill*. Feightner had been engaged in a dangerous solo photo mission over the Saipan beaches, taking pictures of the beaches to be assaulted by the Marines.

Feightner and VF-8 followed up with a mission over Tinian. The island was close enough to Saipan for its artillery to toss shells at the American invasion fleet when it moved into position for the prelanding bombardment of Saipan. The sixteen F6F-3s took off from the *Bunker Hill* with instantaneous fused depth bombs. They brought along a pair of Helldivers from VB-8 that provided some navigational aid and toted additional rescue gear. From the *Cabot*, like the *Bunker Hill*, a member of Task Group 58.2, VF-31 flew cover for the bombers and strafing runs by VF-8. The *Monterey*, from the same group, supplied air cover for the Helldivers. The entire operation bespeaks the abundance of carriers and aircraft that was available.

VF-8 opened the action at Tinian with a bombing attack on the Ushi Point airfield, spreading its explosive wares over the service apron at the end of a runway. A fuel dump erupted in a fierce fire, and a building also blazed up. Explosions rent the parking area, but dust and debris obscured the extent of damage to airplanes on the ground.

During his dive from 5,000 feet, Commander William M. Collins, the squadron's top dog, saw his port wingtip shot away by AA. He retained control of the aircraft, and after he pulled up, he noticed Japanese planes at nearby Gurguan airfield. With his wingman, Lieutenant (j.g.) Ralph Rosen, Collins initiated strafing runs. Rosen set afire one Irving (twin-engine Nakajima J1N night fighter) at the end of a runway and then lit up another as it was turning off. A third Irving, just coming in for a landing, perceived the threat and attempted to lift off. Collins blew it up when the plane was 30 feet off the ground. Collins then caught another enemy plane in the air and destroyed it with a burst into the starboard wing root.

Rosen pursued an Irving as it retracted its wheels and sprinted for cloud cover. The Navy pilot ignited fire in the port engine, but the plane managed to escape into the overcast. Below, Collins passed directly over the ground AA as he chased a target. Although 20-mm shells sprayed shrapnel about the cockpit, cutting Collins's face and ravaging his F6F-3, he downed his third Japanese night fighter.

The commander and his wingman joined in a run at still another

Irving. Collins started the starboard engine smoking, and Rosen finished the job with hits that exploded the port engine. A crewman parachuted to safety as the flaming plane smashed to the earth. During this encounter, Collins was jolted by more AA. As he began the return to base, a last burst of flak started a fire beneath his wing and tore away a flap. The flames subsided, however, and Collins reached the *Bunker Hill* for a successful no-flaps landing.

Others from VF-8 fared worse. Lieutenant Carney led his division to Ushi Point behind Collins. As Carney released his bomb and began to pull out at 2,500 feet, AA caught him and the Hellcat started to burn between the belly tank and the oil cooler shutters. Carney dropped the belly tank, but the fire raged on. He tried to blow it out with several high-speed dives, but soon the entire underside was ablaze. In the midst of a ninety-degree drive, Carney fell from the cockpit at 1,000 feet, his body turning end over end. His parachute never opened before he hit the water. Ground guns mauled another plane so badly that the pilot was forced to ditch. He was picked up by a destroyer.

The frequently intense AA almost ended the career of Alex Vraciu, now with VF-16 aboard the *Lexington*, part of Task Group 58.3. He volunteered to replace a pilot unable to make a flight to Saipan. During the mission he shot up a seaplane ramp. "I caught some flak in my engine. This was where the F6F Hellcat's ruggedness was really appreciated. Fortunately, our fleet was real close, only ten, twelve miles offshore. I was able to get my plane back to the *Lex*."

On one visit to Saipan as a companion for bombers, Vraciu glanced up and saw a Japanese Betty at about 18,000 feet. "I requested permission from the leader of the bombers to go after it and he said, 'Go get him.' I promptly dropped my belly tank, went to full power and raced my division up there. I climbed up in its blind spot, directly underneath it, at a sharp angle. As I reached its altitude, all of a sudden, the Betty's left wing cocked up steeply. Somebody had just spotted me.

"My division was straggling behind me. The Betty quickly lowered its nose and started diving to build up speed. I made one pass and burned him. One of the guys in the division—it wasn't my regular one, sometimes you have a pick-up flight—didn't even get to fire. He was unhappy with me. He yelled on the radio, 'Vraciu, you son-of-a-bitch!' "

Vraciu's practice in skip bombing quickly paid off on a target in the Saipan harbor. "There was still enemy shipping around and from time to time they would strap a 500-pound bomb on our fighters. Skip bombing to me, for a fighter pilot, seemed a hell of a lot wiser than dive-bombing. I took a section down, picking the back half of the ship [a cargo carrier of perhaps 6,000 tons]. I brought us in on a low approach with a lot of speed and lobbed my 500-pounder into the side of the vessel—hitting it right at the waterline. It went down quickly."

Kent Lee, with VB-15 and flying an SB2C, endured an experience that explained his disenchantment with the Helldiver: "I was out with a flight of six SB2Cs and we spotted a Japanese merchantman. He was about a 10,000 tonner—not a big ship. We thought, 'Oh, great, we've got ourselves a good target.' Six of us—I was an ensign and probably the sixth man on the flight—made a dive on this ship. I doubt that its beam was more than sixty feet and it was maybe 300–400 feet long. We dived from about 12,000 feet and each of us released a bomb on him. Not one hit. That was sort of standard for the SB2C. Not a very good dive-bomber.

"We then strafed with our 20-millimeter guns, and that was also a problem with the SB2C. It had two 20-millimeter guns, one in each wing. They were prone to jam. I dare say the 20-millimeter guns jammed fifty percent of the time. Six SB2Cs [dived] on one lone ship and we all missed him. We then strafed him but he was still steaming along when we left."

As the first site in the Marianas scheduled for invasion, Saipan drew the most concentrated air efforts. On June 13, Lieutenant Commander Bill Martin, the skipper of VT-10, brought his TBFs for another whack at the island's defenses. But the skilled ground gun crews were ready for the Avengers. Martin's account in Walter Karig's *Battle Report* reads, "Our specific target was AA installations near a radio station at the Charan-Kanoa airstrip. We could see our target blinking at us when we pushed over in a . . . glide attack from about 8,000 feet. Two black bursts appeared almost in the line of our dive when [William K.] Williams, the radio gunner, called out '4,000.' At 3,500 I pushed the electric bomb release and was pulling the emergency manual release when there was a teeth-shattering jolt. The plane seemed to tumble around its lateral axis and I was on my back being forced out against the safety belt. I knew we were crashing. I felt a heat wave go past me and thought the plane was in flames. I groped for the microphone to tell Williams and [aviation machinist's mate Wesley] Hargrove to jump, but couldn't find it.

"At this point involuntary reactions and instinct went to work; on the count of one I released the safety belt; on the count of two I pulled the rip cord; on the count of three I felt the parachute take up the slack in my harness and on the count of three and a half I hit the water. Our speed had been in excess of 300 knots, at which 3,000 feet are covered in less than six seconds. I do not believe that the parachute opened until I was within a few feet of the water. As there had been no abrupt jerk in the parachute, I was not sure it had opened at all."

Apparently, the chute had ripped and Martin endured a near free fall for about half a mile. As he plummeted through the air, Martin said, he recalled a Marine pilot who claimed to have fallen from 2,000 feet and preserved his life by straightening his body and keeping his toes pointed down. In fact, Martin miraculously survived a descent from 3,000 feet into a mere four feet of water. He said that when he revived from the stunning impact with the water, he found himself mumbling the Twenty-third Psalm aloud. Neither Williams nor Hargrove had gotten out of the falling TBF, whose burning wreckage lay only ten yards away.

A new peril threatened his life. As he floated about 300 yards offshore in a reef-girded lagoon, Japanese soldiers, exultant over shooting down an airplane, now picked up rifles and fired at him. "I started a bit of submarine navigation toward the seaward edge of the reef, coming up only when my lungs ached for air. Once when I came up, I saw two boats moving toward me. At this point, with invasion obviously imminent, the Japs would have stopped at nothing to extract information from a prisoner. My output of energy was extended to the limit." He paused on the inner slope of the reef.

"Upon arrival . . . the firing had ceased and feeling quite secure I sat on a slope with my nose and eyes above water and peeked over the raft back at the shore. Having studied the charts meticulously in reparation for carrying out the duties of Air Co-ordinator, I recognized the shore line in front of me as the landing beaches. So I took cross bearings for an accurate fix of my position and began taking mental notes. It was hard to keep from thinking of Williams and Hargrove. They had been flying with me since the summer of 1942. They were like brothers to me."

Satisfied that he had acquired as much knowledge as he could and spurred by the splashes of several 20-mm shells in his proxim-

ity, Martin collected his gear and dashed across the reef. He leaped
into the breakers off the seaward edge, screened by the surf and the
ridge. He felt secure enough to inflate his life raft, and he contrived
a sea anchor with his parachute and seat pack. Filling the raft with
enough water to make it ride low in the sea, he shoved off.

Using a mirror and a dye marker, he caught the eyes of Navy pilots coming over the island. While they did sentry duty over Martin,
two Seagull float planes from the cruiser *Indianapolis*—Spruance's
flagship—escorted by VF(N)-101 Corsairs arrived from the *Enterprise*. One of the biplanes landed and taxied up to Martin on the reef.
He climbed into the rear cockpit, and they took off despite some
fire from the frustrated enemy onshore. The weary VT-10 skipper
subsequently related to Spruance and his staff his unplanned reconnaissance of the beaches. Still later, he traveled by breeches buoy to
the destroyer *McDonough* for a return to the *Enterprise*. En route,
the warship received orders to blast the western beaches of Saipan
with discretion to pick its targets. Martin requested the skipper to
shell the AA installation that had brought down his TBF. "If our
bombs didn't knock out those Jap guns, the *MacDonough's* main
battery did, and I wished that Williams and Hargrove might have
known of it."

Saipan had been marked off in some three hundred grids. Key
installations such as the Aslito airfield, known antiaircraft batteries,
towns, and villages were shown on the grid map. One mission not
only pounded the artillery locations but also used incendiaries to ignite fires in cane fields. One observer reported a cessation of gunfire
from the areas attacked: "There was plentiful evidence of the success the Bbs [battleships] were having in bombarding the island.
Large oil fires could be seen in several places . . . an ammunition
dump blew up merrily throughout the period in which planes were
on station."

In its quest for more effective weapons, the Navy had begun to
experiment with rockets, already in use by the British Royal Air
Force against submarines. Lieutenant Commander Robert Isley, Jr.,
squadron commander of the *Lexington's* VT-16, had been dubious
about their effectiveness. The rockets, if anything, tended to reduce
the speed and maneuverability of an Avenger. However, Isley agreed
to try them against Aslito Field on Saipan. He led a flight of three
rocket-armed TBFs into the maw of the antiaircraft. During the
glide toward the target, Isley's plane and the one immediately behind it ignited into balls of flame, crashing with the loss of both

crews. The third Avenger, although hit, escaped destruction. At the considerable cost of six skilled aviators, air officers grasped the reality that a slow-moving platform such as a TBF was ill suited to such duty.

As June 15 dawned, the offshore fleet continued its three-day barrages against Japanese positions defending the Saipan beaches. Overhead, Seagulls and Kingfishers, scout-spotter planes catapulted from the bigger warships, coached the gunners. Eyewitness Samuel Eliot Morison described it as a gaudy spectacle: "There are few things prettier than a naval bombardment, provided one is on the sending not the receiving end . . . and has lost all feeling of compassion for the human victims. Nearby ships belch great clouds of saffron smoke with a mighty roar. Distant ones are inaudible, but their flashes of gunfire leap out like the angry flick of a snake's tongue. Planes drop white phosphorus bombs which explode in clouds white as new-fallen snow, and throw out silver streamers which ignite canefields, whence clouds of yellowish sugar-cane smoke arise."

The first leathernecks from the Second and Fourth Marine Divisions raced toward the shore aboard armored amphtracs shortly before 9:00 A.M. Overhead, the initial wave of air support, seventy-two planes from the escort carriers *Kitkun Bay*, *Gambier Bay*, *Coral Sea*, and *Corregidor*, swooped and dived upon the defenders. One group of aircraft dropped smoke bombs to create a fog in the hope of obscuring the beaches temporarily. The invaders quickly learned that many enemy emplacements had survived the prelanding bombardment. While the first amphibious craft may have been invisible, the Japanese gunners showered the area with preregistered mortars and light artillery, scoring some deadly hits. The need for quick redress summoned the full weight of the aviators. At the same time, the gunners aboard the close-in amphibious force were jittery after a previous night's air raid. While six of the attackers were knocked down by AA, the exchanges of gunfire with the low-flying enemy inflicted casualties on several ships.

Jim Ramage, with VB-10, recalled, "Killer Kane, our CAG, was to be the air coordinator of all of the aviation over the beach for the actual target time. I was to be the *Enterprise* strike leader. We took off on a pre-dawn launch and Killer was going on ahead with his wingman King [Lieutenant (j.g.) Karl] Kirchwey. All of a sudden Killer got on the air saying 'Stop it! You're shooting at me.' What had happened was our own amphibious force, which was in position off the beach, was shooting at him. He finally said, 'Well, damn it, you've shot me down now.' Killer was a casualty of our own anti-aircraft fire."

Kane's plea for a cease and desist went unheeded because the ships below him were on a different radio frequency. Unable to continue flying, he stalled his Hellcat into the water. The force of the impact smashed his head against the gun sight. Nevertheless, he recovered enough from the blow to exit the sinking plane. Picked up by a nearby ship and returned to the carrier, Kane nursed a bloody head and black eyes.

Ramage automatically assumed the role of coordinator for all aviation over the target, while Lieutenant Louis Bangs became the strike leader for the *Enterprise* team. Ramage said, "I watched the tremendous power of this fleet putting those people ashore. The big carriers were pre-targeted into areas, and the CVE [escort carrier] planes would go in to strafe just ahead of the beach. Their fighters were strafing just ahead of the troops as they landed. We had carrier aircraft orbiting down to the south and my job was to call them up as targets developed. We simply had so darn much air power over the area that it was hard to find targets for them. I was looking around down in the area, and unfortunately I got too low. I had inherited Killer's wingman [Kirchwey] and this wingman was shot off my wing by AA. This really was kind of dumb on my part because I didn't need a wingman and he simply shouldn't have been with me. I felt very badly about that."

According to Gerald Bogan, the rear admiral commanding Carrier Support Group One who had shifted his flag from the *Fanshaw Bay* to the *White Plains* after a bomb from an enemy plane wrecked the stern of the former, the Marines on Saipan said they had never received better-coordinated air support.

Around dusk on the night of June 15, the VF(N)-101 Corsairs took off to forestall a force of eight Nakajima Francis bombers, new two-engine aircraft with more speed than the Betty. Several Zeros danced attendance around the Francis group. Chick Harmer and his wingman, Lieutenant (j.g.) Rob Holden, attacked. The escorts moved in to deflect them, and several bullets struck Harmer's Corsair. Holden, however, shot down one of the enemy fighters, and the engagement broke off without further incident.

Air Group Ten continued to hit not only on Saipan but also on the other islands to prevent any support for the 17,500 Japanese soldiers on Saipan from arriving. Hearing that there was a ship afloat in a Guam harbor, Ramage led a strike there. "We went in, got hits on it and as we came out I circled to rendezvous. I saw that one of my planes had become a flamer. It was [Lieutenant J.] Leonard and his gunner [Aviation Radioman Second Class R. P] Wynne. He went straight in, right off the ship in the harbor. We were out far enough so we were out of the way of the antiaircraft fire. I detached myself and turned the strike over to Bangs. I went back to see if I could find what had really happened to Leonard. There was just no question he had gone straight in and there was no way of possibly saving him, no chute, no nothing. I made a tour of the harbor and let them take a few shots at me.

"I came back and landed aboard late, which never makes you very popular, and reported to Admiral Reeves [John W., commander of Carrier Task Group Three]. I told him that we had lost a plane and also that I had gone back and there was absolutely nothing that we could do about it. He said, 'Well, that's fine. Now, what I want you to do is get yourself a couple of planes and go on back into the harbor and make absolutely sure that there is no way that pilot can be alive.' It's that type of thinking that we knew that our admirals did. We knew darn well that if there was any time that there was any chance whatsoever of being rescued they'd come after us. Whereas I thought it was a rather useless mission, it still was a very fine thing to know that those admirals knew you were out there too." Reeves was a qualified aviator, having won his wings in 1936. Whether a black-shoe admiral would have ordered such a compassionate mission is questionable.

The *Gambier Bay*'s VC-10, in the air at 8:00 A.M., struck at a stronghold, the sugar mill at Charon Kanoa. Commander Edward Huxtable, the air group leader, brought in the TBMs, while Lieutenant John Stewart led the fighters. The raiders were pleasantly surprised by the light antiaircraft fire, and everyone except Stewart reached the carrier without incident. The lieutenant's engine began to misfire after ground fire struck the plane. He tenderly maneuvered the Hellcat out to sea and then landed beside a destroyer, which quickly plucked him from the water.

Lieutenant (j.g.) Henry Pyzdrowki, who had completed his first solo flight under Civilian Pilot Training on December 7, 1941, posted to a scouting assignment in his TBM, flew over Marpi Point, a steep cliff on the north end of Saipan. He and his radioman, Jerry Fauls, gaped in amazement as they watched men, women, and children, altogether some nine hundred civilians, leap from the 900-foot cliff to their deaths. They committed mass suicide, duplicated in other islands where the resident population considered themselves an integral part of Japan, rather than accept surrender.

On D plus 1, some of the *Gambier Bay* TBMs carried ammunition and supplies for the 20,000 Marines on the island. They also performed interdiction missions. Pyzdrowski's radioman, Fauls, noticed four small guns at the points of a square. He told his pilot that perhaps a big gun, well camouflaged, occupied the middle. Pyzdrowski nosed over, followed by two other bombers. Flak whizzed by them, but three 500-pounders crushed the emplacement. The men of the *Gambier Bay* ran into even thicker squalls of antiaircraft when they sought to obliterate the airdromes on Guam and Tinian. The pressure of the ground forces and the constant hammering of the fleet at Saipan quieted the guns there, but on the other islands, the defenders remained resolute and well prepared.

Under the "New Operational Policy" of Japan's Imperial Command, the strategy called for its fleet to confront the American Pacific naval forces when an opportunity arose to smash the enemy in one massive blow. According to Samuel Eliot Morison, the Japanese command, deciphering the history written in the skies, recognized the supremacy of the aircraft carrier to the battleship. Morison insisted that the United States had adopted that stance with the nomination of Mitscher, an air admiral, to command Task Force Fifty-eight, even though the battleship commanders in TF-58 held that the seniority was not quite correct. The Fifth Fleet, which included Mitscher's group, remained under overall command of Spruance.

While nine carriers, in three divisions, sailed with the Mobile Force, the commander, Admiral Jisaburo Ozawa, was not himself an aviator, even though he had relied heavily on flattops in earlier engagements. Ozawa also had a formidable array of capital ships: the pair of oversize battleships *Yamato* and *Musashi*, both of which mustered 17-inch guns and displaced one and a half times that of anything in the U.S. fleet. In addition, the Mobile Force included four older battleships, eleven cruisers, and a retinue of thirty destroyers plus the usual support vessels. The AGO strategy plotted a fight in the Philippine Sea, where the Americans would be subject not only to Ozawa's carrier-based planes but also to aircraft drawn from the Marianas, the southern Philippines, and other outposts. As Ozawa approached, U.S. submarines tracking the Mobile Force exacted a nagging toll—three tankers and four destroyers—even as the armada sallied into the Philippine Sea on June 15, D-Day at Saipan.

To meet the threat while maintaining support for the Marines still engaged in a savage struggle to enlarge their toehold on Saipan, the invasion of Guam, scheduled for June 18, was postponed. Instead, the U.S. Fifth Fleet dispatched Task Force Fifty-eight to the Philippine Sea and a confrontation with the Mobile Force.

FIFTEEN

THE GREAT MARIANAS TURKEY SHOOT

A s Task Force Fifty-eight steered for a rendezvous with the Mobile Force, the odds on the water favored Mitscher. His flotilla outnumbered the enemy in carriers fifteen to nine, in battleships seven to five (although the gunpower of the superdreadnoughts *Yamato* and *Musashi* compensated for the numerical disparity), twenty-one cruisers to thirteen (though the Japanese had an edge in heavy ones), and sixty-nine destroyers to twenty-eight. But it was in carrier aircraft that the Americans had the greatest superiority. Mitscher commanded at least double the available Japanese planes in every category. His fighters, dive-bombers, and torpedo bombers totaled almost 900.

Ozawa counted on other factors to balance the equation or even provide an advantage. The Japanese planes, absent the added weight of protective armor plate and self-sealing gas tanks, could range 200 miles farther than their counterparts. That enabled them to attack from a distance beyond the striking power of Task Force Fifty-eight. If the airfields in the Marianas remained viable, the Japanese carrier planes could even land there, refuel, rearm, and return to battle. Furthermore, the Nipponese admiral expected strong support from 500 or so airplanes already operating out of the Marianas and islands in the vicinity. The prevailing winds also favored Ozawa for launch and recovery.

To reduce the Mobile Force's support from more distant bases, U.S. fighter sweeps ranged as far as Iwo Jima. In the early afternoon

of June 15, the *Yorktown's* VF-1, loaded with 135-pound fragmentation bombs, set a course for the tiny volcanic island that would become a battle holocaust nine months later. Cruising at a leisurely
pace, they covered the 135 miles in about an hour. Led by Commander Bernard "Smoke" Strean, the first Hellcat division screamed
down upon the airfield at a speed of 350 to 380 knots before releasing their hardware at 2,000 feet. The dives continued to 500 feet to
unleash fusillades from the .50-calibers. Strean reported that his
bomb had exploded in a cluster of eight aircraft, starting several
fires. As he triggered his machine guns, he aimed at soldiers running
for cover, a fighter taxiing, another in a revetment. At an altitude of
only 300 feet, he destroyed a Zeke as it attempted to take off.

Others from VF-1 related similar tales about their bombing
runs. As the flight recovered from its attacks, enemy fighters accosted them. In Strean's division, Lieutenant (j.g.) J. F. Hankins
turned inside a Zeke, and a burst from his guns produced a swirl
of fire as the enemy spun into the water. Lieutenant (j.g.) M. M.
Tomme, Jr., poured bullets from a position behind a fighter before it
turned on its back and nosed into the sea. Lieutenant (j.g.) R. A.
Bechtol scored a fourth victory for the quartet.

Two pilots in another division performed photographic runs
while Lieutenant R. T. Eastmond and Lieutenant (j.g) LaBoutillier
bombed a couple of bombers at the end of a runway. Both started to
burn. Eastmond, joining up with Strean's group, flamed a Zeke, and
then, when he closed in, his stream of fire blew up the Zeke.

Ensign A. P. Morner, in a division intercepted by the enemy before the bombing run, jettisoned his ordnance and engaged the foe.
He shot down a pair, but he had neglected to dump his belly tank.
The Zekes outmaneuvered him, and machine-gun bullets tore up his
wing; a 20-mm shell knocked out the firewall behind the engine; and
shrapnel sliced into his left big toe, the arch of his foot, and his skin.
Two more shells hit above the starboard wheel well, another rock-
eted into the starboard wing, and an oil line leak spouted fluid inside
the cockpit. One blast knocked his radio cord from his helmet, and
a large hole appeared in his starboard elevator. With his altimeter,
airspeed indicator, and gyro compass nonfunctional, Morner threw
his F6F-3 into a 6,000-foot dive to evade a Zeke seeking the kill. At
100 feet over the water he leveled out, jinked violently, and tried to
outrun the persistent Zeke. It followed him for 20 miles before making a slow roll around him, then breaking off contact. The enemy
had probably exhausted his ammunition.

Morner groped his way back to the *Yorktown*, aided by an anti-submarine patrol returning home. Holding a strong port rudder, Morner kept his wobbly right wing from falling off. Over the carrier he lowered the tail hook by vigorously rolling his wings. The starboard wheel descended only partially. He was waved off on his first try, and his windshield was blanketed with oil. Morner achieved a successful belly landing.

Lieutenant R. A. Shireman, Lieutenant (j.g.) G. W. Staeheli, and Lieutenant (j.g.) Tukey, who had collaborated in shooting down an Emily four days earlier, knocked down five fighters confirmed and two probables. Altogether, VF-1 claimed destruction of twenty in the air with three probables. In addition, VF-1 believed it had smashed ten bombers and four fighters on the ground. Two men were lost. One simply disappeared; the other, Ensign Hogue, was last seen in his life raft a half mile offshore but drifting toward the Japanese island.

Fighters from the other flattops in the fast carrier fleet also banged away at Iwo Jima's resources. Eight Hellcats of VF-2 from the *Hornet*, with a pair of SB2Cs from VB-2, scrambled for the island. They were jumped by a far superior numerical force of Zekes, as many as thirty-five to forty. Appraising the ensuing dogfights, the Americans said scornfully, "Their tactics were erratic and disorganized. They would attack single planes when they had altitude advantage but failed on numerous occasions to press home an advantage. One F6F-3 pilot climbed from the water to 7,000 feet, bracketed by four Jap fighters. He turned repeatedly to port and to starboard and they refrained from attacking him until he had sufficient altitude to resist. In several instances, Jap fighters got on the tail of our pilots and the tracer fire from their guns was the first warning received of their presence. Despite this fact, only two F6Fs were damaged in combat and these only slightly."

Lieutenant Lloyd G. Bernard distinguished himself by shooting down five of the foe within a space of twenty-five minutes; in fact, two went down within a thirty-second interval. After his group pushed over for their run, Barnard reported, "We saw eight to ten coming in below us. I made a head-on run from above. I turned as I passed to see him blow up. Wings and debris went everywhere."

For victim number two, he said, "I pulled up and winged one and a Zeke pulled in front of me at 9,000 feet. I fired on him from six o'clock at the same level. He blew up and I went right through his fire. I turned around and there was a Zeke on an F6F's tail. I fired a full deflection shot from nine o'clock, below, and he blew up. By this time they were blowing up all over the place." Bernard spotted another victim low on the water, perhaps 200 feet. He came down and rolled it into the sea. He then chased a Zeke that had taken a run on a fellow American. He followed his quarry down to the water. Just before other Hellcats could bring their guns to bear, Bernard shot it down for his fifth victory

Lieutenant (j.g.) Myrvin Noble chipped in with three confirmed downed Zekes, one probable, and a possible. Lieutenant (j.g.) Charles H. Carroll said he had pursued a Zeke for 20 miles before he put a burst into the cockpit. As the enemy faltered, Carroll polished him off with another spurt. Subsequently, he knocked down two more. The seven pilots from VF-2 registered seventeen confirmed kills. Numbers aside, the experiences of the Navy flyers in the run-up to the battle reveal a crucial weakness in the Japanese. Their pilots demonstrated an inexperience that augured poorly in their bouts with the Americans. Most of the air groups fielded by Task Force Fifty-eight contained veterans of many combat missions. While the minimum for U.S. airmen ordinarily amounted to two years of training, their Japanese opposites tended to be only six months out of flight school or less. Japanese planes continued to have extended range, but that meant they still had not added the weight of armor to protect either their pilots or their machines. In addition, the radar installations in Task Force Fifty-eight and its aircraft had improved greatly, while the Japanese detection devices remained at a primitive level.

On June 18, the *Yorktown*'s combat air patrol from VF-1 intercepted a flight of some thirty-five Zekes and Tonys providing high cover for an even larger congregation of enemy bombers below them in the vicinity of Guam. Since other Hellcats appeared about to engage the bombers, Bernard Strean, leader of the pack from Fighting One, jumped the fighter escorts. The commander directed his fire into the cockpit and wing roots of a Tony, and it headed straight down. Lieutenant (j.g.) R. A. Bechtol confirmed the kill. Strean then added a Zeke to his credits while Bechtol destroyed both a Tony and a Zeke. Lieutenant (j.g.) J. F. Hankins scored three victories, while Lieutenant R. T. Eastmond knocked out four more. Eastmond remarked that when he looked around he saw seventeen aircraft burning. The fracas ended with a dearth of targets; VF-1 listed twenty-six enemy airplanes shot down and four probables.

One pilot, Ensign C. R. Garman, vanished during the dogfights, presumably a victim of the Japanese. Another F6F-3 was forced to make a water landing when an overeager destroyer crew downed it with antiaircraft guns.

According to Alex Vraciu, "On the 18th, the Japanese fleet was still unlocated—they couldn't find them. They sent search planes. They sent torpedo planes with a couple of fighters out on search vectors, each carrying a 500-pounder. If they found the Japanese task force, they were supposed to all concentrate damage on one ship to at least slow it down so that our fleet would be able to sink it later in a following attack. There were a lot of things transpiring that we didn't know about in the ready rooms."

While the admirals contemplated an imminent meeting with the enemy, the flyers doubted any serious response from the Japanese. A few days before June 19, Vraciu recalled, "Gus Widhelm [Mitscher's air officer] came to our squadron ready room and bet our squadron $1,000 that we would have a fleet engagement in seven days. I was on combat air patrol at the time and when I came down, there was only $125 left of that $1,000 bet. So I took it and lost, like everybody else in the squadron."

What appeared at first to be a contest between two well-matched opponents, however, turned into a debacle for the forces of Admiral Ozawa. On June 18, Mitscher determined that his foe was some 350 to 400 miles off. Jimmy Thach, the Midway hero and tactical genius now serving as operations officer directly under Mitscher, recalled, "We knew approximately the distance that the Japanese fleet was. We knew they would come in to throw their strike at maximum range and then withdraw a little bit to keep away from our search planes. The wind was blowing from the direction of Saipan . . . away from the direction of the enemy. I talked to Arleigh Burke very urgently to tell him that we would never catch those people if we didn't run toward them, especially since the prevailing wind was such that when we launched and recovered aircraft, we would have to be going away from them. That night I wanted to run all night long toward them, and that's what I thought Mitscher would do, and what Mitscher thought he would do too.

"All night long, Arleigh Burke and I sat up writing messages for Mitscher to send to Spruance to try to get him to let us run toward the enemy so that the next day we could afford to run into the wind which would be away from the enemy and toward Saipan, launch a strike and we'd be close enough to them to be within our combat radius."

If Task Force Fifty-eight steamed toward the Mobile Force, the stage could be set for a night encounter. Spruance, in his role as overall commander, had directed the battleships to take the lead in the belief that in a surface battle, the Americans would outnumber the enemy in big ships, a dubious proposition considering the power of the *Yamato* and *Musashi*. Mitscher prudently inquired of Vice Admiral Willis A. Lee, who commanded Task Group 58.7, the battleship unit, how he felt about meeting the Japanese at night, adding that it might be possible for his carrier planes to make contact late in the afternoon and in a night attack. That too was a highly risky notion, and Lee demurred, believing that darkness would offset his force's numerical superiority.

The argument, at least from Thach and Burke, intensified. "We wrote dozens of [messages]," said Thach, "some stronger than others, and finally we wrote one that said, 'You can have my job if you won't let me run toward the enemy.' " Mitscher, who'd sent two or three pleas, refused to present his superior with the ultimatum. In Thach's word, Spruance was "adamant." He vetoed a movement west and a possible attack just before or after dark. The Fast Carrier Task Force resumed its position about 40 miles west of the Marianas and still 400 miles away from the Mobile Force. According to Thach, "This was a case, in my opinion, of being overcautious and coupled with a lack of understanding that an aircraft carrier doesn't protect an amphibious force by being within sight of it, or within gun range of it. It will do better to go out and find the enemy and hit him because we had such a wide span of search operations that nothing could do an end run around us and get to the amphibs. But that's what Spruance was worried about, [that] they'd do an end run, get in between us and the amphibious force and somehow we couldn't catch them. They'd [the Japanese] already spent most of their strike capability. They had very little left except the ships. They were relatively harmless because they had lost control of the air."

The decision by the Fifth Fleet commander set the conditions for the fight that ensued. On June 19, there occurred one of the greatest air battles of World War II, and the Japanese were indeed overwhelmed. Ozawa threw what he considered his best punch, launching his aerial armada before dawn. The American fleet lay 350 miles off, but Ozawa's scenario envisioned his raiders hammering Task Force Fifty-eight, stopping at Guam to refuel and rearm, then pounding the enemy on the way back to the Mobile Force. To guarantee that his attack would be coordinated with the planes and installations in the Marianas, Ozawa broke radio silence to advise his cohorts on the islands of his intentions.

The Americans, through their knowledge of the code and radar, consequently located the Mobile Force, and all hands stood alert for the coming onslaught. A four-engine Mariner patrol plane's radar also registered the position, approximate size, and rate of advance of the Mobile Force. Unfortunately, for reasons never precisely determined, Spruance did not receive the intelligence from the Mariner. He dithered over possible feints by the enemy, derived largely from his reading of history. As Thach indicated, he feared a raid in which the Mobile Force would slip around Task Force Fifty-eight and batter the invasion fleet off Saipan, and thus he delayed Mitscher's armada from closing with the enemy. Truman Hedding, serving as a staff officer under Arleigh Burke, chief of staff for Mitscher, remarked that while Nimitz had decreed the mixture of air and sea admirals, the naval aviator chosen to become Spruance's chief of staff had not yet reported when Spruance made his decision.

As June 19 dawned, Task Group 58.7, behind a picket screen of destroyers, U.S. battleships flanked by cruisers and more destroyers stood farthest west of the Marianas with three carrier groups, 58.1, 58.3, and 58.2, in a north–south line about 15 miles behind 58.7 and separated from one another by 12 to 15 miles. Northeast of the great battleship circle was Task Group 58.4.

At 5:30 A.M. that day, the first Japanese aircraft showed on the radar screens of 58.2. Hellcats from the *Monterey* promptly blew away one of a pair of Judy dive-bombers while the other fled. Thirty minutes later, a lone dive-bomber, a Val, made the mistake of coming within range of the destroyer screen for 58.7 and paid the ultimate price. Combat air patrol, in the neighborhood of Guam, confirmed a humming swarm of aircraft, a maximum effort. The Navy pilots signaled a hurry-up call for reinforcements. Aboard the carriers, a profusion of blips spattered the radar scopes, denoting a large number of the enemy assembling for their role. On the TBS (talk between ships), the voice of Mitscher himself squawked the traditional rallying cry of the circus, "Hey, Rube!" Immediately, the loudspeaker on every one of the fifteen flattops ordered, "Pilots, man your planes." The great aerial battle started slowly, but the tempo picked up rapidly to culminate in an all-out melee. Eight separate Hellcat squadrons rose to stymie the Japanese thrust at the task force.

Again, the Americans would profit hugely from their intercepts of Japanese communications. A Japanese air coordinator loitered in the sky, giving specific instructions to various units on their targets and courses. Lieutenant (j.g.) Charles A. Sims, who spoke Japanese, listened to the air coordinator and furnished Task Force Fifty-eight with detailed intelligence that enabled fighter direction to advise the Hellcat squadrons where to head.

Vraciu said, "On the morning of the 19th, the *Lexington* had twelve Hellcats—wings spread [not folded], on the deck ready to go. Just climb aboard; don't even kick a tire. We were on standby alert to supplement the combat air patrol already aloft.

"We had a lot of fighters out there—a lot of planes. They got the bomber and torpedo planes out of the way. Some of them were kept on the hangar deck, but most of them were positioned off to circle south away from the prospective battle area so as not to clutter up the radar screen and likely be considered targets themselves—by our own people. At approximately 10:20 our group was launched. I heard the FDO [fighter direction officer] saying, 'Vector 250, climb to Angels 25, pronto!' [A heading of 250 degrees, climb to 25,000 feet at full power.] It was a running rendezvous on the climb.

"Our skipper—Lt. Commander Paul Buie, a tall, lanky southerner—was leading our flight of twelve. He led the first division. I had moved up to division leader when I joined Air Group 16 and led the second division of Hellcats.

"Overhead, converging contrails of fighters from other carriers could be seen heading in the same direction. After a while, the skipper, who was riding behind a brand-new engine, began to pull ahead steadily until he was out of sight. We had seen his wingman drop out. The full power climb was too much for his engine, and his propeller froze [seized up], causing him to ditch in the water. Luckily he was picked up twelve hours later by a destroyer.

"On the way up, my wingman, [Ensign Homer] Brockmeyer, kept insistently pointing toward my wing. Thinking he had spotted the enemy. I attempted to turn the lead to him, basically by tapping my head and pointing at him—that's the standard signal for 'Take the lead and direct us to the bogey'—but he would only shake his head negatively. He [continued to] nod his head sideways and then point toward my wing. I finally shook him off to concentrate on the immediate task at hand. Later I found out that my wings weren't fully locked in place—the red safety battle locks were showing—hence Brock's frantic pointing. I gulped after I got down and found out what he was trying to tell me. I had flown the whole hop, unaware of the wings not being fully locked. The emergency safety pins were not inserted into the main locking device. I suppose it really wasn't as dangerous as I had thought."

Unaware of that problem, Vraciu concerned himself with a more troublesome matter: his engine was spraying oil on his windshield, and of necessity he eased back on the throttle. His division stuck with him. "When I found my tired engine would not go into high-blower [supercharger], our top altitude became 20,000 feet. This limitation was reported to the FDO." He attributed the mechanical defects not to errant care but to the normal hard wear and tear, particularly from landings.

The initial summons to battle, however, was canceled; someone else dealt with that wave of attackers. Vraciu and company returned to orbit over the task group at 20,000 feet, the limit for his Hellcat. "We had barely returned when the FDO directed us to Vector 265. There was something in his voice that indicated that he had a good one on the string. The bogeys were seventy-five miles away when reported and we headed out, hopeful of meeting them halfway. I saw two other groups of Hellcats converging from the starboard side—four in one group and three in the other.

"About thirty-five miles away, I 'tallyhoed' three 'bogeys' and closed toward them. In the back of my mind, I figured, 'There's got to be more than three planes,' as I remembered the seriousness in the fighter director's voice. Spot-gazing intently, I suddenly picked out a large, rambling mass of at least fifty enemy planes 2,000 feet below, portside and closing. My adrenaline flow hit 'high C.' I remember thinking, 'This could develop into a once-in-a-lifetime fighter pilot's dream.' Then, a little puzzled and suspicious, I looked about for the fighter cover that normally would be overhead of them, but there did not seem to be a top cover. By this time, we were in perfect position for a high-side run. Giving a slight rock to my wings, I began a run on the nearest inboard straggler, a Judy dive-bomber.

"However, peripherally, I was conscious of another Hellcat that seemed to have designs on that Jap, also. He was too close for comfort, almost blindsided me, so I aborted my run. There were enough cookies on this plate for everyone, I was thinking. I streaked underneath the formation, getting a good look at their planes for the first time. They were Judys, Jills [torpedo bombers], and Zeros. I radioed an amplified report.

"After pulling up and over, I picked out another Judy on the edge of the formation. It was doing some wild maneuvering, and the rear gunner was squirting [firing] away as I came down from the stern. I worked in close and gave him a burst. He caught fire quickly and headed down to the sea, trailing a long plume of smoke.

"I pulled up again and found two more Judys flying as loose wings. I came in from the rear, sending both down burning. Dipping my Hellcat's wing, I slid over on the one slightly ahead and got it on the same pass. It caught fire, also, and I could see the rear gunner still peppering away at me as he disappeared in an increasingly sharp arc downward. For a split-second, I almost felt sorry for the little bastard.

"That made three down, and now we were getting close to our fleet. The enemy planes had been pretty well chopped down, but a substantial number of them still remained. It didn't look like we would score a grand slam. I reported this information back to base. The sky appeared to be full of smoke and pieces of planes, and we were trying to ride herd on the remaining attacking planes to keep them from scattering.

"Another 'meatball' broke formation up ahead, and I slid over onto his tail, again working in close because of my oil-smeared windshield. I gave him a short burst, but it was enough; it went right into the sweet spot at the root of his wing tanks. The pilot or control cables must have been hit, also, because the burning plane twisted crazily, out of control.

"In spite of our efforts, the Jills were now beginning to descend to begin their torpedo runs, and the remaining Judys were at the point of peeling off to go down with their bombs. I headed for a group of three Judys in a long column. By the time I had reached the tail-ender [of the trio] we were almost over our outer screen of ships but still fairly high. The first Judy was about to begin his dive and as he started to nose over, I noticed black puffs beside him in the sky. Our 5-inchers were beginning to open up. Foolishly, maybe, I over-took the nearest one. It seemed that I barely touched the trigger and his engine started coming to pieces. The Judy started smoking, then torching alternately, off-and-on, as it disappeared below.

"The next one was about one-fifth of the way down in his dive, appearing to be trying for one of the destroyers—before I caught up with him. This time a short burst produced astonishing results. Number six blew up with a tremendous explosion right in front of my face. I must have hit his bomb. I had seen planes blow up before but *never* like this! I yanked the stick up sharply to avoid the scattered pieces and flying hot stuff, then radioed, 'Splash number six! There's one more ahead, and he's headed for a BB, but I don't think he'll make it.' Hardly had the words left my mouth than the Judy caught a direct hit that removed it immediately as a factor to worry about in the war. He had run into a solid curtain of steel from the battlewagon."

Vraciu, while cognizant of the inability of the blizzard of anti-aircraft shot and shell to distinguish between friend and foe, nevertheless flew through the maelstrom. When he looked back, he said, he saw only Hellcats still in the sky. "Glancing backward to where we had begun, in a pattern thirty-five-miles long, there were flaming oil slicks in the water and smoke still hanging in the air. It didn't seem like just eight minutes—it seemed longer. But that's all it was—an eight-minute opportunity for the flight of a lifetime."

Any emotions of triumph and personal payback for Pearl Harbor or the death of Butch O'Hare yielded to fear and anger when Vraciu homed in on the *Lexington* for his recovery. "Although my IFF was on, and my approach was from the right direction and I was making the required 360-degree right turns, it didn't seen to matter to some of the trigger-happy gun crews in the heat of this fleet battle. I would like to think that the choice words I uttered on the radio stopped all that nonsense, but I know better."

Safely aboard, Vraciu flashed his "six" by holding up six fingers to the bridge as he taxied up the deck. And in the ready room, he was joined by comrades whose excitement included "the liberal use of hands to punctuate aerial victories." Since the carrier was Mitscher's flagship, it served as host to war correspondents, who eagerly copied down the pilots' chatter.

Only in the postmortem did Vraciu learn of the problem with his wing locks. He had expended only 360 rounds of the 2,400 in a fully armed Hellcat. He credited the oil film over his windshield with having forced him to work in close and the flammable nature of the Japanese planes.

Other fighter squadrons also wreaked havoc upon the Japanese attackers. David McCampbell, the 1933 USNA graduate who had temporarily been denied a commission because of a poverty-stricken Navy, had spent the first years of the war as a gunnery officer and then as landing signals officer aboard the *Wasp* until torpedoes sank it in September 1943. He finally received command of a fighter squadron and then took over Air Group Fifteen aboard the *Essex* early in 1944. One of his pilots was his nephew-in-law Wayne Morris, a film actor. Morris had taken a shortcut to his role: he had possessed a private pilot's license before entering the Navy and after a short course at Pensacola had obtained his golden wings and commission. Morris would get credit for seven and half victories by the end of the war.

When McCampbell first trained his squadron and then assumed command of the air group, he abandoned the tactic of the Thach Weave except for special circumstances. In the increasingly crowded skies the maneuvers heightened the possibility of midair collisions. McCampbell realized that Thach had designed it at a time when the Wildcat, the basic Navy fighter, had been inferior to the enemy's Zero. The Hellcat's performance qualities obviated that disadvantage.

On June 19, McCampbell recalled, "I led the second group of fighters to take off from the *Essex*. The fighter squadron commander led the first group and they did quite well." Actually, Lieutenant Commander Charles Brewer, the skipper, knocked down five, while his wingman, Ensign R. E. Fowler, dropped four, and the second division leader, Lieutenant (j.g.) G. R. Carr, destroyed four bombers. Involved in the early devastation inflicted upon the Japanese were fighters from the *Cowpens*, *Bunker Hill*, *Princeton*, *Essex*, and *Enterprise*.

McCampbell's flight received word of incoming aircraft some 120 miles off. "We had plenty of time to launch to go out and attack them. I guess we must have hit that second strike out about sixty miles. We simply tore into them. They had Zeros, and they had Jills, and Judys, which was a beautiful little bomber. For some reason I missed the fighters. I never saw them. I picked up the first of the Judys, concentrated all my attention on that. The last division that was with me, of the four planes, they picked up the fighters and had a good time up there with them. But I led the rest of my people down on the Judys.

"I had so much altitude advantage, that when I dove down, I would estimate we were maybe 20,000 [feet] above, and they were probably 15,000 or 16,000. I dove down on them and I had so much speed, I couldn't hit the leader, but I did hit one of the tail-end Charlies. I attacked him, thinking that I would knock him off, and then go under him, go over to the other side and come back with altitude advantage and hit them from the other side. But the Judy [that he first attacked] blew up in my face and I pulled up above him to avoid the debris. I went across on top and I remember thinking at the time, 'Gosh, will I ever get across this formation?' Because I figured they were all shooting at me. There was no one out there waving binoculars or a sword at me, but I had that feeling.

"I went across the other side [and] made an attack on another plane and I worked my way up, finally got the leader with just one gun firing. I'd burned out the barrels on five of them. I still had one gun firing and with that, I dropped down to the flight of Jills, the torpedo planes below, and shot a plane down. I shot at a plane, the leader down there with the Jills, but I didn't claim him. I think I claimed him a a probable because he didn't blow up in my face. I went on back to the ship."

Like a number of its predecessors, McCampbell's air group had debuted with runs on Marcus and Wake islands, where they had met no aerial opposition. Walter Lundin, who had enlisted in the Royal Canadian Air Force in the spring of 1941 and been trained in Wellington bombers, had transferred to the U.S. Navy. He had become a fighter pilot and eventually received orders to join VF-15 under McCampbell. He recalled the strikes at Marcus and Wake, where the squadron had incurred some losses to ground fire before their first encounter with enemy aircraft on June 11.

"June nineteenth," remembered Lundin, "had started out in an unusual way. CAPs were usually handled by junior officers, as the flights were mostly boring. On this morning, Lieutenant Commander [Charles] Brewer led a flight of twelve of us on a CAP. Someone must have been aware of something about to happen. [Obviously, junior officers such as Lundin were not aware of all of the intelligence reports and scouting data collected by the likes of Mitscher and the squadron and group leaders.] After a predawn launch, we were on station at about 10,000 feet and given a vector to fly. We climbed to 25,000 feet and encountered the first wave of aircraft. The turkey shoot was about to start. Their aircraft were layered at 15,000, 20,000, and 25,000, flying singly, and seemed to stretch from horizon to horizon.

"At this point, all the fighters were being launched from their respective ships, and the traffic on the radio was almost overwhelming. We only had four channels to work with, one emergency channel, one HF [high frequency] and two VHF [very high frequency]. The two VHF were the only ones available to us, and with all the planes taking off, joining up, and being vectored to the target, it was understandable that the radio was overused. This was in contrast to the radio silence we were accustomed to.

"The flight leader picked out his target, and as was customary, the division split up into two sections, since four planes were much too unwieldy in combat. Off to the side a Zeke fighter was approaching, and I was able to make a beam run on it. They had no armor protection and no self-sealing tanks, so a two-second burst caused a fire and explosion. Upon getting in range of another fighter, as I was about to fire, a friendly F6F slid in front of me and took out the target. Had I started firing, he would have flown right into my tracers. Lucky guy. Later, at a much lower level, a torpedo bomber was encountered and a short firing run caused it to crash into the sea.

"Since this was my first encounter with enemy forces, I was a little in awe of what was going on around me. It was natural to think about what your opponent was going to do, what you would do to counter it. Would the training I received permit me to measure up? I later realized that if a pilot could get through his first four or five engagements his longevity options would increase considerably."

Commander Ernest Snowden, boss of Air Group Sixteen on the *Lexington*, reported, "We could see vapor trails of planes coming in with tiny black specks at the head. It was just like the sky writing we all used to see before the war. The sky was a white overcast and for some reason the planes were making vapor trails at much lower altitude than usual. That made it easier for our boys to find the incoming Japs. The air was so clear you could see planes tangling in the sky. Then a flamer would go down. We would hope it was a Jap and from the radio chatter we could hear from the pilots, it seemed that the Japs were getting the worst end of it.

"One of our newest members of the fighter squadron, Ensign Bradford Hagie, shot down three Japs while ferrying from one carrier to another. Hagie had joined up with us as a replacement. On the day before he had motor trouble and couldn't land aboard *Lexington* because we were launching planes. A carrier cannot land and launch planes at the same time. [However, on this particular day, some flattops managed to deal with two-way traffic.] Hagie put down on another carrier about 3,000 yards away. He slept on her the night of the 18th. Next morning he took off about 9:30 to fly back to his carrier. While he was in the air, he heard the report about the Japs coming in and decided to go for a little hunt. He shot down three, which ain't bad for a 3,000-yard ferry flight."

Back aboard the *Essex*, ordnance technicians installed new gun barrels, and David McCampbell took off again as the fourth wave of Japanese sortied. As Admiral Ozawa had planned, Guam dispatched and replenished hordes of aircraft. Throughout the day, combat air patrols reported the furious activity around the island, and Air Group Fifteen's commander flew into the nest. He said, "They had gotten over near Guam by the time I got into them and that was quite a melee. They were scattered somewhat preparatory to landing and we blasted into them. I managed to get two planes out of that group. I guess we probably had only seven planes on this flight but I'd say we got about eight planes out of that bunch near Guam.

"As I was coming home, I saw this seaplane down on the water that was trying to pick up one of the downed pilots and a couple of Japs were strafing him. My wing man and I went down and ran them off. We didn't claim either one. We circled a little bit and I ran into one of my pilots, Ray Nall, who had been damaged. He couldn't make anywhere near full speed and there was at least one Jap attacking him. I ran him off and that's one of the few occasions that I ever used the weave. I was weaving with him, trying to protect him from this Jap or two and got him back to the ship." Although McCampbell, in his oral history, glossed over his exploits in the Marianas, he was credited with having destroyed five planes in the air.

Walter Lundin expected to meet the foe again. "In the late afternoon, an eight-plane fighter sweep was briefed to attack Orote Field on Guam. In Commander Brewer's absence I was the division leader. He was present at the briefing, and when we received the order to man our planes, as I was about to go from the ready room to the catwalk, he stopped me and said, 'Jake, I'm going to take your place and lead this flight.'"

Brewer fell victim to an ambush over Guam when he and his wingman, Ensign Thomas Tarr, dived down at a low-flying Zeke only to be overwhelmed by a number of enemy fighters. McCampbell said he had warned Brewer of the presence of many Japanese aircraft and not to sacrifice altitude for a crack at an enemy. Indeed, one of the principles inculcated by McCampbell in those who flew under his leadership was never to follow a plane down to confirm its destruction. "You've got an advantage and you want to keep that advantage as long as you can. Those are planes that we claim as probables. You know you hit him, you knocked him out of the formation and he's run off or spiraled down, smoking."

VF-2, the squadron tutored by Butch O'Hare before his death, now operated off the *Hornet*. According to *Odyssey of Fighting Two*, by Lieutenant Thomas L. Morrisey, on June 19, the aviators "awoke to an ominously placid sea—the night had passed peacefully enough, but the morning dispatches carried with them forebodings of busy and hectic hours ahead."

That anxiety stands in contrast to Lundin's lack of knowledge. Still, the ship had just secured from a general quarters stance when the first warning of intruders sounded at 7:15 A.M. Only a few pilots were in the ready room when the flight orders were announced. Throughout the remainder of the day, however, VF-2 launched all hands. Well out to sea, Lieutenant (j.g.) Eugene D. "Red" Redmond disposed of a pair of Zekes and registered a probable on a third. Lieutenant Art Van Haren, Jr., and Ensign Paul A. Doherty also destroyed two.

Hellcats from VF-2 escorted torpedo bombers and dive-bombers to Guam, where they caught a flock of Vals about to land at the Orote base. Ensign W. B. "Spider" Webb had been hovering over a downed American pilot when he saw the dive-bombers approaching the field. Said Webb, "All I did was enter the traffic circle at Orote Field and slip in behind a division of three. No. 1: I fired on the port plane first from six o'clock level. It burned. No. 2: I shifted to the center one and did the same thing and it burned. No. 3: Then I shifted to the starboard one and did likewise. I saw the pilot of this latter plane bail out. All three planes exploded. Than I whipped around over the field and got in behind another division of three.

"No. 4: I fired at the one to port; he made a quick flipper turn to the right and the pilot bailed out. His chute opened. No. 5: I came back to the one in the center but it pulled away and I got the one to starboard. No. 6: By this time the Vals were gaining altitude and the Zekes came in above them. I made a head-on run on one from below at 1,500 feet. I fired and saw pieces fly from the plane. It returned fire. A few seconds later, a parachute was in the air and the plane crashed."

By the time he shot down his sixth plane, only one of his guns was working. He still managed to attack two more Vals, causing both of them to smoke, but he was unable to list them as anything more than probables.

Lieutenant Russell Reiserer, ordinarily with VF(N)-76, the night fighter squadron but for the occasion under the VF-2 command, had already made two strafing passes at Orote Field, targeting the AA positions, when he saw a man in the water. He contacted an F4U Corsair escorting a rescue seaplane and directed the pilot to the downed flyer. Reiserer, like Redmond, then noticed the incoming bevy of Japanese dive-bombers. He sprang upon them. With one already down, Reiserer chased another for five miles before knocking it down. He pursued a third for several minutes through the clouds until it was within range. The fourth and fifth victims fell quickly, as Reiserer avoiding overrunning them by letting down his wheels and flaps. Two others from VF(N)-76, Lieutenant (j.g.) Fred L. Dungan and Ensign William H. Levering, added three and two enemy planes, respectively, to the total. Ensign Leroy Robinson vanished during the tumult in the skies, only to surface after landing aboard another carrier with two Zeros confirmed. For the day, VF-2 claimed an astonishing fifty-one downed.

Lieutenant Commander E. S. McCuskey, with eight Hellcats of VF-8 from the *Bunker Hill*, met enemy Zekes and Hamps over Guam. In contrast to other accounts, he described his opposition as "the most skillful encountered by this squadron. It was only by superior team work that our pilots were able to overcome them." The VF-8 group claimed ten enemy planes destroyed, but it was not as simple as a shooting gallery.

McCuskey reported that the aviators in the cockpits of the Hamps seemed able to take evasive action at the exact second McCuskey had opened fire, perhaps by reacting to the muzzle flash rather than tracers, thus limiting the Americans to extremely short bursts. Their escape maneuvers threatened to dunk the pursuing Hellcats in the water. McCuskey recommended firing a short burst from out of range to trick an enemy pilot into committing himself prematurely. One F6F-3, hit in the fuel and oil lines, attempted to ditch, but the aircraft broke up on striking the water and the pilot was lost.

Dan Rehm led a CAP of four F6F-3s from VF-8 off the *Bunker Hill* in the early morning. "Fighter Direction on the *Bataan*," said Rehm, "vectored me at Buster speed to intercept a large group of enemy aircraft. I climbed to twenty-five thousand feet and, after a short period, gave a very excited tallyho of about ninety-five enemy aircraft. I put my flight in a right echelon and began a high-altitude, high-speed pass on the left side of that formation. I fired at a Zero and hit him in the wing root of the plane and he just blew up. I pulled out at blackout speed and came around for another pass. I burned another and later got one more." In his brief account, Rehm telescoped the passage of minutes, even hours. "By this time the airspace was full of Navy fighters and burning Japs. You had to watch out that one of these did not fall on top of you. By this time I had been in the air almost seven hours. As I passed the island [superstructure of the carrier] I held up three fingers and the crew went wild."

The *Hornet's* VF-2 hunted in the skies around the Orote airfield on Guam. Ensign William H. Vaughan, Jr., drilled one Zeke from astern at 6,000 feet. His second prey exploded after a tail-level run at only 700 feet. In Vaughan's third confirmed kill, the pilot tried to bail out, but his plane broke in two, tearing his parachute.

Lieutenant Warren "Andy" Skon, who had accompanied Butch O'Hare on his final mission, working alone, reported knocking down a pair of Vals. Lieutenant (j.g.) Charles Carroll entered a circle of Vals seeking refuge at Orote. While a rear gunner desperately tried to drive him off, Carroll burned the dive-bomber. He sprayed a Hamp, which abruptly plunged into the water; a bullet had probably killed the pilot. Carroll reported, "The water was covered with fires from burning planes." He and his associates were responsible for fourteen destroyed.

The *Enterprise* dispatched VF-10, the Grim Reapers. Three divisions of twelve aircraft discovered four bomb-toting Zeros. Lieutenant (j.g.) Donald "Flash" Gordon nailed one at 3,000 feet, and his wingman, Lieutenant (j.g.) R. W. Mason, disposed of a second. Lieutenant Marion Marks led his division against a pair of torpedo bombers heading for a battleship. Marks missed, but his wingman, Ensign Charles D. Farmer, blew up one.

The Grim Reapers sat out waves two and three of the battle but returned to combat with the fourth and followed the enemy planes seeking refuge on Guam. The battered Japanese aviators, unable to land quickly because of the runway craters produced by Navy TBFs and SBDs, were easy targets. Fifteen assorted planes, ranging from Zeros to an old-style fixed-gear fighter, went down under the VF-10 guns.

Night fighter pilot Lieutenant Commander Chick Harmer, in a Corsair, and VF-10's executive officer, Lieutenant Hank Clem, at the controls of a Hellcat, rode shotgun for a pair of Seagulls endeavoring to retrieve some downed airmen off the west coast of Guam. The two float planes set down and because of the added weight of the passengers elected to taxi rather than fly to the nearby U.S. ships. The SOCs were about five miles apart, and the fighter pilots split up to watch over them individually. A Zero snarled in for a strafing attack on one Seagull. When Clem whipped his F6F-3 around to drive off the intruder, he spun into the water and was killed. Harmer fired on the Japanese plane and drove him off.

From the *Cabot*, a light carrier with Task Group 58.2, Air Group Thirty-one mustered its two dozen fighters, among them that of Lieutenant (j.g.) Arthur Hawkins. "I was with my division," said Hawkins," on combat air patrol at 25,000 feet, sitting there, waiting for them to come. The first wave were mostly fighters; they came in ahead with the big fighter-bombers coming in later. It must have been a good flight of 40 or 50, some Judys, some bombers but not very many.

"Our division was vectored out to hit on that first wave. We were in perfect position about 3,000–4,000 feet above them. As they came in, we dove into them from above. My division accounted for thirteen airplanes on that particular hop. I got three. Everybody got three except one guy, [Lieutenant (j.g.) John L.] Wirth, who got four. He was one of the combat veterans from before. [Wirth was actually a former enlisted pilot.] They hit us with three waves that day. It was so timed that when we finished and were getting low on fuel, we could not land back on our own ship. I landed on the *Monterey* [a sister ship of the *Cabot*] and so did the rest of my flight. They refueled us, replenished us, re-ammoed us, and back in the air we went as soon as they could get back into the wind and launch again.

"We were climbing back out. By that time the last wave had come through. Of course the ships had launched all the planes they could get into the air; they cleared the decks. They had launched bombers, everything. They had sent all the bombers over to orbit out near Guam, just to get them out of the way and leave the decks clear for the fighters to be able to cycle through the decks while this was going on. They [the U.S. Navy] had fighters protecting the bombers as they were circling. All the Japanese planes that had lived through the dogfights headed over to Guam to land. Some fighters were there protecting our bombers that were in the area. Here came all these Japanese planes into the Guam airfield to land. They were low on fuel, low on everything, and they were in a traffic pattern. I think one guy got about six or seven that day in the traffic pattern. It was a bad day at Black Rock for the Japanese that day."

The Hellcats from the *Lexington*, VF-1, which had slaughtered a host of enemy fighters the day before, engaged the Japanese strike force. Commander J. M. Peters, the leader of an eight-plane combat air patrol, lost two of his flight when one plane's F6F-3 engine began cutting out and the pilot, with his wingman, was ordered to return to base. Peters himself almost aborted when his motor started to miss, but when it recovered, he ventured out some 40 to 50 miles beyond the fleet. There he encountered a pair of Zekes, both of which he set ablaze. His remaining associates accounted for another five enemy fighters.

Although the fighter squadrons did most of the damage to the Japanese airpower, other units chipped in. Jim Ramage, leader of VB-10 on the *Enterprise*, noted that his SBDs had left the carrier well after all the Hellcats had been scrambled. "We didn't have fighters with us; they were all up topside. I put my dive bombers into the fluid four formation rather than the tight division that we used, because I thought possibly some of the Japs would break through and we might be able to get a shot at them. We would jettison our bombs and go after them.

"After about two or three hours, we received a message to go on in and drop our bombs on the fields on Guam, the Orote Peninsula. We were to get down there and see if we couldn't keep the field at least temporarily knocked out in case some of the Japs got through and tried to land. We got over there in time to see several shoot-downs. Our F6Fs were right down at treetop level chasing these poor guys up and down the landscape. I don't know if any Jap ever landed. I think there were some enemy pilots that either force landed or actually were so scared they just landed right in the water. It was a real massacre."

To the east of the Marianas, well away from the Japanese assault waves, the escort carriers continued to support the troops on Saipan. From the *Corregidor*, Composite Squadron Forty-one sent fighters and torpedo bombers to attack objectives on Saipan and Tinian. They blasted shipping, gun installations, and troops in the field. When four Zekes appeared, the VC-41 fighters destroyed them. The *Gambier Bay* narrowly escaped destruction. During the afternoon of June 18, an estimated hundred torpedo bombers approached the fleet at Saipan. Combat air patrols splashed several, but a significant number of torpedo bombers sifted through the screen. Flattops such as the *Gambier Bay* faced a difficult situation. Their fighters, having been in the air as long as four hours, needed to land, refuel, and rearm. But that meant aircraft on the deck with gas hoses exposed. Still there was no alternative.

The first fighters were refurbished and ready to start their take-offs when the Japanese planes arrived, 4 miles off, as the carrier gunners started shooting long-range. The opening tracers burned out well before the targets, but as the lead attacker came closer, shells began to strike home. At a quarter mile out, its two engines erupted in fire. Whether the doomed pilot intended to expend himself in a final suicidal blast or not, the torpedo bomber continued on a crash course for the *Gambier Bay*. In the final seconds, the fiery aircraft barely sailed over the flight deck before its final seaward plunge. A second attacker followed the same path, skimming low toward the deck, until it also burst into flames and then dived into the water.

Lieutenant Richard Roby, in his fighter on the after end of the flight deck, saw a strafing airplane fire a shell that passed through the folded wing of a TBM without exploding. Nearby, the sister carriers *Kitkun Bay*, *Coral Sea*, and *Corregidor* endured the same harrowing experience of having armed fighters on deck amid a cacophony of strafing and antiaircraft.

The first of the *Gambier Bay*'s planes lifted off, but Ensigns Charles Dugan and Joe McGraw barged into a hail of AA from the surrounding ships that was focused only on deterring the marauders. Both of the Wildcats (the escort carrier still fielded F4Fs) absorbed hits but remained viable. Lieutenant Gene Seitz hardly had time to charge his guns as he cleared the deck when, with wheels and flaps still down, he saw an enemy plane converging on him. He banked left and fired, and the Japanese bomber winged over into the water.

The chaotic scene continued until darkness neared. McGraw, some thirty holes in his Wildcat, no flaps, no radio, and no lights, could not land until the other less damaged aircraft were recovered. He was at great risk of crashing, and if he fouled the flight deck, no one else would be able to get down. The skipper of the *Gambier Bay* directed McGraw to try the *Kitkun Bay*. The landing officer there waved him off twice; he preferred not to mess up his flight deck.

McGraw returned to his home base when it was almost totally dark. Captain Hugh H. Goodwin decided to chance making his ship a prime target and ordered the lights switched on. The landing signals officer, dressed in shiny coveralls, held iridescent paddles as

McGraw edged toward the deck at 90 knots, 20 faster than normal. The Wildcat banged into the deck, bounced, and then crashed into the barrier. McGraw walked away from the wreckage.

On June 19, while Mitscher's Fast Carrier Task Force grappled with the massive Japanese air armada, those aboard the escort carriers to the east knew little if anything about the cataclysmic events on the other side of the Marianas. A few enemy aircraft tried to attack the four small flattops, but none penetrated the aerial screen. For their part, the Americans flew limited missions against Tinian to the north.

The converted tanker hulled *Suwannee* joined in the general defense of the area around the landing sites and organized the required patrols. Ensign Guy Sabin from Air Group Sixty, in an Avenger, as he broke through a cloud at 1,500 feet, saw a Japanese submarine on the surface. Sabin immediately dived on the U-boat while ordering his radioman to arm the depth bombs and his gunner to man the turret. The sub, having seen Sabin's TBM, began to slide under the water in a crash dive. But instead of running a zigzag course, the undersea boat steered a straight line. Sabin, following the wake, loosed his bombs from about 150 feet. Two of them threw up a shower of white foam, and the final explosions threw up geysers of black oil, signifying a ruptured hull. An oil slick spread over several hundred feet atop the water. Sabin and his crew had sunk Japanese submarine I-184.

The victory of Task Force Fifty-eight's fast carriers, however, dwarfed any achievements by the smaller ships. The AGO plan, which predicated a substantial victory by the Japanese air forces, had not considered the superiority of the American planes and the quality of those who flew them. The losses to Ozawa's resources added up to a staggering 315 aircraft (early U.S. claims posted exaggerated figures of between 400 and 500), while the Navy counted twenty-three of its own felled in combat and another six lost for other reasons. The American casualties numbered twenty pilots and seven air crewman killed, along with four officers and twenty-seven sailors dead aboard ships hit or near missed by Japanese raiders. Most of the shipboard losses occurred when a bomb struck the battleship *South Dakota*.

According to Arleigh Burke, when the shooting finally died away and the helpful Japanese air coordinator, whose messages had all been intercepted, signed off to return to his base, someone on Mitscher's staff asked if they should take him out. The admiral replied, "No, indeed! He did us too much good."

The June 19 event became known as the Great Marianas Turkey Shoot. Although Samuel Eliot Morison credited the label to Commander Paul D. Buie of VF-16 on the *Lexington*, Vraciu said the originator of the title had been one "Ziggy" Neft, a junior lieutenant of VF-16. "He apparently came from a hunting background and just happened to use that hunting jargon phrase in his post-flight briefing, saying, 'It was just like a turkey shoot!'"

SIXTEEN

THE BATTLE OF THE PHILIPPINE SEA

The Great Marianas Turkey Shoot was basically a defensive action as the Navy thwarted the enemy's efforts to strafe, bomb, and torpedo Task Force Fifty-eight. Had the Japanese thrust succeeded, the warships and planes could have then smashed the support for the Saipan campaign. With the Mobile Force repulsed, on June 20, Mitscher and company turned to the offense. Ozawa's ships had already been hurt, not by aircraft but by U.S. submarines, free to take action after having been restricted to tracking the movement of the fleet components.

The skipper of the sub *Albacore*, Commander James W. Blanchard, in the early morning of June 19, peered through the periscope at enemy carriers launching their planes. From the vast fleet on the surface, Blanchard picked out his target. Six torpedoes whooshed from the *Albacore* as it quickly submerged to avoid enemy destroyers. A huge explosion jolted the crew. The sub's torpedoes had rammed into Ozawa's flagship, the carrier *Taiho*. The detonation converted the sleek flattop into a giant floating firecracker. Ozawa had hardly abandoned the shattered, burning hulk before a sister carrier, *Shokaku*, reeled from tin fish loosed by the American sub *Cavalla*. Like the *Taiho*, it did not survive, and, although depth-bombed by destroyers, both of the U.S. submarines escaped.

Because of the enormous losses in the Great Marianas Turkey Shoot, the carriers were not needed to recover the handful of aircraft that returned from the debacle over the Philippine Sea and

Guam. The Mobile Force began what Ozawa considered less a retreat than a strategic withdrawal that would allow him to regroup and engage the Americans again. He had only about a hundred planes left, but reinforcements could come from the bases in the Philippines and on Iwo Jima, Yap, and Truk if the fleet could get near enough before the Americans struck. A catastrophic intelligence failure misled the Japanese into believing that many of their carrier-launched planes had landed at Guam and Rota.

Task Force Fifty-eight, minus Task Group 58.4, detached to buttress the amphibious operation in the Marianas, sped deeper into the Philippine Sea in pursuit of the highly vulnerable enemy. Although the Americans maintained a pace of better than 23 knots to the Mobile Force's 18, the Japanese had turned tail several hours before the task force started pursuit. Absolute radio silence helped mask the location of Ozawa's warships, and the limited probes by Navy search planes did not find them. Morison blamed Mitscher's reluctance to conduct full-scale night aerial searches on his affection for aviators. The historian deemed the admiral reluctant to risk the lives of the tired pilots and disdainful of the available night fighter units.

The hunt for the Japanese continued throughout much of June 20, with the Japanese committing their remaining torpedo bombers to a mission after one of their scouts reported the American position. The airplanes, however, never could find the U.S. carriers. Nor did the American searchers turn up the Japanese until Lieutenant Robert "Stu" Nelson, in an Avenger from the *Enterprise*, discovered the enemy warships about 275 to 300 miles from the task force. The Mobile Force traveled very slowly, refueling from tankers. Nelson listed the enemy strength as consisting of three separate task forces, one with six fleet oilers and a number of destroyers, another with battleships and destroyers, and the third with three large and four small carriers.

The time was almost four in the afternoon. Sunset would come by 7:00 P.M., and Mitscher faced a difficult decision.

In a subsequent report he said, "Taking advantage of this opportunity to destroy the Japanese fleet was going to cost us a great deal in planes and pilots because we were launching at the maximum range of our aircraft at such a time that it would be necessary to recover them after dark. This meant that all carriers would be recovering daylight-trained air groups at night, with consequent loss of some pilots who were not familiar with night landings and who would be fatigued at the end of an extremely hazardous and long mission. . . . It was estimated that it would require about four hours to recover planes, during which time the Carrier Task Groups would have to steam upwind or on an easterly course. This course would take us away from the position of the enemy at a high rate. It was realized also that this was a single-shot venture, for planes which were sent out on this late afternoon strike would probably not all be operational for a morning strike."

His fondness for his airmen and the risks notwithstanding, Mitscher issued a brief message to the aviators—"Give 'em hell, boys; wish I were with you"—before the first planes lifted off just prior to 4:30 in the afternoon. From the carriers *Hornet, Yorktown, Bunker Hill, Wasp, Enterprise, Lexington, Belleau Wood, Bataan, Monterey, Cabot,* and *San Jacinto,* full deckloads—a total of eighty-five fighters, seventy-seven dive-bombers, and fifty-four torpedo bombers, bearing belly tanks to cover the extra miles—roared off toward the Japanese.

Alex Vraciu recalled that the night before, over numerous cups of coffee in the wardroom, the talk had veered around to Gus Widhelm's prediction and the wager. "We told Gus that he didn't win his $1,000 bet yet, because a fleet engagement meant that we had to hit them also." On the twentieth, Vraciu said, "Our squadron had been in and out of ready rooms all day long, anticipating a launch, and we had just been released from ready alert when we received word of the search plane contact. All the ready rooms were busy preparing, primarily on our plotting boards. The flight was so long that we had to go half-scale on plotting boards. We figured that our Hellcats would have enough fuel for this mission, but seriously doubted that the bombers would be too pleased. They would be running on fumes on the return. After a few last-minute aborts, we ended up launching nine fighters which escorted fifteen SBDs and six TBMs. The latter carried bombs instead of torpedoes.

"This was at 4:24 in the afternoon. We knew that by the time we got there and back, it would be pitch-black. I wasn't worried about landing aboard at night because of my night-fighting 'Bat Team' training with VF-6, but a lot of the other guys had never made a night landing aboard."

Jim Ramage, commander of VB-10 off the *Enterprise,* said he had taken off with twelve SBDs, five torpedo planes, and sixteen fighters. After the Hellcats and Avengers preceded them, Ramage and the dive-bombers headed in the direction of the Japanese. "We didn't have the luxury of doing a normal rendezvous. We called it the running rendezvous. We finally got all the bombers together. I was flying along about 5,000 feet and climbing when all of a sudden I got a cloud of smoke in my cockpit. I thought, 'Oh, God, I'm on fire. Here's my big time and here this damn thing is happening to me.'

"Cawley, my rear-seat gunner, said, 'I think it might be just spilled oil.' He said that one time previously that the plane captain had spilled oil around the engine and when it got heated up, the oil burned off the cylinders, causing smoke. That's apparently what happened, because within three or four minutes, the smoke cleared out."

Instead of his own narrative of what followed, "because of my mother's admonition that self-praise stinks," Ramage quoted a first-person account by Lieutenant (j.g.) Donald "Hound Dog" Lewis. "That afternoon . . . I manned my plane and wondered for the hundredth time of the merits of this poor, old, tired-out SBD Dauntless dive bomber, if it still had any place in the war where planes were slow if they cruised at less than 250 knots. I'm ashamed now of my doubts. I was to have ample proof before that day was out that tenacity and the ability to keep going can sometimes make up for speed and show. Of course, the behavior of the plane depends a lot on its pilot, its crew and its squadron. It can be handled rough and it will probably balk. We handled ours gently that day.

"My crew consisted of one John Mankin, once a good citizen of Wyoming. He was both radioman and gunner. He represented I thought the best there was. I had confidence in the other squadron members. I felt that they, too, were the best, and I know to this day that my story would be a lot different if our skipper had merely gone by the rules.

"Lieutenant Commander Ramage, our skipper, was different. Sometimes in this business the rules are inadequate and things happen so quickly there isn't time to consult an admiral's committee about some new ones. They have to be made right on the spot. The skipper made quite a few that night. The Jap losses which we had helped to inflict and the fact that twelve pilots and twelve air crewmen went up that night and all returned to their ships speaks more for his leadership than anything I might write.

"My regular place in the division was flying number two position in Lieutenant Bangs' division. He had at one time been an instructor for Wayne Morris. By 1630, all of our planes were in the air. We were rendezvoused with Commander Bill Martin's Avenger torpedo planes; this flight being led by the exec of the squadron, Lt.

Commander Van Eason; our Hellcat fighter escort was under Commander William Killer Kane, destined to become an ace with five planes to his credit as a result of this day's work. On a heading of 290 degrees and throttle back to the maximum to ensure the most economic fuel consumption, we started out after the Jap fleet. "

Ramage commented, "We thought at that time the Jap fleet was out 260 miles and after we were launched, we got a correction in the position report. Nelson's position was one degree off in the wrong direction. In other words, it was about sixty miles further out. The radius of action of the SBD was about 250 miles and it was as plotted about 260 miles, which wasn't a bad chance to take. But when you add on the extra fifty or sixty miles, which takes you well out over 300 miles, it becomes pretty much a one-way mission as far as SBD's are concerned."

Lewis recalled, "I burned out my left auxiliary tank, 52 gallons gone already, I thought and we were scarcely at the halfway mark. We were at 6,000 feet and it was 1800 [hours]. I could see more air groups from some of our other carriers to one side and headed at the same target. It felt good to see them here.

"At 11,000 feet, I put my engine in high blower, adjusted my oxygen mask, and called my gunner to see how he was doing. John said he was cold. For days while we had been aboard the ship, I had been too hot, but now because of the altitude, the pure oxygen I was breathing, and the nervous drain on my energies, I was beginning to feel cold too. Not even the heat from my engine seemed enough to kill the chill. We were now at 14,000 feet. I had just run out of gas on my right wing auxiliary tank. It was 1845. I was thinking to myself that if we would only go into our dives right now, my chances of a hit would be best, as with my gas tanks evened off, the plane would trim up just about perfectly. I wanted to have as many things in my favor as possible. I knew that once over the target there would be quite a few things decidedly not in my favor.

"I decided to keep my two main tanks of fuel, approximately 250 gallons, exactly equal up to the moment I actually did nose into my dive. I imagine some of the other pilots of my flight were worrying about the same thing, as it meant changing tanks every five minutes. It was now almost 7:00 . . . and we had already covered 225 miles. I thought of my gunner again and knew he was almost frozen to death. The back seat of an SBD is a pretty exposed place, and he must make it even more so in order to keep his guns ready for quick use. I think the real credit of naval aviation goes to those rear seat gunners. Their job is the hardest and requires more downright nerve and guts than anything I can think of.

"We were at 15,000 feet when I heard our fighters tally-ho the Jap force. The first report gave their positions as fifteen miles to our port. This force consisted of six fleet tankers and a half a dozen destroyers. Even as the report was given, I could see several thin strips of white far below, the wakes of those ships. They were moving fast with everything they had.

"I heard my skipper on the air, '41 Sniper to 85 Sniper. We will not attack. We will not attack. Where are the Charlie Victors [CVs, the designation for large carriers]?' I think he must have been exasperated that anyone would even suggest that we would come 300 miles to dump a load of bombs on a few oilers when there were carriers around. I started to get squared away. I took notice where the wind was from in relation to the direction we were now heading. I changed my gas tanks again, checked my bomb release, flipped on my gun switches and bomb sights and did as many things as could be done this much in advance of the dive.

"Then I heard another contact report. More ships had been seen still further north, about 20 miles. There were many cruisers, some battleships and best of all, my heart turned over when I heard this, seven carriers, four small CVs and three large CVs. I started to get ready in earnest now. I was scared. I couldn't really believe this was happening to me. I went over my check-off list again, closed my formation. In a few minutes I could see them. I could make out several black forms ahead, way below and partly concealed by some clouds. They were alreay starting to maneuver. Some were going in circles, others were zigzagging. Their formation was well spread out, just the opposite battle procedure from our task force. '41 Sniper to all bombers,' I heard my skipper call again. 'The first division will dive on the largest CV. The other sections will dive on the small jobs unless the big one is still not hit. Out.' "

Because of the long distance to the Japanese fleet and the problems of fuel conservation and the approach of darkness, the strike forces could not organize a coordinated attack. Instead, they would have to go all out without the usual preliminary suppression of AA by strafing, and followed by an orderly sequence of dive-, glide-bombing, and torpedo drops. As Lewis remarked, the enemy fleet was somewhat strung out, largely because of the refueling process (not due to faulty tactics). Some carriers were exposed, with little protective screen, while other ships formed a tight circle to maximize their antiaircraft power. Aware of the menace from the skies, the warships had begun to defend themselves. One Navy pilot said that the reaction resembled "Fourth of July fireworks around the Washington Monument. The puffs contained more colors than a rainbow—white, pink, red, yellow, orange and black puffs. Thermite shells were all around, throwing white hot metal."

A report from Bombing Eight reported particularly intense barrages at 8,000 and 14,000 feet with bursts of many hues: blue, yellow, lavender, pink, red, white, and black. "Accuracy was very good and planes were hit over the target." In addition, from the flattops, about thirty-five fighters, manned by skilled flyers, rose to intercept the raiders.

Lewis continued, "We were beginning to spread a little now. From 16,500 feet we started what was to be a high-speed break-up into our dive. Three carriers I could see plainly trying to take cover under a cloud. Another large one, I'm sure, of the *Shokaku* class was on my left without a cloud near it. We had 200 knots now. I checked everything. Once more my gas seemed to be evened up, the plane well trimmed. When I came back to low blower because of the natural decrease in power at this altitude, I had lost a little distance.

"[Lieutenant (j.g.) Cecil] Tip Mester, the other wingman in my section, filled in quickly, keeping the interval between planes just about right. We had agreed before the flight to make a close-in diving interval as that keeps the men on the gun crews on the deck below taking cover most of the time—so quickly does one bomb follow another. I glanced quickly at my altimeter. I saw 13,000 feet. For the first time now I took notice [of] AA fire. I couldn't help thinking how unlike our ships those Japs were, for I knew we would never let two divisions of dive bombers get as near as we were now without sending out every available fighter and throwing up a virtual barrage as well.

"I saw a pair of our fighters on the other side of my cockpit. One of them was Lieutenant (j.g.) John Shinneman. He had been just off my starboard, watching the other bombers steepen up into their dives. Now he would go down with me. I was the last plane to dive and I knew there was little chance of anything besides an F6F Hellcat getting on my tail. There were great black puffs all over now and smaller white ones, looking for all the world like small balls of cotton. Things started to happen fast. It was a blur from here on in.

Now it was 10,000 feet. I was starting to overspeed and then overshoot the carrier I had picked out. That meant the last thing on my check-off list, dive flaps. I pushed the actuator, glancing out to see if they had operated successfully, saw a plane smoking horribly away on my port, wondered if it was one of ours.

"I heard Japs talking on our radio frequency. They were counting, then more talk. They were excited. Who wasn't? I heard someone tally-ho again, 'Enemy aircraft, 4:00 clock, Angel 5.' It seemed to take an eternity. Never had a dive taken so long. The wind was from my right. I was overshooting. I corkscrewed toward the left and then back again. It helped. The carrier below looked big, tremendous, almost make-believe. I had a moment of real joy. I had often dreamed of something like this. Then I was horrified with myself. What a spot to be in. I must be crazy. I was straight up and down now in my dive. I was right in the middle of all those white puffs and for the first time I could see where they were coming from.

"Each side of the carrier below seemed to be a mass of flashing red dots. It had been turning slowly to port. It stopped and I noticed a larger red flash which was a bomb hit on the side and well forward but unmistakably a hit. I figured it must have been scored by 'Banger' as we called Lou Bangs. The carrier below had stopped moving. Who could ask for more? I thanked whoever it was who laid on the last one, as it had stopped the carrier right up and down in my sights. I kept trying to move my point of aim to the right to allow more for the wind. First I could move so that it rested squarely on the side of the carrier. That wouldn't be enough, I knew, but it was too late to do any of the violent maneuvers to move it more. I could allow for the error in one other way, however, and that would be by going lower.

"The last time I glanced at my altimeter it registered 3,000 feet. Stopped below, the big carrier looked even larger. It was completely enveloped in a sort of smoke haze. It was hard to stay in my dive this long. Under some conditions, a person can live a lifetime in a few seconds. It was time. I couldn't go any lower. Now! I pulled my bomb release, felt the bomb go away, started my pull-out. My eyes watered, my ears hurt, and my altimeter indicated 1,500 feet. Too low, I thought, but what had I done? I turned back to see that there was more smoke and flame on the same side as the first hit, the first hit I had seen, only this was way aft. That could be mine, but even with my low pull-out, the wind had apparently carried it way to the starboard side. I experienced a momentary disappointment. I had expected much more of a conflagration to follow a direct hit on something as vulnerable as a carrier.

"Then I remembered that our section carried semi–armor piercing bombs which would, of course, pierce the flight deck and burst below. My ears still hurt. I had already closed my dive flaps and had 280 knots, but I couldn't seem to go fast enough. There were ships all about. They were all shooting far above the carrier, which was dark with smoke and its own AA. I saw a plane burst into flames and then slowly float downward. I saw a smaller carrier off my other wing with its flight deck a mass of flames. A torpedo plane flying at only a few thousand feet left a vicious path of black smoke and dark flames before it plunged into the sea. I wondered if I would get out of this yet. I had felt good and a little surprised after pulling out of my dive still unhit. Now I had to do it all over.

"For a moment I was almost panic-stricken. Everywhere I looked there seemed to be ships with every gun blazing. The sky was just a mass of black and white puffs and in the midst of it planes already hit, burning and crashing into the water below. It's strange how a person can be fascinated even in the midst of horror. I'd see orange bursts from some ships, a moment later a billowy puff would blossom out too nearby, a second later another, still nearer. They were getting the word. I was employing the wildest evasive tactics possible. I would be down low on the water and then pull up quick and hard rudder one way, hold it for a moment, then kick rudder the opposite way. I had decided it didn't make any difference which way I went. Our pre-arranged retirement course was 090 degrees. I would take that. Any direction I went, I would still have to run the gauntlet.

"I saw now the Japs' advantage in spreading out their formation of ships. I would no sooner exceed the range of one ship than I would fall into the sights of another further along. I seemed to spend an eternity in the midst of their AA. I began to think that real low on the water was the best place. I flew there for a few seconds, a temporary lull. Suddenly a tremendous geyser ahead, another to starboard. I pulled up quickly and realized that a cruiser was using its large deck guns to drop shells in front of us, hoping we would run into the columns of water, even if the shell itself did miss.

"There were other planes all about now. I saw a Helldiver flying low over the water, as I had been a moment before, lose a wing and disappear almost instantly without either smoke or fire, scarcely a ripple on the sea below. I found myself with a cruiser on one side and a destroyer on the other. Resulting crossfire was effective. I believe they were closer to getting me than any of the other little yellow men I had been a target for. Some of the shells burst so near that the concussion would lift my plane a few feet higher in the air. A few times I was surrounded by black bursts and I could hear the hollow metal sound that concussion makes when it comes against metal fuselage.

"The Japanese should have had one more SBD Dauntless to their credit that day. If it had been our gun batteries, they would have. I saw a bomber, one of our own, it was Lieutenant (j.g) William Schaefer and his rear seatman [George] Santulli. I joined up on him. My own gunner called, 'Jap fighters, high starboard.' I looked to my right and saw half a dozen fighters fighting off in that position. I saw one literally blown to pieces in the air and another catch fire and slowly descend, disappearing in a cloud. Schaefer and I joined on some other planes. We were about out of the AA now, except for an occasional burst. I began to feel better. These were planes from the *Lexington*. I wondered where my own bombers were. There was no other interference from the Jap fighters. They apparently had been well taken care of. My attention was [drawn] by a tremendous explosion and fire off on the horizon. I looked, seeing the remains of one of the fleet tankers we had seen going in. Some other group had decided to concentrate on that task force after all."

Ramage himself said of his own experience, "It was dusk but there was plenty of visibility. The Japanese ships were making high speed so the wakes were very visible. I dove on the carrier easily, a nice clean dive. I went much lower [as Lewis did] than we normally did. We wanted to make sure we got a hit. I put my pipper [the indicator on the gun sight] on the port bow, which was the way I figured the ship's motion and the wind at the time."

Ramage noted that there was considerable confusion over exactly which ships VB-10 had bombed. "Apparently Bangs, Mester and Lewis dived on *Junyo* while Grubiss, Bolton and one of the VB-16 fellows, Jack Wright, went down on *Hiyo*. *Hiyo* was the one ship sunk in this strike, primarily by CVL torpedo planes, but she also sustained bomb damage."

He recalled, "As we approached the fleet, I would say about 20 miles out, when we were still in a fairly tight formation, we got a tally-ho on a number of Zeros. My gunner, Cawley, again, said Zeros up at 4 o'clock. But because of our fighter escort, and VF-10 was darn good at this, they would not in any way ever leave a strike group in order to shoot down an enemy airplane. They hung right in there, and every time the Zeros would start an attack towards us, Killer [Kane] and his guys would nose into them, and the Zeros would back off. They weren't very determined on getting us before the time of break-up.

"As I dived, the Zeros began to come after me, and I think two of them went down with me, one in particular, and with my dive brakes out, he zipped past me so fast that I could hardly see him. Cawley called out to me that he was coming and was trying to shoot at him. He was afraid the Jap would hit us, and it could be very possible that he might have been a kind of kamikaze plane, trying to knock me out of the sky, because he missed me by a matter of just a few feet. It didn't disconcert me too much. By this time I had that pipper right where I wanted it. There wasn't anything going to stop me. The triple A was coming up, and it was shallow, going under my belly. A dive bomber coming down is nearly vertical and it's awfully hard to shoot straight up."

The action report after the battle said that Ramage and a junior lieutenant named DeTemple had aimed at a *Zuiho*-class carrier. The statement declared that their bombs had scored near misses just aft of the stern, causing smoke to pour from the stern and a conflagration on the hangar deck. Another pilot dropped his bomb into the water close to the port side. The final SBD in the echelon, flown by Lieutenant (j.g.) Schaal, supposedly planted his 1,000-pounder on the port side of the stern. Smoke and fire belched from the explosion.

Bangs, as cited by Lewis, scored directly on the fantail of a *Junyo*-class CV. The bomb blew a group of planes into the water. Mester's ordnance exploded on the starboard stern, while Lewis's hit the starboard side of the ship aft of the island. A giant sheet of flame erupted, and the flattop was dead in the water, down at the stern, listing to starboard. While VB-10 believed it had sunk the carrier, it survived the damage inflicted.

Making his getaway—in Navy parlance, retirement—after releasing his bomb, Ramage said he had depended upon Cawley: "My trusty gunner would call it out and I would respond to what he said. I would either go up or down, depending upon what he could see was going on. When we finally joined up, there was still some Zeros in the air and they were doing slow rolls and various things around the area. I don't know why. This was not unusual for Zeros, but they were doing it even at this time when the whole world was falling apart on them. Kane and his group by this time were right with us, and they knocked down two or more of them."

The fighter component of Air Group Ten was commanded by Killer Kane. Because of the wound on his head from his water landing June 16 after friendly fire had brought him down, Kane was wearing a special helmet. He and his wingman, Ensign Jerry Wolf, combined to knock down a Zero, and four other defenders went down from the machine guns of VF-10.

The combat action report noted that six Zekes, shadowing the SBDs, had attacked but "with little aggressiveness and had no effect. Anti-aircraft fire from target carrier was extremely intense but appeared to be going flat as dives, which were commenced from 9,000 feet, were steepened."

The *Enterprise* strike included eight TBFs, each of which bore four 500-pound bombs. Lieutenant Van Eason led the group, which claimed eight hits and then escaped from both the antiaircraft and the enemy fighters.

The Air Group Two contingent from the *Hornet*, which included VT-2, reduced from eight torpedo bombers to six because of lack of gas, a misfiring engine, and hydraulic malfunctions, located the enemy fleet a few minutes before 7:00 P.M. As the ships below them started to turn, dive-bombers from VB-2 began their assault while the torpedo planes circled for their runs. Heavy AA broke up the TBF serial, and the pilots embarked on separate courses for different targets. The torpedo planes attacked the large carrier *Zuikaku*, which adroitly dodged the tin fish. Avengers bearing 500-pound bombs registered several hits plus some near misses. The explosions ignited fires, leading to an "abandon ship" order that was rescinded after damage-control parties restored the working conditions.

The *Bunker Hill*'s Air Group Eight mounted a strike of twelve SB2C Helldivers, twelve TBF Avengers, and fourteen F6F-3 Hellcats. The expedition was joined by eight more Avengers off the *Monterey* and the *Cabot*. VB-8 claimed four hits with its 1,000-pounders, along with a scattering of near misses upon a carrier. Additionally, the flight said that at least seven of its 250-pound general-purpose bombs had struck the carrier. The Japanese damage reports, however, indicated far fewer punches landed, with only one blast set off on the carrier *Chiyoda* and the battleship *Haruna* having shaken off another.

VB-8 encountered as many as a half-dozen Zekes while leaving the scene. Two SBDs, one with pilot Lieutenant (j.g) James O. McIntire and radioman-gunner Robert N. Varmette, the other with pilot Lieutenant (j.g.) Charles D. Smith and radioman-gunner Kenneth E. Bartlebaugh, were seen headed for the water after the attacks. Others in the flight absorbed some hits but continued to fly. Nine from the squadron assembled at the rendezvous point.

Air group leader Commander Ralph L. Shifley, in a Hellcat, bagged a Hamp and a Zeke as well as a probable Zeke. Others from VF-8 scored a kill and several probables among those who attempted to intercept the dive-bombers and torpedo planes.

Lieutenant (j.g.) George B. Brown, of VT-24 from the *Belleau Wood*, commanded four Avengers equipped with torpedoes. Brown chose the flattop *Hiyo* as ideal for his purposes. He had allegedly remarked before takeoff that he would torpedo a carrier at any cost. Lieutenant John D. Walker, in Karig's *Battle Report*, recounted, "Brown found his section had been left alone. The other planes were headed for a glide bombing attack. He hoped to get enough protection from a huge black cloud to get to the level of attack unnoticed, but when the boys came out of the cloud they saw with consternation that they had 5,000 yards to go in the clear, with a gauntlet of battleships, cruisers and destroyers to run—three TBFs [one of the Avengers had apparently turned back] against a big chunk of the Japanese Fleet.

"The tracers were so thick they wondered if they had room for their wings. At night you see them all. Black streaks of oil and bonfires on the water showed them the graves of their comrades and their enemies.

"Brownie broke up his group for the attack. Each was to come in on a different angle. The carrier, now fully alerted, began to circle tightly as the massed fire of her guns was brought to bear. Explosions rocked the three planes and tore into the sturdy TBFs, [Lieutenant (j.g.) Benjamin] Tate ducked as the tracers cut through his cockpit, but one of them burned through his hand. A larger shell smashed his fuselage. Still they headed on.

"Brown's plane took the brunt of the Japanese fire; shell after shell struck home and suddenly it began to burn. He pulled up slightly and his crewmen, unable to live in the white-hot flame, bailed out." The fire in the center of the plane had forced turret gunner George H. Platz to seek refuge in the bombardier compartment, where he found radioman Ellis C. Babcock stuck in the escape hatch. Platz lunged at the door, and it opened; both men, their clothes smoldering, tumbled out above the enemy fleet. On their parachutes, they drifted down to the water. Floating in their life jackets, they watched the air-sea battle raging about them.

The stricken TBF, with Brown now the sole occupant, continued to fly, and the flames, after blackening the aircraft and burning away its recognition marks, died out. Walker reported, "He [Brown] reached the dropping point and released the torpedo straight and true.

"Not on the target, Tate and [Lieutenant (j.g.) Warren] Omark still had to penetrate the murderous head-on fire through which Brown had persevered and Brown knew it. He didn't hesitate. Comparative safety for his plane lay straight ahead. With his attack completed he could get away while the gunners concentrated on the incoming planes. But he had brought the boys in there and he would get them out if he could, so he turned his plane straight into the carrier and then flew straight down the length of the ship. The surprised Japanese instinctively concentrated their fire on him and in that moment of immunity the others sped their two torpedoes straight to the mark." The postmortem analysis indicated that while the missiles loosed by Brown and Omark had probably struck home, Tate's had most likely missed.

The trio headed for home. Tate's Avenger had absorbed considerable punishment, and he barely evaded enemy fighters by scurrying into a cloud. He caught up with Brown, now at a low altitude and visibly wounded and bleeding. He appeared to have trouble controlling his plane. Tate lost contact with Brown, but Omark overtook him and tried to lead him home through the night sky. According to Walker, "Brownie waved a shattered arm to his friend. His khaki shirt was splattered with blood. Then his plane wavered and plunged nose first into the darkness below."

The Yorktown's Air Group One launched two divisions of F6F-3s, one led by Lieutenant Commander Bernard Stream, the other by Commander John Peters. Stream's people would conduct a fighter sweep while those with Peters guarded fifteen dive-bombers and nine torpedo bombers. Stream thought he laid a 500-pounder on a large carrier, and several of those who followed him believed they also had dropped their bombs on the flattop.

Al Vraciu from VF-16 on the Lexington remarked that the slow cruising speed of the bombers required the Hellcats to frequently make S-turns or weave to compensate for the torpid pace of their charges. "Our group was attacked almost immediately upon arrival by many Zekes, and my wingman and I had our hands full trying to keep the enemy fighters off the bombers, which were preparing to push over. Our group leader's flight course as we arrived over the Japanese fleet took us alongside a huge cumulus cloud buildup, which separated our top-cover from those down below.

"The top cover—apparently mesmerized by the clouds and rapidly developing events—lost sight of us. 'Brock' [his wingman, Brockmeyer] and I were the only planes remaining with the bombers at that time and we appeared surrounded. Glancing down, I saw that one of the TBMs had just been hit by a Zeke. It was on fire and the crew parachuted out of the TBM and ended up in the water in the middle of the battle down below. They were picked up by one of our float planes.

"By that time we were fighting to keep the Zekes off the bombers and these Japanese pilots were good. You'd turn into them, take a fast shot, just to ward them off, and they'd come down from the other side. Then you'd turn into them, and these guys would pull up and the other guys would come down. But then it came to a point where we weren't holding formation anymore. Somebody from the top cover later said that they saw some planes, and they were in what looked to be a tail-chase, doing acrobatics. I said, 'Yeah, God-damn it! That was us, fighting for our lives down there!' It was one of those things. It was a botched-up hop, as far as our fighters were concerned—our performance for the bombers.

"While we were doing our scissoring [Thach Weave]—they could have picked the tail of my wing man or myself. They picked his tail and he must have been hit because he didn't turn back like he should have on the weave. I got the Zeke behind him, but the Zeke got him first. I had the sad experience of seeing 'Brock' going down. I still think I hear him faintly say, 'I'm hit.' I was able to get in another good burst at one of them, but I couldn't tell whether he went down. I damaged it, I'm sure.

"But at that point, I had to use my last-ditch defense and dive out. I went to the rendezvous area and I joined up on a damaged TBM that had been shot up. I don't know what carrier he was from. His bomb bay doors were dragging. I pulled up alongside him. I'm sure he felt better, having at least a fighter with him. But he gave me the signal [through gestures] for gas—we used no radio communication. He signaled to me that he didn't have enough to get back. How badly else he was hit I'm not sure, because it was getting dark by that time. The sun had already started to disappear on the horizon. He stayed right down low and didn't climb up for altitude. His wing lights were flickering, so his electrical system must have had troubles.

"I kept hearing voices on the radio. It hadn't gotten real bad yet, but the TBM seemed to head toward a group of seven planes that were circling low on the water. I could hear voices, guys saying, 'I've got only twenty-five gallons of fuel left! I've got to ditch.' Another one said, 'I've got about thirty-five myself. I might as well go down with you.' The TBM seemed to join this group. I figured that they all just landed in the water. It was dark by that time, and I gave them all a heart-felt salute.

"Some of the guys were real cool, coming back that night, but some of them were breaking down—sobbing—on the air. It was a dark and black ocean out there. I could empathize with them, but it got so bad that I had to turn my radio off for a while."

The worst of Mitscher's expectations were being fulfilled. The strike force sent after Ozawa was indeed not only terribly low on gas, but also the blackness of night had smothered the sea. Truman Hedding was present when the plight of the returning pilots became painfully apparent. "When they were coming back, he [Mitscher] was sitting in flag plot [the seagoing war room]. He didn't even get out on the bridge. He just sat there. I would go into the CIC [Combat Information Center]. The radar screens were just covered with emergency IFF. These kids were lost and trying to find their carriers. The first thing we did was tell them just to land on any carriers. Then we told the carriers to light up. We didn't mean for them to do what they actually did, but once the word got out, they just lit up everything, 24-inch searchlights and all."

The first Grim Reapers of VF-10 who came back to the *Enterprise* learned that it was too crowded to take them. Four pilots found refuge on the *San Jacinto*. Two others set down on the *Lexington*. When Killer Kane spotted the *Enterprise*, he was waved off because of its fouled deck. His head throbbing from his previous injury, exhausted by exertion and nagging pain, Kane flew into the water, smacking his head on his gun sight once again. He had the dubious distinction of having ditched twice in the space of five days.

A destroyer flashed its signal light, spelling out, "How much ice cream is Killer Kane worth?" The price was evidently satisfactory, for he was transferred to the *Enterprise* by a high line. He told his squadron, "Everyone else was running out of gas, but I ran out of altitude." Jim Ramage remarked, "He had black eyes under black eyes when they finally sent him back from the destroyer."

Lieutenant (j.g) E. J. Lawton, from VT-10, described the chaotic scene as he sought his home on the *Enterprise:* "We had almost reached the force when we saw the lights come on. It is clear that the task force did all in its power to make it easier for us to get home. Lieutenant [Van] Eason led us in over the *Enterprise* but her deck was fouled for some time. We circled for a few minutes watching the lights of the planes below fan out in the pattern of the landing circle. But there had been too much strain in the last five hours to reduce things to patterns now; and inevitably, landing circles became crowded, intervals were lost and deck crashes occurred. Many planes—too many—announced that their gas was gone and they were going in the water. Others were caught short in the groove. Seen from above, it was a weird kaleidoscope of fast-moving lights forming intricate trails in the darkness, punctuated now and then by tracers shooting through the night as someone landed with his gun switches on and again by suddenly brilliant exhaust flames as each plane took a cut, or someone's turtleback light [canopy bulb] getting lower and lower until blacked out by the waves closing over it. A Mardi Gras setting, fantastically out of place here, midway between the Marianas and the Philippines.

"I made one pass at the *Lexington* and was cut out there, one at the *Enterprise*, just as her deck became fouled again. I climbed to 500 feet, picked out a CVL close by the *Enterprise*, found her circle clear and accepted her invitation to 'Charlie.' It was the *Princeton* and I was the last plane she had room for. Small as that deck had looked, I was awfully glad to see it."

Lawton's superior, Eason, used up his last bit of gas as he approached the ramp of the *Lexington*. He yanked his wheels up and turned off, plopping into the water alongside the flattop. A destroyer scooped him up. An SB2C ignored a wave-off from the landing signals officer on the *Bunker Hill* and crashed onto the deck. With the Helldiver's prop dug into the flight deck, a torpedo bomber from the *Cabot* also disregarded frantic warnings. The Avenger smacked into the Helldiver, killing two sailors and injuring four others engaged in trying to clear the wreckage of the first aircraft. In the massive confusion, at least one pilot even mistook the lights on a destroyer for those of a carrier and only at the last moment realized his error and splashed down next to the tin can.

A third member of VT-8, Lieutenant (j.g.) Cummings, had agonized over the target when his bomb bay doors refused to open on his first dive at a carrier. He "roller-coastered" into a second plunge, which jarred the portals open for his release. As he pulled out, a portion of the canopy glass behind him blew out, but not from an enemy shell. He and his rear-seat crew blamed the damage on "suction." Worse, when he looked back he saw three splashes well ahead of the target and his fourth bomb still hung up in its rack.

En route to the designated meeting place, a few Japanese fighters danced attendance but several F6F-3s interfered, sending one down in flames. Then Cummings entered the panic zone surrounding the recovery phase of the mission. "By the time we arrived, there was bedlam. It was too pitiful to be disgusting. Planes made passes at anything floating. I circled too long myself and was forced to go down to find a carrier. I squared away on the starboard side of the *Enterprise* and seemed to be part of a four-plane landing circle. My center-face gauge registered five gallons less than empty. I felt I could make one pass. I didn't get the chance. The *Enterprise* informed me her deck was foul.

"I remember a carrier calling up and announcing she was sending up some star shells and I saw fresh ones go up. The engine still ran beautifully and I went beyond the screening vessels and forward of the *Enterprise*. Just as I reached the promising lights, I saw it was a large ship, possibly a battleship searching for survivors with her searchlight.

"The engine on gallant old [number] 52 gave us fair warning that she had started burning the hydraulic fluid by coughing violently." He continued for another 2,000 yards and then tried a dead-stick landing. "We were very slow but it was not perfect, slid off the right wing and the nose dropped. We hit somewhat nose down. I felt an impact equal to a rugged carrier landing."

He and his crew speedily exited, although the tail nearly snagged one of his crew, Lindsay. Cummings said he found the "water pleasant" and after he and Lindsay, the radioman, and the rear gunner settled themselves on the raft, he was bemused to see the his turret gunner, Terry, playfully paddling about in his Mae West. The pilot signaled with his waterlogged flashlight, and the cruiser *Baltimore* pulled them from the sea. They had been in the water only fifteen minutes.

Ensign William Vaughan, of VF-2 from the *Hornet*, had achieved
a near miss on a carrier with his bomb drop. "We came back immediately but didn't reach the fleet until three quarters of an hour after
darkness had closed. There was no moon and no horizon. All along
the way I could hear bombers calling that they were out of gas and
going in. When we finally reached the fleet, I was unable to distinguish our carrier. My flight became separated. Planes were milling
around carriers, displaying their red and green wing lights, turtleback lights and tail lights. My artificial horizon was not working. My
first mistake was to have taken that plane off the deck with no artificial horizon as I should have realized the possibility of returning
after dark.

"I finally found our carrier by means of the searchlight they sent
up. There were about eight planes in the traffic circle when I entered
it. I had about fifty gallons of gas at this time. I observed a deck
crash, circled, saw another deck crash, circled four more times and
sought out another carrier. I observed a deck crash there, too, and
I then went to a CVL [light carrier]. I entered its traffic circle at
very low altitude, lowered my wheels and flaps and discovered for
the first time that I couldn't extend the tail hook. I tried the circuit
breaker and emergency handle, observing at the same time less than
twenty gallons of fuel. I heard several transmissions over VHF to the
effect that all planes were dangerously low on fuel. I decided to get
as much altitude as possible ahead of the force and bail out. Upon
reaching 400 feet, my engine began to detonate. It starting doing
this at 200 degrees which is not normal.

"I immediately turned into the wind and prepared for a water
landing. I unhooked the radio cord, checked my shoulder straps and
hood and waited until my plane was what I estimated to be close to
the surface. I used the red lights of a DD [destroyer] 500 yards away
as an altitude reference point. When I felt I was on the water, I put
it [the Hellcat] in a landing attitude. It took about thirty seconds. My
power plant was by this time on fire and it cut out just before I hit.
There was ample time to get out of the plane; it stayed afloat as long
as a minute and a half. After getting out, I unfastened my parachute,
taking it off and holding it with my right arm. I then separated the
life raft from the harness. The chute kept its buoyancy for about
three minutes. After that I inflated my Mae West. It was very dark,
and before I knew it, boat, parachute and sea anchor line had become tangled together from the wash of the swell. Fortunately, it
was a very calm sea.

"I took out my waterproof pack light from my pocket and flashed it at three ships nearest me. Then I tried for twenty minutes to untangle my raft and inflate it. I didn't have a knife with me, having lost it prior to the hop. It probably would not have helped me, as I would have hesitated cutting lines for fear of damaging the raft. The whole process exhausted me and I finally abandoned the raft. I then observed that my light also was gone. I now had a whistle, dye marker and revolver.

"I lay back and rested, floating, for five minutes. Then a DD headed for me, attracted by a light buoy dropped by a passing CV. The DD turned to starboard and away from me so I took off my shoes and started to swim toward it. It was making three to four knots. I blew my whistle at frequent intervals. They finally heard me and picked me up after I'd been in the water about a half hour."

VB-8's Helldivers, accompanied by several fighters and torpedo planes, flew a loose formation in the black sky. Lieutenant (j.g.) Harwood Sharp, who had lost his two wingmen and incurred hits in his propeller and carburetor, struggled with acrid fumes that filled his cockpit, forcing him to wear his oxygen mask. His engine quit five times, only to restart as he nosed over and pumped fuel. His compass and electrical gear stopped functioning. Lieutenant Arthur D. Jones maneuvered without full use of his tail controls, and Lieutenant (j.g.) Warren Pilcher had no hydraulics and his propeller stuck at 1,600 rpm.

Lieutenant (j.g.) Kenneth Holmes, the only one not struck by fire over the target area, landed on the *Cabot*. He was the sole member of VB-8 whose plane survived intact. Seven others went into the water near enough to the fleet for all hands to be saved. The SB2C flown by Lieutenant (j.g.) Perry W. Huntsman, blinded by a squall, ditched just a few miles away. But not until Huntsman and his radio-gunner, Edward Houstoun, had endured thirty-nine hours on a raft were they picked up.

Vraciu believed he had navigated successfully to the vicinity of the fleet when the searchlights lit up the sky. "I said, 'My God! I'm heading for Yap Island.' I kept thinking about the revolting things bomber pilots used to say, that fighter pilots couldn't navigate. I thought it's coming home to roost now.

"Then I could hear voices on our radio frequency and they were saying, 'Land at nearest base! Land at nearest base!' I wanted to get back to the *Lexington* and my own sack that night. I was dehydrated and thirsty as hell. As I arrived close enough, I knew that I was at the correct task group because I recognized the broad stack on the *Enterprise* as the carrier alongside the *Lexington*. I circled a few thousand feet above the melee below. I figured, 'Hell, Al, you've got enough fuel, and you're not worried about the landing part of it, so let the ones short on fuel get aboard first.' After a while it thinned out a bit. Then I waited until my fuel gauge indicator reached as low as I dared, and I let down to get aboard the *Lexington*.

"But it was a constant wave-off with flags; the flight deck was unclear for landing to all who wanted to land aboard the *Lexington*. One of the SB2C Helldivers from another carrier had made a crash landing aboard the carrier. He was running on fumes, battle-damaged and fighting to maintain low-speed control of his airplane. He ignored the wave-off and piled into and through the barrier, fouling the deck. He ended up crash-landing on the plane ahead of him, killing and wounding a number of men. As expected he caught holy hell from the flight department and a few other people. It posed a tough choice, if you put yourself in the shoes of the pilot involved. A wave-off is mandatory but he figured he no longer could wave-off successfully. They said, 'Yes, but you could have landed in the water.' I'm sure he's going to spend the rest of his life agonizing over it.

"They couldn't take me aboard the *Lexington*, so I went next door to the *Enterprise* and got aboard on my first pass. I taxied forward of the barrier, and then I heard the crash horn which told me that somebody had crashed behind me. The SBD behind me had taken a wave-off earlier and the pilot forgot to put his wheels back down for his next pass. He went into the barrier. I was urged, after parking my plane, to get off the flight deck as quickly as possible.

"I went down to one of the ready rooms and the only guys that I recognized were some of the SBD pilots from our carrier. Thoughtfully, the ship provided us with medicinal brandy to relax us."

Don Lewis, like everyone else, endured a torturous return, his gas depleted, his eyes tired, his head aching, his back stiff, his stomach protesting the lack of food. Around him he heard planes falling from the sky as the pilots tried to tell their wingmen they were going into the water. "At 9:20 I thought I could see star shells off the starboard, but I wasn't sure. There was also lighting. A moment later there was no mistaking it. They were star shells and the searchlights as well. We were still a long ways off but it made me feel good. I realized that a tremendous concession was being made in our favor. I heard pilots express the opinion that the admirals looked upon the fliers as quite expendable, and they must be to a certain extent. But I shall never again feel they wouldn't do everything conceivable in their power to bring a pilot back.

"When we approached the outer screen of our fleet, it seemed that almost every ship had a light of some kind on. In the utter darkness, the intensity of some of the lights was blinding. The largeness of the carriers seemed to stretch off into infinity. Every group seemed to get over the fleet at the same time and everyone being low on gas wanted to land immediately. We were told to land on any base available, that is, which had a clear deck. The skipper [Ramage] found a carrier landing planes, the first two sections broke up. I could see them break away and head down for the landing circle. It was a little before 10:00. . . . I figured I had about fifteen minutes more fuel, then I would have to make preparations for a water landing too.

"My best bet I thought would be to circle, for I was at 1,500 feet and try to spot a carrier not only with a clear deck but with no one in the landing circle, for I thought if I once put my wheels and flaps down and started operating at full power, the little gas I still had left would be gone in no time. Some carrier was on the air; their deck was clear, they said.

"I decided if I could find a carrier shortly, I would have enough fuel for one pass. Surely, I thought, there must be one carrier with a clear deck around. I saw more lights further ahead. I gained on them slowly. It was another carrier, and what luck, I was approaching from its stern. For a moment my impulse was to let my wheels and flaps down and immediately come right in for a landing, a very unorthodox procedure. I decided against, mostly because I had lost sight of the landing signal officer. I went by the port side and looked down. He was giving me the wheels-down land signal. The deck looked clear, it was a big carrier of the *Essex* class.

"I got squared away once again. This would be my last chance, as I must be at the very end of my gas. Again I was on my cross leg and got in the groove, picking up the signal man. He was giving me a high and fast [indication of the plane's position and speed relative to the carrier]. I dropped my nose, took off a little throttle, picked up with a little back stick pressure and now I was right over the ramp and there it was at last, the cut. The deck looked big after so many landings on our smaller E. I dropped my nose and guided her down, felt the hook catch a wire. It was all over. I was taxiing on the deck, following the plane director's lights, cutting my engine. I heard myself talking as in a dream. Everyone seemed friendly. What carrier was this? The *Yorktown*, I was told.

"From the side, I watched the next plane land. It was an SBD also, and a good landing followed. I saw the number on the side. It was the skipper's plane. We were glad to see each other. It had only been seven hours since I had seen him last, but it seemed like a year. He had done a swell job that day. I told him so, but he scarcely heard me he was so glad just to be back. I was grateful to my old SBD, still the most dependable plane in the fleet, grateful to my skipper for a fine job in leading us out and back, to every admiral and captain who willingly took 1,000 risks to help us back and last but surely not the least to my God who knows when a fellow needs help."

Speaking of the return to the task force, Ramage said, "I was very unhappy with the air discipline of the other air groups. We went back very slowly because we planned it that way. But a lot of them became frustrated and I think they went into the water unnecessarily. Some of the people actually dived into carrier decks when they got wave-offs. They showed poor air discipline by doing that—knocking the carrier out. I had a lot more with me than just the SBDs and TBFs of Air Group Ten. I had quite a few stragglers and I was the last one in there against the Jap fleet. They all joined up, so I don't know how many planes I had. We came back directly over the *Enterprise* because I wanted to get back to my own ship and my first break-up, when I came back and went around the first time, I could see somebody had gone into the *Enterprise* and they had a wreck on the deck.

"We had broken up by that time. It was kind of every man for himself because the air discipline had just gone apart. I was lined up for a straight-in approach on a CVL, and was coming in, and just ahead of it I saw one of these large, fat carriers. I just kind of pulled my nose up and dropped it again and made a pass at the *Yorktown*.

"Getting aboard the *Yorktown* was great but it was a real unhappy situation because they had an SB2C squadron aboard and I think every one of them went in the drink. In my opinion, there's no excuse for this type of thing, in that the SB2C had far greater range than we did in the SBDs. I just think they hadn't planned their flight correctly."

Based on information to which he was privy, Ramage modified some other statements on the circumstances involved in lighting up the fleet. "The turning on the lights was planned in the afternoon.

Admiral Arleigh Burke, who was Mitscher's chief of staff, had described the fact that they knew they would possibly have this affair going on in this manner and he had separated the task groups by a greater distance. They had prepared ahead of time to turn on the lights, so it wasn't any spur of the moment operation. It was a well considered plan.

"The drawback was that if the signal had been for only the carriers to turn on their lights, it would have been absolutely perfect, but in that mass of ships it was very, very difficult to tell the carriers apart from other surface ships."

With the darkness perforated by a galaxy created by hundreds of shipboard and aircraft lights, every carrier seeking a heading into the wind, radios crackling with desperate calls from pilots pleading priority, destroyers and cruisers dodged about trying to pick up downed airmen. Deckhands, ducking as planes skittered to barely controlled crashes, hacked through tangled cables to shove wrecked aircraft over the side. Aviators floating in Mae Wests or on rafts, some of which sailors had pushed over the side in hopes that swimmers might come across them, blew their emergency whistles and blinked their flashlights. The scene resembled a water carnival gone berserk.

Hedding remarked, "The normal landing lights were usually adequate. But the kids were all upset, so turning on all the lights was a great thing because they were able to find the ships. They landed on any ship; it didn't make any difference. On some they'd take the crew out and push the plane over the ramp until they just couldn't take any more. A lot of them went in the water, 80-some. We recovered all but about sixteen pilots and thirty crewmen." Destroyers spent the night plucking exhausted flyers from the sea. George Brown's two companions, Platz and Babcock, were both rescued the following day as Task Force Fifty-eight steamed into the waters from which Ozawa had now retreated.

The Battle of the Philippine Sea saw considerably less damage to the Japanese fleet than many of the Americans claimed. But the two blows struck by the submarines *Albacore* and *Cavalla*, coupled with the loss of more than half of the hundred carrier planes left from the Great Marianas Turkey Shoot and the hits that were recorded on June 20, convinced the Japanese to retreat. Task Force Fifty-eight reported six Hellcats, ten Helldivers, and four Avengers presumably lost in combat and an additional seventeen Hellcats, thirty-five Helldivers, and twenty-eight Avengers destroyed through either ditching or crashes while coming aboard flattops. The initial tally declared a staggering 100 pilots and 109 air crewmen involved in the lost planes. However, with all of the rescues that night and the subsequent day, the casualties fell to sixteen pilots and thirty-three crewmen.

The aviators blessed Mitscher for his decision to light up his fleet. While the two-day battle erased any threat from the air, the Japanese submarines might have inflicted terrible damage upon the illuminated carriers. Jimmy Thach, who had wholeheartedly endorsed the light show, offered a caustic last word: "I kept thinking what a shame. We didn't have to have this happen, if we'd done the right thing last night." He added, "Any damage done to Ozawa's large task force by our pilots was not because of anything Admiral Spruance did, but in spite of what he did."

SEVENTEEN

NIGHT FIGHTERS
AND GROUND SUPPORT

Although the preliminary reports suggested a severe blow to the Japanese armada, there were some aviators who realized that the Americans had not achieved a huge win in the Battle of the Philippine Sea. Among them was Jim Ramage, who on the *Yorktown* met his former commander, "my old hero," John Crommelin. "He came down to the wardroom where I was having a late dinner and asked me about the strike. He was quite exuberant. He said, 'We finally got to them.'

"And I said, 'Captain, I think these reports that you're getting are very exaggerated. I think we got two carriers out there.' One of the ones I thought we got, which we may not have gotten, was the one when we were pulling away, my gunner Cawley said, 'Can you look back? You've got to see it. It's burning from asshole to appetite.' I never did see it.

"I think Bangs and his group got one and there were other carriers beaten up but it really wasn't that good. I just didn't want to have the same thing happen as in the past where the senior officers got carried away with the idea that this had been a great, great victory. It was a victory, there's no question about it, but it wasn't the way it looked at first."

Some postevent historians such as Morison argue that the use of more torpedo-armed planes instead of dive-bombers might have accomplished more. The one flattop sunk, *Hiyu*, was apparently the victim of a tin fish. Ramage complained of a failure to concentrate the strikes. He noticed a flight of SB2Cs converging on the oilers and said he had questioned them: "Unknown air group going on the oilers. What are you trying to do, sink their merchant marine? Their carriers are up ahead about twenty or thirty miles." Later he was told that the strike group commander had claimed he had gone for the tankers because he was low on fuel. "Hell," snapped the VB-10 commander, "so was everybody else."

When the Japanese forces retreated to the relative safety of the waters around Okinawa after the battering in the Philippine Sea during June 19 and 20, Admiral Spruance, the commander of the Fifth Fleet, permitted Mitscher and Task Force Fifty-eight only limited pursuit of the wounded enemy. Spruance's defenders argue that his lack of aggressiveness stemmed from a primary obligation to protect Operation Forager, the landings in the Marianas. In addition, the speed of the U.S. ships was not enough to narrow the distance sufficiently for further air strikes, much less for a seaborne battle engaging battleships. After search planes could not find any "cripples" or vessels so badly injured that they were straggling behind, Spruance ordered the task force to retire to the east.

Before the warships reversed course, the voyage west did enable the Americans to find some survivors of the previous day's battle. And mindful of what had happened, the Navy now required all pilots to perform nighttime Carquals. With the air groups heavily involved in operations, the policy could not be implemented speedily.

Discontented with the failure to obliterate the Mobile Force, Rear Admiral Joseph B. "Jocko" Clark, commanding Task Group 58.1, a qualified aviator and an aggressive sort, obtained permission for another blast at the Volcano Islands, Iwo and Chichi-Jima, 600 miles south and slightly east of Tokyo. He had the two big carriers, *Hornet* and *Yorktown*, along with the light ones, *Bataan* and *Belleau Wood*, accompanied by the customary screen of cruisers and destroyers for the mission.

From the *Yorktown*, sixteen F6F-3s from VF-1 took off, half of them loaded with incendiaries and the others with 500-pounders. The assault did not come as a surprise to the residents of Iwo. Patrol planes had seen Clark's force approaching. An enemy combat patrol intercepted the Americans before they could reach their objective, an airfield. In the furious dogfights that ensued, VF-1 said, it destroyed eighteen Japanese fighters with five additional ones listed as probables.

The fifteen fighters from VF-1 aboard the *Hornet* hammered the

Japanese at least as hard. According to the squadron history, the intensive air action ended with thirty-three of the enemy vanquished. Lieutenant (j.g.) Conard Elliot disappeared during the skirmishes, and a 20-mm shell exploded in the cockpit of Lieutenant H. R. "Stinky" Davis, obliterating his instrument panel and cutting a big toe. Davis, however, was one of four men who scored four victories apiece, while another quartet received credit for three each. Japanese torpedo planes sallied forth in a costly endeavor to retaliate. Eight fighters from the *Hornet* disposed of eighteen torpedo bombers.

The low-level raids on the airfields in the Volcanos—Iwo and Chichi-Jima—involved heavy risks. After one attack by VF-1, the action report stressed, "It is almost impossible to destroy planes on the ground unless fire is held to 1,000 or 1,200 feet. Any claims from pilots above these altitudes are imagination or wishful thinking. AA accuracy and intensity increased considerably over that of the Gilbert and Marshall Islands. [While] strafing is necessary at lower altitudes, the hazards are increasing and seriously underestimated."

For the moment, however, the chief objective was to secure the Marianas. Marine and Army troops on Saipan were still heavily engaged against stiff resistance, and the invasions of Tinian and Guam, both predicted to be difficult operations, lay ahead. The obduracy of the defenders was brought home to aviators over Saipan, who watched as several thousand men, women, and children threw themselves off a cliff.

In somewhat of a grim sideshow, the Navy began to use a captured airfield on Saipan for operations in the vicinity of the Bonins. Isley Field, named for Lieutenant Commander Robert F. Isley, killed in the ill-conceived effort to fire rockets from Avengers, served as a base for a foray by a pair of VB-109 PB4Y-1 bombers, the equivalent of the Army's twin-tailed B-24 Liberator. Lieutenants T. R. Clark and J. M. Welsh were the senior pilots.

Their search for enemy shipping was rewarded with the sighting of some cargo vessels accompanied by destroyers. Well aware of the futility of high-altitude bombing against moving targets, the PB4Y-1s approached only 10 feet above the water. When they came within 500 feet of the vessels, the planes lifted to masthead level before unloading four 500-pounders. Both of the ships attacked started to founder; one was last seen about two thirds underwater, while the other broke in half.

Unfortunately, the path taken by Clark brought his aircraft directly between two destroyers, which threw up a blizzard of antiaircraft fire. The crew with Welsh saw their companion plane losing altitude and at least one engine smoking. Clark's voice came over the radio: "So long, fellows." The big bomber slammed into the sea and sank immediately. No survivors were seen. The absence of fighter cover that might have suppressed AA from the warships is hard to excuse.

During the forays against Iwo, some Americans observed renewed skill in their adversaries, who exploited altitude and maneuverability. They spoke of aggressive behavior, which had previously been lacking, and one flyer reported, "They used the same weave we use."

The Navy night fighters had become increasingly effective. By the summer of 1944, three squadrons of Hellcat night fighters, VF (N)-76, VF (N)-77, and VF (N)-79, were dispersed throughout the Pacific Fleet. The F6F-3Ns performed "heckler" missions, lurking over enemy air bases in the dark and savaging Japanese planes taking off or returning during the night. The tactic kept the foe off balance and added a worrisome threat to his operations.

Army and Navy night fighters also seriously crimped the capacity of the Japanese to perform reconnaissance on the location and disposition of the U.S. fleets. In the absence of effective radar systems, the Japanese relied heavily on observations by their after-dark scouts. But the American night fighters had begun to either shoot them down or drive them off before they could accomplish their missions.

In Bill Odell's book on night fighters, he reports that on July 4, the *Yorktown* sent out Lieutenants (j.g.) Fred L. Dugan and John W. Dear to locate enemy shipping at Chichi-Jima and attack with 500-pound bombs. Launched shortly after midnight, they remained on station for four hours. As dawn broke, the pair spotted a vessel leaving the harbor. Dear had just dumped his ordnance on a destroyer when a breathless Dugan radioed for help: "Three Rufe float fighters are on my tail!"

An additional six or seven were in the air, but Dear with his much faster, more maneuverable Hellcat immediately knocked off two. Freed of pursuit, Dugan jumped into the ensuing dogfight, shooting down four while Dear brought down another. However, the Rufes had inflicted some injury. A bullet lodged in Dugan's shoulder, and both F6F-3s were riddled. Nevertheless, the two night fighters reached the *Yorktown* safely.

During Operation Forager, on July 7, radar on the *Hornet* picked up blips with sinister intentions. Around 7:00 P.M., the *Yorktown*, cruising approximately 100 miles southwest of Guam, launched Lieutenant Dear, Ensign William Levering, and Lieutenant Russell Reiserer to intercept. Levering pursued the first intruder, which started dumping "window," the confetti-like foil that confuses radar. Fighter Direction lost track of the bogey, and Levering never saw him. It was believed that one of the Black Widows, an Army P-61 night fighter based on Saipan, later shot it out with the enemy but with no discernible results. Dearing also drew a blank when in pursuit of a second plane he mistook the lights on Guam for the raider. He never caught up with the stranger.

Still roaming the night skies, Levering, now controlled by Fighter Direction on the *Yorktown*, hunted a third airplane, which apparently was unaware it was being stalked. Levering changed course three times until he actually saw the Betty a mere 300 to 400 yards away. Levering tried to open fire twice, but in his excitement he had failed to trip the master switch. By the time he had recovered and readied his guns, the crew of the twin-engine bomber had realized it was being chased. The pilot threw the plane into a dive, while the tail gunner unlimbered his guns. Levering shot up the right engine, which gave off sparks. The enemy tried desperately to escape, executing a climbing turn and then a dive. After two more bursts from Levering's .50s, which probably hit the pilot, the plane rolled over and began a steep dive. Levering followed it down until it exploded in the sea.

Reiserer, vectored out by the *Hornet*, caught up with a Betty after boring through the night for almost two hours. At an altitude of 20,000 feet, Reiserer poured bullets into the root of the left wing. Flames sprouted, but, under control, the bomber headed down and made a successful water landing. On the following day, a destroyer retrieved a bag packed with charts and data about Marianas landing strips. Another tin can subsequently retrieved the bodies of the five crewmen and their personal effects.

The night fighter units struggled for recognition and respect. Ship commanders and ship crews groused about the problems of night recoveries' disturbing the work being done to ready the air groups for the daytime operations. The electronics packed into the night fighters demanded intensive maintenance, and while the radar worked well enough against high-altitude bombers, it was questionable whether it would detect torpedo bombers skimming the water.

Still, the concept had gained sufficient believers for the brass to approve the activation of a full-time night air group working from a carrier dedicated to that kind of operation. Lieutenant Commander Turner F. Caldwell, a 1935 USNA alum and a former dive-bomber commander during the Guadalcanal campaign, took charge of VF(N)-79 and transformed it into Air Group Forty-one, which trained exclusively for night combat, gaining proficiency in instrument flying, navigation, and radar use. They even labored to improve their night vision through a technique of exercising their peripheral sight, and eventually they could distinguish forms better than details in darkness.

Air Group Forty-one, composed of nineteen F6F-5Ns and eight radar-equipped Avengers, found a home on a newly overhauled light carrier, the *Independence*. According to Odell, the skipper, Captain Edward C. Ewen, expressed his doubts, wondering if it was "a new experiment in suicide." He quoted a steward who had said, "Man was never made to fly, nohow. And if he was made to fly, he was never made to fly off a ship. And if he was made to fly off a ship, he was never made to fly off a ship at night."

With the garrison on Saipan finally subdued, the next objective was Tinian, a much smaller island whose chief asset lay in a finished airdrome with lengthy runways, ideal for the proposed B-29 base that would serve the long-range bombers assaulting the home islands of Japan. The escort carrier *Suwannee*, a veteran of the North African campaign now featuring its latest organization, Air Group Sixty, provided aircraft for strikes at Saipan, Tinian, and Guam.

One of the *Suwannee* fighter pilots, Roy "Tex" Garner, was a refuge from VF-2 while it was stationed in Hawaii. "They had issued me a .45 automatic with a batch of shells. Even though the first time I picked the .45 up, I shot four rounds, hit four bullseyes and qualified, I wasn't comfortable with it. I knew I'd have to practice up if I ever was going to defend myself with it. At the crack of dawn on Hawaii, I went out the Bachelor Officers Quarters, walked out to the trees and saw a bunch of coconuts. I wanted to see if I could hit them. I began to fire at them at about 5:00 A.M. I got about half a clip out and I was surrounded by Marines. I was taken to the commandant. I told him I'm here to fight a war; they gave me a pistol and I wanted to see if I could hit anything with it. That didn't go over very well and he released me to my air group CO. I knew I wasn't going to do well in that group because they had no shortage of pilots. I thought it would be wise to move on and got to the *Suwannee*."

Garner got an even bigger bang out of a few bullets while working over Tinian. "I was hunting for a radio tower. We knew there was one because they had been bringing in airplanes. I spotted an antenna sticking up through the palm trees. I made a pass at it and noticed a shack at the bottom of a cliff. I destroyed it and immediately went across the island, keeping below the cliff so that the guns on top couldn't get me.

"It was then that I spotted two doors at the base of the white coral cliff. They had canvas pulled over them. I had been flying only twenty feet from the cliff all this time. I called the boys and told them I found something and was going to make a run right across the airstrip, then at those cliffs, to shoot at those doors in the cliff.

"I made my run and headed for one of the two doors with the idea of shooting directly into it. I stayed low, and had to pull to the right a little to get in line with the second door. The first door was at about two o'clock. I never got a chance to shoot at the other because when I touched off those six .50 caliber guns they hit the door immediately. I don't think I got five rounds from each gun when the whole damn cliff went up in my face. I immediately yanked up on my stick. I don't know what I hit but it had a store house full of explosive. It was just like I got hit with a baseball bat, or running into a brick wall. It actually knocked me out. When I came to, I was in a climbing-type turn. It had blown me 10,000 feet into the air. I eased the plane into a level position to assess the damage.

"A piece of coral from the cliff had been blown clear through the plane. The engine, the wings, and me, were hit, but we seemed to be OK. However, I could hear the boys talking, but I could not talk to them. They were saying, Ol' Tex had just flew right into that cliff. And here I was 10,000 feet above them trying, and hoping, to keep the engine running to get back to the carrier. I had to fly back by myself without any chaperone to guide me. I couldn't talk to anyone by radio. I knew I wasn't going to be able to make a normal landing with this engine and its lack of power. There would be no such thing as a wave off. If I didn't make it on the first run, it would be the drink for me.

"I finally made it back, so I put my hook and flaps down and tried to lower my landing gear. They wouldn't lock in place. I knew that if I didn't lock them in place, I couldn't land on the carrier. By the same token, if they were stuck down, I couldn't land on water. I mentally reviewed the Hellcat wheel system. It had an air bottle, a one shot deal to blow your wheels down. I knew my problem, the hydraulic line to put my wheels down had been ruptured. I took my canteen of water, which was only about half full, and urinated in it to fill it. I needed all the fluid I could get. There is a reservoir [for the hydraulic system] down at my side. I took the cover off and dumped the canteen into it. I hoped that when I hit that air bottle, it would activate enough pressure to put the landing gear in a locked position. If it didn't it would be swim time for Ol' Tex.

"I hit the air bottle and the gear locked down. I came into the ship's view with plenty of altitude but falling continuously. Bob Misbach, the Landing Signal Officer, evidently knew my problem. He kept me right in position until I finally landed safely aboard the *Suwannee*. Later a few of us looked over the plane and concluded there was no way anyone was going to fix that plane, especially after pouring that junk into the hydraulic system. The plane was pushed over the side."

Guam housed some 19,000 fighting men, a formidable defense with which to greet the invasion forces. An enormous preinvasion bombardment blasted positions detailed from photo reconnaissance and the general environs of the chosen beaches. The *Bunker Hill's* Air Group Eight lambasted sites on the Orote Peninsula. They bombed and strafed machine guns and trenches, revetments around an airfield, a heavy AA battery, buildings described as officers' quarters, storehouses, and other installations.

In a summary of its operations on July 18 and 21, VB-8, flying various models of the SB2C Helldiver, reported hauling 290,200 pounds of bombs to Guam. Of this total 274,550 were dumped on targets; the remainder was jettisoned or brought back to the carrier. Malfunction of systems connected with bomb releases and racks, as well as other weapons defects, were attributed mostly to the "unusually dirty, neglected and mechanically unsound condition" of the aircraft, which had been brought aboard the flattop only four days before the squadron struck at Guam.

VC-10, from the *Gambier Bay*, could launch only nineteen fighters because of the declining condition of its aircraft. Half of the planes on the flight deck qualified as technically nonoperational. There was an urgency for replacements, but that too could bring problems. The haste with which aircraft, as well as new pilots, were being fed into the war obviously generated problems, but the imperative to maintain the pace overrode consideration for the welfare of men and machines. On the other hand, the newest version of the

Hellcat, the F6F-5, had begun to replace older models. With water injection, its speed and rate of climb made it even more competitive with the Zeke.

Fatigue constantly plagued airmen. John Smith, a replacement fighter pilot detailed to Air Group Sixty aboard the *Suwannee*, noted that the heavy flight schedules frequently launched him twice a day. On one occasion, he logged almost nine hours flying both CAP and a strike. The tiredness manifested itself sometimes in a failure to switch off guns before landing, with potentially disastrous consequences. Other times, the aviators did not adjust their props after a wave-off or forgot to retract their wheels once in the air. In the delicate moments of takeoff and landing, errors due to sluggish reactions led to accidents. Some airmen talked to the flight surgeons about their stress, and while a good night's sleep could be restorative, a number of men found it difficult to shut down. The *Suwannee's* flight surgeon, Dr. Phil Phillips, while offering soothing words, in the absence of barbiturates also doled out his own prescription: two ounces of brandy with lemon and sugar in a steaming glass of hot water.

Drained by arduous long hours in the air, returning from missions with their aircraft shot up, seeing their wingmen lost, the aviators stayed tense throughout Operation Forager. Phillips noted, "The flyers especially need rest. The strain of combat had taken its toll among the flyers and their maintenance crew. Malaria was rampant and fifteen-pound weight loss per man was not considered too bad."

The inability to target enemy defenses precisely while carrying out ground support led to use of Marines as flight controllers over Guam. Four of them were detailed to Air Group Sixty on the *Suwannee*. John Smith wrote in his book, *Hellcats over the Pacific*, "They would fly in the TBMs, low and slow over the heavy fighting, to get a clear view before calling in strike aircraft. No one aboard the ship envied the TBM crews. The greater speed and lesser maneuverability of the TBM when compared to the L-5 [the standard single-engine Piper Cub type of observation plane] combined to make the TBM inferior for the intended role. However, until there was a place for the L-5s [a landing strip] to operate, there was no option.

"Pilot Bill Keller could attest to the fact that these flights were not 'plum' assignments. A Japanese hit in the engine of his TBM had resulted in his plane—and everyone in it—getting a saltwater bath, including Keller and the Marine controller. Indeed, they were fortunate to have enough altitude and control to make it off the island.

Ralph Hennings, the turret gunner, heroically pulled a stunned and half-drowned radioman, Stewart Neasham, from the belly of the plane before it sank."

Those on the *Suwannee* learned firsthand of the fragile nature of ground support missions. Given coordinates one morning for their bombs, a flight set out and plastered the zone with their 500-pounders. When they returned to the ship, an unhappy intelligence officer met them with the terrible news that during the night, Marines had advanced into the targeted area. No one, however, had relayed word of this change of boundaries to the bombers.

On July 21, the first leathernecks of the Third Marine Division and the First Provisional Marine Brigade surged onto the beaches on either side of the Orote Peninsula. While the big guns offshore, aided and abetted by their spotter planes, banged away at the defenders overhead, Air Group One from the *Yorktown* and Air Group Fourteen from the *Wasp*, with aircraft from Carrier Division Twenty-two—the escort flattops *Suwannee*, *Sangamon*, *Chenango*, and *Santee*—hunted for targets of design and opportunity.

During the landings, Ensign John Shea in an F6F-3 from Air Group Sixty on the *Suwannee* took direction from the air coordinator, who instructed him, "Number 5, there are four heavy batteries in area 285, just below the ridge. Out." Shea responded simply, "Roger, out." After a few minutes of silence, the air coordinator impatiently declared, "I say again. There are four heavy guns in Number 285. Over." Shea replied, "There were four. There are now one. We're working on it now. Out."

Even during Forager, routine changes in personnel occurred. Air Group Sixteen, Al Vraciu's parent organization, completed its tour on the *Lexington*, and this time Vraciu decided to go home. To replace the unit, Air Group Nineteen, which had been training in Hawaii for more than a year, flew from Eniwetok to the *Lexington*. Theodore Hugh Winters, Jr., the 1935 USNA graduate and an alumnus of Operation Torch, an executive officer of VF-9 on the *Ranger*, was in command. Winters reported his experiences in his book *Skipper*.

Winters realized that the extended period in Hawaii away from combat had possibly made some of his pilots overanxious to achieve glory. Shortly after they arrived on the flattop, he spoke about coming escort missions into enemy territory and then laid down the law: "I will say here and now if any one of you *ever* leave the bombers or torpecker you are escorting to go after an enemy plane that is not taking position to attack you or yours, not only will you not fly again in this squadron—you will be grounded, and your flight status re-evaluated. There will be plenty of fighter sweeps and combat air patrols for going after planes."

Instead of having the luxury of a shakedown cruise to refine techniques and tactics, the *Lexington* sailed for Guam with Air Group Nineteen, honing its skills during the three-day voyage before its first combat mission. To his chagrin, Winters found the conditions fraught with extra peril. "We were eager to drop our VF brass [the .50-caliber cartridge shells from fired machine guns] on the hats of the Marines as that was *something* we knew we could do, but the surface fleet threw us a curve. They had been steadily shelling Guam for two solid weeks and didn't want to quit while the Marines were landing, whether we were there or not. So orders came down to us to support the Marines, but stay above 1,500 feet or be knocked down by the stuff the ships were throwing in—up to 16-inch shells. How the hell do you drop brass on them at 1,500 feet? Orders are orders, so we farted around at 1,500, which is a suicide altitude to level off, and tried to hit targets well hidden by then or destroyed."

The group lost three torpedo pilots, five air crewmen, and Ensign D. W. "Duke" deLucca, a fighter pilot. All of the casualties came from ground fire. Winters described the sensations when passing through the AA meat grinder: "They usually load one tracer to three or four rounds in the belting, but the rate of fire is such that it appears to be a steady stream, like water out of a strong hose. The tracers are tiny orange balls, growing in size to that of tennis balls as they come straight up at you; then just as they get almost to you, they bend quickly under your plane as if controlled by some powerful magnetic field, or by a giant magic hand. And if they don't bend down under you at the last moment, you've bought it, as Duke did, and all the experience in the world would not have helped. When you have to go in against AA, it's like rolling the dice, and we hated it. The fact that Pasko [Lieutenant Joseph Paskoski] destroyed the 40 mm nest that hit Duke didn't help at all; and you can be sure he didn't do it at 1,500 feet."

On July 24, three days after the first American troops stepped onto the Guam sands, the Fourth Marine Division began the conquest of Tinian. As on Guam, the Navy aircraft carried Marine and Army observers over the island to improve tactical support for those on the ground. The offshore barrages from ships and the attacks of flattop-based planes, aided by the aerial spotters, backed up the overwhelming firepower of the amphibious troops. The campaign inaugurated the use of incendiary napalm dropped from the air. By August 1, Tinian was declared secured, and Guam followed suit on August 10, although deadly pockets of defenders remained in place for several weeks.

As the Allies debated and prepared for the next campaign in the Pacific, a small number of naval aviators participated in Operation Dragoon, the invasion of southern France that began the night of August 14–15 with airborne troops flown from Italy and dropped behind the French Riviera. Because Normandy was a short hop from the airfields in Great Britain, Operation Overlord had relied upon the Army Air Corps and the Royal Air Force to fly air cover and ground support. The distances from Allied bases to the targeted sites in Dragoon, however, were greater. In addition to bringing in seven Jeep carriers from Great Britain and Australia, the strategists assigned the escort carriers *Kasaan Bay*, with VF-74 on board, and *Tulagi*, the home of an observation fighter squadron, VOF-1, to deal with expected opposition from the German Luftwaffe. However, the prelanding bombardment aimed at destroying railroads and bridges in the area remained the responsibility of the Mediterranean Allied Air Forces.

Fighting Squadron Seventy-four had actually been formed and trained for the mission, although the aviators were not informed of their destination until just five days before D-Day. The squadron members on the *Kasaan Bay* had been issued a new version of the Hellcat, the F6F-5, but nine pilots and seven aircraft were detached temporarily as a night-fighter unit.

Initially, the seven nocturnal Hellcats with their nine pilots operated from a field at Solenzara, Corsica. Command lay with the Twelfth Tactical Air Force. The Navy flyers on Corsica checked in on July 25 and needed a week of practice to familiarize themselves with the local air traffic jargon. But once it was operational, to the disappointment of the outfit, the Germans seemed to reduce or even discontinue the nightly reconnaissance missions for which the unit had prepped. On D-Day two of the after-dark specialists landed aboard the *Tulagi* in case the Germans showed, but no strikes developed.

Lieutenant H. H. Basore, the acting commandant of VF-74 on the *Kasaan Bay*, expressed disappointment when his fighters encountered a total absence of enemy aircraft on D-Day. Allied intelligence had vastly overestimated the strength of the Luftwaffe in the area. Intensive bombing of the airfields before D-Day may have driven them away.

On August 16 and 17, the Germans sent Dornier 117s and

Junkers-88s against the fleet offshore. VF-74 claimed one of each destroyed in the air. After these sorties, it became apparent that the Luftwaffe planes had been evacuated from the area. The Allied command pressed Fighting Seventy-four into tactical air missions. For close to two weeks the Hellcats fired rockets, dropped bombs, and strafed.

In his report Lieutenant Basore noted, "The squadron was used as fighter bombers and for armed reconnaissance. This was something that had not been reckoned with, and for which the squadron had not been trained . . . rocket projectile launchers were installed just prior to leaving the States and the pilots had been given little training for using them.

". . . in nearly every instance strafing attacks had to be carried out with more Army-type than Navy-type tactics, i.e., using a comparatively small angle glide and continuing low. This type of attack was necessitated, rather than the usual type of steep glide (45 to 60 degrees) because of the Germans' effective camouflage and because the tree-lined roads on which nearly all motor transport concentrations were found made aiming difficult."

In addition to the pair of aircraft downed, VF-74 listed 338 trucks destroyed by strafing or bombing, 25 locomotives destroyed or seriously damaged, 207 casualties inflicted, and a host of other achievements. German antiaircraft gunners were rated quite effective, and five pilots were killed or missing during VF-74's brief sojourns over France.

In the Pacific, the completion of Forager moved the Philippine archipelago to the head of the list of objectives. For some time the top brass and the political leaders had debated whether to honor the strategy of Douglas MacArthur's return to the Philippines or that of Chief of Naval Operations Admiral Ernest J. King, who proposed bypassing the archipelago in favor of Formosa. As much as it was a matter of strategy, it was also about command. Formosa lay within the Navy's territorial obligations, while the Philippines belonged to the Army and MacArthur. When Admiral Halsey broke ranks to side with MacArthur on the grounds that absent control of the Philippines, any moves against Formosa and the home islands of Japan could be risky, the Joint Chiefs opted for MacArthur's choice.

During the first six months of 1944, control of the skies became too important for the American military to allow the traditional total subjugation of aviation to either land-based or sea-surface commanders. The Army Air Corps now operated with such independence that at times it seemed engaged in a separate war. In the Navy, the air admirals had gained the confidence of the new secretary of the Navy, James V. Forrestal, himself a former pilot. Chief of Naval Operations Ernest J. King, a dubiously qualified flyer, remained more or less on the fence when it came to the division of power between the black-shoe admirals and their aviation-minded counterparts. However, some concessions toward airpower had come with the appointment of several gold-winged veterans to key positions on his staff. Aircraft carrier building became a priority. Furthermore, the number of graduates of flight school who had advanced to the rank of admiral in 1943–1944 leaped from thirty-four to fifty-four, a gain among flag officers from 20 percent to 26 percent.

In the command sphere, a system of rotation of the top officers reflected a shift in favor of the air admirals. When Vice Admiral Raymond Spruance was at sea, he would lead the Fifth Fleet while Vice Admiral William F. Halsey plotted the next campaign. Then Halsey and Spruance would change jobs, with Halsey in charge of the Third Fleet. Similarly, Marc Mitscher, as part of Spruance's Fifth Fleet, bossed Task Force Fifty-eight. Under Halsey, it would become Task Force Thirty-eight, governed by another aviator, Vice Admiral John Sidney "Slew" McCain. The two-platoon arrangement was not wholly fulfilled when in August, Mitscher, who had been in the Pacific for seven months, balked at following Spruance to Hawaii. A disgruntled McCain had to be content with command over a task group for three months before he could replace Mitscher at Task Force Thirty-eight. During this period, King issued his ukase that all nonaviator fleet and task force commanders must have flyers as their chiefs of staff, with the appropriate rank of either commodore or rear admiral. At the same time, an airman like Halsey would have a nonflyer as his chief of staff, just as Arleigh Burke served Mitscher.

Bull Halsey now led the Third Fleet, which included Mitscher's Task Force Thirty-eight, on a series of raids that scourged the Philippine Islands. Air strikes on September 12–13 ravaged the Visayas, the central islands in the archipelago. VF-8 fighters from the *Bunker Hill* escorted VT-8 Avengers and VB-8 Helldivers from the carrier as all three organizations ravished several airfields. They counted thirty-two enemy who attempted to intercept them. VF-8 claimed a dozen destroyed, two probables, and four damaged. Strafing runs burned four planes on the grounds, and a sub chaser sank after it had been machine-gunned and then bombed by VB-8.

Lieutenant (j.g.) John Vanderhoof dove down on Luzon's Legaspi airfield. Suddenly, he realized that a Zeke off his port wing had all four guns blazing away at him. Vanderhoof's Hellcat seemed to him to be flying almost normally, but a wingman yelled over the radio, "Van, you're smoking very badly." Within seconds, Vanderhoof's instruments advised him that he was indeed in deep trouble: his oil pressure was dropping toward zero while the propeller ran wild.

"I got out a few miles off shore," said Vanderhoof, "and the engine began to vibrate terrifically. I was at about 700 feet and at that time just about to bail out. But I decided, maybe I can ride on down into the water." For a few moments he endured the shaking, but then the engine seized up and the prop stopped turning. He notified his wingman that he was going to ditch, and the other pilot assured him he would stick around until a rescue plane arrived.

"I set it down in the water. It skipped and bounced a few times and finally settled in. I unfastened my safety belt, had my parachute strapped on tight and tried to get out. My foot slipped and I fell back in the plane, but I finally got out, jumped off into the water and inflated my life jacket. With the parachute and everything on you, your tail end is very light and your head's very heavy. Consequently, your fanny is floating up in the air and your head's down in the water. I found the thing to do was hold my breath, unfasten the two straps that fasten the link at the chest. As soon [as you do that] the parachute and life raft float free and you can bring it right around in front of you. There you can open it and get in.

"I looked up and the F6Fs were circling me, so I was feeling all right. I opened the jungle pack. The first thing I wanted was some sunburn lotion. There wasn't any sunburn lotion in the pack. I thought if the sunburn lotion was missing, maybe something else. I found that my compass and my waterproof match-case, the jackknife and the mirror reflector, were all gone from the seat-pack. Evidently stolen by men aboard ship."

To protect himself against the sun, Vanderhoof improvised, smearing a boric acid ointment over his face, ears, neck, and hands and putting his helmet back on to cover his head. When he checked the drift of the raft, he discovered he was drifting back toward the Japanese-occupied shore. He tossed out the sea anchor and did whatever he could to thwart the wind and tide. From his perch he could see planes whacking the airfield, plumes of smoke arising. Whatever satisfaction Vanderhoof drew from the sight gave way to dismay as the guardians above him departed.

In the vicinity of the harbor, boats under sail moved about, but they seemed uninterested in him. However, he heard the sound of engines and watched several launches leave a pier. They headed in his direction, and he quickly hauled in his sea anchor and started to paddle, trying to hide himself under a blue sailcloth. Patrol craft skittered around the bay. One approached so close that the downed flyer could see the space between the legs of a man standing atop the pilothouse.

After nearly six hours in the water, he had begun to despair of rescue when three airplanes zoomed toward him, only about 300 feet off the water. "I immediately took one of the cans of dye marker and started sprinkling that over the side, uncovered my raft, and got my Very pistol out. One fighter came within 100 feet of me and I fired [a flare] right at him. I thought surely he would see me, but he kept right on going. They worked the harbor in close to Legaspi Town."

As the flight methodically covered the area, the dye thrown into the sea by Vanderhoof spread over a wider sphere. Commander Pete Aurand of VF(N)-76 saw the raft and dropped a smoke light. A Kingfisher float plane soon slid onto the water. After three tries, including one dunk back into the water, Vanderhoof climbed aboard. On the trip back to the cruiser *Miami* he watched two accompanying night fighters fall upon a Betty, which blew up as it slammed into the sea.

A second member of VF-8, Lieutenant (j.g.) S. F. Czekala, exploded a Zeke before realizing that enemy fire had thumped his Hellcat. "My plane really felt ragged. I was somewhere off the northwest shore of Negros Island. I felt pretty lonely there. I could see planes bursting into flame and plunging to the ground; brownish green Japanese planes flying around with a big meatball on them. I got somewhat nervous. I knew I'd been hit pretty badly."

A VF-8 mate, Lieutenant (j.g.) Tom O'Boyle, radioed, "You look as if you'd had your tail shot away. Your motor hasn't been hit."

The damage to the engine may have been invisible to O'Boyle, but oil began to spew back toward Czekala. "The oil was really spreading, just as if somebody had taken a big black paintbrush and painted my windshield and cockpit enclosure. I couldn't see a thing. This forced me to open my cockpit to get some visibility."

A Japanese army fighter, known as an Oscar, attacked O'Boyle, who called, "He's on my tail." Barely able to control his floundering Hellcat, Czekala still tried to help, firing blindly with his two machine guns that were still working. The Oscar quit the scene, but O'Boyle informed Czekala, "Your plane's on fire."

They were now nearing Cebu Island as the flaming aircraft started a death dive. "I knew I couldn't make a water landing," said Czekala, "so I just unsnapped my safety belt. Next thing I knew I was standing in midair, looking down at my plane. I could see it hit the water. I pulled the ripcord; it gave me a nauseating feeling when that ripcord came out so easily. I was afraid that it didn't work. I went to grab at it again when I heard a swish and then a pop. I looked up and saw that umbrella.

"I had made about a swing and a half when I hit the water. I went down under before I had time to get organized. I started to unbuckle my harness under the water. When I came to the surface, I was entangled in my shroud lines. I tried to untangle myself, found it pretty difficult, so I hacked at the shroud lines with my knife and got clear of them.

"Then I pulled up my life raft, snapped it open, spread it out and pulled the pin on the CO_2 bottle and turned the handle to the right; nothing happened. I started twisting it to the left, but it just worked freely and still nothing happened.

"I inflated my life jacket, got on my back and floated for a while to get my wind back. I tried my life raft once more but couldn't get it to work. My jungle pack, made in the form of a seat-pack, was dragging me down under and my shoes and clothes were getting heavy. I had to release the pack, shoes, helmet, gloves and socks. After swimming a while I started removing my flight suit. I took it off, but decided to keep it. Clothes would be very handy if I had to spend any time ashore.

"I couldn't see any land except to the east, where there was a range of pretty high hills. That was Cebu. I started swimming for it. It was a great distance away, for any fellow out of condition for swimming. It was at least eight miles. The fear of drowning got pretty strong. I told myself that it just couldn't be, that this was a hell of a way to die and I couldn't die that way. I just gave up all fears and swam on for the island."

O'Boyle faithfully stayed overhead, and Czekala worried that at his low altitude he would be easy prey to an enemy fighter. None appeared, and then a flight of bombers with fighter escort, heading back to base, came within range. O'Boyle contacted them, and one managed to drop a life raft near enough for the downed pilot to grab it. He carefully read the instructions and then inflated it. "I crawled onto the raft and practically collapsed. I hadn't realized how tired I was."

He recovered quickly and resumed his passage toward the island, paddling the raft. O'Boyle and another F6F-3 were finally
forced to leave because of dwindling gas supplies. In the distance,
Czekala saw a fishing boat slowly traveling toward him. He fretted
that it might be someone anxious to collect a reward from the Japanese for retrieving an American.

A quartet of American aircraft approached him, and Czekala attracted their attention by flashing his mirror at them. As the fishing
boat came nearer and nearer, he figured he might drive it off by
threatening to throw a smoke bomb. Salvation arrived suddenly in
the form of a Kingfisher. It plopped down neatly beside Czekala, and
they took off. Seated in the rear, Czekala had no communication
with the pilot. But he was not yet safe. When the OS2U landed and
taxied up to the cruiser *Houston*, it missed the hook. The plane was
sucked under the stern of the cruiser and a wing dipped down.
Thinking the Kingfisher was about to capsize and go under, the pilot
and passenger jumped into the water.

"I didn't even have a life jacket with me," remembered Czekala,
"so the OS2U pilot called to me to come over and hold onto him. I
swam over and he introduced himself to me as Lieutenant Parkin-
son. I gave him my name and we shook hands in the water. He held
my head up and we both paddled around." They considered hanging
on to the plane, but it seemed about to turn turtle. At that moment
a destroyer pulled alongside and took the two men aboard.

A fighter pilot with VF-31 on the light carrier *Cabot*, Arthur
Hawkins, the former enlisted man who had earned his wings of
gold, had already become an ace after he shot down five enemy
during the July raids on Iwo Jima. He had also gone on missions
against the southern Philippines. He recalled that after they hit Mindanao, they moved on to the next group, including Los Negros. "As
we approached the field with our large flight of bombers, two Oscars
made a pass on the formation. They came right through the formation, firing as they went through. They didn't hit any of our bombers.
But in support, you couldn't get them because they were coming
straight down and went through with the force. With us on the low
cover for the bombers, the air group commander called my flight
leader [Lieutenant James S. Stewart] and released him. He said, 'Go
get 'em Stew.' The four of us did a split-S and followed the two Oscars down to the ground. We caught one of them. We lost the other
one in a dive; we don't know where he went.

"I was able to get in position on the first one and come on in, straight down. I hit him with all six of the .50 calibers going at him. It just thrust him in the ground. As we pulled out from this dive, we were right over four fields. Other planes were taking off with the four of us down there. We pulled straight up to get a little altitude, and then started picking these guys off as they were coming out. I had gotten a couple and the flight picked up three or four more. They stopped coming off the field, so we pulled up. We were sitting there, waiting for them to get going again and not paying too much attention.

"You've got to keep your six [the area right behind the aircraft] covered and we forgot about that because there was so much fun down there. I was sitting there, looking down and waiting for somebody to get brave enough to start off again. I had a feeling there was something over here, so I looked and there sat an Oscar in perfect position to make a high-side run on me.

"I'll never forget that Oscar. He had the markings of the Marine squadron, which was their famous group. It was just a beautiful airplane. Boy, was it shining. The thing was polished up so much that it made the Blue Angel planes of today look like dirt." Ordinarily, Hawkins would have enjoyed the protection of his wingman, but the latter happened to be on the other side of the airfield, like his partner awaiting takeoffs from below.

"My first instinct was just to turn into him, even though I knew he could outmaneuver me. I got the jump on him. When I turned, here he came. But it was too late because I had already started my turn, which gave me the edge. As we pulled into each other, I was shooting with my firepower and he just flew into it. We did the turn to come back and he torched up and went off. I'll always remember, in that particular case I did out-turn him in the F6F because I got the jump on him."

He expressed some puzzlement about the lack of change in Japanese tactics: "We started hitting the Philippines at Mindanao. We hit that for three days. We'd pull off, replenish, move up to the next island and hit that for three days. Pull out, go up, hit the next one. We moved up to Clark Field [on Luzon, near Manila]. That was about the fourth set of raids. You'd think they'd be ready. They know you're coming. I went in on the fighter sweep, the first one to hit Clark Field. We went in there, dived in, dropped our bombs on the field, got close to the runway and pulled back. We were getting ready to hassle whoever was around and here it is, smoke and burning where all these bombs went off.

"Then here came a big old Emily, their big flying boat. It was approaching from out at sea and coming straight in at Clark Field. We were in there just bombing the hell out of it, and here he came, straight in. We took care of him, and then got back up. We were circling over Clark Field and here came a flight of twelve Topsys, which were similar to our DC-3s. They flew right across Clark Field and came under where we were orbiting, just as if they had no communications. Those things didn't last very long at all."

Killing the enemy might seem to have come easier for Hawkins, since his brother had been shot down by the Japanese. He admitted to initially having had a hatred because of his brother's death. "I guess it was revenge. But when I shot down a guy, I just felt, 'Well, I bested him. He would have gotten me, but I bested him.' There was no hatred. We'd have reports of them shooting at some of our guys in parachutes, to build up a little hate and discontent. But we had only one case where a guy was strafed after he got in the water. Other than that we had no reason to hate them, because they hadn't done anything other than [fight for their side]."

Hugh Winters, with Air Group Nineteen, expressed somewhat stronger sentiments: "It had been common knowledge in the fleet that Jap AA gunners and pilots repeatedly shot our pilots in their chutes, and it was squadron doctrine in VF-19 to delay pulling the rip cord till the last minute. It was left to a pilot's discretion whether or not to reciprocate. Joe Kelley had an opportunity to strafe a Judy pilot shot down by our CAP and confessed a bit shamefacedly to me and the torpedo skipper that at the last minute he just could not squeeze the tit. I said lightly, 'That's okay, Joe. You know the sharks got him anyway.' "

Halsey's flyers met surprisingly little air opposition from the expected nearest Japanese bases on Mindanao, the large southern-most island of the Philippines. Hugh Winters brought VF-19 from the *Lexington* on a hunt over Mindanao. "We covered all our targets in the southern sector," said Winters. "But finding nothing, and having plenty of gas and full ammo, we went north into our neighbor's territory and hit pay dirt. I don't know whether the planes we found on two fields had been flushed by our next-door fighters or not, but they had landed and were refueling when we got there. We burned twenty-seven of them, making flat strafing runs.

"We had the hard loss of A. N. Ruffcorn here. I had strafed ahead of him, and pulling up, saw the emplacement of about three guns that hit him. It looked like 40 mm. I got four of us together and we went into a spread attack on the guns and poured 4,000 or so rounds into the gunners. As we left, the emplacements were covered with dust and smoke and it looked like some ammo was going off. That didn't help Ruff, but it relieved just a mite of our seething rage at the time, and sadness later."

The run-up to the invasion of the Philippines required the neutralization of areas that might threaten the amphibious forces and troops engaged in the landings. The Bonins, from which the Japanese might draw aerial reinforcements and stage a seagoing thrust, drew the attention of a carrier group that included the *Enterprise*, *Franklin*, and *San Jacinto*. The *Franklin* was the latest addition to the Pacific task fleet, and the *San Jacinto* was a light carrier.

Hosting Air Group Twenty, the replacement for Air Group Ten, the *Enterprise*, after a fifteen-day voyage from Pearl Harbor, threw twenty-eight fighters and a dozen bombers against Chichi-Jima. In their combat debut, on the final day of August 1944, the Hellcats, equipped with rockets, blasted targets and streamed .50-caliber bullets from their machine guns at hangars, maintenance shops, and equipment depots. The Helldivers, SB2Cs, unloaded 500-pounders and added to the devastation with their own .50s installed in the wings.

For the next two days, the aircraft from all three carriers visited havoc upon the Bonins. Other than ground fire, there was no real opposition. But from Air Group Fifty-one, on the *San Jacinto*, a young ensign named George H. W. Bush, piloting a torpedo bomber, was knocked out of the sky by ground fire. His two crewmen were both killed, but Bush survived the ditching. The sub *Finback* rescued him.

Along with others from Task Force Thirty-eight, the Big E steered to the southwest. The script called for reduction of the enemy forces on Yap, Palau, and Ulithi. Yap had already been battered, its airfields were out of commission, and the mission seemed relatively as easy as the strikes on the Bonins. But the ground gunners at Yap ripped into the Air Group Twenty fighters, burning at least one fighter. Two others went down; either they were hit by a single burst of AA or the damage to one sent it tumbling into the other. Palau, also bereft of aircraft, literally harbored deadly antiaircraft emplacements. Several ships, sunk in the shallows, served as bunkers. Their guns flamed the Helldiver flown by the exec of VB-20, which crashed in the lagoon, killing the pilot and his gunner. Another rear-seat crewman died from a machine-gun bullet.

Although the Army Air Corps continued to expand its night-fighter capacity, the Navy's nocturnal unit, Air Group Forty-one, lost valuable assets in late August, once it went to war. Authorities, worried about the loss of a Hellcat bearing a radome with the most sophisticated electronic air intercept gear, ordered Caldwell to remove the radomes. To add to the humiliation, the group routinely flew daylight combat patrols that required none of their special training. And their modified Hellcats, without the bulbous radome on the starboard wing, no longer trimmed easily. Pilots were required to forcibly hold the stick off center. The disappointment was only moderately assuaged by the September 12 shoot-down of one enemy bomber just after dawn and the destruction of another after dark, the first of the rare night actions.

The Navy also made some tactical changes. Kent Lee, the dive-bomber pilot with VB-15 on the *Essex*, recalled, "In mid-August, after my first combat experience, our part of the fleet went into Eniwetok Atoll for rest and recreation. After we had been in for three or four days, we were called into the ready room by Commander [James] Mini. We were told that the fleet commander had decided to reduce the number of SB2Cs on each of the carriers and increase the number of fighters. If we did that, we would have some extra pilots in VB-15." Undoubtedly, the increasing effectiveness of bomb-laden F6F-3s, coupled with the disappointing performances of the SB2C, influenced the decision.

Lee said, "The thinking was that we should train some of our SB2C pilots in the F6F on Eniwetok, while we were in, and take them back to sea as fighter pilots. These pilots all had two or three months of combat experience, a number of carrier landings. They could partially solve VF-15's problem of getting additional pilots and also VB-15's of having extra pilots.

"Commander Mini asked for volunteers, nine SB2C pilots to check out in the F6F and go over to VF-15. There were six volunteers and I was one. I think Mini hesitated a moment about letting me go since I'd been in the squadron only about two months. I think if there'd been more than six, I wouldn't have been allowed to go."

Asked his motivation for the switch, Lee remarked, "More action, I suppose. I often think I was very foolish to volunteer for such a thing—not having all that much experience, all that much flight time. I think it was the idea of, 'I've seen what flying a dive bomber is like. And that's pretty exciting, but I'd like to try a fighter plane. Maybe I'd get myself a Japanese plane.'" He dismissed the notion that it was his unhappiness with the SB2C, although he later came to see it as "the dog of all dogs." "The grass is usually greener on the other side and I wanted to fly the F6F. I think it was just a challenge. At 21 years old, a young man wants a challenge."

Although Group Commander David McCampbell strongly voiced his own ideas on tactics—he regarded the Thach Weave as unnecessary and even undesirable once the high-performance Hellcat met the Zero and the Zeke—his attitude apparently had not led his immediate subordinates to train their newcomers. Lee said, "I was absolutely amazed at the contrast between VB-15 and VF-15. We got absolutely no indoctrination and no training in VF-15. We had enough experience in VB-15 to know the things we ought to learn, so we had our own little training sessions—more of a do-it-yourself thing. The commanding officer and the department heads organized nothing for us. I got four carrier qualification landings in the F6F in four flights. That was the extent of our training. We then went to sea as fighter pilots."

The campaign to protect the advance into the Philippines brought a major strategic blunder. Nimitz and his closest advisers believed it necessary to capture the Palau group's Peleliu Island for use as a base. In retrospect, Peleliu offered no threat. It lacked any real airpower and was already too isolated to offer a springboard for a Japanese thrust. However, the resident Japanese, drawing on their experiences with previous U.S. invasions, substituted a defense in depth rather than relying on an outer ring to keep an enemy off the beaches. The strategy sharply reduced the effectiveness of the usual American barrages from ships and the air targeted on the landing sites.

Ignorant of the shift, Kent Lee and VF-15 arrived over Peleliu on September 8, one week before A-Day (Assault Day, rather than the customary D-Day, which by now had become so associated with the Normandy invasion that some in the military were choosing a different label). Lee recalled, "On September 8 I was sent over to bomb and strafe with Lieutenant Kramer, also from VB-15. I flew wing on Lieutenant Kramer on this particular mission. We got to Peleliu, and there was lots of fire, smoke, bombs going off and so forth. We made an attack in our assigned area, dropping bombs, and strafed.

As we pulled out, Lieutenant Kramer was hit in the right wheel well. We pulled up to 2,000 or 3,000 feet and I told him that he was on fire and to get out. But he never opened the canopy, never made a move. He just rolled to the left and went right in. His only combat flight in the F6F was at Peleliu."

The thunderous cannonades from the battleships and cruisers at Peleliu barely dented the defenses created by the Japanese, who burrowed into caves and timed their aboveground movements to the intervals between salvos. Similarly, the carrier-based flight operations like that described by Lee aimed at surface targets and had little impact. Only after the Marines pushed far enough to capture an airfield from which they could fly F4U Corsairs bearing 1,000-pounders and napalm did airpower begin to make a difference on Peleliu.

Douglas MacArthur's forces, advancing in the southwest, focused on Morotai in the Moluccas, a group of Dutch East Indies islands between New Guinea and Mindanao. The Navy lent its support from the air, and prior to the actual invasion, one pilot was shot down while making a safe water landing inside a harbor reachable only through narrow, crooked channels. In his rubber boat, the flyer paddled furiously, but a strong wind blew toward the beach while a frustrated lifeguard sub stood outside the harbor, unable to see a way to navigate the uncharted, cramped openings.

Flying an F6F, Lieutenant Art Downing, who became a fighter ace, heard about the situation and flew over the area. He spoke to the submarine and, according to Thach, radioed, "You can get in and get him." The sub captain answered, "If I can get through the channel."

"Downing," recounted Thach, "says, 'I'll get you through the channel. I will con you through the channel.' The submarine skipper was apparently a similar type to Art Downing because he said, 'All right. Come on. We're going to get this man.'

"The submarine started in. Art Downing, flying his fighter would tell him so many degrees right, now you've got a sharp turn coming to the left, and he just coached him right into the channel, conning tower up, not submerged. All the time the wind was blowing this poor little raft with the pilot in it closer towards the beach.

"By the time the submarine got in there, they were shooting at him with machine guns from the beach. The submarine got in there and went between the beach and the pilot and picked him up. Art Downing coached him back out again. As soon as the submarine got clear, he called Downing and said, 'I don't know whether you noticed it or not, but there were two Japanese planes flying above you. I didn't want to tell you about it because I was afraid you'd leave me in the harbor.'

"Art Downing said, 'I saw them, but I figured that they were too curious about what you were doing to bother me.' "

EIGHTEEN

THE BATTLE OF LEYTE GULF, ACT I

During the second week of September 1944, from Fighting Two off the *Hornet*, Ensign Thomas Tillar escorted TBFs and SB2Cs on a mission to a target on Cebu. While the bombers were completing their runs on an airfield, Tillar and Lieutenant (j.g.) C. P. Spitler jumped a pair of Zekes. Although an enemy fighter started to ride in on Tillar from behind and the American saw tracers zip by his cockpit, he pursed a Zeke in level flight, gradually overtaking him. "He apparently was aware of this, and when I was within 2,000 foot range, he went into a wing-over to the left. I turned inside him and followed him around in the turn, firing at five-second intervals. One half his wing and part of his tail came off. By that time we were going straight down to the water from 2,000 feet. I pulled out about 100 feet off the water and saw him splash—he did not bail out or burn. He just crashed."

In his recovery mode, Tillar discovered a pair of Zekes blasting away at him head-on. He returned fire and smoked one but lost track of them. He had climbed to 9,000 feet before he discovered trouble. An oil film began to cloud his windshield, and the oil pressure dropped gradually. Although his engine labored, Tiller even joined his companions in a strafing run before the return to the *Hornet*.

But the Hellcat's oil pressure fell to ominous levels and he could not maintain his airspeed or altitude. When the engine started to overheat, Tillar realized he had no alternative but to ditch. He landed softly, and in the twenty seconds before the F6F-3 sank, he left the cockpit and inflated his rubber boat. Overhead, a pair of comrades circled for his protection. He drifted calmly perhaps ten miles from Leyte, awaiting rescue.

After he had been meandering for about an hour, several outrigger canoes from a small island close to Leyte approached. "An elderly man and a boy were in the leading canoe and a single man in each of the others. They seemed suspicious of me and I was even more so of them. They stopped about twenty yards from me. They were jabbering in a foreign tongue, which I presumed to be Filipino [Tagalog in many different dialects was the language of the indigenous residents]. I was unable to understand. All this time I had my revolver in my lap as I was unable to determine whether they were native or Jap, friendly or unfriendly."

The canoeists and the pilot exchanged gestures, and the locals came very close to the raft. Tillar offered his razor blades from his emergency kit to curry favor. The items were passed about and studied. When they motioned for the pilot to get into one of their canoes, he agreed, having decided they meant him no harm. He waded ashore to a festive reception.

"There was a native village and many people—about 200—were waiting for us. They whole population had turned out. They were scantily clothed, those with anything wore a tough type of cloth that resembled burlap. The men were about five feet, four inches tall, all of dark yellow complexion with almond-shaped Filipino type of eyes and straight, black hair."

To his relief, one young man spoke broken English. He became Tillar's interpreter. The aviator explained that he was an American flyer but the people did not understand what either "Navy" or "aircraft carrier" meant. Tillar handed out more razor blades, and when the chief's wife expressed a desire for his silken parachute he immediately presented it to her. She was astounded when he held a mirror up to her face, and he won more appreciation after he bandaged the finger of a man who had been experimenting with his razor blades.

Tillar learned that the people had had no contact with the Japanese but, because of what they had heard, regarded them as unfriendly. His hosts fed him well and he reciprocated, dishing out his emergency rations and the gear from his life raft. He tried to attract attention when another carrier strike passed overhead. But no one seemed to see his mirror reflection signals. However, a pair of F6Fs, flown by squadron mates Andy Skon and Les Sipes, began circling the area. "I used the mirror—and they came down close. Then I shot a .38 tracer right in front of them. They must have seen it because they joined up and came down still closer. I ran back to the chief's cabin and got the Very pistol out of my seat pack."

Just after he fired the Very pistol, which Skon and Sipes saw, an outrigger arrived from a little island in the south. The interpreter recognized its occupant and said he was a lieutenant in the Filipino army. He spoke fairly good English and understood when Tillar described himself and the carriers offshore. "He asked how many carriers we had out there and I said a great many. He seemed quite pleased with this. He told me—in answer to my questions—that there were no Japs on Leyte."

Moments later a Kingfisher droned toward the island while the two Hellcat pilots directed it toward Tillar. Not until he fired a second Very shell did the rescue plane find him. It landed 75 yards off the beach. Tillar bade his hosts farewell and paddled out to it. Fighting Two on the *Hornet* received a most gratifying dispatch that reported Tillar's rescue and then said, "Natives state there are no Japs on Leyte, Bosol, Apid or small islands in the area." An hour after he returned to the flattop, Tillar flew over the island carrying a specially prepared parachute rig. Attached to it was a box of cigars, a delicacy he had learned that his friends on Apid Island savored. He dropped the item along with a thank-you note in Spanish.

Tillar's report that the local people had seen little or no evidence of a Japanese presence heavily influenced a strategic decision. But either something had been lost in the translation, or its source, the Filipino army man, was distributing misinformation: Leyte actually housed a strong enemy force. With MacArthur's forces in the southeast poised to advance to Morotai, leapfrogging over Halmahera, Halsey argued that the meager air resistance he had met and the intelligence about the absence of enemy forces suggested that Leyte was a better objective than Mindanao. Leyte was farther up the archipelago and closer to the main island of Luzon.

With A-Day, the scheduled return of Douglas MacArthur to the Philippines via the island of Leyte, set for October 20, Task Force Thirty-eight, guided by Marc Mitscher, steamed into the China Sea. Under Mitscher's command were seventeen carriers of various sizes and more than a thousand aircraft. One of the task groups sailed under the command of John Sidney McCain, Mitscher's designated replacement. Their superior, Bull Halsey, hoped that the Japanese might be tempted to confront the armada with their remaining carriers, but the Japanese refused the bait. The carrier planes first sacked targets on Okinawa, ruining more than a hundred planes, and sank nearly a score of small warships at a cost of twenty-one U.S. aircraft. Most of the airmen were rescued by lifeguard subs.

Next on the agenda came crippling any air opposition that might come from Formosa. As TF-38 sailed ever deeper into hostile waters, Mitscher ordered the night fighters from the *Enterprise* to deal with snoopers seeking the location of the fleet. Commander Jim Gray had four F6F-3 night fighters, and he and wingman Ensign Ed Boudinot drew the duty. The two Hellcats, which still retained the radar housings fastened to their starboard wings, sifted through the darkness, listening to their flattop's Combat Information Center (CIC). While Boudinot stuck by the fleet, Gray followed a vector toward a suspicious blip.

Gray listened intently as the fighter director officer relayed information. He pursued a course until he was 50 miles away from home before he heard "Bogey two o'clock level five miles." Guided by the FDO, Gray slid into position behind the fast-moving twin-engine aircraft. At full throttle, the Hellcat slowly gained on its quarry until, through a pair of binoculars hung about his neck, he made out a dim shape. The Betty, still searching for the ships and unaware it was being stalked, began a shift of path until it had completely reversed direction. To Gray's delight, the change silhouetted his target against the afterglow in the western sky. He closed the range to a few hundred yards and then opened fire. The tracers, a sharply limited load to avoid blinding Gray, stitched the fuselage and then spread over the wing roots into the engines. In four seconds, the Betty became a flaming coffin for its crew as it exploded.

Eight days before the first landings on Leyte, VF-8, from the *Bunker Hill*, with more than half of the newer F6F-5 Hellcats, some bearing 500-pounders, struck Formosa. They rendezvoused with the *Intrepid*'s VF-18. The honors for the first strike against Shinchiku Airfield went to the VF-18 while VF-8 flew cover. Two enemy fighters quickly succumbed to the Navy fighters.

The raiders moved on to the Taien airfield. Commander William Collins from VF-8 reported seeing several Nicks, twin-engine fighters with a crewman manning a single gun, taking off. They were quickly shot down. Suddenly, some fifty enemy fighters, according to Collins, dived from high altitude and attacked the Americans, who instantly jettisoned their bombs. In his action report, Collins laconically noted, "I shot down two Zekes and two Oscars. My plane was hit during the engagement, evidently damaging my port guns. My oil pressure dropped to zero and I entered the nearest cloud to avoid a Zeke making a run from above. The loss in oil pressure had undoubtedly been [due to] a previous maneuver that caused me to be on my back for a few seconds. On emerging from the cloud, a Betty was slightly above and directly ahead of me. This plane was shot down." In this single sortie, Collins had destroyed five airplanes.

Lieutenant (j.g.) Ralph Rosen, wingman for Collins, jumped into the melee. "I saw an Oscar making a run on Lieutenant [Whitey] Feightner and got a bead on him and fired a burst of about four seconds. As I followed through, still firing, the plane started to smoke. Just as I passed it, the pilot bailed out." Unable to find Collins, who had slipped into a cloud for a temporary respite, Rosen said he had joined up with a fighter from the *Intrepid*. When an Oscar, intent on F6Fs below, flew in front of Rosen, he quickly took a position on the enemy's tail. His machine guns cut into the wing root, igniting a massive fire.

"Just about that time I felt an explosion in the after part of my fuselage and saw tracers going by my wing. I glanced back and saw an Oscar on my tail about fifty feet behind me. I did a violent diving turn to the left which threw him off for a moment. There was no friendly plane near me, but I headed for some F6Fs higher and to the south. One of these, piloted by Lieutenant (j.g.) Lamoreaux, shot the Oscar off my tail but not before it had cut my radio and filled my cockpit with smoke. I believe some 20 mm went off just in back of my seat. Since I didn't know how badly I was damaged, I headed for the sea and the rendezvous point, flying at full throttle. Two F6Fs were about 1,000 feet below me, and I thought they were going [there also]. However, I saw they were trying to catch an Oscar that was above them and outdistancing them. I had enough speed to close and since I didn't see the other two Hellcats firing, I got on the Oscar's tail and followed it through some half-hearted rolls and split-8s almost down to the water before I got in a good burst. The Oscar started to level out but then did a nose-down turn to the right and hit the water, wing and nose first." His aircraft apparently functioning well, Rosen flew home alone.

As Lieutenant (j.g.) Dan Rehm, who had burned three enemy planes during the Great Marianas Turkey Shoot, recalled, during the action at Taien, "About six to eight Nicks were tally-hoed here and I picked one out that was not being worked over at the time and burned him after a short burst. The group then began to rendezvous at about 8,000 feet. About this time, Zekes were tally-hoed above and I looked to see about twenty-four of them. I immediately began to climb. I spotted one Zeke making a pass at me and I went into a flipper turn. I could see him shooting. As he went past me, I rolled over and tailed in on him. Just at this time I noticed another Zeke on my tail, and McCormick tailing in on him. I gave up the idea of getting the one I was after and concentrated on getting that bastard off my tail. I went into a flipper turn to the left and began kicking my rudders. I didn't dive away because I thought Mac would take care of him. I could feel his breath on my neck, as a matter of fact. I got tired of playing tag so I dived away. Just after this, I was climbing to get a Zeke when he saw me coming and dived over. I tailed in behind him and he went down about 1,000 feet after a short chase. I finally set him on fire and he went straight in."

Whitey Feightner, who had achieved the status of ace during the grim days of Guadalcanal in 1942 with Air Group Ten, had come back to the Pacific with VF-8. He said, "I was watching the boys knocking off planes below us on the Taien Airfield and feeling pretty happy about the whole situation when my wingman reported many bogeys starting an attack. I looked up and saw fifty to sixty fighters in two groups with four or five already in their dives and heading for Division One, the only planes not down around the field. We immediately pushed over in a dive to gain speed and as the first plane got within range, pulled into a steep climbing left turn across the Skipper's [Collins's] bow. The first two planes had so much speed and were so close they were unable to bring their guns to bear and rushed on past. But number three was just getting into range when the Skipper fired on him. The Zeke split-sed and I did not see him any more, just as I spotted a Zeke on the tail of an F6F which was turning into me. I got a burst into his engine, which burst into flames, and the plane spun slowly. I immediately pulled up and found another F6F scissoring with me with a Zeke on his tail. I got almost a head-on shot from his port bow, hitting near the wing root, and the Zeke exploded."

Feightner reported that he had started to climb to join other Hellcats when he glimpsed another enemy fighter maneuvering toward the tail of a Navy plane. "I immediately dived for him and gave him a short squirt, whereupon the Zeke rolled to my left. I didn't see him again. A moment later I saw an *Intrepid* plane with a Zeke [behind him]. I dived for the Zeke, got a short burst around his engine, which smoked, passed over him and did not see him again. The fight had slowed down by this time and all I saw was about ten to twelve Zekes high above us and a lot of F6Fs all around. Several parachutes were still in the air below."

Cruising the area, Feightner drew a bead on another foe. "Just before I got in firing range, the Zeke suddenly pulled out in a right turn and [the pilot] bailed out." Far below him he saw Lamoreaux dueling with an enemy fighter, then gunning the Zeke into the ground. Pilot after pilot from VF-8 and others in the task force told similar stories. The fight, which lasted only about twenty minutes, ended with VF-8 alone claiming to have destroyed thirty-two in the air, three probables, and thirteen damaged. The squadron lost not a single plane.

Air Group Twenty from the *Enterprise*, composed mostly of combat rookies, threw its contingent of fighters and bombers at Formosa. Commander Fred Bakutis, leading a six-aircraft division, looked down at the Einansho airdrome and then after circling saw the opposition climbing to meet him. These were Tojos, snub-nosed fighters vaguely resembling the Army Air Corps's P-47. Bakutis aimed at the lead plane, assuming it to be flown by the enemy flight commander. A single burst ignited both wing roots, and the Tojo went into a death spin. In no more than ten seconds after Bakutis opened fire, five Tojos burned, floundered, and tumbled to the ground.

While Bakutis and the other F6F-3 pilots shot it out with the Tojos, VT-20 and VB-20 worked the airfields over. Hangars blew up, fuel depots exploded, and grounded aircraft were reduce to wreckage. Unlike the flyers of VF-8, those from the *Enterprise* sustained casualties. Antiaircraft knocked down two dive-bombers and a torpedo bomber. The submarine *Sailfish* picked up both Helldiver crews, but the three-man Avenger crew perished.

Lieutenant (j.g.) Fred "Shorty" Turnbull, from VF-20, pulled up from a run that strafed parked aircraft and installations after being hit by ground fire. Turnbull joined three others for the trip home, but his airplane showed increasing distress. He elected to bail out and in his parachute drifted down to the water, only 20 yards offshore. His companions dropped life rafts, but they saw him dragged from the surf by Japanese, then wrapped in his chute and driven off in a truck. On the ground, someone shot Turnbull twice while he lay wrapped in his silk. He attempted to walk to the truck, prodded with a bayonet that drew blood. Despite his wounds, he survived interrogation, a Japanese hospital, and a prison camp.

Hugh Winters moved up to the post of commander, Air Group Nineteen, aboard the *Lexington* after his predecessor incurred severe burns from a fire ignited while he was in the process of ditching. Assigned a new F6F-5, named *Hangar Lilly* because Winters's plane captain stashed the Hellcat in a corner of the hangar deck, Winters volunteered to accompany the air groups striking Formosa as an observer. Air group commanders ordinarily did not fly CAP missions.

With Ensign Paul O'Mara as his wingman, Winters lolled high in the sky over the harbor during an afternoon strike. "We started our turn back toward where the squadron should be," recalled Winters, "and down below I saw four Hellcats closing fast on three Zeros. One burst into flames. As we circled above them, 'observing' the uneven fight, suddenly twenty Zeros jumped the four Hellcats, changing the odds. One Hellcat commenced to smoke.

"Diving, I used the throat-mike. 'Hey Rube, Hey Rube! [the carney's traditional yell for help] All *Mohawk* [his group's moniker] chickens from Ninety-Nine, over harbor, Hey Rube!' " Winters recalled in a semi-stream-of-conscious memoir, "Release belly tank, double-check all gun switches, wing-span growing through outer gunsight ring—squeeze it gently, and *hold* the pipper just on the top of his cowling, throttle back so as not to overrun too fast. Pilot dead over the stick. Full throttle, two Zekes in range, both on a Grumman's tail and firing. As my tracers poured into the rear Zero, another stream of tracers joined my own and I felt the shuddering jar of bullets cracking through *Hangar Lilly*. I jerked away and almost into another Zeke ahead on my right. There was time for a good burst, and pieces of his canopy tore off and passed by my wingtip. Approaching four planes with belly tanks (looked just like Hellcats, and I needed friendly company at the moment), I had to shoot down their tail-end Charlie—all wore the bright red-orange meatball.

"During this *long, long* three to four minutes, Toby [Lieutenant Franklin Cook, Jr.] arrived with the rest of the squadron, so they tell me, but I was unaware of it. Once again two Tonys on my tail, firing into me—O'Mara on their tails, everyone firing and nothing now in front to shoot at! I was swimming in an avalanche of tracers and all the bullets in between—some might have been the Kids's [O'Mara's] but that was perfectly OK with me. Cockpit full of smoke, *Hangar Lilly* again shuddering from those deafening cracks of bullets—something had to give."

Winters shoved his Hellcat into a series of gyrations and dived down to 1,000 feet, where he leveled off, pleasantly surprised to find himself without hostile company. He headed out to the position of the lifeguard sub, readying himself to bail out. O'Mara showed up and, after a quick pass underneath *Hangar Lilly's* belly, signaled Winters by hand (the radio was out) that the fire was diminishing. O'Mara led his commander back to the *Lexington* for a successful landing. His plane captain reported forty-seven holes in shot-up *Hangar Lilly* before it was pushed over the side. Minutes later, another member of VF-19 checked in with forty-eight bullet holes.

Toby Cook, however, did not return. After succoring the embattled Winters, he returned to strafing duties. He was last seen headed straight down. The squadron received credit for twenty-seven confirmed kills.

Now a fighter pilot with VF-15, Kent Lee flew a scout mission in company with an SB2C, also from the *Essex*. Their mission was to search for enemy ships or planes. Toward the end of their sector, Lee saw a Betty. "I alerted my SB2C partner [Lieutenant (j.g.) Dave Hall]. I told him, 'Let's catch that Betty.' The Betty had sighted us and made for the clouds. I went to full power and the SB2C couldn't keep up with me. I was going to give him a shot at it too. SB2Cs don't get many chances to shoot a Japanese plane.

"I didn't want to let the Betty get away. But before I could catch him, he'd gone into a cloud. I went in right behind him. He came out the other side, I was right behind him. I started right on his tail, but he opened up with that turret [machine gun atop the fuselage]. I would see tracers going by me. I decided that wasn't such a good idea. I pulled up to an altitude about 1,500 feet higher than the Betty and made what aviators call a high-side run.

"I turned all six guns on and when I got within range, I let all six go, and hit him in the starboard wing root. His wing root and engine caught fire, and then he spiraled down to the ocean. The plane hit the water, there was a big flash of fire, followed by black smoke."

Lee admitted a sense of exhilaration with his first kill. "The adrenaline was flowing freely. Having cornered this Betty and shot him down first pass, I thought I'd accomplished a great deal. The SB2C pilot was just about as excited as I was."

On the following day, Lee was assigned to do a fighter sweep over Formosa. After his flight assaulted airplanes on the ground, tank trucks, vehicles, people, and buildings, a gang of enemy fighters attacked the outnumbered Navy bunch. The division leader led the Hellcats into a cloud, but Lee lost contact with him. "When you're flying wing on another pilot and not looking at your own instruments, when you lose him, you've lost your point of reference. It's very difficult to regain your orientation from the instruments in your cockpit.

"Next thing I knew I was pretty much out of control, dropping out of those clouds. I could see those Zeros heading for me. I got my plane straightened out, went to full power and right back into those clouds. I must confess I wasn't much of a hero that day. But I think the true heroes are those who know when they've been licked and live to fight another day." He managed to find his way home; the others in his group thought he had been shot down.

As the American fleet withdrew, Japanese torpedo planes, at heavy cost to themselves, penetrated the combat air patrol and scored hits on the cruisers *Canberra* and *Houston*. A small task group, formally designated "Cripple Division I," assumed the responsibility for towing the damaged ships, with the light carriers *Cowpens* and *Cabot* providing air cover. The enemy dispatched torpedo planes, dive-bombers, and fighters, sixty-five to seventy-five aircraft, to finish off the limping cruisers. The *Cabot* launched its fighters from Air Group Twenty-nine to meet the threat. In a furious midafternoon donnybrook, eight Hellcats lit into the multitudes of predators. Three *Cabot* pilots—Lieutenant Robert L. Buchanan, Lieutenant Alfred J. Fecke, and Ensign Robert E. Murray—achieved ace status within fifteen minutes as each of them accounted for five planes. Altogether, the original interceptors from the *Cabot*, aided by comrades hastily summoned from antisnooper patrol, destroyed thirty-one. One Hellcat went down, but a Seagull rescued him.

Willard Eder, elevated to the rank of lieutenant commander, now skippered VF-29 on the *Cabot*, which, with the *Cowpens*, escorted the crippled vessels away from the east-of-Japan area. "VF-29's score was terrific," said Eder. "My eight planes on combat air patrol attacked seventy-five Japanese carrier-type attacking aircraft. The enemy force was routed with thirty-one kills by *Cabot* pilots. I was launched from the deck just as the enemy was met by our combat air patrol, and I found only one Jap plane in the area. He was good and finally got in position on my tail at fifty-foot altitude. I flew straight, and he settled in firing at me from very close range until my wingman swung in and shot him down. I returned aboard the *Cabot* with 101 holes—7 mm in my Hellcat."

During three days of missions against Formosa and in the immediate aftermath, the Japanese suffered an appalling defeat, reminiscent of the Great Marianas Turkey Shoot, with roughly five hundred aircraft lost. Aside from the sailors killed or wounded aboard the two torpedoed ships, the United States lost seventy-six aircraft in combat and thirteen more due to noncombat incidents. Sixty-four aviators were added to the dead-or-missing list. The air war had become for the Navy fighters almost a shooting gallery, except that occasionally the targets returned fire. Increasingly, the most deadly opposition lay in the antiaircraft.

In the final five days before A-Day on Leyte, the Third Fleet concentrated upon the Philippines themselves. About 9:00 A.M. on October 15, the first of the *Enterprise's* now-blooded air group took off for a 230-mile hop to Manila, the Philippine capital. The Big E's team included nine dive-bombers, eight torpedo bombers, and sixteen fighters. As they approached Manila Bay with the intent of ravaging the local airfields, coveys of Japanese fighters sallied forth.

From their tactics, it was obvious that the interceptors wanted to lure the fighter cover away from the bomb carriers, but the Americans in the Hellcats maintained their ranks. When their ploy failed, the enemy had no choice but to attack the formations. Ensigns Doug Baker and Chuck Haverland blasted five of them in a wild rumble. Baker discouraged a quintet of Oscars with his air-to-ground rockets before shooting one down.

A veritable curtain of antiaircraft fire greeted the bombers and strafers over the air bases. Nevertheless, they unloaded on and machine-gunned the many parked aircraft. Not a single fighter went down. Commander Emmett Riera, of VB-20, reported, "Escort was superb; not one enemy fighter approached to within gun range of the bombers and torpedo bombers, either during approach or upon retirement. Every plane that attempted an attack was either shot down or driven off."

The Visayan Islands, the southernmost components of the archipelago, rocked under daily assaults by Task Force Thirty-eight, complemented by U.S. Army bombers. By A-Day, the customary overtures of sustained bombardment from battleships and sorties off the carriers rained down upon the Leyte beaches and inland. Unlike most of the previous island invasions, the ground troops all came from the Army. The air support involved both the Air Corps and the Navy. The latter contributed air sweeps against installations on Leyte as well as the neighboring islands of Mindanao, Cebu, Negros, and Panay. The 24th Infantry Division troops reached their beaches near Tacloban, where they encountered stiff opposition from bunkered Japanese backed by well-directed artillery. Still, the GIs quickly pushed inland far enough for Douglas MacArthur to wade ashore in his ultimate triumph. At a second site a mile or so north, the 1st Cavalry Division was pleasantly surprised by the absence of sustained, forceful resistance. Two more Army outfits, the 7th Division and the 96th Division, waded ashore seven to ten miles south. The Japanese all along the line soon retreated to their well-prepared defenses in depth.

During the first three days of the Leyte invasion, the Japanese air arm remained largely out of sight. In this period, the task force's aviators pummeled ground bastions and wrecked 125 planes caught on the ground. The enemy brought down only seven American aircraft, and all except two of their pilots were rescued.

The surge of Americans onto Leyte inspired the Japanese command in Tokyo to change strategy. Instead of defeating the enemy on Luzon, massive reinforcements would come to the aid of the beleaguered garrison on Leyte, the Japanese air forces would contest for control of the air, and the remnants of the Imperial Navy would whip the U.S. fleet. Morison quoted a comment by a Major General Tomochika, who said, "We were determined to take offensive after offensive and clean up American forces on Leyte. . . . We seriously discussed demanding the surrender of the entire American Army after seizing General MacArthur."

On October 24, the hitherto dormant Japanese aircraft sortied with vengeance. They buzzed almost incessantly over the warships standing close in to support the GIs. In particular, they sought out the escort carriers from which fighters and bombers threatened the Japanese soldiers on Leyte. From the deck of the *Suwannee*, Tex Garner, who had shot down his first enemy, a twin-engine Lily bomber, a month earlier, took off on a predawn patrol. "We had been on station about four hours and were ready to return to *Suwannee*," said Garner. "A radio reported, 'Tally-ho. Eight bombers reported at ten o'clock heading towards Leyte.' I swept the sky and spotted a formation of Lily bombers. I tally-hoed them. We dropped our empty belly tanks and climbed to intercept them.

"Lip Singleton and I set up one line of the formation while Edgar Barber and Ralph Kalal set upon the other wing of the Vee. We all rolled in at the same time. It was perfectly coordinated and four Lilies were knocked down on the first pass. Each pilot had a bullseye.

"After that run we whipped the Hellcats around for another target and for an instant all four fighters had the same bomber and fired at him—so long Lily. All four scrambled for another bomber. Lip burned one. Kal exploded one and the last bomber pushed over, hell bent for our landing ships. I called on my Hellcat to give her all, closing very slowly. I was trying to get to him before he got to the fleet because there was no way he would miss 'em. I began to realize some of our AA was trying for him too. I either had to break off or go for him into our ships' AA.

"I bore in firing all six .50 caliber guns. He began to smoke. I notice the bomb bay doors open. There was no way he should have done that because that slowed him down enough for me to catch him. I closed to within four feet. I thought I'd ram him. I came across from his left engine, left wing spar, cockpit, right spar, right engine. On the sweep back, as I crossed the cockpit area, I saw like an accordion door open and the pilot appeared. The six guns cut him in half. The plane exploded with the bombs still on board.

"I knew I was in a tight spot with all those ships still firing and if I pulled up I was a dead man. I pushed over, leveled off at about eighteen inches off the water and went zigging through the ships like a scared rabbit, hunkered down behind the armor plating and praying. I was amazed when I reached the other side, wringing wet but still alive, with eighteen holes and nothing serious."

Dave McCampbell, CAG for Air Group Fifteen on the *Essex*, recalled that after the Great Marianas Turkey Shoot, Rear Admiral Ted Sherman, commander of Task Group Three, had told him he did not want McCampbell to take part in "scrambles or purely fighter-type missions: He wanted me to lead the deckloads of fighters, bombers and torpedo planes on missions." Along with everyone else in the Third Fleet, McCampbell knew that the Japanese fleet was on a course to confront them and they could expect hostile visitors on the twenty-fourth. The earliest strike from the *Essex* left without McCampbell, who planned to lead one in the afternoon.

After the aircraft had left, however, those manning the radar reported an enemy flight approaching. "We were just right off Luzon," said McCampbell. "We had only seven planes left flyable. So we scrambled all the fighters we had left. The *Lexington* was short too. I had told my plane captain to get my plane on the catapult. He had to bring it up from the hangar deck. Then word came I was not to go." Apparently, Sherman had instructed Captain C. W. Weiber to ground McCampbell. Crestfallen, McCampbell said he had begun removing his flight gear when over the loudspeaker came the message "The group commander is to go." He believed the change of heart was due to the realization of how few fighters remained ready to meet the enemy.

"When I got the word to go, he [E. E. Carroll, the plane captain] had to get the plane on the elevator and get it topside. When we were told to man our planes, mine was on the catapult, ready to go, except it wasn't full of gas. We'd always degas it when we'd put it below, in case of bomb attack, the fire hazard. They were gassing it when I went out and manned the plane. Pretty soon, word came down, 'If the group commander's plane is not ready to go, send him below.' With that I waved away the fueling detail. I looked at my gauges and saw that my main tanks were only half full. What they had done was gas the belly tank full. Of course, the first thing you do when you get in combat—you drop that belly tank.

"Anyway, I waved the gasoline detail away and I told them I was ready to go. They launched me and the other six planes followed. We made a running rendezvous. The first fighter direction [said] the enemy was twenty-two miles away at 14,000 feet." Indeed, some sixty bandits, twin-engine Bettys and dive-bomber Vals, escorted by a large flock of fighters, were headed for the task force. "We intercepted them," said McCampbell. "Five of the fighters went down and attacked the bombers and left Roy [Ensign Rushing] and I topside.

"We'd gotten the altitude advantage, and they [some fighters] quickly went into a Lufbury circle. We saw that was not very fruitful, although I think we did get a couple of planes. So Roy and I just preserved our altitude, got up about 3,000 feet above them and circled, figuring that at some point they'd have to come out of this Lufbury circle. Then we could go to work on them. We had a cigarette apiece, about ten to fifteen minutes. Then they broke out of this circle and headed for Manila and got strung out, later formed up in a nice neat formation, Vee-type. That's when we went to work on them.

"We had the altitude advantage all the time we attacked the Japanese. We would zoom down, shoot at a plane or two. Roy and I each would take one. I'd tell him which I was going to take, whether it was to the right or left. By telling him this, that allowed him to know which way I was going to dive and then allowed him to pull out after the attack, which gave me freedom to go either way I wanted.

"This worked very successfully. We'd make an attack, pull up, keep our altitude advantage, speed and go down again. We repeated this over and over. We made about twenty coordinated attacks. In the meantime, a third pilot joined up on us and he made, he said, two attacks, getting a plane on each one. Then he said he ran out of ammunition, and went back to the ship.

"Pretty soon, Roy called me. He says, 'Skipper, I'm out of ammunition.'

"I called back, 'Roy, I've got a little left. Do you want to go down with me for a couple more runs, or do you want to sit up here and watch the show?'

" 'Oh, no. I'll go down with you.' He followed me down for a couple more attacks. Then I looked at my gas gauges and saw I'd emptied one main tank and was down on the second one, running pretty low. By then I was out of ammunition too. I called him and said, 'We'll go back to the ship.' Having followed this flight away from the task group towards Manila, we'd gotten pretty far away from the ship. I'd estimate maybe 100 miles, give or take a few."

McCampbell navigated successfully back toward the *Essex*. En route, he and Rushing passed the *Hornet*. "They started shooting at Roy and me. I counted twelve bursts from the five-inch guns. Fortunately, they were all behind us. Also they directed their combat air patrol down on us. I saw them coming down and called on our frequency and they must have been on the same [one] although they weren't in our task group. I said, 'For chrissake, call off the dogs! We're friendlies!' Somehow they got the word.

"We proceeded back to the *Essex*. We passed the *Princeton*, which was in the throes of sinking [a lone Judy glide bomber, a survivor from interceptions by the *Princeton*'s own CAP, had planted a bomb that smashed through three decks and created explosions that doomed the ship]. When McCampbell neared his carrier, he called in, asking if they could take him as soon as he got back. When they replied affirmatively, he continued to head for the carrier. But when he flew over it he saw a flight deck full of aircraft, requiring him to wait a good twenty minutes. His fuel would not last that long.

"I called the ship and told them that. The admiral [Sherman] called the *Langley* and directed them to launch nine torpedo planes so they could give me a clear deck, which they did. I came around and made a pass, but the LSO didn't cut me on that first pass. They still hadn't cleared the deck properly for landing. I made a quick turnaround, came back again and landed safely. But when I tried to come out of the landing gear, I gave it near full gun. The engine conked out on me. I ran out of gas there on the deck. They had to push me out of the area. From the mechanic that regunned me, reammunitioned the guns, I [learned] I had exactly six rounds left in the starboard outboard gun, and they were all jammed." (His wingman had enough gas to await clearance and safely came aboard the *Essex.*)

"I went down to the fighter ready room. I remember the air group commander [Commander M. T. Wordell, Air Group Forty-four] who had just come back from a flight. I was having a sandwich and some milk and he was all excited. I knew him. He said, 'Dave, I just got five planes! How many did you get today? How many did you get today?'

"I was almost embarrassed to say. I said, 'Well, I think I got eleven,' because I had a couple of possibles thrown in there, probables. 'You'll have to wait and talk to Roy Rushing.' That took the wind out of his sails." McCampbell explained that after he and his wingman had shot down five of the enemy, he had started to mark them down with pencil and paper, which is how he had kept account. Rushing was credited with six and McCampbell with nine. For his achievements he received one of a handful of Medals of Honor awarded to Navy pilots. By the end of the war he had shot down a total of thirty-four, the highest score in the Navy.

Walter Lundin, a Hellcat pilot with VF-15 who had destroyed two enemy planes during the Great Marianas Turkey Shoot and added a pair during September missions over the Philippines, was one of the handful who took off that afternoon with McCampbell. He recalled, "The weather was heavy rain and clouds almost to the water. I watched Commander McCampbell take off; he waited for his wingman and then disappeared into the clouds. I was next off (on a plane that was marked in chalk, 'flyable dud,' which meant it was flyable but needed an overhaul) and waited for my wingman. We went into the clouds on a vector to the approaching enemy aircraft. At about 25,000 feet we came out on top in broken clouds of a group that numbered twenty-three assorted dive-bombers in a loose formation with eight Zekes covering. I told my wingman that the leader was my target and that he should take the wingman on the right.

"We were unobserved at this point. We commenced our attack, taking out our targets. While regaining altitude, a Zeke passed in front of me, which I was able to dispatch immediately. Speed was lost regaining altitude, so we were bracketed by the Zeros. Turning left [or] right or going up would have made us sitting ducks, so we pushed over, outran them, and lost them when we went through a cloud layer. When we came out on the bottom, we made a 180-degree turn and then back up through the clouds to encounter them head-on. However, not a plane was in sight. We searched for a while but could not come in contact with them. In hindsight, they probably headed for the deck, where their chances were better."

During these maneuvers, McCampbell and Rushing had gone off after the group headed toward Manila. Lundin and his companion flew back to the carrier. He too saw the burning wreck of the *Princeton*. "I often wonder if a plane in the group we attacked was responsible."

Late in the afternoon, Lundin, leading a four-plane CAP, was preparing to land when the Combat Information Center stopped them and directed the flight toward a contact detected on radar. "At 28,000 feet we caught up to aircraft that turned out to be one of their newest high-speed reconnaissance aircraft, named 'Myrh.' I gave it one small squirt, and it went up in flames. CIC directed us on another vector. Shortly after, we [found] and destroyed two Bettys. It was already dark below, which resulted in a night landing. It was the first night landing for the four of us, but no difficulty was encountered."

NINETEEN

THE BATTLE OF LEYTE GULF, ACT II

The punishing blows administered by the carrier aircraft as well as land-based Army units gave the United States the first rounds in the Battle of Leyte Gulf. The successes of the ground forces on Leyte itself further worsened the Japanese situation. However, the Imperial Navy still packed considerable punch and the amphibious landing force just offshore, and Halsey's Third Fleet expected to be tested severely.

Steaming from several ports, the entire Japanese armada divided into what American intelligence labeled the Northern Force or Main Body, the Center Force, and the Southern Force. In the Northern Force sailed the big flattop *Zuikaku* and three light carriers, *Zuiho*, *Chitose*, and *Chiyoda*, along with a pair of battleships converted for aircraft, *Hyuga* and *Ise*. However, the disastrous campaigns of the previous months had reduced the Japanese resources so much that the four regular carriers could operate only a limited number of planes—116, or half the normal complement. *Hyuga* and *Ise*, with no aviation units, were present only as decoys. Destroyers and light cruisers made up the rest of the Northern Force.

The most lethal power lay with the Center Force, whose first section boasted the two superbattleships *Musashi* and *Yamato*, both of which far outweighed and outgunned anything in the American fleet. Accompanying the behemoths was a third battleship, *Nagato*, and a retinue of heavy cruisers and destroyers. That same group's second half boasted two more battleships, as well a number of cruisers and tin cans. The overall strategy predicated a pincer movement by the Center and Southern Forces against the Third Fleet, with some of Halsey's resources seduced by the decoys of the aviation-bare *Hyuga* and *Ise* from the Northern Force.

The smallest aggregation, the Southern Force, split into two parts, had a pair of battleships plus supporting cruisers and destroyers as well as a troop transport unit scheduled to embark soldiers on Mindanao and land them on Leyte to reinforce that island's garrison.

Although the Japanese fleets themselves possessed only modest airpower, they expected to draw strong support from planes based in the Philippines. Additionally, Vice Admiral Takajiru Onishi of the First Air Fleet was ready with a secret weapon, the first graduates of a special program, the kamikaze, or "divine wind"—suicidal pilots who borrowed their name from a fortuitous typhoon that had annihilated a Mongol flotilla about to invade Japan.

Vice Admiral Jisaburu Ozawa, commander of the Northern Force, which would lure away a portion of the American fleet, fully expected his group to be destroyed. But the aim was for the other warships and aircraft to inflict enough damage to disrupt the Leyte invasion and cause Halsey's Third Fleet to retire. The Japanese admirals, for the most part, no longer thought in terms of victory. But there was always the hope that prolonged attrition and heavy losses might lead the Allies to accept less than unconditional surrender.

The departure of the massive fleet from Japan had not gone unnoticed. A pair of U.S. subs, *Dace* and *Darter*, acting as a mini–wolf pack, had been prowling waters close to the home islands, hoping to torpedo cargo and transport vessels on their way to Leyte. But when they picked up radar contacts they realized this was not a convoy of merchant ships but a large task force of warships. The submarines flashed word of their sightings to their command, and the news was relayed to Halsey. After tracking the enemy for a period, *Darter* went on the offensive. It fired six torpedoes into the heavy cruiser *Atago*. Huge fires arose, billowing black smoke, and the ship sank with a loss of 360 officers and men. Among those pulled from the water was Vice Admiral Takeo Kurita, commander of the first section of the Center Force. *Darter* blasted a second cruiser, which remained afloat but was forced to head home for repairs. *Dace*, the companion sub, blew up the heavy cruiser *Maya*. It was hardly an auspicious start for the Japanese operation.

The course taken by the Center Force would snake among the Philippines from west to east, passing through the narrow San Bernardino Strait between Samar and the southern tip of Luzon, then continuing southward toward Leyte Gulf. The Southern Force was to approach from the west and steam through the archipelago's Sibuyan Sea and via the Surigao Strait into Leyte Gulf. Ozawa's Northern Force was to head south from the eastern side of Luzon and then reverse course, dragging with it the bulk of Halsey's fast carriers.

Having lost his flagship, *Atago*, Admiral Kurita had moved to the battleship *Yamato*. Search planes from Task Group 38.2, commanded by Rear Admiral Gerald Bogan, an aviator since 1925 who before Pearl Harbor had sneered at the Japanese as too puny to last more than nine months, located Kurita's Central Force. The report, radioed at about 8:00 A.M., came from a two-plane team including a fighter manned by Lieutenant D. L. Watts, Jr. A Helldiver piloted by Max Adams, from Air Group Eighteen on the *Intrepid*, listed "13 DD, 4 BB, 8 cruisers off the southern tip of Mindoro . . . speed 10 to 12 knots." Bogan, aboard the *Intrepid*, ordered air strikes launched against the enemy.

From the *Intrepid* and the *Cabot*, the first wave of twenty-one fighters, twelve dive-bombers, and a like number of torpedo bombers struck Kurita's warships in spite of fierce antiaircraft fire. Group Commander William Ellis led his organization's dozen fighters, an assortment of torpedo planes and dive-bombers, which took off at ten minutes before nine. They sighted the enemy fleet as it passed through the Tablas Strait along the east coast of Mindoro in the Sibuyan Sea. There were actually five battlewagons along with the cruisers and destroyers, divided into two groups.

Ellis said, "The Japs opened up on our formation at very long range, using everything they had, including their turret guns, and the cumulative effect was terrific. Pilots [described] some of the AA bursts as pink with streamers, others, purple with white tracer, and an abundance of white phosphorus and one shell that burst and ejected silvery pellets."

The weather conditions were ideal for the attack, and the bombers pushed over first, screaming down from 12,500 feet at angles of 65 to 80 degrees before releasing their bombs at 2,500 feet. As they pulled out at 1,500 feet, they jinked violently to avoid the enemy fire. The action report said that eight of the Helldivers had gone after a "BB of the *Yamato* class" (or possibly the sister ship *Musashi*).

VB-18 claimed four possible but unconfirmed hits and three near misses with a mixture of armor-piercing, semi-armor-piercing, or general-purpose 1,000-pounders. One bomb failed to drop. The other members of the squadron attacked a *Kongo*-class battleship and told of two confirmed hits amidships and one possible.

The Hellcats followed the dive-bombers, strafing the biggest battleship and working over several in the destroyer screen. They started their runs at 10,000 feet, roaring down at a steep 70-degree angle to climb back up at 1,500 feet. The torpedo planes coordinated with the bombers and fighters to reach their release points. VT-18 reported that two tin fish had stabbed the *Yamato*-class battleship and one had exploded against a cruiser. Two torpedo planes were hit and presumably crashed in the Tablas Strait.

Lieutenant (j.g.) Bill Anderson, a former chemical engineering student in Rhode Island, had been a torpedo-bomber pilot on the *Santee* off North Africa, then flown antisub duty before joining Air Group Twenty-nine on the *Cabot*.

"There were five of us from the torpedo squadron who took off the morning of October 24. Our commander was Irvin McPherson, an experienced pilot who occasionally did odd things. For example, he always flew wearing leather bedroom slippers because he said if he was shot down in the water and he had to swim for it, he did not want to be burdened with flying boots." Also on this mission were the exec, Lieutenant John Williams, and two of Anderson's close friends, Lieutenants (j.g.) Howard Skidmore and John H. Ballantine, Jr.

"Somehow we became separated from McPherson and Williams and we never saw them when we reached the Japanese fleet or on the way back. Williams was shot down and rescued but he never rejoined the squadron. The three of us came over the Japanese fleet at about 15,000 feet. We circled them, looking for a target, and we started down. Our Hyannis training [where they had undergone special instruction on torpedoes] kicked in. I automatically adjusted speed and altitude. The ideal was about 270 knots and an altitude between 150 and 300 feet. The only way you could get that kind of speed in a TBM was through a steep dive at full power and when you leveled off you might be at about 315 mph. You would rapidly slow down, but if you could pick up your aiming point and drop the torpedo from 300 feet up, chances were good for a good torpedo entrance [into the water]. It was a fairly restricted envelope in which to work. You also had to have wings level, not nose up or down, when you released or else the torpedo might not have the proper attitude when it hit the water.

"The torpedoes were armed through two wires. One wire ignited a mixture of alcohol and water to provide the steam that drove the torpedo. The other was for a fuse in the nose which activated the exploder. It needed a run of 500 feet to fully arm the torpedo."

Over the Center Force, Anderson selected a battleship as his target and began the attack. "There were bursts of antiaircraft fire all around but not close enough to rattle anything in the aircraft. We lost sight of the our other planes. The Japanese fleet started evasive maneuvers and it was necessary for me to pass over the battleship and pick up a cruiser target on the other side. They were shooting at us with their major-caliber weapons. A sixteen-inch shell is not a proper weapon against aircraft; the chances of being hit are like those of being struck by a lightning bolt. They did throw up geysers of water and you'd turn so as not to be hit with falling water. The water would be full of color [from the exploding shell]; the Japanese did this in order to tell how close they came.

"We got in pretty close, straight and low, opened the bomb bay doors, and pickled off the torpedo. Any torpedo pilot who says he saw where it went after he dropped it is probably dreaming because after you fire it, you're so busy making a hard turn to get out of there you can't stop to look over your shoulder. My gunner, Richard Hanlon, said he saw it drop and head for the cruiser before he lost sight of it. The radioman, Joe Haggerty, said he saw it hit the cruiser. I was credited with having hit the cruiser and got a Navy Cross but I'd be hard-pressed to swear to the fact."

Anderson's friend Howard Skidmore, in another Avenger, made a run on the lead battleship. He unleashed his torpedo while passing through a curtain of hot flying metal. A hole opened up in the starboard side of the fuselage. Through the gap, Skidmore could see the ocean beneath him. As he pulled up, tracers illuminated his pathway in the sky. Over the crackling voices on the radio, Skidmore heard a report of a TBM afire. Because he smelled no smoke, he reasoned that the problem involved someone else. But some years later he learned from his gunner, Don Hambidge, that it had been his aircraft; the flames subsided, however. Hambidge busied himself tending to the wounds of radioman Danny McCarthy, who had been struck by fragments from a battleship's 5-inch shell.

Because he had a wounded man aboard, Skidmore received priority when the *Cabot* began to recover its planes. An oil film staining his windshield barely allowed Skidmore to see the landing signal officer. Still he touched down safely, although his wing missed the port catwalk by a bare three feet. He believed his torpedo had hit one of the two superbattleships.

By the early afternoon, the *Musashi*, which in fact was the massive battleship badly wounded by earlier Navy assassins, was already lagging behind the fleet. The heavy cruiser *Tone* paced the stricken battleship. New assailants from the *Franklin* and *Enterprise*, along with return visits from the two organizations on the *Intrepid* and *Cabot*, arrived to administer the coup de grâce. Nine SB2Cs, eight TBMS, and twelve fighters comprised the deckload from the *Enterprise*. They left the carrier around 1:15 P.M. and arrived over the Center Force shortly before 3:00 P.M. Commander Daniel F. "Dog" Smith, in a Hellcat, directed the mission, and he chose the *Musashi*, which, although moving at reduced speed and trailing oil, seemed fire-free.

The other Japanese warships opened up with all their firepower but other than providing pyrotechnics inflicted no injury. Smith assigned the fighters, with their rockets and machine guns, to the cruiser and a destroyer while the Helldivers and Avengers focused on the massive battleship. According to Edward Stafford in his book *The Big E*, "The bomber pilots, suspended over *Musashi*'s growing deck, had never had such a target—big, fat and steady as a tidal rock. They stayed late in their dives, released both bombs low and pulled out sharply as only the SB2C could do, retiring low and fast, and under heavy fire. . . .

"As the last Helldiver dropped and pulled out, the first torpedo from an Avenger slid into the quiet waters of the Sibuyan Sea. Four of Prickett's [Lieutenant Commander Samuel, VT-20's leader] planes came in on either bow, spread out so that the torpedo wakes ran straight and parallel, as though an invisible rake had been dragged through the sea. The torpedo pilots, like the dive bombers, pressed in close and released late, knowing that in all the history of war at sea, few men have had opportunities like this one, and grimly determined not to muff it."

Stafford's account lists few misses, stating that eleven out of eighteen 1,000-pound bombs smashed into the hapless warship and all eight torpedoes struck home. Fountains of fire and black and white smoke obliterated sight of the *Musashi* temporarily, but when she became visible again, she lay dead in the water, her bow beginning to slide beneath the sea. All of Air Group Twenty returned to the flattop without sustaining serious damage.

Navy flyers, unhampered by any Japanese aircraft, delivered lethal ordnance almost at will, until, butchered by a total of nineteen tin fish and seventeen assorted bombs, the giant rolled over and sank. About 1,500 men were rescued by elements of the Japanese fleet and more than a thousand sailors perished.

Before October 24, sporadic kamikaze attacks had already claimed some victims. On this day, a massive strike of perhaps one hundred Philippine-based planes included several kamikaze flights. Ken Hippe, who, as a flight instructor at Pensacola, had bragged that not a single student of his ever failed his check flights, had become a member of VC-3, a composite squadron, when it formed. From the escort carrier *Kalinin Bay* he had flown missions for the Saipan and Guam landings and then in the Palaus. His aircraft was an FM-2, a replica of the F6F-5 Hellcat manufactured by General Motors rather than the fighter's creator, Grumman.

"We seldom saw enemy planes," said Hippe. "The big carriers knocked them out ahead of the landings." Now he and others from his squadron met a wave of oncoming aircraft, some of which were on suicide missions. "They were Army Kawasaki K148, twin-engine Lily bombers, twenty-one of them in V formations, and they flew the formations well. There wasn't time to make runs on them, so I got in back of them and started to shoot." In a few brief moments, Hippe achieved ace status, destroying five of the Lilys.

When he had emptied his machine guns, Hippe said, he considered trying to chew off the tail of a Lily with his prop. "We were at 8,000 feet, and I was afraid the propeller might splinter. I didn't want to parachute at that height with all of the AA below me." In contrast to kamikazes, the Japanese bombers were fully manned with a crew of three, and the rear gunner fired a .30-caliber machine gun at Hippe. However, the only damage he incurred was a thick spray of oil from his victims that covered his windshield. The first large effort by suicide bombers was thus not a success. The single Navy casualty was the *Sonoma*, a fleet tugboat.

Despite the death of the *Musashi* and two other battleships, *Yamato* and *Nagato*, which had to cope with a pair of bomb hits on each, the Central Force remained a serious threat to the Leyte campaign. The ability of the enemy to shake off a strong air attack that proceeded with virtually no aerial opposition raised doubts in some minds about the supremacy of the carrier. Halsey issued a statement: "The most conspicuous lesson learned from this action is the practical difficulty of crippling by air strikes, alone, a task force of heavy ships at sea and free to maneuver."

Samuel Eliot Morison, who would never completely give up the surface ship for the flattop, while underscoring this precept, also noted that it had been sheer folly for the Japanese to sail within range of enemy carriers without benefit of air cover. Actually, Kurita had pleaded for support by the land-based planes in the Philippines, but the admiral in command there had insisted on using his assets to hit at the task force rather than protect his brother in arms.

The interception of the Center Force and the battle in the Tablas Strait caused the Japanese commander to pause to succor to his wounded vessels and then to hesitate further while the aircraft in the Philippines struck at the Americans. Unfortunately for his side, the delay threw off the precise timetable that was necessary for successful execution of the plan to squeeze the Americans between the two Japanese fleets.

As the Center and Southern Forces, now out of sync, steamed toward their rendezvous, Admiral Ozawa, with his Northern Force, vainly tried to entice the Americans to send their carriers after him. He had launched nearly three quarters of his aircraft in the direction of Task Group 38.3, commanded by Rear Admiral Ted Sherman, and when there was no response, the planes landed in northern Luzon rather than return to their carriers. Ozawa then broke his armada into two parts, keeping his best flattops with him while Group A, with the two converted battleships, trolled farther south.

Halsey snapped at the bait. In the afternoon of October 24, patrol planes from the Third Fleet finally spotted Group A. The admiral explained that the sighting "completed the picture of all enemy naval forces. As it seemed childish to me to guard statically San Bernardino Strait, I concentrated TF-38 during the night and steamed north to attack the Northern Force at dawn. I believed that the Center Force had been so heavily damaged in the Sibuyan Sea that it could no longer be considered a serious menace to Seventh Fleet [responsible for the Leyte amphibious operations]."

Halsey was victimized by the credence given to the reports of the destruction wreaked upon the Main Force. The aviators coming home said that Kurita's fleet was now reversing course, away from the Leyte Gulf. However, it was not actually in retreat, merely hesitating. Halsey claimed he had been informed of "at least four and probably five battleships torpedoed and bombed, one probably sunk; a minimum of three heavy cruisers torpedoed and others bombed; one light cruiser sunk, one destroyer probably sunk and four damaged." Overestimation of damage, aircraft shot down, and enemy casualties is a common phenomenon of war, and in this case the misinformation threatened grave consequences.

Before the Leyte Gulf action ever began, Halsey had created Task Force Thirty-four, replete with battleships and cruisers, to serve as reinforcements in the event of a confrontation with enemy seapower. But it was a paper organization, one not specifically charged with responsibility for blocking the San Bernardino Strait, through which an aggregation like the Main Force would come. Without a direct order from Halsey, Task Force Thirty-four remained a phantom. He saw no need to activate it; believing the Center Force so badly battered, he felt that the warships in Vice Admiral Thomas Kinkaid's Seventh Fleet should be up to the job.

Kinkaid, apparently ignorant of the Third Fleet's hasty dash after the Northern Force and the opening up of an unimpeded passage through the San Bernardino Strait into Leyte Gulf, deployed his armada to handle only the Southern Force, which was approaching in two sections through the Surigao Strait. The Seventh Fleet's six battleships, four heavy cruisers, four light cruisers, and almost thirty destroyers, commanded by Vice Admiral Jesse Oldendorf, paraded back and forth across the twelve-mile-wide mouth of the Surigao Strait, prepared to lambaste any warships coming through. On the opposite end of the channel, where the foe would enter the strait, Oldendorf stationed a school of forty-five PT boats, which, in the absence of night-flying, radar-equipped aircraft, could sound the alert while harassing the enemy with their torpedoes. Tracking of the Japanese indicated that they could be expected after dark, when they would be safe from serious attacks launched by the small carriers belonging to the Seventh Fleet.

When the Main Force plowed into the Surigao Strait, a sound-and-light show erupted. PT boats fired thirty-four torpedoes (only one found its mark). Japanese warships lit up the scene with searchlights and exploding shells. The first fracs hardly slowed the Nipponese. They swatted the mosquito boats aside and then raced through the strait toward Leyte Gulf.

A thunderous battle ensued between the surface vessels as the surging Southern Force's lead section encountered a destroyer squadron, the advance element of Oldendorf's fleet. In the Battle of Surigao Strait, the Japanese fought off this first barrier to their advance and came within range of the main body of the Seventh Fleet. Searchlights, star-shell bursts, muzzle flashes, red, white, and green tracers, and fiery, deafening detonations splintered the night. The duel, which began shortly before 3:00 A.M., continued perhaps two hours. It ended with the Southern Force shattered and in retreat. The Japanese, lacking a coordinated attack by the Center Force, withdrew, minus two battleships and two destroyers sunk and with major damage to other vessels. The Americans chased the fleeing flotilla and blasted several more ships, notably the cruiser *Mogami*. Morison said that the Battle of Surigao Strait marked the last naval battle in which airpower played no part.

While Oldendorf's fleet relished its victory, about 100 miles to the northwest lay the unguarded San Bernardino Strait. Southeast of this area, off the coast of Samar Island, the Seventh Fleet's Task Group 77.4, with sixteen of the unit's escort carriers, monitored the Leyte Gulf area. The carriers and surface vessels provided support for the landing forces. The air groups pounded enemy airfields, attacked their ground forces, and staved off their aerial attacks. On the morning of October 25, the flattops, broken into three groups— Taffy 1, Taffy 2, and Taffy 3—began to catapult planes into the air to hunt for enemy warships, perform routine antisub patrols, and watch over the Leyte beaches for targets of opportunity.

Aboard the carriers, lookouts reported the puzzling sighting of distant antiaircraft shells. On the *Gambier Bay*, assigned to Taffy 3, the skipper, Captain Walter Vieweg, heard an excited voice from a plane with another group, shouting that the Japanese fleet was beneath him, 40 miles from Taffy 2 but 10 miles closer to Vieweg's unit. Over the radios sounded Japanese voices, but no enemy ships were believed to be within 100 to 150 miles. Suddenly, an antisubmarine plane reported sighting four Japanese battleships, eight cruisers, and a herd of destroyers. A disbelieving Rear Admiral Thomas L. Sprague, the CO for the task group, ordered a recheck, thinking that the flyers had simply confused the sighting with elements of Task Force Thirty-eight. But to the observers' horror, the distinctive pagoda-like superstructures of Japanese battleships poked above the horizon and a salvo of brightly colored explosions announced hostile intentions.

Admiral Kurita and his Center Force had sailed, totally unnoticed, through the opening left in the San Bernardino Strait by

Halsey's chase after Ozawa to the north. The Japanese armada men-
aced both Task Group 77.4 as well as the thin-hulled tankers, cargo
vessels, and troopships engaged in the reinforcement of the troops
on Leyte. While Kurita possessed no air cover, in a surface fight his
guns packed a much more powerful wallop than anything in the
task group's destroyer screen.

As the *Gambier Bay* crews and aviators frantically scrambled
to ready their planes, the enemy's first shells could be seen in the
distance. The fighters and torpedo bombers on deck still had not
been loaded with bombs or torpedoes. The situation for the rest of
Taffy 3 was about the same. All of the vessels began to churn out
smoke in a desperate attempt to hide. On the *Gambier Bay*, Lieutenant (j.g.) William Gallagher and his crew quickly climbed aboard
their Avenger as it came up the elevator with its torpedo in place.
The TBM rolled to the catapult position, but the plane captain ran
alongside, yelling that it needed to be gassed. The command "All
carriers, launch all aircraft" forced Gallagher to signal himself ready
to be hurled into the air, even though he knew his forty-five gallons
of fuel would keep him flying for only five minutes. Two more TBM,
both fully armed and fueled, followed to the catapult. The first one
took off. As the *Gambier Bay* maneuvered to avoid the enemy salvos,
it turned downwind, while an Avenger piloted by Lieutenant [j.g.]
Henry Pysdrowski was yoked for a launch.

In his book *The Men of the Gambier Bay*, Edwin Hoyt wrote, "Pyzdrowski got the 'cut' signal. He shut off the engine of the TBM, jumped
out and ran for the bridge. 'What's the matter?' he shouted. 'The catapult is charged.' Commander Borries [Fred 'Buzz' Borries, the air
officer, who had been an all-American football player at the Naval
Academy] held up his fist. 'Wait.' Pyzdrowski ran back to the plane
and ordered Fauls and Jensen [Gerald and Robert, his crew] out. He
intended to fly this one himself, alone. The signal was to hold up. He
jumped out and again ran to the bridge, calling to Borries. 'We can
take off without wind.' . . . While the ship was in harbor at Espiritu
Santo, the torpedo bombers had been fitted with new twin-barrel
Honeywell carburetors which were promised to increase engine efficiency. Carrier doctrine, however, said you must not take off except
into the wind, and with salvoes falling all around the ship, Commander Borries was not about to argue with the captain.

" 'Sure, sure,' he said to Pyzdrowski, and then he pointed to the
catapult. The TBM was just then being shot off, pilotless. It took off
beautifully, just as Pyzdrowski had said it would. It climbed for a

moment, then flipped over on its left side and went into the water. The *Gambier Bay* had launched its last plane. It was 7:50 A.M."

The Center Force blew away two destroyers and a destroyer escort attempting to shield the vulnerable carriers of Taffy 3. The flattops tried to run and hide in a rain squall, but when it passed, they saw four heavy cruisers overhauling them. One shell hit the *Gambier Bay*, killing some of the crew and setting a fully loaded TBM in the elevator well afire. Then a near miss knocked a hole in the thin-plated hull, reducing power. The Japanese, having found the range, zeroed in. Salvo after salvo burst upon the doomed carrier. Flying shrapnel decapitated one sailor, ripped off the arm of another, paralyzed a third man. Some died instantly; others lingered briefly with their wounds. A similarly vicious shower of shells battered the *Kalinin Bay* and *Fanshaw Bay*, but both remained afloat. The *Kalinin Bay* also absorbed a kamikaze crash, but fortunately the suicide's bomb did not explode. However, the damage removed the Jeep carrier from the battle, and Ken Hippe's war was over. The *White Plains* reeled from one hit, and the *Kitkun Bay* shuddered from a series of near misses.

But aboard the *Gambier Bay*, the situation was dire. Water flooded in through the holes; engines, pumps, and steering shut down. At 8:50, the captain ordered, "Abandon ship." Some of those who survived spent two full days drifting in rafts before being rescued. Pyzdrowski was among the lucky ones who were picked up.

A flight of eight fighters who had left the *Gambier Bay* before dawn to strike at the ground forces on Leyte knew nothing of the battle at sea. When the mission was over and they sought instructions on returning to the carrier, they were told of an attack off Samar. The Hellcats were instructed to land at the Tacloban field, controlled by the Americans. But it was a muddy mess. Some hundred refugees from the Japanese bombardment of their home carriers orbited Tacloban as those who attempted to land combated the boglike runway. Some nosed over, others bumped hard enough to crumble their landing gear, and a few even started to burn. Eventually, a number of them were directed to the field at Dulag.

While their base settled beneath the water and shipmates went over the side, the aircraft launched earlier by the *Gambier Bay* fought with their meager weaponry. Several Avengers had only their machine guns, and the TBM was not well suited for strafing. Nevertheless they dutifully pushed over and fired their weapons, hoping to discourage the Japanese ships. Ensign William Shroyer happened to

have two 500-pound bombs, and he scored a pair of hits on the fantail of a cruiser. Shroyer's was the only confirmed hit by a pilot off
the *Gambier Bay*.

Lieutenant Gallagher, who had taken off with a severely limited
amount of gas, wasted no time in unloading his torpedo at a cruiser
before turning toward the shore. His engine was seen smoking, and
when it died, Gallagher ditched. A companion observed all three of
the crew climb into a rubber boat. But they were never seen again.

To reinforce the efforts of its besieged partner, Taffy 2 dispatched fighters and bombers, and now it became the turn of the
Center Force to pay the penalty for its lack of air cover. Taffy 2 put
up three strikes, utilizing thirty-six fighters and forty-three torpedo
bombers. Composite Squadron Sixty-Five (VC-65), from the *St. Lô*,
and VC-68, from the *Fanshaw Bay*, located elements of the Central
Force. The planes, some of which had been engaged in dropping
supplies by parachute to the Leyte Island GIs, had not been toting
torpedoes when launched. They landed aboard the nearest carrier,
Marcus Island, which quickly loaded tin fish on seven TBMs. Lieutenant T. B. Van Brunt from VC-65 hastily diagrammed a plan of attack, and the group took off. Cloud cover dispersed the Avengers,
but Van Brunt descended until he saw a battleship. From an altitude
of 300 feet and 1,200 feet distance, he launched his torpedo. As he
pulled out, he saw a trail of oil behind the warship, suggesting a hit.

Intense and accurate AA, however, ripped into Van Brunt's tail,
destroying his rudder and smashing into the tail wheel, landing
hook, and rear fuselage. A 40-mm shell shook up his radioman. Believing he could not make a successful carrier landing, Van Brunt
put down at the Dulag strip. He was handed a rifle, assigned to a foxhole, and instructed to fire on the enemy, who were expected to
counterattack at any moment.

VC-65's Ensign W. C. Brooks, Jr., in an Avenger, peeled off from
a trio of TBMs and picked out a *Nagato*-class battleship for his
quarry. He released his torpedo at 500 feet, some 1,000 yards from
the target. His gunner observed a hit forward of the bridge, a large
orange explosion with a geyser of water. Brooks then landed un-
scratched by AA on the *Fanshaw Bay*. The aviators from Taffy 2
claimed torpedo and 500-pound bomb hits on a battleship and several cruisers. The damage inflicted by the escort carrier planes and
the smaller guns of the surface ships was substantial but not crippling. However, mindful of the losses incurred before arrival at the
San Bernardino Strait and worried by confused, largely erroneous

intelligence that suggested he might be beset by other forces, Admiral Kurita seemed to have lost heart. On October 25, he remained strong enough to have fulfilled the mission of an attack upon the amphibious force at Leyte. Instead, he turned about and retreated.

Taffy 1, the southernmost carrier outpost of the triumvirate, some 130 miles from Taffy 3, that morning had launched Avengers and Hellcats to chase the fleeing Southern Force in the Surigao Strait. When Taffy 3 called for help, the flattops of Taffy 1 were mostly recovering and rearming aircraft. About twenty minutes or so before 8:00 A.M., the spotters saw four enemy planes breaking out of the clouds some 10,000 feet up. Gunners manned their weapons, tracking the attackers. Aboard the *Santee*, Gunner's Mate Third Class John Mitchell, who captained a 40-mm position, said, "I ordered the crew to load and cock both guns. Before we were able to bear on the target, the bogey was in a dive and strafing the stern deck. I watched it come in all the way. I could not believe that the plane was not coming out of its dive. I was screaming, 'Pull out, you bastard! Pull out!'

"It came in so fast and with such surprise we didn't get off a single round. The plane used our aft elevator as a target and crashed just a few feet forward and to port of the elevator." The kamikaze had made its debut—or at least its first successful mission. Actually, Rear Admiral M. Arima, on October 15, had tried to crash into the *Franklin*, but watchful combat air patrol had shot him down during his approach.

Antiaircraft blew up the second and third kamikazes from the original quartet, but the last member penetrated a wall of shrapnel and bullets to drill into the flight deck of the *Suwannee*. Leaving the impression of its front silhouette in the flight deck, the plane's nose dug through three decks, halting just shy of the aviation fuel stores. Although numerous sailors and some aviators on the flattops were killed or wounded, both remained afloat, even though a sub's torpedo also racked the *Santee*. Kamikazes inflicted greater injury when they jumped Taffy 3. A Zeke smashed into the *St. Lô*, igniting fires below the flight deck. Torpedoes and bombs exploded, and the carrier sank within half an hour. Two more of the suicide corps smacked into the *Kalinin Bay*, but the crew quenched the fires.

Oblivious to the events south of his Task Force Thirty-eight, Third Fleet, Halsey, seduced by Ozawa, drove north. David McCampbell, the CO of Air Group Fifteen on the *Essex*, recalled being awakened in his bunk at about 2:00 A.M. by a staff officer who had called to say he was assigned to lead a flight at 7:00 A.M. That meant arising at about 5:00 A.M., which deprived McCampbell of further sleep.

Buoyed by a couple of cups of coffee, McCampbell received instructions from Mitscher to fly about 100 miles and then circle about in search of the enemy. Although McCampbell expected to meet the strike from the *Lexington*, it was Air Group Twenty from the *Enterprise*, under Commander Dan Smith, that tagged onto the tail end of McCambell's formation.

"We proceeded out a little ways," remembered the Air Group Fifteen leader, "and I sighted the Jap fleet. I called the [air group trailing behind him] and told them, 'I have the fleet in sight.' I gave them the approximate location, about forty miles from where we circled. I gave them the disposition and approximate speed, and laid out a plan where the first group to attack would hit a ship on the starboard side and the second group would hit one on the port side of the formation, to keep them from trying to go in at the same time and get all mixed in there.

"When I got a little closer, I could see this one ship, the *Chitose* [a light carrier], was pulling out of formation as if to launch planes. I communicated this to the bombing squadron flight leader and told him to attack that ship, which he did. [McCampbell, by orders of Mitscher, acted as target coordinator.] I circled over them, my group, while they attacked the *Chitose*. Of the eleven 1,000-pound bombs that were dropped, they got nine direct hits on her. They also carried 250-pound bombs, one on each wing in each plane. I didn't count those. Some hit, some didn't.

"Shortly after, or almost the same time, we came in with torpedo planes. I called the flight leader, [Lieutenant Commander] V. G. Lambert, and told him if it was not too late, if he could see his way clear, to divert his attack on the battleship next door, the *Ise*, converted with half a flight deck on the after end of the ship. He called me back and said no; he was too much committed to the *Chitose*. I didn't actually see or count any torpedo hits, although he claimed later they had five or six."

The concentration upon the *Chitose* continued in spite of McCampbell's best efforts. As target coordinator he directed Smith and Air Group Twenty toward another carrier, but instead the ordnance all fell upon the already doomed *Chitose*. In *The Big E*, Edward P. Stafford wrote, "The dive bombers dropped straight and true and released low above the empty flight deck with its unfamiliar markings over a clever shadow camouflage intended to make her resemble a battleship. The Avengers, skimming in over a sea torn with splashes of all sizes, the tracers smoking and the shells bursting around them, saw the big bombs punch into the target, the smoke puff out and pieces fly before they dropped their torpedoes in close and began jinking wildly down among the viciously spitting warships, on their way out."

At this point, McCampbell said, Air Group Nineteen from the *Lexington*, under Commander Hugh Winters, arrived. McCampbell turned over responsibility for target coordination to Winters while he took his brood home. McCampbell, in his oral history, failed to mention the contributions of aircraft from the *Intrepid* and *San Jacinto*. The former dropped one bomb on the carrier *Zuiho*, and a torpedo from either an *Intrepid* or *San Jacinto* TBM hurt the flattop *Zuikaku*.

Winters explained in his memoir, *Skipper*, "I soon found he [McCampbell] had flushed the task force, sunk a small CV, damaged another, and sent the rest hellbent over the horizon. . . . It developed rapidly that there were three carriers—*Chitose* . . . *Zuiho* . . . and our old friend *Zuikaku* speeding north." *Chitose* actually sank a few minutes after 9:30 A.M. and rather than that flattop, it was the sister ship *Chiyoda* that Winters pursued, along with a limping *Zuikaku* and the slightly damaged *Zuiho*.

"I divided the strike and of course took the *Mohawk* group down with me on the *Zuikaku*. I had better results leading them into the attack than staying up with the high cover and directing things from there, at least with the first wave. There was rivalry between *Lexington* and *Essex* [a phenomenon obvious in the memoirs of both McCampbell and Winters]—there always is in any force—and Dave had had his way on the first strike of the morning. I was glad he had left the *Zuikaku* for us and had only nicked her, as indicated by the long thin line of oil in her wake." (Morison said that the one earlier torpedo had caused the carrier to list 6 degrees and made steering so difficult that Ozawa had shifted his flag to another vessel.)

"A few of our high-cover fighters, as in practice, lingered back, and came in with the slow torpedo carriers, who must drop their weapons flying straight and level over the water instead of a fast dive and pullout. The ships were using new anti-aircraft stuff with wires and burning phosphorus shells which put up all different-colored fire and smoke around our planes. It looked like Fourth of July laid on by the Chamber of Commerce at Virginia Beach. But we had faced so much deadly AA lately for so many lousy targets that it didn't bother us too much hunting this big game. The boys were as cool as any professionals working in [a] hospital or law office.

"The *Zuiho* limped on, burning, but the *Zuikaku* stopped and started to die on one side. She needed no more, but hung in there for awhile and her AA battery was nasty. In the excitement, I stayed down too long (not very professional) and got some holes in my left wing."

Having unloaded his 500-pounder, Winters and his wingman lingered over the scene. New waves of Navy attackers from the *Franklin, San Jacinto,* and *Enterprise* arrived. "I assigned them to *Zuiho,* which was still maneuvering at fairly high speed. She went down within an hour." *Zuikaku* also succumbed, sliding under the water without any big explosions, fire, or smoke, just a collection of huge bubbles. Winters rebuked several other strike leaders who sought to usurp his prerogative by choosing their own victims. He also reported continually to Jim Flatley, Mitscher's staff operations officer. When D. F. "Dog" Smith returned for a final blast by the *Enterprise* warriors, Winters turned control over to him and headed for the *Lexington.* On the way home he passed a burning light carrier, which he identified as *Chitose.* The hulk was in fact the *Chiyoda,* which remained afloat until cruisers from the task force reached the area and sank it.

The Northern Force had succeeded all too well in drawing off Halsey's Third Fleet. While that may have opened the passage for Kurita and his Center Force, the Japanese lost four carriers and a destroyer. Only a scattering of fighters tried to prevent the slaughter, but these were either shot down or driven off.

During the time the fast carriers of the Third Fleet were demolishing Ozawa's Northern Force, Halsey received several urgent pleas for assistance against the Central Force, which had sailed through the San Bernardino Strait. He first detached McCain's Task Group One to aid the Seventh Fleet and later the battleships of Task Group Three. Finally, the entire Third Fleet, except for a batch of cruisers that continued to hunt the enemy, headed south. However, the cavalry steamed into position too late to confront the retreating Center Force.

TWENTY

CARRYING THE FIGHT
TO THE HOME ISLANDS

As 1944 drew to a close, the Japanese military was inundated by overflowing rivers of destruction, its once-mighty navy reduced to a paltry few ships, its air force largely consigned to suicide missions, and its soldier garrisons facing inevitable bloody annihilation. The Hamp, the newest version of the Zero and the Zeke, occasionally tangled with American fighters, and the first really competitive plane, the George, was about to debut. But production of these was limited. The Imperial Navy still had five carriers but very few planes or pilots for them, as well as a shortage of fuel. American aviators henceforth would combat land-based enemy airmen.

On October 30, Rear Admiral John Sidney McCain succeeded Marc Mitscher as commander of Task Force Thirty-eight under Halsey's Third Fleet. McCain's air officer was Commander Jimmy Thach. Proceeding according to plan, MacArthur's soldiers slowly ground up the defenders on Leyte, who fought to the bitter end. Having secured airfields on Leyte, the Army expected to assume all responsibilities for air operations. MacArthur even directed that the fast carriers dispatch no more air strikes against land targets unless specifically requested by the Army. However, the soggy ground frustrated efforts to establish enough squadrons to carry out the Air Corps's mandate. Behind the scenes American ground forces grumbled about the lack of air support from the Air Corps and regarded the Navy as far better at tactical aid for the foot soldiers.

A major source of help for the Japanese garrison on Leyte originated on the big island of Luzon with Manila as the spigot. Halsey's Third Fleet struck targets on Luzon frequently during the weeks after the landings on Leyte. David McCampbell, from the *Essex*, recalled runs on the airfields of Luzon and on Manila, whose anti-aircraft defenses impressed him. Nevertheless, he and companions from the *Lexington* and *Enterprise* helped turn the harbor into a graveyard of ships.

Kent Lee, the dive-bomber pilot who switched to fighters in VF-15, flew over the Philippine capital. "Our assigned area was the waterfront. We [four Hellcats] arrived over Manila and lo and behold, there was a Japanese destroyer out into the stream, doing twenty to twenty-five knots hoping to escape. We each had one 500-pound bomb. Of course our six .50-caliber machine gun magazines were filled. We dived on this destroyer and the three people in front of me released their bombs and all three missed. I figured I had him. I had him right in my sights, pickled the bomb and nothing happened. I pulled out and my division leader saw I hadn't dropped my bomb. I could just see him thinking, 'That dumb-assed ensign.'

"I persuaded him, 'Let's make another run. Let me drop my bomb.' I double-checked all my switches and we went in again on this destroyer. He was smoking a little bit where we were hitting him with the .50-calibers. Another run, released it—was just positive I had a hit, no explosion, pulled out. About this time the division leader had had it. We didn't make any more strafing runs on [the destroyer]. We then made some runs on shore-based targets and headed back to the ship,

"I tried to jettison my bomb, which is the procedure because you don't like to land aboard with a bomb on, but it wouldn't [drop]. Back aboard ship, I inspected the airplane with the ordnance man. The bomb rack was not hooked up. Otherwise I would have gotten myself a destroyer."

In the midst of the Leyte campaign, the fast carriers hustled off for strikes on Formosa when the Army asked for their help. Convoys of Japanese transports and cargo ships had been bringing reinforcements and fresh supplies into Ormoc Bay. The waterlogged airfields held by the Americans on Leyte could not handle the heavier bombers, and the Army's fighters were inadequate to the task. Task Force Thirty-eight mounted 347 aircraft to deal with the convoy.

David McCampbell was again assigned as target coordinator. "I took in about sixteen fighters, maybe twelve bombers and six or eight torpedo planes. We hit them around 9:40. There were four troopships, one *Teruzuki*[-class] destroyer and four or five destroyer escorts. [The account from *The Big E* lists three destroyers.] We, my air group, made the first attacks and we sank three of the troopships real quick. I believe the *Lexington* air group had joined up with mine.

"About that time, Dog Smith's outfit [from the *Enterprise*] came in and I directed them to hit the *Teruzuki*. He was doing about 30–35 knots around in the bay, and so far he'd dodged every bomb successfully. There hadn't been a lot of strafing of the destroyer so there wasn't too much antiaircraft opposition. Dog Smith's outfit started dive-bombing on them and they got him with two or three direct hits which finished him off. I think there was only one of their destroyer escorts that escaped being sunk out of that whole convoy."

Commander Smith complained that so many planes crowded the sky that day, he and his companions were forced to circle for twenty minutes before their turn to attack came.

When Japanese planes, stashed liberally around the Philippines, increased the frequency of their raids upon U.S. troops and installations, MacArthur reversed himself and asked that both the fast and the escort carriers remain on the scene. Their presence exposed them to further depredations by kamikazes, with *Franklin*, *Belleau Wood*, *Intrepid*, *Cabot*, and *Essex* all feeling the weight of the suicide corps.

Gerald Bogan, who had qualified as a pilot in the 1920s, was commander of Task Group 38.2, with his flag on the *Intrepid*, when a kamikaze struck the flattop. He counted eighteen aircraft bearing down on his ships, which included the battleship *Iowa*. "Two planes came in about 660 feet," said Bogan, "and passed over the *Iowa*. They shot one down and it landed in the ocean, a mass of flames. The other one had a slight flame on one wing, but instead of shifting to that one, the *Iowa* with all these antiaircraft guns, kept firing at this flaming mass in the water. The one that was on fire, came up and we were shooting at it with 40-mms and 20-mms, all we had at that range, and we didn't hit him.

"When he was about 400 feet off the starboard bow, he did a wing-over and dived right into the center of the flight deck, just before the flag room. He had a big bomb that created a helluva lot of damage in the area under the flight deck. While this whole thing was obscured by smoke, a few minutes later, [another] one came in just as if he were making a carrier landing, and landed in the arresting gear, nose down. His bomb exploded in the hangar deck. The body of the pilot and the engine rolled all the way forward and stopped near the bow. A few minutes later I was down there. I saw the Jap pilot and said to this kid standing there, 'At Guadalcanal I understand the Marines used to knock out their teeth and get the gold.' He reached in his pocket and said, 'I heard that, too. Here they are.' "

For two hours, the ship's crew on *Intrepid* fought the inferno created by the kamikaze blasts until they gained control. Hours before the suicide planes smashed into the *Intrepid*, it had launched his air group. Although the fires had been suppressed, the flight deck could not recover any planes. According to Bogan, McCain, as head of the task force, said, "When these planes come back, we'll land them on the *Hancock* [his flagship], take the pilots off and throw the planes over the side.

"That was about $4 million worth of airplanes," said Bogan. An officer on his staff, Lieutenant Ben Sturges, suggested, "They're over near the Philippines now. Don't you think they could land at Tacloban [the Leyte airfield]?"

Bogan said he thought that a splendid idea. "I called McCain and [Wilder] 'Rowdy' Baker, who was his chief of staff. I couldn't talk to the planes because my communications had been burned up. Tell those planes to land at Tacloban instead of trying to return to the task group. He [Baker] said, 'The field isn't ready.' I said there are 100 Army planes on it right now. Tell them to land there and don't give me any argument on it.

"Baker said, 'This is your boss's chief of staff.' I said, 'I'm commanding this task group. Tell them to land there.' " Baker yielded to Bogan's demand, and all of the aircraft managed to set down on Leyte without any casualties. He recommended a Bronze Star for Sturges. Bogan added, "Pete Mitscher, in my opinion, was a consummate master of naval air power and when he ran Task Force 58 or 38, it was a professional outfit, doing a professional job. When McCain ran it, it was a Goddamn circus." He was not the only high-ranking officer to find McCain less proficient than his predecessor.

According to Jimmy Thach, the command situation deteriorated into a dangerous turf war. "One thing that MacArthur did," said Thach, "was to draw a line just north of a place called Legaspi [on Luzon], an east–west line, and said, . . . 'the carriers will take care of the enemy air north of the line and the Army Air Corps everything south of the line. Don't attack anything south of the line and the Air Corps won't attack anything north of the line.' This would have been all right except we never believed in lines that restrict our operations when the carrier task forces had this great mobility and can hit something that might do some good. We ought to be able to hit something that might do some good, no matter who else is hitting it. We [the task force] went in there several times and got hit by kamikazes." Thach said he believed there were as many as eighty sites in the Philippines, from full-scale airdromes down to tiny strips, where the Japanese hid kamikazes.

"One time one of our carriers was hit, one of the *Essex* class, and had its flight deck out of action, burning. They finally put it out but the airplanes couldn't land aboard in all those flames. There wasn't room for them on the other carriers. We caught them en route and told them to go back and land in the Philippines [at an Air Force base]. They flew over Legaspi and saw all these [Japanese] airplanes. They landed at this base and talked to the squadron commanders, the Air Corps operations officers, and told them about these airplanes." According to Thach, the astonishing response was along the lines of "They're not bothering anybody, are they?" The Navy pilot said, "That's the reason we're here [at the Air Corps field]. We got hit by a kamikaze and we think maybe it came from Legaspi. We're not permitted to hit it and we would like for you to hit it."

"They said, 'All right. We'll take off tomorrow morning and we'll give you some bombs and you can go with us.' That was fine. They loaded bombs on the Navy planes as well as the Air Force ones and said, 'You lead us up there and show us these airplanes.'

"Away they went. They flew pretty high but the Navy always like to fly lower. They said, 'We don't see any.' Of course you couldn't see them from that altitude. The torpedo planes were going in, winding around the trees and picking out an airplane and dropping a little bomb on it. One of the strike leaders of the Army planes said, 'We'd better get up higher. There's a lot of antiaircraft going off down there.' They couldn't even see our torpedo planes either.

"That got straightened out and they all went in, got quite a few of the airplanes and some photographs. We finally made room for them [the Navy pilots whose flattop had been struck] on other aircraft carriers. We sent a blistering message on the basis of this. We argued against the line but we didn't get to MacArthur and he was the one who [established] it.

"Halsey immediately saw the problem and he argued with MacArthur against the line. He finally told MacArthur that when his carriers were called in to do a job, they had the right to protect themselves and to hit any airfield that was within range because the kamikazes were undoubtedly coming from airfields that had not been properly attacked. [Halsey] didn't argue anymore. He just told him and we didn't hear anymore about it." The black-shoe admirals versus the air admirals and the rivalry between the carrier air groups mentioned by Hugh Winters paled in comparison with the bitterness and strife among the branches of the American military, occasionally to the serious detriment of those under fire.

Following the script, troops, virtually unopposed, landed on the island of Mindoro, southwest of the main objective, Luzon, in mid-December. Much of the Third Fleet had debouched to Ulithi for refurbishing on the first of the month, and on their return voyage nature delivered a stinging blow in the form of a typhoon. Glenn Elstrom, a replacement pilot with VF-29 on the *Cabot*, recalled, "The waves broke ten feet over the deck, which was sixty feet above the water. Steel cables anchored the planes to the deck. I saw chiefs with twenty years in the Navy who were seasick. The escort carriers really took it. They had water up to their knees in the wardroom."

Three destroyers foundered in the storm, and the carriers lost 146 airplanes as they rocked, rolled, and pitched in the mountainous seas. Because Halsey apparently failed to appreciate the threat of the weather, he drew considerable criticism for the disaster. A court of inquiry said that he had committed "errors in judgment under stress of war operations and not as offenses."

The kamikazes posed a more sustained threat as the Navy ships supported the campaign in the Philippines. Again Thach innovated tactics to suppress the menace. In a small notebook he wrote, "Offense to spoil kamikaze raids on the task force, three-strike system, will provide a holey blanket over enemy known operational airfields, a holey blanket, but only small holes, I hope."

Though he realized that the Navy could not maintain cover over every field all day long, he hoped to come close. "We'd launch the first [planes] at 6:00 A.M.—I called the strikes A, B, and C. [We'd] launch A with bombs, B with no bombs, both together, two-thirds of [our] strength. They'd take off at six o'clock, en route to the target about an hour and fifteen minutes. Both A and B arrived at 7:15. The reason for sending that much strength on the first [strike] was we weren't sure how much they'd been able to feed in during the night and what opposition [we would] find. We'd double our strength so that A and B could both fight them. Then A would depart at 7:30. It was only over the target fifteen minutes. B would remain there. Then at eight o'clock C would take off, and then at 8:35 A would land and re-arm.

"At 9:20 strike C would arrive over the target, but at 9:10 strike B would have departed. That's only a ten-minute gap between the departure of one strike and the arrival of the next one. We would split these people up and cover all the airfields and just watch them. Many times, [the Navy flyers] would see airplanes being towed out from under the trees just as they arrived. They had been uncovered for ten minutes—they'd try to get this airplane out, on the field, and here would come the next strike."

Under Thach's system, A, having rearmed, would take off again to relieve C. Aircraft without bombs were armed with rockets and of course machine guns to deal with any enemy planes exposed or in the process of trying to take off. Although the kamikazes continued to ravage U.S. ships, the "holey blanket" worked well enough for Thach to earn a Legion of Merit.

Another tactic designed to keep the enemy off balance was night hecklers, two- and four-plane raids that harassed men engaged in work after dark, interrupted sleep, inflicted damage when installations became visible, and provided information on ground and shipping targets for the first morning strikes.

According to Robert Pirie, who acted as CNO Admiral King's representative in the Pacific Fleet, the Navy strategists recognized that the Japanese were transferring aircraft to the Philippines from mainland Japan in flights designed to arrive at places such as Clark Field just at daylight, thereby avoiding the Americans. "We discovered that in the early part of the game," said Pirie, "through our night fighter flyers on the *Independence*, who were going in as single airplanes, not making any major attacks. But they observed this habit they had of arriving at night. Also there were considerable numbers of take-offs of combatant planes going out of these fields at about the same time.

"We said that if we could get a significant number of our fighters over that field at that time [dawn] we could really have a field day. We devised a plan to take sixteen fighter aircraft off each one of our carriers at roughly 2:00 to 2:30 or 3:00 in the morning, so that at 4:30 or 5:00, when the sun came up, they would be over those fields and let them have it, then come on home. We didn't have in the aircraft any radar, any method of rendezvousing, other than just by sense or feel. It was black as a stack of cats and you couldn't have anything except a minimum of light to show."

Pirie allowed that there was a "terrific" danger of collision, but he said the risk was worth it. "In the *Lexington*, we had Freddie Bakutis, who was one of the great air group commanders. He was a fighter squadron commander. And in the *Hornet*, we had Emmet Riera. They would rendezvous sixteen of their boys and go in over these fields. How those guys did it I don't know. Riera and Bakutis were the first ones off the catapult every damned time. They never delegated that to anyone. We caught a lot of high-powered Japanese officials and bumped them off in transport airplanes, causing real havoc.

"They finally caught on to it, but we'd done a tremendous amount of damage."

As the final year of World War II neared, Navy pilots prepared for their role in the conquest of Luzon, the logical next step in the Pacific Theater. Seizure of Luzon not only would bring MacArthur back to Manila but also would completely block off the Japanese route to the Dutch East Indies, with their vital resources of oil and rubber.

McCampbell noted that Manila was a wasps' nest of antiaircraft. When the *Yorktown*'s VF-3 brought napalm-thickened gasoline fire-bombs to the city's harbor, it knew in advance that the opposition from the ground would be fierce. The pilots dived down from 12,000 feet to lay their incendiary eggs at rooftop level between the Pasig River and the walled city. "They were picked up by gunners from a [cruiser] and several [destroyers] and [armed cargo ships] as well as by dozens of gunners located on rooftops an in vacant lots," read the combat action report. "They were intensely and accurately fired upon from all sides throughout their run across the city and harbor with utter disregard for safety of personnel, buildings and ships. The only time when they were not under the most intense and accurate fire was during the time pilots could fly down behind and between buildings.

"One pilot was shot down in flames before reaching the target area, one had his belly tank fire bomb shot off and all returning pilots expressed utter amazement at the good fortune which let them through this extreme and determined opposition."

For all of that, the attack rendered minimal damage. "In view of the extreme hazard involved and the disappointing results [two out of seven electrical and two out of three manual releases functioned] it is recommended that further study be made of the belly tank release mechanism on the F6F-5 traveling at high speed. Fires did not appear extensive. . . . The extreme hazard of the deck level attack is considered unacceptable unless absolute surprise is achieved or AA is very weak."

The experiences over Manila with the latest form of napalm weapons underscored the major threat to naval aviators: antiaircraft. Far more airmen were shot down, killed, or wounded by ground- and ship-based defenses than by enemy fighters, particularly as the war entered its late stages. One weakness of the F6F-3 was that its underbelly was not armored, making that section of the fuselage highly vulnerable.

The long-awaited invasion of Luzon began on January 9, 1945, with support from Seventh Fleet escort carriers backed up by Task Force Thirty-eight's strikes on Formosa and the Ryukyu Islands, from which the garrison on Luzon might draw help. Kamikazes sank the flattop *Ommaney Bay* and hammered both *Manila Bay* and *Savo Island* in spite of the best efforts of shipboard gunners and the combat air patrol. Three more of the Jeep flattops writhed under the sting of the suicide bombers the following week.

The kamikazes and the responses to them demanded a shift in deployment—additional fighters assigned to combat air patrol. But with more of them performing that duty, fewer Hellcats could escort bombers, which might then be vulnerable to the remnants of the enemy air arm. Naval aviation, drained by the attrition through combat and operational losses as well as the need for air crews to be rotated and recharge themselves, required a heavy infusion of skilled flyers. Although replacements flowed to the flattops, they lacked expertise as well as experience.

Air Group Twenty-seven, on the *Savo Island*, complained about the quality of the replacement flyers. During the flattop's efforts on behalf of the Lingayen Gulf invasion of Luzon, the commander reported, "It is the opinion of this squadron that the work involved could easily have been handled by the fifteen TBM pilots aboard and that three additional green pilots was an unnecessary and undesirable assignment. These pilots, a lieutenant and two lieutenants (j.g.) were entirely unfit for combat operational flying through no fault of their own. They were operationally dormant from doing a minimum amount of flying in the pool [replacement unit] and were rusty both in their flying and their thinking. To make matters worse, these pilots qualified aboard a training carrier on August 12, 1944, and had had one period of field carrier landings between that time and coming to this squadron at the end of December 1944.

"Since they were permanently assigned to this squadron it was decided we might as well try to train them. The results were disastrous! All three committed major blunders resulting in the loss of three lives, and two aircraft. . . . It is felt that the blunders committed by these pilots was a contributing factor to the series of deck crashes which accumulated over a period of a few days in this operation [the support for the Lingayen Gulf invasion].

"Since this squadron has been in the combat theater, eighty-five percent of the accidents have been caused by so-called replacement pilots. If these pilots are to be fed into operating squadrons they must have better training by the pools. . . .

"Radio discipline is still very weak. Possibly this was due to the many new squadrons being on their first combat assignments. Unless a squadron takes pride in being heard the 'least' in the air, this condition will continue."

The criticism of too much chatter over the limited number of channels was one that had been voiced from the start of the war. Even with the opening up of additional wavelengths, the problem persisted.

As early as August 1944, well before the advent of the kamikazes, the Marine Corps, which had abandoned carrier training, now asked for its own flattops. At the time of the Guadalcanal campaign, the Marines were content to operate from land bases. But the war had now moved far beyond the range of their air groups on Guadalcanal, and the Corps found itself flying almost milk runs to isolated and unimportant targets. There was a desire to provide tactical support for their fellow leathernecks engaged in the amphibious assaults of far-off islands.

Navy brass such as Marc Mitscher and his former deputy Rear Admiral J. J. "Jocko" Clark voiced support for adding Marines to the carrier-based mix. Mitscher, who had finally taken leave of Task Force Thirty-eight and yielded command to McCain, lobbied in Washington for Marines on carriers. The idea won approval, and Marines started to practice carrier landings with their F4U Corsairs, a somewhat more difficult task than setting down a Hellcat. (The F4U was very slowly being phased in as a Navy fighter beginning in the spring of 1944.) The first squadrons would report to the fast carriers rather than their own flattops. The addition of trained Marine pilots meant that the need for extra fighter jockeys to combat the kamikazes could be met. The initial costs proved high. After the first Marines started to work off flattops in January 1945, seven pilots were killed when thirteen F4U Corsairs crashed on flight decks.

As more carriers entered the war, the newest air groups mixed virgins to combat with veterans. In April 1944, Willard Eder, who had started out as a novice under Jimmy Thach and Butch O'Hare, in his second tour had assumed command of Air Group Twenty-nine, and he was still aboard the *Cabot* when the New Year began.

Fighter pilot Thomas Harris, with VF-18 from July 1943 until March of the following year, resurfaced with VF-17, stationed on the *Hornet*. Air Group Ten, with its fighter component, the Grim Reapers, enlisted an entirely fresh batch of airmen. The Reapers now worked with F4U Corsairs. Whitey Feightner, an alumnus of the dismal days with VF-10 on Guadalcanal, now flew a Hellcat with the reconstituted VF-8. Another change was the creation of eighteen bomber-fighter squadrons, VBFs, to satisfy the shifting combat requirements.

Task Force Fifty-eight again sortied into waters close to the enemy's homeland. Strikes against the Indochinese coast as far south as Saigon devastated the foe's shipping as well as docks, oil storage depots, buildings, and of course the dwindling supply of aircraft, mostly on the ground. VF-7 took off from the *Hancock* for a coordinated strike with aircraft from the *Hornet* and *Lexington* with points of call that would become familiar names to Americans during the 1960s and 1970s. VF-7 reported making landfall at Camranh Bay and proceeding to an airfield at Nha Trang.

The F6F-5s bore rockets rather than bombs, which they used to burn three small tankers. At Camranh Bay, they spotted eight Jakes—seaplanes—lined up beside a ramp. A trio of runs devastated all of the Jakes. Antiaircraft gunners forced Lieutenant (j.g.) W. B. Bahr to eject from his flaming Hellcat. Bahr plopped down in the water. When a launch started out to capture him, Ensign W. R. Hearne, Bahr's wingman, strafed it, and the boat began to smoke and was beached. Other pilots discouraged a destroyer escort from approaching Bahr.

"The air was so full of transmissions of all types," said the action report, "mostly repetitive messages of no consequence that the flight could not get through to the base and inform it of Bahr's plight or even contact the succeeding strike. They left the area with two planes from the *Wasp* circling Camranh Bay and returned to base to obtain help.

"Immediately upon their return, the Task Group Commander was contacted and given the facts. Two Kingfishers were sent out under the escort of Lieutenant G. M. Sullivan and Ensign Hearne. . . . They left the OS2Us outside the Bay while the fighters proceeded to reconnoiter the terrain and investigate the rescue. Several low runs were made with the planes strafing to prevent enemy interference with their work. While Ens. Hearne was pulling up in the low clouds to make another run, Lt. Sullivan disappeared. In spite of repeated efforts on the part of Hearne to make contact with his flight leader, no trace of plane or occupant was ever found. A large fire, which might have been caused by a crashed plane, was observed near the seaplane base."

Nor were they able to effect a rescue of Bahr. The action report attributed the failure in large measure to the "blocking of the VHF and HF radio circuits." The incident is concrete evidence for the lament by Composite Squadron Twenty-seven.

Hong Kong proved a tartar, as half a dozen forays met ferocious antiaircraft reactions. In a two-day period in January 1945, the task force listed thirty planes lost in combat and another thirty-one in operational mishaps, again evidence of poorly prepared aviators or machines. Still, on January 20, the task force chalked up another 104 of the foe's airplanes destroyed on the ground.

Jean Balch, a native of Abilene, Texas, who enlisted on December 8, 1941, at age seventeen while a student at Hardin-Simmons College, was a radioman-gunner on an SB2C that attacked Hong Kong. His unit was VB-9, based on the *Yorktown*.

"For some reason or other, the fighters didn't make it and the torpedo bombers and the dive-bombers went in [without the customary preliminary strafing of the fighters]. We got hit right at the bottom of the dive, by what I assume was 20 millimeter antiaircraft fire. The last time I had looked at the altimeter it showed 600 feet. I was told that if she showed 600 feet, we probably had 350 feet." Balch tried to contact his pilot but got no answer and believes the man in the cockpit was killed.

"We were dead in the air. The engine was dead. There was no noise. It's deafening—the silence of a single-engine aircraft when the engine quits." He thrust himself up and out of the cockpit. "The next thing I knew I was looking at twenty-three feet of silk. I was real low and that turned out to be fortunate because the Japanese were shooting [at me] with pistols and rifles. They got thirteen bullet holes in the parachute canopy, and none in me."

Balch drifted over the water and then landed in a bombed-out building. While he was trying to conceal his parachute, a Chinese man entered the building. When Balch showed him a small American flag with Chinese writing on it and a tiny Chinese flag, the civilian helped him hide the chute. He also gave the downed airman clothes to cover his dungarees. Other people appeared, and a discussion among them followed. The benefactor attempted to secret Balch at another site, but a squad of Japanese soldiers soon seized the American.

Balch endured a series of beatings and interrogations over a period of weeks as he was moved first to Formosa, then to Okinawa, and finally to Tokyo from where he was bundled off to a POW camp near Yokohama. He lived on a starvation diet, perhaps 500 calories a day. "Things just got worse," recalled Balch. "Imel died; Hunt died; Flynn died. A bunch of guys died. It got to where you could tell who was likely to die. When you give up, you die. I never gave up.

"There were several guys, including Sage Johnson, who think I saved their lives. I would go by his cell and say, 'Are you still alive? I figured you had died last night.' I kept on ragging him and get him mad until he could get up. If he couldn't get up, I would pick him up." When finally liberated at the end of August 1945, Balch said, he had pneumonia, pellagra, scurvy, beriberi, hepatitis, and amoebic dysentery. He was hospitalized for months. More than a year after he left the service, he learned that the Japanese had murdered the Chinese man who had tried to help him. However, other Chinese who had betrayed him to the Japanese were facing a war crimes trial in Hong Kong.

Army B-29s had bombed the Japanese home islands using unoccupied China as a base beginning June 14, 1944, but the extreme distance and the advances by enemy land forces in China reduced the effort to symbolic rather than hurtful. With the capture of the Marianas, the superforts had started to raid from Saipan on November 28, 1944. Now, in February, Task Force Fifty-eight—with Mitscher again in charge, prepared to hurl its weight at Japan. It also was assigned to help the Marines evict the Japanese from Iwo Jima, an ideal site to station Army P-51 fighters assigned escort duty for Marianas-based B-29s headed to Japan and for distressed superforts during the Saipan-to-Tokyo runs and return flights.

For all of the ships, planes, and trained people produced, the resources of the Navy still could not fulfill the needs on all of the fronts. The Marines of the Iwo Jima amphibious force requested a full ten days of heavy bombardment of the volcanic island's defenses by ships and planes. Admiral Spruance allowed only three days, arguing that the sustained shelling and bombing from the sea and air during the previous ten weeks should be adequate. Furthermore, Spruance wanted to put the Navy over the Tokyo airspace through the fast carriers. He partially justified his decision by asserting that the attacks there would pin down any Japanese aircraft that might interfere with the Iwo invasion. Spruance originally promised the unhappy Marines that he would leave two of his battleships behind to continue the bombardment, but when Task Force Fifty-eight headed for the waters off Tokyo, all eight battleships sailed with it. While the heavyweights would undoubtedly contribute greatly to the antiaircraft protection of the carriers, the task force just as obviously was not likely to see a surface fight since the Japanese had no fleet left.

On February 16, from a distance of about 120 miles to the target, Mitscher's flyers manned several hundred planes bound for Tokyo and the airfields in the vicinity. The first wave of VF-9, from the *Lexington*, headed for the target area at 6:45 A.M. and less than an hour later encountered airborne opposition. The Japanese, who had husbanded their shrinking number of aircraft, made a desperate attempt to ward off the Navy planes. They were badly overmatched, however. VF-9's initial group counted fourteen fighters shot down, seven probables, and twenty-two damaged. In the air, working with VF-9, were fighters from the *Hancock*'s VF-80 and the *San Jacinto*'s VF-45. VF-80 said that it alone had wiped out eighty of the enemy. Some Navy pilots noticed that during these operations their machine guns occasionally froze, a phenomenon never observed before in the tropical climes of the Pacific Theater.

A division of four fighters from Air Group Four, led by Commander F. K. Upham and operating from the *Essex*, left the carrier at 7:30 A.M. with the expectation that Upham would coordinate a massive assault upon the Nakajima Tama aircraft factory just west of Tokyo. But bad weather delayed the arrival of the aircraft assigned to the task and Upham, short on fuel, left the scene. Over Japan, Lieutenant L. M. Boykin, of VT-4, now directed an attack that deployed fighters and torpedo bombers from his own unit, as well as Corsairs, Avengers, and Helldivers from Air Groups Eighty-four and Forty-six, from the *Bunker Hill* and *Cowpens*. In addition, Marine Corps Corsairs from VMF-124 and VMF-213 joined in the raid.

VF-4 flew high cover for the others and quickly dissuaded a handful of Tonys that sought to interrupt them. Another dozen enemy fighters prudently kept their distance. Rockets and 500-pound bombs exploded on the manufacturing plant.

Four hours after the first Hellcats from the *Lexington* hit the Tokyo area, a second dozen from that ship, again coordinated with VF-80 and VF-45, ranged over the Imba Lake region, site of the Imba airdrome. Zekes, Tonys, Tojos, and Oscars all sought to stop them. Seven of them were destroyed, a half-dozen damaged. But during the running battles, air group leader Commander Phil Torrey, who a year earlier had spearheaded the strike at Truk, disappeared, and the cockpit of another Hellcat, jumped by six Zekes, exploded from a direct hit.

Thomas Harris, now piloting an F6F-5 with VF-17 on the *Hornet*, strafed the Hamamatsu and Tateyama airfields. A Zeke intercepted him over Tokyo, with the result that Harris, in his logbook, drew in red ink another replica of a rising sun. It was the second such symbol in the notebook. He also noted that part of his starboard elevator had been shot away and Ensign Gene Fetzer had been killed.

The *Enterprise*, transformed into a night carrier, flew only combat air patrol over the fleet until the late afternoon, when Night Air Group Ninety scrambled a dozen Hellcats. The mission was a "zipper" patrol, designed to lock down enemy air bases from which bombers and torpedo planes might sortie in quest for the task force.

Initially, as twilight deepened, all remained quiet except for the roar of the twelve engines. But when they commenced their strafing runs, the enemy guns sprang to life. The flak was described as intense, accurate, and continuous. The Americans poured bullets into parked aircraft, although only one ignited. The Japanese had learned not to leave gassed or armed planes exposed. The after-dark marauders concluded their onslaught by shooting up freighters, radar stations, and trains. Later, the Big E also sent off a flight of Avengers equipped with radar. For hours they scanned the ground and sea below to make certain that no one was trying to approach the carriers under cover of darkness.

Task Force Fifty-eight delivered a second round of slings and arrows upon the Tokyo area on the morning of February 17. The weather soon worsened considerably. Spruance and Mitscher canceled plans for afternoon raids and charted a course for Iwo Jima. The futile but valiant effort to defend the homeland cost the Japanese hundreds of airplanes—the unconfirmed estimates ranged from 300 to 400— that got airborne and half again that number on the ground. Some sought out the task force only to be knocked down by accurate gunners on destroyer picket ships. However, the Navy losses from a total of 2,761 sorties, including the CAP for the task force, added up to sixty planes, a higher percentage than incurred during the raids on the Philippines. Too often American fighter pilots broke from their formations or assigned responsibilities to chase Japanese planes and fell into traps. Clark Reynolds, in *The Fast Carriers*, quoted Commander F. J. Brush, of the *Wasp's* Air Group Eighty-one, whose ranks had been depleted by five pilots: "The old lesson was learned the hard way again."

TWENTY-ONE

IWO AND OKINAWA

From its location off the shore of the Japanese island of Honshu, the entire Fifth Fleet with its fast carriers steamed south toward the volcanic island bastion of Iwo Jima. The Japanese outpost had been a target for heavy bombardment for eight months, with raids from flattops as well as sweeps by Army fighters and bombers, including B-29s. Between December 8, 1944, and February 15, 1945, B-24 Liberators from the Seventh Air Force struck daily with the intent of eliminating the Iwo airfields from the defenses. For all of their effort, the Japanese had managed to restore the runways and conduct several hit-and-run forays that had inflicted serious damage upon the Saipan-based bombers.

With the Fifth Fleet in attendance, the cacophony of shot and shell upon Iwo reached a crescendo during the three days before February 19, the date set for the first leathernecks to splash ashore. On the sixteenth, the cruiser *Pensacola* hovered offshore, pounding targets with the aid of an OS2U spotter plane piloted by Lieutenant (j.g.) Douglas Gandy and a Marine officer acting as the guide. A Zeke threatened to put out these eyes of the *Pensacola*. To his utter amazement, Gandy, in the slow, fragile seaplane, actually outmaneuvered his adversary and with his single .30-caliber forward gun hit the fighter in a vital area. Afire, it fell into the sea. But on the following day, the shore batteries gained some revenge as their shells rocked the *Pensacola* six times, killing seventeen men and wounding ninety-eight. More than enemy fighters, the U.S. spotter planes faced more danger from the raging storm of naval ordnance blanketing the small island as well as the heavy volume of AA from defenders in concealed, protected emplacements.

The bombardment of Iwo continued for the planned three-day period. Although at first enemy planes sortied from Japan itself with the ambition of attacking the amphibious force, the U.S. attack substituted the carrier forces to the north. No real aerial opposition harassed the landings, but the best the American flattops could offer was not up to the task. Buried deep in reinforced bunkers with a maze of connecting tunnels, the defenders were immune to the bombs, rockets, and bullets from aircraft. Napalm dropped from the air was not effective, and many of the incendiary jelly bombs simply did not explode. The conventional explosives dumped from fighters, TBMs, and SB2Cs lacked the ability to penetrate the hardened Japanese installations.

VT-82 launched from the *Bennington* waited forty-five minutes above the island for instructions on a target. Finally vectored toward a "suspected concentration of dual-purpose gun positions," the Avengers straddled the area with their 500-pounders. "Meager and inaccurate tracer fire was observed over the target," commented the action report, "but no planes were holed, and pilots agreed this was a relatively safe and unpleasant way to log that green ink Combat Time." But it was also obvious that the raiders had no sense of having accomplished anything of significance.

A second strike from Air Group Eighty-two knocked down most of what were described as concrete blockhouses. The combat action statement for this effort said, "There is little doubt that the bomb load laid into this small area sealed up quite a few rat holes and jarred a number of Japanese brains loose, but the difficulties of finding an attractive target, and absence of any spectacular results, left the crews rather unenthusiastic about the mission." Iwo, because of its impervious volcanic rock and the diligence of the commander in fortifying the site, would have to be subdued in an agonizingly bloody campaign by ground troops without benefit of much aid from the air.

Although the amphibious force supporting the ground troops slugging it out on Iwo Jima faced no enemy aircraft, things were different for the carriers assigned to deter any interference via air. On the night of February 21, the *Saratoga*, furnishing a combat air patrol thirty-five miles northwest of the island, dutifully sent out six fighters to investigate bogeys. The Hellcats from Sara soon triumphantly called in, "Splashed two Zekes." But at about 5:00 P.M. half a dozen would-be kamikazes plunged out of the low-hanging clouds. The carrier's antiaircraft guns actually knocked down a pair, both of which nevertheless skidded across the water and slammed into the *Saratoga*'s side. Their bombs penetrated the hull and exploded below deck. Two more kamikazes struck the carrier, and a pair of bombs also fell upon the sorely maimed ship during an ordeal that stretched over two hours.

Fire control crews doused the flames while other sailors shoved burning aircraft over the side. With her power plant still in full operation, the *Saratoga* remained afloat and able to limp to Eniwetok and then to the United States for repairs. Less fortunate, the Jeep carrier *Bismarck Sea* succumbed to a suicidal assault. It exploded, burned, and sank.

For a number of weeks after the invasion of Iwo, the carrier aircraft engaged in desultory activities. Task Force Fifty-eight anchored at Ulithi for replenishment and a breather before revisiting Japan itself. On this occasion, the primary targets were the airplanes on Kyushu, the southernmost island. The first arrivals, after a dawn takeoff, found few planes. The enemy, alerted to the imminence of raids, had literally flown the coop for safer precincts.

On the *Franklin*, nine Helldivers from VB-5 and eight Corsairs from VF-5 had departed a few minutes after 7:00 A.M. Gerald Bogan, temporarily an observer with Task Group 58.2, said, "A Jap [a Judy-type dive-bomber] flew out between holes in a cloud barrier at 2,200 feet and over the deck at about an altitude of 200 feet and dropped two 500-pound bombs. The flight deck was loaded with planes in the process of taking off, fully armed, and the force of the explosions threw them on their backs or off their landing gear so they could not be moved to salvage or jettison. In a very few minutes the forward part of the ship was an inferno."

Many of the Corsairs on deck were armed with "Tiny Tim" rockets that cooked off and screamed in all directions from the burning aircraft. Heroic efforts by firefighting parties preserved the *Franklin*, which would crawl first to Pearl Harbor and then to New York for repairs. However, 724 men were killed or missing, 265 wounded, and some 1,700 rescued after they abandoned ship because of the heat and flames. The blasts and fires wrecked fourteen TBDs, sixteen F4Us, and five SB2C dive-bombers.

The intense antiaircraft, directed at the lone conventional rather than kamikaze bomber before it hit, had scattered the VB-5 and VF-5 airplanes attempting to form up with colleagues from the *Hancock* and *San Jacinto*. Commander E. B. Parker pounced on the Judy and shot it down.

While the *Franklin* struggled for its life, the fighters and bombers continued the missions to sites around Kobe and Osaka, major cities on Kyushu. They encountered no opposition en route and reached their targets to find thick haze and smoke due to smoldering fires created by B-29 incendiary raids. While AA opened up, the Navy fly-ers aimed at a carrier lying anchored between a breakwater and the docks. According to the *Franklin*'s airmen, their predecessors from the *Hancock* had missed, but they scored several hits. Because the *Franklin*'s flight deck was shredded, its planes, on their return, dis-persed to other carriers in the task force.

Tommy Harris, in the cockpit of an F6F-5 for VF-17, on March 18 flew a mission to Kyushu bent on neutralizing the Chiran and Takayama airfields. He downed two Zekes while scrubbing the bases. A day later, over the Kure naval base on Honshu, he added two more rising suns, denoting another Zeke and a Tony, to his log-book. He reported thirty-five of the enemy knocked out of the sky on the eighteenth and, on March 19, twenty-five more. But three com-rades were also lost, although one was later found alive in a prison camp.

On March 21, VF-17's Jim Pearce, the former Kingfisher scout plane pilot, led two divisions vectored toward "a large group of enemy aircraft steering straight for the fleet." Pearce and his flight intercepted eighteen Betty bombers with fighter cover. "I sent the other division—Hal [Lieutenant Henry B.] Mitchell was [that divi-sion's] leader—out wide, and we intercepted the bombers after mak-ing a crossing 180 degrees over them so we were heading the same direction as the bombers with a division on each side of them.

"When we were all in proper position for excellent intercepts, I gave the order to 'go get 'em.' We proceeded on to the attack one af-ter another from both sides of the bomber formation. In no time we had burning Bettys all over the sky. Some of them were carrying small airplanes under their open bomb bays. Their wings went from nacelle to nacelle of the Bettys. These, we were later informed, were manned rocket-powered bombs called Bakas. We destroyed all of the bombers (proven by postwar data), and Hal lost one plane and pilot to a defending fighter." In his pilot's log, Harris noted, "Turkey shoot for Jim Pearce."

Said Pearce many years later, "When I was lucky enough to be victorious in an air battle, I really didn't think a lot about what it meant for the other guy. War was war; we won and lost, they won and lost. I was always very careful to stay away and keep my division members away from an enemy in a parachute. That seemed a little more personal. I vividly remember one Betty bomber we shot down just over the water. The pilot was running full power and turning left and right to try to avoid our attacks. Soon the side hatch was opened and things, including machine guns, came flying out into the sea, shortly followed by a man, who bounced about thirty feet high as he hit the water. I felt a bit bad for him, but a few seconds later the plane banked sharply, dipping its right wing into the water, and exploded into pieces."

With Iwo Jima secured, the start of Operation Iceberg, the conquest of Okinawa, the next objective, loomed. Considered a part of Japan and only 350 miles from Kyushu, the southernmost of the Japanese homelands, Okinawa, as the largest island in the Ryukyu chain, offered excellent harbors and airfields from which to stage the invasion of Japan itself. Because of Okinawa's strategic value, the Japanese had invested heavily in its defenses in terms of both fortifications and well-armed troops. The location meant that the American fleet would be within easy flying distance of kamikazes stationed in Japan and Formosa.

Love Day, the first landing of Operation Iceberg, was scheduled for April 1, April Fools' Day, which also happened to be Easter Sunday. During the prior week, pilots such as Tommy Harris flew combat air patrol daily as the massive fleet of 1,457 ships crowded around the Ryukyus and bombarded all visible installations and possible beach defenses. Task Force Fifty-seven, composed of British flattops, scourged the Sakishima Islands, south of Okinawa, which might serve Japanese aircraft flowing from Kyushu and Formosa.

Henry Miller now commanded a reconstituted Air Group Six based on the *Hancock*. "It may have been the biggest air group in the Navy. I had 186 officers, 162 pilots and 103 airplanes. With my first air group on the *Princeton*, I had one extra pilot for my planes. But this second time out I had pilots coming out of my ears. I had all the airplanes I wanted. The war machine was really grinding 100 percent and turning out everything we wanted.

"We supported the landing on Easter Sunday. It was a beautiful morning when we took off. I looked back and I watched a pilot who didn't make it with those belly tanks of napalm. They hit the water and blew up. There was fire all over. The guys just burned up." However, VF-23 from the *Langley* boasted of effective use of the weapon on a gun position near the Yontan airfield, reporting an inferno erupting after they dropped napalm.

Miller said, "We went in with the air group. I was one of the air support coordinators, and I watched the landing on West Beach. I looked out at all the boats coming in. We had shot up the planes on the field [there was no aerial opposition] and everything else. I said, 'This is a hell of a way to spend Easter, to watch everybody shooting everybody else.' It looked easy."

Indeed, the only casualty among the ground forces during the landings was a Marine who broke a foot stumbling on the beach. The Japanese had recognized the folly of trying to stop the invaders at the shore. But while Love Day was almost a day at the beach, subsequent operations became more of a visit to hell because of defenses in depth, pillboxes, cave fortifications, deeply excavated systems of tunnels, and weapons emplacements. The ferocity of the Japanese resistance on Okinawa would match that shown on Iwo Jima.

During the first few days of Operation Iceberg, a lull, partially attributable to weather conditions, delayed the kamikazes. Having now gained considerable if painful experience with the suicide corps, the Navy had developed a strategy to thwart the threat. Tom Hamilton, flag secretary to Rear Admiral Ingolf Kiland, commander of Task Group 51.1 of the Western Islands Attack Force, described the arrangement as "nested layers." Hamilton explained, "The first and most effective layer was the Combat Air Patrol, projected over the carriers assigned for that purpose. Navy fighters [and Marine airmen as well] would intercept kamikazes as far from their targets as possible. The CAP were guided by the picket screen. These were destroyer-type ships stationed at strategic points around the area perimeter [from 15 to 100 miles from Okinawa] whose radar would locate incoming attackers and whose air controllers [fighter-director teams] would vector CAP fighters to their targets." After ground troops secured airfields on Okinawa, land-based interceptors and night fighters became part of the combat air patrol mix.

Hamilton said, "Kamikazes which broke through to the ships were engaged at medium range by the next layer, five-inch guns on destroyers and larger screen vessels. [The first warships put on the picket line were smaller, lacking sufficient firepower to fight off kamikazes.] By 1945, five-inch anti-aircraft shells were equipped with proximity fuzes which greatly increased their effectiveness. At short range, attackers were engaged by the innermost layer, 40 mm and 20 mm anti-aircraft guns, usually in multiple mount gun tubs. These rapidly firing weapons could put up a withering curtain of fire. Each of these layers was effective, and together they defeated a lot of kamikazes." But not all of them.

At Okinawa, Picket Station Number 1 was closest to Japan and the stations were numbered in order as they neared the Ryukyus. According to Hamilton, "The average life of a destroyer on Picket Station # 1 turned out to be about six hours before getting hit; some of them would sink and others would come limping back. I remember one that had stayed up there and we ordered him back. He sent us a signal that said, 'I have been on Picket Station # 1 for eight hours and am returning. This is better than par for the course.' And he was right."

In the Japanese military lexicon, the word *tennozan* applied to any critical campaign. For the Okinawa *tennozan*, they mobilized a massive onslaught under the code name Operation Ten-Go. On the afternoon of April 6, in the argot of the kamikaze legions, the *kikusui*—"floating chrysanthemums"—in a series of ten flights deploying 355 kamikaze aircraft and an equal number of conventional bombers, bore down on the Americans. That battle was the first of many that started on April 6 and lasted into the morning of the following day.

VF-82, operating off the *Bennington*, put up eleven Hellcats at 3:15 P.M. for the final combat air patrol for the day. As the fighters flew over Okinawa, they heard over their radios the sounds of an aerial battle to "north of Ie Shima," a smaller island off the west coast of Okinawa. The action was in the vicinity of the more advanced picket stations.

Lieutenant R. E. Britson led the group toward the area. The squadron action report noted, "Arriving on the scene at about 1630, the flight participated in what every pilot dreams about. For the next hour and fifty minutes, Jap planes by the score coming in just right for nice runs on them. In that time, 11 VF-82 pilots accounted for 25 Jap planes definitely destroyed with several more probables. Every pilot shot down at least one enemy plane. Exact number of Japs sighted is impossible to determine, but best estimate is 35–40. Most of them came in low (1,000 feet or less) from the north and were heading directly toward our force supporting the invasion of Okinawa. . . . Of all the enemy planes encountered, *not one returned fire* [report's italics]; all remained on course, boring in toward the surface vessels. The only evasive action offered was jinking, and the majority of the a/c were obsolete models as can be seen by the list destroyed.

"Primary danger to our pilots was collision or getting in the path of a friendly plane's fire. Three Japs were seen to blow up when hit; 14 burned and crashed in the water, and 8 dove in the water before breaking into flame. A sample of the action was told by Lieutenant [H. A.] Gregory, who kept a tally of planes he observed crashing on his plotting board. There were 28 marks on it when he returned to base. Of these 28, Gregory estimates he had 20 in his sights during the action and actually fired on 12 or 15 but found it necessary to break off to avoid hitting our planes which were near." The statement concluded, "Special comment on the excellent direction of the following Fighter Director ships was expressed by all pilots: *USS Colhoun USS Bush USS Panamint.*"

The compliment was an unknowing but ironic tribute. While the aviators clashed in the skies above them, the destroyers *Bush* and *Colhoun* waged a desperate struggle to fend off the deadly kamikazes. Their antiaircraft splashed some, but even in their death throes, flaming kamikazes careened into the picket ships, gouging large holes in hulls, wrecking machinery, and severing pipes that spit out superheated steam. The burning fuel ignited infernos, and the crews abandoned their doomed destroyers.

The *Belleau Wood* scrambled fourteen F6F-5s from VF-30 just before 3:00 P.M. After they had been in the air for about half an hour, enemy planes began to appear. "Not as large groups," said the action report, "but in small groups of about four planes each. As one pilot put it, 'It was like an Easter egg hunt—look under any cloud and there would be a Jap plane or two.' Vals, Tojos, Zekes and Oscars were seen."

The drill for kamikaze pilots was to focus on their targets and not to engage the interceptors. The VF-30 postmortem said, "Pilots report that the fighter planes encountered did not return fire and appeared very inexperienced. [The suicide corps had begun to fill its ranks with men who knew only the rudiments of flying.] When two were caught together they split instead of trying to protect each other. They used no evasive maneuvers except speed in an attempt to dodge into clouds. No slow rolls or other maneuvers were generally resorted to." As others who engaged the kamikazes also noted, the VF-30 airmen reported that none of the enemy bombers carried the customary rear gunners.

"Any attempt to describe the individual exploits of pilots, or to detail the maneuvers leading to the destruction of individual planes, would draw this report out to interminable lengths. . . . Probably the most spectacular 'Kill' occurred when Ensign Ward followed a Zeke into a loop and, firing bursts at every opportunity, finally exploding the Zeke at the very top of the loop." Altogether, with a second flight launched early on the morning of April 7, VF-30 claimed forty-seven of the foe destroyed. Ensigns E. F. Dawes and Carl Foster each received credit for six aircraft shot down. The squadron counted about seventy enemy aircraft sighted during the running two-hour battle. Some of the others were knocked down by units from other carriers or land-based Marines.

The estimated carnage among Japanese aviators that afternoon and night totaled nearly three hundred who were stopped either at the picket line, by AA fire, or by the American fighters, including Tom Harris, with VF-17, who inked another rising sun in his logbook. But two dozen kamikazes survived long enough to fling themselves at ships, and all but two succeeded. In addition to the *Bush* and *Colhoun*, a third destroyer, *Emmons*, was also fatally wounded. Two ammunition ships were blown up, an LST was sunk, and several other vessels were damaged so badly they barely remained afloat.

In the late afternoon of April 6, two U.S. submarines, the *Hackleback* and *Threadin*, lurking around the Bungo Strait exit from the Inland Sea, spotted ten warships, including a very large one. In the dim light through the periscope, a sub skipper guessed that the biggest enemy vessel was an aircraft carrier. In fact, it was the last remaining pride of the Imperial Navy, the mighty battlewagon *Yamato*, under full steam. Escorted by a light cruiser and eight destroyers in the East China Sea, the *Yamato* could only be bound for the American anchorage off Okinawa. The Japanese task force was under the command of Vice Admiral Seiichi Ito, with Rear Admiral Kosaku Ariga in command of the *Yamato*.

Under orders to report but not attack, the submarines advised the Pacific Fifth Fleet headquarters of their sightings. Alerted by a radio message, Rear Admiral Morton Deyo, commander of the American gunfire and bombardment forces off Okinawa, prepared to execute a battle plan that would dispatch six battleships, seven cruisers, and twenty-one destroyers to intercept the *Yamato* and its cohorts. Deyo's superior, Vice Admiral Richmond K. Turner, advised, "Hope you will bring back a nice fish for breakfast." But even as

Deyo scribbled his reply, "Many thanks, will try to," the radio crackled news that Task Force Fifty-eight, Vice Admiral Marc Mitscher's
fast carrier group, had picked up the scent and was already launching an airborne attack. Deyo then added the comment, "If the peli-
cans haven't caught them all."

Displacing 68,000 tons and with nine huge 18.1-inch guns that
measured 70 feet in length, the oversize *Yamato* dwarfed any vessel
in the U.S. Navy. Built in secrecy to evade treaties restricting the size
of the Japanese fleet, the *Yamato*, along with its sister heavyweight,
the *Musashi*, which had been sunk by American carrier planes in the
Sibuyan Sea, boasted armor plate more than 25 inches thick.

Since the defeats in the Philippine waters, *Yamato* had stuck
close to its home base at Tokuyama. But now, with the enemy
ashore on Okinawa, at the doorstep to the home islands, the high
command ordered *Yamato* on what even the most optimistic considered to be a suicidal mission. Strategists hoped that the battleship's vast firepower would distract the Americans enough to allow
a massive kamikaze strike to penetrate the U.S. defenses and destroy the fleet off Okinawa.

One preposterous scenario proposed that if the *Yamato* could
stagger through the enemy gauntlet and the ship could empty its arsenal of 3,200-pound shells at the American troops, it might then
beach itself. The nearly three thousand crewmen would then surge
ashore to act as ground soldiers. Some reports claim that the *Yamato* had enough fuel only for a one-way voyage, but author George
Feifer reported in *Tennozan* that the vessel held enough for a return,
unlikely as the possibility was.

With the discovery that it had left its sanctuary, the race to sink
the *Yamato* was on. The contest pitted the seagoing U.S. warships
against the American dive-bombers and torpedo planes from its flattops. But Admiral Deyo's men-of-war would never have a shot at the
target. A prowler from the carrier *Essex* caught sight of the Japanese
warships. Then, early on April 7, a pair of Marine twin-engine flying
boats, hovering just out of range of the enemy antiaircraft guns,
tracked the prey for five hours.

When the distance from Task Force Fifty-eight narrowed to 250
miles, Marc Mitscher launched his planes, some 280 dive- and torpedo bombers making up the initial waves. The sky was congested
with aircraft. Ensign D. H. Crow advised VF-10's leader, Lieutenant
Commander Walter E. Clarke, that he thought he saw a Japanese
fighter. When Clarke advised Crow to pursue the bogey, the ensign

sought to turn under Clarke's section. He cut it too fine, and the prop on Clarke's Corsair tore off Crow's tail. The F4U spun into the sea; Crow, who had survived an earlier ditching, was gone. Clarke settled into the water near an American destroyer and was rescued.

The initial flight from VB-82, on the *Bennington*, amounted to nine dive-bombers under Lieutenant Commander Hugh Wood. Through a gumbo soup of clouds, they, among the other would-be ship killers, hunted for the small fleet. Wood's radar suddenly made contact with the Japanese forces, saving essential minutes that would otherwise have been consumed by a search. The warships were some 25 miles from their previously estimated position.

Pittsburgh native Ensign Harry Jones, in an Avenger from Torpedo Squadron Seventeen aboard the *Hornet*, recalled, "Scuttlebutt on the ship had it that the battleship admirals who outranked the air admirals wanted to shoot it out with the Japanese. But the *Yamato*'s guns were bigger than anything we had, and the air admirals won out. We would intercept them.

"We took off from the *Hornet*, seven torpedo bombers plus fighters and dive-bombers. The torpedo planes, which had search radar, did the navigation, and it was a poor day for flying, rainy, misty, a lot of scud, not much ceiling. The flight leader from another carrier developed engine trouble and turned the lead over to our air group, bossed by Commander E. G. Konrad, a Naval Academy graduate.

"The lead pilot said they ought to be in range, but we couldn't see anything on radar. Konrad said, 'Stay on course.' One plane radioed he saw a blip off to starboard about fifty miles out, and we turned right. Then we saw them. Holy mackerel! The *Yamato* looked like the Empire State Building plowing through the water. It was really big. We orbited around out of their gun range. They opened up with main batteries, eighteen-inch guns. What was surprising to us was that there were no Japanese aircraft around even though we were very near their home island."

Another Navy flyer, Lieutenant Alan Turnbull, recalled, "We couldn't see the entire Jap force at one time, because the clouds hung between 3,000 and 5,000 feet."

In a fatal decision for the *Yamato* and its companions, the Imperial Navy had reserved almost all available aircraft for kamikaze missions. Less than half a dozen Japanese fighters appeared on the scene, and they were quickly overwhelmed. In its own defense, the *Yamato* possessed awesome weapons. Extra guns had been added to an already prodigious array of antiaircraft firepower: six 6-inch secondary batteries, twenty-four 5-inch antiaircraft, and 150 machine guns, along with all that the escorts could throw up. A special new shell equipped with a time fuse exploded into six thousand deadly pieces. To ward off low-flying torpedo planes, the battleship's big guns blasted giant waterspouts. But none of these defenses could deal with so many punches thrown by so many aircraft manned by skilled airmen.

At 12:32, the *Yamato* opened up on the approaching aircraft. According to Avenger pilot Harry Jones, "The air boss gave us the order of attack. He said, 'Shasta,' meaning those from the *Hornet* go in first. Then he read off the order in which the planes from other carriers would attack." Over their radios, the VB-82 crews heard the strike leader direct "Sugar Baker Charlies [SB2C dive-bombers], take the big target." Similar instructions governed the torpedo planes.

Jones commented, "We didn't have too much ceiling. I was at twelve thousand feet at most and usually like to start at eighteen thousand feet for a torpedo run, a steep approach, and then right over the water, drop the torpedo, and then get the hell out there. Meanwhile, the bombers are supposed to be going down, so we all hit the ship simultaneously."

The guns of the warships began to speak, but the rounds fell short. When the squadron's SB2C-4s emerged from the clouds, six of them saw that they were no longer in a position to effectively drop on the *Yamato*. They then switched their attention to the cruisers or destroyers.

Wood plus Lieutenants (j.g.) F. Ferry and K. A. Sieber, however, remained lined up on the battleship. Sieber, who followed Wood, saw an extensive explosion amidships. After his pullout, Wood reported two other hits, one forward of the bridge and the other aft of the mainmast. Ferry confirmed these observations. Gunner H. H. Reed, in Wood's rear seat, said he watched three of the 1,000-pounders blast the *Yamato*. VF-82 had committed six F6F-5s to the assault, and with the exception of a photo plane, they toted 1,000-pound bombs. Their instructions before they left the *Bennington* specified the destroyers as their targets. The pilots who focused on the cruisers and destroyers believed they also scored with their ordnance.

Confusion continues about who actually scored the initial hits. Some accounts report that bomb-laden Hellcats from the *Hornet* struck first, targeting the destroyers and the light cruiser *Yahagi* that formed a diamond shape surrounding the battleship. The fighter-bombers claimed two hits, and Lieutenant Commander M. U. Beebe, the squadron honcho, whose plane bore no bomb, zoomed in for a strafing run at the *Yahagi*. Hellcats from other ships also pounded the escorts. Their mission was to suppress and draw off fire, enabling the other attackers to zero in on the main target, *Yamato*.

In the assault upon the cruiser *Yahagi* and the destroyers, a swarm of Avengers, armed with torpedoes set to only a twelve-foot depth, zeroed in on the smaller ships. Within a few minutes, the *Yahagi* lay dead in the water. Seven torpedoes and twelve bombs eventually devastated the cruiser. It foundered with only a handful of survivors left to tread water while hoping for succor.

Hornet Avenger pilot Lieutenant Robert L. Mini, separated from others in his flight because of cloud cover, glimpsed a destroyer. He dropped his tin fish while dodging flak bursts. "Bingo!" an exultant gunner shouted over the intercom. Aviation Machinist's Mate Third Class William A. Baker saw the Mark 13 slam into the tin can with a fiery explosion.

Mini is credited with having shattered the destroyer *Hamkaze*. It sagged amidships, broke in two, and finally flashed its crimson underbody as it disappeared beneath the water. Three more of *Yamato*'s accompanying warships, battered beyond repair, were abandoned and scuttled. The surviving quartet of destroyers, all nursing serious wounds, would hang about long enough to pluck out some of those who were in the sea and flee to safety.

It was not, however, a day at the seaside for the American Navy. Lieutenant Norman A. Weise, from the *Hornet*'s VT-17, concentrating upon his destroyer quarry, accidentally passed within range of the *Yamato*'s antiaircraft batteries. Shrapnel from 25-mm shells burst in the vicinity of his Avenger just as he released his torpedo. Jagged shards of metal ripped through his windscreen and into the cockpit. One splinter dug into his scalp while gasoline from a ruptured fuel gauge sprayed his face, temporarily blinding him. Fragments from another shell wrecked the radio compartment, wounding his gunner. His rudder and vertical stabilizer absorbed two more hits. Weise managed to guide his crippled plane back to a safe landing on a carrier.

Nine minutes after the opening salvo from the *Yamato*'s defenses, dive-bombers plunged down on the battleship at 400 knots per hour. A pair of 1,000-pound bombs exploded near the mainmast, obliterating a radar room and a fire control station. Avenger pilot Harry Jones recalled, "We spread out, and I kept diving toward different puffs of smoke, where shells had already exploded. There shouldn't be any damage there. There were two fighter planes in front of each of the torpedo planes. They were supposed to strafe the destroyers and probably draw some of the fire. I saw one of our replacement pilots in a plane take a direct hit and explode in the air. Down he went. I went down, dropped my torpedo, and went right across the bow of *Yamato*. The ship was turning, but in our attack we always dropped in a fan shape, so no matter which way a ship is turning, it is going to get hit. Our group was credited with two torpedo hits from the seven planes, but the gun camera that showed my angle on the bow didn't credit me with a hit." From Jones's VT-17, Lieutenant Thomas C. Durkin, the executive officer, registered the initial torpedo hit on the target.

When the first tin fish exploded against the battleship's hull, however, it did little damage. The squadron's Mark 13 missiles had been set to explode ten feet below the surface, striking the *Yamato* where its armor was thickest. One of the reasons Mini and those in his squadron settled on the more lightly shielded cruiser and the destroyers had been the knowledge of their vulnerability to even shallower depth torpedoes. Aware of the problem, VT-84, from the *Bunker Hill*, reset its weapons to dive deeper into the water, bringing them home below the protective iron plates.

Lieutenant Commander Chandler W. Swanson led VT-84, from the *Bunker Hill*, and instructed his people at the pretakeoff briefing, "This squadron will attack the battleship and only in case of necessity will any pilot drop on any other target." When they came within range of the *Yamato*, Swanson broke his fourteen Avengers into two flights for an anvil-like approach. As they closed to drop their torpedoes, the Americans separated into groups of two and three, making a five-pronged assault.

Swanson reported, "As soon as we started diving from the overcast, they threw everything at us, including a barrage from the *Yamato*'s 16-inch [*sic*] guns. Puffs of purple, red, yellow and green flak blanketed the sky. It would have been beautiful if you didn't know it was so deadly. Our planes were crisscrossing over the target from all directions. That was the most dangerous part of it. We had to keep from running into our own planes. There were so many of them and so little room to maneuver. It was surprising we had no collisions."

For Lieutenant (j.g.) Jack Speidel, from VT-29, assigned to the "baby" flattop *Cabot*, this was his second crack at the *Yamato*, since he had been among the aviators whose swipes at the ship during the battle of Leyte Gulf had failed to inflict serious damage. Now, in the

East China Sea, he arrived on the scene after the first blows at the dreadnought and its escorts. "When we took off for the *Yamato* on April 7, we had one drop tank that gave us an extra hour of flying time. There was an overcast and one group never did find the *Yamato*. Everybody had to go through a single hole in that overcast, and there was so many planes it was incredible.

"I remember colored bursts in front of us and splashes in the water from enemy ships. We came in on the port side, not real low. Others had probably already hit the ship. After we dropped the torpedo and turned away, my radioman was watching and he screamed, 'We hit it! We hit it!' " The history of the *Cabot* claimed that Speidel's tin fish struck "directly under the bridge, causing a terrific explosion."

A pilot from the *Belleau Wood*, Lieutenant (j.g.) W. E. Delaney, made his attack at 1,400 feet, dropping four 500-pounders. As his plane passed over the battleship, he said, "There was a loud explosion under the fuselage. The cockpit filled with smoke and fumes. One wing was on fire. I was afraid the plane would explode and ordered my crew [a gunner and radioman] to jump. They bailed out five miles southwest of the Jap task force. I watched their parachutes open, then I jumped." Unfortunately, although Delaney saw their chutes deploy, both crewmen apparently drowned.

Delaney, after hitting the sea in the midst of the enemy vessels, managed to inflate his rubber raft. However, he stayed in the water, hanging on to the raft and hiding from the Japanese. A destroyer came within 100 yards but veered off, apparently thinking there was no American survivor. "At first I was so cold," said Delaney, "when the Jap can approached, I thought of giving up. But I decided they might shoot me. So I stayed behind the raft."

The pilots from the two Marine flying boats, Lieutenant James R. Young and Lieutenant (j.g.) Richard L. Simms, still on station, saw him floating amid Japanese sailors who had abandoned their sinking ships and clung to bits of wreckage. While Simms acted as a decoy to draw off any fire from the remaining enemy vessels, Young set down his patrol plane, took Delaney aboard, and flew him to safety on Okinawa.

According to Harry Jones, observation or scouting planes, ordinarily launched by catapult from the decks of battleships or cruisers, had been ordered to tag along to perform rescues like that which saved Delaney. "I remember a pilot from one of these came on the radio and said he was getting low on gas and was going to turn around. I heard what must have been a fighter pilot say, 'If you turn around, you son of a bitch, I'm going to shoot you down.' "

From the *Intrepid*, Air Group Ten, under the command of John J. Hyland, the prewar Annapolis graduate, an aviator since 1935, and a veteran of the grim retreat from the Dutch East Indies in early 1942, arrived on the scene. An Avenger from the group connected with a torpedo, and the Grim Reapers' Corsairs believed they planted eight 1,000-pounders on or near the battleship.

One plane, hit by fire from the battleship, suddenly nosed down and then blew up when it smashed into the ocean. Undaunted, the others, jinking now and then to throw off enemy gunners, a mere 500 feet above the water, homed in. The final thrusts came from a swarm of TBMs belonging to VT-9, on the *Yorktown*. When the squadron first observed the *Yamato*, in spite of all the earlier blows, burning amidships and trailing oil, she sped through the water at an estimated 20 knots. But the blows from the *Intrepid* appeared to have inflicted critical wounds. The battleship's list had hiked her starboard side high out of the water, leaving the thinner lower hull exposed.

Lieutenant Thomas Stetson, in charge of the VT-9 assailants, split his team, directing some to go after a cruiser and destroyer while he and five others would finish off the faltering *Yamato*. Stetson instructed his flight to adjust their torpedoes. The Avenger tunnel men reset the tin fish, doubling their original ten-foot depth when they slipped into the water. They would now explode below the thick armor plate.

From a distance of less than a mile, torpedoes flopped smoothly into the sea and then darted swiftly toward the ship. The vessel swerved in a vain effort to avoid the onrushing Mark 13s. But at 1:37, an hour or so after the action began, at least three if not four torpedoes from the attack led by Stetson ripped into the *Yamato*. Moments later another pair hammered the faltering battlewagon. One observer commented, "It looked like Old Faithful geyser erupting when the torpedoes hit the *Yamato*."

Seawater rushed into the gaping holes, and the ship began to list badly. Rear Admiral Kosaku Ariga was forced to order flooding of the starboard-side engine and boiler rooms. A warning to sailors in those areas arrived too late, and several hundred men drowned at their posts. While the maneuver temporarily prevented the ship from capsizing, its pace slowed drastically with only a single screw still churning.

The *Yamato*, considered a luxury ship by Japanese sailors ordinarily confined to fetid, spartan quarters, could only be described now as hell on water. Amid the continuing explosions of torpedoes and bombs, American planes methodically hosed the stricken ship with machine guns. Steam from ruptured pipes scalded some sailors; fire incinerated others; corpses and body parts littered the blood-soaked decks.

It was apparent to those in command that the *Yamato* was doomed. Amid the wreckage and bodies strewn about the bridge, Seiichi Ito, as task force commander, signaled the other ships to abort the mission. Those still afloat would try to pick up some of the men floundering in the water and then head for port. He saluted, shook hands with some other officers, then locked himself in his cabin. He would go down with the ship.

The *Yamato*'s skipper, Kosaku Ariga, rather than permit the ship's hallowed portraits of the emperor and empress to suffer the indignities of capture, arranged for an officer to secure himself in a room with the artwork. Having take care of that final piece of business, Ariga ordered a seaman to bind him to a binnacle on the bridge. There he chewed on biscuits, awaiting his inevitable fate.

In the bowels of the battleship, fire cooked off ammunition magazines, inducing shattering convulsions of the infrastructure. The subterranean blasts erupted up through the steel decks into a six-thousand-foot tongue of fire stretching into the sky. A four-mile pillar of smoke trailed the *Yamato*. At 2:23 in the afternoon it rolled over and sank, dragging some 2,500 sailors down with it. Only 269 survived.

The hopeless excursion by the Japanese task force ended with as many as 3,750 of its crews dead. Mitscher counted ten aircraft and twelve airmen lost. The last remnants of the once-powerful Japanese navy had been vanquished. The results left no doubt that the carrier had triumphed over the battleship.

For Henry Miller and his shipmates, the triumph was muted. "When we got back I'd been in the air for four hours and a half. As I circled the carrier coming in for a landing, I thought, 'The air officer promised me he'd clean the flight deck, get all that grease off it. Boy it looks funny.' Then as I looked further, here was a great big bomb hole in the deck. The carrier *[Hancock]* had been hit by a kamikaze. They said come aboard. We landed, taxied right around the bomb hole, surveyed the damage, asked how many people had been killed." Seventy-two were dead, another eighty injured.

TWENTY-TWO

THE ENDGAME

The fatal voyage of the *Yamato* and its consorts did not seem to dampen the kamikazes' ardor. They flooded over the American fleet around Okinawa, exacting a frightening toll of sailors and ships, albeit at the ultimate cost to themselves. Their lemminglike plunges continued even though the carrier airplanes, aided by night fighters on Okinawa and the dense curtains of antiaircraft, knocked them down at a staggering rate.

The Japanese had paused after the death of their superbattleship, but on April 12 and 13 floating chrysanthemums descended en masse upon American warships. The impact upon the picket destroyers was devastating, and some of the suiciders penetrated the screen to hit the bigger ships. There were too many for the combat air patrols to handle.

As awful as the carnage wrought by the kamikazes was, they presented easy targets to fighters. John Hyland, the head of Air Group Ten, remembered, "One of our younger pilots, who was an undisciplined youngster and generally speaking a problem in the air because he ws relatively inept, by himself ran into a group of seven kamikazes. They were just droning along and he got in behind them and shot down six Nates and a Val. He shot down the last two when he had only one gun left. The seven pilots never made any evasive effort. They simply stayed in straight and level flight. Apparently, their attitude was that if they didn't get to where they could see something to dive into, they'd just keep going. If they were knocked down, that was okay.

"It always burned me up that this very poor pilot got seven airplanes in one flight. It burned everybody else up too—that they weren't likely to run into such a situation."

Lieutenant Commander Walter Clarke, the head of Fighting Squadron Ten, expressed some exasperation with the rookies assigned to his air group: "Frequently, the inexperienced pilots with this squadron expended a great deal of ammunition on even the vulnerable Val without knocking it down on stern shots. The squadron doctrine has been to always try for a minimum of fifteen degree deflection shot in order to hit the most vulnerable spots, especially on the newer protected planes, but this doctrine has too often been forgotten by over-zealous pilots. This waste of ammunition has also been reflected in the number of guns that have jammed, possibly due to overheating.

"The older type Bettys burn rather easily and the wings are prone to break off outboard of the engines when hit, but the newer type are very difficult to shoot down with a stern shot, and, in addition, the pilot attempting such a shot places himself in a dangerously exposed position to the enemy rear gunner. Because of the lack of enemy fighter opposition encountered, pilots have become careless . . . resulting on one occasion in a plane of this squadron being shot down by a Judy."

At the same time Clarke remarked on the inferior performance of the foe: "Japanese pilots encountered have generally appeared to be inexperienced. Poor evasive tactics and poor use of cloud coverage has been usual. . . . Very few aggressive attacks have been made by the Japs, even by the fighter cover when their bombers are under attack. The usual preponderance of friendly fighters in the air, coupled with this lack of aggressiveness on the part of Jap pilots, has tended to make our pilots throw caution to the winds insofar as sticking together and making follow through runs against enemy planes is concerned. This must be guarded against because the Jap still has good pilots somewhere and someday will cause this indiscretion to be costly. While most Jap pilots seem intent only on diving on surface vessels, all are not strictly kamikaze. On several occasions pilots have bailed out and on other occasions have been observed trying to jump out before the plane crashed."

A. B. "Chick" Smith, with VBF-12 on the *Randolph*, reached the waters off Okinawa a bit later than the others in Task Force Fifty-eight. In mid-March, the carrier was at Ulithi, explained Smith. "I was in my stateroom, having just returned from Mog Mog Island [part of the Ulithi atoll], the recreational center, feeling no pain due to many enjoyable drinks. VBF-12's skipper, [Lieutenant Commander J. C. Lawrence,] and I were talking about the coming operation— I was the squadron executive officer. We felt the ship shudder. From officers' country, hangar deck level, we ran to the hangar deck, where we saw flames aft." A lone kamikaze had sifted through the defenses to smash into the *Randolph*.

Repairs had delayed the flattop's journey to Okinawa, but once it arrived, Smith immersed himself in what he described as "my longest and most intense battle. Once there in April and May I flew thirty-six combat flights. The two kamikazes I shot down April 29 were very easy, except for going after them among our own AA. They certainly weren't in the league with their team at Pearl Harbor or Midway." Nor were they as skillful as those he had previously encountered, successfully, over Rabaul and Truk.

Although his adversaries presented less of a threat, the constant exposure to death built up a residue of fear. "At the end of any combat mission, you felt relief that you survived. This was particularly true of strafing or bombing attacks. Although I flew as a fighter pilot, always anticipating aerial combat, at least half of my missions were attacks against ground targets. For me close air support missions were most worrisome. I always worried about hitting our own troops.

"I didn't dwell on taking someone's life. However, at the end of my combat time, I did tend to question my own survivability. I fought a long war. Every year of the war except 1941, I was in combat. Still, it's worth noting that in 1945, while flying with VBF-12, the casualties were usually the 'youngsters.' "

Lieutenant Al Bolduc, also a member of VBF-12 on the *Randolph*, flew the latest-model Hellcat, the F6F-5. "It was different from the F6F-3 in the following respects: the skin had flush rivets in all those areas that would cause drag with the 'dimple' rivets—worth 15 knots. It weighed a little more, and the stalling speed was two to four knots higher." He noted that its engine had more power, and with its water-injection system, the F6F-5 could probably fly 50 knots faster than any published reports. With a belly tank the plane could stay in the air as many as seven hours.

But there was one new wrinkle that spelled trouble: the Mark 23 gun sight, which required a pilot to reset the aiming reticle for each type of enemy plane. "This was the last kind of sight we needed in a dogfight," said Bolduc. "Our guns were bore-sighted to cross at 1,500 feet with this sight instead of the usual 900 feet." Fortunately, said Bolduc, when he flew a mission on May 4, he had a replacement plane with the old Mark 8 sight.

The target was Kikai, a small island about 100 miles northeast of Okinawa and a refueling and regrouping point for Japanese aircraft headed south toward Okinawa. Task Force Fifty-eight habitually stationed eight or twelve fighters over Kikai from dawn to dusk to prevent the enemy from using the airstrip. On May 4, three four-plane divisions from VBF-12 drew the duty.

"In the ready room," remembered Bolduc, "the briefing was routine. We had been to Kikai so many times, we hardly listened to the details. The weather would be clear. The radio frequencies were noted. Navigation was already on the chart boards. We had our maps with the new targets of opportunity marked. Search-and-rescue details were listened to very intensely, as always."

Launched at dawn, they rendezvoused inside the screen of destroyers and headed north. "Twelve planes, not eight as usual," remarked Bolduc. "I couldn't help thinking something was up. Someone knew more than I did about this hop. I thought this over for about ten minutes and called the leader of the flight, suggesting that my division take the first turn at the high-altitude station at 25,000 feet. Since the first division to go to altitude had the longest stay on oxygen, it was the least desirable assignment. Lieutenant Jemison readily agreed to my request.

"As we continued along our course, the sun became very brilliant and visibility increased to about seventy-five to one hundred miles. I moved my division to a stepped-up position on the leader so I could watch across the other planes to the sun line. He questioned my position, but when I told him I was watching his tail he concurred. After a few more minutes we could see Kikai very clearly, about twenty-five miles ahead. It was two to three miles wide and about seven miles long. Our approach was made at 10,000 feet from the eastern side so we could come down out of the sun. At a couple of miles from the beach the AA opened up—never very accurate at this distance, but the black puffs were disturbing. I looked over at Joe's [Mangieri] plane and got the thumbs-up along with his famous grin. Jim [Funsten] on the other side did the same. About this time the leader rocked his wings and down we went on our targets, some buildings making up the Jap headquarters on the island. The AA was intense, with red balls passing upwards over and under wings and on each side. As we dropped lower, the white streaks of the 20s and 40s added hundreds of shells trying to knock us out of the air. We each dropped our two 500-pound bombs and headed for the rendezvous point east of the island.

"Miraculously, no one got hit. After this feverish welcome by the AA and the dropping of the 500-pounders, my division bid adieu to the other two and started climbing to our assigned altitude of 25,000 feet over Kikai. This was no time to give the enemy the altitude advantage. I decided to climb into the sun as high as I could go and as quickly as possible. Having determined from previous encounters with enemy planes that four guns were enough, I turned off the two outboard guns, saving them to go home on. The altimeter finally read 36,000 about fifteen miles northeast of Kikai. After about one circle at this altitude, the radio crackled with a cry for help from our fellow pilots. This was it! We started down, diving towards Kikai, trying to spot the other eight planes. We were indicating well over three hundred knots. No planes in sight. I called for a position. A clear and calm voice said, 'Ten miles southeast of Kikai.' Another voice said, 'Hurry!' A slight left turn, and there they were! A big ball of planes at 16,000 to 18,000 feet, well ahead and below us. I dropped my belly tank. The four of us were spread out about a hundred feet apart.

"We leveled off slightly above the ball of planes, and I went through them from east to west in the same direction they were moving. It seemed as if all the planes, both Japs and F6Fs, were in slow motion. Tracers were floating through the air. I came up behind a Jap plane. He made a slight turn to the left, unaware that a plane was behind him. From about two hundred feet I let go a burst, and the incendiaries sparkled all over the cockpit and engine. Thank the Lord I had an MK-8 gun sight! Immediately, I did a steep chandelle to the right into the sun gaining about 4,000 feet. I dove back into the pile, fortunately behind another Jap. Another short burst into the cockpit and engine. Two down. Another chandelle. Still never slowing down except at the top of the chandelles. This time I noticed several burning planes spiraling down."

Bolduc fired again and noted, "Three down. Another chandelle, four down. I'm all by myself. There are now six or eight columns of smoke from falling planes. Somehow I know they are not F6s. I then spotted a lone Jap plane headed due north for home. Since I had the altitude advantage, I decided to give it a try. About ten miles north of

Kikai I closed up to a mile behind him, and I guess he spotted me because black smoke started pouring out of his exhaust. I firewalled the F6 with everything it had, including water injection. This gave me a fifty-knot edge, and as I closed in behind he made a sharp turn to the left. This is when I discovered that the F6 could easily turn inside a Zero at high speed. I pulled back on the stick until it hit the stop and was outturning [him] by such a margin that I had to reduce [speed] by a substantial amount. Again a burst into the cockpit and engine that no one could survive. Splash number five. As I sped by and turned south, I could see him burning in a graveyard spiral down to the deep blue water, 11,000 feet below.

"Heading south at a somewhat reduced speed, I spotted the rest of our planes chasing a lone Jap easterly in a huge circle at about 8,000 feet. I cut across the circle and got right behind him when tracers streamed past me from behind. I had cut in front of another F6 so quickly that he didn't have time to quit firing. Whew! I dove out of there in a hurry. That was evidently the last of the enemy planes. The dogfight was over. Time to join up and go home.

"I called Joe, my wingman, whom I hadn't see since the second run on the Japs. A miracle! He answered. He was about three miles south of us at about 500 feet. He was a 'sick chick' and couldn't put on more than half power without the engine cutting out. I headed towards his position, losing altitude, and another miracle occurred. I spotted his plane silhouette against the gleaming sunlit water from 3,000 feet and five miles' distance. We flew the remaining ninety miles or so back to the *Randolph* and were the first of the flight back aboard the ship. While crossing the flight deck on the way to the ready room, Joe said he had got one for sure and perhaps two before his engine began cutting out."

According to Bolduc, "The next thing I knew, I was up on the bridge talking to Admiral Bogan [the task group commander] about the flight. At debriefing the [intelligence] officer asked me what kind of planes they were, and I said 'Zeros, they all had big red meatballs on the wings.' Joe said they were all Jacks. Later, from the gun camera film, we found out they were Franks and Zekes." Had Bolduc been equipped with the Mark 23 gun sight, he might have achieved far less while attempting to adjust for the different types of planes.

During the postcombat review, Bolduc learned that his friend Joe's engine had had a cylinder head shot off. "Joe, who had a jigger of Navy 'tension reliever,' said he didn't think the guy could hit him and was surprised when his engine began to cut out. This is when I learned he had shot a plane off my tail and probably saved my life. Our training really paid off. Joe said, 'I knew exactly what you were going to do when we started down.' "

Inspection of Bolduc's guns found he had used fewer than five hundred rounds to destroy five enemy planes, and together the three divisions from the *Randolph* had accounted for all fourteen of the enemy planes they had encountered. VBF-12 lost not a single Hellcat, although a number of them had bullet holes.

Throughout the last half of April and into May, the Japanese continued to send waves of suicide planes. During May, four two-day raids aimed at the fleet off Okinawa sank five ships and damaged thirty-four but at a staggering cost of six hundred aircraft of all types. At the same time, advances of GIs and leathernecks on Okinawa reduced their dependence upon a huge offshore fleet to support them. The subsequent redeployment of ships devalued the area as a target for kamikazes. During the three months of Operation Iceberg, Japanese airpower declined by 7,830 airplanes and 12,000 aviators. The United States counted 763 airplanes lost, less than 10 percent of the enemy's losses, and an even smaller price in terms of people. The inevitably accelerating attrition among kamikaze pilots, however much death and destruction they inflicted, diminished the ability to germinate full-flowering *kikusui*, but smaller bouquets bedeviled the Allied vessels.

A particular insult to Task Force Fifty-eight saw two kamikazes grind through the avalanche of ship gunfire to crash the *Bunker Hill*, Task Force Fifty-eight's flagship, with Marc Mitscher aboard. The explosions and fire killed 402 and wounded 264. Mitscher himself transferred by breeches buoy to a destroyer. To forestall further such assaults, Task Force Fifty-eight steamed a course that put it in position to hammer Kyushu, a major source of enemy raids. Reminiscent of what Thach had promoted during the early days of the Philippine campaign, Task Force Fifty-eight threw serial fighter sweeps at airfields in southern Kyushu. Taken by surprise, the Japanese could muster only a small number of interceptors; twenty-nine of them were shot down, while another fifty-one planes on the ground were destroyed.

The *Randolph* launched its torpedo and bomber squadrons together with two fighter squadrons for a strike at Usa, a field at the extreme northeast corner of Kyushu on the Inland Sea. Al Bolduc was in a Hellcat on this mission, and he reported that as they neared the spit of land that separates the Inland Sea from the ocean, the antiaircraft grew intense. "We were at about 16,000 feet, with the bombers and TBFs a couple of thousand feet below. I looked over to the right at Joe, about fifty feet off my wing, and he gave me his usual thumbs-up. About this time, on the radio I heard the words, 'Camel Hump 105.' " Two of the TBMs had special gear for interfering with enemy radar, and the phrase heard by Bolduc was a code communication instructing one of the torpedo bombers to adjust its jamming gear to a certain frequency. At the same time the TBMs talked to each other about throwing out "window," strips of aluminum foil that confuses radar detectors.

After the first message the black puffs of the ground guns fell behind the torpedo planes. But when they came closer, a voice on the radio called, "More window, hurry!" The cycle was repeated several times before the Navy planes neared the target. On signal Bolduc and company spread out, dived down, picking up targets, and released their 500-pounders. "Just as the other planes of my division joined up," said Bolduc, "an SB2C made a steep dive down past us towards a 150-foot vessel anchored several hundred feet offshore. The pilot opened up with his two 20 mm cannon, and the vessel literally exploded. I couldn't help thinking that the 20s were a powerful weapon for strafing.

"After rendezvousing with the rest of the planes, we heard that one of the SB2Cs had been hit by antiaircraft fire and its engine had quit. It landed in the Inland Sea, about ten miles southeast of Usa. I received instructions to circle the downed pilot and crewman until relieved or until rescue planes arrived. Lieutenant Commander Mike Michaelis, skipper of the VF squadron, also stayed and circled the rubber boat." The crew of the dive-bomber, John Morris and Cletis Phegley, had inflated the craft as their airplane sank.

"Mike suggested that I stay at about 6,000 feet," said Bolduc, "and he would stay down a little lower. After a while, Mike called up and said his gas was low and he was leaving and for me to stay as long as I could with my division. It wasn't long after he left that things began to get a little exciting. Evidently, Mike's being pretty low made him visible to quite a few of the Japs in the area and no one made a move toward the two in the rubber boat. Shortly after he left, we spotted what appeared to be a 250-foot tanker about one and a half miles northwest of the life raft. The tanker was on a course in the general direction of the rubber boat.

"After a few minutes it became obvious that the crew had spotted our chaps in the life raft because it made a sharp course change, heading directly to their position. Decision time again. We'll make a coordinating strafing run and see if that will persuade them to go somewhere else. Down we came, all four of us, Joe and I on the right and Jim and Frank [Ness] on the left of the stern. We filled the after section, the bridge, [the] wheelhouse, and the surrounding super-structure full of holes with some good long bursts. After pulling up and rendezvousing, we circled to see if the strafing persuaded the tanker to go somewhere else. It slowed down but continued on course.

"About this time, Jim Funsten, my section leader, called on the radio and said he had a 500-pound bomb. My reply: 'Go ahead and drop it.' We could see the bomb gracefully arc down towards the tar-get. We observed the most beautiful splash but not blast about five feet from the tanker's railing amidship." Funsten had probably been too low when he loosed the bomb for its arming propeller to turn the required eight hundred revolutions necessary to arm the ordnance.

"Another voice said, 'I also have a bomb.' Frank Ness, Jim's wingman and an ex–bomber pilot, now had a turn at the tanker. I cautioned him to drop it from a thousand feet and to be sure it was armed. Again we watched as the bomb made its way down. This time, at about the same location that Jim's had landed, there was a tremendous blast and the tanker seemed to rise about five feet out of the water. The tanker immediately started an uncontrolled circle and within a minute or two began to leak oil and spew steam from various areas around the after section, where the wheelhouse and stack were located.

"Frank evidently got their attention because after a few more minutes the tanker headed away towards the shore, about a mile or two away. The crew on board the tanker had been popping away at us with a 20 mm and what looked like about a three-inch gun, but after the bomb blast they quit shooting and were probably trying to save the ship."

Bolduc and the other resumed cruising above the downed air-men as clouds began to build up. He continued his account: "A few more minutes, and *oops*! A tugboat approaching the rubber boat from the northwest. Guess we'll have to strafe this one. Using alti-tude to gain speed and save gas as much as possible, the four of us made a circling approach, and as we made our last half-mile straight-in run, I could see a 40 mm cannon popping away from the fore deck, but to no avail. After that pass by the four F6Fs, the tug was finished. White steam, black smoke, and oil coming out in all directions. It headed slowly over toward the beach." The quartet climbed to 6,000 feet, anxiously checking their dwindling gas.

"Jeepers!!" Bolduc noted. "What the heck is that about five miles northeast? Looks like two PT boats coming our way at full speed. I started easing up that way. Suddenly there are big orange flashes from the bows of the PT boats. PT boats don't have five-inch guns, and therefore they must be destroyers. Sure enough, after getting a little closer and a little abeam, my conclusion becomes valid. We don't have enough gas to fly around at full throttle and made a decent coordinated attack. I put out a call for friendly planes. Immediately the photo planes from our ship answer that they are in the area and volunteer their services. We talk it over, and I suggest they continue above the overcast to conceal their approach. I'll stay under and draw the fire so they can get a good start in their dive before being observed. Just as they started their dive, the AA went up through the overcast but fortunately was behind them. Radar-controlled AA.

"The photo planes made repeated runs, strafing both destroyers. The result was that both ships headed northerly about two miles to the nearest land and beached themselves on the shore of Honshu [the largest of the home islands]. This attack by the photo planes was made in the face of intense antiaircraft fire and was one of the bravest acts I observed during the entire tour."

Once again the Hellcats stationed themselves above the rubber raft in the Inland Sea. When their gasoline supply fell to a critical level, leaving them barely enough to return to the *Randolph*, the four reluctantly waggled their wings and headed toward their carrier. From the radio chatter they heard that some sort of rescue effort was in motion. Aboard the ship, while being debriefed on their very successful attack on Usa, they heard that a pair of Kingfishers, with a twenty-four-plane escort, had picked up the downed pilots.

Enterprise, as host to night marauders and now Mitscher's flagship, dispatched heckler flights on May 12 after dark. Lieutenant (j.g.) Charles Henderson flew a TBM toward the airfield at Kanoya. The Japanese, though tracking him on radar, left all of the base's lights on, apparently thinking it was a friendly plane. Henderson was quoted in *The Big E* as saying, "They were so nice, I hated to drop my bombs." After he did and the explosions began, the enemy turned out the lights. Two other Avengers struck at other airfields with both bombs and rockets, smashing parked aircraft and igniting fires.

On the second night of these excursions, the Japanese, now

aware of the imminent danger, kept their bases dark. Unlike the previous day, they instantly threw up vicious streams of AA and used radar-controlled searchlights to blind marauders. Nevertheless, *Enterprise*'s Avengers denied the foe any sleep, pounding away throughout the night. When dawn broke and Japanese aircraft attempted to go after the task force, combat air patrols were already on stations and fell upon them when they were at their most vulnerable. Mitscher, who had always been skeptical of the value of night missions, praised the achievements of the carrier's air group.

Neutralization of the Kyushu bases was still in progress on May 14, when early in the morning the radar detected sinister bogeys. The CAP splashed some, but one Zeke, popping into and out of clouds, evaded both aerial interception and the fireworks from the ships. The pilot, in a series of skillful maneuvers, slipped through the AA screen and dived into the *Enterprise*'s forward elevator. His bomb hurled the elevator 400 feet into the air. In spite of the enormous damage, which knocked the Big E out of the war, only thirteen were killed and sixty-eight wounded.

Third Fleet Commander Bull Halsey relieved Raymond Spruance on May 17, and Task Force Fifty-eight reverted to the control of John McCain as TF-38. In June, Halsey and company ventured toward Japan for renewed strikes. For the second time, they sailed into the path of a typhoon. The howling gale inflicted severe injuries, ripping off a cruiser's bow, forcing two destroyers to retire from the task force, and collapsing portions of the flight decks on both the *Bennington* and *Hornet*.

Jim Pearce, the Hellcat pilot with VF-18 on the *Hornet*, said, "The typhoon tore up a third of the aircraft on board as they rolled around the hangar deck and flight deck. After that, Jocko [Rear Admiral John J. Clark, a choleric and highly opinionated officer] decided to launch the aircraft over the stern with the carrier going backwards. Being the flagship of the fleet, of course this screwed up the entire fleet, with everybody going everywhere as the flagship slowly came to a halt and started steaming backwards. It took thirty minutes to stop its forward motion and another twenty minutes to get it going as fast as it could backwards to launch the planes.

"Chaos! Then after a few hours of flight the aircraft had to be brought down to refuel, so the entire charade had to happen again to get the thing going forward so the planes could be landed. This foolishness went one cycle when a bigger admiral must have gotten word of it and immediately sent the *Hornet* home."

A court of inquiry sat in Guam on June 15 to examine the responsibility for the Third Fleet's second encounter with a typhoon. The findings criticized Halsey for not following recommendations that had grown out of the February experience. The investigating body also placed some guilt on McCain, Clark, and Rear Admiral Donald Beary, who had been in charge of the service squadron. Halsey, who blamed inadequate weather information, escaped being relieved because of morale considerations.

Jim Pearce, who obviously was not impressed with Clark, favored Mitscher over others: "The entire complexion of the fleet changed every time command shifted from Halsey to Mitscher and back [actually, the former commanded the entire Third Fleet while Mitscher ran only a part of the Fifth Fleet, Task Force Fifty-eight]. With Mitscher in command, the fleet headed towards the target after launching to make the trip home easier, especially for the wounded people or planes. With Halsey in command, the ships turned away from the target after launch, a tactic not appreciated by the airplane drivers."

Although Pearce was measuring a fleet leader against the boss of a task force, the comparison is valid in that Mitscher had much more independence than his counterpart, McCain, serving under Halsey. McCain, according to Clark Reynolds in *The Fast Carriers*, while personally likable, "issued not only vague communications but often contradictory ones."

Personalities could and did influence single events and even campaigns, but they meant less as the war wound down. By the summer of 1945, the Japanese had lost control of the Pacific right up to their shoreline and the merciless bombardment by the Army Air Corps on Japan, supplemented by the strikes from Navy carriers, was beginning to transform rubble into dust.

The *Hancock*'s Air Group Six, commanded by Henry Miller, spoke of the difficulty of finding enemy aircraft: "As we moved on up to the Japanese mainland," Miller noted, "when we would go in to hit, we would hunt for camouflaged airplanes around the fields. When you found one or two, it led you to a whole bunch of them. You'd form a circle and start firing at all these airplanes. We got hundreds of planes on the ground. The Japs were saving them. They hadn't given up." Miller named three targets that were off limits. One of them was Kyoto, which he had learned was "a city of culture." The other two forbidden places were Hiroshima and Nagasaki.

John Hyland remarked, "In the later months, it was hard to find anything in the air. People were trying to steal them from one another. You could listen to the fighter directors and you could realize that there were some Japanese airplanes over there and maybe you'd be lucky if you could get a crack at them before the fellow who was being directed to them would get there."

With Okinawa secured and the crushing of the Japanese forces in the Philippines in its final stages, starting toward the end of July, the fast carrier airmen paid their last calls on the Kure naval base. On the morning of July 24, thirteen planes from VB-1, off the *Bennington*, bearing 1,000-pounders, participated in a Task Force Thirty-eight strike against the remaining warships of the Imperial Navy. Heavy cloud cover partially obscured the target area, but Lieutenant Commander A. B. Hamm placed his 1,000-pounder squarely amidships of the 28,000-ton aircraft carrier *Unryu*. Lieutenant F. G. Mulvihill, leading a division that aimed at an *Ise*-class battleship, scored a direct hit that was enhanced by a pair of 250-pound fragmentation bombs. VB-1 Helldivers also damaged a cruiser. During the afternoon, aircraft from the *Bennington* again struck at the Kure anchorage. They registered explosions on a carrier and a battleship. For the first day of the campaign to wreck ships in the harbors of Kure and Kobe, Task Force Thirty-eight put up 1,747 sorties.

After four days of continuous battering, the battleships *Haruna*, *Ise*, and *Hyuga* were reduced to hulks squatting in the mud of the harbors. Cruisers and an aircraft carrier suffered the same fate. Having ravaged the naval bases, Task Force Thirty-eight shifted its operations to wipe out a concentration of planes on northern Honshu.

Two weeks earlier, on July 16, the Manhattan Project, at Alamogordo, New Mexico, had successfully detonated a prototype of an atomic bomb. Frederick Ashworth, who had both a practical and an academic background in the use of ordnance and had commanded a torpedo-bomber squadron during the Guadalcanal days, following his tour in the South Pacific, had been assigned to the Manhattan Project as an assistant to the Navy's Captain William Parsons, directing the ordnance division.

Ashworth remarked, "Groves [General Leslie M., who headed the program] was certain that he would require a member of the crew on the bomb-carrying aircraft who had at least a general background on the bomb's technical characteristics, so that proper decisions could be made should they be required. Groves always wanted spares for everything. I would be Parsons' spare."

Although the role of Navy experts rarely appears in accounts of the atomic bomb's development, Ashworth credited his boss, Captain Parsons, with having contributed considerably to the technique of implosion worked out with John von Neumann (one of the civilian scientists). While Ashworth could add little expertise to the actual building of the weapon, he supervised much of the in-flight testing of components. He was also charged with recruiting military personnel whose knowledge would add to the work.

"In February 1945," said Ashworth, "I was designated to carry a top-secret letter to Guam and hand it personally to Admiral Nimitz. This letter would inform him for the first time that there was under development an atomic bomb which would be about 8,000 tons of TNT equivalent, and that support of his command would be required. He was authorized to inform only one officer on his staff. If he had any questions, the bearer of the letter would be able to answer them. It directed Admiral Nimitz to give me what support I might need in selecting a site for the operation.

"I traveled from Washington direct to Guam, wearing the ordinary cotton khaki uniform of that period. I carried the letter in a money belt around my waist next to my skin. When I arrived on Guam I went directly to the headquarters of Admiral Nimitz and told his aide I had an important letter to deliver to the admiral. He said okay, he would carry it in. I said that wasn't okay. I was required to hand the letter directly to the admiral. With some reluctance he went into the office to find out if the admiral would see me, coming out in a moment with word I could go in. The aide followed me. I told Admiral Nimitz that I had been ordered to hand the letter direct to him and that no one else could be present. Admiral Nimitz told the aide to leave and I proceeded to break out the letter.

"I opened my uniform jacket, unbuttoned my shirt enough to extract the money belt, all to the amusement of the admiral. After the long trip, the money belt was a bit the worse for wear and its contents a little stained and damp from sweat. However, it was in good enough shape for the admiral to open and read it."

Nimitz informed Ashworth that in order to provide the kind of services required, he would need to clue in his operations officer. He also wanted to know why the weapon was not available immediately. After Ashworth described the status in the development of the bomb and said that Groves believed it would be ready for use in August, he said, "He [Nimitz] turned in his chair and looked out the window for several seconds, turned and said, 'Thank you, Commander. I guess that I was born just about twenty years too soon.' I felt he had sensed the magnitude of the thing. Perhaps he also saw that the bomb might have a possibility to end the war."

Ashworth was charged with exploring the Pacific for the space needed to house the Army's 509th Bomb Group, which was training to use the device, and the scientists and engineers who would accompany the weapon as it went to war. He chose Tinian in the Marianas because of its air operations facilities, even though Saipan was closer to Japan.

The vital element of the bomb, a hunk of U-235, the active ingredient for the first bomb, known as Little Boy, arrived on the cruiser *Indianapolis*. Ashworth commandeered an LCM for the delicate job of picking up the package from the warship. After the LCM docked, a truck carried the U-235 to the Tinian airfield. After sailing from the Marianas, the unlucky *Indianapolis*, several days later, was torpedoed by a Japanese sub. The Navy apparently did not realize the cruiser was missing, and only 316 sailors of the more than 850 crewmen were rescued.

Technicians loaded Little Boy onto the *Enola Gay*, the B-29 commanded by Colonel Paul Tibbets. Amid some ceremony, camera flashbulbs popping, at 2:45 A.M. on August 6, the plane took off with Captain Parsons on board as "weaponeer" to arm the bomb after they were airborne. The first nuclear explosion then devastated Hiroshima.

Three days later, without any pomp, the second nuclear weapon, Fat Man, went into the bomb bay of *Bock's Car*, flown by Major Charles Sweeney. On this occasion, Ashworth had the task of weaponeer. Once in flight and well away from Tinian, Ashworth and his assistant, Army Lieutenant Phil Barnes, replaced the green-painted plugs that isolated the arming and firing systems from other electrical components with red ones that readied the firing and fusing systems to activate after the bomb dropped.

Everything went smoothly except that only one of two B-29s assigned to accompany them arrived at the rendezvous point. Ashworth persuaded Sweeney to delay for forty-five minutes. "I told Sweeney that it was particularly important that we have the plane carrying bomb-yield measuring instruments with us before we proceeded to the primary target. I wasn't worried much about the plane carrying the observers, but very much wanted to be able to attempt measurement of the bomb yield."

When the missing Superfortress did not show, Ashworth advised

Sweeney that they should continue as planned and hope the B-29 with them contained the instruments rather than spectators. When *Bock's Car* reached the primary target, Kokura, the bombardier reported that too much smoke and haze covered the area. Ashworth suggested approaching from different angles, but none of these improved visibility. The delay waiting for the second B-29 and the three tries over Kokura had consumed considerable fuel.

Unable to drop on the primary target, Sweeney flew toward Nagasaki, the secondary target, which appeared to be hidden by a solid cloud cover. Said Ashworth, "We would have one and only one attempt at a successful drop and that appeared to be impossible by visual bombsight in view of the clouds beneath us. I informed Sweeney that we would make our approach by radar and if necessary drop the bomb by use of the electronic bomb director which would be operated by the navigator. The approach continued."

As they reached the city, the overcast broke up into patches with the ground showing beneath large holes in the clouds. The bombardier called out, "I have the target." He then dropped visually. *Bock's Car* quickly executed a sharp banking turn to put itself the maximum distance from the blast.

"About forty-five seconds after release and the time of fall of the bomb," said Ashworth, "we were able to see through heavy welders' goggles a brilliant flash of light. When we were about eight miles away, the detonation, the first shock wave arrived, followed immediately by a second and to my recollection a third. The evidence of these shock waves was more one of noise than anything else. I have always characterized it as if someone had struck an empty metal trash can with a baseball bat. There was a minor movement of the plane, no worse than a sharp bump frequently experienced when flying in a commercial aircraft in clear air turbulence."

The crew looked back on the mushroom cloud composed of smoke and pink- or salmon-colored fire. But the plane escaped contact with what was a toxic radiation plume. Short on gas, Sweeney elected to land at Yontan on Okinawa.

Once there, the Army Air Corps staff, ignorant of the atom bomb mission, refused to transmit a message from Ashworth to his superiors on Tinian. However, he managed to gain an audience with General Jimmy Doolittle, who, with the war in Europe ended, now commanded the air operations focused upon Japan. After Ashworth described what had happened, Doolittle said, "Son, I am sure that

General Spatz [Lieutenant General Carl, his superior] will be much happier that the bomb exploded where it did, over the industrial area and not the city. There will be far fewer casualties. Now, I'll help you send your report."

Henry Miller and his air group had been traveling as far as Hokkaido, the most northern of the Japanese islands. But on August 15, he brought a task group of planes from three carriers to bomb and strafe a familiar target, an electronics plant southeast of Tokyo.

"All this time everybody was sweating it out, saying, 'Is the war over?'" said Miller. "I got about forty miles from the electronics plant and the task group [Combat Information Center] called me and said, '99 Jamboree. This is Christopher. Over.'

"I said, 'This is 99 Jamboree. Go ahead with your message.'

"He said, '99 Jamboree, have all your planes drop their bombs in the water and return to base. Do not attack, repeat, do not attack any targets in the Tokyo area. Call and get acknowledgments from the three fighter sweep leaders and tell them not to strafe or bomb anything, but to come back, return to base. Watch out for rats in the air (those were Jap pilots). They've taken off to give it the go for just one last try. Watch out for rats in the air.'

"I asked if the war was over. He said he didn't know but them were your orders. I repeated back and about that time the pilots started singing, 'When the war is over, we will all go USN.' I said, 'Get the hell off the air. I've got to get this message across,' which they did. I got acknowledgments from my three fighter sweep leaders. I told everybody to return to base. People were dropping their bombs, they were doing loops.

"About that time, my fighter sweep leader, Neff Bigelow, called me. We had code names but he wanted to be sure. He said to me, 'Hank, this is Neff. There are seven Japs over me and it looks like they're going to attack. What do?'

"I thought, gee shizz, I don't want to start World War III, but I don't want to lose any of my kids. I said, 'Neff, this is Hank. If it looks like they're going to attack, shoot them down gently.' He got four out of seven. That quote later was in *Reader's Digest*. My wife said, 'Hey look what they have here,' and they attributed it to Admiral Halsey." Sometime later, Miller met Bigelow, who affirmed, "it wasn't Halsey. It was between you and me."

When Miller began to circle his carrier for a landing he received information that justified his instructions to Bigelow. Over his radio he heard another pilot speaking to the flattop: "Tomcat one. This is 311 Zebra. Is the war over?"

"311 Zebra. This is Tomcat one. We don't know if the war is over. We got the same message as you. Return to base."

"Tomcat one. This is 311 Zebra. If the war is over, some Jap bastard didn't get the news because he just shot my ass off." However, Miller reported, the pilot managed to land safely.

World War II's shooting phase ended on this day. A cease-fire preceded the September 2 surrender ceremonies on the battleship *Missouri*. Navy planes, along with those from the brother services, began dropping food over prisoner-of-war camps. On August 30, the first Navy planes began landing on Japanese fields and U.S. warships tied up in the harbors. Those who wore wings of gold stood down, a respite that would last six years before the Korean War once again demanded their services.

TWENTY-THREE

THE LAST TALLYHO

The final figures for the achievements of those who wore wings of gold set the number of Japanese aircraft destroyed in the air by Navy flyers—not including the Marines—at well over 7,000. They also claimed more than another 5,800 planes destroyed on the ground, although this statistic necessarily involves a certain amount of guesstimation. Losses from combat were more than 600 to enemy planes and about triple that number due to antiaircraft. Operational losses—which cover accidents, malfunctions, and situations such as the many who ditched during the after-dark recovery while pursuing Ozawa—totaled 1,001. The Japanese also destroyed nearly a thousand planes through attacks on carriers or at bases hosting Navy fighters. (None of these totals includes the counts for Operations Torch and Husky or antisubmarine patrol in the Atlantic.)

The figures compiled show that the flights from flattops, by themselves, sank five battleships, eleven carriers, a dozen cruisers, and twenty-eight destroyers. Working in combination with other forces, the Navy airmen helped sink another thirty warships, including a battleship and two more carriers. Also destroyed by bombs, torpedoes, and rockets were 275 merchant ships.

From its inauspicious debut in the war, marked by half a dozen F4Fs from the *Enterprise* shot down by friendly fire over Hawaii on December 7, 1941, naval aviation obviously contributed an enormous amount to the prosecution of the war. Its success must be attributed not only to the technical and mechanical achievements that produced more and vastly improved machines but also to the young men who flew them. They had some special qualities. All of them, including those who had chosen the service as a career via the USNA, were highly motivated; they volunteered to fly. Furthermore, the skills required meant that when they entered the service, they tended to be better educated than their contemporaries. Learning to handle an airplane added to their knowledge. Like their opposite numbers in Army or Marine squadrons, they received extra money through flight pay, and the romance of their service gave them cachet with civilians. Carrier life—a regimen of clean quarters, laundry, hot food, and few duties other than missions—was certainly far more pleasant than that of the ground-pounders or even the land-based aviators who in the Pacific outposts occupied barracks with few amenities. An army or a navy may not travel only on its stomach, but it is certainly a plus to be well fed.

In common with other combat airmen, Navy people, except when their ship was struck by a bomb, torpedo, or kamikaze, had limited exposure to the carnage of war. They did not have foxhole buddies die in their arms or witness the awful wounds inflicted by shrapnel or bullets. Infantrymen and armored troops would literally be soaked in gore. Airmen never saw bodies, in the cliché of the day, "stacked like cordwood." Advancing on the ground, GIs would walk over earth littered with the enemy dead. While a few of those wearing wings of gold professed hatred for the Japanese enemy, there was an almost antiseptic attitude toward the deaths they caused. That is true for all combat airmen, who do not see the bloodied, maimed corpses they manufacture. Army Air Corps crews engaged in strategic bombing undoubtedly realized that they killed civilians, many of whom were not engaged in war factories. Some of them may have experienced pangs of remorse. But except for the limited number of strikes at plants in the home islands, the Navy assaults rarely touched civilians. One does not get a sense of the horror of war in the oral histories or interviews with naval aviators. There was plenty of emotional stress, but it was more a product of moments of high terror, when their own planes and lives were in jeopardy, they lost friends, or they were exhausted because of overwork. Very few instances of battle fatigue seem to have occurred. Similarly, airmen who said they could not continue, or aborted missions without good reason, were rare. Undoubtedly the camaraderie from having trained together, the teamwork required when engaged in combat, and the intimacy of shipboard life for long stretches of time provided emotional stability and support. Aviators in all branches of the military enjoyed one boon not granted to the ground forces: they flew a certain number of missions or endured combat tours with the knowledge that they would eventually be rotated. That too bolstered their morale.

The conflict between the battleship and air admirals seeped down to those directly in the line of fire. There were complaints that uncaring top officers arbitrarily extended combat tours and sent aviators back for a second taste of war. Some flyers noted that only six naval aviators received the Medal of Honor, while the Marines pinned on eleven of the nation's highest decoration, even though the Corps flew nearly 20 percent fewer missions. The difference was ascribed to admirals, prejudiced against naval aviation, who refused to approve recommendations for the award.

The U.S. Navy, like its brothers in the American military, entered World War II poorly prepared for the kind of conflict it faced. In the field of aviation, its aircraft were at best marginally adequate. The Japanese, the most obvious opponent, were superior in the number and quality of their planes. They also had the advantage of combat experience, albeit against an almost nonexistent Chinese air force. The Imperial Navy also boasted more carriers and heavyweight warships.

The assault upon Pearl Harbor buckled the Navy's knees, and during the first months of 1942, much of the responsibility for maintaining an American presence in the Pacific devolved upon the flattops and their air groups. By sheer happenstance, naval aviation gained an opportunity to demonstrate its capability as a weapon, culminating with the Battle of Midway, which in retrospect signaled the eventual decline of the Japanese forces.

Much has been made of the failure of the battleship admirals to recognize the strength inherent in aircraft carrier operations. This was due to a lack of imagination, just as the debacle at Pearl Harbor was a failure to think beyond the conventional wisdom on strategy and tactics. It should be remembered, however, that until the United States plunged into World War II, there was no history of carrier warfare. Aviation itself had been a minor part of World War I; the Navy had flown seaplanes, and the carrier experiment by the British is hardly worth a footnote in an account of World War I. At least those young Army officers who were part of the American Expeditionary Force in France learned something about modern combat. The Navy people, other than on convoy and submarine duty, did not fight sea battles, much less deal in any significant way with the air. Those destined for senior positions could only draw their inspiration from hearing or reading about surface-ship confrontations, such as the Battle of Jutland, in which the United States did not participate.

As Noel Gayler observed, senior commanders steeped in the technology, tactics, and doctrine of earlier days develop a mind-set that blinds them to the reality of the present day. That hardened attitude hinders advances accruing from learning on the job, which in itself can be costly enough.

The oft-quoted comment by George Santayana, "Those who cannot remember the past are condemned to repeat it," is one more leaky truth, counterbalanced by the equally sound observation that generals and admirals tend to fight a current war with the mind-set of the previous one. In the case of the Navy, with the exception of a few senior individuals such as Marc Mitscher and Gerald Bogan, it was the younger men—such as Thach, Flatley, and O'Hare, those who flew the planes—who grasped the potential of their weapon. They were rebels—Hegelians, if you will—who met thesis with their own antithesis, and from this came the winning synthesis of the aviation units.

BIBLIOGRAPHY

PUBLISHED WORKS

Bergeraud, Eric. *Fire in the Sky*. Boulder, Colo.: Westview Press, 2000.

Buchanan, A. R. *The Navy's Air War*. New York: Harper & Bros., 1946.

Costello, John. *The Pacific War*. New York: Rawson & Wade, 1981.

Cressman, Robert J., and Michael Wenger. *Steady Nerves and Stout Hearts*. Missoula, Mont.: Pictorial Histories Publishing Company, 1990.

Dacus, W. R., and E. Kitzmann. *As We Lived It*. USS *Suwannee* Reunion Association.

Feifer, George. *Tennozan*. New York: Ticknor and Fields, 1992.

Hamilton, Robert. "Reflections of an Amphibious Force Staff Officer in the Second World War." Sunnyvale, Calif.: Privately published manuscript, 1993.

Hammel, Eric. *Guadalcanal: The Carrier Battles*. New York: Crown Publishers, 1987.

Hoyt, Edwin. *The Kamikazes*. Short Hills, N.J.: Burford Books, 1983.

———. *The Men of the Gambier Bay*. Middlebury, Vt.: Paul S. Eriksson, 1979.

Hudson, J. E. *The History of the USS Cabot*. Hickory, N.C.: 1986.

Johnston, Stanley. *The Grim Reapers*. New York: E. P. Dutton & Co., 1943.

Karig, Walter. *Battle Report* (6 vols.). New York: Farrar & Rinehart, 1944–1952.

Layton, Edwin T., with Roger Pineau and John Costello. *And I Was There*. New York: William Morrow and Company, 1985.

Morrisey, Thomas L. *Odyssey of Fighting Two*. Privately published by the VF-2 Association.

Morison, Samuel Eliot. *History of United States Naval Operations in World War II: Aleutians, Gilberts and Marshalls*. Boston: Little, Brown and Company, 1951.

———. *History of United States Naval Operations in World War II: The Battle of the Atlantic*. Boston: Little, Brown and Company, 1984.

———. *History of United States Naval Operations in World War II: Leyte*. Boston: Little, Brown and Company, 1958.

———. *History of United States Naval Operations in World War II: North African Waters*. Boston: Little, Brown and Company, 1984.

Prange, Gordon. *At Dawn We Slept*. New York: McGraw-Hill Book Company, 1981.

———, with Donald M. Goldstein and Katherine V. Dillon. *Miracle at Midway*. New York: McGraw-Hill Book Company, 1982.

Reynolds, Clark. *The Carrier War*. New York: Time-Life Books, 1982.

———. *The Fast Carriers: The Forging of an Air Navy*. New York: McGraw-Hill Book Company, 1968.

Smith, John R. *Hellcats over the Philippine Deep*. Manhattan, Kans.: Sunflower University Press, 1995.

Spector, Ronald H. *The Eagle Against the Sun*. New York: Free Press, 1985.

Stafford, Edward P. *The Big E*. New York: Random House, 1962.

Van der Vat, Dan. *The Pacific Campaign, World War II*. New York: Simon & Schuster, 1991.

Van Wyen, Adrian O., and Lee M. Pearson. *United States Naval Aviation, 1910–1980*. Washington, D.C.: U.S. Government Printing Office, 1981.

Winters, T. Hugh. *Skipper*. Mesa, Ariz.: Champlin Fighter Museum Press, 1985.

Wordell, M., and E. N. Seiler. *Wildcats over Casablanca.* McLean, Va.: Brasseys, 2003.

ORAL HISTORIES AND INTERVIEWS

Anderson, Bill. Interview with author, June 10, 1995.

Anderson, George W., Jr. Oral history. Annapolis, Md.: United States Naval Institute, 1980.

Ashworth, Frederick. Oral history. Annapolis, Md.: United States Naval Institute, 1990.

Balch, Jean. Oral history. Denton, Tex: University of North Texas, 1996.

Bender, Chester. Oral history. Annapolis, Md.: United States Naval Institute, 1976.

Berree, Norman. Interview with author, March 23, 2002.

Billo, Jim. Interview with author, March 30, 2002.

Bogan, Gerald F. Oral history. Annapolis, Md.: United States Naval Institute, 1969.

Bolduc, Al. Interview with author, March 5, 2002.

Davis, Robert. Interview with author, March 17, 2002.

Duncan, Robert. Interview with author, March 20, 2002.

Eder, Willard. Interview with author, April 25, 2002.

Elstrom, William. Interview with Michael Bak, March 18, 1991.

Feightner, Edward. Oral history. Annapolis, Md.: United States Naval Institute, 2002.

Foley, Francis. Oral history. Annapolis, Md.: United States Naval Institute, 1985.

Gallery, Dan. Oral history. Annapolis, Md.: United States Naval Institute, 1970–1974.

Gayler, Noel. Oral history. Annapolis, Md.: United States Naval Institute, 2002.

Griffin, Charles. Oral history. Annapolis, Md.: United States Naval Institute, 1970.

Harris, Thomas. Interview with author, April 15, 2002.

Hawkins, Arthur. Oral history. Annapolis, Md.: United States Naval Institute, 1983.

Hedding, Truman J. Oral history. Annapolis, Md.: United States Naval Institute, 1971.

Hippe, Kenneth. Interview with author, March 25, 2002.

Hyland, John J., Jr. Oral history. Annapolis, Md.: United States Naval Institute, 1972.

Jackson, Andrew. Oral history. Annapolis, Md.: United States Naval Institute, 1972.

Jones, Harry T. Interview with author, August 12, 1998.

Lee, Fitzhugh. Oral history. Annapolis, Md.: United States Naval Institute, 1992.

Lee, Kent. Oral history. Annapolis, Md.: United States Naval Institute, 1987–1988.

Lundin, Walter. Interview with author, April 25, 2002.

McCampbell, David. Oral history. Annapolis, Md.: United States Naval Institute, 2000.

Michaelis, Frederick. Oral history. Annapolis, Md.: United States Naval Institute, 1981–1982.

Miller, Henry L. Oral history. Annapolis, Md.: United States Naval Institute, 1971.

Minter, Charles. Oral history. Annapolis, Md.: United States Naval Institute, 1979.

Moorer, Thomas H. Oral history. Annapolis, Md.: United States Naval Institute, 1975–1976.

Murray, Robert. Interview with author, April 23, 2002.

Odell, William C. *Those Few Who Dared.* Colorado Springs, Colo.: Unpublished manuscript.

Ogden, James R. Oral history. Annapolis, Md.: United States Naval Institute, 1982.

Pearce, Jim. Interview with author, June 23, 2002.

Pirie, Robert B. Oral history. Annapolis, Md.: United States Naval Institute, 1972–1974.

Pownall, Charles A. Oral history. Annapolis, Md.: United States Naval Institute, 1970.

Price, Arthur W. Oral history. Annapolis, Md.: United States Naval Institute, 1978.

Pride, Alfred M. Oral history. Annapolis, Md.: United States Naval Institute, 1970.

Ramage, James D. Oral history. Annapolis, Md.: United States Naval Institute, 1985.

Rehm, Daniel. Interview with author, May 10, 2002.

Richardson, David C. Oral history. Annapolis, Md.: United States Naval Institute, 1992.

Riley, Herbert D. Oral history. Annapolis, Md.: United States Naval Institute, 1971.

Robinson, LeRoy. Interview with author, August 21, 2002.

Russell, James S. Oral history. Annapolis, Md.: United States Naval
Institute, 1974.

Smith, A. B. Interview with author, May 28, 2002.

Stanley, Onia B. Unpublished typescript, undated.

Stroop, Paul D. Oral history. Annapolis, Md.: United States Naval
Institute, 1969–1970.

Thach, John S. Oral history. Annapolis, Md.: United States Naval
Institute, 1970–1971.

Thorn, Floyd. Oral history. Denton, Tex.: University of North Texas,
2000.

Vraciu, Alex. Oral history. Denton, Tex.: University of North Texas,
1994.

OFFICIAL NARRATIVES AND STATEMENTS

Action with the Enemy (VB-3), June, 4, 1942.

Report by Torpedo Squadron Six, June 21, 1942.

Narrative by Ensign Albert K. Earnest, Squadron Eight
Detachment (after Battle of Midway).

Action Report of Fighter Squadron Eleven, May 18, 1942.

Report VF-49, November 8, 1942.

Air Command Solomons Intelligence, June 7, 1943.

Report of Antisubmarine Action by Aircraft, June 12, 1943.

Report of Antisubmarine Action by Aircraft, June 15, 1944.

Air Command Solomons Intelligence, June 16, 1943.

Report of Antisubmarine Action by Aircraft, August 12, 1943.

Aircraft Action Report, November 21, 1943.

Aircraft Action Report (VT-17), November 23, 1943.

Aircraft Action Report (VF-2), June 11, 1944.

Aircraft Action Report (VF-1), June 15, 1944.

Aircraft Action Report (VF-2), June 15, 1944.

Aircraft Action Report (VF-1), June 18, 1944.

Aircraft Action Report (VF-2), June 19, 1944.

Aircraft Action Report (VF-10, VB-10), June 20, 1944.

Aircraft Action Report (Air Group Eight), June 20, 1944.

Aircraft Action Report (Air Group Ten), June 20, 1944.

Aircraft Action Report (VF-1), June 24, 1944.

Aircraft Action Report (VF-74 Night Fighter Detachment), July 25–
August 20, 1944.

Aircraft Action Report (VF-8), September 13, 1944.

Aircraft Action Report (VF-8), October 12, 1944.

Aircraft Action Report (Composite Squadron Five), October 31, 1944.

Aircraft Action Report (VT-3), November 13, 1944.

Aircraft Action Report (VF-9), February 16, 1945.

Aircraft Action Report (VF-82), April 6, 1945.

Aircraft Action Report (VF-30), April 6, 1945.

Aircraft Action Report (VB-9), April 7, 1945.

Aircraft Action Report (VB-1), July 24, 1945.

INDEX